W9-AGE-813

GREAT PEOPLE OF THE BIBLE AND HOW THEY LIVED

GREAT PEOPLE OF THE BIBLE AND HOW THEY LIVED

THE READER'S DIGEST ASSOCIATION, INC.

PLEASANTVILLE, NEW YORK   MONTREAL   LONDON   SYDNEY

The Scripture quotations in this publication are from the
Revised Standard Version of the Bible, Copyright 1946, 1952 and © 1971
by the Division of Christian Education of the National Council of
the Churches of Christ in the U.S.A. and used by permission.

The acknowledgments and credits that appear on the facing page and page 432 are
hereby made a part of this copyright page.

Copyright © 1974 The Reader's Digest Association, Inc.
Copyright © 1974 The Reader's Digest Association (Canada) Ltd.
Copyright © 1974 The Reader's Digest Association Pty. Ltd., Sydney, Australia
Copyright © 1979 Reader's Digest Association Far East Ltd.
Philippine Copyright 1979 Reader's Digest Association Far East Ltd.

Reproduction in any manner, in whole or in part,
in English or in other languages, is prohibited. All rights reserved.

Library of Congress Catalog Card Number 73-86027
ISBN 0-89577-015-6

Printed in the United States of America
Sixth Printing, August 1979

Acknowledgments

The editors are grateful to the many individuals
and organizations that have generously helped in the creation of this book.
Our particular thanks are due the following scholars:

Principal Adviser and Editorial Consultant:
G. ERNEST WRIGHT
Chairman, Old Testament Department, Harvard Divinity School
President, American Schools of Oriental Research

Consultants:
VAUGHN E. CRAWFORD
Curator, Department of Ancient Near Eastern Art, Metropolitan Museum of Art, New York

Rev. Fr. STEPHEN J. HARTDEGEN, O.F.M.
Director, U.S. Center for the Catholic Biblical Apostolate

The Reverend Dr. LATON E. HOLMGREN
General Secretary, American Bible Society

ROBERT H. JOHNSTON
Dean, College of Fine and Applied Arts, Rochester Institute of Technology

JAMES B. PRITCHARD
Associate Director of Biblical Archeology, University Museum
Professor of Religious Thought, University of Pennsylvania
President, The Archeological Institute of America

NAHUM M. SARNA
Chairman, Department of Near Eastern and Judaic Studies, Brandeis University

Msgr. PATRICK W. SKEHAN
Professor of Semitic Languages, The Catholic University of America

Rabbi MARC H. TANENBAUM
National Director, Interreligious Affairs, The American Jewish Committee

The Reader's Digest is also indebted to the National Council of the
Churches of Christ, particularly to Howard N. Woodland, for permission to quote
extensively from the *Revised Standard Version of the Bible*

Contents

Preface: A Journey Into Biblical Times

As seen from outer space, the Holy Land is mainly an empty sweep of barren deserts, mountains and valleys. In the midst of this apparent desolation is the dark oblong shape of the Dead Sea. Most of the cultivated land seems to be on a strip of narrow coast between the Mediterranean Sea and the cloud-covered hills that form the spine of Israel. Yet this is the Promised Land. Through the lens of the satellite camera that photographed it, it appears to be a small, barely fertile place. In the eyes of the great people of the Bible, it was "a land flowing with milk and honey"—the land the Lord had given to them alone. Those people, from the Patriarchs down to the apostles, lived most of their lives in this tiny spot on the vast globe of Earth. The last of those great people lived almost 2000 years ago, the first almost 4000 years ago. Time, aided by both man's and nature's destruction, has obliterated most of the material things the people of the Bible created. But the book written about their experiences lives on, as does the faith in the Lord that inspired its authors to write it. Essentially, the Bible is the record of God's dealings with man, yet we are understandably curious about the everyday life of Biblical times.

Today, many archaeologists and other scholars, students, laborers and even tourists carefully work at the excavation of the ruins of Biblical towns and cities. (These ruins are for the most part buried in the numerous man-made mounds, or "tells," that are found in the area.) Guided mainly by the Bible itself, they seek to learn how the people of the Old and New Testaments lived their lives. Biblical archaeology, which was in its infancy at the start of this century, has become a bewilderingly complex science. Every year, new and often significant discoveries are made. As a result, in recent times we have learned much more about Biblical life than was known by our ancestors. With each discovery, our knowledge of the great people of the Bible becomes a little fuller and our understanding of the Holy Scriptures becomes a little clearer.

It is the purpose of this book to show the ages of the Bible as we now see them in the light of modern scholarship. It describes the settings in which the men and women of the Old and New Testaments experienced their times. The personalities—and the faith—of Moses, Elijah and Jesus, of Ruth and Mary, and all the others, are described matchlessly in the Bible itself. But the way in which these people probably lived their everyday lives is not always clearly understood by those who read the Bible today. We need to understand the times in which they lived in order to appreciate more fully the problems and tasks they faced. Their way of thought, the food they ate and the clothing they wore, what their houses looked like and how their tools worked—these and a thousand other facts are not only interesting in themselves, but are helpful in fully comprehending the meaning of the Bible.

Just one example of how a knowledge of the everyday life of the time can help us more fully understand the stories of the Bible can be seen in the account of the arrangements for the Last Supper. As related in the Gospel of Luke, Jesus tells Peter and John to prepare a Passover feast. When they ask him where to prepare it, Jesus replies, "Behold, when you have entered the city, a man carrying a jar of water will meet you; follow him into the house which he enters . . ." (Luke 22.10). Since the city of Jerusalem was full of Jesus' enemies, secrecy was necessary. Only if we know that in that time no man would normally be seen carrying a water jar—that was women's work—can we realize that this was probably a secret, prearranged sign. Thus, something of the ominous danger surrounding Jesus and his disciples is revealed in a seemingly innocuous detail. It is through such details that we can more fully know the great people of the Bible and how they lived.

The Old Testament

A unique new faith dawned in the Near East almost 4000 years ago, unnoticed by the great civilizations of the time. Inspired by the Lord at Mount Sinai, it moved the Israelites to find a homeland and establish a vigorous religion that outlived all those of the ancient world.

THE LIVES OF THE GREAT PEOPLE of the Old Testament span almost 2000 years, from the time of Abraham to the time of the Maccabees. It was an era that saw the Hebrew people emerge from a wandering nomadism to a proud nationhood. Though the technology of civilization developed relatively slowly compared to our own age, ideas and customs developed considerably over the course of time. During those two millennia of Old Testament life, many important changes occurred in the ways the people of the Bible lived, worked, thought, played, worshiped, loved, fought and died. Moreover, each period of the Old Testament era had its own special influence on the people who lived in it. The life of a semi-nomadic Israelite of Jacob's time, for instance, was considerably different from that of a city-dwelling Jew of Judas Maccabeus' time. Only recently have we learned how vast their differences were. Their everyday activities, their ways of looking at things and even their conceptions of God were sometimes dissimilar.

Since the Bible developed over a period of many centuries, it makes assumptions that were shared by people at the time a particular passage was written, but not necessarily at an earlier or later time. The marriage customs of the Patriarchs were not familiar to later Jews, and the Patriarchs themselves would have been puzzled by the concepts of heaven and hell. When the people of the Bible are seen in real historical settings, their actions, beliefs and words become more meaningful. In our own century, archaeologists, historians, linguists, theologians and scientists have enabled us to see these settings more clearly than ever before. The Bible itself tells the stories incomparably better than any book about the Bible, but to modern readers, many of the details seem mysterious or unclear. By placing the great people of the Bible in their historical settings, as discovered by modern scholars, we can more fully understand the Bible's meaning and its relevance to the time in which it was written.

Abraham is the first of the great people of the Bible who can be placed in a historical period. Some modern scholars put the Patriarch's birth as early as the twentieth century B.C., almost 2000 years before the birth of Jesus and almost 4000 years before our own time. The early figures of the Old Testament who appear before Abraham—Adam, Eve, Cain, Abel, Noah and others—cannot be related to any specific historical time because the Bible offers us no real clues to when they lived. Only with the story of Abraham do we begin to get the telling details of place, custom and event that enable historians to guess at an approximate date.

Then, from Abraham through the stories of Isaac, Jacob, Joseph and Moses, more and more historical facts appear to place these great men in particular times and places. By the time of the Judges and Kings—Saul, David and Solomon—the Bible is full of datable events and people, and it remains so right up to the end of the Old Testament. Moreover, the Bible is the only great religious book which is generally historical. This is so because the men who wrote it devoutly believed that by recording the history of Israel, they were recording the acts of God. Thus, for the people of the Old Testament times (as well as for many today) the Bible was literally the book of the acts of God, a holy record of his dealing with man. In it, historical events are seen as expressing the Lord's will and purpose, so to believe the history in the Bible was to confess one's faith. History was important to Biblical man because it not only recorded the past but indicated the direction of the future: the kingdom of God.

This unique belief in the relation of history to religion had its origin in the time of the Egyptian captivity in the middle of the second millenium B.C. To the enslaved Hebrews, as to many other oppressed peoples of the ancient world, it seemed that the gods of the world were only interested in the welfare of the masters, not of the slaves. They recalled the Lord's promise of a land to their forefathers, the Patriarchs Abraham, Isaac and Jacob. Then, under Moses' leadership, came the miraculous liberation from Egyptian slavery. The subsequent covenant with the Lord in Sinai (when the Ten Commandments were delivered), the Conquest of Canaan and, finally, the achievement of David's kingdom seemed to confirm the Lord's power and purpose. Those five great "faith events" became the foundation of Israel's religious belief.

Their faith also made the Jews look closely at the world and their society in the light of their beliefs. If they did not do so themselves, their prophets reminded them. Since there was almost always some conflict between personal and national desires on one side and religious beliefs and duties on the other, these prophets were often unpopular. But the faith of Israel endured.

Originally the history of the early days of Israel—from the stories of the Creation through the time of the Patriarchs and Moses—was probably preserved in memory and expressed in spoken verse and song. With their attainment of a written language sometime after the Conquest, the Israelites may first have begun to write down those early accounts. More stories of early Israel may have been transcribed in the times of Saul and David, but it was not until the tenth century B.C., during the reign of Solomon, that priests of the Jerusalem temple began systematically to copy and preserve the sacred texts. Those texts were probably the nucleus of the first five books of the Old Testament, or "Pentateuch" as they came to be known. These books (Genesis, Exodus, Leviticus, Numbers and Deuteronomy) contained the histories of the Patriarchs, the story of the Exodus, and all the laws and commandments of the Lord. Throughout the next 800 years of Biblical history additional books were added, until the Old Testament was ruled closed to new additions by Hebrew scholars in the second century A.D.

The Bible in History

Until recent centuries, there was little curiosity about how the great people of the Bible may actually have lived, because men did not have the sense of historical development and cultural differences that we have today. It was assumed that people had always lived in approximately the same way: the basically agricultural and feudal world of peasants, priests, warriors and kings. Moreover, as the Bible was a sacred text, it was not subject to critical analysis.

In the eighteenth and nineteenth centuries the discoveries of science and scholarship began to put the Bible in a new light. Such influential books as William Smith's on fossils (1799) and

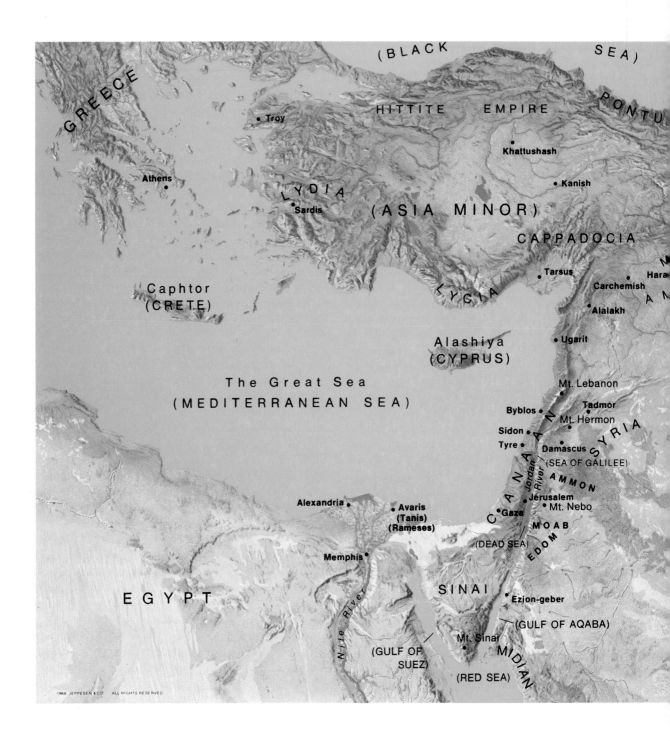

Sir Charles Lyell's on geology (1830–33) seemed to indicate that the earth was considerably older than had been traditionally calculated from the Genesis account of the Creation. (Until the beginning of the nineteenth century, most people accepted chronologies such as that of the Irish Archbishop Ussher (1581–1666), who concluded that man was created in the year 4004 B.C.) The realization that the earth was vastly older than the Bible suggested caused some people to begin to doubt the truthfulness of the Old and New Testaments. This mood of skepticism was reinforced by such controversial books as Thomas Huxley's *Place of Man in Nature* (1863) and Charles Darwin's *Descent of Man* (1871), which offered biological rather than theological explanations of the

(ARMENIA)

BACTRIA

(Lake Van)

(CASPIAN SEA)

Mountains

(Lake Urmiah)

NNI

ITES

ASSYRIA

Nineveh•

Asshur •   • Nuzi

• Ecbatana

PARTHIA

MESOPOTAMIA

Euphrates River

Tigris River

ari

MEDIA

AKKAD

Babylon •

• Susa

ELAM

BABYLONIA

SUMER

• Ur

P

E

R

S

I

A

CHALDEA

(ARABIAN

• Persepolis

(PERSIAN
GULF)

DESERT)

The World of the Old Testament

The map above shows the vast stage upon which 2000 years of Biblical history were enacted. Canaan, in the corridor between Asia and Africa, was the ultimate settling place of the Israelites. Canaan's geographic position brought the Israelites into contact—and often conflict—with powerful Egypt to the southwest and the dominant kingdoms along the "Fertile Crescent" to the north and east. The "Crescent" is the fertile green area that extends northwest from the Persian Gulf along the Tigris and Euphrates rivers, then dips into Canaan.

origin of man. By the end of the century many people, including some prominent Biblical scholars, felt that much of the history related in the Bible was probably myth.

It was the discovery of the remains of the ancient civilizations mentioned in the Bible—the cities and monuments of the Babylonians, Egyptians, Assyrians, Persians and Greeks—that eventually began to reverse the tide of skepticism. Throughout the nineteenth century, linguists in many countries worked to decipher the mysterious languages of these civilizations, which they found inscribed on tablets of clay and on ancient buildings and monuments. By the end of the century a number of them were understood, and scholars began to piece together the history of the ancient Near East. It soon became apparent that many of the events mentioned in the Old Testament were, in fact, true. But these discoveries also revealed that the great ancient empires themselves usually took little notice of ancient Israel. The land of the Patriarchs and Prophets was a very small one, squeezed between the giant empires of Egypt and Mesopotamia. Not until this century, when Biblical archaeology was developed as a scientific method, did the everyday life of Israel begin to reveal itself.

Archaeology and the Bible

Archaeology has been technically defined as "the science or study of history from the remains of early human cultures as discovered chiefly by systematic excavations." Palestine (and most of the Near East, as well) is dotted with mounds or "tells" which are not natural but man-made. They were formed over hundreds, even thousands of years, by the successive building of one settlement over the ruins of another. It is in these tells that archaeologists have sought to unearth the daily lives of ancient peoples.

Early excavators of tells in Palestine and elsewhere were often more treasure hunters than archaeologists. They indiscriminately dug straight into a mound in search of gold or other valuable artifacts. They often disregarded such valuable clues to everyday life as simple pottery, weapons and tools, and they made no attempt to determine where one level ended and another began.

In the past 80 years, archaeology has become a careful science, largely through the efforts of such eminent scholar-excavators as Sir Flinders Petrie, W. F. Albright, Roland de Vaux, G. Ernest Wright, Kathleen Kenyon, Nelson Glueck and Yigael Yadin. Modern archaeologists do frequently find treasures, but their goals and methods are much different from those of their predecessors. With the aid of trained teams of laborers and scholars, they carefully excavate one level at a time, photographing and drawing plans of the whole level before beginning on the next. The location of each found object—vase, tool, jewelry, weapon, etc.—is carefully recorded and each is cleaned and labeled. Even the humblest utensil is a clue to the life of the man or woman who used it. When the excavation is completed, it is possible to reconstruct the entire mound on paper and trace its history from the earliest settlement (bottom level) to the most recent (top level).

The two main methods of archaeology are stratigraphy (the careful excavation and examination of levels, or strata, of a tell) and typology (the classification of the objects uncovered by excavation). Frequently, specialists such as paleobotanists (who can determine ancient crops and diets from the evidence of dried seeds and fossil plants found at sites) and engineers (who can guess at ancient methods of construction) are also present at the excavation site.

Biblical archaeology is the special field of study which seeks to illuminate the historical and cultural backgrounds of Biblical events. Archaeology cannot "prove" miraculous events described in the Bible, any more than science can prove the existence of God. (These are matters of scholarship, not faith.) What archaeology can do is discover the true settings in which the events of the Bible took place. It tells us, for instance, that there was a destructive invasion of Canaan during the twelfth century. Whether this destruction was caused by the conquering Israelites under Joshua is a matter of speculation. The fact of a conquest having taken place is the evidence of archaeology, and in this fact we can see what seems to be the historical background of the Book of Joshua. As one eminent archaeologist has written, "Our ultimate aim must not be 'proof,' but truth." Briefly, then, these are the discoveries of archaeology and modern scholarship about the history of great people of the Bible.

Ages of the Old Testament

The first great historical period of the Old Testament was that of the Patriarchs of Israel: Abraham, Isaac, Jacob, Joseph and his brothers. The time was within the Middle Bronze Age (about 2000 to 1500 B.C.), when most men still relied on tools and weapons of copper and bronze. Iron was known, but rare, the secret of its smelting carefully hidden by the peoples (like the Hittites) who knew it. The great cities and civilizations of

Canaan: Small Land of Great Contrasts

Though only 150 miles long and 54 miles across at its greatest width, Palestine (or Canaan as it was known in Biblical times) includes extreme varieties of scenery. Within the land's 6000 square miles are deserts, verdant farmlands and towering mountains.

The Dead Sea is 1290 feet below sea level—the lowest point on the earth's surface. Water draining down into it by way of the Jordan River can escape only by evaporation, which leaves behind high concentrations of mineral salts.

The Sea of Galilee is actually an inland lake 696 feet below sea level, fed primarily by the Jordan River. Hills slope down to the water's edge except in the northwest where a fertile plain (above) has been cultivated since ancient times. During the days when Jesus lived, the fishing industry on the lake was substantial.

The Jordan River Valley winds southward from the Sea of Galilee to the Dead Sea, a fertile green strip amid barren hills on either side. The Jordan Valley is part of a major geological fault, the Great Rift Valley, that runs along the eastern border of Canaan, down through the Red Sea and into the eastern part of Africa.

Olive trees cover the hillsides in Samaria near the geographic center of Canaan. Some peaks rise to more than 3000 feet in this region, but most of the land is made up of gentle, low-lying hills and spacious, productive valleys.

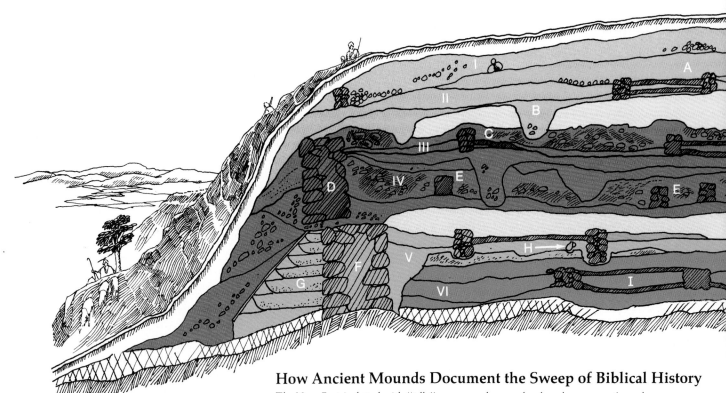

How Ancient Mounds Document the Sweep of Biblical History

The Near East is dotted with "tells"—man-made mounds whose layers were formed over thousands of years by successive construction on top of the ruins of older settlements. The tell above has typical features and is shown in cross-section as an archaeologist might draw it, after he had carefully excavated all its levels. Each of the successive historical levels, or strata, is a different color, keyed to the diagram of the stratum pottery below, at left.

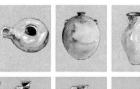

Stratum I—modern times to A.D. **100.** *The top layer of this typical tell near Jerusalem has stone farm walls from Roman times. Pottery (left) in this layer is simple and utilitarian.*

Stratum II—625 B.C. **to 700** B.C. *More than five centuries pass before the next evidence of habitation appears. At location (A), a house with stone walls and dirt floor was built during the days of the prophet Isaiah. A second floor, laid when the house was rebuilt later, lies above the first. Dirt was excavated from a pit (B) in order to level the foundation of the house. The decanter, perfume jug and oil lamp of this period also have a simple, utilitarian design.*

Stratum III—1100 B.C. **to 1200** B.C. *Below a layer of wind-blown sand from another long period of abandonment comes a brief interval of habitation in which two stone houses (C) were built on top of a layer buttressed by walls (D) from an earlier time. Scattered debris in the stratum indicates a violent attack, possibly by Philistines. The Philistine swan motif (left center) in pottery fragments found in the area gives positive evidence of their presence.*

Stratum IV—1200 B.C. **to 1450** B.C. *At the time of the Exodus (about 1290* B.C.*), the tell was in Canaanite territory and heavily guarded by walls (D) against possible attacks by marauders from nearby city-states. Extensive rubble around building walls (E) indicates a very heavy destruction between 1350 and 1400* B.C. *During this period, traders from Greece and Cyprus flooded Canaan with elegant, strikingly decorated pottery from many other lands.*

Stratum V—1500 B.C. **to 1800** B.C. *The tell was also fortified shortly after the days of Abraham and Isaac. Walls (F) not only rested on bedrock, but were also protected by smooth slopes (G) which made it difficult for attackers to maintain their footing. At location H, a burial urn beneath the floor of a house contains the remains of an infant who died at birth. Artisans of this period had learned to use the potter's wheel to produce elegant designs with greater ease.*

Stratum VI—2400 B.C. **to 3000** B.C. *The site of the tell was only a rocky, low-lying knoll at the time the great pyramids of Egypt were being built. A satellite village associated with a larger, fortified town was located here. One of its principal structures was a stone house (I) which was later rebuilt with a new floor above the old one. The elegant quality of the pitchers and large jar of this period reflect an art that was possibly 2000 years old by this time.*

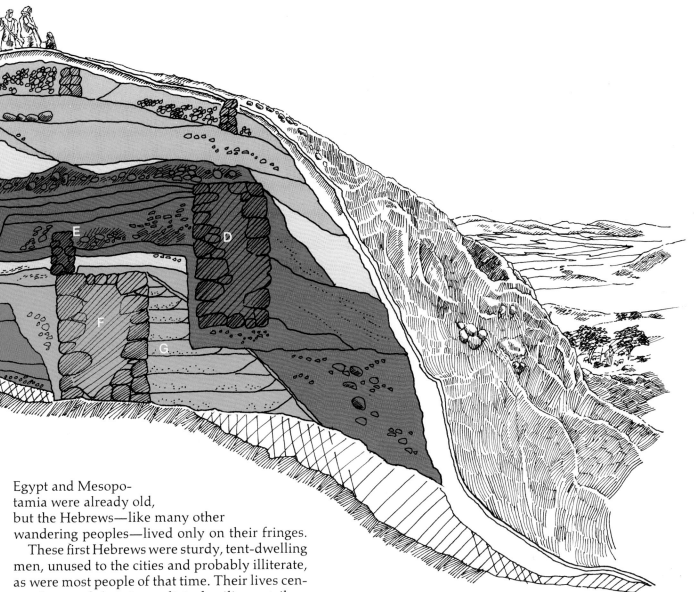

Egypt and Mesopo-
tamia were already old,
but the Hebrews—like many other
wandering peoples—lived only on their fringes.

These first Hebrews were sturdy, tent-dwelling
men, unused to the cities and probably illiterate,
as were most people of that time. Their lives centered around their immediate families or tribes,
rather than a city or nation. Their everyday work
was mostly with the flocks they owned and
tended: these were their main wealth and source
of food, fuel and cloth for garments and tents.
They worshiped the Lord as their god exclusively
and their special relation to him was expressed in
a covenant, or agreement, which resembled the
form of a contemporary political treaty. This
guaranteed the Lord's protection and guidance in
return for obedience and exclusive loyalty. According to the Book of Genesis, it was during this
time that the Lord first promised the Hebrews a
land of their own.

In time the tribes of Israel became slaves of the
Egyptians. They were rescued (about the thirteenth century B.C.) by the Lord through his
chosen prophet Moses. With that escape, the subsequent giving of the Law and Commandments

on top of Mount Sinai and the
molding of the tribes into a confederation dedicated to the Lord, a new period began.

The next period (about 1200 to 1020 B.C.) of the
Old Testament saw the conquest and settlement
of the Promised Land of Canaan under Joshua
and the Judges. This was a time of heroes who,
the Bible says, were chosen by the Lord to save
Israel from the many enemies that surrounded it.
After the conquest of Canaan's central hills by
Joshua, the seminomadic Hebrews learned to
grow crops and settle in towns. They also faced
the challenge and temptation of foreign gods.

The period witnessed battles and massacres
in the name of the Lord. To the Israelites, this
bloodshed was justified by a belief in divine purpose and righteousness, even though Israel rec-

ognized evil within itself. The loose confederation of tribes that formed Israel eventually proved inadequate to defend itself against the powerful Philistines, and the people were soon asking for a king. It was the great Prophet and Judge Samuel who anointed Israel's first king, Saul.

The age of kings Saul, David and Solomon (about 1020 to 922 B.C.) is probably the best-known part of the Old Testament. This was when the nation of Israel reached the zenith of its ancient splendor. It was a time which later Israelites looked back upon as a golden age.

Under Saul, Israel finally began to defend itself effectively against the Philistines and other enemies, but it was under the great David that Israel became a true kingdom. Aided by the decline of Egyptian and Mesopotamian power, David expanded Israel's land by conquest and treaty until it reached from Syria to Egypt. During his reign the Philistine monopoly of iron smelting and smithing was broken, and the city of Jerusalem was captured from the Canaanites and made the capital of Israel. David's personality and brilliant leadership made him Israel's greatest king.

Solomon, David's son, was the first hereditary king of Israel. Under his rule Israel became the most prosperous kingdom in the Near East. Not a warrior like his father, Solomon was a businessman and diplomat. Through marriages and treaties he further enlarged the legacy of David. The first temple in Jerusalem was erected by him and became the spiritual center of Israel. But the country could not support Solomon's lavish expenditures and his large court. There was popular resentment of the taxes he levied and conservative religious anger at his tolerance of foreign religious cults in Jerusalem. This strain and discontent, together with the long-standing rivalry between the tribes of northern and southern Israel, brought about the division of Solomon's kingdom after his death.

For the next 300 years (about 922–587 B.C.) the two Hebrew kingdoms—Judah in the south and Israel in the north—fought to maintain their independence against the reviving might of Egypt, Assyria and Babylonia. A series of great prophets —Elijah, Elisha, Isaiah and Jeremiah—warned the Israelites that the Lord had sent these enemies to punish them for their lack of faith and attraction to foreign gods. Their warnings were in vain, for first Israel and then Judah fell to the foreign invaders. Jerusalem itself was left a desolate ruin.

It was during their exile in Babylonia (sixth century B.C.) that the Jews learned to preserve their faith by studying the scriptures and discussing them in local meetings, or "synagogues." The prophet Ezekiel was instrumental in this development: by his writings and actions he vividly reminded his fellow exiles of their religious heritage and instilled in them a hope for a future return to the Promised Land. This return was actually made possible by the enlightened policy of the Persians, who had succeeded the Assyrians and Babylonians as the Israelites' captors. The Persians were the first great nation known to have granted religious freedom and considerable self-government to subject peoples. Men like Ezra and Nehemiah were sent back to the province of Yehud (Judah) by their overlords, and they furnished exceptional leadership in critical times. The temple was rebuilt and a new Jewish nation began to rise on the ruins of the old one.

Exile influenced the Jews deeply. Many became absorbed in the life of their captors' lands and chose to remain away from Israel. These first Jews of the Dispersion became the founders of the worldwide colonies that have flourished ever since. Worshiping the Lord in their foreign towns and cities, they nevertheless continued to look to Jerusalem as the center of their faith; from all over the known world, Jews sent contributions to their temple. But soon began the first of the waves of religious persecutions that were to plague the Jews throughout their existence abroad as well as in Israel itself. The story of Esther—set in Persia—was a popular account of a rescue from that kind of persecution.

By the time of the great Judas Maccabeus (around 160 B.C.), the Hellenistic civilization brought to the Near East by Alexander the Great in 330 B.C. threatened to absorb and extinguish Jewish religion and culture. The heroism and leadership of Judas, his father and brothers, succeeded in freeing Israel from the foreign rule. The Maccabees themselves then established a dynasty of priest-kings who ruled from Jerusalem until the Romans conquered Palestine in 63 B.C.

Though the history in the Old Testament ends with the Maccabees, the world of the Old Testament really died in A.D. 70, when the Roman army under Titus sacked Jerusalem, destroyed its temple and killed or dispersed its Jewish citizens. Titus celebrated the event by erecting a triumphal arch in Rome; a relief sculpture on the arch showed Roman soldiers carrying away the sacred candelabrum of the temple as a prize of war. He also issued a commemorative coin which bore on its face the legend *Iudaea capta* ("Judea captured") and the figures of a standing man and a weeping woman beneath a palm tree. The woman, seated and despondent, represented the mood of the conquered Jewish population of rebellious Judea.

Today the arch and the coin are all that remain of the Emperor Titus' triumph. The faith of the city he destroyed continues to command the reverence of many millions throughout the world. The history of that faith and the people who lived it is the story of the Old Testament.

Jericho: A Town for 10,000 Years

Excavations at Jericho, located near the northern tip of the Dead Sea, have uncovered surprising evidence of the complex beginning of settled life. By 8000 B.C. Stone Age hunters had built the first permanent settlement there and had learned to cultivate crops.

Finely plastered skulls with eyes of shell were ancestral clay images, the first portraits in history. This example from Jericho is approximately 9000 years old.

Ancient Jericho today is a mound of rubble (above left) formed from countless generations of occupation. This first walled town, reconstructed at right, was built about 6000 B.C. It covered 10 acres and had about 2000 inhabitants. A massive stone wall encircled the town, surrounded by a dry moat. Part of the wall was a defense tower 30 feet in diameter. People lived in rounded, mud brick huts with leather roofs. Grainfields outside the town were irrigated by spring-fed ditches. Archaeologists probed some 60 feet into the mound to find the ruins shown here.

Part One
Seekers of
the Promised Land

"And Abram took Sarai his wife, and Lot his brother's son, and all their possessions . . . and they set forth to go to the land of Canaan" (Gen. 12.5). In Canaan, the presence of towns in the valleys and "dolmens," or prehistoric tombstone structures like that on the ridge at center, reminded Hebrews they were sojourners in an ancient culture. The Canaanites were sometimes hostile, but pasturage was plentiful on the sparsely settled hillsides where Patriarchal tribes pitched their tents and grazed their flocks. Within camp, the women churned butter in goatskin bags or did other chores, while the younger men tended the tribe's sheep and goats, led their donkeys on trading expeditions and stood guard. From the elders of the tribe came social and religious leadership that enabled Patriarchal Hebrew culture to survive and flourish in alien lands.

"Go from your country and your kindred and your father's house to the land that I will show you" (Gen. 12.1). This command by the Lord to Abraham began the great age of the Patriarchs, seven-centuries that culminated in the founding of a new nation by Moses.

THE FOUNDING FATHERS of ancient Israel were the Patriarchs, leaders of Hebrew clans that settled in Canaan some 1800 years before the birth of Jesus. The first of them—Abraham, Isaac and Jacob—made covenants, or agreements, with the Lord: in return for their complete faith in him, he promised his protection and favor, and a land of their own. The 12 sons of Jacob, including Joseph, were considered patriarchs, too, and became the ancestors of the 12 tribes of Israel. Later, the prophet Moses welded these tribes into a nation and set the stage for the conquest of the "Promised Land."

Compared to the Canaanites, the Hebrews who first appeared sometime after 2000 B.C. were primitive, seminomadic herdsmen to whom the settled routine of farming was an entirely new way of life. The established nations of the Near East had seen wandering peoples come out of the surrounding mountains and deserts for centuries. Sometimes the nomads came in great, warring hordes, leveling the civilized societies in their path. Sometimes they came in relative peace, trading (and occasionally robbing), driving their flocks and herds before them, avoiding the towns.

In Abraham's time there were numerous Semitic* tribes migrating from Mesopotamia into Canaan, and the Hebrews numbered only a few among many. It is understandable, then, why there were no references to them in the records of the Amorites, Hittites, Canaanites and Egyptians, through whose lands they passed. These power-

* A group of originally nomadic peoples whose languages have similar basic characteristics. Arabic and Hebrew are both Semitic languages.

ful nations had more important problems to contend with than the incursion of a relatively small band of herdsmen and caravaneers.

In the more than 5000 years before Abraham's birth, the peoples of the ancient Near East had witnessed the rise of the world's first civilizations. Men and women in Mesopotamia and Egypt had started that rise by gradually abandoning the cave-dwelling, animal-hunting life their people had led for untold thousands of years. Instead, they now began to live in small towns, to grow crops and to domesticate animals.

Eventually, they cooperated with each other to perform such great tasks as the draining of the marshes in lower Mesopotamia and the irrigation of the lands adjoining the Nile River. That cooperation led to the development of the first cities. Within those cities the arts and crafts of civilization began to emerge: writing, building, trade, transportation and organized religion, among others. The first true civilizations were those of Sumer, in Mesopotamia, and Egypt.

When Khufu raised the great pyramid of Giza as his monumental tomb, Egypt was still relatively isolated. But in Mesopotamia empires were already beginning to succeed one another. In the twenty-fourth century B.C. the Akkadians, a Semitic people with whom the Sumerians had coexisted for centuries, conquered their neighbors. Sargon extended Akkadian power throughout most of Mesopotamia. But in the northwest he encountered the influence of Ebla. From their city in northern Syria astride the main trade route leading from Palestine and Egypt, the Eblites held economic sway from Gaza (southwest on the Mediterranean) to Mari (northeast on the Euphrates). The Egyptians lost their Asian markets as Palestine and most of Syria became dominated by Eblite merchants. And the people of Akkad also lost markets until Naram-Sin, Sargon's grandson, destroyed Ebla around 2250 B.C. in a war over Mari, a commercial center vital to both kingdoms.

Shortly before the year 2000 B.C. the whole Near East entered a dark, turbulent period. All across the Fertile Crescent waves of people known to us as "Amorites" invaded and overturned the old centers of power. The Amorites were Semitic tribesmen, seminomads who had been living on the fringes of northwest Mesopotamia and making frequent raids against city-states throughout the area. By the beginning of the second millennium, Amorite kings gained control over most of the north, and within two centuries nearly every important city in Mesopotamia was ruled by Amorites.

Throughout these turbulent years there were great population movements across the Near East, many originating in the early Amorite centers in northern Syria and Mesopotamia. Around this time Amorite tribesmen poured into Canaan, causing the abandonment of towns across the countryside and destroying major cities like Jericho, Megiddo and Ai.

The disorders gradually declined, and the armed invasions gave way to more peaceful migrations of nomadic clans. Some of these settled in Syria, where they eventually founded a group of powerful city-states headed by Ugarit, Carchemish, Aleppo and Qatna. Others wandered farther south into Transjordan, Palestine and even Egypt. Among these wanderers, seeking grazing ground for their flocks, were the Patriarchs.

In later times ancient Israelite schoolchildren were taught to recite their nation's history, beginning with the words, "A wandering Aramean was my father." The Bible records that Abraham came to Canaan from Haran, in northwest Mesopotamia. It was from around Haran that the Aramean clans—part of the Amorite population—set out on their migrations.

Though Abraham made his journey during the same period, we can't be certain that his ancestors came from near Haran. Indeed, one passage in Genesis (11.31) says that Abraham's father, Terah, moved his family to Haran from Ur, the Sumerian capital in southern Mesopotamia. However, the oldest existing text of the Bible—a

Greek translation from the third century B.C.—makes no mention of Ur at all, and many experts believe the passage was a later addition or, at best, that Ur was simply a major stop during the nomadic travels of the Amorites. Moreover, the findings of archaeologists and scholars indicate that Israel's roots were not in southern Mesopotamia, but in the north.

Several members of Abraham's family—including his brothers Haran and Nahor—had names almost identical to the names of towns in the Aramean region. Other names, including Abraham and Jacob, were simply variations of Amorite personal names. The customs of the Patriarchs described in the Bible are also of this region in northern Mesopotamia.

Thanks to a fascinating group of clay tablets found in the ruins of Nuzi, a city in the north, we can now explain some of the incidents in the Patriarchal stories that have perplexed readers for years. The Nuzians were a people who took over most of northern Mesopotamia in the sixteenth and fifteenth centuries B.C. They preserved many old Amorite laws and customs and recorded some of them on the clay tablets. From these we have learned, for example, that it was common (and respectable) for a man whose wife was barren to use her maidservant for childbearing, as Abraham and Jacob both did. The kind of deathbed blessing by which Jacob became Isaac's heir was also common, and it was apparently irrevocable even when obtained under false pretenses, as when Jacob stole Esau's.

Abraham's Canaan

The people Abraham led into Canaan were a clan of seminomads, probably numbering no more than a few hundred, who depended on their sheep, goats and cattle for a living. Abraham remained in the hills and southern region of Canaan, leading his tribe and flocks through the countryside between Dothan in the central hills and Beer-sheba on the edge of the Negeb. This hill country was a good area for the newcomers. Though rugged and heavily wooded, it offered adequate grazing land and was only sparsely settled, lowering the chances of friction with the native population.

In other parts of Palestine there was a great upsurge of commerce and urban life in the nineteenth century B.C., at about the time of the He-

Mesopotamian civilization began along the Euphrates River near the Sumerian capital of Ur, where the Bible says the Hebrews originated. Here, about 2500 B.C., houses and ingenious boats were woven from frail reeds, while on the river, goods were transported by the first merchants. As the city grew, the ziggurat (temple) of Ur rose above it, its top a shrine to the city's god. The Sumerians wear the typical scalloped sheepskin skirts of that time. Below is a contemporary gypsum carving of a Sumerian citizen.

brews' arrival. Cities destroyed many centuries before were rebuilt, and new towns founded, as the incoming tribes settled down. Within a short time the newcomers had adopted the language of Canaan and much of its culture.

When the Patriarchs arrived in Canaan, two of the more important cities were Gezer, which dominated the Aijalon Valley leading into the highlands from the coast, and Megiddo, which commanded the northern plain as it guarded the vital pass through Mount Carmel. There were other flourishing towns along the revived trade routes running up the coast and through the valleys into the heartland. Southeast of the Dead Sea were the notorious "cities of the plain," including Sodom and Gomorrah.

Life of the Seminomads

As long as they remained in Canaan, Abraham's people clung to their seminomadic ways. They continued to move from place to place, always in search of fresh pastures and a reliable water sup-

ply. They lived in tents and whenever possible they set up their camps near larger towns like Dothan, Shechem and Bethel for security. Their main base was the purchased burial ground at Machpelah, where they planted grain each spring. This sort of existence was not really as austere or difficult as it might seem to a modern reader. A contemporary Egyptian story, about a youth who fled to Canaan, gives us a good idea of what life was like for the early Hebrews:

It was a good land . . . Figs were in it, and grapes. It had more wine than water. Plentiful was its honey, abundant its olives. Every (kind of) fruit was on its trees . . . There was no limit to any (kind of) cattle . . . Bread was made for me as daily fare, wine as a daily provision, cooked meat and roast fowl . . .

Another source, a tomb painting at Beni-hasan in southern Egypt, has added further details to our knowledge of the Patriarchal way of life. The painting dates from about 1900 B.C. and shows a family of Semitic seminomads entering Egypt. Their colorful clothing, weapons, tools and other belongings all show that, while not on the advanced level of Egyptian civilization, they were certainly no band of ragged barbarians. They had knowledge of the crafts of sheep herding, metal working (copper) and pottery making.

Though the Patriarchs never really settled down, each of them came to be linked with one or two particular places. After Lot's departure from Bethel, for example, Abraham found a new site about 25 miles to the south—"So Abram moved his tent, and came and dwelt by the oaks of Mamre, which are at Hebron . . ." (Genesis 13.18). He continued to wander, but he always returned to Mamre. There he bought a tract of land surrounding the cave of Machpelah, which he had chosen to be his family's burial place. With this the nomad became a landowner, and in so doing Abraham planted the roots of a tradition that would draw his descendants back to Canaan some 600 years later.

Abraham's son Isaac and his grandson Jacob also established ties with particular places in the hill country. Isaac's wanderings were centered in

The only evidence of how the Hebrews may have looked and dressed in Abraham's time comes from this Egyptian tomb painting found at Beni-hasan. The scene shows a Semitic chieftain taking his tribe to Egypt around 1900 B.C. Leading are men with spears and bows, followed by donkeys bearing household goods, children and what may be bellows for metalworking. Following the women, the last man carries a lyre.

the neighborhood of southern Canaan near Beer-sheba, while Jacob roamed farther north, most often around Shechem and Bethel.

Religion of the Patriarchs

Stone altars and pillars of the kind that both Abraham and Jacob erected to the Lord were frequently raised in the Near East. They were often memorials to a covenant or sacred vow, sometimes between two men, but more often between a man and a god. Such covenants were basically private agreements or contracts, similar in phrasing to political treaties of the day. In them a man would vow to worship a particular god in return for aid and protection. This concept of a personal god was the foundation of the Hebrews' early faith. The covenant between the Lord and Abraham is described in chapters 15 and 17 of Genesis: "And I will establish my covenant between me and you and your descendants after you . . . for an everlasting covenant, to be God to you and to your descendants after you. And I will give to you, and to your descendants after you . . . all the land of Canaan, for an everlasting possession; and I will be their God" (Genesis 17.7–8). In return, Abraham and his descendants were to signify their fidelity to the Lord by the ritual of circumcision: "So shall my covenant be in your flesh an everlasting covenant" (Genesis 17.13).

Although the early Hebrews worshiped the God of Abraham, they did not deny the existence of other deities. On one occasion Abraham made an explicit oath to El Elyon (God Most High), the creator-god of both Amorite and Canaanite be-

lief, and it seems the Patriarchs' religion was often practiced side by side with local cults. In fact, the idea of a covenant described in terms of a family relationship with a god is Canaanite.

To later Israelites the figures of Abraham, Isaac and Jacob embodied the distant past from which their nation had emerged. In the course of many generations, the Patriarchs' stories were shaped and written to emphasize the spiritual destiny that made Israel different from other nations—a destiny summed up in God's promise to Abraham. These stories gave Israel a feeling of continuity with the past, re-creating the nation's origins from the earliest days in Haran to the arrival of Joseph and his brothers in Egypt.

Joseph in Egypt

Joseph, Jacob's favorite son, was sold into slavery in Egypt by his brothers around 1700 B.C. He quickly rose from adversity to become the most powerful minister of the Pharaoh. His story is full of details that modern scholars have been able to connect to historical facts.

The idea that Joseph, a Hebrew slave, could have become the Pharaoh's highest governing official, is not as fanciful as it might sound. About the time of his arrival, between 1720 and 1700 B.C., Egypt was invaded by a Syro-Canaanite alliance called the "Hyksos" by the Egyptians. These invaders established their own line of Pharaohs and ruled the country for about 150 years. Hated foreigners themselves, it was likely that the Hyksos might trust someone like Joseph sooner than they would a native Egyptian, and the ac-

tement of discovery

GIVE someone else the chance to step back in time . . . to meet the remarkable men and women of the Bible . . . to see their world and share their warm and human stories . . . to RELIVE the greatest story ever told!

Great People of the Bible and How They Lived is sure to attract much attention from the guests in your home, many of whom may wish to have their own copies.

That's the reason for the Order Card attached below: it entitles a friend or relative to receive Great People of the Bible and How They Lived for just $13.95 payable in three monthly installments of $4.65 each (plus $1.25 postage), with no interest or charge for credit or handling. Give someone else the chance to receive Great People

of the Bible and How They Lived for the same low price you enjoyed; pass along this Order Card to a friend . . . or use it yourself to give a unique and welcome gift for a birthday, "thank you," farewell, house-warming, congratulations—for any occasion, any time.

TO ORDER: have your friend fill in their name and address on the Order Card, then drop in the mail (we've already paid the postage).

Or, if you would like an additional copy for gift-giving, just fill in your own name and address.

Either way, someone you care about will enjoy the same opportunity you did . . . the opportunity to meet the great people of the Bible and step into the world THEY lived in.

Detach and mail Order Card today! No postage necessary.

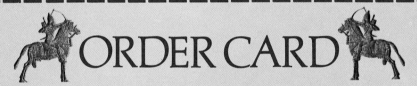

ORDER CARD

YES, send my copy of Great People of the Bible and How They Lived and bill me for just $13.95. I understand that I may pay in three monthly installments of $4.65 each (plus $1.25 postage, and applicable state tax, if any, which will be added to the first installment) and that there is no interest or charge for credit or handling. Price and postage subject to change without notice. Order subject to acceptance and credit approval by Reader's Digest. Money-back guarantee from Reader's Digest.

NAME _____
(please print)

ADDRESS_____ APT. # _____

CITY _____

STATE _____ ZIP _____

29603

Here's your chance to let a friend turn back the pages of time with the greatest story ever told...

▲ Ruins of an ancient church at Nicea, in Asia Minor.

◀ The Philistines held the monopoly of metalworking.

▲ At the spring of Herod.

The temple court was the scene of ▶ Isaiah's conversion to the role of Prophet.

(If Order Card has been detached, please write to Reader's Digest, Pleasantville, N.Y. 10570.)

Detach and mail Order Card today! No postage necessary.

No Postage
Necessary
If Mailed
In The
United States

Business Reply Card
First Class Permit No. 1 Pleasantville, New York 10570

POSTAGE WILL BE PAID BY ADDRESSEE

Reader's Digest
Pleasantville
New York 10570

Invite a friend to meet...

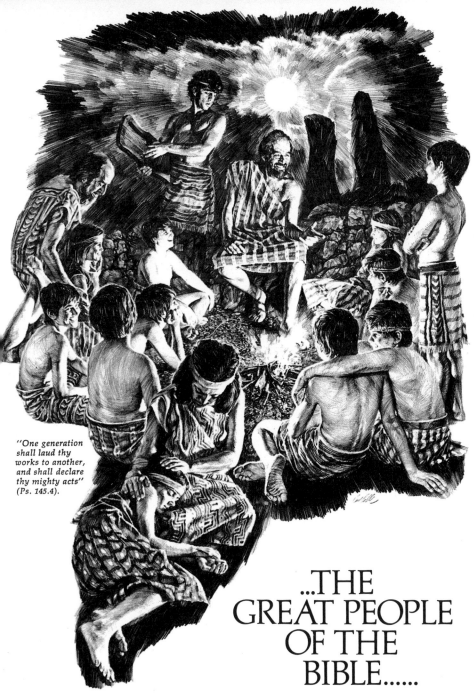

"One generation shall laud thy works to another, and shall declare thy mighty acts" (Ps. 145.4).

...THE GREAT PEOPLE OF THE BIBLE......

...Share the exc

count of Joseph's rise to power has an undeniably authentic flavor. Another part of the narrative, in which the Pharaoh acquired most of the country's land during a famine, would be easy to understand if Egypt had been under the Hyksos.

Joseph's ability to interpret dreams would certainly have attracted attention in Egypt, where the ancient arts of magic and divining were highly respected. Also, the various titles given Joseph by Potiphar and the Pharaoh are exact translations of the Egyptian offices, and the description of Joseph's swearing-in as prime minister came from someone familiar with such ceremonies.

Joseph's reunion with his brothers is another event that mirrors historical conditions. It was a period of famine throughout the Near East—"the famine was severe over all the earth" (Genesis 41.57)—and, according to an Egyptian text, certain of the foreigners "who know not how they should live, have come begging a home in the domain of Pharaoh . . ." There was often surplus grain in the Pharaoh's storehouses, and in time of hardship or famine it was apparently an old Egyptian policy to allow nomads from other countries into the land. The region of Goshen in the fertile Nile Delta could sustain great numbers of people and their flocks, and would have been the logical place for the Hebrews to settle. "Thus Israel dwelt in the land of Egypt, in the land of Goshen; and they gained possessions in it, and were fruitful and multiplied exceedingly" (Genesis 47.27).

According to the Bible, Joseph lived to be 110 years old—the traditional length of a full and happy life in Egyptian lore. Nearing his death, Joseph called his brothers together: "I am about to die," he told them, "but God will visit you, and bring you up out of this land to the land which he swore to Abraham, to Isaac, and to Jacob" (Genesis 50.24). Here again the great promise was repeated. This had been the basis of the Patriarchs' faith, the covenant God had made with them. Now they were in Egypt and could only wait for the Lord to make good his vow.

Slaves of the Pharaoh

The Book of Exodus opens after an interlude of some 400 years. It was the beginning of the thirteenth century B.C. The Hyksos had long since been driven out and Egypt was profoundly changed. The powerful landed aristocrats of Joseph's time no longer existed, their place taken

What School Was Like 3700 Years Ago

Because of their seminomadic way of life, few of the Patriarchs and their descendants learned to read or write. But these skills were common among more settled peoples. For example, at Mari, an Amorite capital on the Euphrates River, some 20,000 clay documents have been discovered, along with the ruins of an ancient school. Students sat on backless stone benches (immediately below) and wrote with styluses on heavy clay tablets. When a student finished a lesson on his tablet, he could erase his work by simply kneading the clay until it was smooth again. To protect or preserve a piece of writing, the tablet (below right) could be stored in a clay envelope (left).

by a new class of royal officials and bureaucrats. Nearly all the land in Egypt was owned by the Pharaoh, and the great number of people who lived and worked on it were entirely at his mercy.

During the period leading up to the Exodus, Egypt was ruled by two Pharaohs—Seti I (1308–1290 B.C.) and his son Rameses II (1290–1224 B.C.). It was apparently Seti who enslaved the Hebrews and other foreign peoples living in Egypt. During his reign Egypt was asserting itself again as a major power. Seti quelled a series of local rebellions that had fragmented Egypt's empire in Canaan and Syria. He also began to rebuild the old Hyksos capital, Avaris, in the Nile Delta. The Pharaohs who succeeded the Hyksos had moved their capital back to Thebes in the south, but Seti —whose family came from the delta—chose to revive Avaris as the seat of his government.

The First Wagons Came From the Near East

One of the earliest uses of the wheel, which originated in Mesopotamia around 3500 B.C., was in covered oxcarts similar to the Sumerian type above. The ponderous, unspoked wooden wheels were simple to make and gave ancient traders their first efficient means of transporting loads that were too heavy for pack animals. Seminomadic tribes, such as the Israelites, encountered these wagons frequently as they migrated along the trade routes of the Near East, but for carrying their goods over rough terrain they preferred the agile pack donkey.

This work could only be done by forced labor, and the task undoubtedly fell hardest on the foreign population—including the Hebrews living in the Nile Delta. "So they made the people of Israel serve with rigor, and made their lives bitter with hard service, in mortar and brick, and in all kinds of work in the field . . ." (Exodus 1.13–14).

Seti's policies were continued vigorously by Rameses II, whose reign marked Egypt's last

flourish of real power in the Near East. Rameses finished subduing Canaan, fought the mighty Hittite Empire to a stalemate in Syria, and enjoyed great prestige and relative peace for the last 50 years of his life. At home he planned numerous building projects to glorify his kingdom, including the completion of rebuilt Avaris, which was renamed Raamses in his honor. The splendor of the finished city soon became legendary. The most striking creation was a magnificent temple, flanked by two colossal granite statues of the Pharaoh that stood 40 feet high.

All this grandeur took a heavy toll in human suffering. The Hebrews and other foreigners were conscripted into the labor battalions, condemned to the brick-fields and stone quarries for as long as it pleased the Pharaoh. "And the people of Israel groaned under their bondage, and cried out for help . . ." (Exodus 2.23). The time seemed to have come for Israel's God to reveal himself, to deliver the Hebrews out of bondage and redeem his ancient promise.

So it was that Moses, reared in the court of the Pharaoh, but then a Hebrew shepherd herding his flock in the Sinai Peninsula, was called to lead his people out of Egypt. Here began the dramatic story of the Pharaoh's refusal to release the Hebrews and the succession of plagues which God sent down in reprisal—the last one killing all the first-born children in Egypt but miraculously passing over those of the Hebrews. The Jews later celebrated this event in the Passover holiday.

With this, the Bible says, the terrified Pharaoh summoned Moses and his brother Aaron and told them: "Rise up, go forth from among my people . . . Take your flocks and your herds, as you have said, and be gone . . ." (Exodus 12.32).

Moses and the Exodus

Organizing a motley crowd of perhaps 3000 to 5000 people, Moses set out across the marshes of the Reed Sea, escaping the charioteers that the Pharaoh had sent in a last-minute change of heart. He then turned south toward the region of Mount Sinai (where he had first received the Lord's call) to avoid the Egyptian fortresses in the northern part of the peninsula.

It was here that Moses went up on a mountain to receive the Law and make the covenant binding Israel forever to "the God of the Fathers." It is impossible to judge the accuracy of the details

Busy Caravan Routes Created Channels for Biblical Migrations

By the time of the Patriarchs, well-established and heavily traveled trade routes linked kingdoms and settlements from one end of the Fertile Crescent to the other. The distance from Ur in the Tigris-Euphrates Delta (see lower left) to Tanis in the Nile Delta was about 1500 miles. Woolen textiles and grain from the rich farmland of Mesopotamia moved up the Tigris and Euphrates rivers by boat, then were carried overland by wagons or pack animals whenever a waterway was lacking. Coming from the opposite direction was a rich variety of trade items—metal implements from the Hittite Empire, superior pottery from Asia Minor, gold from Egypt, cedar lumber from the forested hills of the Lebanon. This trade brought prosperity all along the Crescent—and it also created a tradition of hospitality to all strangers who came in peace. During stable times, migrating tribes suffered little harassment as they trekked up and down the Crescent; in fact, Abraham and other Patriarchs usually prospered as they made the journeys traced on the map at right.

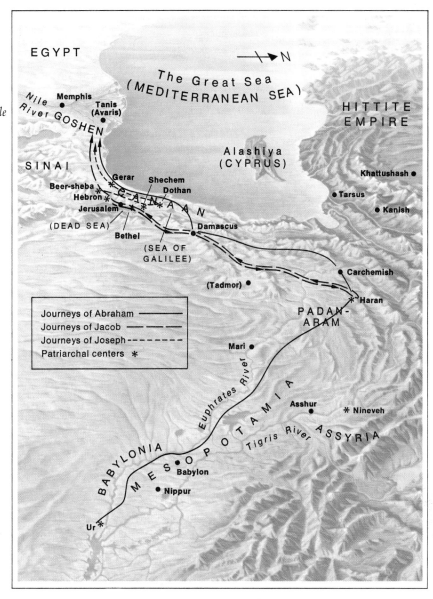

in the Exodus story. The Biblical account we have was not actually written down until 400 years later. (Until then, the story had been passed down by word of mouth.) Egyptian records of Moses' time make no mention of the Hebrews' escape, but ancient kings were not in the habit of recording their defeats. It seems likely that the group which escaped from Egypt included other slaves as well as the Hebrew descendants of Jacob. These others would not have been familiar with the promise the Lord made to the Patriarchs. Nevertheless, most of them were absorbed into the Israelite tribes and religion.

There is no reason to doubt that the Hebrews did escape from Egypt during the reign of Rameses II, and this "Exodus" was a crucial event in the faith of Israel. The faith of the Patriarchs had been based on a divine promise, and the Exodus was interpreted as a divine act which would lead to the fulfilment of that promise.

With the Exodus, the real history of Israel as a nation began. Egypt was behind them, and the Promised Land lay ahead. Most important, the Lord had shown the Hebrews that his power was equal to the ancient pledge he had made to Abraham: ". . . I will make of you a great nation, and I will bless you, and make your name great so that you will be a blessing" (Genesis 12.2).

Chapter 1

*Following the Lord's command, the Patriarchs settle
in Canaan, ancient land of fertile valleys and rugged hills.*

Pioneers in the Promised Land: Abraham and Isaac

*Abraham and his son Isaac were the first Patriarchs of
Israel. The covenants, or pacts, which these founding fathers made with the Lord were the beginnings of Israel's
religion. Their story, which begins in the early second
millennium B.C., is not only one of faith; it also gives us
an authentic glimpse of the nomadic life from which the
nation of David and Solomon eventually sprang.*

Abraham, descended by 10 generations from
Noah, was born between 2000 and 1850 B.C. in
southern Mesopotamia, near the Euphrates
River. His family would have been indistinguishable from those of the many other seminomadic
tribesmen who had temporarily settled near the
cities of the Fertile Crescent. These dusty caravaneers and herdsmen were relatively uncivilized,
by Mesopotamian standards. They lived in tents,
surrounded by their flocks of sheep and goats and
herds of cattle. Tough, self-sufficient men and
women, they had arrived sporadically from the
northeast and southwest. Many of them had re-
spectfully adopted the native religions, but they
were never fully absorbed by the carefully struc-
tured Mesopotamian society.

Though it is unlikely that Abraham and his
brothers attended the cities' schools (only a privileged minority did), they were undoubtedly impressed by the written tradition of law and myth
that the Mesopotamian civilization had developed. They may even have heard the awesome
story of the Great Flood read from incised clay

tablets by a scribe. Abraham was also doubtless
familiar with the wonders of Ur, already ancient
and much celebrated in his day. Although hardly
the area's largest city in the time of the Patriarchs,
it did have a sizable population, perhaps as
many as 24,000. It also boasted not one but two
harbors. Its crowning achievement, however, was
its towering ziggurat, a man-made mountain with
temples and altars to the moon-god, patron deity
of the city. Did the sight of sacrifices on this great
ziggurat burn into Abraham's memory, later
prompting his near sacrifice of Isaac?

Settled with other nomads on the edge of the
city, Terah's family grew as his three sons, Haran,
Nahor and Abraham, came of age and married.
Haran died and left a son, Lot, and a daughter,
Milcah. Milcah later married her uncle Nahor.
This kind of marriage—of niece and uncle—was
not yet prohibited by Hebrew law. It had a practical purpose: the orphaned girl and her property
were cared for within the family. Abraham and
his wife Sarah probably loved their nephew Lot
as a son, for they had no children of their own.

From Abraham, Lot learned the age-old arts of
the shepherd. He must have marveled at Abra-

*In Abraham's time, the Negeb was a hospitable region that was
heavily settled, affording cities and pasturage to the Patriarch
and his tribe as they followed a seminomadic way of life. Centuries of conflict and neglect have since turned the Negeb into
a huge barren area that covers nearly half of modern Israel. At
right, a flood of rainwater has provided some temporary ponds.*

ham's seemingly magical ability to summon his sheep and goats simply by the sound of his voice. The shaggy creatures would obey no other command. When the flocks of Abraham and Nahor and their father, Terah, were led into the common sheepfold for the night and counted, young Lot (and every new shepherd boy) would despair of ever separating the various flocks. Standing within the rough, rock-walled enclosure, the hundreds of animals looked totally indistinguishable to Lot's untrained eyes. So it was with wonder that the boy saw each flock go surely to its own shepherd when the gates of the enclosure were opened at dawn.

Migration to Haran

As Lot grew older, his uncle Abraham taught him the other duties of a shepherd. Under Abraham's watchful eyes, Lot proudly performed the tasks of his elders: the constant look-out for predatory lions, jackals and bears; the continual commanding of the wandering flock; separating sick sheep and goats from the main herd with crooks; carrying very young lambs and kids; and the endless search for more abundant grass and water. The shepherd's tasks were all the more difficult because there were no sheep dogs then.

Terah's clan probably did not own their pasturage, but rented it from the Mesopotamians by the regular payment of a certain number of their animals. It was partly the desire for more fertile land that caused the clan to migrate north to Haran, several hundred miles up the Euphrates Valley. In addition, the cities of southern Mesopotamia were declining as the power of Babylonia grew. What we do know is that eventually Terah took all of the families of his clan to Haran.

The route that Terah and Abraham followed to Haran was the eastern leg of the greatest caravan trail of the ancient Near East. Cutting through the center of the Fertile Crescent, it arched from the Persian Gulf up through the valleys of the Tigris and the Euphrates rivers to Haran, then southwest through Damascus and Canaan into Egypt.

The prosperous town of Haran was a gathering point for trade caravans. The walled city, surrounded by distinctive beehive-shaped huts, was ruled by a great Semitic people, the Amorites. Their capitals were at Haran and at Mari on the Euphrates, 250 miles to the south.

"I Will Make of You a Great Nation"

The Hebrews probably camped outside the city walls, where they could graze their animals and pitch their goat-hair tents. There they stayed for many seasons, and each year their numbers increased. It was a good place to settle, for the land was fertile and the trade brisk. Terah died at Haran, and Abraham, his eldest son, assumed the leadership of his tribe.

Abraham and his family might well have looked like this group of Hebrew seminomads when they left Haran for Canaan in the 19th century B.C. Surrounded by their donkeys and flocks of goats and sheep, these caravaneers wear the characteristic Semitic costumes of the period. Stacked brick "beehive" houses can still be found in northern Syria.

Eventually, Abraham and his tribe began to long for land of their own. They were weary of being tenants of the Amorites. It was then that the command of the Lord directed Abraham toward Canaan: "Now the Lord said to Abram, 'Go from your country . . . to the land that I will show you. And I will make of you a great nation, and I will bless you, and make your name great . . . I will bless those who bless you, and him who curses you I will curse; and by you all the families of the earth shall bless themselves.' So Abram went, as the Lord had told him; and Lot went with him. Abram was seventy-five years old when he departed from Haran. And Abram took Sarai his wife, and Lot his brother's son, and all their possessions which they had gathered, and the persons that they had gotten in Haran; and they set forth to go to the land of Canaan."

Following the Lord's instructions, the tribe of the Patriarch headed west, the men leading their flocks and donkeys, the latter burdened with all of the portable possessions: tents, blankets, food, cooking utensils and tradable goods. They must have stopped in Damascus, for at that time its amply watered location made it the main caravan city on the trail from Haran to Canaan.

Damascus—"city of the asses," as the Assyrians were to call it—was where caravans bound west for Canaan and Egypt were outfitted. Situated on a plain that is startlingly fertile by Near Eastern standards, the city must have impressed Abraham. Here, surrounded by flowering fields, rushing streams and productive farms, was an exciting center of trade, news and novelty. In the large open squares and dark narrow streets, men and women of dozens of different tribes and nations jostled each other and spoke in many languages. Haughty Egyptians with numerous slaves and attendants bargained with bearded Aramean caravaneers while Phoenician traders bartered dyes and spices for goods imported by Hittite merchants. Everywhere were the large Damascus donkeys. Heavy-shouldered and colored dark brown, these intelligent beasts were the essential component of every caravan.

Abraham left Damascus at the head of his family and flocks, leading his burdened donkeys. He also had a supply of money (precious metals) and goods to barter with. At first he might have traveled with one of the large donkey caravans that regularly left the city. One caravan might include up to 3000 donkeys, but 500 or 600 were more common. Abraham and Lot noticed the care with which the caravan leaders planned their route to be sure that there would be fresh water for the animals every night. The journey to Haran had been up a river valley, but this route was another matter. Except for the Jordan Valley, fresh water was available only at jealously guarded wells and springs. The right to use them had to be delicately negotiated. Abraham learned this lesson well as they traveled on.

Grinding Grain With Portable Millstones

Whether settled or on the move, the day's work for the women of Abraham's tribe began with the grinding of meal for the daily bread, a mainstay of the nomadic diet. The tools for cracking wheat and maize, such as the two stones below, were easily carried and quickly set up. After the grain was cracked, it was further refined into flour with a mortar and pestle, then moistened and shaped into flat loaves and baked on hot stones.

Covering almost 15 miles a day, the Patriarch's caravan headed southwest toward Canaan, the land promised to them by the Lord. Camped amidst their tents at night, their donkeys tethered and their flocks enclosed, Abraham, Sarah and Lot could see the signal fires of scattered Amorite settlements flashing in the dark. The settled Amorites tolerated their wandering cousins but kept careful track of them by the use of signal fires, for some of the bands of travelers were not as peaceful as Abraham's. There was, for instance, a tribe of "Benjaminites" that was suspected of being in collusion with marauding bands of robbers.

Abraham's caravan had long since left the tilled fields surrounding Damascus and the river that watered them. Within sight of the 10,000-foot heights of Mount Hermon, the fields had given way to a series of relatively barren grayish hills outlined by dry riverbeds. This region, in turn, merged into the forbidding Syrian desert where greenery disappeared. Suddenly, several

days after their departure from Damascus, Abraham saw the hills of Canaan appear behind a ridge. They were at last at the frontier of the Promised Land.

Arrival in the Promised Land

Abraham, Sarah and Lot continued to make their way through Canaan, keeping to the central highlands that ran from north to south. Behind them to the west lay the coastal cities of Tyre and Sidon. To the east in the Jordan Valley were other Canaanite cities. There were Canaanite strongholds in the highlands, too, but they were less powerful or less jealous of their lands than the kingdoms in the plains. All of the cities of the Canaanites owed nominal allegiance to Egypt, as Abraham well knew before he entered the country. The Egyptian peace in Canaan, like the peace in Mesopotamia, gave him the freedom to travel as he did.

Despite the peace, it was best for the Hebrews to stay in the highlands. The Canaanites were continually feuding over land and trade. Many of their ancient cities had already been destroyed by the Egyptians and invaders from the east, and new cities were slowly being built.

Abraham and his descendants were in awe of the remaining towns. Some of them, like Jericho and Megiddo, were ruins surrounded by the remains of immense fortification walls. The Canaanites had bronze armor and weapons, as well as more advanced warfare techniques. This made them formidable to the Hebrews, so Abraham was wise to avoid their strongholds.

Abraham led his family on until they came to Shechem. There, between Mount Ebal and Mount Gerizim, ". . . the Lord appeared to Abram, and said, 'To your descendants I will give this land,'" reaffirming the original promise he had made in Haran.

From Shechem, they made their way south to the rich pasturelands between Bethel and Ai. In these hills they pitched their tents, grazed their flocks, and it was there Abraham built an altar to the Lord. There the Lord appeared to him once more and again renewed his promise of land and prosperity. Abraham and his family probably stayed there for several months, letting their flocks fatten on the grasses that grew around the many springs in the area. Then a famine swept through Canaan, and once again the Patriarch and his family packed their tents. They headed south in search of water and pasturage.

Near Egypt, both Abraham and Lot prospered. Their flocks increased tremendously, and Abraham, perhaps by trading sheep for silver and gold in the northern Egyptian markets, became rich by nomad standards. At any rate, when Abraham and Lot returned to Bethel some years later, they found their numbers so increased that the land there could no longer support them all. "So Lot chose for himself all the Jordan valley, and Lot journeyed east; thus they separated from each other. Abram dwelt in the land of Canaan, while Lot dwelt among the cities of the valley and moved his tent as far as Sodom," near what was then the southern end of the Dead Sea.

From that time on, Lot's fortune dwindled. Not long after he settled in Sodom, an army led by a coalition of four chieftains—possibly seeking control of the copper mines in the area—captured and ransacked the cities on the southern shores of the Dead Sea. The soldiers took many prisoners, including Lot. When Abraham learned of the disaster, he recruited a small army from among his own people and pursued the fleeing soldiers to the foothills of Laish, far to the north, and then east toward Damascus. After a night attack and battle, he rescued Lot. Soon, however, Lot's area experienced a great catastrophe.

"Then the Lord rained on Sodom and Gomorrah brimstone and fire . . . and he overthrew those cities, and all the valley, and all the inhabitants of the cities, and what grew on the ground." Because of his relation to Abraham, Lot and his family were warned to escape. As they fled, Lot's wife disregarded a divine command not to look back and she "became a pillar of salt." The Dead Sea then overflowed and flooded the valley, cov-

The Mystery of Sodom and Gomorrah

The exact location of the sinful cities that the Lord destroyed with "brimstone and fire" has long intrigued Biblical scholars. The dominant theory now places them under the southern waters of the Dead Sea, the "Salt Sea" of the Old Testament.

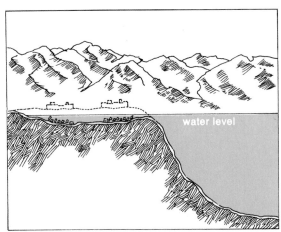

What is now shallow bottom at the southern end of the Dead Sea may once have been the fertile valley of Siddim, where Sodom and Gomorrah were situated. Geologic evidence indicates that some kind of cataclysm—probably an earthquake—occurred in this area during the early part of the 2nd millennium B.C. The floor of the valley may have dropped abruptly and been submerged as in the illustration above. Today, dead trees encrusted with thick layers of salt rise from the shallows, and at the great salt mountain at the southern end of the Sea one may still see formations reminiscent of the pillar of salt that Lot's wife became when she turned to look back at the city.

ering the cities' ruins with over 10 feet of water.

For a long while Lot and his two daughters lived in a remote cave, seeing no one else. Both daughters worried that they would never have children of their own to raise. The older girl suggested to her sister, "Come, let us make our father drink wine, and we will lie with him, that we may preserve offspring through our father." This was done, and each of Lot's daughters bore a son; Moab became the ancestor of the Moabites, and Ben-ammi, of the Ammonites.

Abraham eventually settled near Hebron, an unusually fertile area about 20 miles south of Jerusalem. There he was able to plant crops of barley and wheat in the fields beyond the camp. At Hebron the Lord appeared to Abraham once again. Up to this time he had been called Abram (exalted father), but now the Lord renamed him Abraham.* His wife's name was changed from Sarai to Sarah. The Lord also established a covenant sign with Abraham. "Every male among you shall be circumcised . . . in the flesh of your foreskins," directed the Lord. "So shall my covenant be in your flesh an everlasting covenant."

A Son for the Patriarch

Despite more than 30 years of marriage, Abraham and Sarah had remained childless, a bitter misfortune at a time when family and tribal leadership was passed from father to son. Thirteen years earlier, when the aging Sarah decided she would never bear a son, she had given her Egyptian maid Hagar to Abraham. According to Amorite custom, Sarah could claim any children Hagar might have as her own, and they would become Abraham's legitimate heirs. Hagar promptly bore Abraham a son, Ishmael, now a young boy about 12 years of age.

So when the Lord announced to Abraham that Sarah would bear a son within the year, both he and Sarah laughed in disbelief. But Abraham also worried about his first son Ishmael's fate, for if the Lord's prediction were true, Ishmael would no longer have a right to Abraham's inheritance. The Lord reassured him, ". . . I will bless him and make him fruitful and multiply him exceedingly . . . and I will make him a great nation. But I will establish my covenant with Isaac, whom

* Abram and Abraham mean exactly the same thing: "My (divine) Father is exalted." Later editors of the Bible incorrectly translated Abraham as "father of a multitude."

Sarah shall bear to you at this season next year."

Abraham probably thought nothing more about the Lord's promise of a son. One hot afternoon shortly afterwards, he saw three men approaching his tent. Immediately he rose and greeted them, offered them cool water to wash their tired feet, and a shady spot to rest from their journey. Here on the borders of the wilderness, hospitality to strangers was an essential part of nomadic life—Abraham knew he could rely on that same hospitality whenever he traveled. Hurriedly he ordered Sarah to prepare three cakes from her finest ground meal, and then he picked out a tender calf from among his cattle. While a servant prepared the tasty meat, Abraham set milk and goat cheese before his guests and stood aside while they ate.

When the men had finished their meal and were preparing to leave, the Lord suddenly appeared to Abraham in their midst and said, "I will surely return to you in the spring, and Sarah your wife shall have a son." Sarah was doubtful, and she laughed once again, amused by the idea that an old woman like her could bear a child.

But in fact a year later Sarah gave birth to a son. The child was named Isaac. The two aged parents were delighted and Sarah exclaimed joyfully, "Who would have said to Abraham that

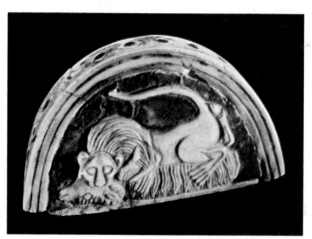

"The lion has roared; who will not fear?" (Amos 3.8). Lions, bears and other predatory beasts were a constant threat to the flocks of early Near East shepherds like Abraham and his brothers. They were also a frequently recurring subject in art. The Sumerian ivory cosmetic box lid (above) shows a lion devouring a ram. The female lion, however, usually made the kill, as in the scene at right, and shepherds, carrying cumbersome goatskins of water and armed only with spears and slings, had difficulty protecting their flocks. Lions were common in Palestine during Biblical times, but became extinct in this region toward the end of the Middle Ages.

Sarah would suckle children? Yet I have borne him a son in his old age." Then, when the infant was eight days old, Abraham circumcised him as the Lord had instructed.

As Isaac grew older, Sarah became more and more hostile to Hagar and Ishmael. Frightened for her own son's future, and jealous of Abraham's affection for his firstborn son, she said to him: "Cast out this slave woman with her son; for the son of this slave woman shall not be heir with my son Isaac." The Lord directed the unwilling Abraham to do as Sarah wished, and Hagar and Ishmael were sent into the desert with only a goatskin filled with water and a small supply of bread. But ". . . God was with the lad, and he grew up; he lived in the wilderness, and became an expert with the bow." Indeed, Ishmael was destined to be the legendary ancestor of all the Bedouin tribes of northern Arabia.

A Sacrifice for the Lord

From their camps up in the hills Abraham and Isaac watched the settled Canaanites work their land. Their agricultural year began in late September when they harvested the olive crops. The oil from that fruit was used for cooking, as medicine and in perfumes. When the winter rains began in late October, wheat and barley were planted on terraced fields carved out of the hills. Women scattered seed in furrows dug with flimsy bronze-tipped wooden plows.

After four rainy months, the first spring harvest began: in March, flax was cut down to be dried and spun into linen fiber. By late April the rains had ended and the barley harvest began. One month later the wheat crop was ready for cutting. The golden stalks of grain were expertly cut with flint-edged sickles and gathered in wicker baskets. The crop was taken to a communal threshing floor where it was beaten with stones and trampled to separate the grains from the stalks. The grain itself was then stored in earthenware containers.

During the summer months, figs, pomegranates, dates, lentils, chickpeas, cucumbers, onions and leeks ripened and were harvested. Then, in late August, the annual grape harvest began. It was a time of joy for all, for it signaled the end of the hot summer weather. Some of the grapes were eaten fresh from the vines, some were dried into raisins that would last throughout the winter, but most were used to make rich, potent wine.

Continuing his search for pasturage, Abraham moved to Beer-sheba, some 20 miles southwest of Hebron. There he and his men dug a well of their own. A short time later, a dispute arose between Abraham and a local chieftain, Abimelech, whose servants had wrongfully captured the well. The two men finally came to an agreement, which they confirmed by taking an oath. According to tradition, Beer-sheba, or "well of the oath," was named for that pact.

Then, unexpectedly, ". . . God tested Abraham, and said to him . . . 'Take your son, your only son Isaac, whom you love, and go to the land of Moriah, and offer him there as a burnt offering upon one of the mountains of which I shall tell you.'" Abraham was stunned. Offerings to the Lord were nearly always rams or young lambs—a human being was never sacrificed.

The grief-stricken father loaded a donkey with several days' provisions and enough wood to burn an offering. Then, with Isaac and two servants, he began the journey. On the third day they reached the place the Lord had chosen. Perhaps Isaac sensed his father's anguish, for the absence of an animal indicated that his father would not be making a regular offering. His father had assured him, "God will provide himself the lamb for a burnt offering, my son," but there was no animal to be seen.

Isaac watched apprehensively as Abraham built a crude altar and laid the wood they had brought on top of it. Then the Patriarch tearfully bound the terrified boy and placed him on the altar. Abraham held his knife, bracing himself to sacrifice Isaac. "But the angel of the Lord called to him . . . 'Abraham, Abraham! . . . Do not lay your hand on the lad or do anything to him; for now I know that you fear God, seeing you have not withheld your . . . only son, from me.' And Abraham lifted up his eyes and looked, and . . . behind him was a ram . . . and Abraham . . . offered it up as a burnt offering instead of his son." Thus Abraham's faith was tested by the Lord. His unswerving loyalty was rewarded by yet another divine blessing.

He and Isaac returned to Beer-sheba and resumed the routines of the shepherding life, moving their camp whenever better pasturage or water could be found elsewhere. Eventually, Abraham resettled his family in Hebron, where they had lived for so many years.

Warriors from the North: The Hittites

The first piece of land owned by the Israelites in Canaan was purchased from a Hittite tribesman. The Hittites were a non-Semitic people who established an empire in present-day Turkey. Their power was felt in the Near East for 500 years of the 2nd millennium B.C.

The Hittites, like the Egyptians, became expert in the use of battle chariots such as the one in the frieze at right. With this weapon they dominated the region north of Canaan until 717 B.C., when the Hittite chariots were routed by more maneuverable Assyrian cavalry units in a battle fought at Carchemish.

The ruins of Khattushash, the ancient Hittite capital, are still guarded by menacing stone lions on either side of the fortress-city's western gate. Located near the center of the Hittite Empire (at present-day Boğhazköy, Turkey), Khattushash flourished from 1600 to 1200 B.C. through its military power and its control over the richest silver and iron mines in all of Asia Minor.

As the Hittite Empire expanded, some of its people drifted south and settled peaceably in Canaan. The Bible records that Abraham bought a burial place for his wife Sarah from "Ephron the Hittite" for 400 shekels worth of silver. The silver was probably in the form of jewelry—rings or bracelets—whose weight was measured on a scale as in the transaction depicted at left.

The years passed, and Abraham's love for Isaac grew. He taught Isaac the same things he had learned from his own father, Terah: the duties and skills of shepherding, the use of the plow and the history of his ancestors. In addition, he raised the boy to believe in the covenant the Lord had made with Abraham and his descendants. They had reason to be grateful to their God: the land he had directed them to was a good one.

At Hebron, Sarah died at the age of 127, "and Abraham went in to mourn for Sarah and to weep for her." Having no burial land of his own, he appealed to some neighboring Hittites to sell him a plot of land containing a cave which he could use as a tomb. At first the Hittites offered him the free use of their tombs, but eventually Abraham persuaded Ephron the Hittite to sell him his plot of land with the cave of Machpelah. This—a burial site—was the first property the Hebrews owned in the land the Lord had promised them.

The time came for Isaac to marry. Abraham had no desire for a Canaanite daughter-in-law, but neither did he want Isaac to leave Canaan in search of a wife. So Abraham sent his steward to Haran, where his brother Nahor and his family still lived, in hopes of finding a wife for Isaac among his own kin.

When the steward arrived at Haran, a lovely young girl offered him water from the earthenware jug she carried, and took him to her parents' house, where he was given food and lodging. The girl was Rebekah, granddaughter of Abraham's brother. On learning who she was, the steward told her parents and her brother Laban the reason

"And Isaac sowed in that land, and reaped in the same year a hundredfold" (Gen. 26.12). At planting time, oxen were yoked to wooden plows to break the ground. Following after them came the sowers with their bags of seed. Boundary markers—often nothing more than stones placed one atop another—marked off each farmer's plot and helped the plowmen line up their furrows.

for his journey, and they quickly decided that Rebekah should marry Isaac. Then the steward gave Rebekah and her family the gifts he had brought from Hebron—gold and silver rings and bracelets, fine clothing and other costly ornaments. The next day the steward and Rebekah, accompanied by her maids, departed for Canaan.

Several days later, "Isaac went out to meditate in the field in the evening; and he lifted up his eyes and looked . . . And Rebekah lifted up her eyes, and when she saw Isaac, she . . . said to the servant, 'Who is the man yonder, walking in the field to meet us?' The servant said, 'It is my master.' So she took her veil and covered herself . . . Isaac brought her into the tent, and took Rebekah, and she became his wife; and he loved her,'' from that moment on.

Abraham also took another

Royal boundary stones of Babylon were elaborately inscribed, unlike the simple markers in the fields of Canaan.

wife, Keturah, who bore him many sons. As they reached maturity, Abraham rewarded them with gifts—probably flocks of their own—and sent them away from Canaan, so that Isaac remained his only heir.

The Peaceful Patriarch

When Abraham was 175 years old, he "breathed his last and died . . . and was gathered to his people." His son Ishmael returned from his wilderness home and was reunited with Isaac for the last time. The two brothers buried their father next to Sarah at Machpelah. Then Ishmael returned to his own people.

As head of the tribe, it was now Isaac's responsibility to provide adequate pasturage and water for his people's flocks. During the next years of his life, he and his tribe traveled from place to place, from one oasis to another between Beersheba and Gerar, 20 miles to the northwest. They usually settled long enough in each place to dig a well near the camp and to raise crops of grain nearby. Sometimes disputes arose between the Canaanite and Hebrew shepherds over the

use of wells already dug. When that happened, Isaac usually chose to move on rather than to argue with the more heavily armed Canaanites. He was a peaceful man, blessed by the Lord, and dedicated to the God of his fathers.

During Isaac's wanderings, he frequently came across wells his father had dug, now blocked because of neglect or the maliciousness of the local Canaanites. "And Isaac dug again the wells of water which had been dug in the days of Abraham . . . and he gave them the names which his father had given them."

Later in his life, Isaac returned to his former home at Beer-sheba. There the Lord renewed the promise of land he had made to Abraham, and Isaac in turn built the Lord an altar to commemorate that promise. Abimelech, the local chieftain who had befriended Abraham, then approached Isaac with a plan to restore the peace between the Hebrews and his own people. "We see plainly that the Lord is with you; so we say, let there be an oath between you and us . . . that you will do us no harm, just as we have not touched you and have done to you nothing but good and have sent you away in peace. You are now the blessed of the Lord." So the two men took an oath of peace which remained in effect for many years.

Despite the Lord's blessings and his friendly relations with the local Canaanites, Isaac's family life was far from tranquil. Rebekah had borne twins: Esau, the elder by only a few minutes, and Jacob. The two boys could not have been more unlike each other—Esau was a boisterous outdoorsman and Jacob was the quiet one. Toward the end of Isaac's life, when he had become frail and nearly blind, he was cruelly tricked into giving his blessing, which rightfully belonged to Esau, to his younger son, Jacob. The blessing could only be given once, and Esau's fury was such that Jacob had to flee Canaan for his life.

Finally, at the end of 180 years, Isaac died near Hebron where his father had lived and died before him. Jacob and Esau, now at peace with each other, buried him near his parents, Abraham and Sarah. Since childhood, he had been protected by the Lord, his life "full of days."

The story of Abraham and Isaac is told in the Book of Genesis, Chapters 11–35.

The Canaanites: Worshipers of Baal

When the Hebrews first entered Canaan around 1900 B.C., they found the region occupied by Semitic peoples like themselves who had lived there for many years. These "Canaanites" had built fortified cities on the coastal plain and in the fertile valleys. Their superior weapons and numbers forced the Hebrews to keep to the sparsely populated hills of the central highlands. But it was the Canaanites' religion that presented the greatest threat to the children of Abraham. A ritual that included music, magic and sex offered a seductive challenge to Israel. All of the great prophets from Samuel to Malachi denounced such pagan rites, often defying a king when they feared the people were being corrupted.

This Canaanite's heavy beard is typically Semitic. The Canaanites were of eastern origin and their culture was similar throughout Palestine and Syria during the time of the Patriarchs, from which this portrait dates.

The agricultural nature of Canaanite society emphasized the importance of fertility. Gods such as the male Baal and the female Astarte were worshiped as both creators and destroyers linked to the forces of nature. The crowned figure above, covered with gold and silver, possibly represents Baal ("the lord"), king of heaven and earth. The plaque at right shows a female deity resembling Astarte. Dressed in little more than her jewelry, she holds lotus blossoms symbolic of the fertility which was central to the Canaanites' sensual religion.

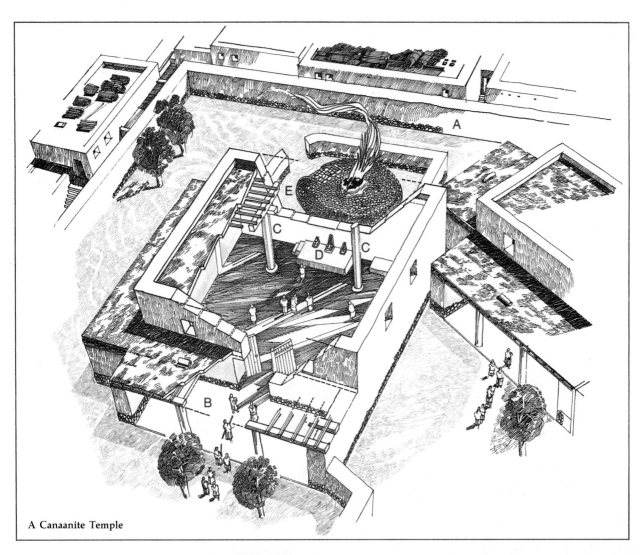

A Canaanite Temple

Isaac built only a rough stone altar to the Lord, whereas the Canaanites maintained large temple compounds in which to worship their many gods. Three temples were contained within the walls of the complex at Megiddo, built around 2500 B.C. Believing that a god lived in his temple, the Canaanites based its floor plan on the design of a house. Walls (A) separated sacred grounds from the rest of the city. The temple itself, an enclosed room about 30 feet wide and 45 feet long, was entered through a covered porch (B). Two sturdy wooden pillars (C) supported a clay-straw roof over the main room, and at the far end a stone podium (D) held images of the gods. Outside the Megiddo temple, sacrificial animals were burned atop a huge stone altar (E) reached by the steps at right. Religious rites conducted here were varied according to the seasons of the year and the cycles of nature.

Chapter 2

*By means of a stolen birthright, Jacob emerges as the leader of the tribe
of Abraham and Isaac during a period of bitter family quarrels and intrigues.*

Twelve Tribes for a New Nation: Jacob and His Sons

Third of the Israelite Patriarchs, Jacob is portrayed in Genesis as a strong, thoughtful man, capable of foxlike cunning as well as deep emotion. Like his father, Isaac, and grandfather Abraham, he made a pact with the Lord, who renamed him "Israel." His 12 sons were the founders and namesakes of the tribes that formed the ancient nation of Israel.

Jacob and his twin brother, Esau, were born around the nineteenth century B.C. near Beer-sheba, in the Negeb region of southern Canaan. Their father, Isaac, was the prosperous owner of substantial herds of sheep and goats, which he moved around the arid, hilly land in a seasonal search for water and pasturage. In early spring he planted fields of grain, before rains evaporated under the summer's sun. He and his servants plowed the soil with a metal-tipped wooden plow drawn by sturdy oxen. It was a pleasant pastoral life, governed by the changing seasons and the fluctuating supply of water. The times were peaceful throughout the whole Near East.

Isaac had been married for 20 childless years to Rebekah, when at last she became pregnant with her twin sons. "And Isaac prayed to the Lord for his wife, because she was barren; and the Lord granted his prayer, and Rebekah his wife conceived. The children struggled together within her; and she said, 'If it is thus, why do I live?' So she went to inquire of the Lord. And the Lord said to her, 'Two nations are in your womb, and two

peoples, born of you, shall be divided; the one shall be stronger than the other, the elder shall serve the younger.'" To later Israelites his prophecy proved to be true: Rebekah's sons became the founders of the Israelites and the Edomites.

When the time came, Rebekah gave birth to the twins in the privacy of her tent. At the first pangs of labor, she straddled two cushioned stones above a space intended for the newborn infants. Rebekah herself—and countless generations before her—had been born in the same way. "The first came forth red, all his body like a hairy mantle; so they called his name Esau. Afterward his brother came forth, and his hand had taken hold of Esau's heel; so his name was called Jacob [he takes by the heel]."

Maidservants assisted with the delivery, probably aided by a midwife. The women cut the umbilical cords with a copper knife and washed the babies with water. Then they rubbed them with cleansing salt and oils, and wrapped them firmly in clean strips of woolen cloth. Soon afterward Rebekah began nursing her sons.

Isaac—delighted to be the father of sons—was consulted about what names the boys should be given, and eight days after the birth, he circum-

Jacob grew to manhood among pastoral scenes, such as the one at right, near Beer-sheba, focal point of tribal life in the Negeb region of southern Canaan. The land around Beer-sheba was ill-suited for agriculture, but had just enough water and pasturage to support the flocks of Jacob's family until the time of the great droughts which drove them to look for food in Egypt.

which you lie I will give to you and to your descendants; and your descendants shall be like the dust of the earth, and you shall spread abroad to the west and to the east and to the north and to the south; and by you and your descendants shall all the families of the earth bless themselves.'"

Jacob awoke from his dream, filled with awe for the place where he had slept and for the God he had seen. He named the spot Bethel (house of God). Before leaving, he swore a personal oath, reaffirming the covenant of Abraham and Isaac.

Jacob continued his journey northward, and at length he approached Haran. This city, a busy junction point on the great caravan routes between Mesopotamia and the Mediterranean, lay on a plain between the Tigris and Euphrates rivers. As Jacob neared Haran, he saw first the colorful tents of Laban and his people. Beyond these lay the beehive-shaped, mud-brick huts of the settled inhabitants, and, beyond these, the gates of the great city itself.

While still on the outskirts of Haran, Jacob came to a well. This was a popular meeting place

Household gods, such as those stolen by Rachel from her father, Laban, were small, portable clay statuettes of ancestors or family deities. The possession of these images symbolized the holder's claim to family leadership and property. Those above are Syrian.

The women of Jacob's era were responsible for making, mending and pitching tents. Below, a group of women prepare a new camp. Their tents—made of woven strips of black, brown and red-brown goat hair—differed little from Bedouin tents of modern times. Inside, curtained partitions separated the living areas. There was hardly any furniture; woven mats served as rugs, seats and beds.

among shepherds, who watered their flocks there at the end of each day. A large, flat stone slab, too heavy for one man to move, usually covered the opening. This was to insure that all got their fair share of water. Jacob went up to some nearby shepherds and asked where he might find Laban. As the men were talking, Laban's younger daughter, Rachel, came up with her sheep.

When Jacob saw his shapely and beautiful cousin, he fell in love with her on the spot. He went up to her, explained who he was and helped her water the sheep. Then, unable to hide his feelings any longer, he kissed her and wept with happiness. His love for Rachel never wavered after that moment.

Rachel ran quickly to tell her father the news. Laban, delighted to see his sister's son, welcomed Jacob heartily and invited him to stay. Jacob could not have come at a better time. Since Laban had only two children, both girls, he was looking for a capable son-in-law who would eventually take over the family holdings.

Earning a Bride

Jacob told Laban of his desire to marry Rachel. It was customary for the prospective husband to present a gift to the family of the bride. The gift was generally made in livestock or material goods, but as Jacob had brought little with him, he offered to look after Laban's flocks for seven years instead—an accepted custom of the time. At the end of his servitude he would marry Rachel. Laban agreed, and "Jacob served seven years for Rachel, and they seemed to him but a few days because of the love he had for her."

Laban had a problem, however. His elder daughter, Leah, was a plain girl, while Rachel was a natural beauty. It would be difficult to make an advantageous marriage for Leah, particularly if Rachel married first. The wily shepherd made his plans with this in mind.

When the seven years were up, Jacob reminded Laban of their agreement. Laban immediately prepared a great wedding feast, and many guests gathered for the usual week of celebration. There was no religious ceremony: the customary formalities had already been arranged by Laban and Jacob. The marriage was usually consummated (and thus made legal) on the first night. The bride was brought to Jacob's darkened tent late at night, her face hidden behind the traditional veil. Jacob rejoiced that at last he had won his beloved Rachel, and it was not until morning that he discovered he had married Leah instead. He had been fooled by Laban in much the same way he himself had fooled Isaac.

Jacob was furious. He went immediately to Laban and demanded an explanation. But the old shepherd shrugged it off, explaining that it was the custom of the land to marry the older daughter first. Laban then calmly suggested that Jacob marry Rachel at the end of the week of feasting and serve seven more years as a second marriage gift. Jacob had to agree.

Sons for the Shepherd

Leah bore Jacob four sons: Reuben, Simeon, Levi and Judah. But Rachel remained childless. Because of this, a serious rivalry developed between the two sisters. Children, especially sons, were of prime importance in tribal society, since they worked in the fields and helped protect the herds and other possessions of the family against marauders. Even more important, male children carried on the family line. The tribal ancestry was traced through the men of the family, and a boy was always identified by his father's or even his grandfather's name.

It's not surprising, then, that childlessness was a great calamity. If there were more than one wife, the one with the most children would feel superior. In fact, a childless wife might well fear her husband's rejection.

"When Rachel saw that she bore Jacob no children, she envied her sister; and she said to Jacob, 'Give me children, or I shall die!' Jacob's anger was kindled against Rachel, and he said, 'Am I in the place of God, who has withheld from you the fruit of the womb?'"

Desperate, Rachel resorted to a legal arrangement Jacob's grandmother Sarah had used. Laban had given Rachel a maidservant, Bilhah, as a wedding present. Rachel gave Bilhah to Jacob and asked him to treat her as a wife, "that she may bear upon my knees, and even I may have children through her." Any child born would be regarded as Rachel's. But Leah, not to be outdone, gave her maid, Zilpah, to Jacob.

By the time the 14 years of Jacob's servitude were nearly over, he had a daughter, Dinah, and six more sons—Dan, Naphtali, Gad, Asher, Issachar and Zebulun—by Leah and the maidservants. Moreover, Rachel had finally conceived. She gave birth to Joseph, Jacob's eleventh son. Shortly thereafter, Jacob informed Laban—who by now had sons of his own—that his servitude was completed and asked to take his wives and children and return home to Canaan. It took Jacob another three years to extricate himself from Laban's domination, but during this time he accumulated many sheep and goats of his own.

Flight to Canaan

Jacob, sensing the growing hostility of Laban and his sons to his prosperity, made up his mind to leave Haran, and waited for an opportunity to do so. Fearing that his departure would be opposed, Jacob decided to leave while Laban, his sons and his servants were away shearing their sheep.

As soon as Laban and his sons had departed, Jacob hastily assembled his wives, children, servants, flocks and possessions and stole away. They traveled southward, forded the Euphrates and headed as rapidly as possible toward Canaan.

But, unknown to Jacob, Rachel had taken Laban's household idols with her. These were small clay images, perhaps of family ancestors. They were symbols of the right of inheritance. If Jacob possessed Laban's idols, he might legally claim to be Laban's heir. This may have been the reason Rachel took them from her father's house.

Laban was outraged when he returned and found Jacob's family—and the idols—gone. He and his retainers pursued and caught up with the fugitives just east of the Jordan. Jacob insisted that he was innocent of the theft, but Laban insisted that the idols were with him. "So Laban went into Jacob's tent, and into Leah's tent, and into the tent of the two maidservants, but he did not find them. And he went out of Leah's tent and entered Rachel's." There Rachel sat upon the saddle in which she had hidden the images.

Laban frantically searched about her tent, for he may have suspected that his younger daughter was the thief. But she remained seated. "And she said to her father, 'Let not my lord be angry that I cannot rise before you, for the way of women is upon me.'" The ruse worked and Laban, his anger lessened, gave up the search. Laban and Jacob parted after swearing a ceremonial friendship, a covenant of peace. Even Esau—now prosperous

A Potter's Wheel Driven by Toe Power

Portable stone wheels for turning pottery were sometimes carried by seminomadic families. The simplest type of wheel (below) consisted of a pivot (right) set in the ground and an indented stone (left) that revolved on the pivot when it was pushed by the potter's big toe. Clay was placed on top of the rotating stone and shaped by hand as it was turned, a slow method, but one with which lovely forms were often created.

himself—greeted his estranged brother with friendship when he and Jacob met again.

The night before meeting Esau, Jacob wrestled with a stranger. Bravely, against all odds, he fought with his opponent until daybreak, and he won. In the course of the struggle, Jacob, recognizing the stranger as a divine emissary, refused to release him until he had received a blessing. The stranger blessed Jacob and gave him a new name, Israel, "for you have striven with God and with men, and have prevailed." The nation descended from Jacob would bear his new name.

Jacob now headed westward into Canaan and settled near Shechem, a new Amorite town about 70 miles north of his childhood home, Beersheba. Shechem controlled the central passes through the northern hill country of Canaan. In the verdant valley outside the town, Jacob bought

"One generation shall laud thy works to another, and shall declare thy mighty acts" (Ps. 145.4). *Few, if any, Hebrew leaders knew how to read and write during the Patriarchal era. Instead, history, family relationships, laws and traditions were handed down by word of mouth from one generation to another. Stories were sung or told in rhyme to make them easier to remember, and often were accompanied by the music of a lyre, as in the scene above.*

pastureland and settled down. He also built an altar of rough stones and dedicated it to his God, the God of Israel.

But trouble followed. A quarrel between Jacob's sons and the Shechemites resulted in a massacre of the Shechemites. When Jacob learned of his sons' treachery, he was furious. As a newcomer to Shechem, he had wanted to make peace between his family and the surrounding people, but his sons had provoked hostility.

Wandering Patriarch

Again following a command of the Lord, Jacob and his family left the area and traveled south toward Bethel. Here the young Jacob had dreamed of angels and heard God repeat to him the promises made to Abraham and Isaac. Here, too, he had promised to build an altar. To prepare for this sacred task, he now ordered his family and servants to bury all their household gods, to purify themselves and to put on new clothes. These actions symbolized the decision that from that time on, only the God of Abraham and Isaac was to be revered and worshiped by Jacob's people.

In addition to the altar, Jacob erected a pillar of stone as a memorial to the God of his fathers. Then he and his household continued southward. They were nearly at Ephrath (Bethlehem) when the caravan had to stop. Rachel, who was pregnant for the second time, began to feel the pains of childbirth. Jacob's beloved wife did not survive the birth of her second son, and she was buried beside the road to Bethlehem. In deepest grief, Jacob took up his twelfth and youngest son, Benjamin, his only child to be born in Canaan.

Soon afterward, Jacob traveled to Mamre, near Hebron. A short distance to the south was the cave of Machpelah, the burial place of Abraham. In Mamre, Jacob visited Isaac for the last time. Isaac died there, and together Jacob and Esau buried their father in the family tomb and then parted forever. Centuries later their descendants, the Israelites and the Edomites, would meet as enemies on the soil of Canaan.

Jacob and his family passed the next years in peace, moving their tents and flocks from place to place among the hills of southern Canaan between Hebron and Beer-sheba. Every spring they planted fields of barley, as Isaac had done when Jacob was a boy. Jacob's sons grew to be men; and his household, possessions and flocks increased.

In his old age the Patriarch was troubled by a great sorrow. His favorite son was Joseph, the firstborn of Rachel, and he made no attempt to hide his great love for the boy. He even gave Joseph a long, sleeved robe to wear instead of the sleeveless, knee-length tunics the other sons wore. "But when his brothers saw that their father loved him more than all his brothers, they hated him, and could not speak peaceably to him." One day, when all the brothers were out in the fields with their flocks, they decided to get even with Joseph and sold him to a passing caravan.

"Then they took Joseph's robe, and killed a goat, and dipped the robe in the blood; and they . . . brought it to their father, and said, 'This we have found; see now whether it is your son's robe or not.' And he recognized it, and said, 'It is my son's robe; a wild beast has devoured him; Joseph is without doubt torn to pieces.' Then Jacob rent his garments, and put sackcloth upon his loins, and mourned for his son many days. All his sons and all his daughters rose up to comfort him; but he refused to be comforted, and said, 'No, I shall go down to Sheol [the underworld] to my son, mourning.' Thus his father wept for him."

Jacob remained inconsolable until he was miraculously reunited with Joseph in Egypt years later. There he and his family settled in the easternmost section of the Nile Delta, a place they then called Goshen.

The years of Jacob's old age in Egypt were the happiest and most peaceful of his life. He had never thought he would see his favorite son again, yet he saw not only Joseph but Joseph's two sons, Manasseh and Ephraim, as well.

Near the end of his life, Jacob summoned all his sons, blessed each in turn, and described their future inheritance in the land of Canaan. "When Jacob finished charging his sons, he drew up his feet into the bed, and breathed his last, and was gathered to his people."

A great procession carried his body back to Canaan, where he was buried near Hebron in the tomb of his father and grandfather. Despite his early and all-too-human failings, Jacob had grown to become the venerated founder of a people, as the Lord had promised at Bethel.

The story of Jacob and his sons is told in chapters 25–50 of the Book of Genesis.

Chapter 3

*Under Joseph's protection, the Israelites migrate into Egypt
in a prelude to the great drama of the Exodus.*

Egyptian Interlude: Joseph and His Brothers

*One of the Patriarchs and favorite son of Jacob, young
Joseph was sold into slavery by his jealous brothers.
From that calamity he rose to become the most powerful
minister of Egypt and rescuer of his people. To later Israelites, Joseph's life demonstrated that the Lord could
reveal his purpose through adversity as well as success.*

Joseph was born near Haran in northern
Mesopotamia during the eighteenth century B.C.,
Jacob's eleventh son. Shortly after his birth, the
family moved to Canaan, where his mother,
Rachel, soon died following the birth of her second son, Benjamin. Jacob had had two wives and
two concubines, but his deepest love had been for
Rachel and he made no secret of it or of his extraordinary love for her firstborn, Joseph.

Jacob led a seminomadic life, much as his forefathers had, tending livestock and cultivating
small fields when the land was available. When
his older sons were grown, they assumed most of
the shepherding duties. Their life was not easy,
for the flocks required constant attention.

Young Joseph had his own responsibilities. If
his older brothers were grazing the sheep near the
main camp, he carried fresh bread and goat
cheese to them. He also helped to herd the animals into the stone-walled sheepfold in the evening. As he grew older, he took turns standing
night watch over the flocks, armed with a sling
and a club. By the time he was 17 he was sharing
all the duties of a shepherd with his brothers.

Joseph's older brothers resented the youngster,
and their jealousy intensified when their father
gave Joseph a luxurious, long robe with sleeves
instead of a short, sleeveless tunic such as they
wore. Moreover, Joseph's sometimes arrogant
behavior did nothing to lessen their anger.

Jacob kept a small field of wheat or barley near
the main camp at Hebron. Each year his sons assisted in harvesting the grain, reaping it with
flint-edged scythes, then tying it into bundles, or
sheaves. One day, during the harvest, Joseph began to tell of his dreams.

"Hear this dream which I have dreamed," he
said to his brothers, "we were binding sheaves in
the field, and lo, my sheaf arose and stood upright; and behold, your sheaves gathered round it,
and bowed down to my sheaf."

In those days, people regarded dreams as divine prophecies of future events. The brothers
saw the meaning of the dream clearly enough and
responded angrily.

" 'Are you indeed to reign over us?' " they demanded, and ". . . they hated him yet more for
his dreams and for his words."

Some time later, Jacob's older sons were pas-
turing their father's flocks in Shechem, about
60 miles north of their home. Jacob sent Joseph to

*By the time Joseph reached Egypt as a slave, 14 centuries had
elapsed since the First Dynasty, and the majestic pyramids
at Gizeh (right) had been standing for over 700 years. Medieval
pilgrims to the Holy Land called the pyramids "Joseph's barns,"
believing them to be the granaries the Patriarch had erected.*

find out how they were. Taking a few days' supply of bread with him, the youth headed north through the highlands around Hebron.

Sold into Slavery

When Joseph finally arrived at the Plain of Shechem, he looked for his brothers there until a man told him, "They have gone away, for I heard them say, 'Let us go to Dothan.'"

Joseph wearily headed another 20 miles northward until he reached the large plain where Dothan was located. Through this plain ran one branch of the main intercontinental highway, connecting Asia Minor and Mesopotamia with Egypt. Several wells and cisterns—bottle-shaped pits—had been dug in the area to provide water for the many travelers who passed that way.

When Joseph was still at a distance, his brothers recognized him by his long robe. The sight angered them. Said one: "Here comes this dreamer. Come now, let us kill him and throw him into one of the pits; then we shall say that a wild beast has devoured him . . ."

Only Reuben argued against killing Joseph. He had seen, among the wells, one nearby that had dried up. "Let us not take his life," he said to his brothers. "Shed no blood; cast him into this pit . . . but lay no hand upon him."

The brothers did what Reuben had suggested. Instead of killing Joseph, they seized him, stripped off his robe and cast him into the pit. Then, apparently satisfied with what they had done, they sat down to eat their bread and cheese. In the pit beneath them, Joseph contemplated the slow death that almost certainly awaited him.

Far in the distance, a caravan was approaching Dothan from the east. When it came closer to them, Joseph's brothers looked up and saw a line of nearly 100 donkeys bearing loads of gum, fra-

An Egyptian nobleman and his wife inspect the workrooms of their estate. An overseer (pointing) accompanies them just as Joseph might have, as Potiphar's steward. In the beer-making process, at left, barley dough is shaped into loaves, which are placed over low heat. After the loaves rise, they are mashed underfoot in water and strained through baskets. The yeasty liquid ferments in jars sealed with Nile mud. At the right, workers crack grain in a mortar and grind the kernels in a mill, supplying flour for the brewery and the preparation of bread for eating, far right.

grant balms and rare spices. The caravaneers were Ishmaelites from Gilead, distantly related to the Hebrews through Abraham's oldest son, Ishmael. They were headed for Egypt.

As the caravan drew near, a thought crossed Judah's mind: he remembered that occasionally the Egyptians bought slaves from Asiatic traders.

"What profit is it," he asked his brothers, "if we slay our brother and conceal his blood? Come, let us sell him to the Ishmaelites . . ."

Judah's argument seemed reasonable enough, and the brothers agreed. They lifted Joseph out of the pit and sold him to the traders for 20 shekels of silver in the form of ingots.

The transaction was time-consuming, for a shekel was not then a simple coin that could be counted quickly, but a unit of weight. The brothers watched the Ishmaelites very carefully as the silver ingots were measured against the bronze and stone weights the traders carried with them.

"And Joseph's brothers came, and bowed themselves before him with their faces to the ground" (Gen. 42.6). This gesture of homage was commonly used in the nations of the Near East in Patriarchal times. In the stone carving above, two Egyptian courtiers make their obeisances to a Pharaoh or some other powerful royal figure.

Egyptian priests often used magic in their religious ceremonies. A stone statue of the falcon sky-god Horus (above) has a hole drilled in it from base to a movable beak as indicated in drawing. This passage may have contained cords that enabled the priests to manipulate the beak while the "god" was delivering a message.

Satisfied with the bargain—for 20 shekels of silver could buy 10 good rams for the flock—the brothers carried out the rest of their scheme: they slaughtered a goat, dipped Joseph's robe in the blood and brought the robe to their father in his camp at Hebron.

Recognizing Joseph's robe, Jacob was grief-stricken. He went into mourning for many days longer than the customary seven, for the death of his favorite son had killed the joy in his life.

Joseph, however, was very much alive. At that moment he was traveling with the Ishmaelite traders across the barren northern coast of the Sinai Peninsula toward Egypt.

The caravan was stopped at one of the forts guarding the Egyptian frontier: travelers to Egypt were inspected and questioned until the border guards were satisfied that they were peaceful. Joseph was impressed by the guards' weapons,

their strong bows made from wood and horn, their body armor and especially by their light-weight, mobile chariots. These formidable vehicles had been brought to Egypt only a few years before, when the Hyksos, a Semitic people, had conquered the country.

An Egyptian Estate

The Ishmaelites then traveled north to the delta city of Avaris, the Hyksos capital. From within this stronghold, the Hyksos Pharaoh ruled his country. His personal guard was stationed there as well, and it was the captain of the guard, Potiphar, who bought Joseph from the Ishmaelite traders and took him to his estate inside the city.

Never before had Joseph seen such a large and magnificent home. It was surrounded by a wall to guarantee safety and privacy for the household. Just inside the main entrance stood a small temple and, beyond that, formal gardens and an artificial pond. In the middle of the grounds was the main house, a large square building of thick mud-brick with small windows near the ceilings for ventilation and light. The ground floor contained storerooms and the servants' quarters. On the second floor were the main entrance (reached by a flight of stairs), a central hall, a dining room and the bedrooms. Potiphar's family lived here and on the roof garden above. The furniture—tables, chairs and beds—must have seemed strange to Joseph, who had sat and slept on simple mats and goatskins all his life.

Behind the main house was a group of one-story sheds containing the slaughterhouse, stables, bakery and brewery, grain silos, kitchen and slaves' quarters. There, too, was the service entrance where tradesmen delivered whatever fresh vegetables and dairy products the estate could not produce itself.

Joseph probably began his service to Potiphar in this section of the estate. He may have worked in the bakery, kneading dough and shaping it into loaves, some of which were baked. Other loaves were sent to the brewery, where they were mashed and mixed with water, then allowed to ferment into a bitter beer in large stone crocks. Perhaps he worked in the slaughterhouse, butchering cattle. At any rate, Potiphar quickly spotted Joseph's honesty and efficiency and gave him more responsible duties, eventually promoting him to overseer of the entire estate. But Joseph's comparatively happy situation soon came to an abrupt and dramatic end.

"Now Joseph was handsome and good-looking. And after a time his master's wife cast her eyes upon Joseph, and said, 'Lie with me.'" Joseph refused, but Potiphar's wife persisted. One time she caught hold of Joseph's white linen loincloth and pulled it from him. Joseph hurriedly ran from the house, his garment still in his mistress's hands. Furious, she summoned the men of the household and said that Joseph had tried to seduce her. As proof, she showed her husband the loincloth Joseph had left behind. Potiphar was enraged and had Joseph thrown into jail.

Interpreter of Dreams

Despite his situation, Joseph's faith and spirit were not dampened, and even in prison his talent for organization was quickly recognized. In a short time, the warden put him in charge of his fellow prisoners. Some time later, two of those prisoners had disturbing dreams. The Egyptians, too, took dreams seriously and believed they were communications from the gods. The average man often had to consult a professional interpreter to have his dreams explained. Prisoners could not do so. When Joseph saw their distress, he recalled the prophetic dreams of his youth, and he said, "Tell them to me, I pray you."

One of the prisoners had been the Pharaoh's chief butler; the other, his chief baker. When Joseph heard their dreams, he predicted that in three days the butler would be restored to his office, but the baker would be hanged.

Joseph's reading of the dreams proved to be accurate. Three days later his predictions came true. The butler had promised to tell the Pharaoh about Joseph's ability to interpret dreams, but once out of prison he forgot his promise.

One night about two years later the Pharaoh himself was troubled by two dreams. He summoned the court magicians, royal priests who had been trained in the interpretation of dreams, and asked them for an explanation. When they failed to explain the meaning of the dreams, he called on other magicians in Egypt, but they failed, too. Finally, the Pharaoh's butler remembered Joseph and told his master how accurately the Hebrew had interpreted his and the baker's dreams. Joseph was immediately summoned to the royal palace, where the ruler told him of his dreams:

". . . I was standing on the banks of the Nile," he said, "and seven cows, fat and sleek, came up out of the Nile and fed in the reed grass; and seven other cows came up after them, poor and very gaunt and thin . . . And the thin and gaunt cows ate up the first seven fat cows, but when they had eaten them . . . they were still as gaunt as at the beginning."

Cosmetics Became a Fine Art in Egypt

The Egyptian noblewoman used a wide assortment of sophisticated beauty aids to create a "look" that was popular for centuries. She probably began a session at her dressing table by

trimming eyebrows and hairline with a razor. She darkened her eyes with shadow, then accentuated their almond shape with a black substance, such as kohl, applied with a small stick dipped into a jar like the one at right. Rouge and lip coloring also made a contribution. Potiphar's alluring wife probably possessed all these means of enhancement.

The second dream had a similar tone, but it concerned ears of grain rather than cattle. Both dreams, Joseph explained, had the same meaning: there would be seven years of plenty in Egypt, followed by seven years of famine.

He advised the Pharaoh to "select a man discreet and wise, and set him over the land of Egypt," and to "take the fifth part of the produce of the land of Egypt during the seven plenteous years. . . . That food shall be a reserve . . . against the seven years of famine . . . ."

The Pharaoh was so impressed by Joseph's advice that he asked him to be the vizier, or prime minister, of all Egypt. So that everyone would recognize Joseph's authority, the Pharaoh had him dress in a fine white linen gown and wear a ceremonial gold necklace and a signet ring bearing the Pharaoh's official seal. When Joseph had to travel, he rode in his own splendid chariot. The Pharaoh also gave Joseph a wife—Asenath. She later bore two sons, Manasseh and Ephraim.

Joseph was suddenly a man of high position, related by marriage to the nobility. Indeed, at the age of 30 he had become the second most powerful person in Egypt.

Grain for the Hungry

As he had foreseen, Egypt enjoyed seven years of plenty, when the Nile overflowed its banks and irrigated the land and food grew abundantly. Meanwhile, to prepare for the predicted famine, Joseph sent overseers throughout the country to collect a fifth of the produce of every farmer. Huge granaries were built in every major town to hold this contribution. The reserve built up was so great that Joseph "ceased to measure it, for it could not be measured."

Then, after seven years of plenty the Nile suddenly failed to overflow, and Egypt was devastated by famine. Everyone came to the Pharaoh to buy the grain essential to survival. At first they used money, but when that ran out, they were forced to trade their cattle, the principal source of meat. Eventually there were no more cattle to trade, so the Egyptians began to exchange their land for grain. (Only the priests were given free supplies and allowed to keep their lands.)

Each man was allowed to live on his former property, but he had to agree to give one-fifth of whatever he produced in the future to the Pharaoh. By the end of the famine, Joseph had obtained nearly all the land in Egypt for his master.

The famine affected neighboring countries as well. In Hebron, Jacob heard there was food in Egypt, and sent all of his sons but Benjamin there to buy grain. He did not know, of course, that it was Joseph who controlled the distribution.

The 10 brothers set out for Egypt. With them were their donkeys, carrying empty sacks to hold the grain they hoped to receive. On their arrival in Egypt, they were sent to the Pharaoh's vizier, who was directing the grain distribution.

Finally, it was their turn to plead to the vizier for grain. Joseph recognized his brothers at once and he also saw that Benjamin was not with them. His brothers, on the other hand, failed to recognize the lad they had sold into slavery. Joseph had been only 17 years old then. Now he was close to 40. As the dream of Joseph's youth had foretold, the brothers bowed down before him.

Joseph wondered what had become of his father and why Benjamin had not come with his brothers. Yet he did not ask them and kept his identity secret. Instead, he spoke harshly. "You are spies," he said, "you have come to see the weakness of the land."

"No, my lord," they protested, "but to buy food have your servants come. We . . . are twelve brothers, the sons of one man in the land of Canaan; and behold, the youngest is this day with our father, and one is no more."

Joseph was glad to hear that his father and Benjamin were well but, remembering his brothers' cruel trickery at Dothan, he again accused them of being spies and put them all in jail.

After three days, he softened a bit: ". . . let one of your brothers remain confined in your prison," he offered, "and let the rest go and carry grain for . . . your households, and bring your youngest brother to me . . . ."

Leaving Simeon behind, the brothers returned to Hebron, their sacks filled with grain. They told Jacob everything that had happened, but the Patriarch refused to allow Benjamin out of his sight. "My son shall not go down with you, for his brother is dead, and he only [of Rachel's sons] is left."

But the famine in Canaan persisted, and the

". . . all the earth came to Egypt to Joseph to buy grain" (Gen. 41.57). A Hebrew caravan loads up for its return to Canaan after purchasing a shipment of grain. As Joseph predicted, Egypt produced a surplus of grain for seven years, as symbolized by the "plump and full" stalks in the Egyptian bas-relief at left. This surplus was stored in circular granaries (background above) against the seven years of shortage which Joseph also foretold. After a grain purchase was negotiated, the pack animals were loaded at the granaries, then paraded past an Egyptian official whose scribes tallied up the transaction.

grain that the brothers had brought back was soon gone. At last Jacob reluctantly agreed to let his sons return to Egypt with Benjamin.

Joseph was deeply moved when he saw the boy with his brothers. He turned to his steward and commanded, "Bring the men into the house, and slaughter an animal and make ready, for the men are to dine with me at noon." Joseph freed Simeon, who had been held hostage all this time, and then invited all the brothers to have dinner with him in his palace.

Raising Water From the Nile

Centuries of cultivation taught the Egyptians how to direct precious water from the Nile into irrigation canals on levels above that of the river. Here a peasant of Joseph's time uses a "shaduf" to raise water and pour it into an irrigation ditch. The long lifting-pole of the shaduf, balanced on a crossbeam, has a stone weight on one end and a rope and bucket on the other. After the bucket is pulled down into the water and allowed to fill, the counterweight raises it up to the canal. The peasant empties it into the ditch and begins the process again.

The brothers washed their feet, as was customary, before entering Joseph's house. There they offered him some presents from their father, and "bowed down to him to the ground."

Joseph began calmly, asking, "Is your father well?. . ." But when he looked at Benjamin, he was overcome with emotion. Hurriedly he left his bewildered guests and found a room where he could weep unseen. "Then he washed his face and came out; and controlling himself he said, 'Let food be served.'"

Joseph, as master of the house, sat apart from them all. His brothers were seated according to age, with a small table for food placed near each of their chairs. When everyone was properly seated, the servants served the meal.

The brothers were impressed by the variety of the foods offered them. Juicy figs, dates and grapes grown on Joseph's estate were carried in on alabaster platters. There were also apples, relatively new to Egypt and strange to the Hebrews. Cucumbers, beans, carrots and lettuce dressed in oil were brought in with the main course, which was beef butchered in Joseph's own slaughterhouse. They were also offered duck, pigeon and quail, which Joseph himself hunted. The meat and other dishes were flavored with onion or garlic and accompanied by loaves of bread. There were no knives or forks—the guests ate with their hands, which they washed in basins of water brought by the servants after each course. Red and white wines, sweetened with honey, and beer were served with the food.

Brothers Reunited

The dinner completed, Joseph uttered confidential orders to his steward: "Fill the men's sacks with food . . . and put each man's money in the mouth of his sack, and put my . . . silver cup . . . in . . . the sack of the youngest."

The silver cup was a sacred divining vessel, then commonly used in Egypt for predicting the future. Water was poured in the cup, then oil, and the future was "divined" by interpreting the suggestive shapes the oil made on the water.

Soon after the brothers had begun their long journey back to Hebron, Joseph called for a steward. "Up, follow after the men," he commanded, "and when you overtake them, say to them, '. . . Why have you stolen my silver cup? . . . You have done wrong in so doing.'"

The servant quickly caught up with the brothers and accused them of taking the cup. The brothers, dismayed by the dramatic turn of events, protested their innocence, but the cup was found in Benjamin's sack, and they were all brought back to Joseph's house. There, Joseph told the terrified brothers: "Only the man in whose hand the cup was found shall be my slave; but as for you, go up in peace to your father."

Judah pleaded with Joseph. "[If] I come to . . . my father," he explained, "and the lad is not with us . . . he will die . . . Now therefore, let [me] . . . remain instead of the lad as a slave to my lord; and let the lad go back with his brothers."

When Judah stopped speaking, Joseph, no longer able to control his emotions, cried, "Make every one go out from me!" Everyone left the room except his brothers. Then, alone with them, he said: "I am your brother, Joseph, whom you sold into Egypt. And now do not be distressed, or angry with yourselves, because you sold me here; for . . . it was not you who sent me here, but God; and he has made me a father to Pharaoh, and lord of all his house and ruler over all the land of Egypt." Then he embraced and kissed his astonished brothers, and they all wept.

Settlers in Goshen

The Pharaoh, hearing of the reunion, was pleased. He summoned Joseph and told him to say to his brothers, ". . . load your beasts and go back to the land of Canaan; and take your father and your households, and come to me, and I will give you the best of the land of Egypt . . . take wagons . . . for your little ones and for your wives, and bring your father, and come."

The brothers set off once again for Canaan. This time they rode in two-wheeled Egyptian carts that were filled with provisions and drawn by pairs of oxen. When they arrived in Hebron they told their amazed father, "Joseph is still alive, and he is ruler over all the land of Egypt."

Jacob, his children and all their children excitedly packed their tents and possessions in the wagons and, with their flocks, made the long trip to Egypt. There Joseph welcomed his aged father with joyful embraces and tears. Then he took Jacob before the Pharaoh. The ruler invited them to live in the land of Goshen, a fertile region in the northeast Nile Delta not far from Avaris. It was an excellent grazing area, well suited to the semi-nomadic life of the Patriarchal families. Jacob blessed the Pharaoh. "Then Joseph settled his father and his brothers, and gave them a possession in the land of Egypt, in the best of the land . . ."

For many years Jacob's family grew and prospered in their new home. When Jacob knew that he would soon die, he called his sons together and

Papermaking Began With Reed Strips

Joseph's scribes kept their grain distribution records on papyrus, the earliest form of paper. It was made from the pith of the papyrus plant, a common Egyptian reed. In the picture above, the man at right is slicing papyrus pith into strips. His partner covers layers of these strips with cloth. Next he will pound the covered pith into a sheet and press it under a heavy stone. The pressed sheet will be polished with a small, smooth stone, then pasted with other sheets to form a continuous scroll.

blessed each one in turn. After his death, Joseph's physicians embalmed the corpse, the Egyptians' customary procedure for preserving the bodies of the dead. Jacob was mourned for 70 days, and then his body was carried to Canaan, where it was buried in the family tomb, the cave in the field at Machpelah near Mamre. After the funeral, the family returned to Egypt.

Joseph lived long enough to see another generation reach adulthood. He had long since forgiven his brothers and continued to provide for them and their families. Near the end of his life, he called his family together and told them: "I am about to die; but God will visit you, and bring you up out of this land to the land which he swore to Abraham, to Isaac, and to Jacob. . . . and you shall carry up my bones from here."

When Joseph died, his body was embalmed as Jacob's had been, but it remained in Egypt, waiting for burial in the Promised Land.

The story of Joseph is told in chapters 37–50 of the Book of Genesis.

Ancient Egypt: House of Bondage

The descendants of Joseph and his kinsmen lived their lives outside the mainstream of Egyptian culture from the time of his death until the Exodus some 300 years later. As long as the Semitic Hyksos dynasties ruled Egypt, the Israelites were permitted to farm their Nile Delta holdings in peace, undisturbed by the bitter power struggles among Egypt's wealthy, aristocratic families. But when the Hyksos were overthrown around 1500 B.C., a purge of foreign elements was begun. Soon the Israelites were reduced to the status of slaves. Egypt reached the peak of her power following the Hyksos' overthrow. The foundation of this era of grandeur and opulence was the exploitation and forced labor of the Israelites and other subjugated minority peoples.

These lifelike wood figures were placed in the tomb of a wealthy Egyptian more than 3000 years ago. They depict a cattle owner inspecting his animals as slaves drive them past his viewing stand. The continuation of life after death was an important element in Egyptian religion; thus those who could afford it furnished their tombs with all the trappings of their life-style—clothing, jewelry, paintings, sculpture, furniture, even real food and drink.

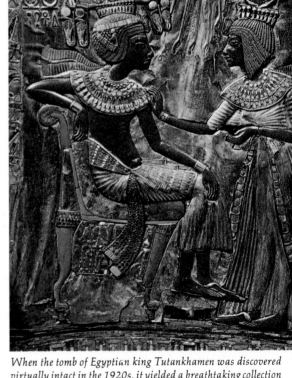

When the tomb of Egyptian king Tutankhamen was discovered virtually intact in the 1920s, it yielded a breathtaking collection of art objects from the 14th century B.C.—just a few years before the Exodus. Above is a panel from Tutankhamen's throne showing the youthful king speaking to his adoring queen.

The exquisitely engraved bronze relief at left shows a pharaoh hunting ostriches from his horse-drawn chariot. This carving once formed the base of a royal feathered fan similar to the one appearing behind the chariot in the scene portrayed.

During the long years of Egyptian prosperity, many aristocratic families acquired sufficient wealth to emulate the Pharaoh's opulent and luxurious style of living. The imposing villa modeled above, for example, based on excavations of an estate at Tell el'Amârna, may resemble the kind of home Joseph worked in as an overseer. A guest passing through the main entrance (A) would come first to a chapel (B) and would next be treated to the sight of an oasislike garden (C) with an artificial pond. He would be given quarters in the main house (D), where the family and principal servants lived, and perhaps be entertained on the roof garden of the main house in the evening. The tradesmen's entrance (E) led to grain silos (F), stables (G), additional servants' quarters (H) and a kitchen (I). A well (J) provided drinking water for the people and animals in the compound.

In times of political stability, Egyptian trading ships ventured far down the Red Sea in search of luxuries that were unavailable along the Nile Valley. The stone relief at left is one of a series that documents an ambitious trade mission to the African kingdom of Punt, an almost legendary land that probably lay at the mouth of the Red Sea in what is now the nation of Somalia. In this panel the Egyptian ship has arrived. Its sails are down and its captain is supervising the unloading of gifts for the rulers of Punt. These will be exchanged for cargoes of ivory, ebony, animal skins and myrrh, an aromatic gum frequently used in Egyptian religious rituals and by embalmers.

Chapter 4

Towering above all the great Old Testament personalities is the commanding figure of Moses, the man chosen by God to lead the escape from Egypt, to hand down the Law, and to shepherd the children of Israel to the gates of the Promised Land.

Moses: The Lord's Prophet

Moses was Israel's greatest spiritual leader. Though raised as an Egyptian prince, he never forgot his Hebrew origins. With the Lord's guidance he led his people out of Egyptian bondage into the wilderness of Sinai. There he forged a zealous nation out of a band of rebel slaves and founded a religion that has flourished for over 3000 years since his death on the border of the Promised Land.

At the time of Moses' birth, about 1350 B.C., the descendants of Joseph and Jacob had lived in Egypt for nearly four centuries. Most of those years had been good ones. The Israelites had lived peacefully, raising their families and tending their flocks in the fertile Nile delta region the Bible calls Goshen. Then, about 1580 B.C., the native Egyptians revolted against their alien rulers, the Semitic Hyksos who had been friendly to Joseph and his descendants. After destroying the Hyksos capital at Avaris, near Goshen, the Egyptians reunited their country under a native Pharaoh, who ruled from Thebes in southern Egypt.

An Oppressed People

Shortly before Moses was born, Egypt's Pharaoh, by now master of a large empire extending over most of Canaan and Syria, decided to move his capital north to the delta region, where he could more effectively control his foreign vassals. There Pharaoh Seti I and his successor, Rameses II—the Pharaoh of the Exodus—launched an ambitious

building program. Using enormous numbers of slave laborers, they set about reconstructing the old Hyksos capital (renamed Raamses) and other delta cities of Egypt.

Slaves, foreign captives and even alien nomads were pressed into gangs and forced to work at hard labor for the Pharaoh. Among them were the Hebrews. "So they made the people of Israel serve with rigor, and made their lives bitter with hard service, in mortar and brick, and in all kinds of work in the field . . ."

From dawn to dusk every day, Moses' father and other slaves labored to make bricks to build huge palaces, granaries, walls, gates and temples for the Pharaoh. It was grueling work under the hot Egyptian sun. Some of the men mixed Nile mud with water, sand and chopped straw. Others trod upon the mixture for long hours, breaking it up occasionally with wooden mattocks. When the muck was thoroughly blended, another group of slaves troweled it into wooden molds. The formed bricks were left to dry under the sun for eight days. The process was repeated day after day, year after year, under the stern eyes of Egyptian overseers, who stood ready to whip or beat any uncooperative slave.

In spite of this hardship, the Israelite popula-

"And he gave to Moses . . . upon Mount Sinai, the two tables of the testimony" (Ex. 31.18). On a barren summit similar to this, Moses stayed 40 days and nights and received the stone tablets of the Law from the Lord. Although the precise location of Mt. Sinai is unknown, tradition places it near the tip of the Sinai Peninsula.

A typical Egyptian building brick of the Exodus period (above) is stamped with the royal seal of Pharaoh Rameses II and has clearly visible pieces of straw embedded in it as a binding material. To make these bricks, slaves first moistened muddy Nile Delta clay with water brought to the building site in large pottery jugs. The clay was then trampled to the proper consistency (below left). Next, it was shaped into bricks in wooden molds (center). When partly dry, the bricks were re- moved from the molds and arranged in stacks (far left) for final drying in the sun. Straw binding was normally supplied by the overseers and was added to the clay as it was being trampled. But after Moses appealed to Rameses II to permit the Israelites to leave Egypt, the Pharaoh increased the burden on the slaves by forcing them to gather their own straw, while turning out the same number of bricks during their day's work.

tion continued to grow. To check their numbers, the Bible says, the Pharaoh ordered that every newborn Hebrew son be thrown into the Nile. Moses was born soon after this decree was pro- claimed, but his mother managed to hide him from the Pharaoh's officials for about three months. Probably realizing that she could not conceal him much longer, she made a plan to save him. She wove a small basket of bulrushes, laid her infant son in it and placed it among the reeds that grew along the Nile. Miriam, the baby's sis- ter, hid in the reeds to see if her brother would be rescued from the river.

"Now the daughter of Pharaoh came down to bathe at the river . . . she saw the basket among the reeds and sent her maid to fetch it. When she opened it she saw the child; and lo, the babe was crying. She took pity on him and said, 'This is one of the Hebrews' children.'"

Miriam, who had witnessed the scene, came forward and offered to find a Hebrew woman to nurse the child. When the Pharaoh's daughter agreed, Miriam arranged for her own mother to raise the baby. So until he was about three years old the baby lived with his parents, sister and older brother, Aaron, in the family's flimsy reed hut at the edge of the city.

As he grew, Moses gradually became aware of the world around him—a world where men, women and children toiled long hours and had little time or energy for frivolity. Each morning the family rose with the sun and put on their rough woolen clothing. Life was governed by the changing seasons, which brought yearly floodwaters to irrigate the fields and nourish the soil. During the four fall months of flooding, Moses' father and brother worked making bricks for the Pharaoh's monuments, but as soon as the water receded they were sent to the fields to sow grain.

At sunrise each winter morning the Hebrew men yoked two long-eared cows to a crude wooden plow and, carrying a basket of bread and a goatskin of water, headed for the muddy, black fields. All day long the family toiled under the scorching sun. Aaron, or sometimes his mother, walked ahead, holding a rope to guide the cows in one hand. With his other hand he sprinkled seeds. Moses' father walked behind, steering the plow with one hand and lashing the cows forward with a whip, burying the seeds under furrowed soil until the entire field was sown.

The planting finished, the men returned to brickmaking until the grain began to ripen. As soon as the first yellow ears appeared, a group of government agents—scribes, surveyors and civil servants—went out to the fields to estimate the size of the harvest and calculate the amount of taxes owed to the treasury. Then the harvest began. From dawn to dusk for several weeks the whole family—the young Moses was strapped to his mother's back—slashed the stalks with sickles and gathered the grain in reed baskets. Behind them followed the poorest peasants, carrying baskets for gleaning any fallen ears and begging for a bit more. The harvested grain was taken to the communal threshing floor to be treaded by oxen, separated first with forks and brooms, then winnowed by tossing in the air.

Education of a Prince

When he was three years old, Moses' life was completely changed: he was returned to the Pharaoh's daughter, as agreed, and she adopted him as her own son. She gave him an Egyptian name, Moses, and raised him as a prince in the Pharaoh's palace. Moses' home was now an enormous brick building adorned with gold, turquoise and lapis lazuli. Surrounded by colorful gardens fragrant with oleander and jasmine, it was shaded by tall palms and sycamore. With the other royal children and their pet dogs, cats, monkeys and geese, Moses spent his childhood frolicking naked in the sunlit palace gardens.

When he was about six years old, Moses was sent to the temple school to be educated. At about the same time, he began to wear the fine white linen loincloth and girdle of an Egyptian nobleman. Each carrying a basket containing a lunch of bread and beer, the young boys jostled one another as they walked to the huge stone temple of the storm god Seth. There, seated crosslegged on the floor, they learned to draw picture symbols on small, lined slabs of thinly cut limestone under the tutelage of a temple scribe. Once they had mastered these hieroglyphic symbols and memorized passages from Egypt's classical writings, they were allowed to copy their lessons on scrolls of papyrus, using reed pens dipped in ink made of carbon soot and gum.

Until Moses reached his late teens, his world was limited to the sheltered confines of the palace and temple. Only as a young man did he begin to appreciate the bustling world around him. Strolling along basalt-paved streets, he admired the colossal granite statues of the Pharaoh, the enor-

mous public buildings, the crouching red sphinxes and tall gold-domed obelisks which adorned Egypt's new capital. The bustle of activity was everywhere: Phoenician sailors unloaded their cargoes of cedar and ivory along the river; Asian traders displayed their spices, perfumes and slaves in the crowded marketplace; Nubian soldiers and guards patrolled the streets and palace grounds; foreign slave gangs labored on ambitious construction projects.

Moses had grown to be a handsome young man. In outward manner and appearance he seemed an Egyptian nobleman. His skin was clean-shaven and scented with expensive oils and perfumes, and he wore the fine white linen tunic and jeweled collar of a royal prince. In the Pharaoh's court he had quickly mastered the noble skills of war, hunting, athletics and leadership. His only shortcoming was an ineloquence of speech, and his features, though commanding, were not those of a highborn Egyptian. Alone and out of place in this privileged world, Moses wondered why he should live in such luxury while his people suffered the misery of slavery.

One day he was passing by a construction site and saw an Egyptian overseer brutally beating an exhausted Hebrew slave with a leather whip. Infuriated by such cruelty, Moses quickly looked around to be sure no one was watching and then beat the Egyptian to death. He buried the body in the sand and hurried away.

Flight to Midian

The next day Moses learned that someone had seen him kill the Egyptian. Frightened of what might happen to him if the Pharaoh found out, he decided to flee from Egypt to take refuge among the mountains at the southern apex of the Sinai Peninsula. There many foreigners could be found, all seeking copper and turquoise in the red sandstone rocks amid a rugged, inhospitable desert area. Here a lone fugitive could quickly lose his Egyptian identity among the various groups of Asiatic slaves working mines for the Egyptians.

For a man who had never been outside the lush delta region of Egypt, the journey across barren Sinai must have been grueling. The hot desert sun burned his skin as he trudged through the parched, lifeless wilderness, spending long days and nights without food or water between the occasional oases. This was a stark and forbidding

Bushes of thorny scrub are one of the few signs of life in the southern Sinai desert. After killing an Egyptian overseer, Moses fled to this region and married into the family of Jethro, a Midianite tribesman whose forebears had been attracted to the area by its copper and turquoise mines. The Lord appeared before Moses in a burning bush while he tended Jethro's flocks, and commanded him to return to Egypt.

land. Steep, rust-colored mountains, rising in jagged cliffs from the flat desert floor, dominated the landscape. An occasional clump of thorny scrub or a lone acacia tree was the only sign of vegetation. The settled routine of Egyptian farming, governed by the certainty of the Nile's yearly floodwaters, was impossible in Sinai. Here rainfall came only in winter in sudden, violent cloudbursts which disappeared at once into the sandy soil. Life was precarious, a constant struggle against a hostile and unpredictable environment.

One day soon after Moses reached his destination, he sat down at a well. He was tired and hungry and wondered how he could survive in this alien land. The schooling he had received in Egypt was useless here. His dilemma was solved when he met a tribe of Midianites.

The Midianite tribes from southern Arabia had learned to survive in this land. Like Moses' own ancestors, the Midianites were seminomads and lived in portable goat-hair tents. They fed their flocks of sheep and goats on thorny desert plants and dug their wells in porous limestone rocks beneath the brittle soil. Some of their livelihood also came from copper ore, which they hammered into utensils and weapons and traded for grain or other goods.

As he sat at the well, seven young girls, the daughters of Jethro, a Midianite priest, came up to the well with their father's sheep. The girls drew water from the well in goatskin bags and emptied it into nearby troughs where the sheep could drink. Before they had finished watering the animals, a band of shepherds appeared and drove the girls' flock away from the well. Moses quickly leaped up and chased away the shepherds. Then he helped the girls gather their sheep together and finish watering them.

A Voice in the Wilderness

When the girls returned home, they told their father what Moses had done. Jethro, with true nomadic hospitality, asked, "And where is he? Why have you left the man? Call him, that he may eat bread." Moses willingly accepted the priest's invitation and soon afterward he agreed to live with Jethro and his family. In time, Moses married Jethro's daughter Zipporah, and she bore him two sons, Gershom and Eliezer.

Moses lived with the Midianites for several years. Jethro taught him how to care for the flocks

"The heart of Pharaoh was hardened, and he did not let the people of Israel go" (Ex. 9.35). Moses had to plead for his people's freedom before Rameses II, the forbidding monarch portrayed above. The most powerful person in the world, Rameses II was a renowned warrior who ruled Egypt as both a god and a hereditary emperor.

and sent him on journeys to find pastureland. He soon learned to survive in his new surroundings, to find water and food in unlikely places, valuable knowledge that would save his life, and his people's, more than once in future years.

Then, on one journey, Moses came to Mount Horeb. "And the angel of the Lord appeared to him in a flame of fire out of the midst of a bush; and he looked, and lo, the bush was burning, yet it was not consumed. And . . . God called to him out of the bush, 'Moses, Moses! . . . I am the God of your father, the God of Abraham, the God of Isaac, and the God of Jacob.' And Moses hid his face, for he was afraid to look at God.

"Then the Lord said, 'I have seen the affliction of my people who are in Egypt . . . and I have come down to deliver them out of the hand of the Egyptians, and to bring them up out of that land to a good and broad land, a land flowing with milk and honey . . . Come, I will send you to Pharaoh that you may bring forth my people, the

sons of Israel, out of Egypt.' But Moses said to God, 'Who am I that I should go to Pharaoh, and bring the sons of Israel out of Egypt?' He said, 'But I will be with you . . . I know that the king of Egypt will not let you go unless compelled by a mighty hand. So I will stretch out my hand and smite Egypt with all the wonders which I will do in it; after that he will let you go.' "

Moses doubted his ability to fulfill the Lord's wishes. " 'Oh, my Lord, I am not eloquent . . . I am slow of speech and of tongue. . . . send, I pray, some other person.' Then the anger of the Lord was kindled against Moses and he said, 'Is there not Aaron, your brother, the Levite? . . . he is coming out to meet you . . . He shall speak for you to the people; and he shall be a mouth for you, and you shall be to him as God.' "

The Ten Plagues

Moses was electrified by his vision of the Lord and filled with zeal for his new mission. He quickly rounded up his sheep and goats and hurried back to Jethro and explained that he must return to Egypt at once. With Jethro's blessing,

Moses and his family departed for Egypt. On the way they met Aaron—as the Lord had promised—and together they journeyed back to the delta.

They went first to the elders of the Hebrew community in Goshen. Aaron told them the Lord had promised that Moses would lead the Hebrews out of Egypt to a land of milk and honey. "And the people believed; and when they heard that the Lord had . . . seen their affliction, they bowed their heads and worshiped."

Soon afterward, Moses and Aaron petitioned for an audience with the Pharaoh, and their request was granted. At the appointed time a servant ushered the two men into the royal audience hall, a long, high-ceilinged room lined with thick granite columns and painted with vivid scenes of Egypt's military victories. Slowly they approached the Pharaoh, who was enthroned at the far end of the room on a raised platform. When they were a few feet away, the Pharaoh indicated with a slight movement of his hand that they had come close enough.

For a moment the two men gazed in wonder at the figure before them. Less than 10 feet away sat the world's most powerful monarch, a tall, hand-

"Stretch out your hand over the sea, that the water may come back upon the Egyptians, upon their chariots, and upon their horsemen" (Ex. 14.26). A group of fugitive slaves (background above, far right) makes its escape as the heavy war chariots of the Egyptians are mired in a swamp and trapped as the water rises. Biblical translations made many years ago gave the impression that the Israelites escaped their Egyptian pursuers when the water of the Red Sea parted. More recent research shows that they probably crossed the "Reed Sea," which was located in the swamps (right) that now border the Suez Canal just north of the Bitter Lakes.

some man clothed in sheer white linen and wearing the high red and white crown of Egypt. A heavy jeweled collar hung around his neck, and his arms and fingers were wrapped in brilliant bracelets and rings. Golden slippers adorned his feet. In his right hand he held an inlaid gold shepherd's crook, symbol of his great authority. Sardinian bodyguards, Arabian handmaidens with long, feathered fans, priests and court officials clustered around his gilded throne. At his feet lay a royal pet, a male lion.

Aaron and Moses bowed low before the Pharaoh. Then Aaron, speaking for Moses, quickly explained their mission. "Thus says the Lord, the God of Israel, 'Let my people go, that they may hold a feast to me in the wilderness.'" The Pharaoh, who had expected to receive gifts and praise, was insulted by the men's audacity. "Who is the Lord, that I should heed his voice and let Israel

go?" he asked. "I do not know the Lord, and moreover I will not let Israel go."

Instead, after he had dismissed Moses and Aaron, he commanded his overseers to increase the burden of the Hebrew slaves. "You shall no longer give the people straw to make bricks . . . let them go and gather straw for themselves. But the number of bricks which they made heretofore . . . you shall by no means lessen . . ." In effect, the Hebrews' work was almost doubled by the Pharaoh's harsh order, for they could not make strong bricks without straw.

Moses felt responsible for the new hardships inflicted on his people. In anguish, he cried out to the Lord, "O Lord, why hast thou done evil to this people? Why didst thou ever send me? For since I came to Pharaoh to speak in thy name, he has done evil to this people, and thou hast not delivered thy people at all." But the Lord reassured him, ". . . I will bring you out from under the burdens of the Egyptians . . . Go in, tell Pharaoh . . . to let the people of Israel go out of his land."

Once again Moses and Aaron visited the palace and made their request to the Pharaoh. This time the Pharaoh demanded that the men perform feats of magic to demonstrate the power of their God. Magic, at that time, played an extremely important part in Egyptian daily life. The Egyptians believed that illness, accidents, bad omens and enemies could be controlled by means of magical charms and incantations. The Pharaoh required a large number of magicians to protect him from disease and other evils. Each magician carried a staff with an image of the head of a serpent as a symbol of his powerful office.

In answer to the Pharaoh's demand, Aaron threw down the shepherd's staff he carried, "and it became a serpent. Then Pharaoh summoned the wise men and the sorcerers; and they also . . . did the same by their secret arts. For every man cast down his rod, and they became serpents. But Aaron's rod swallowed up their rods."

The Pharaoh was still not convinced of the power of the Hebrew God. Only after Moses had demonstrated the Lord's power, by bringing down 10 destructive plagues on the Egyptians, did the Pharaoh finally agree to let the Israelites leave his country. First the waters of the Nile turned blood-red. Then the land was overrun by frogs. The other plagues followed in swift succession: swarms of gnats and flies; a severe cattle blight; skin boils; hail and thunderstorms; clouds of locusts; and thick darkness. But each of these plagues had occurred naturally in Egypt from time to time, and the Pharaoh refused to believe they had been caused by a supernatural power. Then God sent down his final plague, which killed the eldest son in every Egyptian family.

To protect the Hebrew children from this last plague, God had told Moses to order the Israelites to prepare a special meal. Each family was to kill an unblemished year-old male lamb in the evening and roast and eat it that same night with unleavened bread and bitter herbs. Then the head of each household was to daub the doorposts of his house with a bunch of hyssop that had been dipped in the lamb's blood. When the Lord came to a house so marked, he would "pass over," leaving its occupants unharmed.

When the plague struck, death came to every house in Egypt, even the Pharaoh's. Only the sons of the Hebrews were spared. Finally convinced of the power of the Israelite God, the Pharaoh summoned Moses and Aaron and begged them, "Rise up, go forth from among my people, both you and the people of Israel . . . Take your flocks and your herds . . . and be gone . . ."

In great haste, Moses and his people gathered up their belongings and began their flight from Egypt to Canaan, the Promised Land. Many of the Hebrew families chose to follow Moses, but some preferred to remain behind in Egypt, where at least they knew what the future held. A number of non-Hebrew slaves and malcontents, hoping to escape from their miserable way of life, also joined Moses and his followers. They formed an awkward, unwieldy caravan: several thousand

"Every male among you shall be circumcised . . . it shall be a sign of the covenant between me and you" (Gen. 17.10-11). For the Israelites, circumcision, shown here on a stone bas-relief from an Egyptian tomb, came to represent their covenant with the Lord. It was an ancient rite practiced by many other Near East peoples.

men, women and children on foot, herding their flocks of sheep and goats, their tents, pottery, mats and utensils strapped to the backs of donkeys. Progress was slow because the motley caravan could cover only five or six miles a day.

Escape to Sinai

After several days the caravan reached Baalzephon, on the shores of the Reed Sea, a marshy, often flooded area near the Sinai border. By that time the Pharaoh had decided to pursue the Israelites. Breaking his promise, he sent a contingent of charioteers to capture them.

When the Israelites caught sight of the fast-approaching Egyptian chariots, they panicked. Their forward path of flight was blocked by the shallow, muddy waters of the Reed Sea, and the Egyptians were closing in fast on their rear. Moses alone remained calm. "Fear not, stand firm, and see the salvation of the Lord," he cried out to his people, "for the Egyptians whom you see today, you shall never see again."

Then, at God's command, "Moses stretched out his hand over the sea; and the Lord drove the sea back by a strong east wind . . . and made the sea dry land, and the waters were divided. And the people of Israel went into the midst of the sea on dry ground, the waters being a wall to them on their right hand and on their left. The Egyptians pursued, and went in after them into the midst of the sea, all Pharaoh's horses, his chariots, and his horsemen. . . . and the Lord routed the Egyptians in the midst of the sea. The waters returned and covered . . . all the host of Pharaoh . . ."

Safely on the other side, Moses' sister, Miriam, led the Israelites in a song of victory:

"I will sing to the Lord, for he has
    triumphed gloriously;
    the horse and his rider he has
    thrown into the sea."

For the moment, the Israelites rejoiced at their good fortune. At last they were free from bondage, but many arduous trials lay ahead.

Survival in the Desert

From the Reed Sea, Moses led his followers southward into Sinai's Wilderness of Shur, a barren, waterless desert. About the only plants able to survive in that harsh climate were an occasional tamarisk tree or acacia bush. For days the caravan trudged through the seemingly endless, parched expanses. Each night they shivered in their goathair tents, for the scorching heat of the day disappeared with the setting sun, and the temperature dropped greatly.

After three waterless days the Israelites reached the oasis of Marah. Finding the water there bitter and undrinkable, they complained to Moses. "What shall we drink?" they cried. Moses quickly remedied the situation. He took a small tamarisk tree, threw it into the water, and the water became sweet. The Israelites and their flocks drank their fill of the cool water and filled their goatskin bags with it. Then they continued their journey southward until they reached the oasis of Elim, where they wearily pitched their tents and rested for several weeks before continuing their journey.

Refreshed by their stay at Elim, the caravan set out across the vast Wilderness of Sin toward the Sinai mountains and Mount Horeb, where Moses had talked with God and where he would return to make a covenant. But after several days the people began to complain of hunger. Remembering the plentiful vegetables and meats they had enjoyed in Egypt, they groaned, "Would that we had died . . . in the land of Egypt, when we sat by the fleshpots and ate bread to the full; for you have brought us out into this wilderness to kill this whole assembly with hunger."

Attack of the Amalekites

Enraged by the grumblings of the Israelites, Moses called them together and angrily chastised them for their lack of faith in God. "At evening," he shouted, "you shall know that it was the Lord who brought you out of the land of Egypt, and in the morning you shall see the glory of the Lord, because he has heard your murmurings . . ."

As Moses had promised, the Lord demonstrated his great power by providing food for his hungry people. ". . . and in the morning dew lay round about the camp. And when the dew had gone up, there was on the face of the wilderness a fine, flake-like thing, fine as hoarfrost on the ground. . . . Israel called its name manna; it was like coriander seed, white, and the taste of it was like wafers made with honey."

Their hunger satisfied and their faith in the Lord restored—at least for the time being—the Israelites continued their journey across the Wil-

"And he received the gold . . . and made a molten calf"
(Ex. 32.4). The golden idol that Aaron made while Moses was
on Mount Sinai likely resembled this bronze bull which was
found in excavations of a Phoenician temple at Byblos. The bull
was associated with worship of the Canaanite gods Baal and El.

named Joshua to lead them into battle. He himself, accompanied by Aaron and a man named Hur, climbed a nearby hill to watch the progress of his novice army. Miraculously, the Israelites won the battle. "Whenever Moses held up his hand, Israel prevailed; and whenever he lowered his hand, Amalek prevailed. But Moses' hands grew weary; so they [Aaron and Hur] took a stone and put it under him, and he sat upon it, and Aaron and Hur held up his hands, one on one side, and the other on the other side . . . And Joshua mowed down Amalek and his people with the edge of the sword."

That night there was great rejoicing in the Israelite camp, and Moses built an altar of rough stone and sacrificed a lamb upon it in honor of the Lord. Not long thereafter the caravan finally reached Mount Horeb, also called Mount Sinai. The Israelites pitched their tents on a narrow plain at the foot of the tall granite mountain.

The Tablets of the Law

"On the morning of the third day there were thunders and lightnings, and a thick cloud upon the mountain, and a very loud trumpet blast, so that all the people who were in the camp trembled. Then Moses brought the people out of the camp to meet God; and they took their stand at the foot of the mountain. And Mount Sinai was wrapped in smoke, because the Lord descended upon it in fire . . . And as the sound of the trumpet grew louder and louder, Moses spoke, and God answered him in thunder. And the Lord came down upon Mount Sinai, to the top of the mountain; and the Lord called Moses to the top of the mountain, and Moses went up."

There on the top of Mount Sinai, the Lord spoke in thunder to Moses: "I am the Lord your God, who brought you out of the land of Egypt, out of the house of bondage. You shall have no other gods before me."

Moses listened in awe as the Lord revealed to him all the commandments and laws which were the conditions of his covenant with Israel. Then Moses came down from the mountain and told his people all he had heard. When he had finished, "all the people answered with one voice, and said, 'All the words which the Lord has spoken we will do.'"

The next morning Moses built an altar at the foot of the mountain. The altar was encircled by

derness of Sin. But now another problem presented itself. A band of Amalekites—fierce, seminomadic traders from northeastern Sinai —met the Israelites at Rephidim and attacked them. Most likely, the Amalekites wanted to prevent the Israelites from occupying territory along their trade routes between Egypt and Arabia.

The Israelites had never before been tested in battle, and they were poorly equipped. The men carried mostly simple weapons used by shepherds to protect their flocks—slings, staffs, crude spears and simple bows and arrows. The Amalekites, on the other hand, had bronze-tipped arrows, spears and swords.

Moses quickly rounded up a band of his most able-bodied men, equipped them with every available weapon and chose a zealous young man

12 pillars, one for each son of Jacob, whose descendants formed the 12 tribes of Israel. "And he sent young men of the people of Israel, who offered burnt offerings and sacrificed peace offerings of oxen to the Lord. And Moses took half of the blood and put it in basins, and half of the blood he threw against the altar." Then he read the Lord's commandments, and the people promised to obey them. "And Moses took the blood and threw it upon the people, and said, 'Behold the blood of the covenant which the Lord has made with you . . .'"

Later that day the Lord again summoned Moses to the top of the mountain, where he said: ". . . I will give you the tables of stone, with the law and the commandment, which I have written for their instruction." Moses obeyed. "And Moses was on the mountain forty days and forty nights," while his people waited below.

The Israelites grew fearful during Moses' absence. They felt they had been abandoned by their God as well. Forgetting the terms of their covenant with the Lord, they appealed to Aaron, "Up, make us gods, who shall go before us; as for this Moses, the man who brought us up out of the land of Egypt, we do not know what has become of him." Aaron, no doubt sharing their anxiety, agreed to make them an idol and fashioned a golden bull. When the people saw the statue, they immediately claimed it as their god. Aaron built an altar and placed the bull-god upon it, and many Israelites made burnt offerings, and sang, drank and danced before the golden bull.

Suddenly, in the midst of the celebration, Moses came down from the mountain carrying the stone tablets on which the Lord had written his commandments. At the sight of his people dancing before a golden idol—in defiance of God's first commandment—Moses grew hot with anger. In his rage he hurled the tablets to the ground, where they shattered. Then he seized the bull, melted it in the fire on the altar Aaron had built, ground the gold into powder, mixed the powder in water and made the Israelites drink it.

The next day Moses called the people together and said, "You have sinned a great sin. And now

The Exodus and the Approach to Canaan

"The Way of the Land of the Philistines" was the best route from Egypt into Canaan, but along it were Egyptian forts. So the Israelites traveled southeast to Mt. Sinai, then northeast to Kadesh-barnea in northeastern Sinai, where they remained for 40 years. After failing in their attempt to penetrate Canaan from the south, they circled back to approach it from the east. The Israelites then detoured to Ezion-geber in the hope of traveling up the "King's Highway." Refused permission to pass through both Edom and Moab, they had to parallel the highway, then swing eastward again and circle around Moab to Mt. Nebo overlooking the Jordan.

I will go up to the Lord; perhaps I can make atonement for your sin." Then he returned to the mountaintop, and he stayed there another forty days. When he returned to his people, "the skin of his face shone because he had been talking with God." With him he brought two new stone tablets bearing the Lord's commandments.

Building the Sanctuary

On the mountain, God had commanded Moses, "Speak to the people of Israel . . . And let them make me a sanctuary, that I may dwell in their midst." And he described to Moses how the sanctuary was to be built.

For many weeks all the Israelites worked to

Weaving Cloth for Tents and Curtains

"The shaft of his spear was like a weaver's beam" (1 Sam. 17.7). Two Israelite women move the "weaver's beam" forward on this large vertical loom as they make fabric for tents and clothing. The beam creates a space between the two sets of warp (vertical) yarn so that a shuttle with the woof (horizontal) yarn can be passed through from side to side. Then the back yarn will be brought forward and the shuttle passed through again from side to side. Finally the woof yarn will be pushed upward and firmly pressed against the other horizontal yarns.

build the movable dwelling place for their Lord. Women wove yards of fine linen and goat hair. Men hammered utensils out of gold, silver and bronze and sawed acacia wood for tent poles. Soon the sanctuary began to take shape. It stood at the center of a courtyard, which was enclosed by a high wall of linen curtains embroidered with purple, blue and red. Before the sanctuary stood the stone altar for sacrifice and a bronze laver where the priests could wash. The sanctuary, or tabernacle, itself was a colorful linen tent, embroidered with cherubim and protected by another tent of goat hair. Inside, the tabernacle was divided by a veil of fine, embroidered linen. In the outer room stood a gold lampstand, a table and an altar for incense. In the inner room stood the ark of the covenant, a small wooden chest decorated with cherubim and containing the Ten Commandments, which symbolized the covenant and the vows the people of Israel had made.

When the sanctuary was completed, Moses sacrificed a lamb and bull on the altar and filled the bronze laver with water. Thereafter, Moses was forbidden to enter the sanctuary because God had chosen Aaron and his descendants to be his sole high priests. Only they, dressed in fine purple linen robes decorated with gold, jewels and semiprecious stones, were allowed to perform the sacred rituals of offering and sacrifice inside the sanctuary.

Miraculous Meals

Now that the Israelites had renewed their covenant with the Lord and had built a sanctuary to him, it was time to leave the sacred mountain and head northward to Canaan. They took down their tents, packed their belongings on the backs of their donkeys, collected their flocks and resumed the trek. They carefully dismantled and packed the sanctuary as well. Then they placed the sacred ark of the covenant on two long poles, which the priests carried at the head of the caravan.

Slowly they made their way northward toward Canaan. Several weeks later they came to the Wilderness of Paran, a forbidding chalk and limestone plateau stretching for about 80 miles along the eastern edge of the Sinai Peninsula. In these bleak surroundings the Israelites soon became restless and discouraged again. Day after day many of the people complained of hunger. "O that we had meat to eat!" they whined, "We remember the fish we ate in Egypt for nothing, the cucumbers, the melons, the leeks, the onions, and the garlic; but now our strength is dried up, and there is nothing at all but this manna . . ."

Exasperated, Moses went off by himself and cried out to God. "Why hast thou dealt ill with

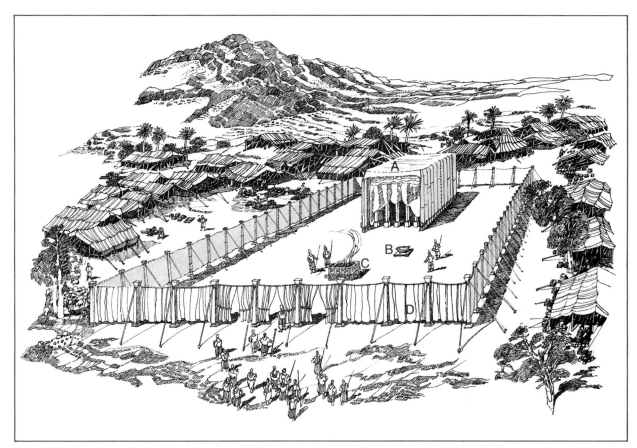

So that the Lord "might dwell in their midst," he gave Moses detailed instructions as to how the Israelites should build him a portable sanctuary. After three months the structure was finished. The heart of the sanctuary was the tabernacle (A) which housed the ark of the covenant, a chest containing the stone tablets of the law. Directly in front of the tabernacle was a bronze laver (B) for priests' ablutions during the ceremonies. Next came the altar (C) for burnt offerings. Linen curtains (D) on poles formed the courtyard.

thy servant?" he asked. "And why have I not found favor in thy sight, that thou dost lay the burden of all this people upon me? . . . I am not able to carry all this people alone, the burden is too heavy for me. If thou wilt deal thus with me, kill me at once, if I find favor in thy sight, that I may not see my wretchedness."

And the Lord said to Moses, "Gather for me seventy men of the elders of Israel . . . and bring them to the tent of meeting . . . and I will take some of the spirit which is upon you and put it upon them; and they shall bear the burden of the people with you, that you may not bear it yourself alone. And say to the people, 'Consecrate yourselves for tomorrow, and you shall eat meat . . . the Lord will give you meat, and you shall eat. You shall not eat one day, or two days, or five days, or ten days, or twenty days, but a whole month, until it comes out at your nostrils and be-

comes loathsome to you, because you have rejected the Lord . . . and have wept before him, saying, 'Why did we come forth out of Egypt?'"

The Lord soon made good his promise: "And there went forth a wind . . . and it brought quails from the sea, and let them fall beside the camp . . . And the people rose all that day, and all night, and all the next day, and gathered the quails . . ." Soon they had had their fill.

Spies in Canaan

At last the caravan reached the edge of the wilderness and stopped to rest at Kadesh-barnea, a large oasis just north of Paran. Here they were almost within sight of the southernmost part of Canaan, so Moses chose 12 spies to gather information about the land, its people and its defenses. One of them was Joshua.

"Go up into the Negeb [southern Canaan] yonder," Moses instructed them, "and go up into the hill country, and see what the land is, and whether the people who dwell in it are strong or weak, whether they are few or many, and whether the land that they dwell in is good or bad, and whether the cities that they dwell in are camps or strongholds, and whether the land is rich or poor, and whether there is wood in it or not. Be of good courage, and bring some of the fruit of the land."

Some weeks later the men returned from their mission laden with grapes, figs and pomegranates. Moses called together all the Israelites to hear the news. "We came to the land to which you sent us," the spies reported, "it flows with

---

Sinai: Land Where the Lord Spoke

"The Lord spoke to Moses in the wilderness of Sinai . . ." (Num. 1.1). Israel's faith and national unity were forged more than 3200 years ago in the searing deserts and windswept mountains of the Sinai Peninsula. A triangular wasteland approximately 23,000 square miles in area, Sinai stretches 150 miles along its Mediterranean seacoast. It is almost 260 miles from the Mediterranean to the southern tip on the Red Sea. There are deserts in the north, limestone and gravel plateaus in the middle and jagged granite mountains in the south, where Moses received the tablets of the Lord. From amidst those peaks, the Israelites made their way north to oases in the wildernesses of Paran and Zin.

"And Moses . . . struck the rock with his rod twice; and water came forth" (Num. 20.11). At arid sites such as Meribah (above), porous limestone rocks trap rainwater beneath their surfaces.

"Pharaoh's Bath" on Red Sea coast is where Bedouin legend places the Israelites' escape from the Egyptians. A sulphurous odor in this region was believed caused by bodies of drowned Egyptians.

milk and honey, and this is its fruit. Yet the people who dwell in the land are strong, and the cities are fortified and very large; and besides, we saw the descendants of Anak [a giant] there."

When they had heard the report, the people were disheartened. "Would that we had died in the land of Egypt!" they moaned. "Or would that we had died in this wilderness! Why does the Lord bring us into this land, to fall by the sword?"

Only Joshua and Caleb, another of the spies, were convinced that Israel had the strength and power to conquer Canaan. "Let us go up at once, and occupy it," they advised. But the other spies were adamant. "We are not able to go up against the people; for they are stronger than we," they insisted. "The land through which we have gone

Waterless stretches of sun-scorched rock and sand dominate the northwest Sinai landscape. Only the hardiest plants and animals can survive in this hostile climate. Rainfall is less than four inches a year. Summer temperatures climb above 100 degrees F.

Lush, palm-fringed oases—rare sights in parched Sinai—provide water for nomads and their flocks, as well as fruit, vegetables and shelter from the sun. Soon after fleeing Egypt, the Israelites pitched their tents at the Elim oasis (above), where the Bible says they found 12 springs of water.

Springing forth from the barren Sinai desert, the acacia—called the "tree of life" by Semitic tribesmen—thrives in the Wilderness of Paran, where the Israelites camped. Moses placed the tablets of the Lord in the ark of the covenant which was made of wood from the acacia tree (right).

... devours its inhabitants; and all the people that we saw in it are men of great stature ... and we seemed to ourselves like grasshoppers, and so we seemed to them."

A mood of anger and resentment swept through the assembly, and the Israelites talked of rebellion. "Let us choose a captain," they cried, "and go back to Egypt."

Joshua and Caleb tried to calm them. "The land, which we passed through to spy it out, is an exceedingly good land," they assured them. "If the Lord delights in us, he will bring us into this land and give it to us, a land which flows with milk and honey. Only, do not rebel against the Lord; and do not fear the people of the land ... the Lord is with us ..."

"Moses sent them to spy out the land of Canaan" (Num. 13.17). From these barren outskirts of Kadesh-barnea, Moses sent his spies into Canaan.

The Gulf of Aqaba comes to a point at the oasis of Elath, which was also known as Ezion-geber. Elath was visited by the Israelites after they crossed Sinai and then again when they headed northward on the last leg of their long journey to Canaan.

Inscribed tablets from an ancient Egyptian temple still stand at the turquoise mines of the Pharaohs which were along the Israelites' route to Mt. Sinai.

But no one seemed to hear their words, and the hostile crowd decided to stone them. Suddenly they stopped as "the glory of the Lord appeared at the tent of meeting to all the people of Israel. And the Lord said to Moses, 'How long will this people despise me? And how long will they not believe in me, in spite of all the signs which I have wrought among them?'"

Moses pleaded for forgiveness, but this time God would not forgive the Israelites so easily. "How long shall this wicked congregation murmur against me?" he asked. "I have heard the murmurings of the people of Israel, which they murmur against me. Say to them, 'As I live,' says the Lord, 'what you have said in my hearing I will do to you: your dead bodies shall fall in this wil-

Before arriving at Mt. Sinai, Moses' successor, Joshua, distinguished himself by defeating the Amalekites in a fierce struggle near Rephidim.

The empty vistas of the Sinai wilderness are relieved now and then by the sight of a magnificent terebinth tree, a species of oak that has adapted to the harsh environment. According to one legend, Jesus was crucified on a cross made of wood from the terebinth.

The Arabah, a trough running between the Dead Sea and the Gulf of Aqaba, is part of the Great Rift Valley, a major geological fault that extends from Asia Minor into Africa. The Israelites were forced to follow the Arabah north from Elath, rather than travel the easier "King's Highway," when they were refused permission to enter the kingdom of Edom. Visible in the background are the mountains of Edom.

derness; and of all your number, numbered from twenty years old and upward, who have murmured against me, not one shall come into the land where I swore I would make you dwell, except Caleb the son of Jephunneh and Joshua the son of Nun. But your little ones, who you said would become a prey, I will bring in, and they shall know the land which you have despised. But as for you, your dead bodies shall fall in this wilderness. . . . I, the Lord, have spoken . . .'"

Punished by the Lord

Thus the Israelites were condemned to wander in the wilderness of Sinai for a generation. The men who had set out from Egypt would never set foot on the Promised Land of Canaan.

The Israelites were stunned by this harsh sentence, and many refused to believe that they would never enter the Promised Land after coming so far. Before long, a few of them formed an armed band and tried to invade Canaan from the south. They marched into southern Canaan and

headed for the central hill country but they were turned back by a combined army of Canaanites and Amalekites. It would be many years before the morale of Israel grew strong enough to invade Canaan successfully.

The time passed. For a generation Moses and his people pitched their tents and pastured their flocks in the area near Kadesh-barnea. One by one the older members of the community died. A new generation of zealous, stouthearted men and women gradually replaced the weak, suspicious, complaining band who had followed Moses out of Egypt. Nurtured from childhood on the Lord's laws and commandments, they eagerly awaited the day when they would at last conquer the beautiful land he had promised them.

But Moses would not lead his people into Canaan. Near the end of the long sojourn at Kadesh-barnea, he had shown that even his faith in the Lord was not firm enough to save him from the fate of his generation. The Israelites had run out of water one day, and Moses had sought the Lord's counsel. ". . . and the Lord said to Moses,

*On a rock outcropping opposite Mt. Nebo, Israelites look down
on their encampment. There, on the Plains of Moab, Israel's
tents surround the courtyard of the tabernacle. West of the mountain, beyond the Jordan River, lies Canaan. For the new generation
of Israelites, this was the last way station before the Promised
Land, but for Moses, their leader, it was where his life would end.*

'Take the rod, and assemble the congregation,
you and Aaron your brother, and tell the rock before their eyes to yield its water; so you shall
bring water out of the rock for them . . .'

"And Moses and Aaron gathered the assembly
together before the rock, and he said to them,
'Hear now, you rebels; shall we bring forth water
for you out of this rock?'" Moses lifted up his
hand and—instead of speaking a command as the
Lord had ordered—struck the rock twice with his
rod; water gushed out and the people and their
cattle drank. But the Lord was affronted and said
to Moses and Aaron, "Because you did not believe in me . . . you shall not bring this assembly into the land which I have given them."

The King's Highway

It must have been a bitter disappointment to
Moses to be punished so severely for his mo-
mentary lapse of faith, but he accepted his fate
without question. Soon afterward, with a heavy
heart, he gathered his people together and began

the final leg of his long journey. He would lead
the Israelites to the edge of Canaan and there take
leave of them forever.

This time, however, the Israelites did not try to
enter Canaan from the south. Instead, they
marched to the Gulf of Aqaba and joined the
King's Highway, an ancient caravan route that lay
to the east of Canaan. They planned to follow the
highway through the kingdoms of Edom and
Moab and then cross the Jordan River and attack
Canaan on its more vulnerable eastern border.

According to the Bible, the people of Moab and
Edom were related to the Israelites. The Moabites
were descendants of Moab, the son of Lot and
grandnephew of Abraham. The Edomites were
descendants of Esau, the hairy brother of Jacob.
For this reason, Moses may have hoped to pass
through the two kingdoms in peace.

If so, he was mistaken. The king of Edom refused to grant Moses permission to travel through
his land. "You shall not pass through," he threatened, "lest I come out with the sword against
you." And he sent a division of soldiers to pre-

Catching Quails With a Weighted Blanket

Exhausted after a long flight over the Mediterranean, migrating quails were easy prey for Israelite hunters who may have caught them by simply trapping them with a weighted blanket. The birds were then preserved for later use by drying

in the sun. These tasty game birds fly south each fall from Europe to Arabia, North Africa and to Egypt especially, where their presence has been noted in artworks, such as the relief at left, for thousands of years. Twice during the Exodus the Israelites feasted on quails. The second time, though, they overate and suffered a severe illness.

vent the Israelites from crossing into his country.

Unwilling to go to war over the matter, Moses led his people up the trough of Arabah, a wide canyon stretching from the Gulf of Aqaba to the Dead Sea along Edom's western border. To the east and west rose the rugged mountains of red granite and porphyry for which Edom, meaning "red" in Hebrew, was named.

Reaching the southern border of Moab, Moses sent to the king for permission to enter his country, but again his request was denied. So the Israelites were forced to bypass Moab, marching instead through the desolate wilderness to the east. Farther east lay the boundless Arabian Desert.

At the northern frontier of Moab, the caravan finally turned westward toward Canaan. But still another obstacle lay in their path. Sihon, the king

of the territory directly north of Moab, also refused to let the Israelites pass through his land and sent an army to stop them. Finally forced into battle at Jahaz, the Israelites defeated Sihon's army and continued their journey westward.

Their path sloped gradually upward, across a limestone plateau. Climbing the high central ridge of the plateau, the caravan caught its first glimpse of the snakelike Jordan River and the land of Canaan beyond. A cry rang out amid the weary band and they raised their voices in praise of the Lord. With heightened spirits, they began their descent to the rolling "Plains of Moab," where they would pitch their tents and begin their final preparations for the assault on Canaan.

Moses could not share wholeheartedly in his people's elation. He knew that his arduous journey had come to an end and that very soon he would die. Sadly, he called his people together and spoke to them for the last time.

The young nation of Israel gathered at the feet of their beloved leader. The man who stood before them was very old. His hair was white, and his face and hands lined with age and care. The long years of wandering, the endless bickering, the disappointments, the burden of responsibility—all had left their imprint. Yet his eyes still flashed with youthful spirit, and his words held force and conviction.

Slowly, he recounted for this new generation the saga of his people's flight from Egypt and their pilgrimage to the mountain of God. Then he repeated all the words God had spoken to him on Mount Sinai and urged them to keep the commandments and the laws. "If you obey the commandments of the Lord your God which I command you this day," he explained, "by loving the Lord your God, by walking in his ways, and by keeping his commandments and his statutes and his ordinances, then you shall live and multiply, and the Lord your God will bless you in the land which you are entering to take possession of it. But if your heart turns away," he warned, "and you will not hear, but are drawn away to worship other gods and serve them, I declare to you this day, that you shall perish . . ."

The prophet paused and took a last look at the attentive young faces looking up toward his. Then he continued. "I am a hundred and twenty years old this day," he told them. "I am no longer able to go out and come in. The Lord has said to me, 'You shall not go over this Jordan.' The Lord your God himself will go over before you . . . so that you shall dispossess them; and Joshua will go over at your head, as the Lord has spoken. . . . And the Lord will give them over to you . . . Be strong and of good courage, do not fear or be in dread of them: for it is the Lord . . . who goes with you; he will not fail you or forsake you."

Death of the Prophet

When Moses had finished speaking, he picked up his shepherd's staff and turned to leave. He walked alone across the plain to the foot of Mount Nebo. Slowly he climbed up the steep rocky mass, higher and higher, until he finally reached the summit.

Looking back, he could see his people camped far below him on the plain. The sun had begun to set, and the evening fires flickered among the tents. His eyes finally came to rest on the sacred tabernacle, which stood in its place of honor at the center of the large square encampment. Smoke was rising in black clouds from the altar, where the priests were sacrificing a lamb.

Reluctantly he turned away and looked westward, out over the far side of the mountain. There in the light of the setting sun lay the land of Ca-naan. Directly below he could see the fertile green valley of the Jordan River and, just beyond, the Canaanite town of Jericho. To the south he saw the waters of the Dead Sea, glimmering red and gold in the sunset, and the purple Judean hills rising steeply westward toward Jerusalem. His eyes followed the winding course of the Jordan northward to the blue waters of Lake Galilee and then looked westward over the rough, rocky hills of central Canaan. This was the land that was soon to belong to the young nation of Israel.

Moses gazed out upon this panorama for a long time, until the last rays of the sun had disappeared. Then he closed his eyes and, with the image of the Promised Land still before him, the great man died. "And there has not arisen a prophet since in Israel like Moses, whom the Lord knew face to face, none like him for all the signs and the wonders which the Lord sent him to do in the land of Egypt, to Pharaoh and to all his servants and to all his land, and for all the mighty power and all the great and terrible deeds which Moses wrought in the sight of all Israel."

The story of Moses is told in the Books of Exodus, Leviticus, Numbers and Deuteronomy.

"The Lord your God is bringing you into a good land . . . a land of wheat and barley, of vines and fig trees . . . of olive trees" (Dt. 8.7–8). Grapes (above left) and olives (right) on Egyptian reliefs represent the "abundance" the Israelites left behind when they escaped from bondage. Not until they crossed the Jordan under Joshua's leadership did they encounter a fruitful land again. But they would enter the Promised Land with a divine warning: "Take heed lest you forget the Lord your God . . . when you have eaten and are full" (Dt. 8.11–12).

Part Two
Conquerors and Settlers

"So Joshua took the whole land, according to all that the Lord had spoken to Moses . . . And the land had rest from war" (Jos. 11.23). The Israelite army that invaded Canaan around 1250 B.C. was primitive compared to its opposition. The Canaanites had large, fortified cities, advanced weapons and swift chariots, while the Israelites had to rely on their lightly armed infantry and the great cunning of Joshua. Surprise attacks were often mounted in the early light of dawn, before enemy chariots could get through the city gates in sufficient numbers to counterattack successfully. A blast from rams' horns would sound the charge, and spearmen, slingmen and archers would then assault the high walls. Despite his great victories, Joshua's conquest was not total. He by-passed some strategic cities and left them for later generations to subjugate.

"Hear, O Israel; you are to pass over the Jordan this day, to go in to dispossess nations greater and mightier than yourselves" (Dt. 9.1). But the Conquest proved difficult, and for over two centuries, Israel's tribes fought to maintain their foothold in the hills of Canaan.

ISRAEL's life as a nation began when Moses led his people from Egypt in the early thirteenth century B.C. From the start, the Israelites saw their great Exodus as the first step in the fulfillment of God's promise that they would be given a land of their own. But before the Israelites could enter the Promised Land they would have to spend 40 arduous years in the wilderness.

For Moses and his followers, those years of struggling to survive in the arid deserts of the Sinai Peninsula were vitally important. During that time the embryonic nation became unified, shaped its society and hardened its determination to establish itself in its own land.

For Canaan and much of the Near East, they were years of fragmentation and deep unrest. Two great empires, the Egyptian and the Hittite, had for centuries controlled Canaan and neighboring Syria. But from 1250 onward the stability of their rule began to crumble under the pressure of land-hungry invaders from the west, east and north. The Hittite Empire finally succumbed and had disappeared by 1200 B.C. The Egyptians fared better, but about 1220 the Pharaoh Merneptah found his empire attacked simultaneously by a Libyan army and a group known as the Sea Peoples, who probably belonged to the same coalition that destroyed the Hittites. Merneptah repelled the invaders, but growing resistance to Egyptian rule in Canaan forced him to mount a campaign there, too.

According to Egyptian records, the campaign was a brilliant success, but the Pharaoh did not live long enough to see its results. Between 1215 and 1200 B.C. a series of four incompetent Pharaohs could not maintain Merneptah's fragile control of the empire. Soon a new wave of invasions by the Sea Peoples—in Canaan and Egypt—all but destroyed Egypt's power. In Canaan there was also unrest that stemmed from the decadent and fragmented nature of its society. The departure of the Egyptians only aggravated this condition.

Canaan was dominated by a network of city-states that derived their wealth from the export of textiles, dyes and other goods. While the ruling classes lived in comparative luxury, most of the population endured virtual slavery and crushing taxes. Alongside these two groups, there existed a sizable class of landless people known as the "'Apiru" (a name related to the word Hebrew). The 'Apiru had been present in Canaan for over a century, and were regarded as outlaws and troublemakers. By the time of Moses, they had settled in and around the city of Shechem, which they used as a base of operations. Some were traveling merchants and peddlers, while others lived a haphazard life in loosely organized bands that roamed about the countryside, occasionally raiding villages for food. This social fragmentation made the land especially vulnerable to the invasion the Israelites were about to mount. The social equality of Mosaic law would have a strong appeal to the dispossessed and discontented people of Canaan. Thus, many non-Hebrews may have joined the forces of the invading Hebrews led by Joshua.

Poised for Conquest

The Israelite warriors who invaded Canaan were tough, dedicated soldiers, united by a zealous belief in the Lord. In the years that followed the Exodus, the Israelites had grown and changed considerably. The original "rabble"—the Bible's own word for those who followed Moses out of Egypt—had been united more by devotion to the leadership of Moses than by blood ties. Moses organized them into the 12 tribes, naming each according to the largest family in its ranks. Many scholars think that this was the origin of Israel's tribal system. As the first generation of the Exodus died off, they were replaced by strong, zealous youths who grew up in the wilderness and longed for a more fertile land of their own. The promise of the Lord was foremost in their minds.

Not only had the Israelites become organized and dedicated, but their numbers had swelled as well with the many offspring born to the original fugitives. On their way the wanderers had also probably been joined by new followers, social outcasts like themselves, who were attracted by Moses' message of faith and hope. The commitment of these newcomers was invaluable to the Israelite cause. Without them Joshua's army could scarcely have survived the early battles in Canaan. What did they find so compelling in the Israelite religion?

They found, in an era when the gods of every nation seemed to care only for the rich and powerful, a God who was the conspicuous champion of the weak. This God had miraculously delivered an oppressed people from slavery and had helped them survive in the desert. He seemed able to control worldly events as he wished.

In return for his favor, the God of Israel demanded absolute fidelity not only to a set of rituals but to a basic system of laws. Stemming from the Mosaic covenant between the Lord and Israel, many of these laws—those dealing with government and land ownership, for example—were specifically designed to promote justice and personal freedom among the Israelites. Such laws were unusual among the religious and social codes of the day. To those who had previously known nothing but oppression and poverty, their appeal was great. The Law could also be harsh, particularly in the matter of religious war. The Conquest was such a war.

The Israelites' first victory west of the Jordan was at Jericho, where "As soon as the people heard the sound of the trumpet, the people raised a great shout, and the wall fell down flat" (Joshua 6.20). The remains at Jericho show that its walls did suffer a sudden, violent destruction, but archaeologists have established that this disaster took place about a hundred years before the Israelite Conquest. Unlike most of the other Conquest stories, the Biblical account of the victory at Jericho is told as a miraculous event. Its significance may be more religious than historical.

In general, though, archaeology seems to have confirmed the Biblical version of Joshua's campaign against the Canaanites. Among the more important finds is an Egyptian inscription of Pharaoh Merneptah's campaign in Canaan in 1220, which lists the name of Israel among the peoples defeated there. This is the earliest mention of Israel outside the Bible, and it confirms that the Israelites were present in Canaan as early as the year 1220 B.C.

Herem—The Holy War

Although the Israelites won many peaceful converts to their cause, the Conquest of Canaan was an undeniably bloody affair, and as such has left some readers of the Bible deeply perturbed. How could the Lord ever condone such brutal slaughters as those described in Joshua?

The answer, an important one in understanding the early Israelites, is that the Conquest was conducted as a *herem*, or holy war. According to the rules and principles of this ancient institution, a holy war was believed to have been proclaimed and led by the Lord himself. His followers were promised victory as long as they obeyed his commands exactly. A cardinal command was that no booty be taken, because the victory belonged to God alone. Since booty included prisoners as well as goods and livestock, no captives were ever taken in a holy war. In practice, this meant that none of the defeated enemy population could be left alive. The war against Canaan was waged solely to gain a home for the Israelites, and the land could be purified only by the extermination of those who had occupied it: "Not because of your righteousness . . . are you going in to possess their land; but because of the wickedness of these nations the Lord your God is driving them out from before you" (Deuteronomy 9.5).

Joshua's military campaign established a firm foothold for Israel in Canaan's central hills, though a few powerful city-states remained. An era of continual strife with surrounding enemies lay ahead, but the new nation would survive. The symbolic culmination of God's promise was the division of the land among the tribes of Israel.

However, since the victory had been God's, so was the land: "The land shall not be sold in perpetuity," God had commanded, "for the land is mine" (Leviticus 25.23). The Bible says the land was distributed among the 12 tribes of Israel by lot, so that God's will could manifest itself in the casting. Actually, the larger tribes (Judah, Manasseh, Ephraim) took the most land, and the smaller tribes were left to claim what they could.

New Settlers in Canaan

After years of a marginal seminomadic life in the desert, the Hebrew tribes now had their own country, limited though it was. Settling onto the land was not an easy task for the newcomers. They were suddenly faced with problems that had never concerned them before, such as building permanent homes and towns, and digging wells. Even the basic skills of farming, long known to the Canaanites, were new to them. The Israelites had to learn how to clear a field, plow, seed and fertilize it, how to terrace a hillside, what crops to plant and when to rotate them. In fact, Israel was the first people to turn the hill country of Canaan into a center of national life. Two inventions in particular made this possible: the lavish use of slaked lime to create water-holding cisterns under almost every home; and the elaborate terracing of hillsides for crops, vines and fruit trees.

All this took time, and in the first years the Israelites had a very meager existence, at least compared with life in the cities of Canaan. Many of them lived in flimsy goatskin huts rather than solid houses like the Canaanites'. Their tools and weapons were also far inferior to those of the Canaanites, and their small, poorly fortified towns and villages were barely able to withstand aggression.

During the early years in Canaan, Israel bore little resemblance to other nations in the Near East, states ruled by powerful monarchs. The 12 tribes formed a loose confederation, each more concerned with its own problems than with those of its neighbors. There was no central government to bind them together—no king, capital city or unified administration. Problems of mutual concern were settled by a council of elders representing the separate tribes. Even the geography of the land weighed against its unification. The northern clans in Galilee were isolated from the others by Canaanite-held territory in the Plain of Esdraelon. The deep Jordan Valley separated the eastern and western tribes, and in the central hills the rugged terrain divided the people into small, self-contained units.

What did usually hold the tribes together was their covenant with God. Shortly after the Conquest, Joshua summoned all the tribes to Shechem for a religious ceremony. After recounting the origin and fulfillment of the Lord's promises, he called upon the people to reaffirm their allegiance to the Lord. "The Lord our God we will serve, and his voice we will obey" (Joshua 24.24).

False Gods

About eight miles southeast of Shechem the Israelites constructed a shrine at Shiloh, and a simple tabernacle to house the ark of the covenant. The ark, a small wooden chest containing the tablets of the law (the Ten Commandments), symbolized God's presence among his people. It was the most sacred object in Israel. The tribes gathered at Shiloh periodically to celebrate the major festivals, renew their commitment to the covenant and discuss matters of mutual concern.

"They smote them with the edge of the sword, and utterly destroyed every person" (Jos. 10.39). *In hand-to-hand combat, Joshua's lightly armed warriors quickly learned to take advantage of enemy troops, who were encumbered with heavy, metal-studded leather shields and suits. The Israelites also lured Canaanite chariots into the hills where they could not maneuver effectively. Weapons during the Conquest were in a transitional state: the dagger above has a handle of bronze and a blade of iron. The double-pronged spear end, at left, was used to stand a spear upright in the ground.*

Even in religious affairs there was no unified authority. Although the central shrine was at Shiloh, there were lesser shrines scattered throughout the tribal territories, and most festivals and religious ceremonies were local ones. Nonetheless, the young nation was unified by its faith in the covenant with the Lord.

Those Israelites whose faith had been tested in the wilderness and rewarded by the Conquest were fiercely committed to the covenant. But later generations, taking their homeland more or less for granted, "did not know the Lord or the work which he had done for Israel" (Judges 2.10). Many of the Israelites now did "what was evil in the sight of the Lord, forgetting the Lord their God, and serving the Baals . . ." (Judges 3.7), of neighboring Canaanite communities.

A fairly large Canaanite population still remained within the tribal lands, and many Israelites intermingled with them. "So the people of Israel dwelt among the Canaanites . . . and they took their daughters to themselves for wives, and their own daughters they gave to their sons; and they served their gods" (Judges 3.5-6). It was a common practice in the ancient world for newcomers to an area to worship the local gods as well as their own, and the Canaanite religion had undeniably attractive features.

Compared with the strict demands of the Mosaic covenant, the Canaanite gods were easy to please. They also seemed more related to the agricultural kind of life that the Israelites were now adopting. Canaan's gods each controlled a part of the nature cycle which brought rain and fertility to the land. The Israelites were inexperienced as farmers and naturally imitated the successful agricultural methods of the Canaanites, including the worship of their gods. Canaan's chief god was El, whose female counterpart was the mother-goddess Asherah, but the most popular deities were "the Lord Baal," god of storms and rain, and the fertility goddess, Astarte. The Canaanite religion was chiefly a fertility cult, whose practices included ritual prostitution (both male and female) and whose large pantheon of gods and goddesses required the support of many priests. Although the Israelites could and did embrace many aspects of Canaanite religion, there were certain practices—particularly the sexual rites—that violated the relatively austere Mosaic code. This contrast was to lead to conflict among the Israelites.

The Judges of Israel

During these formative years, national leadership was provided by a few individuals who came to Israel's aid in times of crisis. These heroes, the Judges, were not born leaders but men believed to be infused with a divine spirit that made them capable of extraordinary deeds. Thus, Ehud found the courage to kill the Moabite king, Eglon, in his own palace, and Gideon the cleverness to rout a Midianite encampment with only a handful of brave men.

Some of the Judges seemed ill-suited for their heroic roles. Jephthah was a bastard and a notorious outlaw, and Samson was a man of murderous rages. Gideon was the son of a farmer and Deborah was a woman. Each became a leader not through birth or popular acclaim, but through enormous physical strength or bold, imaginative leadership, both of which were accepted as spiritual gifts conferred and withdrawn by God according to his will.

The Judges served primarily as military leaders, championing the Israelites against ene-

Drying Flax on a Canaanite Roof

The story of the fall of Jericho tells how two of Joshua's spies escaped notice when a woman of the city "hid them with the stalks of flax which she had laid in order on the roof" (Jos. 2.6). After flax stalks were soaked and their fibers loosened, Canaanite women spread them out on rooftops to dry. Dried fibers were separated by beating and combing, spun into fine yarns and threads and woven into linen fabrics. The roller was for the purpose of packing down the earthen roof after a rain.

mies who sought to drive them from their hard-won homeland. During the twelfth and eleventh centuries B.C., the tribes were attacked by enemies on all sides: by the kingdoms of Ammon, Edom and Moab to the east of the Jordan; by the nomadic Midianites from the Arabian desert; by Canaanite city-states which still remained in power; and by the Philistines along the coast. For the most part, the hasty tribal coalitions summoned by the Judges during emergencies were sufficient to fight off or defeat Israel's enemies. However, one foe—the Philistines—was too

The Pleasures of Sophisticated Canaan

When the Israelites invaded Canaan, they came in contact with a worldly style of life comparable to that of Egypt, though less grand in scale. As the Israelites settled down there, they adopted many features of Canaanite dress, furnishings, custom and language.

Attended by a slave, a wealthy Canaanite couple enjoys a leisurely drink. Their beverage is probably beer, and the long straws are both a convenience and a way of straining out any husks that might remain after brewing. The elaborately carved benches and the decorated vessel from which the couple drink are typical of those used in upper-class Canaanite homes at the time of the Conquest. Within a few decades, similar furniture and pottery could be found in Israelite homes.

An ancient Egyptian carving (left) of a captured Canaanite nobleman shows how these people looked and dressed. He wears a long-sleeved undergarment, over which a decorative fringed cloth is wound around his body to end in a shoulder-length cape.

Beads and a star-shaped golden pendant (right) might have adorned the wife of the nobleman above, along with earrings, metal bracelet and signet ring. The style of gathering the hair into locks and then curling it at the ends seems to have been common to both men and women in this period.

powerful for the Judges. Their constant aggression threatened to destroy Israel entirely, and this great crisis forced the Israelites to abandon the tribal confederation and unite under a powerful central government. This decision changed the course of Israel's history forever.

Not long after the Israelite Conquest the Philistines were settled along the southern coast of

Serenade for a Canaanite Nobleman

This formal scene is derived from an ivory carving that was found at the Canaanite stronghold of Megiddo. The man, to judge from his apparel and the sphinx-chair on which he sits, is a nobleman, possibly a prince. As he drinks from a small bowl, a woman wearing a tiara offers him a lotus blossom and the end of her shawl to use as a napkin. Behind her, another woman plays on a nine-stringed lyre. A performance such as this would be typical of the Canaanites, who, during Biblical times, were celebrated for the superiority of their musicianship.

Canaan as a mercenary elite of the Egyptian Pharaoh. They were a disciplined, energetic people with a long military tradition and a formidable record of victories on land and sea. Though divided into several independent city-states, their rulers frequently joined forces and campaigned with devastating effectiveness. They had also acquired the secret of iron smelting, which gave their weapons and tools a vast superiority over the bronze implements of the Israelites.

Throughout most of the twelfth century the two peoples apparently coexisted with occasional conflict but no major confrontations. (The story of Samson illustrates the friction between the dominant Philistines and the tribe of Dan, whose

territory lay directly east of the Philistines.) Metalworking was monopolized by the Philistines and Israelite farmers were forced to rely on Philistine blacksmiths to repair their bronze plow points and tools.

As their numbers increased, the Philistines gradually began to push northward and eastward, forcing the tribe of Dan to migrate northward and seizing Israelite towns and villages farther inland. By the early eleventh century they posed a threat unlike any that Israel had faced before.

Finally, some time about 1050 B.C., there was a battle that effectively marked the end of Israel's tribal confederation. During an engagement on the edge of the western hills, near Aphek, the ark was brought from Shiloh in the hope of rallying Israel's beleaguered forces. Instead, the Israelites were decimated, the priests from Shiloh were killed and the ark itself was captured by the Philistines. Within a short time the shrine at Shiloh had been destroyed and much of Israel's central territory was occupied.

It was against this background of defeat and demoralization that the imposing figure of Samuel appeared in Israel's history. Remembered as both the last of Israel's Judges and the first of her great Prophets after Moses, Samuel was the bridge between the old tribal league and the monarchy that replaced it.

The continuing Philistine occupation convinced a majority of Israelites that their nation's only chance for survival lay in stronger, more effective leadership. This sentiment was finally voiced by a delegation of tribal elders, who journeyed to Samuel's home and called on the holy man to "appoint for us a king to govern us like all the nations" (1 Samuel 8.5).

Under the circumstances, the request seemed entirely sensible to most Israelites. To Samuel, however, it was little short of blasphemy. In his view the Philistine invasion was not so much a political or military crisis as a moral one. Israel had turned away once again from her sacred covenant with the Lord, and the Philistines were merely the agents of his judgment. What was needed was not a new form of government but repentance and faith. God was Israel's sovereign, the only one she would ever need.

The elders continued to press the issue, however, and Samuel finally gave his reluctant consent, anointing a young Benjaminite tribesman, Saul, as Israel's first king. Samuel expected Saul's rule to be limited: he was to be a kind of elevated Judge. Early in his reign he was referred to not as a "king" (*melek* in Hebrew) but as a military leader (*nagid*). Only later was the royal title applied to him. His domain would be the entire country rather than one area, and he would remain in office for life, not merely until the Philistine crisis was over. However, he would not be governing on his own behalf, like the other Near Eastern kings, but as God's agent. Only in this way, Samuel believed, could the covenant principle of God's sovereignty remain intact.

In practice, this concept of a limited monarchy posed one important dilemma: how would the secular ruler receive God's instructions? In answer, Samuel formalized the role of the Prophet, a wholly new position that was to become a potent force in Israel's history. The true Prophet would literally be a spokesman for the Lord, and his words would be directed at the king as well as

the people of Israel. Samuel, the first to exercise this office, organized the various bands of religious visionaries—known as "sons of the prophets"—into communities who roamed the countryside singing, dancing and prophesying. These sons of the prophets were also zealous patriots who sought to give their fellow Israelites the inspiration and courage to fight for independence against the Philistines.

In a sense, Samuel was dividing the traditional role of Judge into two parts: Israel's commander would now receive his inspiration and guidance through the Prophet rather than directly from God. This at least was the theory of Samuel's plan, but in fact he soon found himself in a bitter rivalry with Saul. So began a tension between king and Prophet that came to characterize much of Israel's history. From this time on the nation's spiritual history would be shaped in the often stormy relations between them.

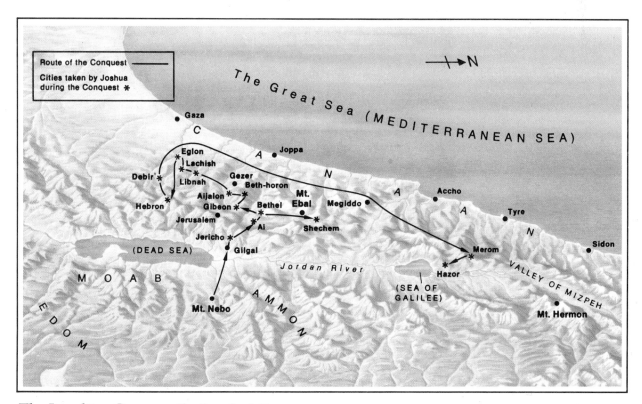

The Israelites Conquer the Land of Canaan

Joshua's strategy of conquest was a great sweeping operation, beginning in the central hill country, moving south into Judah, then northward into the hills of upper Galilee. Once he had made this initial thrust, it was possible for the 12 tribes of Israel to occupy the land and become, for the first time, the nation of Israel. In the time of settlement which followed, however, the Books of Judges and Samuel tell of the Philistine threat from the coast, troubles with remaining Canaanites and conflicts with Moabites, Ammonites and others across the Jordan. True consolidation would arrive later, during the time of the Kings.

Chapter 5

Led by one of the greatest warriors in the Bible, the Israelites attack Canaan in a fierce invasion that reduces many of the Canaanites' central hill cities to rubble.

A Gift of the Lord: Joshua and the Conquest of Canaan

Though his personal life remains something of a mystery, the public, Biblical Joshua was clearly an instrument of the Lord. Through him, God fulfilled his promise of a land for the landless Israelites. To the people of the Bible, Joshua's story was inspiring proof of the Lord's power.

About the year 1250 B.C. a large band of armed men forded the Jordan River into Canaan. They were followed closely by their women, children and livestock. The shallow ford they crossed was located several miles north of the Dead Sea and about the same distance southeast of the ancient town of Jericho.

On the western bank, the band paused and gave thanks to their Lord: at last they had entered the land he had promised them. The people were the Israelites. They had finally returned to Canaan after almost 400 years of exile and hardship. In the past 40 years they had been forged into a nation by their leader and prophet, Moses. The man who was leading them into the Promised Land, however, was Moses' successor, Joshua.

Canaan itself was ripe for invasion. For centuries the land had been controlled by a handful of small, quarrelsome city-states, each ruled by its own king. Most of these petty monarchs owed nominal allegiance to Egypt, but in Joshua's time Egypt, preoccupied with its own internal weaknesses, had withdrawn its military support from Canaan. Warfare between these petty kingdoms was common and chaos prevailed in many parts of the country. Bands of discontented peoples called "'Apiru" roamed the hills of central Canaan, raiding towns and villages and joining with friendly kings in wars against rival city-states. Moreover, Canaan's rigid social structure, made up of a small, landowning upper class and a landless, semislave lower class, was beginning to crack. In many towns the rebellious masses longed for release from centuries of oppression.

Joshua may not have been aware of all these things, yet he never doubted that his campaign would end in triumph. Had not the Lord ordained it? The ancient city of Jericho, which lay in the Jordan Valley and guarded the major route into central Canaan, would be the first target of his invading army. Before crossing the Jordan, Joshua and the Israelites had camped at Mount Nebo in Moab. From there Joshua sent two spies across the Jordan. "Go, view the land," he charged, "especially Jericho."

Under cover of night, the spies crossed the plains of Moab and forded the muddy, rushing waters of the Jordan. They swiftly traversed the Jordan Valley, verdant from the recent spring floodwaters, and approached Jericho. In the gray morning light, the fabled oasis of date palms came into view.

"The sun stayed in the midst of heaven, and did not hasten to go down for about a whole day" (Jos. 10.13). The sun is said to have stood still over the Valley of Aijalon (at right) so that Joshua could have extra hours of daylight to pursue retreating Amorites. "There has been no day like it before or since" (Jos. 10.14).

"Go over this Jordan . . . as I was with Moses, so I will be with you" (Jos. 1.2, 5). As Moses led the Israelites across the Reed Sea, so Joshua led a new generation across a dry riverbed, possibly when a landslide a few miles north stopped the Jordan's waters.

Like most other cities in Canaan, Jericho lay atop a steep mound—or tell—composed of the debris of all its earlier settlements, which even then dated back thousands of years. (Although the Bible states flatly that Jericho at that time was a thickly walled city, archaeologists have found no evidence of these walls. It seems that Jericho was a thinly populated border outpost. The town had been violently destroyed about a century earlier, and the people who reoccupied it apparently did not bother to completely restore its fortifications.)

The spies had no trouble slipping through the gateway and entering the town undetected. They found lodging at the house of a harlot named Rahab. Since Rahab was accustomed to receiving strange men, their presence probably did not arouse curiosity. Her house, like many others in Jericho, was built into the remains of the city wall. From there the spies had a good vantage point from which to view the city and evaluate the strength of its resistance.

Before dawn the next morning, the spies may have wandered through the crooked, narrow streets of Jericho. What they saw would have seemed strange to them. Alongside the earthen streets ran clay trenches designed for draining off water and sewage. Makeshift, one-story houses of mud brick huddled side by side at the streets'

edges, and in their midst stood the comparatively solid two-story palace of the king and his chapel, a temple of Baal, the Canaanite storm god.

When the men returned to Rahab's house, she hid them among the stalks of flax that were drying on her roof and advised them to wait until evening to make their escape. Someone must have noticed their presence, because later that day soldiers came to Rahab's door and demanded that she hand the spies over to them. But the woman refused. "True, men came to me," she explained, "but I did not know where they came from; and when the gate was to be closed, at dark, the men went out; where the men went I do not know; pursue them quickly, for you will overtake them." The soldiers hurried away. Rahab hastily climbed up to the rooftop and told the men what had happened. Bewildered, they asked her why she had taken such a great risk to save them.

"I know that the Lord has given you the land," she confessed, "and that the fear of you has fallen upon us, and that all the inhabitants of the land melt away before you. For we have heard how the Lord dried up the water of the Red [Reed] Sea before you when you came out of Egypt, and what you did to the two kings of the Amorites that were beyond the Jordan, to Sihon and Og, whom you utterly destroyed. And as soon as we heard it, our hearts melted, and there was no courage left in any man . . ."

Crossing the Jordan

The two men, in gratitude for her valuable help and information, readily agreed to spare Rahab and her family when the Israelites attacked Jericho. Then she fetched a rope and lowered the men down from her roof outside the wall, cautioning them to hide in the nearby hills for three days to be sure they would not be arrested by the king's soldiers.

The spies returned across the Jordan with an encouraging report: "Truly the Lord has given all the land into our hands; and moreover all the inhabitants of the land are fainthearted because of

"When your children ask their fathers in time to come, 'What do these stones mean?' then you shall let your children know, 'Israel passed over this Jordan on dry ground' " (Jos. 4.21–22). After the Israelites had crossed the Jordan, Joshua directed men from the 12 tribes to set up 12 stones in Gilgal to commemorate the event. From their encampment at Gilgal, the Israelite army marched on the strategic Canaanite town of Jericho to begin the great conquest.

us." At once Joshua gave orders to break camp. "Sanctify yourselves;" he commanded, "for tomorrow the Lord will do wonders among you."

At daybreak the Israelites assembled near the edge of the camp and took their appointed places, forming a long, solemn procession with the ark of the covenant carried at their head. At the Jordan the flowing waters miraculously "stood and rose up in a heap far off," allowing the Israelites to pass over on dry ground.

At long last the Israelites had set foot in the land of Canaan. With great solemnity, they gathered 12 stones from the Jordan and placed them in a circle at the river's edge to commemorate the miraculous crossing. They named the place Gilgal, which means "circle of stones" in Hebrew. The circle designated the solemn vows of the covenant (treaty) which bound them to their divine Lord; each stone represented a tribe. As a final act of sanctification, Joshua commanded the Israelites to take flint knives and circumcise every man as a symbol of his membership in the Lord's covenant community. While the men were recovering from that painful operation, the nation celebrated the Lord's passover with a ritual meal.

A City Falls

Meanwhile, the people of Jericho had detected the Israelite encampment and had made ready for the inevitable attack. To their surprise, the Israelites did not attack. Instead, in obedience to divine instructions, they performed a strange and terrifying rite: for seven days they solemnly circled the town, carrying their ark before them and blowing on trumpets. "On the seventh day they rose early at the dawn of day, and marched around the city in the same manner seven times: it was only on that day that they marched around the city seven times. And at the seventh time, when the priests had blown the trumpets, Joshua said to the people, 'Shout; for the Lord has given you the city. And the city and all that is within it shall be devoted to the Lord for destruction; only Rahab the harlot and all who are with her in her house shall live . . .' As soon as the people heard the sound of the trumpet, the people raised a great shout, and the wall fell down flat, so that the people went up into the city, every man straight before him, and they took the city. Then they utterly destroyed all in the city, both men and

women, young and old, oxen, sheep, and asses, with the edge of the sword."

When they had completed their slaughter, the soldiers lit torches and set fire to the palace, temple and houses. Only Rahab and her family were spared. That night, from their camp at Gilgal, the jubilant Israelites watched the crimson flames rising from Jericho as they celebrated their victory with songs and sacrifices. By morning Jericho had become a black, smoldering wasteland.

Ai: The First Defeat

Early that same morning spies were sent from the camp to explore the country beyond Jericho, particularly the city of Ai (probably the nearby city of Bethel), which lay to the northwest of Jericho. They crossed the Jordan Valley behind Jericho and climbed an ancient road across a wide ridge in the desolate, saffron-colored hills of the Judean wilderness. Toward evening the men reached the edge of the desert and entered the open, stony moorland bordering Canaan's central hills. In a short time they came upon Ai.

No natural barriers provided protection from approaching armies, but the city was well fortified by a tall, stone rampart about 11 feet thick. The steep slope, or glacis, below the wall was faced with clay to prevent enemies from undermining the foundations beneath the wall. Two tall towers guarded the entrance, and other towers stood at intervals along the wall. Just inside the gates was a sturdy stone garrison.

Perhaps the Israelite spies could not guess the strength of these elaborate fortifications. Perhaps, with the memory of their smashing victory at Jericho still vivid, they overestimated the capability of their fledgling army. Or perhaps they felt that Ai's location was so vulnerable that their army could easily take the city.

Whatever their reasoning, the spies returned to Gilgal and advised Joshua to send only two or three thousand men against Ai, because the defenders "are but few." But they suffered a humiliating defeat, the men of Ai chasing the survivors into the Judean wilderness.

When Joshua learned of the disaster, he prostrated himself on the ground before the ark of the covenant and beseeched the Lord for an explanation. "Alas, O Lord God," he cried, "why hast thou brought this people over the Jordan at all . . . to destroy us? Would that we had been content to

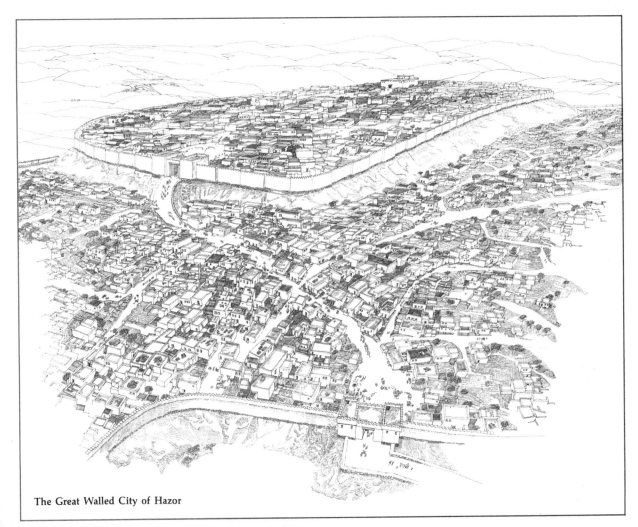

The Great Walled City of Hazor

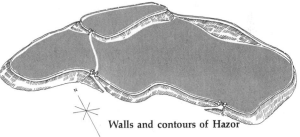

Walls and contours of Hazor

To win control of northern Canaan, Joshua had to take Hazor, a powerful and heavily fortified metropolis about 10 miles north of the Sea of Galilee. Hazor's inner city stood on a tell—a mound built up on the ruins of earlier settlements. Thick stone walls surrounded this stronghold. Below the walls were steep, rocky slopes to prevent attackers from gaining a secure foothold near the base of the walls. Similar walls and slopes protected the larger lower city which sprawled out on a plateau below the tell. The soldiers of Hazor used swift and highly maneuverable battle chariots like the one depicted at left on a golden bowl from Ugarit in northern Canaan. But in a night raid outside the city, Joshua "hamstrung their horses, and burned their chariots" (Jos. 11.9) and then conquered the city with little difficulty.

dwell beyond the Jordan! O Lord, what can I say, when Israel has turned their backs before their enemies! For the Canaanites and all the inhabitants of the land will hear of it, and will surround us, and cut off our name from the earth; and what wilt thou do for thy great name?"

"The Lord said to Joshua, 'Arise, why have you thus fallen upon your face? Israel has sinned; they have transgressed my covenant which I commanded them; they have taken some of the devoted things; they have stolen, and lied, and put them among their own stuff. . . . I will be with you no more, unless you destroy the devoted things from among you.'"

Apparently someone in the Israelite camp had violated the rule of holy war and kept booty for himself. The next morning Joshua summoned the Israelites and ordered a search. The booty was found in the tent of a soldier named Achan: a beautiful mantle, 200 shekels of silver, and a heavy bar of gold. Achan was seized and brought before his angry general. "Why did you bring trouble on us?" Joshua demanded. "The Lord brings trouble on you today." He summoned Achan's wife and children, and the Israelites stoned the entire family to death for their sin and burned their bodies along with the loot Achan had hoarded.

"And the Lord said to Joshua, 'Do not fear or be dismayed; take all the fighting men with you, and arise, go up to Ai; see, I have given into your hand the king of Ai, and his people, his city, and his land; and you shall do to Ai and its king as you did to Jericho and its king; only its spoil and its cattle you shall take as booty for yourselves; lay an ambush against the city, behind it.'"

Ambush and Deception

This time Joshua himself led his entire army across the Judean wilderness. In the dead of night, the main part of the army positioned itself across a ravine north of the city. A small force lay in ambush in a valley to the west. At daybreak Joshua led his men in a charge against the city, and the king and soldiers of Ai came out to pursue them, leaving the gate open and the city undefended. Meanwhile, the small force of Israelites circled around the city, marched up the roadway, stormed through the gates and set the city on fire. As the terror-stricken women and children ran from their flaming homes into the streets, the soldiers cut them down with their swords and daggers.

Smelling the smoke, the men of Ai looked back in the direction of their city. When they saw the flames and black clouds rising above the walls, they panicked and turned back. But now they found they were trapped between the two flanks of the Israelite army with no hope of escape. Savagely, the Lord's warriors swept into their midst, dealing deathblows to every soldier of Ai.

"But the king of Ai they took alive, and brought him to Joshua." Like other Canaanite kings, he was probably an imposing man, dressed in gleaming bronze armor over his royal finery.

Yet even so proud a figure as the king could not deter Joshua from his divine purpose. The Lord had commanded him to spare no man's life. "And he hanged the king of Ai on a tree until evening; and at the going down of the sun Joshua commanded, and they took his body down from the tree, and cast it at the entrance of the gate of the city, and raised over it a great heap of stones, which stands there to this day."

The Covenant at Shechem

There is no account in the Bible of a conquest of the central hills of Canaan in the area surrounding the city of Shechem. Yet this area later became the core of the nation of Israel, and in the time of Israel's Judges it was the home of the dominant tribes of Manasseh and Ephraim. At the time of the Conquest, Shechem was a large, prosperous settlement commanding the ancient pass between Mount Ebal and Mount Gerizim, at the geographical center of Canaan.

Centuries earlier, the Patriarchs of Israel had made peace with the people of Shechem. Abraham and Jacob had built altars to the Lord near the town, and Jacob had purchased land there. There is a record in Genesis of an ancient covenant between the people of Shechem and Jacob's family. Perhaps for that reason, the Shechemites did not resist the Israelite army. Instead, the city and its surrounding territory seem to have been incorporated peacefully into Israel.

Shortly after the conquest of Ai, Joshua and his followers gathered at Shechem. "Then Joshua built an altar in Mount Ebal to the Lord, the God of Israel . . . and they offered on it burnt offerings to the Lord . . . And all Israel, sojourner as well as homeborn, with their elders and officers and

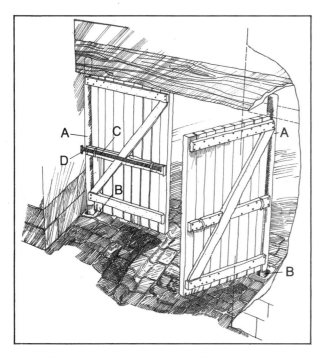

The Weakest Point in a Wall

Any break in the continuity of a wall was a source of danger in an attack; thus the Canaanites built gates to their cities with great care. The double doors of the main entrance were usually large enough to let chariots through. They swung on posts (A)

recessed into a wood lintel at the top and set into stone sockets (B) at the bottom. At right is one type of stone socket, a round version from the Philistine city of Beth-shan. To reduce wear, stone sockets were often protected with bronze sheathing. Doors were locked with metal bolts (C), which slid into holes (D) when doors were in a wide-open position.

---

their judges, stood on opposite sides of the ark before the Levitical priests who carried the ark of the covenant of the Lord, half of them in front of Mount Gerizim and half of them in front of Mount Ebal . . . And afterward he read all the words of the law . . . before all the assembly of Israel, and the women, and the little ones, and the sojourners who lived among them."

The people of Gibeon, a rich Canaanite town about seven miles southwest of Ai, soon heard about Israel's victories and the covenant at Shechem. Hoping to escape the fate of Jericho and Ai,

the elders of Gibeon thought of a clever ruse. Dressed in tattered clothes and patched sandals, their bodies covered with dust and their bread moldy and dry, they approached the Israelites at Gilgal. "We have come from a far country," they lied, "so now make a covenant with us."

Joshua quizzed them at length until he was convinced of their sincerity. Then he made a covenant with them, and together they swore a solemn oath in the name of the Lord. Three days later Joshua learned he had been tricked. Ready to do battle, he marched his army to Gibeon and summoned the elders. Angrily, he demanded to know why they had deceived him.

"Because," they answered, "it was told to your servants for a certainty that the Lord your God had commanded his servant Moses to give you all the land, and to destroy all the inhabitants of the land from before you; so we feared greatly for our lives because of you, and did this thing. And now, behold, we are in your hand: do as it seems good and right in your sight to do to us."

Joshua stood by his covenant and spared the lives of the Gibeonites. Meanwhile, the kings of five powerful city-states to the south of Gibeon—Jerusalem, Hebron, Jarmuth, Lachish, and Eglon—heard of Israel's league with Gibeon and combined their five armies. In full battle formation, they marched northward and surrounded Gibeon. The frightened Gibeonites sent to Gilgal for aid, and Joshua acted at once.

He led his men into the hill country in a night-long trek and surprised the coalition army at dawn. The startled enemy troops fled in disarray, but the Israelites and Gibeonites gave chase and slew a great number of them that day. Gradually the sun sank lower in the west, and darkness threatened to give the enemy refuge. "Then spoke Joshua to the Lord in the day when the Lord gave the Amorites [Canaanites] over to the men of Israel . . . 'Sun, stand thou still at Gibeon, and thou Moon in the valley of Aijalon.' And the sun stood still, and the moon stayed, until the nation took vengeance on their enemies."

Those who escaped the Israelites fled down the Valley of Aijalon from the hills toward the lowland plains. Near Makkedah, another Canaanite royal city southwest of Gibeon, the five enemy kings took refuge in a cave. On Joshua's orders, his men entered the cave, captured the kings, and brought them before him. Raising his sword, Joshua killed them one by one, and had their bodies strung up on a tree. Then the victorious army attacked the fortress cities of the Judean foothills—Makkedah, Libnah, Lachish, Eglon, Hebron and Debir—avoiding the powerful city-states of Jerusalem and Gezer.

The Charioteers of Hazor

Joshua's soldiers next headed northward. At that time most of the petty kingdoms of northern Canaan were united under the powerful city-state of Hazor, situated in the Jordan Valley about 10 miles north of the Sea of Chinnereth (Galilee). Unlike the armies Joshua had encountered in the south, the armies of northern Canaan fought with horse-drawn chariots.

Chariots had been introduced into Canaan and Egypt nearly 500 years before by the Hyksos, mysterious Semitic warriors who had ruled Egypt

and Canaan for about 150 years. The chariots had revolutionized Near Eastern warfare by greatly increasing maneuverability, speed and firing power. But they could only be used effectively on level ground or gentle hills, like those around Hazor. In the steep, hilly terrain of central Canaan, they were clumsy and virtually useless.

Joshua realized that in head-on combat the Israelite foot soldiers would be at a great disadvantage against the archers of Hazor's chariot corps. With divine guidance, he devised a scheme to eliminate the enemy's advantage. The king of Hazor had brought his army to meet the Israelites' northward advance and had pitched camp on the banks of the Merom River, near the Sea of Chinnereth. In the dead of night Joshua's army stormed into the sleeping camp, and the startled Hazorites fled in confusion. While most of the Israelites pursued the fleeing enemy, Joshua and a

According to some archaeologists, this may be the actual stone erected by Joshua at Shechem more than 3000 years ago as witness to the Israelites' renewal of their covenant with the Lord. Shechem no longer exists as a city, but is the site of an important tell where the stone was found in ruins of an ancient temple. Its continued use as a witness to vows is well known from the Bible and other sources.

handful of soldiers tied up the horses and set fire to the wooden chariots. Joshua soon caught up with his men and they all turned towards Hazor.

Under ordinary circumstances the Israelites would never have been able to capture that mighty stronghold. Hazor was probably the largest and best-fortified city in all of Galilee at that time. Within its powerful stone ramparts lay a double city covering 175 acres and housing about 40,000 people. Above the larger, lower section of the city rose a second mound, protected not only by the wall of the lower city but by its own wall as well. The steep slopes of the upper city mound were plastered with limestone; and as at Ai, the gateway was approached by an angled roadway.

But Joshua had rendered Hazor defenseless. He had decimated its army and destroyed its formidable chariots. The Israelites easily captured the mighty city and set it ablaze. "And they put to the sword all who were in it, utterly destroying them; there was none left that breathed . . ."

With the destruction of Hazor, the northern coalition collapsed, and Israel gained a foothold in Galilee. By that time Joshua and his army could claim control of major portions of Canaan's central hills. Now that a part of the Promised Land was firmly in Israelite hands, the Lord instructed Joshua to ". . . allot the land . . . for an inheritance . . ." one portion for each of the 12 tribes. This he did, and each tribe claimed its own district and began to settle there.

Joshua's Last Days

Some years later, ". . . when the Lord had given rest to Israel from all their enemies round about, and Joshua was old and well advanced in years, [he] . . . gathered all the tribes of Israel to Shechem, and summoned the elders, the heads, the judges, and the officers of Israel; and they presented themselves before God." In the hazy afternoon sunlight they gazed out over the golden wheatfields, the dark-green olive groves and vineyards and the stony brown hills of the land that had become their own. Then they turned to Joshua.

"I am now old and well advanced in years," he explained, "and you have seen all that the Lord your God has done to all these nations for your sake, for it is the Lord your God who has fought for you. . . . Therefore be very steadfast to keep and do all that is written in the book of the law of Moses, turning aside from it neither to the right hand nor to the left, that you may not be mixed with these nations left here among you, or make mention of the names of their gods, or swear by them, or serve them, or bow down yourselves to them, but cleave to the Lord your God as you have done to this day."

Joshua then recounted the miracles that the Lord had performed for Israel. He repeated the Lord's promise to Abraham, Isaac, Jacob and Moses—that he would give their people a homeland—and he reminded them that the Lord had fulfilled that promise. "Thus says the Lord, the God of Israel . . ." he told them, "'I gave you a land on which you had not labored, and cities which you had not built, and you dwell therein; you eat the fruit of vineyards and oliveyards which you did not plant.'"

But, Joshua continued, the Lord's gift was conditional on the Israelites' faith—if they lost that, they would lose the land. The people responded with a pledge to serve only the Lord.

"So Joshua made a covenant with the people that day, and made statutes and ordinances for them at Shechem. And Joshua wrote these words in the book of the law of God; and he took a great stone, and set it up there under the oak in the sanctuary of the Lord. And Joshua said to all the people, 'Behold, this stone shall be a witness against us; for it has heard all the words of the Lord which he spoke to us; therefore it shall be a witness against you, lest you deal falsely with your God.' So Joshua sent the people away, every man to his inheritance.

"After these things Joshua the son of Nun, the servant of the Lord, died, being a hundred and ten years old. And they buried him in his own inheritance at Timnath-serah, which is in the hill country of Ephraim . . .

"And Israel served the Lord all the days of Joshua, and all the days of the elders who outlived Joshua and had known all the work which the Lord did for Israel." Yet the time would soon come when the valiant, zealous men who had carried out the Lord's conquest of Canaan would die as well. And the generation raised on the soil of the Promised Land, lacking the burning faith of Joshua and his cohorts, would begin to turn away from the Lord.

The story of Joshua is told in the Book of Joshua.

The Philistines: People From the Sea

Less than a century after the Israelites crossed the Jordan River, their claim to the heartland of Canaan was threatened by new intruders. These were the Philistines, one of the "Sea Peoples" who migrated from the Aegean Sea region for unknown reasons in the 13th century B.C. The Philistines settled on the coast of Canaan in the vicinity of Gaza, then marched inland. Hired as mercenaries by Egypt, they quickly became a menace to Israelite towns and fields, even forcing some tribes to give up their land. With superior arms and an aggressive military policy, the Philistines impeded Israel's development as a nation and made life miserable for her people for almost 200 years. Tales of heroism, such as that of Samson, were passed down to later generations from this troubled time.

The shapes and painted decorations of Philistine pottery were closer to the pictorial styles of the Aegean area than to the plainer Near East forms. This example came from the Philistine town of Gaza on the coast of Canaan.

A feathered helmet identifies a warrior of the "Sea People" on an Egyptian monument commemorating the defeat of a major Philistine invasion of Egypt around 1175 B.C. The clean-shaven chin and copper decoration of the helmet indicate skills superior to the Israelites' in making and using metal implements.

The Philistines, like the Egyptians, decorated the coffins of prominent people with human figures. The photograph at right shows the head end of a clay coffin about six feet long. It was discovered at Beth-shan and dates from the period when this city in upper Canaan was under the control of the Philistines.

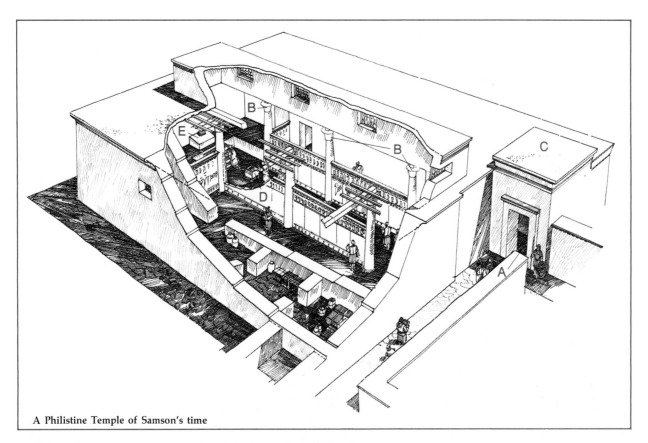

A Philistine Temple of Samson's time

In just such a temple at Gaza, the Bible says, Samson brought the roof tumbling onto the heads of the Philistines, "so the dead whom he slew at his death were more than those he had slain during his life" (Jg. 16.30). The drawing above is reconstructed from excavated ruins of a temple at Beth-shan in which the fertility god Dagon was probably worshiped during the 11th century B.C. The Philistines frequently assimilated what they liked from native culture; thus this temple seems to have been rebuilt from older Canaanite structures. The Canaanites, in turn, were culturally dominated by strong influences from Egypt. This can be seen in many architectural details such as the entrance (A) and the capitals (B) atop the interior columns. Worshipers entered the temple through a small antechamber (C). The main hall, lined with wooden pillars that suggest the ones that Samson pulled down, had a tablelike altar (D) which might have held incense burners. Against a wall stood an altar with a slanted upper surface (E) where stone or metal figures of deities could be placed. This temple at Beth-shan is said to be where Saul's head was taken after his death on Mt. Gilboa.

The Philistines' seafaring background and their contacts with many nations throughout the eastern Mediterranean area gave them a worldly culture, which they brought with them into Canaan. The young bull at left, so different in mood from less sophisticated Canaanite designs, decorates a vase from Cyprus found in the Philistine area of Canaan.

Chapter 6

A generation after the Conquest, the Israelites in Canaan are threatened by foes from all sides. Yet timely and inspired leadership preserves the new nation.

The Judges:
Warriors for God and Israel

The Judges were Israelite heroes who lived in the two centuries after Joshua's conquest of Canaan. Their colorful and daring deeds became part of the young nation's folklore. In those unsettled years, the new nation was threatened by enemies on all sides, and bitter feuds flared up among the tribes themselves. The Bible describes it as the period when "there was no king in Israel; every man did what was right in his own eyes." Yet, in times of great danger, brave figures like Ehud, Gideon, Barak, Deborah, Jephthah and Samson rose to wage victorious battle against Israel's enemies.

After Joshua's death (about 1200 B.C.), the Israelites began the difficult transition from a wandering to a settled way of life. They now wanted to be farmers and settlers, and to abandon the seminomadism that had characterized their lives for so many years. Gradually they cleared forests, plowed fields, terraced hillsides and built permanent homes. New towns and villages appeared atop the rubble of Canaanite settlements that the newcomers had destroyed, and also in places where towns had never before existed.

Their first villages were makeshift in comparison to the well-built Canaanite settlements they replaced. The new settlers built rough, flimsy dwellings of unfitted stones, with rooms arranged in an irregular design. Their household tools and implements were strictly utilitarian as well. Instead of the graceful pottery jars the Canaanites had used for storage, the Israelites used large goatskin bags or rough earthenware crocks. Wealthy Canaanites had eaten and slept on wooden benches, tables and beds, but the new settlers used only coarse reed or woven mats for furniture. Canaanite women wore gold hair ornaments, earrings and bracelets, mixed their own cosmetics and carried aromatic oils in elegant ivory boxes. Gold plaques served as amulets, magic charms to avert evil.

Perhaps inevitably, the Israelites, who had no distinct culture or knowledge of settled life, gradually absorbed many aspects of Canaan's sophisticated culture. The architectural style, pottery, furniture and literature of later Israel were all borrowed from those of Canaan. In many ways this borrowing was beneficial. The Israelites were able to profit from the techniques of construction, farming and craftsmanship which had taken the Canaanites centuries to develop.

But in the eyes of Israel's religious leaders, the pagan ways of the Canaanites posed a continual threat to the integrity of the nation. The Israelites' only strength lay in their common covenant. Any weakening of this basic loyalty left the individual tribes without the strength that comes from unity. When misfortune came, it was blamed on the faithlessness of the people, who again and again turned away from the Lord.

At the spring of Harod, Gideon reduced his inexperienced army from several thousand to 300 reliable men before marching against the Midianites in the Valley of Jezreel. Defeating the enemy with such a small force convinced the Israelites that they were victorious through the will of God, not because of superior numbers.

Many Israelites readily embraced the new religion and openly worshiped Canaan's gods. Yet to do so was a direct violation of the Lord's first commandment: "You shall have no other gods before me."

Faithful Israelites believed the Lord had sent the Judges to save them in times of great need. Unlike her neighboring nations, Israel had no central government, but was loosely organized into a tribal confederacy, each tribe in control of a specific area. Every town had a local council made up of the community elders, and the tribal representatives were selected from these leaders. What held the nation together was its common heritage and its covenant with the Lord. For that reason the central sanctuary at Shiloh, which housed the tabernacle and the sacred ark of the covenant, served as Israel's capital. There tribal leaders would gather in times of emergency.

The young nation was beset by trouble from the very beginning. Its new territory in Transjordan and in Canaan's central hills was surrounded by hostile enemies. In the hill country, Canaanite strongholds like Gezer and Jerusalem divided Israel into separate enclaves, and the kings of these cities allied themselves from time to time in attempts to drive the newcomers out. On Canaan's coastal plain, a group of invaders from across the Great Sea, the Philistines, had recently seized territory and were beginning to press inland toward Israel's new villages. To the east of the Jordan, the kingdoms of Moab, Ammon and Midian were threatening Israel's holdings on both sides of the river. Among the tribes of Israel themselves, there were occasional quarrels and sometimes even open warfare.

Deborah: "A Mother in Israel"

Israel had no standing army to defend itself in times of crisis. Instead, each tribe would call up a militia of all able-bodied men. Each tribe fought most of its battles alone, but at times neighboring tribes would combine against a common enemy. Occasionally, a local leader would appear and lead his troops to victory. The entire nation never made a united stand, but it came close to doing so in the time of Deborah, a prophetess and Judge from the hill country of Ephraim.

The Canaanites of the northern and central hills had gathered a huge army, led by the great general, Sisera. The Canaanite forces had assem-

bled on the strategic plain of Esdraelon, a wedge-shaped valley cutting across Canaan's northern hills. According to the Bible, Sisera's army had "nine hundred chariots of iron," each one manned by crack archers armed with long-range bows. Most likely, his foot soldiers were equipped with iron spears and shields and wore protective iron helmets and coats of mail. As in the days of Joshua, the Israelites still fought on foot, with bronze and copper daggers, swords, slings and short-range bows and arrows. They probably carried leather-covered wooden shields, but they had no armor.

When Deborah heard that Sisera's army was preparing to attack, she immediately sent out a call for help to the leaders of the tribal league for their quota of fighters. At her request the Israelite

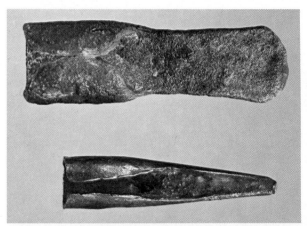

"But every one of the Israelites went down to the Philistines to sharpen his plowshare" (1 Sam. 13.20). The Philistines held a monopoly on metalworking, which forced Israelite farmers to work their land with inferior tools. Bronze points (top) that fitted a wooden plow and bronze daggers molded in a slot cut in a stone (bottom) were soft and often needed repair. The smith at his forge at right tempers a dagger of iron for a Philistine warrior, while Israelites wait to have their bronze tools repaired. The Philistines kept iron-smelting and forging methods secret so their weapons would remain superior to those of their neighbors.

The plains below Mt. Tabor (background) were the scene of the victory celebrated in the famous "Song of Deborah," the oldest extensive fragment of Hebrew literature in the Bible. Here an army of 10,000 men swooped down from the mountain and routed a powerful Canaanite force equipped with battle chariots.

general, Barak, of the Naphtali tribe in the north, assembled an army from the tribes of the northern and central hills.

Barak stationed most of his new troops on the fortress hill of Mount Tabor, which guarded the northern entrance to the plain. Meanwhile, Deborah and a small detachment of troops lured Sisera's army to low land near the Kishon River. Suddenly, at a prearranged signal Barak's army swept down from the hill and surrounded Sisera's men, driving them to the river's edge. There, Sisera's chariots were immobilized in the mud and many soldiers were swept away by the torrential floodwaters of the river; others were cut down by the Israelites as they tried to flee. Only Sisera

escaped, but he was killed by Jael, a Kenite woman from whom he sought refuge.

A poem written soon after, the "Song of Deborah," describes the action in vivid detail:

"In the days of Shamgar, son of Anath,
  in the days of Jael, caravans ceased
  and travelers kept to the byways.
The peasantry ceased in Israel, they ceased
  until you arose, Deborah,
  arose as a mother in Israel . . .
Tell of it you, who ride on tawny asses,
  you who sit on rich carpets
  and you who walk by the way.
To the sound of musicians at the watering place
  there they repeat the triumphs of the Lord,
  the triumphs of his peasantry in Israel.
Then down to the gates marched the people of
  the Lord . . .
Then down marched the remnant of the noble;
  the people of the Lord marched down for him
    against the mighty . . .
The kings came, they fought;
  then fought the kings of Canaan,
at Taanach, by the waters of Megiddo;
  they got no spoils of silver.
From heaven fought the stars,
  from their courses they fought against Sisera.
The torrent Kishon swept them away,
  the onrushing torrent, the torrent Kishon.
  March on, my soul, with might!
Then loud beat the horses' hoofs
  with the galloping, galloping of his steeds . . .
Most blessed of women be Jael,
  the wife of Heber the Kenite,
  of tent-dwelling women most blessed.
He asked water and she gave him milk,
  she brought him curds in a lordly bowl.
She put her hand to the tent peg
  and her right hand to the workmen's mallet;
she struck Sisera a blow,
  she crushed his head,
  she shattered and pierced his temple.
He sank, he fell,
  he lay still at her feet;
at her feet he sank, he fell;
  where he sank, there he fell dead . . .
So perish all thine enemies, O Lord!
  But thy friends be like the sun as he rises
    in his might."

Deborah and Barak's victory was of great importance to the Israelites, for it gave them control of the important Plain of Esdraelon and thus eliminated the threat of northern Canaan's armies. The great kingdoms of Sidon and Byblos remained in firm control of Canaan's northern coast, but the northern and central hills were Israel's. In the south, Jerusalem and Gezer would remain in Canaanite hands until David's time.

Ehud: Slayer of a Tyrant

Another foe was the kingdom of Moab, which lay to the east of the Dead Sea. The Moabites, according to the Bible, were descendants of Lot, Abraham's nephew. They had become enemies of Israel when they had refused to let Moses and his followers pass through their land, and in retaliation the Israelites had occupied the plains of Moab. In the period of the Judges, Moab's king, Eglon, reconquered the plains and, with the help of the neighboring Ammonites and Amalekites, pushed westward across the Jordan. There his army ". . . took possession of the city of palms," Jericho, and may also have taken Bethel. This area had been assigned by Moses to the Israelite tribes of Ephraim and Benjamin.

The Moabite occupation lasted 18 years. "But . . . the Lord raised up . . . a deliverer, Ehud, the son of Gera, the Benjaminite, a left-handed man." Ehud devised a clever scheme: "The people of Israel sent tribute by him to Eglon the king of Moab. And Ehud made for himself a sword with two edges, a cubit [1½ feet] in length; and he girded it on his right thigh under his clothes." He was thus able to conceal his sword because he carried it on his right side instead of his left, where men usually carried their weapons. "And he presented the tribute to Eglon king of Moab. Now Eglon was a very fat man. And when Ehud had finished presenting the tribute, he sent away the people that carried the tribute. . . . [He] said, 'I have a secret message for you, O king.' And he commanded, 'Silence.' And all his attendants went out from his presence. And Ehud came to him, as he was sitting alone in his cool roof chamber. And Ehud said, 'I have a message from God for you.' And he arose from his seat. And Ehud reached with his left hand, took the sword from his right thigh, and thrust it into his belly; and the hilt also went in after the blade, and the fat closed over the blade, for he did not draw the sword out of his belly. . . . Then Ehud went out into the vestibule, and closed the doors of the roof chamber upon him, and locked them.

"When he had gone, the servants came; and when they saw that the doors of the roof chamber were locked, they thought, 'He is only relieving himself in the closet of the cool chamber.' And they waited till they were utterly at a loss; but when he still did not open the doors of the roof chamber, they took the key and opened them; and there lay their lord dead on the floor."

Meanwhile, Ehud had escaped from Eglon's Jericho quarters to Se'irah in the hills of nearby Ephraim. There he rallied a makeshift army from among the tribes, and to the sounds of a trumpet, he led them in a charge down the hills and across the plains surrounding Jericho. "Follow after me; for the Lord has given your enemies the Moabites into your hand," he cried. "So they went down after him, and seized the fords of the Jordan against the Moabites, and allowed not a man to pass over. And they killed at that time about ten thousand of the Moabites, all strong, able-bodied men; not a man escaped. So Moab was subdued that day under the hand of Israel."

Gideon: The Farmer Judge

Ehud's exploits eliminated Moab's hold on Israelite land west of the Jordan, but another enemy soon appeared—the Midianites. These were fierce nomads from the desert, who may possibly have been related to the Kenites, a family of smiths which had united itself to Israel by covenant. By the time of Israel's conquest of Canaan, the Midianites from Arabia had tamed the camel. The awkward-looking but surprisingly fleetfooted beasts were used in the Midianites' armies, greatly increasing their mobility and striking power. With incredible swiftness, soldiers mounted on the tall animals could swoop down on Israelite towns and villages at harvest time, steal the annual crops, and ride off before the townsmen could organize an effective defense.

The Midianite raids created a terrifying hardship for the Israelites, who were struggling to eke out an existence from the stony soil of Canaan's hills. The people of Manasseh, descendants of Joseph who lived to the west of the Jordan just north of Benjamin, suffered especially. They were finally saved by Gideon, a farmer from the town of Ophrah. Like the other farmers in his region, Gideon spent the entire year toiling from dawn to dusk in the fields surrounding his village.

The farmer's year began in September with the

The camp of a Midianite raiding party is thrown into confusion as a small torch-bearing band of Israelites shouts in the darkness amid the sound of trumpets and shattering crockery. Such tricks were necessary to rout the Midianites, who had the advantage of a new tactical weapon—the camel. Riding these newly domesticated beasts, they could move rapidly out from the desert in marauding bands, sending the Israelites into the hill caves for protection. "For they would come up with their cattle and their tents, coming like locusts . . . both they and their camels could not be counted; so that they wasted the land as they came in" (Jg. 6.5). Four centuries later, camel raiders were still troublesome, as shown in a relief (below) which depicts the Assyrians fighting against them.

olive harvest. Then, when the winter rains began in late October, he planted wheat and barley. The barley was harvested in late April when the rain ended, the wheat a month later. Fruit and vegetables were picked in the summer, and in late August came the joyous time of the grape harvest.

The farmer's life was hard and, at best, precarious. He was faced with constant uncertainties and threats to the safety of his animals and crops: drought, flooding, locusts, mildew and beasts of prey. Another potential enemy was the sirocco, the hot, stifling wind from the Arabian desert that lasted for as long as a week and wrung all moisture from the air, causing plants to wither and die.

The Canaanites had devised elaborate rituals and offerings to their gods to help ward off these evils and these were adapted by many Israelites. Gideon's own relatives and neighbors at Ophrah had built an altar to Baal and dedicated a sacred tree (called the Asherah in the Bible) to his consort, Astarte, the goddess of all fertility.

wheat in the wine press, to hide it from the Midianites. And the angel of the Lord appeared to him and said to him, 'The Lord is with you, you mighty man of valor.' And Gideon said to him, 'Pray, sir, if the Lord is with us, why then has all this befallen us? . . .' And the Lord turned to him and said, 'Go in this might of yours and deliver Israel from the hand of Midian; do not I send you?' And he said to him, 'Pray, Lord, how can I deliver Israel? Behold, my clan is the weakest in Manasseh, and I am the least in my family.' And the Lord said to him, 'But I will be with you, and you shall smite the Midianites as one man.'"

A Night Victory

One night, following the Lord's command, Gideon pulled down the Canaanite god's altar and erected one for the Lord. The men of the town were furious when they discovered the deed. Joash intimidated them: "Will you contend for Baal? Or will you defend his cause? Whoever contends for him shall be put to death by morning. If he is a god, let him contend for himself, because his altar has been pulled down."

Meanwhile, the Midianites had crossed the Jordan and encamped in the Valley of Jezreel, a fertile plain in Manasseh's territory, not far from Gideon's home. Gideon sent out an urgent call for help throughout Manasseh and to the neighboring northern tribes of Asher, Zebulun and Naphtali. The tribes responded immediately and sent all their able-bodied men.

Gideon, however, acting on the Lord's advice, decided not to face the Midianites with a novice, undisciplined army. Instead, he handpicked 300 men who seemed the most valiant and sent the others back to their homes.

That same evening Gideon and his servant, Purah, went to the edge of the enemy camp to evaluate the military situation and plan their strategy. Stealthily they approached the large tent-city, lit here and there by the flickering light of campfires. The herds of camels and most of the nomads lay sleeping. As the two men took in the scene before them, they overheard a conversation between two Midianite guards.

One of the guards said, "'Behold, I dreamed a dream; and lo, a cake of barley bread tumbled into the camp of Midian, and came to the tent, and struck it so that it fell, and turned it upside down, so that the tent lay flat.' And his comrade

For seven years the people of Manasseh suffered from the raids of the Arabian Midianites. "And the hand of Midian prevailed over Israel; and because of Midian the people of Israel made for themselves the dens which are in the mountains, and the caves and the strongholds. For whenever the Israelites put in seed the Midianites and the Amalekites and the people of the East would come up and attack them; they would encamp against them and destroy the produce of the land, as far as the neighborhood of Gaza, and leave no sustenance in Israel. . . . For they would come up with their cattle and their tents, coming like locusts for number; both they and their camels could not be counted; so that they wasted the land as they came in. And Israel was brought very low because of Midian; and the people of Israel cried for help to the Lord. . . .

"Now the angel of the Lord came and sat under the oak at Ophrah, which belonged to Joash the Abiezrite, as his son Gideon was beating out answered, 'This is no other than the sword of Gideon the son of Joash, a man of Israel; into his hand God has given Midian and all the host.'

"When Gideon heard the telling of the dream and its interpretation, he worshiped; and he returned to the camp of Israel, and said, 'Arise; for the Lord has given the host of Midian into your hand.' And he divided the three hundred men into three companies, and put trumpets into the hands of all of them and empty jars, with torches inside the jars. And he said to them, 'Look at me, and do likewise; when I come to the outskirts of the camp, do as I do. When I blow the trumpet, I and all who are with me, then blow the trumpets also on every side of all the camp, and shout, 'For the Lord and for Gideon.'

"So Gideon and the hundred men who were with him came to the outskirts of the camp at the beginning of the middle watch, when they had just set the watch; and they blew the trumpets and smashed the jars that were in their hands. And the three companies blew the trumpets and broke the jars, holding in their left hands the torches, and in their right hands the trumpets to blow; and they cried, 'A sword for the Lord and for Gideon!' They stood every man in his place round about the camp, and all the army ran; they cried out and fled."

Suddenly awakened by the noise of the trumpets, the breaking of jars and the shouts of Gideon's warriors, and seeing the camp surrounded by torches, the Midianites assumed they were being attacked by a huge army. In panic and confusion, they ran from their tents and into the swords of the waiting Israelites. Many of the Midianites escaped and fled toward the Jordan, but there they were stopped by a large contingent of soldiers from the tribe of Ephraim, who had massed at the river's edge under Gideon's orders. Trapped between the Ephraimites and Gideon's pursuing soldiers, the Midianites were easily routed, and the severed heads of their leaders were soon brought before Gideon.

Jephthah and His Daughter

Other enemies still remained. The Ammonites, a seminomadic people east of the Jordan, north of Moab, were hostile to Israel. They wished to expand their territory into Israel's fine farmlands, especially Gilead, the tribal area of Gad.

The people of Gilead mustered a strong oppo-sition to the Ammonites under the command of a mighty warrior and Judge, Jephthah. On the eve of the battle, Jephthah made a vow to the Lord: "If thou wilt give the Ammonites into my hand," he promised, "then whoever comes forth from the doors of my house to meet me, when I return victorious from the Ammonites, shall be the Lord's, and I will offer him up for a burnt offering."

The next day Jephthah's forces won a decisive victory against the Ammonites and drove them back across the frontier. But the victory brought Jephthah only short-lived happiness, for he had yet to fulfill his vow to the Lord.

"Then Jephthah came to his home at Mizpah; and behold, his daughter came out to meet him with timbrels and with dances; she was his only child; beside her he had neither son nor daughter. And when he saw her, he rent his clothes, and said, 'Alas, my daughter! you have brought me

A Strong Vehicle for Simple Work

The sturdy carts of the Philistines followed a simple, efficient design still used in many places around the world today. A wheel's main pieces were cut from wood sections as shown below, then joined so that the curved pieces fastened against the center section to form a strong unit. The Philistine laborer on the left fits a heated metal rim on the wood; as it cools, it will shrink and grip the frame tightly. The Philistines used such vehicles for transporting property, but did not employ them in battle, as some of their Canaanite enemies did.

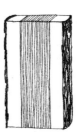

very low, and you have become the cause of great trouble to me; for I have opened my mouth to the Lord, and I cannot take back my vow.'" His daughter answered that he must fulfill his vow to the Lord. She asked only that he allow her two months to "'wander on the mountains, and bewail my virginity. . . .' And he said, 'Go.' And he sent her away for two months; and she departed, she and her companions, and bewailed her virginity upon the mountains. And at the end of two months, she returned to her father, who did with her according to his vow which he had made. She had never known a man. And it became a custom in Israel that the daughters of Israel went year by year to lament the daughter of Jephthah the Gileadite four days in the year."

Samson: A Lone Hero

The most famous figure of the period of the Judges was Samson, a man of the tribe of Dan whose feats of physical strength became legendary. His earthy and clever personality also made him a popular figure. Unlike the other Judges, Samson waged a one-man battle against the Philistines, relying solely on his own great strength. His fatal weakness was Philistine women. The stories of his deeds paint a colorful picture of life in those troubled times.

Samson's people lived in the southwestern part of Canaan's hill country, on the border of the southern coastal plain. The nearby Philistines were organized into a loose confederation of five city-states—Ekron, Ashdod, Ashkelon, Gath and Gaza—each ruled by a "tyrant," or lord. During Samson's lifetime the Philistines virtually controlled the tribal territory of Dan, and Israelite resistance to their rule was ineffective. Samson's exploits reveal the deep bitterness and tension between the two peoples.

Samson was born in the town of Zorah, a farming village on a low hillside. The village faced south and was usually bathed in warm sunlight and aired by balmy Mediterranean breezes. Below the town, wheatfields and olive groves sloped gently down to the grassy valley of Sorek, opposite the Philistines.

Before Samson was born, his mother had made a vow to the Lord that she would consecrate him as a Nazirite. This meant that he would practice certain forms of abstinence, including not cutting his hair nor drinking alcoholic beverages, as an

When Samson set out from his home to court Delilah, the Philistine, he walked through this countryside in Canaan's lowland region. Conflicts with the Philistines ultimately compelled Samson's people, the tribe of Dan, to leave this region and move north.

expression of his special loyalty to Israel's God.

Young Samson's adventures with the Philistines began when he fell in love with a woman from Timnah, a Philistine-controlled settlement that lay across the valley from Zorah. When he returned home from Timnah one evening, Samson presented his startled parents with an urgent request. "I saw one of the daughters of the Philistines at Timnah; now get her for me as my wife." His parents objected strongly. "Is there not a woman among the daughters of your kinsmen, or among all our people, that you must go to take a wife from the uncircumcised Philistines?"

Samson ignored their protests and went ahead with his plans. Since his parents would not let him hold the traditional wedding feast at their home, he started back to Timnah to arrange to hold the feast at the bride's home. "And behold, a young lion roared against him; and the Spirit of the Lord came mightily upon him, and he tore the lion asunder as one tears a kid; and he had nothing in his hand. . . . Then he went down and talked with the woman; and she pleased Samson well. And after a while he returned to take her; and he turned aside to see the carcass of the lion, and behold, there was a swarm of bees in the body of the lion, and honey. He scraped it out into his hands, and went on, eating as he went . . .''

A Riddle for the Philistines

Samson had invited 30 Philistines to be his groomsmen, and during the wedding feast he began to taunt them with a riddle. "And Samson said to them, 'Let me now put a riddle to you; if you can tell me what it is, within the seven days of the feast, and find it out, then I will give you thirty linen garments and thirty festal garments; but if you cannot tell me what it is, then you shall give me thirty linen garments and thirty festal garments.' And they said to him, 'Put your riddle, that we may hear it.' And he said to them, 'Out of the eater came something to eat. Out of the strong came something sweet.' And they could not in three days tell what the riddle was.''

The Philistines then coerced Samson's wife into enticing the answer from him. "Then she told the riddle to her countrymen. And the men of the city said to him on the seventh day before the sun went down, 'What is sweeter than honey? What is stronger than a lion?' And he said to them, 'If you had not plowed with my heifer, you would not have found out my riddle.' And the Spirit of the Lord came mightily upon him, and he went down to Ashkelon [a large Philistine city] and killed thirty men of the town, and took their spoil and gave the festal garments to those who had told the riddle. In hot anger he went back to his father's house.''

Some time later, during the annual wheat harvest, Samson returned to Timnah to visit his wife, bringing her a young goat as a gift. But her father refused to let him see her. "I really thought that you utterly hated her," the old man explained, "'so I gave her to your companion. Is not her younger sister fairer than she? Pray take her instead.' And Samson said to them, 'This time I shall be blameless in regard to the Philistines, when I do them mischief.' So Samson went and caught three hundred foxes, and took torches;

and he turned them tail to tail, and put a torch between each pair of tails. And when he had set fire to the torches, he let the foxes go into the standing grain of the Philistines, and burned up the shocks and the standing grain, as well as the olive orchards. Then the Philistines said, 'Who has done this?' And they said, 'Samson, the son-in-law of the Timnite, because he has taken his wife and given her to his companion.' And the Philistines came up, and burned her and her father with fire. And Samson said to them, 'If this is what you do, I swear I will be avenged upon you, and after that I will quit.' And he smote them hip and thigh with great slaughter; and he went down and stayed in the cleft of the rock of Etam.''

The Philistines quickly organized a raiding party and went up into Dan to capture Samson. When the Danites saw the armed men approaching, they sent a delegation to Samson's hiding place to capture him, hoping to appease the Philistines by turning him over to them. "So they bound him with two new ropes, and brought him up from the rock.''

His captors led him away. "When he came to Lehi, the Philistines came shouting to meet him; and the Spirit of the Lord came mightily upon him, and the ropes which were on his arms became as flax that has caught fire, and his bonds melted off his hands. And he found a fresh jawbone of an ass, and put out his hand and seized it, and with it he slew a thousand men.''

Samson and Delilah

Samson continued his daring harassment of the Philistines, but he was finally betrayed by a beguiling Philistine woman named Delilah, who lived in the Valley of Sorek. Having learned that Samson had fallen in love with Delilah, a group of Philistines came to her one day. "Entice him," they urged, "and see wherein his great strength lies, and by what means we may overpower him, that we may bind him to subdue him; and we will each give you eleven hundred pieces of silver.''

Delilah readily agreed. "And Delilah said to Samson, 'Please tell me wherein your great strength lies, and how you might be bound, that one could subdue you.' And Samson said to her, 'If they bind me with seven fresh bowstrings which have not been dried, then I shall become weak, and be like any other man.' Then the lords of the Philistines brought her seven fresh bowstrings which had not been dried, and she bound him with them. Now she had men lying in wait in an inner chamber. And she said to him, 'The Philistines are upon you, Samson!' But he snapped the bowstrings, as a string of tow snaps when it touches the fire."

Twice more the crafty Delilah tried to coax Samson into revealing the secret of his phenomenal strength. Twice more Samson evaded her questions and gave her false answers. But Delilah was not yet ready to abandon her promise to the Philistine nobles.

"And she said to him, 'How can you say, "I love you," when your heart is not with me? You have mocked me these three times, and you have not told me wherein your great strength lies.' And when she pressed him hard with her words day after day, and urged him, his soul was vexed to death. And he told her all his mind, and said to her, 'A razor has never come upon my head; for I have been a Nazirite to God from my mother's womb. If I be shaved, then my strength will leave me, and I shall become weak, and be like any other man.'

"When Delilah saw that he had told her all his mind, she sent and called the lords of the Philistines, saying, 'Come up this once, for he has told me all his mind.' Then the lords of the Philistines came up to her, and brought the money in their hands. She made him sleep upon her knees; and she called a man, and had him shave off the seven locks of his head. Then she began to torment him, and his strength left him. And she said, 'The Philistines are upon you, Samson!' And he awoke from his sleep, and said, 'I will go out as at other times, and shake myself free.' And he did not know that the Lord had left him. And the Philistines seized him and gouged out his eyes, and brought him down to Gaza, and bound him with bronze fetters; and he ground at the mill in the prison. But the hair of his head began to grow again after it had been shaved."

Destruction of Dagon's Temple

Samson's strength gradually returned, and the time came when he got his revenge. The Philistines were holding a great religious festival in honor of their chief god, Dagon, who seems to have been an agricultural deity. (Dagon, which means "grain" in the Canaanite language, was originally a Canaanite god.) The citizens of Gaza, colorfully dressed in long, embroidered linen festal garments, had assembled inside the pillared stone temple of Dagon to offer a sacrifice and to celebrate the completion of the harvest with songs and rituals. They were especially thankful that year because Dagon had helped them capture the troublemaking Samson.

"And when their hearts were merry, they said, 'Call Samson, that he may make sport for us.' So they called Samson out of the prison, and he made sport before them. They made him stand between the pillars; and Samson said to the lad who held him by the hand, 'Let me feel the pillars on which the house rests, that I may lean against them.' Now the house was full of men and women; all the lords of the Philistines were there, and on the roof there were about three thousand men and women, who looked on while Samson made sport.

"Then Samson called to the Lord and said, 'O Lord God, remember me, I pray thee, and strengthen me, I pray thee, only this once, O God, that I may be avenged upon the Philistines for one of my two eyes.' And Samson grasped the two middle pillars upon which the house rested, and he leaned his weight upon them, his right hand on the one and his left hand on the other. And Samson said, 'Let me die with the Philistines.' Then he bowed with all his might; and the house fell upon the lords and upon all the people that were in it. So the dead whom he slew at his death were more than those whom he had slain during his life."

Trouble with the Philistines continued after Samson's death, and some years later the tribe of Dan was forced to migrate northward and find a new home. They eventually settled in the very north of Canaan, around the city of Laish, which they renamed Dan.

By the time most of the great Judges of Israel had died, the Israelites had been in Canaan for nearly two centuries. They had secured their homeland from a host of enemies—the Canaanites, Ammonites, Moabites and Midianites—and had settled most of their intertribal disputes. They still lacked the unity of a real nation, though, and it remained for the Judge Samuel to give them the king who would provide it.

The stories of these and all the other Judges are told in the Book of Judges.

Chapter 7

A young widow from the hated land of Moab achieves an honored place among the Israelites by placing compassion and family loyalty above all ties to her homeland.

Ruth: Israel's Gentle Heroine

The story of Ruth's devotion to her family provides a warm and peaceful interlude in the history of an otherwise warlike age. An alien and penniless Moabite widow, she won the love of a prominent citizen of Judah and eventually married him. One of her descendants, David, became Israel's greatest king.

Ruth's tale is set in Judah "in the days when the Judges ruled," about the twelfth century B.C. Many years had passed since the Israelites had crossed the Jordan and formed a loose tribal confederacy in the central highlands of Canaan. As they established their own settlements, they gradually discarded their nomadic traditions and adopted an agricultural way of life.

Yet their position remained precarious. As the story of Deborah shows, friction between Israelites and Canaanites in the north occasionally exploded into warfare; while in the valleys the Hebrews were often at the mercy of marauding Amalekites and Midianites, as the story of Gideon shows. In contrast, Judah, at the southern end of Israelite territory, seems to have been relatively tranquil and not involved in the great wars of the Judges.

The people of Judah regularly battled another sort of enemy: the climate. Judah occupied a rugged plateau in the semiarid lands west of the Dead Sea. Normally, the land was fertile enough to sustain fields of wheat and barley, grape vineyards and groves of olive and fig trees. But occa-

sionally the rains failed, the crops withered and there was famine.

During one such disaster, a Judean man named Elimelech, who lived in the town of Bethlehem, fled the land with his wife, Naomi, and their two sons, Mahlon and Chilion. The family traveled to Moab, a kingdom on the eastern borders of the Dead Sea. The distance was not great—perhaps 30 or 40 miles along the edge of that inland sea. Nevertheless, it was a long journey spiritually.

Both the Israelites and Moabites traced their ancestry back to the family of Abraham, and they spoke dialects of the same language. But the Moabites worshiped a different god, Chemosh, with rites regarded as sinful by the people of Judah. This religious difference, along with political rivalry, was the source of centuries-long friction between the two peoples. Before the Israelites first entered Canaan, attractive Moabite women seduced many of the Israelite warriors and even enticed them into sacrificing to Chemosh. Angered, the God of Israel sent down a plague, killing the sinners and thousands of other Israelites. The people of Israel still spoke harshly of Moabite women.

It is not clear why Elimelech chose Moab as a refuge. Certainly he was aware that it was a fertile

"Is it not wheat harvest today?" (1 Sam. 12.17). Usually, in the Holy Land, wheat is ready for harvesting in late spring. But if the spring rains have been meager, it will not grow as high and as thickly as these stalks, and in times of severe drought, it will not grow at all. Ruth's story begins with such a natural disaster.

land with ample rainfall, where he was likely to prosper. There may also have been some personal or commercial connection that made it possible for him to lease farmland or transact business. At any rate, it was in Moab that he once again took up the broken threads of his life. Ironically, he died soon afterward, leaving his two sons to carry on. Despite traditional enmities, each married a Moabite girl. Chilion was wed to Orpah, and Mahlon married Ruth. For a number of years, life was comfortable for them.

Then the sons died, too, and the three widows, Naomi and her two daughters-in-law, faced a very uncertain future. In those days women could not inherit property directly; they could only hold it in a kind of trust for some future husband or another male relative. Women had virtually no way of earning a living. Without a husband or family, they were sure to become dependent upon the charity of others.

The two younger women, Orpah and Ruth, at least were among their own people and might have had families to look after them. Moreover, both were still young enough to find new husbands among the men of Moab.

Harvest in Judah

Naomi, however, was a stranger in the land and was past the age when she could reasonably expect to bear children. No man was likely to choose her as a wife. When she heard that the Lord had favored Judah with rich harvests once more, she decided to return to Bethlehem. Among her own people there might be more concern for her welfare. Sadly, she gathered her meager belongings and began the trip back.

But the two younger women insisted on going with her. Naomi pleaded with them to turn back, since she knew full well that she could not take

The Israelite woman worked hard and long, but she was fortunate if her toil was for husband and children. A childless widow in Ruth's position depended on the charitable provisions of Mosaic law. According to it, she was allowed to gather grain from a stranger's field. Only after this gleaning could she begin grinding grain and kneading dough for bread—as in this clay model from a tomb in the Galilee area.

care of them. She may also have feared that her daughters-in-law, as Moabite women, would receive a hostile reception in Judah.

Orpah gave in at last and tearfully kissed Naomi goodby. But Ruth would not be swayed. "Entreat me not to leave you or to return from following you," she insisted, "for where you go I will go, and where you lodge I will lodge; your people shall be my people, and your God my God; where you die I will die, and there will I be buried."

Naomi could offer no protest against such devotion, and the two women went on to Bethlehem together. The journey lasted four or five days. After bidding farewell to Orpah on the fertile, rolling fields of Moab, the women continued northward to the southern end of the Jordan River. Near Jericho they forded the river, and headed westward through the hot, desolate Wilderness of Judah. At last the grassy hills of central Judah came into sight. Before them lay the village of Bethlehem, its humble whitewashed houses huddled together on the side of a hill. Below the town stretched fields of ripening grain. The two women entered the town and soon found lodging they could afford.

Their arrival coincided with the beginning of the spring grain harvest, a seven-week period lasting from mid-April to about mid-June. They found that what Naomi had heard was true: the time of famine in Judah was long past, and the rains that year had been particularly plentiful. A large supply of grain waited to be gathered— barley first, then wheat a few weeks later.

Harvesting was difficult work and demanded long hours. Young men moved through the fields grasping handfuls of the grain and cutting through the stalks with sickles. These small bunches of grain were then bound into bundles called sheaves. As the men worked rapidly, a number of stalks fell to the ground. If the men were careful and took the time, these too could be gathered up. However, any stalks that dropped were allowed to remain where they fell. Poor people, following the reapers, were permitted to "glean," or gather, the random stalks—possibly all that stood between them and starvation. In addition, the edges of the field, where the sickle was not as easily wielded, were left unharvested. The poor were welcome to that portion, as well.

The destitute of Bethlehem now included Ruth and Naomi, and Ruth offered to go into the fields

Gathering Grain at Harvest Time

"You shall keep close by my servants, till they have finished all my harvest" (Ru. 2.21). Ruth arrived in Judah when the harvest was in full swing and was encouraged by Boaz to follow his reapers and binders when she gleaned. Reaping was done with wooden sickles (below) which had sharpened pieces of flint embedded in them to form a blade. Binders followed reapers and tied the stalks of grain into bundles called sheaves. Then came the gleaners who gathered stray stalks missed by the binders into the folds of their long veils. Gleaners, including the homeless and the orphans, as well as widows, could keep all they found for their own use.

and glean. It was no light offer. Stooping for the occasional stalks over and over in the hot sun all day was backbreaking labor. There were also the young harvesters, who did not always treat undefended women gently. A Moabite girl would almost certainly be a target for abuse, yet there seemed to be no other way of eking out a food supply. Naomi was simply too old to do it herself, so, with considerable reluctance, she consented to the young woman's wish to join the gleaners.

After the grain was harvested, it was brought in from the fields and dumped on the threshing floor, a leveled area of hard-packed earth. Oxen dragged sleds, weighted by the driver and perhaps a small passenger or two, over the harvest to loosen the kernels of grain and to break up the stalks. Winnowers then tossed the grain into the air so that the breeze would carry the chaff away. Any remaining chaff was sifted out with sieves (far right). Each evening of threshing a feast would be prepared (far left), for a good harvest was a joyous time.

"Now Naomi had a kinsman of her husband's, a man of wealth, of the family of Elimelech, whose name was Boaz. And Ruth the Moabitess said to Naomi, 'Let me go to the field, and glean among the ears of grain after him in whose sight I shall find favor.' And she said to her, 'Go, my daughter.' So she set forth and went and gleaned in the field after the reapers . . .'" As Ruth worked her way through the barley fields outside Bethlehem, she eventually reached the property of Boaz. He had come out from the city to supervise the harvest and noticed the unfamiliar girl working so hard in his fields.

"Whose maiden is this?" he asked of his men. One of them answered, "It is the Moabite maiden, who came back with Naomi from the country of Moab." And the men told him how she had worked without rest since early morning.

They may have related this with a grudging respect. Any girl from Moab would not have appeared admirable in the eyes of these Israelites.

A Prosperous Farmer

Boaz, however, reacted with compassion. He remembered Naomi as the widow of Elimelech, who was his own kinsman, and he knew her story. Perhaps he felt embarrassed that he had done so little for Naomi.

Boaz, obviously impressed by Ruth's devotion, told her to glean only in his fields and to remain with the women he employed. He also promised to warn his men not to molest her. "Now listen, my daughter," he told her gently, "'do not go to glean in another field or leave this one, but keep close to my maidens. Let your eyes be upon the

field which they are reaping, and go after them. Have I not charged the young men not to molest you? And when you are thirsty, go to the vessels and drink what the young men have drawn.' Then she fell on her face, bowing to the ground, and said to him, 'Why have I found favor in your eyes, that you should take notice of me, when I am a foreigner?'"

Boaz reassured her, saying, "All that you have done for your mother-in-law since the death of your husband has been fully told me, and how you left your father and mother and your native land and came to a people that you did not know before. The Lord recompense you for what you have done, and a full reward be given you by the Lord, the God of Israel, under whose wings you have come to take refuge!"

Ruth thanked him with such grace that Boaz invited her to join him and his workmen at the midday meal. As she sat among the harvesting crew, he offered her bread and allowed her to dip it into the wine, a special treat. He himself placed helpings of parched grain before her. When the meal was over, Boaz discreetly instructed his men to drop grain wherever Ruth was gleaning.

By the end of the day, Ruth found that she had collected a surprising quantity of barley. She gathered it up in her veil—the mantle of heavy cloth that women of that time wore draped around the head and shoulders—and took it home to Naomi. The older woman stared at the heap of grain with disbelief. How could Ruth have managed to glean all that? In all, she had gathered half a bushel of grain. Ruth recounted the day's events and Naomi was overjoyed. Boaz, she said, was treating Ruth as a kinswoman.

Naomi must have feared that Boaz would have no interest in caring for an old woman past the age of childbearing. Apparently he was concerned after all. What is more, he did so in such a delicate fashion that there was no humiliation attached to his act of charity.

Levirate Marriage

Naomi was concerned with more than the gathering of grain. She began to think of a practice that then prevailed in Israel called the "levirate" marriage (from a word meaning husband's brother). The custom insured the security of a widow who might otherwise be left destitute and friendless. Under it, any childless widow had the right to expect her dead husband's brother to marry her. If no brother existed, some more distant male relative was required to perform this duty. Whichever relative married the widow became her "go'el" (redeemer or protector). The first son born to the widow by the new marriage was counted as a child of the dead husband and inherited his property.

Naomi, past childbearing age, could not hope for such a marriage. She had not thought it possible for Ruth, either, knowing that a Moabite woman would probably be looked upon with contempt. But now, Boaz' interest in her daughter-in-law might make it possible, after all.

The timing was fortunate. Immediately after the harvest, the farmers assembled to thresh and winnow the grain—a happy time when Boaz might be most receptive to such an idea.

To thresh the grain—that is, to separate kernels from stalks—the workers first scattered the sheaves over a threshing floor (a dry, hard, flat piece of ground). They then beat the stalks with flails or drove a team of oxen over them. The process was often speeded up by hitching the animals to a wooden sledge which had knobs of stone or metal attached to the underside. The scraping of the sledge loosened the kernels and broke the dry stalks into straw bits (chaff).

The men winnowed the mixture of grain and chaff by lifting it on a five- or six-pronged fork or a fanlike shovel and tossing it into the air. Breezes caught the chaff and dust and blew them aside. The heavier grains of barley or wheat fell back to the ground. The winnowing was generally done in the late afternoon and early evening, when the warm breezes from the Mediterranean blew.

When the winnowing was finished, groups of women sifted the grain through sieves to separate the last bits of chaff and other impurities from the grain. The sieves were made of round wooden frames and fine leather mesh, with holes so small that only the purified grain could pass through. Once the grain had been sifted, it was collected in large earthenware pots for storage.

When harvests were good, the time of threshing and winnowing was an occasion for celebration. The grain had been safely gathered, and there would be plenty to eat that year. As the farmers and their workers waited their turns to use the communal threshing floor, they joined in laughing, singing and feasting. And because the labor took several days, they usually planned on remaining overnight.

Since Boaz would take part in these festivities, Naomi felt it would be an ideal atmosphere in which to remind him of his family duty. She told Ruth to: "'Wash therefore and anoint yourself, and put on your best clothes and go down to the threshing floor; but do not make yourself known to the man until he has finished eating and drinking. But when he lies down, observe the place where he lies; then, go and uncover his feet and lie down; and he will tell you what to do.' And she replied, 'All that you say I will do.'"

That night, when all was quiet, Ruth cautiously approached the spot where Boaz slept. She lifted his blanket, uncovered his feet, and lay down there. By lying at his feet she was appealing to him to become her "go'el" and provide the protection due her as the widow of his kinsman.

A Public Agreement

At midnight Boaz awoke. He was startled to find Ruth at his feet. "Who are you?" he asked. "I am Ruth, your maidservant," she replied, "spread your skirt over your maidservant, for you are next of kin." Boaz, who was middle-aged, was flattered that this charming young woman had turned to him for protection, and he was quite willing to do what was required. He was a man of principle, however, and pointed out that there was another kinsman, a closer relative, who took precedence as a "go'el." That man must first be offered his chance.

As morning approached, Boaz insisted that Ruth leave while it was still dark: he did not wish any of the men to see her. As she left he said,

"You must not go back empty-handed to your mother-in-law," and he gave her a large heap of threshed and winnowed barley to take home.

Boaz wasted no time in making good his promise. Later that morning he went to the city gate of Bethlehem, center of the town's public life. Almost anyone could be found there at some time during the day. It was the spot where caravans arrived, where farmers and herdsmen gathered to buy and sell, perhaps just to gossip.

Making an Agreement Legally Binding

The public life of an Israelite village was concentrated at its main gate. It was here that matters of law were brought for adjudication before the elders of the community. They also were the official witnesses for transactions such as the one in which Boaz agreed to marry Ruth if her kinsman would give up all rights to her dead husband's property. A man renouncing property rights removed a sandal and presented it to the new property holder, a gesture that everyone understood and considered binding if witnessed by the elders.

Merchants bartered and tradesmen spread their wares on the ground, sometimes under a canopy.

The city's elders also met at the gate, where they functioned as justices of the peace. They settled property disputes and judged a wide variety of crimes ranging from theft of livestock to murder. If the elders decided the accused was guilty, he was punished on the spot.

Boaz did not have to wait long before the kinsman he sought came by. He called him over and then summoned 10 of the elders to witness the transaction he had in mind. Naomi, he explained, held some land of her late husband's which, out of poverty, she would have to sell. Would the near kinsman purchase it in order to keep the property from passing out of the family's possession? The kinsman readily agreed to do so.

But, Boaz went on, if the kinsman were to do that, he would also be obligated to a levirate marriage with Naomi's daughter-in-law. He would assume responsibility as her "go'el."

The kinsman balked at this. If he married Ruth, the tract of land would eventually be passed along to the first son she might have by him. "I cannot redeem it for myself, lest I impair my own inheritance," he said. "Take my right of redemption yourself . . ."

To bind the matter legally, the kinsman had to remove his sandal and hand it to Boaz—a gesture signifying the transfer of property. Boaz held up the sandal so that the elders could see it and bear witness to the contract. He had acquired all the property that Elimelech and his sons had owned, and Ruth the Moabitess, the widow of Mahlon, was to be his wife.

Boaz soon married Ruth. A loving, devoted wife, she remained a faithful daughter-in-law as well, and Naomi was properly taken care of for the rest of her life. When Ruth bore a son, Naomi proudly held it in her arms for everyone to see. Legally he counted as her grandson. Sons were held in much higher esteem than daughters, so the admiring women of Bethlehem paid Ruth their supreme compliment, saying to Naomi, "your daughter-in-law who loves you, who is more to you than seven sons, has borne him."

The happy ending of the tale of Naomi and Ruth was also an important beginning. Ruth's son was Obed, who was the father of Jesse, and he in turn fathered David, who was to become the Israelites' conquering hero, the leader who himself fostered a line of rulers that would endure for over four hundred years.

Centuries later, after the return of the Jews from their exile in Babylon, the great scribe Ezra demanded that Jewish men divorce foreign wives. This harsh policy was an attempt to "purify" Israel's society of alien influences. The demand caused much sorrow. It was about this time that the Book of Ruth first appeared—a plea for compassion and religious tolerance.

Ruth's story is told in the Book of Ruth.

Chapter 8

A Judge from the tribe of Ephraim guides the new nation toward monarchy, though he insists that the Lord is Israel's true king. Under his leadership, the prophetic movement becomes a potent source of religious fervor and social protest.

Samuel: Prophet for a New Nation

The last of the Judges, Samuel helped bring Israel from loose confederation to unity. Though committed to the ideal of a nation ruled by God, when the people requested a monarch, he reluctantly anointed Saul the first king of Israel. He lived on to the time of David, frequently reminding the Israelites of their first duty to the Lord.

Samuel was born at a critical time in his country's history. By the middle of the eleventh century B.C., the nature of Israel's life had undergone a gradual, profound change. The days of a wandering, rootless existence were long past, and the people of Israel had settled down, built towns, planted grain and vines, and were beginning to prosper. But their hard-won land was being threatened by the neighboring Philistines, who had begun to push eastward into the interior of Canaan from their territory along the Mediterranean coast. This was no band of nomads making occasional forays in the countryside, but a large, well-organized and well-equipped military elite coalition, hired by the Pharaoh to recapture the country for the Egyptian empire. By 1100 B.C., they had control of the coastal plain, the northern Plain of Jezreel and the Jordan Valley as far south as Succoth. This left Israel surrounded and confined to the high central ridge. The next Philistine move followed during Samuel's boyhood: a campaign into the central hills themselves.

The old tribal confederation established by Joshua was unable to meet the heightened demand for military and political unity. It was now divided by tribal rivalry and isolation. Consequently, when it became obvious that the Philistines threatened the independence of Israel, a delegation of elders from each tribe gathered together and journeyed to the town of Ramathaim, or Ramah, in Ephraim. They had come to see the aged prophet Samuel, and their message was straight to the point: "Give us a king . . ."

It was in Ramah that the life of this remarkable man began. The town was similar to many of the new Hebrew settlements in Canaan. A visitor would encounter a modest group of houses gathered on a grassy hilltop, surrounded by cultivated land and terraced hills. Among the small mud-brick dwellings he might find larger, two-story structures that housed several families grouped together under a patriarchal head.

For the people of Ramah and the rest of Israel, one of the great events of the year was the annual pilgrimage to the shrine at Shiloh, some 15 miles to the east. From the time of Joshua, Shiloh had been one of the major spiritual centers of Israel. The sacred tabernacle was there—a simple tent-like shrine that housed the ark of the covenant. To the Israelites, the ark—a small wooden chest decorated with winged creatures and con-

This sunlight-brushed elevation a few miles north of Jerusalem is known as the "hill of Samuel" because the great prophet is thought to have been buried here. High ground was considered holy throughout Biblical times; Samuel first met Saul when he was returning from making a sacrifice on such a "high place."

taining sacred objects—symbolized the invisible presence of God and his covenant with Israel.

The Feast of Booths was held at Shiloh each autumn to celebrate the harvest and to commemorate the covenant Israel made in the Sinai wilderness. For a week the people lived outdoors in small huts fashioned out of branches, bringing in the harvest by day and celebrating late into the night with feasting, music and sacrificial rites.

It was to Shiloh that Elkanah, a man of Ramah, came each year with his wife to make a sacrifice at the time of the fall harvest celebration. His offerings had a special importance to him because his wife Hannah had been unable to bear him a child. During one visit, Hannah went to the tabernacle alone to beseech God to grant her a son. She vowed, if her wish were fulfilled, to give the child's life over to the Lord's service.

Priests of the Tabernacle

Eventually, Hannah bore a son and named him Samuel. As soon as the child was weaned, she fulfilled her vow by delivering him to the shrine at Shiloh, where he was placed in the care of the high priest Eli for training as a Nazirite. He was pledged to the lifelong service of God and was obligated, as a token of this commitment, never to cut his hair or beard nor to consume alcohol.

During his early years at the shrine, Samuel was a firsthand witness to the corruption and decadence that had come to characterize the priesthood at Shiloh. The worst offenders were Eli's own sons, Hophni and Phinehas. They habitually stole food brought by pilgrims as offerings for sacrifice, cooked it contrary to sacrificial law, seduced women who had come to worship there and otherwise profaned their priestly roles. Eli himself was a worthy enough man, but he was very old, nearly blind and unable to deal with the scandalous conduct of his sons. Samuel's years at Shiloh left him feeling that the priesthood was morally defunct—an opinion widely shared in Israel, and one that would profoundly influence the course of his later life.

It was also at Shiloh that Samuel received the vision that launched him on his long prophetic mission. As he lay down to sleep one night, he heard his name called. "Here I am!" he answered, and he ran to Eli to see what he wanted.

"I did not call," said the surprised Eli; "lie down again." So Samuel returned to bed, and

again he heard the voice calling his name. He went to Eli and once more was told to go back to bed. When he heard the voice a third time, Samuel returned to Eli's side, and the aged priest realized that the child had been called by God. "Go, lie down," Eli told him, "and if he calls you, you shall say, 'Speak, Lord, for thy servant hears.'"

When Samuel heard the voice again, he answered as Eli had instructed, and the Lord spoke to him: "Behold, I am about to do a thing in Israel, at which the two ears of every one that hears it will tingle. On that day I will fulfil against Eli all that I have spoken concerning his house, from beginning to end. And I tell him that I am about to punish his house . . . because his sons were blaspheming God, and he did not restrain them."

Thus the fate of Eli's priesthood was revealed to Samuel, and he knew that he had been singled out to announce the Lord's plan to the people of Israel. He himself would provide the spiritual guidance that Eli and his sons had failed to give.

Not long after Samuel's vision at Shiloh, the

In addition to the regular sacrifices prescribed for holy days, priests of Samuel's time also conducted these rituals for families who wished to give thanks or ask for God's blessing on their personal affairs. Animals provided by the family were slaughtered on the altar. A meal of boiled meat was then prepared, in which the priests shared. Cooked fat—the sweetest part of the meat— was not eaten but set aside and burned on the altar to complete the ritual. The "horns," which show up prominently on the 10th century B.C. altar above, were symbols of divine power and were moistened with the blood of sacrificial animals during the ceremony.

Philistines engaged the Israelites in a major battle at Ebenezer. When the day was over, Israel had been badly outfought, and the distraught leaders sent to Shiloh for the ark in hopes of rallying their forces. The ark was brought to the Israelite camp by Eli's two sons, and the sight of it brought a great cheer from the troops as they prepared to join the battle again.

Capture of the Ark

The Philistines were frightened when they learned of the presence of the ark, but their leaders revived their courage. The second day brought disaster to Israel: many men fell, the survivors fled, Eli's sons were killed and the ark itself was captured by the enemy. When Eli heard the news, he collapsed and died.

The ark proved to be an unlucky prize. Wherever the captors took it, a pestilence followed. After seven months, the Philistines decided to rid themselves of the dreadful object. They put it on a wooden cart and placed symbols of the plague, gold images of mice and tumors, beside it as offerings to the God of Israel, and yoked two cows to the cart. "And the cows went straight in the direction of Beth-shemesh," an Israelite town.

Meanwhile, without the ark to bolster their courage, the Israelites had suffered great losses. After their victory at Ebenezer, the Philistines captured and occupied one town after another. The sanctuary at Shiloh was taken and destroyed, and Philistine garrisons were placed at key points throughout the hill country.

The recovery of the ark, however, failed to improve the fortunes of the Israelites. For 20 years the Philistines continued their aggressions, and Israel suffered a bitter and demoralizing period of enemy occupation and sporadic warfare.

In the meantime, Samuel had returned to Ramah and had become a prophet of the Lord. He was no common "seer" of the sort that had proliferated for centuries around the Near East—who for a fee would predict the future and the like. The prophet Samuel was known as a man truly possessed of the spirit of God, called to be the spokesman and agent of the Lord's will.

In addition to his religious duties, Samuel assumed the important role of judge. This included not only the traditional responsibilities of Israel's great Judges, but those of an actual magistrate as well. He traveled in an annual circuit from his home in Ramah to Bethel, Gilgal and Mizpah to preside over local issues and disputes.

Local judges usually settled the easier cases, but every so often more complicated cases arose, and these Samuel heard. Often the disputes concerned buying and renting land, for Israel had a complex series of laws controlling sales and leases. Men who had accidentally killed someone, those accused of slander, perhaps those caught in adultery—such cases were tried by Samuel, whenever an important decision by the local elders and tribal officials was appealed.

With the death of Eli and his sons, the destruction of Shiloh and the continued Philistine oppression, the faith of the Israelites reached a low point. The task of reviving Israel's spirits fell to Samuel. To assist him, he recruited bands of "nabis," ecstatic prophets "touched by God's hand," who roamed about the countryside dancing, chanting, playing musical instruments and falling into trances during which they communed with God. By proclaiming the Lord's intentions for Israel, they rallied the populace and fired up religious and nationalistic fervor.

Samuel was actually establishing a new institution in Israel, that of the Lord's prophets. By placing ecstatics in organized groups, with himself at their head, he gave fresh meaning and power to them. He focused their attention on national rather than local religious issues.

One of the most dramatic triumphs in the struggle against the Philistines occurred at the Benjaminite town of Mizpah, about 10 miles northwest of Jerusalem. Samuel had called a convocation there of all the tribes of Israel to make offerings and pray for divine guidance. When the Philistines learned of this gathering, they prepared for an attack. Samuel continued to pray, however, and the Lord responded. As the Philistines launched their attack, "the Lord thundered with a mighty voice [a great storm] that day against the Philistines and threw them into confusion; and they were routed before Israel."

One victory did not win a war, though, and the Philistine occupation continued with no sign of an end. Israel was tired and disorganized, and Samuel himself was growing old.

What Israel needed, it seemed, was a whole new kind of leadership—one that would provide the unity and direction necessary to expel the Philistines. It was with this in mind that the elders of the 12 tribes went to see Samuel. Other coun-

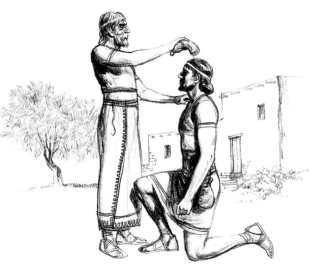

A Simple Ceremony Creates a King

"Then Samuel took a vial of oil and poured it on his head, and kissed him and said, 'Has not the Lord anointed you to be prince over his people Israel?'" (1 Sam. 10.1). Thus Saul was designated as the first king of Israel in a time-hallowed Near Eastern ritual. The sacred mixture used for the anointment usually consisted of a fine grade of olive oil, frequently scented with herbs and perfumes. It was poured from a horn-shaped vessel such as the gold-banded ivory cup at right, which was found in a palace at Megiddo. When Samuel consecrated Saul in this traditional ritual, it served notice to the Israelites that their prophet was carrying out God's will.

tries had prospered under monarchical rule: this was what the people of Israel wanted. "Behold, you are old . . . now appoint for us a king to govern us like all the nations," they said to Samuel.

It was a demand that went deeply against Samuel's beliefs. To ask for a king, he thought, was nothing short of blasphemy, for the simple reason that God *was* their king, on earth as well as in heaven. They needed no human monarch.

Yet when confronted by the elders' demand, Samuel's first thought was for himself—the people were rejecting him as their leader. But then the Lord spoke to him: "Hearken to the voice of the people . . . for they have not rejected you, but they have rejected me from being king over

them . . . only, you shall solemnly warn them, and show them the ways of the king who shall reign over them."

Samuel returned to the elders and warned them of what they could expect from a king: he would conscript their sons into his army, force them to work his lands and make his weapons, take over the best of their farms and their harvests—in short, he would make them his servants. "And in that day you will cry out," Samuel concluded, "because of your king, whom you have chosen for yourselves; but the Lord will not answer you in that day."

In spite of this ominous prediction, the elders stood by their demand, and Samuel finally sent them away with his promise to find them a king. Then he returned to his home and waited for a sign from the Lord.

Soon afterward the Lord told Samuel that he was sending him a man who would be a prince over Israel and who would lead the people to victory over the Philistines. The man would be of the southern tribe of Benjamin, the smallest of the twelve tribes of Israel.

Saul Made King

The next day Samuel traveled to a small town near Ramah to perform a sacrifice at the local sanctuary. Another traveler also arrived there that day: Saul, a young Benjaminite. He had been told that the prophet could help him find some donkeys that had strayed from his father's farm.

As he approached the town, Saul asked a group of young women if Samuel was there. "They answered, 'He is; behold, he is just ahead of you. Make haste; he has come just now to the city, because the people have a sacrifice today on the high place.'" This was a sacred area located on a hilltop near the town.

When Samuel saw the tall, handsome youth coming toward him, he knew at once that this was the man God had chosen to be king. ". . . go up before me to the high place," he told him, "for today you shall eat with me, and in the morning I will let you go . . ."

That night Saul slept in Samuel's house, and at dawn the next day the prophet awakened him. "Up, that I may send you on your way," he urged. The two men walked together to the outskirts of the town, where Samuel turned to Saul and said, "'. . . stop here . . . for a while, that I may make

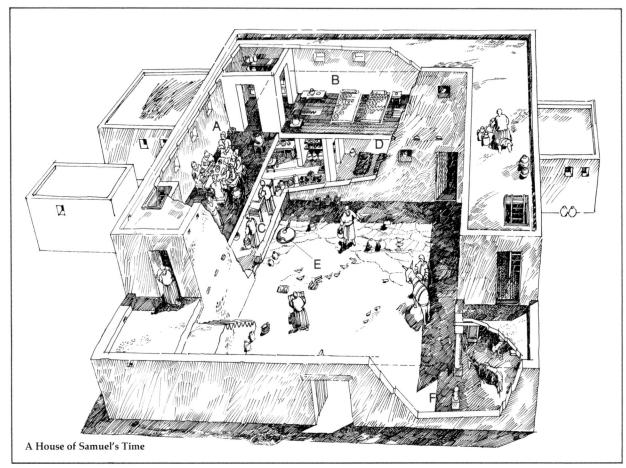

A House of Samuel's Time

"When they came down from the high place into the city, a bed was spread for Saul upon the roof" (1 Sam. 9.25), probably the most comfortable place on a sultry night. City houses took shape haphazardly amid older buildings, but a wealthy Israelite's home would follow the basic plan of the dining (A) and sleeping (B) areas located on the second floor, and the kitchen and storage (C) area and the servants' quarters (D) below. The oven would be in the courtyard (E). The pillars at right correspond to (F) above, in the reconstruction adapted from the remains of a house in Shechem.

known to you the word of God.' Then Samuel took a vial of oil and poured it on his [Saul's] head, and kissed him and said, 'Has not the Lord anointed you to be prince over his people Israel? And you shall reign over the people of the Lord and you will save them from the hand of their enemies round about.'"

Saul soon demonstrated his worth as a leader by bringing enough Israelite troops together to raise the siege of Jabesh-gilead east of the Jordan. On the heels of this unexpected victory, Samuel called the people to Gilgal, and they unanimously proclaimed Saul their king. Samuel then addressed the multitude, recalling times past when God had answered the cries of his errant people. "And now," he concluded, "behold the king whom you have chosen, for whom you have asked; behold, the Lord has set a king over you."

It was not long before trouble arose between Samuel and Saul. Prior to a major battle with the Philistines at Michmash, Samuel, speaking as the Lord's prophet, instructed Saul to assemble his forces at Gilgal and wait there for seven days, at which time Samuel would come to perform a ritual offering to the Lord.

Wrath of the Prophet

The waiting proved too much for many of the soldiers, who began to desert and scatter throughout the hills and caves of the region. Saul was impatient and anxious to get on with the battle while he still had men to command, and when Samuel failed to appear at the appointed time, Saul performed the offering himself. Suddenly Samuel appeared and berated Saul for his disobedience: "You have done foolishly; you have not kept the commandment of the Lord your God . . . But now your kingdom shall not continue . . ." Then Samuel abruptly left Gilgal.

This episode marked the beginning of a lasting antagonism between the man of God and the king. The final break occurred when Samuel, again in God's name, ordered Saul to launch a holy war against the Amalekites, a warlike tribe living in the wilderness south of Judah. Saul's forces were victorious, but they spared the life of Agag, the Amalekite chief, and brought back the best of the enemy's cattle. Both acts were in violation of the concept of "herem," the holy war, which required that the enemy and all its possessions be totally destroyed.

When Samuel learned of these two offenses he confronted Saul angrily: "The Lord anointed you king over Israel. And the Lord sent you on a mission, and said, 'Go, utterly destroy the sinners, the Amalekites . . .' Why then did you not obey . . . ?" When Saul explained that he had brought the animals back only for a sacrifice, Samuel answered, "Has the Lord as great delight in burnt offerings and sacrifices, as in obeying the voice of the Lord? . . . Because you have rejected the word of the Lord, he has also rejected you from being king." Samuel had the Amalekite chief brought before him, drew his sword and

killed him. Then Samuel left the king forever.

Though Saul continued to occupy the throne, he no longer ruled with God's blessing. This fateful turn of events created the need to find a successor among the Israelites.

Once again the task fell upon the Lord's prophet, Samuel. This time God directed him to Bethlehem to seek out and anoint David, the youngest of eight sons of Jesse. It would be many years before David would succeed to the throne. In the interval, Saul persecuted his young rival relentlessly, but it proved beyond his power to alter the course Samuel had set.

After anointing David, Samuel retired to Ramah, where he continued to act as a prophet and judge of his people. Some years later David, fleeing from the jealous Saul, sought refuge in Samuel's house. There he managed to evade Saul's soldiers temporarily, and he probably listened eagerly to the prophet's teachings.

Not long after that, Samuel died at Ramah, but his influence over Israel's destiny continued. Sometime later the Philistines prepared to attack Saul's army near Gilboa. Frightened without Samuel's support and advice, the tormented king went to a witch at nearby Endor and asked her to conjure up Samuel's spirit—in direct violation of an Israelite law forbidding witchcraft. Samuel's spirit appeared and predicted Saul's defeat and death: "The Lord has done to you as he spoke by me; for the Lord has torn the kingdom out of your hand, and given it to your neighbor, David. . . . Moreover the Lord will give Israel also with you into the hand of the Philistines; and tomorrow you and your sons shall be with me . . ."

As Samuel had prophesied, Saul and his sons died the next day in battle against the Philistines. Israel's first attempt at kingship seemed to have met a disastrous end: Saul was dead and the Philistines were again without effective opposition in Israel. Wisely Samuel had prepared for such a situation, and within a short time after Saul's death, David would occupy the throne of Israel. This brilliant young king would rid Israel of the Philistine menace and establish a powerful, united kingdom over his people. Samuel's relations with Saul had set a pattern which would be repeated often throughout Israel's history: the prophet of the Lord at odds with a king.

The story of Samuel is told in Book 1 Samuel.

Part Three

The Golden Age
of the Kings of Israel

"They shall plant vineyards and drink their wine" (Amos 9.14). Israel's "golden age" arrived in the years of David and Solomon, around 950 B.C. The Israelites were no longer newcomers to Canaan, but rulers of a sizable empire. During these years annual festivals were celebrated with special joy. Among them was the grape harvest, held in September or October. Then, farmers and their families would gather for singing, dancing and communal labor on the terraced hillsides. By day, men, women and children cut the ripened grapes. At night, sentries watched for foxes, boars and poachers. Some of the grapes were eaten fresh or dried for later consumption. Wine grapes were trampled in vats hewn from stone, and their juice was run off into smaller vats. The new wine was fermented, then sealed in clay jars and stored in cool rock cellars.

Under the rules of three great kings—Saul, David and Solomon—the Israelites finally realize the Lord's promise of an earthly kingdom. Yet, even during this "golden age," kingly power increasingly clashes with the people's belief in the sovereignty of God.

The tenth century B.C. was the most glorious in ancient Israel's history. During the years 1000 to 922 Israel reached the height of its territorial size and international power. Under David and Solomon the loose tribal confederation was replaced by a powerful central monarchy, and Israel enjoyed an era of peace and prosperity. Ironically, it was also during this time that the seeds of Israel's ultimate division and destruction were planted.

Following Saul's anointment as king in about 1020 B.C., Israel embarked on a century of unprecedented growth. Within the span of two generations a small, embattled group of tribes was transformed into the most powerful kingdom between the Nile and Euphrates rivers, and the austere faith of Moses was given focus by Solomon in the temple of Jerusalem.

Israel's dramatic rise to power involved changes with far-reaching (and to some, ominous) implications for the future. The creation of a centralized monarchy was a necessary step in meeting the Philistine threat, but it also represented a major break with tradition.

Kingship was historically a notion alien to Israel. The original Mosaic covenant nowhere mentioned it, and the tribes themselves had a long tradition of independence. The elders of each village and tribe were the acknowledged leaders, and the average Israelite felt a stronger allegiance to his own clan and patriarchal tribe than to the nation as a whole.

But the threat posed by the Philistines was such that the Israelites thought that only "a king . . . like all the nations" (1 Samuel 8.5) could save their nation from disaster. After its defeat near Aphek in 1020 B.C., and the subsequent destruction of the central tribal-league shrine at Shiloh, much of Israel had fallen to the might of the Philistines. Enemy soldiers occupied the hill country, and it seemed that the nation was doomed. The weak tribal system, based on councils of elders and a loose militia-type army, could not effectively oppose the Philistines, whose army was well organized and equipped with advanced weapons, chariots and armor.

Israel's only hope for survival seemed to be in a new form of national organization. If the tribes could unite under a powerful leader and create a strong army, they might be able to throw off the Philistine yoke. So the tribal elders gathered and went to the aged prophet Samuel and asked him, as Judge of all Israel, to appoint a king.

Samuel told them that Israel needed no king because the Lord was its sovereign, and he further warned of the consequences of monarchy: loss of freedom, military conscription, heavy taxation and forced labor. (This was precisely what happened under Solomon.) Yet when the people still insisted, Samuel reluctantly agreed to find them the king they wanted.

King Saul

So it was that a young Benjaminite whose name was Saul became Israel's first king. Cast in the heroic mold of the earlier Judges, Saul was expected (at least by Samuel) to rule according to the will of God.

But how would God's will be communicated to Saul and his successors? Samuel provided the answer by creating the office of prophet—a position that was to be a potent force in Israel's history. He organized the visionaries who roamed among the people into a new order known as the "sons of the prophets," with himself as their head. The role of Judge was thus split into two parts, king and prophet. The divinely chosen commander would now receive his instructions through the prophet rather than directly from the Lord himself.

This was the theory; in practice, Samuel soon found himself involved in bitter and fateful rivalry with Saul. In his campaigns against the Philistines, Saul proved himself more than equal to any of Israel's former Judges as a tactician and field commander, while his rugged simplicity and lack of princely manners only enhanced his reputation among the people. Samuel remained unimpressed, and when Saul twice disobeyed the prophet's instructions, Samuel withdrew his support of the new king.

From then on, Saul's fortune took a disastrous plunge. "Now the Spirit of the Lord departed from Saul, and an evil spirit from the Lord tormented him" (1 Samuel 16.14). He began to suffer from spells of anxiety and severe depression. Unable to find a remedy, his servants brought a young shepherd from Bethlehem named David, reputed to be a skilled musician, to soothe him with his lyre. Shortly thereafter, during a campaign against the Philistines, David established himself as a warrior in the duel with Goliath.

Rather than fight a full-scale battle, the Philistines had challenged the Israelites to choose one of their men to fight a duel with their huge warrior of Gath. Young David volunteered to accept the challenge, and he killed the heavily armed Goliath with a stone hurled from his shepherd's sling. This and subsequent victories quickly made David a popular national hero.

In Saul's eyes, David's growing popularity seemed a danger to his rule. The king fell prey to jealousy and accused his young protégé of royal ambitions. For the rest of his reign Saul was to dedicate himself to a futile effort to eliminate David and so preserve the succession for his own son Jonathan. But from the beginning Jonathan's first loyalty was to his friend David, even if it meant losing his own claim to the throne.

Inevitably, David was forced to flee, making his way southeast to seek refuge in the Wilderness of Judah. He was joined by a band of outcasts like himself, and together they managed a precarious existence.

The Wilderness was an excellent place to hide from the enraged Saul. Today, as then, it is a narrow strip of land bordering the western coast of the Dead Sea. Innumerable valleys and gulches slice through the area as it falls from the central hills to the edge of the sea—a drop of over 4000 feet. The barren, rough terrain contains many caves, which have offered fugitives safety and shelter for thousands of years.

Saul kept up a relentless pursuit of David, sending forces into the Wilderness in the hope of capturing the young fugitive. Each time, David and his band succeeded in eluding their pursuers. Twice during his forced exile David could have easily killed Saul but refrained, for although Saul was now his mortal enemy, he was also the anointed monarch of the Lord.

Each time he was confronted with proof of David's fidelity, Saul cried out in agonized repentance, but his passions were something he could not predict or control. David realized this, and after nearly three years he left Israel altogether. He and his men journeyed to the Philistine city of Gath, where the king, Achish, accepted them as mercenaries. Achish gave them the city of Ziklag in the Negeb as a base of operations for forays against Saul. In fact, David and his men left the Israelites in peace, fighting instead against the aggressive nomadic tribes in the southern Negeb.

A year later, as David and his followers were resting after a battle with the southern nomads, a messenger reached them with news that the Israelites had just been badly defeated by the Philistines. Jonathan and his two brothers had been killed in the battle and Saul had committed suicide to avoid being taken alive.

David received the news of Saul's death with grief as genuine as that which he felt at the loss of his beloved Jonathan. After a day of fasting and lamentation he and his troops returned to Judah, where the tribal elders promptly proclaimed him their new ruler.

King David

David began his reign as king of Judah only, with his capital at Hebron. Israel was no longer a united kingdom. In the north Saul's general, Abner, made one of Saul's surviving sons, Ishbosheth, king. There followed a period of bitter and sporadic warfare between the northern and southern tribes.

Abner quarreled bitterly with Ishbosheth, and in revenge offered to reunite the northern tribes with Judah under David's rule. But before negotiations were complete, the reconciliation was seriously jeopardized. David's field commander, Joab, murdered Abner over a long-standing blood feud. Joab thereby eliminated Abner as a rival candidate for the post of commander-in-chief of David's army.

Acting quickly to keep from alienating the north, David ordered a state funeral. Then, accompanied by his entire court, he walked in mourning behind Abner's bier. David's gesture was widely admired, and "all the people . . . understood that day that it had not been the king's will to slay Abner . . ." (2 Samuel 3.37). The elders of the northern clans agreed to accept

Playing Leapfrog

Children's games are rarely recorded in the arts and writings of the ancient world, including the Bible. However, the Egyptian carving on which this picture is based shows that some games were not very different from those of modern children.

David as ruler of their people, seven years after Saul's death in battle.

David's most urgent task was to defeat the Philistines and drive them into the coastal region that they had originally occupied. Pushing westward, his army gradually drove the enemy forces out of Israel. The Philistines became vassals of

the new kingdom and, to guard against future aggression from them, David strengthened the defenses at Beth-shemesh and Debir.

He then moved to capture Jerusalem, which lay on the border between Judah and the north. At that time Jerusalem was held by a Canaanite group calling themselves Jebusites. The city commanded the main north-south highway through the central hills, and its capture was essential to David's plan to unite the northern and southern parts of Israel without causing jealousy on either side. By means of a clever strategy, Joab took Jerusalem and David claimed it as his personal holding.

Thus a city with no tribal ties became Israel's capital, the City of David. To further strengthen Jerusalem's position, David made it the religious center of Israel by transporting the ark of the covenant there.

David erected only a simple tabernacle to shelter the ark. Although, as king, he had ample resources to beautify his capital, throughout his reign it remained a small, unimpressive fortress-city, much as the Jebusites had left it.

Other Canaanite cities surrendered to David and became part of his growing empire. At last the entire Promised Land had been delivered into Israel's hands. For the first time in history, all of Canaan was united under one leader.

David, hardly pausing to savor the moment, next turned his armies eastward to the lands across the Jordan River. He quickly subdued the three neighboring kingdoms of Ammon, Moab and Edom. Then he moved north to face his greatest challenge, the Aramean kingdoms of western Syria. Soon afterward, the badly defeated Arameans came to terms.

Israel's sudden expansion came at a time when the traditional powers in the area were preoccupied with domestic problems. Toward the end of Solomon's reign, they were to reassert their dominance in western Asia—with dire consequences for Israel. But for the time being, the field was open, and David stepped in, building up the most powerful state between the Mesopotamian and the Nile valleys.

David's military successes were due in large part to his genius as a commander. Unlike the loose militia of the days of the Judges and Saul, his army was well organized and centrally controlled. At the top was a small core of leaders known as "The Thirty," men who had proved their loyalty and courage during David's outlaw years. Below them was a standing army of 1200 regular mercenaries, and a reserve force of 24,000 men chosen from the Israelite tribes. There was also a royal bodyguard of 600 veterans of David's guerrilla warfare days.

The vast empire David had created was too large and complex to be governed under the old tribal institutions. Israel now needed an efficient, centralized bureaucracy and David, with characteristic foresight, set about creating a new form of government. In Jerusalem he organized an administration loyal to him, creating several important new posts, including a court "recorder," or herald, whose job it was to transmit government policies to the public; and a "scribe," whose duties included foreign correspondence. In addition, David appointed two high priests in Jerusalem representing two dominant (and rival) priestly houses. The conquered territories were administered by court-appointed governors and lesser officials.

In the later stages of his reign, David's great public success was marred by a series of family tragedies brought on, people believed, by his sinful liaison with Bathsheba. Like many oriental monarchs, David had a sizable harem and as he grew older, his court was filled with plots and intrigues. Since there was no Israelite precedent for hereditary succession to the throne, his many sons tried to seize their advantage before David died. One son, Absalom, gathered a large group of supporters and started a rebellion against his father, but his dramatic revolt failed and he was killed by David's general, Joab.

Near the end of his reign David ordered a national census. This was intended as the first step in a long-range program to replace the old tribal system with one based on provinces, administered by royal officials. Such a program represented one more step away from Mosaic tradition and toward a powerful monarchy.

Soon after the census was completed, a plague began to ravage Israel, moving rapidly down through the northern countryside toward Jerusalem. It was widely believed to be a punishment for David's violation of God's will in ordering the census, and the aging king fearfully regretted what he had done. As the pestilence reached the outskirts of Jerusalem, its progress was miraculously halted, and the court seer instructed David to build an altar on the spot where the plague had

Psalms of the Bible Were Sung to a Lyre

The lyre (below in an Egyptian carving) was universally used by the peoples of the ancient Near East. It was light and portable enough for nomadic tribes, yet melodious enough to be used even in performances at court. The player held his lyre either horizontally or cradled in his arms, plucking the strings with his fingers or with a pick. A sound box at the base of the instrument resonated with the strings to produce the music. Perhaps the most famous musician of the Bible was David, who played a lyre—in a way similar to that shown at left—for Saul. To this accompaniment he might have recited traditional poems or stories, sung favorite songs or just improvised.

stopped—a threshing floor on a hill just north of the city wall. David immediately bought the land from its owner, and there he built a sacrificial altar. That ground was to become the most sacred spot in Israel, the site of Solomon's temple.

During David's last days, his eldest surviving son, Adonijah, a handsome and magnetic young man, decided to seize the kingship for himself, and he was accepted as the rightful heir by many, including Joab. But a rival group headed by the prophet Nathan went to the king to remind him of an old vow that Solomon, Bathsheba's son, would inherit the throne. David remembered his promise and willingly designated Solomon as Israel's next king.

In a public ceremony watched over by the royal

bodyguard, Solomon arrived riding on the king's mule and was anointed king. Adonijah now took refuge inside the sanctuary, while his supporters fled. The issue thus settled, Solomon began serving as regent for his ailing father. Finally, as David lay on his deathbed, he summoned Solomon to his side for a final set of instructions that included the necessary but heartrending decision concerning the loyal Joab. Recalling Joab's killing of Abner, David said to Solomon: "do not let his gray head go down to Sheol in peace" (1 Kings 2.6).

What today may seem to have been a needless and ungrateful action was in fact unavoidable in the tenth century B.C. According to the belief in bloodguilt, David had been tainted with it during his own reign because he had left Joab's crime unpunished. If Joab were to die in peace under Solomon, the bloodguilt would be transferred to Solomon and all his heirs. David knew only too well the demands of Mosaic law in such a case: Joab must die bearing his own guilt.

King Solomon

Coming to Israel's throne in about 961 B.C., Solomon wasted little time in putting both Joab and Adonijah to death. And so it was that "his kingdom was firmly established" (1 Kings 2.12).

Solomon reorganized and enlarged David's administrative structure, introducing a nation-wide system of public officials headed by a sort of prime minister. This officer, a man named Ahishar, presided over a council that directed a bureaucracy extending from the palace in Jerusalem down to the rural village level.

At the same time, Solomon eradicated the old tribal boundaries and made 12 new administrative districts in the north. In Judah he retained districts that David had created. Each new district was governed by a royally appointed official. With this, Solomon all but eliminated an ancient and basic aspect of Israel's life; tribal distinctions thereafter remained in force for certain ceremonial and genealogical purposes, but the authority of the clans in local affairs was drastically reduced from that time on.

On the international scene, Solomon's chief concern was to maintain through diplomacy what his father had won in battle. He obtained a treaty with Egypt by marrying the Pharaoh's daughter—important recognition of Israel's new role as a major power. Other alliances were also sealed by foreign marriages, and Solomon acquired a large harem. The new diplomacy was a success, and for the greater part of his 40-year reign Solomon preserved and enriched David's kingdom without large-scale warfare.

Solomon's most beneficial alliance was with Hiram, king of Tyre. At that time Tyre was the dominant power in Phoenicia, a league of maritime cities along the coast north of Israel. With the assistance of Tyrian craftsmen and builders, Solomon embarked on a large-scale construction program. He fortified the important cities of Megiddo, Gezer and Hazor, and built a port at Ezion-geber, on the Gulf of Aqaba. From there Solomon's Phoenician-manned merchant fleet sailed to Red Sea ports, returning with cargoes of gold, precious stones, ivory and spices.

In Jerusalem Solomon built a splendid palace and a beautiful temple for the ark of the covenant. The temple was his crowning achievement. Dedicated in about 952 B.C., its design was similar to contemporary Phoenician temples. The interior measured some 105 feet long, 35 wide and 50 in height, and was divided into two principal areas. The ornate main hall, or "holy place," contained a small altar for incense, behind which a flight of stairs led up to a smaller chamber, the mysterious "holy of holies." It was empty except for two cherubim (mythological animals: lions

Typical Israelite pottery of Saul's time was made in the courtyard of his fortress at Gibeah. First clay and water were trodden together (l. center), and this mixture was shaped on a foot-driven wheel (r. center). Small standardized vessels were mass-produced from a single clay cone by molding each at the top, lifting it off and then repeating the process. A creamy clay coating, or "slip," was applied (foreground) and the vessel was polished with a bone or pebble (center) before firing (rear). Above are samples.

This bronze statue, unearthed at Megiddo, symbolizes the fighting tradition of its citizens, guardians of the strategic pass through Mt. Carmel to the northern plain. The man is armed with a typical scimitar-shaped sword and rectangular shield.

Archaeologists have never been able to find any trace of King Solomon's buildings in Jerusalem, because excavation has never been permitted in the sacred areas on and around the original temple site. In any case, the thorough destruction by the Babylonians and then the Romans would leave very little to discover.

The completion of the temple had a political as well as a religious meaning. It was intended by Solomon to signify the permanence of Jerusalem as God's worldly capital and of the House of David as Israel's ruling family. Through his prophet Nathan, the Lord had anointed the House of David: "Thus says the Lord of hosts [to David]. . . . I will raise up your offspring after you . . . He shall build a house for my name, and I will establish the throne of his kingdom for ever" (2 Samuel 7.8, 12–13).

During Solomon's reign Israel experienced a flowering of the arts. David had begun this process by importing Canaanite musicians to play at court, to compose temple music and to encourage the writing of psalms (hymns). Solomon may even have participated in the literary activity at his court when he fostered the beginnings of a tradition known as the "wisdom school." In later centuries this school of thinking produced the books of Proverbs, Job and Ecclesiastes.

The riches and splendor of Solomon's court were far removed from the life of the average Israelite, yet everyone benefited to some degree from the general peace and prosperity. With the danger of Philistine attack eliminated, people could move out from fortified towns and build new communities in the countryside. Now that the Philistine monopoly on iron had been broken, farmers could use iron plow points in their fields, and could harvest with sharp, iron-bladed sickles. In general, life became a bit easier under the monarchy, and the Israelite population grew from perhaps 500,000 under Saul to 1,000,000 under Solomon.

For most people, however, life remained simple and unpretentious. Traditional ties were strong, and a person's first loyalty was to his immediate family and patriarchal clan. Village life centered around the farming calendar, and the week was divided into six days of work and one day (the Sabbath) of rest. The major annual harvests were celebrated with festivals, which the Israelites also associated with great events from their history.

with human faces and outstretched wings) and the ark of the covenant, which was placed between them during the ceremony of dedication. The cherubim were believed to support the invisible throne of God, whose presence in the temple reaffirmed the eternal covenant with his chosen people.

The idea of a temple was a new one for Israel and was pagan in origin. The thought of the deity actually living in the temple was alien to the orthodox religion of the Israelites: their Lord had always dwelled with them as they moved about the desert. Nor did the Israelites see sacrifice as the daily nourishment of the Lord, as it was for pagan gods; they believed in it as a pious gift from his worshiping people.

Above all, it was a life governed by the needs of agriculture. In 1908 a schoolboy's writing exercise plaque, from the time of Solomon, was found in the ruins of Gezer. Its rhythmic enumeration of the seasons (beginning in the fall) gives us a glimpse of the farmer's year:

"The two months of [olive] harvest,
    The two months of planting [grain],
        The two months of late planting;
The month of hoeing up of flax,
    The month of harvest of barley,
        The month of harvest and storage;
The two months of vine-tending,
    The month of summer-fruit."

In the last years of Solomon's reign there was a general discontentment which grew out of his harsh programs of labor conscription. The Israelites resented being forced to serve for part of each year on huge labor gangs to build the king's palaces and fortifications. Many people also became critical of his toleration of the pagan religions of his foreign wives.

Within a short time after Solomon's death in 922 B.C., Israel's empire disintegrated and the nation was divided into two rival kingdoms. Yet later generations never forgot the brief period when, under David and Solomon, Israel had achieved glorious nationhood. In later centuries, the prophets would look back on that era as the prototype of a triumphant age to come when God would send a new David to rule and to bring peace, not only to Israel, but to the whole world he had originally created.

David and Solomon Establish an Empire

In the relatively brief span of two generations, nearly all of the major states around Canaan became part of the Israelite empire. From Hamath in the north to a southern frontier in the Sinai desert, it included Moab, Edom, Ammon and the important Syrian capital of Damascus—in all, over 10,000 square miles. To govern the newly won territory, David made centrally located Jerusalem his capital. Later, Solomon divided Israel into 12 administrative districts, each required to supply the court's provisions for one month out of the year. With these taxes, and tribute from vassal states, he embarked upon such ambitious building projects as Israel's first seaport at Ezion-geber.

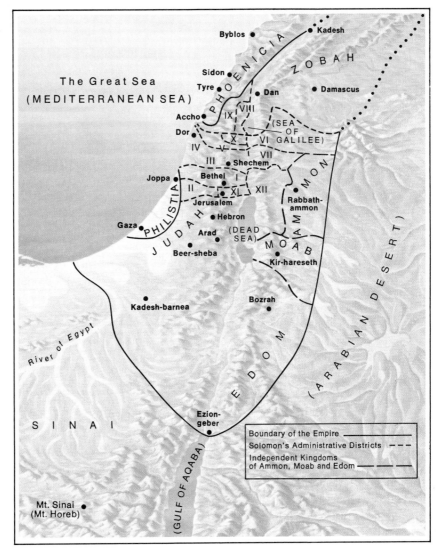

Chapter 9

*Faced with extinction, the tribes of Israel cease quarreling among themselves
and unite in a single kingdom under Saul. His firm leadership wins victories for Israel,
but his conflicts with Samuel and David lead to torment and a tragic death.*

Saul: Israel's First King

*Saul, anointed king by Samuel, began his reign with a
series of triumphs and ended it in tragedy. But, for Israel, it was an era of important political progress. Under
a permanent political leader, disunity—the most serious
weakness of the tribal league—was done away with.
Despite his own personal failure, it was Saul who laid
the groundwork for a united Israel.*

Although the country the Israelites had occupied was only slightly larger than the state of
Vermont, its harsh terrain was a barrier to national unity. Split down the middle by a sharp
rise of craggy hills—with the steeply sloping Jordan Valley to the east and the verdant coastal plain
spreading to the west—the hilly landscape naturally divided Israel into a series of scattered settlements. Within these sharply outlined enclaves,
the tribes remained independent of one another.
They came together as a nation only for the annual renewal of the Mosaic covenant, for certain
festivals and to meet emergencies. This lack of
unity made them highly vulnerable to the enemies that surrounded them.

Here and there some Canaanite strongholds
still existed, but Israel's most formidable opponents were the Philistines. The Israelite militia
was no match for these tough, well-disciplined
warriors, who opposed the copper and bronze
weapons of the Israelites with iron swords and
spearheads. The Philistines also zealously
guarded the secrets of iron smelting they had
brought from their eastern Mediterranean home.

Their swift, heavily armed charioteers easily
crushed any unmounted opponents. Striking
from their cities on the coastal plain of Canaan,
they were gradually swallowing Israel. By 1050
B.C., they had seized most of the central mountain
territory and had destroyed Shiloh, site of Israel's
central shrine. Their powerful army was even
augmented by mercenary divisions of Hebrews.

The Philistines reinforced their domination by
imposing a monopoly on metallurgy, so armed
resistance was stifled because the Israelites had
no access to the sharper, more durable iron
weapons. No Israelite community was allowed to
have its own forge. Farmers were forced to buy
their plow points and other metal implements
from Philistine smiths, and they were charged
exorbitant fees for repairs.

A King for Israel

Israel would soon have ceased to exist if the tribal
elders had not decided on a course that was completely contrary to their traditions: they went to
their spiritual leader, the Prophet Samuel, and
asked him to appoint a king.

Samuel was indignant. God was the only king
Israel had ever acknowledged. He had always

*"There was hard fighting against the Philistines all the days of
Saul" (1 Sam. 14.52). From bases along the coast, the Philistines
occupied key cities as far inland as Beth-shan on the strategic
heights (right) that controlled a major route to the Jordan Valley.
After killing Saul in battle, the Philistines brought his body here.*

brought forth men like Joshua and Gideon to lead the people in times of crisis. But the elders insistently demanded a king "that we also may be like all the nations, and that our king may govern us and go out before us and fight our battles."

Reluctantly, Samuel sought guidance from the Lord, who told him: "Hearken to their voice, and make them a king." Then the Lord instructed him: "Tomorrow about this time I will send to you a man from the land of Benjamin, and you shall anoint him to be prince over my people Israel. He shall save my people from the hand of the Philistines . . ."

The ruler-to-be was already on his way to Samuel. It was Saul and "There was not a man among the people of Israel more handsome than he; from his shoulders upward he was taller than any of the people."

His father, a wealthy Benjaminite landowner named Kish, had sent him to look for a herd of donkeys that had strayed from their property at Gibeah, four miles north of Jerusalem. After an unsuccessful search through the neighboring farmlands and hill country, Saul and his servant arrived at a small walled town on a hillside near Ramah. The servant suggested that they seek the advice of a local wise man. The seer was Samuel.

As Saul approached him, Samuel heard the Lord's voice: "Here is the man of whom I spoke to you! He . . . shall rule over my people."

Samuel took the young man in for the night and early the next morning led him to the outskirts of the city. There Samuel stopped and ordered Saul to send his servant on ahead. Then the prophet drew a vessel made of a ram's horn from the sash of his robe. Raising the horn over Saul's head, he anointed him with oil and revealed the Lord's will, saying "you shall reign over the people of the Lord and you will save them from the hand of their enemies . . ."

Cautioning him to remain silent about the event, Samuel sent the newly anointed king on his way and, several days later, summoned all the tribal elders to Mizpah. There, when the people were ready to acclaim their new monarch, they could not find him. Shy and still not used to the idea of being king, Saul was finally discovered hiding among the baggage.

Generally he was a popular choice and the assembled elders rejoiced. But some had reservations. A number of "worthless fellows" looked on Saul with contempt and refused to accept him

as ruler. "How can this man save us?" they asked. Saul soon had the opportunity to prove that, though he might be humble, he was not meek.

It was Samuel himself who was most reluctant about Saul's elevation. At the convocation ceremony he continued to berate the Israelites for wanting a king. From the start, his attitude toward Saul was one of watchful suspicion.

Tactics of Surprise

Not long after the ceremony at Mizpah, several men from the village of Jabesh-gilead east of the Jordan hastened through the hills with an urgent plea for help. Nahash, king of the seminomadic Ammonites, had crossed Israel's eastern border and laid siege to the community on the eastern edge of the Jordan Valley. Even though the helpless villagers offered to surrender, Nahash was not satisfied. He wanted to humiliate all Israel and demanded that the right eye of each man in Jabesh be gouged out. Confident of his superiority, he granted the village elders a seven-day grace period to seek outside support. Everywhere the messengers traveled, the Israelites wept over the plight of the men of Jabesh, but no one volunteered to help them.

Still a farmer, Saul was plowing his field when he heard the news. Enraged by the cowardice of his countrymen, he slaughtered and dismembered his oxen on the spot, then sent the pieces throughout Israel with an ultimatum: "Whoever does not come out after Saul and Samuel, so shall it be done to his oxen!"

The Israelites quickly fell into line, and each of the tribes contributed troops. Saul mustered a large force and led them on an overnight march toward the Ammonite camp outside Jabesh. The army arrived in the early morning hours when light barely showed over the surrounding hills.

Using whispered commands Saul dispersed his forces into three companies. This three-unit formation was common at the time, and Saul probably used the pattern for fighting most of his battles because it offered great flexibility. He could station one company on a fixed front with the other two flanking it on either side; two companies could remain in frontal position with the other ready to attack from the side; or two groups could attack while the third was held in reserve.

The three units slowly converged on the Ammonites. Only a few dozing sentries were on duty

Saul's Fortress at Gibeah

The double wall and broad towers of Saul's fortress-palace at Gibeah made it the strongest Israelite citadel of its time. Partitions divided the space between the inner and outer walls into chambers, which were used as arsenals and storerooms. These chambers could also be packed with rubble to make one solid wall if an enemy attacked with battering rams. The crenellated design of the parapets enabled soldiers to take aim in the gaps and then take cover behind the projections. Apart from its pillared porch, the palace itself was a relatively simple, two-story building constructed, like the walls, of brick on stone foundations. The royal family lived on the second story and slept on the roof in summer. Some of the servants and palace guards were housed by the fortress gate. At left is a view of the mound, or tell, of Gibeah. But "Gibeah of Saul has fled" (Is. 10.29); all that remain are the stones from one tower and a piece of a wall.

as the Israelites crept silently toward their camp. Suddenly the morning stillness was shattered as rams' horns signaled the order to attack. Brandishing their swords and spears, the Israelite army rushed forward, cutting down many of the sleeping Ammonites before they could reach for their weapons. The Ammonites were totally unprepared for such an attack. Saul's three companies seemed to be coming from every direction. By midday the Ammonites were scattered "so that no two of them were left together."

The tactics of surprise used at Jabesh also became an integral part of Saul's military style, an early form of what we would now call guerrilla warfare. His decisive victory prompted the Israelites to accept him as king without reservation. They wanted to execute those who had initially rejected him, but Saul granted amnesty to the offenders. "Not a man shall be put to death . . . for today the Lord has wrought deliverance in Israel," he declared. At the people's urging, Samuel held a formal investiture at Gilgal. Saul was, in effect, elected king.

The kingdom he established bore little resemblance to the feudal system of the Canaanite and Philistine city-states. Israel kept its tribal structure, and at first, one tribe—Judah—refused to give Saul its complete allegiance. He did not establish a royal bureaucracy to exercise governmental control and he levied no taxes.

The limits of his authority were reflected in the simplicity of his court at Gibeah, where he lived with his wife and their three sons and two daughters. There, amidst olive groves and vineyards, he built his headquarters on a high promontory overlooking the main road that led northward from Judah to Bethel, Shiloh and Shechem. It was more like a military fortress than a royal residence, and although Saul was definitely in command, he did not take on many regal airs. He still planted his fields each season, and he may even have joined his men as they built the rough stone walls of his rugged citadel.

Saul's Court at Gibeah

A subject summoned to Saul's court would enter a sparsely furnished throne room measuring only 15 by 24 feet. He would see none of the lavish silver, gold or ivory ornamentation that decorated the palaces of neighboring monarchs. If the visitor were invited to dine, he would see servants hard at work in the kitchen area next to the throne room. Some might be roasting an ox or a lamb over a large open hearth. Others would be cooking the vegetables in clay pots or pouring olive oil from large clay storage jars.

Bread was baked in stone ovens. The flour was probably ground in the courtyard where another servant drove an ox hitched to a heavy grinding stone. Elsewhere in the building, servants spun wool yarn to be dyed and woven into cloth for the royal family's simple garments. Upstairs were the private quarters of Saul and his family.

Since Saul had not abandoned farming, the between-wall storerooms held plow points and other agricultural tools. And because the palace was a military outpost, the king's personal bodyguards used these rooms to hold their arsenal of sling stones and wooden or bronze-tipped arrows. This group of young men formed the nucleus of Israel's first standing army.

After the inspiring victory over the Ammonites, Saul turned his attention to Israel's chief menace: the Philistines. He gathered 3000 of his best soldiers and dispersed them to three strategic locations. He himself commanded 2000 men—about half at the Benjaminite village of Michmash and the others spread through the hills around Bethel. A thousand remained at Gibeah under Saul's courageous eldest son and second-in-command, Jonathan.

It was Jonathan who struck the first blow of the campaign. He launched a surprise attack on the Philistine garrison at nearby Geba and easily routed the enemy. When the news of the defeat reached Philistine headquarters, the generals mustered a massive army of charioteers, horsemen and infantry to fight against Israel.

Saul waited for the approaching enemy near Gibeah in the hill country, where he knew the Philistine chariots and cavalry would be at a disadvantage. Somehow, Saul and Jonathan had acquired some of the prohibited iron weapons. The vast majority of the Israelites—who furnished their own weapons—were armed with old-fashioned bronze swords, bronze-tipped spears, arrows, pikes and slings.

The slings were made of leather or cloth sewn into a pocket shape to which cords were attached. The slingman would place a stone in the pocket and whirl it around, then release his ammunition by letting go of one of the cords. Long practice made their accuracy deadly.

A few of Saul's men may have had bronze helmets and breastplates and leather shields, but most were probably protected by nothing more than their short cloaks of rough cloth and their leather sandals. Saul was counting on the combination of rugged terrain and his own unorthodox tactics to overcome the superiority of Philistine numbers and their iron weapons.

Following instructions given him by Samuel, speaking for the Lord, Saul withdrew his army to Gilgal, almost 13 miles away in the Jordan Valley. He was to hold his troops there for seven days until the prophet arrived and offered a sacrifice before sending the men into battle.

Meanwhile, the Philistine army had encamped at Michmash by the deep ravine separating that settlement from nearby Geba. The Philistine commanders stationed sections of their forces in a series of garrisons along the edge of the rocky divide. The soldiers marched to their posts with the sun reflecting off their bronze body armor, round shields and feather-topped helmets. The Israelites across the pass watched apprehensively as the enemy troops spread out "like the sand on the seashore in multitude . . ."

The psychological impact of this formidable

sight soon took its toll in Saul's camp at Gilgal. Each time the sun rose during the wait for Samuel, the king saw the size of his army diminished. Tension mounted and, when Samuel failed to appear after the appointed seven days, the men began to desert en masse. They ran to the hills and hid in caves, hoping to escape the expected onslaught. In desperation, Saul offered the sacrifice himself. Suddenly, Samuel arrived in a storm of righteous anger. Saul protested that any further delay would have been fatal, but the Prophet would not listen. "You have done foolishly," he raged; "you have not kept the commandment of the Lord your God . . . the Lord would have established your kingdom over Israel for ever. But now your kingdom shall not continue; the Lord has sought out a man after his own heart; and . . . has appointed him to be prince over his people . . ." Then the prophet departed angrily.

"You will meet a band of prophets . . . with harp, tambourine, flute, and lyre before them, prophesying" (1 Sam. 10.5). The rapt expression on the face of this clay figure, from the time of Saul, could portray religious ecstasy. The Hebraic meaning of prophesy was not foretelling but "telling forth" of the Lord's will.

By this time Saul's army had dwindled to 600 men, and the Philistines had already dispatched three raiding parties into Israelite territory. Seemingly calm despite Samuel's rebuff, Saul returned to Gibeah and readied his forces to meet the invading enemy.

There, a daring two-man raid by Jonathan and a companion startled the overconfident Philistines. Lookouts quickly reported the enemy's confusion to Saul, who immediately seized the advantage and sent his troops up the pass toward the Philistine encampment.

Saul took up his position at the head of his troops, closely shielded by his guards. As the Israelite army surged toward the main Philistine encampment, fear and confusion spread like an epidemic among the enemy. Their well-disciplined ranks crumbled into disarray. Many must have turned and run.

Suddenly, the Hebrew mercenaries in the Philistine army revolted against their masters and joined their Israelite cousins in battle. The Philistines found themselves attacked from all sides. The many Israelites who had timidly deserted Saul took courage when they saw what was happening. They grabbed their weapons and emerged from their hiding places in the hills to rally around their king. Saul's ragged band of 600 had swelled into an avenging army. He pursued the retreating Philistines through the hills and valleys. Mile after mile the slaughter continued as the Israelites fought the foe westward past Aijalon and into the coastal plain. Only when the remnants of the Philistine chariots reached the plain were any of them able to escape. The Israelites sent them on their way with a cry of victory.

Condemned by the Prophet

The victory at Michmash was an enormous success for Saul. With a single stroke he had ejected the Philistine occupation forces from the central mountain territory. The Philistine iron monopoly was shattered, too, and the Israelites were able to forge stronger and more effective weapons and tools for themselves.

Saul and his battle-hardened troops now had more freedom to operate against the Philistines and other enemies that regularly harassed the nation from every side. Before long he marched south through Judah into the desert region of the Negeb, where his army annihilated the surprised

Amalekites. In the course of this successful war against the seminomads, Saul made a fatal blunder: he disobeyed Samuel's command to slay all of the foe and destroy all enemy property as a dedication to the Lord—a custom called "herem." To Samuel, Saul had committed the ultimate sin. He had placed his own judgment above the Lord's. The prophet denounced Saul and said, "The Lord has torn the kingdom of Israel from you this day, and has given it to a neighbor of yours, who is better than you." This breach between the monarch and his mentor was the beginning of Saul's slow downfall.

Saul was under constant political pressure to maintain the unity of the tribes and keep his army intact. Philistine aggression never let up. Such steady stress would have challenged the resources of the most capable ruler. But, to make matters worse, the instability of Saul's own personality now began to emerge and he sank into prolonged periods of deep depression. His servants brought a young shepherd named David to play the lyre for the king, hoping it would cheer him. David's music did seem to soothe Saul's melancholy moods, and the youthful harpist quickly became a court favorite. "And Saul loved him greatly, and he became his armor-bearer."

By Saul's day, many well-to-do Israelite families were beginning to lead a comfortable existence. They now lived in houses rather than in tents and owned true furniture, not just rugs and mats. The clay models of Israelite beds and chairs above are from this period and were found in Lachish and Beth-shemesh. At Gibeah in the summer, evening meals for King Saul were probably served on the rooftop of the palace, with the lights of Canaanite Jerusalem in the distance. Lentil soup was ladled into individual bowls, and a large plate of lamb mixed with parched grain and chick peas was the main course. Cheese, fruit and wine rounded out the meal.

David soon became a national hero following his defeat of the Philistine giant, Goliath. Impressed by David's daring and bravery, Saul gave him command of a division of his troops, unaware that Samuel had secretly anointed the youth to be king.

Saul Grows Jealous of David

David repeatedly trounced the Philistines, and his popularity among the people of Israel grew rapidly. During a triumphant return from battle, Saul heard women in the streets chanting: "Saul has slain his thousands, and David his ten thousands." The king became enraged with jealousy. Doubtless remembering Samuel's ominous prophecy, he thought: ". . . and what more can he have but the kingdom?"

From that point on Saul regarded David as his enemy. Twice his anger erupted so violently that he hurled his javelin at David, who dodged away barely in time. In calmer moments Saul plotted more subtle ways to rid himself of the boy he had once loved as a son. He used his daughter Michal as a ruse. David could have her in marriage—if he battled the Philistines and returned with evidence that he had slain 100 of them. David slew 200. Again and again, Saul dispatched David to fight the Philistines, but David remained victorious.

The more Saul was thwarted, the more his malice deepened. But his children drew closer to David. On one occasion, Michal had to help her husband escape through a window when Saul's agents came to kill him. A deep bond had developed between David and Saul's eldest son; Jonathan alternated between pacifying his father's outbursts of anger and helping his friend avoid murderous traps. His friendship seems especially sincere because he, not David, was the logical successor to the throne.

David, fearing that one of Saul's clumsy plots to kill him might eventually succeed, fled the court. With a small company of renegades and malcontents, he darted from one Israelite community to another, pursued by Saul.

In Saul's tortured mind everyone had become a traitor—including Jonathan and his most trusted servants. Affection for David was equal to treason. The most innocent meeting seemed to be a conspiracy. When he learned that priests in the village of Nob had given shelter to David, Saul ordered all 85 of them executed.

Since Saul trusted no one, he decided he must kill David himself. Accompanied by an armed retinue he hunted his enemy throughout the Judean countryside. The pursuit evolved into a contest of wits between two expert guerrilla fighters. Saul soon had David cornered in the Wilderness of Maon, but he was called away to fight the Philistines before he could slay the fugitive.

That conflict out of the way, Saul quickly returned to his primary obsession. He trailed David into the Wilderness of En-gedi, a bleak region along the western edge of the Dead Sea. The area's pockmarked limestone outcroppings were filled with caves that offered good hiding places. Saul halted his troops at a spot known as Wildgoats' Rocks and went into one of these caverns to relieve himself.

At the entrance of the cave, light seemed to glow from the blue-green moss that cloaked the walls, but within a few feet Saul was surrounded by almost total darkness. He could not know that he had chosen the very cave where David and his little band of followers had sought refuge.

But David recognized Saul in the dim light from the entrance. He crept up silently behind the king, careful not to dislodge any pebbles or slip in the dust of the dry cave floor. He could easily have slit Saul's throat, as his men urged him to do. Instead he cut off the edge of the king's robe and retreated. Saul left the cave and, when he had moved some distance away, David emerged, holding up the piece of cloth.

He called out to Saul. ". . . by the fact that I cut off the skirt of your robe, and did not kill you, you may know and see that there is no wrong or treason in my hands. I have not sinned against you, though you hunt my life to take it."

Saul wept with shame. "You are more righteous than I," he said, "for you have repaid me good, whereas I have repaid you evil . . . I know that you shall surely be king . . . Swear to me therefore by the Lord that you will not cut off my descendants after me . . ." David agreed and they parted company once more.

Shortly thereafter Samuel died and, like all the Israelites, Saul grieved. Once the period of mourning was ended, however, Saul's penitence vanished. His obsession now drove him after David into the Wilderness of Ziph, part of the great Judean desert that extends from the central watershed to the Dead Sea. Near the Dead Sea,

mountains of soft white chalk are cut by deep, craggy gorges, forming natural caves. In these caves the fugitive David found refuge, as had other fugitives throughout history.

When Saul's army camped on the hill of Hachilah by the road to the east of Jeshimon, David was watching. That night he and one of his men stole into the camp and entered Saul's tent. David resisted his companion's pleas to murder the sleeping king. He merely took Saul's javelin and the water jug that sat by his head, and stealthily departed.

The next morning was almost a repeat of the scene at Wildgoats' Rocks. From a distance David produced the evidence that he had refrained from striking the mortal blow and Saul was again contrite, saying, "I have played the fool, and have erred exceedingly." He sent David on his way.

The Final Battle

If David was still at large, so were the Philistines. They again marshaled their armies at Aphek and proceeded north to the Plain of Jezreel. Along the route, they were joined by supporting armies from other "sea peoples" and their allies in the Canaanite city-states.

Saul mustered his troops and went to meet the enemy, marching to a point near the town of Jezreel about seven miles west of the Jordan and 40 miles north of Gibeah. There, they camped at the base of Mount Gilboa, a 1700-foot peak that forms the northeastern spur of the highlands as they drop away into the plain.

When Saul viewed the opposition he was about to encounter, he was struck by fear for the first time in his military career. Thousands of enemy soldiers streamed across the plain toward him. Swordsmen, archers, spear throwers, cavalrymen, charioteers—all of them well protected by armor—were being positioned for the attack.

Absorbed in his manic pursuit of David, he had abandoned his usual strategy and allowed himself to be lured into an indefensible position. In the past the Philistines' superior numbers and heavier equipment were rendered impotent by Saul's lightning attacks in the rugged terrain of the highlands, but here at Jezreel he was forced to fight on their terms. His skilled military eye could see that the chariot corps alone would crush his relatively small force, trained only in the hit-and-run strategy of guerrilla warfare.

The Philistines had all the power they required as well as reinforcements within easy reach at the strongholds of Megiddo and Beth-shan. Even worse, they had aligned themselves so that Saul was cut off from the Galilean Israelite tribes to the north, where he might have sought the additional support he so urgently needed.

Saul's confidence was completely shattered. He prayed to the Lord for assistance. But the Lord did not answer. The king grew so desperate that he broke one of his own laws: he consulted a medium. That "witch," however, conjured up the angry ghost of Samuel, who foretold Saul's death: "Because you did not obey the voice of the Lord . . . the Lord will give . . . you into the hand of the Philistines . . ."

The next morning, with Samuel's death sentence in his mind, Saul grouped his men for a last stand near the summit of Gilboa. Although there was little room in which to maneuver, it was preferable to confronting the enemy on the flatlands. But the hordes that stormed up the slope were more than Saul's forces could cope with. The Philistine archers decimated the Israelite ranks. Jonathan and Saul's other two sons were among the first to die. Saul himself fought valiantly, but suddenly an arrow struck him.

As blood gushed from his wound, he pleaded with his armor-bearer. "Draw your sword, and thrust me through with it, lest these uncircumcised come and thrust me through, and make sport of me." The servant could not bring himself to do it. Saul then grasped his own sword and fell upon it, killing himself. All the remaining Israelites were also slain by the Philistines.

"On the morrow, when the Philistines came to strip the slain, they found Saul and his three sons fallen on Mount Gilboa. And they cut off his head, and stripped off his armor, and sent messengers throughout the land of the Philistines, to carry the good news to their idols and to the people. They put his armor in the temple of Ashtaroth; and they fastened his body to the wall of Beth-shan. But when the inhabitants of Jabesh-gilead heard what the Philistines had done to Saul, all the valiant men arose, and went all night, and took the body of Saul and the bodies of his sons from the wall of Beth-shan; and they came to Jabesh and burnt them there. And they took their bones and buried them under the tamarisk tree in Jabesh, and fasted seven days."

All of Israel mourned the death of their troubled king, but the greatest tribute came from David, the man he had tried so often to kill. When news of the defeat on Gilboa was brought to him, he lamented with these words: "Saul and Jonathan, beloved and lovely! In life and in death they were not divided; they were swifter than eagles, they were stronger than lions. Ye daughters of Israel, weep over Saul, who clothed you daintily in scarlet, who put ornaments of gold upon your apparel. How are the mighty fallen in the midst of the battle!"

The story of Saul is found in Book 1 Samuel 9–31.

"And they mourned and wept and fasted until evening for Saul and for Jonathan his son and for the people of the Lord and for the house of Israel, because they had fallen by the sword" (2 Sam. 1.12). This clay figurine—only 3 inches high—from 12th century B.C. Hazor and probably Philistine, depicts a woman mourning.

Judah: Rugged Wilderness Sanctuary

"Then the prophet Gad said to David, 'Do not remain in the stronghold; depart, and go into the land of Judah'" (1 Sam. 22.5). In fleeing from Saul, David took refuge in the stony hills of Judah, just to the west of the Dead Sea, where terrace farming and water-storage cisterns made the land habitable. Judeans, cut off from northern Israel by Canaanite cities, were strongly unified, having fought the Canaanites for more than two centuries to gain decisive control. They "anointed David king over the house of Judah" (2 Sam. 2.4), and when the Israelite empire later divided, they remained loyal to the Davidic dynasty.

"Now David and his men were in the wilderness . . . to the south of Jeshimon" (1 Sam. 23.24). These deeply eroded limestone hills, in an area the Bible calls the "Wilderness of Judah," begin at Judah's central ridge and run down to the shores of the Dead Sea, a drop of over 3000 feet. Here the rainfall averages only two inches a year, and water soon evaporates in the hot, dry air of the Arabian Desert.

"And David went . . . and dwelt in the strongholds of En-gedi" (1 Sam. 23.29). One of the few oases in eastern Judah, by the Dead Sea, is En-gedi ("spring of the goat"). It lies along the desolate western edge of the sea. Sheer cliffs and sparse vegetation characterize the area, and because of its low-lying situation, its water does not rise up from underground. Instead, water cascades from springs which originate over 400 feet above the arid valley floor.

Michmash, the town in the background above, was the place where Saul "struck down the Philistines" (1 Sam. 14.31). It is located about seven miles northeast of Jerusalem, and in Old Testament times it dominated a strategic pass leading from the Jordan Valley into Canaan's central hill country. In the days of the divided kingdoms, Michmash and other Benjaminite cities formed a border zone between the Israelites and Judeans.

"And the descendants of the Kenite, Moses' father-in-law, went . . . from the city of palms into the wilderness of Judah . . . and settled" (Jg. 1.16). Though generally barren, the wilderness region did have habitable areas, such as these hills (left) northeast of Jerusalem. Crops could be grown successfully because of the mild climate with its sufficient rainfall. The hillsides were terraced to prevent erosion.

Chapter 10

David, Israel's greatest leader, defeated the Philistines and subdued them, breaking their power forever. His gifts as a poet, soldier and statesman make him, of all Israel's kings, the most beloved by his people and the most respected by his enemies.

David: The Lord's Anointed One

A brilliant leader, decisive and just, David transformed Israel from a weak and divided kingdom into a formidable empire. This transformation paralleled his own progress from shepherd boy to king. Throughout his life he was loyal to the Lord and the prophets, a fact which brought him victory against his foes and forgiveness for his very human weaknesses. His colorful Court History, written by a close friend, makes him better known to us than any other Biblical person.

Toward the end of the eleventh century B.C., Israel was finally gaining in its war against the hated Philistines. Under King Saul, a series of victories had given Israel a firm foothold in the hills and valleys of central Canaan. Saul, however, was increasingly at odds with the prophet Samuel. He had, in Samuel's eyes, too often ignored the religious prerogatives of the prophet. Samuel felt it was time to anoint a new monarch for the young kingdom of Israel.

"I repent that I have made Saul king," said the Lord to Samuel, "for he has turned back from following me, and has not performed my commandments." He ordered Samuel to go to Judah "to Jesse the Bethlehemite, for I have provided for myself a king among his sons."

Samuel feared Saul would kill him if he heard of the selection of a new king. The Lord reassured him and, following his instructions, Samuel went to Bethlehem, taking a young heifer with him. The stern prophet's sudden appearance caused a stir in the simple hill town. "The elders of the city came to meet him trembling, and said, 'Do you come peaceably?' And he said, 'Peaceably; I have come to sacrifice to the Lord . . .'" Samuel asked that Jesse and his sons be present at the sacrifice.

But when Samuel saw the seven boys accompanying their father to the altar, he said, "The Lord has not chosen these."

"Are all your sons here?" asked Samuel.

"There remains yet the youngest," responded Jesse, "but . . . he is keeping the sheep."

"Send and fetch him," ordered the prophet, and David, who "was ruddy . . . had beautiful eyes, and was handsome," was brought in.

"Arise, anoint him . . . this is he," said the Lord to Samuel. The prophet did as the Lord commanded, ". . . and the Spirit of the Lord came mightily upon David from that day forward."

David was then sent back to the hills, where he wandered with his flock of sheep and goats during the day, seeking good pasture. When the animals needed water, he drew it from wells in the hills. On summer nights he slept with his animals under the sky, curled up in his rough sheepskin coat. (In the winter months he slept in a tent, cave or stone sheepfold, but always near his flock.) His usual meal was bread, cheese and olives. The hours of labor were long and lonely, but David must have used the time to play his

In the gloom of this Negeb landscape a new era was dawning for Israel. David hid in these hills from the jealous wrath of King Saul. After years as a fugitive, he emerged from them to unite his people and lead them in the eventual creation of a great empire.

A Simple Weapon Won a Mighty Victory for the Israelite Army

"So David prevailed over the Philistine with a sling and with a stone" (1 Sam. 17.50). David killed Goliath in the valley of Elah (above left), thereby checking a Philistine advance into Judah. He defeated the heavily armed giant with a sling, a weapon devised by shepherds thousands of years earlier. Its operation was simple. The slinger took a stone from a supply in his shoulder bag and placed it in a leather patch tied between two cords. One cord was wound about the wrist and the other was held by the hand of the same arm. The stone was whirled rapidly above the head, and at the right moment the hand-held cord was released to eject the stone. Great numbers of slingstones have been found in Palestine, several as large as three inches in diameter.

lyre and compose songs. He also gained an intimate knowledge of the rugged terrain of Judea.

Like other shepherds, David carried a studded club, almost 3 feet long, to protect his flock against any human or animal predator. He also carried a leather sling, which he had made for himself. With it he could throw a stone, sometimes from a considerable distance and always with great accuracy, in front of an errant sheep to bring it back into the flock. He could also fell a marauding wolf or bear—even a lion—with one of the swift missiles.

David continued his life as a shepherd after his secret anointment by Samuel, while at Gibeah, only four miles away, Saul—unaware of David's existence—continued the war with the Philistines. Meanwhile his mental instability continued to worsen, plunging him into depression. At times his mind touched the edge of madness, for "the Spirit of the Lord departed from Saul, and an evil spirit from the Lord tormented him." His servants

suggested that music might cure his melancholy.

"Provide for me a man who can play well, and bring him to me," ordered Saul.

"One of the young men answered, '. . . I have seen a son of Jesse the Bethlehemite, who is skilful in playing . . . and the Lord is with him.'"

David was sent for and brought to Saul's castle at Gibeah. More fort than royal palace in its design, the castle was only two stories tall and very plainly adorned. There young David played his lyre and sang for the king, and, as the servants had hoped, "Saul was refreshed, and was well, and the evil spirit departed from him."

Goliath of Gath

Saul came to love the young musician, and he appointed him armor-bearer. But David's family responsibilities were no less than before, and he regularly "went back and forth from Saul to feed his father's sheep at Bethlehem."

David was again tending to his father's flock when Saul and the Israelites were arrayed for battle against the Philistines at the valley of Elah, in the foothills of the Judean mountains. Three of David's brothers were in Saul's armies, so their father sent David with some parched grain and 10 loaves of bread for his fighting sons, as well as 10 cheeses for their commander. "See how your brothers fare," charged Jesse.

As David entered Saul's encampment, he could hear the excited clamor of the Israelites and the Philistines. The soldiers of the opposing armies were moving into their battle lines. Quickly, he left the gifts he had brought with the "keeper of the baggage" and ran to the ranks. He found his surprised brothers and ignored their commands to leave. When the giant Goliath of Gath stepped out of the Philistine lines to shout his challenge to Israel, David was in the ranks.

"Choose a man for yourselves," said Goliath, "and let him come down to me. If he is able to fight with me and kill me, then we will be your servants; but if I prevail against him and kill him, then you shall be our servants and serve us."

Duels between two warriors, to decide the victory between two opposing armies, were common in Canaan at the time of David, and perhaps before. Sometimes the duels involved only two men; at other times groups of elite fighting men from opposing camps would battle each other. Such contests were looked upon with favor by doubtful military commanders; they could bring about a military decision without great loss to their fighting forces. The Israelites themselves rarely practiced the custom.

Goliath of Gath stood "six cubits and a span" (9 feet 8 inches tall). Formidably armed as well, he wore a bronze helmet and a coat of mail that weighed 5000 shekels (150 pounds). "And he had greaves of bronze upon his legs, and a javelin of bronze slung between his shoulders. And the shaft of his spear was like a weaver's beam, and his spear's head weighed 600 shekels of iron [more than 19 pounds]."

Not one soldier in Saul's army dared to answer Goliath's challenge. "And David said to the men who stood by him, '. . . who is this uncircumcised Philistine, that he should defy the armies of the living God?'" Then, disregarding the warnings of Saul himself, "David ran quickly toward the battle line to meet the Philistine."

To the amazement of the massed armies, the young shepherd swiftly felled the huge warrior with a stone hurled from his sling. He then strode quickly to the giant's prostrate body, took up the great sword and cut off Goliath's head. In a moment, the Philistines had lost a battle and Israel had gained a hero.

Jonathan, Saul's son, was overwhelmed by the shepherd's courage and became his lifelong friend. He gave David his robe, his sword, his bow, his girdle, and he "made a covenant [of friendship] with David, because he loved him as his own soul."

A King's Jealousy

With his victory David immediately became a national hero. Now a full-fledged leader in the army of the king, the number of his victories in the field grew, as did his popularity.

When David returned from a victory, "the women came out of all the cities of Israel, singing and dancing . . . with timbrels, with songs of joy, and with instruments of music. And the women sang to one another as they made merry,
'Saul has slain his thousands,
and David his ten thousands.'"

Saul had made David a leader for his prowess in battle, but so much public adulation for the young hero did not please him. He began to question David's actions and motives. With distrustful eyes, he watched the young man and soon suspected him of an ambition for his throne.

Twice, in fits of madness, Saul hurled his javelin at David. He would have killed him if David had not been agile enough to avoid the weapon. The fearful king, certain that only the Lord's intervention could have saved the youth from the javelin, grew even more suspicious of David's ambitions. He hoped the Philistines would kill the young commander for him, but David continued to be victorious and his popularity with the people continued to grow.

Saul then offered David his eldest daughter, Merab, in marriage, if David won more victories—". . . only be more valiant for me and fight the Lord's battles," he said, hoping for David's death. "For Saul thought, 'Let not my hand be upon him, but let the hand of the Philistines be upon him.'"

David never married Merab, since Saul abruptly decided to give her to another. But Saul's hope for David's death at the hands of the Philistines was revived when his youngest daughter,

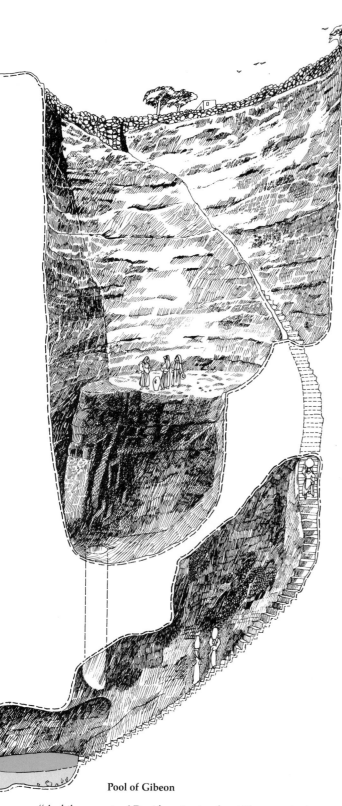

Pool of Gibeon

"And the servants of David went out and met [the servants of the son of Saul] at the pool of Gibeon . . . And the battle was very fierce that day" (2 Sam. 2.13, 17). The probable scene of this encounter—a stair well which led down to the water table near Gibeon—was uncovered in 1956, and appears in the photograph and drawing above. It was a circular pit, 37 feet across, cut from solid rock to a depth of 82 feet. For this engineering feat almost

Michal, fell in love with the hero. In lieu of the usual bride price, Saul demanded 100 Philistine foreskins. He was setting David a task which he thought would surely be impossible. David, however, brought back to his king not 100, but 200 enemy foreskins. The king resignedly gave Michal to David, but his fear of the seemingly invincible young man mounted.

He even called on Jonathan to kill David, but when his son pleaded David's innocence and services, Saul relented. For a short while, there was even a reconciliation between the king and David, but Saul's animosity soon returned.

One night, Michal got word that her father was sending soldiers to take David to the palace, where he was to be slain. She warned David: "If you do not save your life tonight, tomorrow you will be killed."

With his wife's help, David quickly escaped through a window and fled into the night. Hur-

3000 tons of limestone had to be removed. The rock at the bottom (see center of the drawing) shows that digging was stopped for a time, then resumed as a tunnel to the pool at the water table. Getting water must have been an arduous task. Village women descended with jars, filled them, then climbed back up the 79 steps with the jars on their heads. Rubble on the floor of the excavation shows the facility was not used after the 6th century B.C.

riedly, Michal arranged the goat-hair pillows and bedcovers to appear as if her husband were lying in bed. When Saul's soldiers arrived to arrest him, she pleaded that David was ill and could not be disturbed. But the soldiers forced their way in and discovered the ruse.

David, in the meantime, had found shelter with Samuel at Ramah, a few miles away. Saul and his soldiers chased him there; however "the Spirit of God came upon the messengers of Saul, and . . . came upon him also . . ." All were caught up in an uncontrollable fit of "prophesying," or ecstatic religious dancing, and David seized the opportunity to flee once more.

David arranged a secret meeting with Jonathan, whom he asked, "What have I done? What is my guilt? And what is my sin before your father, that he seeks my life? . . . truly, as the Lord lives and as your soul lives, there is but a step between me and death."

"You shall not die," answered Jonathan. He promised to plead again with his father and the two men renewed their vow of friendship.

The next evening was the night of the new moon, a feast day when the entire household dined together. David's place was conspicuously empty, and Saul demanded an explanation. Jonathan replied that he had given David leave to visit his brothers in Bethlehem.

Saul, insanely angry with his son for his friendship with David, hurled his spear at him, but he missed his target. There was no quieting his fury, and Jonathan could only tell David of his father's unforgiving temper. "In the morning Jonathan went out into the field to the appointment with David. . . . David rose from beside the stone heap . . . and they kissed one another, and wept with one another, until David recovered himself." The two friends then exchanged a final farewell, for they both knew that David must now live the life of an outlaw until Saul's death.

Outlaws in the Hills

David moved first to Nob, where the priest Ahimelech gave him the sword of Goliath, which had been left in his care. From there, David fled to the Philistine town of Gath, Goliath's place of birth. It was a desperate move, for he could hardly expect to find asylum among the Philistines. He was recognized immediately and seized by the soldiers of Achish, king of Gath.

They took him directly to their king, before whom David feigned madness. He "made marks on the doors of the gate, and let his spittle run down his beard." Achish reacted as David had hoped he would.

"Lo, you see the man is mad . . ." he shouted at his soldiers. "Do I lack madmen . . . ? Shall this fellow come into my house?"

In David's time, the insane were thought to be touched with the divine, and were therefore inviolable. The ruse had saved David's life. The Philistines released him, and he fled to a cave in Adullam, near the border between Judah and the Philistines' territory. There, a small army of men began to gather around him, "every one who was in distress, and every one who was in debt, and every one who was discontented" with Saul. The ill-sorted but spirited band of rebels roamed from one camp to another, always keeping one step ahead of Saul. They depended largely on the hospitality of local shepherds and farmers for food and water, for the rocky Judean hills provided little sustenance. Gradually, as sympathy for David grew, so did his army.

It was a small army, but it was strong enough to defeat a Philistine force threatening the city of Keilah. Soon, with 400 men under his command, David was able to demand tribute from the settlements in the hills. When Nabal, a rich man of Carmel, refused to pay tribute, David readied his men to march against him. Considerable blood would have been spilled in Carmel if Abigail, Nabal's wife, had not acted swiftly.

Without Nabal's knowledge, she came to the outlaw chieftain with grain, bread, wine, raisins, figs and five dressed sheep. She apologized for the miserliness of her husband, and her quick action saved her household. Nabal, appalled by the tribute she had paid David, apparently suffered an apoplectic stroke and died.

David, on hearing of Nabal's death, sent for Abigail and married her. He was undoubtedly impressed by her wisdom and diplomacy, and grateful to her for having saved him "from bloodguilt and from avenging myself with my own hand!" He would marry again, for in those days a man was permitted many wives. A king's wealth and power were often measured by the number of women in his harem.

All this time, Saul kept to his purpose of hunting down and killing David. In Nob, he had slain the priest Ahimelech and his family for his kindness to the outlaw. He had ordered a siege of Keilah when he heard that David was in the city, saying of the young fugitive, "God has given him into my hand; for he has shut himself in by entering a town that has gates and bars." Earlier, however, one of Ahimelech's sons, Abiathar, had escaped the massacre of his family and had joined David. He advised the leader to abandon Keilah immediately. David and his men managed to escape back into the surrounding hills. Saul followed him to Horesh, thence into the wilderness of Maon and finally to the forbidding wilderness of En-gedi on the edge of the Dead Sea.

There, one day, Saul paused in his pursuit and entered a cave to relieve himself. Coincidentally, David and his men were hidden in the back of that cave. One quick thrust of his sword would have killed Saul, but David held back. "The Lord forbid that I should do this thing to my lord, the Lord's anointed," he said. Instead, he crept up behind the preoccupied monarch and stealthily cut off the skirt of Saul's robe. He then followed the king out of the cave, and called to him from a distance, waving the cloth. Loudly protesting his innocence of ambition for the throne, he shamed the amazed Saul into a tearful but temporary repentance.

Saul could not, however, rid himself of his desire to destroy David and keep the dynasty within his own family. The hunt soon continued.

Later, at Hachilah, David and a companion boldly stole into the center of Saul's camp, where the king lay sleeping. Again it was in David's power to dispatch his tormentor. Again he did not. Instead, he took away Saul's spear, which was stuck in the ground near his head, and a jar of water. On discovering his loss, Saul knew that David had spared his life once again.

Death of Saul and His Sons

There was no hope for a reconciliation. David would not strike at the Lord's anointed and he had no stomach for civil war, which could only weaken all of Israel. He finally took the grave step of leaving his country for Philistine territory and permanent safety from Saul. He returned to Gath and the Philistines, but this time with a band of 600 men. There, in a final effort to disengage himself from Saul's relentless pursuit, he offered the services of himself and his men to the Philistine vassal king, Achish.

Achish undoubtedly had some misgivings, but he accepted the Israelites' presence among the Philistines and established them at Ziklag, on the southern frontier of Judah. From there David was expected to conduct raids against the cities and settlements of his own people.

In fact, David and his army conducted their raids against the seminomadic enemies of Judah, strengthened its borders and distributed the spoils of victory among the people of the Negeb.

Traveling Fighters Pause for a Meager Meal

"Every one who was in distress . . . every one who was discontented, gathered to [David]; and he became captain over them" (1 Sam. 22.2). David and his followers, pursued by Saul, led the life of guerrilla fighters in Judah. They offered protection to those who fed them and seized provisions from the uncooperative rich—sharing the spoils with the poor—while all the time harassing Saul's forces. Here some rebels relax at the house of a Judean peasant, who brings a bowl of lentils and figs. This and goat milk would perhaps be their only meal of the day, for such fighters traveled light and rarely carried much food; weapons and water flasks were burden enough during rapid maneuvers.

At the same time, David was methodically enhancing his own position among the Judeans for the claim he would eventually make to the crown of the nation of Israel.

Achish was unaware of David's surreptitious activities in the Negeb. The vassal king was now occupied with the plans of the five Philistine overlords far to the north. The Philistines had organized a huge coalition army for an all-out assault against Israel. The first objective was to take the entire strategic Plain of Jezreel. Initially, Achish had asked David to join in the assault, but a lingering distrust among the other Philistine commanders kept David out of the battle. David was returning from Jezreel to the Negeb by the time Saul met the Philistines at Mount Gilboa.

"Now when David and his men came to Ziklag . . . they found it burned with fire, and their wives and sons and daughters taken captive." During David's absence, the fierce Amalekites had raided the town, looting and pillaging but apparently killing no one. This time the Lord advised David, "Pursue; for you shall surely overtake and shall surely rescue."

With his band David headed south to the brook Besor, where 200 of the men collapsed, "too exhausted to cross the brook . . ." David and the remaining 400 found the Amalekites, "spread abroad over all the land, eating and drinking and dancing, because of all the great spoil they had taken . . ." At dawn the next day David's army attacked the marauder's camp, and recovered every prisoner and all the stolen livestock. Then David set a precedent by dividing the extra spoils among not only the 400 who had fought with him, but the 200 who had remained behind. "For as his share is who goes down into the battle, so shall his share be who stays by the baggage," he decreed.

Meanwhile, on Mount Gilboa the Israelites were poised for battle, but Saul was no longer a young warrior, confident that the Lord was with him. Before joining battle, he had consulted with his prophets for a sign of the Lord's support, but "the Lord did not answer him."

He then called on a "witch," or medium, at Endor to conjure up the spirit of Samuel, who had died long before. This, too, was against Israelite law. The angry spirit of the prophet appeared and predicted Saul's death and Israel's defeat at the hands of the Philistines.

It was a distraught Saul who fought at Mount

"The Lord gave you today into my hand in the cave. . . but I spared you" (1 Sam. 24.10). In an En-gedi cave like this, David spared Saul's life, even though Saul was trying to kill him. He and his men also hid out in these caves, whose cool recesses offered shelter not only from men but from the blazing heat of the desert.

Gilboa. As Samuel had predicted, the Philistines were victorious everywhere. Jonathan and his two brothers, Abinadab and Malchishua, were killed, and Saul, seriously wounded by the Philistine archers, took his own life.

In Ziklag, when David heard the news he rent his clothes in grief and went into mourning. Jonathan had been David's closest friend, and Saul, though he had persecuted David, nevertheless had been the Lord's anointed monarch, deserving of his utmost loyalty and respect.

War Between North and South

Despite his grief, David soon realized that if he were to take Saul's place as king, he must act immediately. "Shall I go up into any of the cities of Judah?" he asked the Lord. "And the Lord said to him, 'Go up.' David said, 'To which shall I go up?' And he said, 'To Hebron.'"

David did as the Lord commanded. To Hebron "the men of Judah came, and there they anointed David king over the house of Judah." The year was about 1000 B.C. David, now 30 years old, ruled Judah, but Israel, which had been one nation under Saul, was now divided. Abner, Saul's chief general, had established Saul's youngest son, Ishbosheth, as king of the 10 tribes who lived in the central and northern areas of the kingdom: Benjamin, Dan, Ephraim, Manasseh, Issachar, Zebulun, Asher, Naphtali, Gad and the remnant of Reuben which had escaped Moabite and Ammonite pressure. In Judah, the southern half of the kingdom, David ruled over the tribes of Judah and Simeon. For two years the armed forces of divided Israel met in fratricidal skirmishes and battles, the north led by Abner, Judah by David's nephew and loyal general, Joab. But the bloody encounters were never decisive.

A quarrel between Abner and Ishbosheth broke the deadlock. Abner had taken one of Saul's concubines for his own harem, and Ishbosheth interpreted the act as a sign of Abner's ambition for the throne. More likely, Abner saw a brighter future for Israel, and himself, with the charismatic David. Whichever it was, Abner began to negotiate secretly with David for the delivery of the northern kingdom to Judah. As an indication of his good faith, he brought Michal (David's first wife) from Gibeah. Saul had married her off to another man when David fled his palace. In David's harem, Michal established a link between Saul's line and the king of Judah, strengthening David's claim to the throne.

Then Joab, David's general, put an abrupt end to Abner's secret negotiations, about which David had failed to inform him. Abner had killed Joab's brother Asahel in one of the battles between the two kingdoms. Learning that Abner had just left Hebron after one of the covert negotiating sessions—and with no understanding of what was going on—Joab killed him.

The murder was not to David's political advantage and he promptly ordered a period of public mourning in an effort to lessen the anger which was certain to arise among Abner's followers. It was a wise political gesture by David, but apparently it was not essential. Without Abner, Ishbosheth's "courage failed, and all Israel was dismayed." The northerners began to falter in their determination to oppose David.

With the end of the northern kingdom in sight, two of Ishbosheth's captains, perhaps seeking some favor from David, assassinated their king in his sleep. David, appalled by the murder, had the

Until David's time the state of Israelite music was rather primitive. It typically consisted of such instruments as the "sistrum," which was little more than an elaborate rattle. David added to his nation's culture by importing skilled Phoenician musicians.

two captains executed. But the house of Saul, except for Jonathan's five-year-old crippled son, was no more. There was now no one between David and the throne of Israel, and "all the elders of Israel came to . . . Hebron . . . and anointed David king" over all the Israelites. Samuel's prophecy had finally been fulfilled.

A New King for All

The Philistines, who had benefited from the division of Israel, were alarmed. So long as the Israelites fought among themselves, the Philistines would eventually be able to take over all of Canaan. A united Israel, however, under the leadership of the warrior-king David, posed a serious threat.

The Philistines acted quickly. They marched against David, hoping to defeat him before the young king could get any help from the northern tribes. Their immediate objective was to drive a permanent wedge between Judah and Israel by massing in the valley of Rephaim near Jerusalem and then attacking in force. There, however, David defeated them not once, but twice. Then, after taking the Philistine stronghold of Gath, he moved his forces into the rich plain of Philistia and Shephelah where he finally destroyed their armies. The Philistines would never rise again to threaten the kingdom of Israel. Only four of their cities were allowed to retain their identity, one completely surrounded by territory regained by Israel's victorious army.

With the Philistine problem permanently settled, David moved swiftly to consolidate his kingdom. His first step was to establish a capital on neutral ground that could not be claimed by any of the tribes. Jerusalem, the last city in central Israel still controlled by the Canaanites, was built on a high ridge bordered on the east, west and south by steep valleys. With its lofty walls and nearby springs, it appeared to David to be an ideal site for his capital. It was also conveniently close to the border between Judah and the northern tribes of Israel.

Leading his army, David prepared to attack the city, only to be mocked by Jerusalem's defenders, a Canaanite tribe called the Jebusites. "You will not come in here, but the blind and the lame will ward you off," they jeered from atop the formidable walls. David challenged his troops, "Whoever shall smite the Jebusites first shall be chief and commander."

The redoubtable Joab led a contingent of men through a water tunnel leading from the spring Gihon in the eastern valley to a point inside the walls. He attacked the Jebusites from the rear, throwing open the city gates and causing the Jebusites disastrous confusion. The victory was soon complete. "And David dwelt in the stronghold, and called it the city of David." It belonged neither to Judah nor to Israel, but was the personal possession of the king.

It was a masterful stroke. Where Saul held the tribes together in a loose confederacy, David centralized the power of the state in the king, with Jerusalem as the seat of the government of Israel. Those who came to serve David in his capital city, in high government post or low, forgot their tribal allegiances. Their loyalty now belonged to the king and the kingdom of Israel.

David went a step further. He had the sacred ark of the covenant brought to Jerusalem, as well as the prophet Nathan. As the ark was carried into the city, David leaped and "danced before the Lord with all his might . . . girded with a linen ephod. So David and all the house of Israel brought up the ark of the Lord with shouting . . ." Jerusalem was now not only the city of the king, the city of David, it was the city of the Lord.

The effect of these moves was to concentrate the administration of all laws, civil and religious, in the one capital city, with David in incontestable command of his kingdom.

David, of course, had assistants. Jehoshaphat, the "recorder," kept the official records, arranged David's public appearances and acted as liaison officer between David and the people. Seraiah, the "secretary" or scribe, served as the secretary of state. One of the few officers of the court who could read and write, he also handled David's official correspondence. As David had promised, Joab was appointed commander-in-chief of the armies of Israel. Benaiah commanded David's personal bodyguard. To the position of high priest, David named both Zadok, an older priest, and Abiathar, who had served him during his years as an exile.

There were a variety of other ministers, scribes, heralds, clerks and stewards to manage "the treasuries in the country, in the cities, in the villages and in the towers . . . those who did the work of the field . . . the vineyards . . . the wine cellars . . . the olive and sycamore trees . . . the stores of oil . . . the herds . . . camels . . . she-asses . . . flocks . . . All these were stewards of King David's property."

Because of his love for music, David wrote several of the songs now collected in the Book of Psalms, a compilation of supreme religious poetry. These hymns were sung by priests and celebrants at the Tent of the Covenant, to the accompaniment of flutes, lyres and cymbals. They were to become an important part of Israel's religious and literary heritage.

The Might of Israel

Saul had created Israel's first standing army. David developed and enlarged it. The elite of the armed forces were "The Thirty." These were the men who had fought at the side of David in his outlaw days. They formed a kind of honorary army council, framed military regulations and made promotions and army appointments. Under Joab, they commanded the two separate branches of David's regular mercenary army. One branch was recruited from the Sea People, Cretans and Aegeans, among others. The second branch was recruited entirely from among the former enemy: the Philistines. A special bodyguard for the king and palace was formed from a group of David's companions in exile: these were the men of Gath, or the Gittites.

In addition to this army of some 2000 well-trained regulars, David had several territorial contingents, volunteer or conscripted, as the situation demanded. These came from the Israelite tribes in groups of 10, 50, 100 and 1000, each under the command of a veteran soldier.

The standing army was equipped with swords, lances, javelins and spears. A regular soldier's armor consisted of a helmet, breastplate, leg guards and a leather-covered wooden shield. The territorial contingents, who were called on only for temporary service and special campaigns, had to buy most of their own equipment. Only the rich among them were able to carry the two-edged sword. The rest came with ox goads, rough lances, wooden bows and arrows, bludgeons, axes and the primitive but deadly slings.

With this kind of well-organized military power, and with his southern and western borders no longer in great danger from the armies of the Philistines, David marched eastward across the river Jordan and launched a series of ambitious wars of expansion. The time was right for such adventures. Babylonia had for a long time been in a state of decline. The Hittites were no longer a power in the Near East, and the Hurrians had been destroyed by the Hittites and Assyrians, the latter themselves not yet ready for further southern expansion. Torn by priestly dissent, Egypt's weak administration had neither the will nor the force to stop David. He was fully aware of the comparatively free hand he had in the area and he took advantage of it.

In quick succession, he defeated the Ammonites, Moabites and Edomites and completed the destruction of the Amalekites. He was victorious in a number of encounters with the belligerent Arameans. He stretched his kingdom south from Edom, with its copper mines in the Arabah, to the Gulf of Aqaba and the Red Sea. In the latter conquest he gave Israel a potential port. Eventually, under Solomon, Israel would trade from there with Arabia and Africa. His greatest conquest was of the Arameans of eastern Syria: this brought Israel control of all the trade routes to the Euphrates River.

David took a personal part in many of Israel's battles and conquests. More often, however, it was his brilliant commander Joab who led the troops while David remained in his capital. It was during one such campaign that, while walking upon the roof of his palace, he looked down and saw a young woman bathing.

David and Bathsheba

Struck by her beauty, he inquired after her. He learned that she was Bathsheba, the wife of a Hittite soldier, Uriah, who was with Joab, fighting the Ammonites. Nevertheless, he sent for her and "he lay with her" and "the woman conceived, and she . . . told David, 'I am with child.'"

David immediately recalled Uriah to Jerusalem, but the husband would not go home to his wife. To David's dismay, he slept instead with his comrades at the door of the king's house. A soldier in battle, in the time of David, kept himself sacramentally clean. This meant, among other things, that he did not sleep with a woman. David, faced with the collapse of his plan, resorted to legal murder: when Uriah returned to his camp the next morning, he carried a sealed letter from David for his commander, Joab. The letter ordered Joab to put Uriah "in the forefront of the hardest fighting, and then draw back from him, that he may be struck down, and die."

The order was followed, and the betrayed Uriah was killed. Bathsheba went into mourning,

Jerusalem was newly captured from Canaan when David named it Israel's capital. He then had the ark of the covenant brought there, which made the city the nation's religious center as well. The procession (right) escorting the ark probably came up the Kidron Valley, then through the city and out to a tent set up on a threshing floor (top right) on a hill to the north. The rock above, which today is still enshrined there, is thought to have lain under an altar David erected. It was here that Solomon built his temple.

David probably expected Nathan to pronounce his death sentence as expiation for Uriah's murder. Instead Nathan warned him, "The Lord also has put away your sin; you shall not die. Nevertheless, because by this deed you have utterly scorned the Lord, the child that is born to you shall die." The prophet then left David.

"And the Lord struck the child," and for six days the infant lay ill. Hoping to save its life, David prayed and fasted but, despite his efforts, on the seventh day the child died. The king grieved deeply for the loss of the child. "I shall go to him," he said, "but he will not return to me." Bathsheba would later bear David another child, named Solomon.

Absalom's Revolt

Israel had become rich and secure under David, but in time his popularity began to wane. The Israelites, grown comfortable with victories and prosperity, resented the conscription of troops and the persistence of taxes. David's third-born son, the ambitious Absalom, took full advantage of the people's resentment.

His sister, Tamar, had been raped by Amnon, David's eldest son, and Absalom avenged that rape by ordering his servants to kill his older brother. But the killing of Amnon took place two years after the rape. It seemed that the fratricide was more a political maneuver than an act of vengeance. With the death of Amnon and the earlier death of Chileab, David's second-born son, Absalom, became heir apparent.

Following the murder, Absalom—fearing his father's anger—fled from the court. It was several years before he managed a reconciliation, with the help of Joab. Once back in Jerusalem, however, he impatiently began to plot again, hoping a rebellion would give him the kingdom.

Absalom showed himself opulently in public with his chariot and horses, and "fifty men to run before him." Like a present-day political candidate, he was quick to extend his hand and, in the manner of the times, quick to kiss any and all who approached him. He stood in front of the city gate, publicly drawing attention to David's neglect of the office of judge and charging him with injustice. His arguments must have convinced many of his father's subjects, for "Absalom stole the hearts of the men of Israel."

For four years he built an alternately proud and

An Israelite Woman's Bath

"[David] saw from the roof a woman bathing; and the woman was very beautiful" (2 Sam. 11.2). Bathsheba enticingly bathed in the open, but for most upper-class Israelite women the

ritual was done indoors. Following a rinse in clear water, unscented oil was used to rub off excess dirt, much as modern women use cleansing cream. Then scented oil, poured from decorative juglets, was applied. In the clay figure at left, a woman of the time washes herself alone.

and when the period of grieving was over, David married her. Shortly after the marriage, Bathsheba gave birth to a son. "But the thing that David had done displeased the Lord. And the Lord sent Nathan to David."

When the prophet formally visited the king, the story was known throughout the country. Said Nathan: "Thus says the Lord, the God of Israel, 'I anointed you king over Israel, and I delivered you out of the hand of Saul; and I gave you your master's house . . . and gave you the house of Israel and of Judah; and if this were too little, I would add to you as much more. Why have you despised the word of the Lord, to do what is evil in his sight?'" David accepted his guilt and confessed, "I have sinned against the Lord."

humble image of himself. Then he abruptly left Jerusalem for Hebron with 200 of his followers, sending word to his supporters throughout the country that the time was right for rebellion. "As soon as you hear the sound of the trumpet," he ordered, "then say, 'Absalom is king at Hebron!'" Open rebellion had finally come.

When David finally learned of Absalom's insurrection, it was almost too late. His own court was divided in its loyalties and the people of Jerusalem were for the most part with Absalom. The aging king was forced to flee his capital, across the Jordan to Mahanaim. Several hundred people still loyal to David followed him as he made his way east—his servants, runners, soldiers and his household. However, he had shrewdly ordered his high priests, Abiathar and Zadok, to remain behind and report Absalom's plans as they developed.

Once outside Jerusalem, David could gauge the sentiments of the people. An old man named Shimei assaulted him with rocks and curses. But to many Israelites it appeared as if their king was abdicating in favor of Absalom, and they "wept aloud as all the people passed by." Meanwhile, in David's absence, Absalom took Jerusalem without a struggle.

Ahithophel, Absalom's chief adviser in his drive for the crown, urged an immediate attack on Mahanaim, before David could gather his loyal armies around him. Absalom had 12,000 men under his command, enough to insure victory, if he acted at once. But a second adviser, Hushai, suggested that Absalom would be more sure of success if he mobilized all Israel and led them against his father. Hushai too had remained in Jerusalem when David fled. He had sworn allegiance to Absalom, but he secretly remained loyal to his king. He was playing for time, hoping he could give David time to build up his forces.

"You know that your father and his men are mighty men, and . . . your father is expert in war," he warned Absalom. There was enough truth in that thought to deter the son. When he finally did attack, David was ready for him.

There was no match. Joab and the other great commanders who had remained loyal to the king led battle-proven veterans. Absalom had unseasoned, conscripted troops. The rebels were utterly routed: thousands died in the battle and, though David had asked that the life of his son be spared, Joab himself killed Absalom.

When told of Absalom's death, David lamented, "O my son Absalom, my son, my son Absalom! Would I had died instead of you, O Absalom, my son, my son!" Then, instead of praising his victorious army, he pronounced a day of mourning. He retired to his bedroom, and

Foreign Scribes Employed at David's Court

Because few of his people were literate, David used foreigners to record accounts and official correspondence. Above, an Egyptian takes dictation for a letter, using a form of the Phoenician alphabet. He writes on a leather roll held open with a stone, dipping his reed pen in water to moisten cakes of solid black ink—a mixture of gum and soot—on his wood or slate palettes. Oil lamps were used for evening work; below are three similar to those used during Israelite times. They would have burned olive oil, the universal lighting fuel in David's period.

wept inconsolably. David had a great love for his children, whatever ill they did to him. Joab, however, realized that David risked losing the support of his followers by isolating himself. He stormed into the house and confronted the grieving king. "You have today covered with shame the faces of all your servants, who have this day saved your life . . . because you love those who hate you and hate those who love you. For you have made it clear today that commanders and servants are nothing to you . . . if Absalom were alive and all of us were dead today, then you would be pleased. Now . . . go out and speak kindly to your servants; for I swear by the Lord, if you do not go, not a man will stay with you this night . . ." Joab was undoubtedly right.

Shamed by his general's accusations, David left his room and went out again to meet his people. But before he could return to his capital, a new cry of insurrection erupted.

"We have no portion in David,
and we have no inheritance in the son of Jesse;
every man to his tents, O Israel!"

The leader of the new insurrection was Sheba, a Benjaminite. It was the last effort, in David's time, to split northern Israel from Judah and destroy the unity of the tribes under one king. The invincible Joab followed Sheba to the town of Abel, and the people of the town, to save their own lives, cut off the rebel's head and tossed it over their walls. The insurrection—and Sheba—were both dead.

The Final Years

The trials of David's last years were not quite over. Adonijah, his oldest surviving son, was now the heir apparent, but there was no precedent for succession to the throne of Israel. Adonijah had good reason to be concerned with the influence of Bathsheba, the mother of his half brother, Solomon. She had the allegiance of a powerful palace clique behind her ambitions. David was now old and ill, near death and secluded in his chambers. Adonijah, with Joab and the high priest Abiathar in his camp, decided to act. To preclude any other claims to the throne, he performed the required ritual sacrifices and declared himself king of Israel. Then he and his supporters gathered for a festive banquet to celebrate his accession.

When Bathsheba heard of it, she followed the advice of the prophet Nathan and went directly to the bedridden king. There she related the treacherous actions of Adonijah and reminded David of the promise he had made her that Solomon would be king of Israel.

David responded as Nathan had predicted. He at once summoned all the palace supporters of Solomon. Quickly, in a religious ceremony, Bathsheba's son was anointed. During his banquet, Adonijah and his guests learned of the anointment. His followers quickly deserted him, and Adonijah was subsequently tracked down and killed upon the order of Solomon.

By this time, David, the former shepherd, had reigned in Jerusalem for 33 years. Then, in about 960 B.C., "he died in a good old age; full of days, riches and honor," and was buried in his city of Jerusalem. He had broadened the borders of Israel and made her richer with the spoils he had taken. This was the heritage he left to Solomon and the golden age of Israel that was to follow. To the world he left the city of Jerusalem—a center of religious aspirations—and the beloved Psalms.

The story of David is told in 1 Samuel 16–31, 2 Samuel, and 1 Kings 1–2.

"Then David slept with his fathers, and was buried in the city of David" (1 Kg. 2.10). Led by priests carrying incense burners like those shown in the photograph at right, a funeral procession bears a king's casket to its tomb in Jerusalem. Professional mourners, whose presence was necessary for this highly stylized lamentation, weep, raise their arms in unison and perform other ritualistic wails, chants and gestures. Coming after them are the friends and relatives of the king. The procession will be led down a sloping rock-cut shaft to the burial chamber, and there the king's comrades will leave his sword, shield and robes. After the ceremony, the tomb entrance will be sealed with a giant hand-hewn slab of rock.

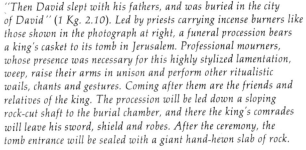

The Phoenicians: Far-reaching Traders

As David advanced and strengthened his borders, the Phoenicians of the Canaanite lands north of Israel were confined to the fertile coast between the mountains of Lebanon and the Mediterranean Sea. These people got their name from the Greek word for "Canaan," which originally meant "land of the purple," referring to a famed dye made from mollusks. Seamen, artisans and merchants, their cultural influence extended far beyond their geographical boundaries. Sidon and Tyre were the most famous Phoenician city-states. Their culture and religion were frequently adopted by Israelites in the time of David and Solomon. By the reign of Ahab in the 9th century B.C., most of Israel worshiped Phoenician gods.

Four sculptures give clues about Phoenician religion and daily life. The bronze figure (left) of a fertility goddess is crowned with symbols of the Egyptian goddess Hathor, whose influence reached the Phoenicians in the second millennium B.C. A Phoenician man of Elisha's time may have looked much like the one (above) in this ivory relief, and the clay statues (right) play a tambourine and double flute, both of which were used in religious services of Jezebel's time.

"The Sidonians and Tyrians brought great quantities of cedar to David" (1 Chr. 22.3), and later to Solomon, transporting them partially by sea. An Assyrian king, Sargon II, had a similar event recorded in this frieze from his palace at Khorsabad.

A Phoenician Temple

The Phoenicians built temples that combined Egyptian influence with their own fondness for ornamentation. The drawing above is based on ruins of a small temple that was part of an extensive palace complex unearthed at Tell Tainat, Syria. Although it dates from two centuries after Solomon's reign, it is important for our knowledge of his temple at Jerusalem (see pages 189, 191), since it is probably the style familiar to Solomon's Phoenician builders. In a ground plan derived from Phoenician architecture, three consecutive rooms lead from the entrance. Each room is progressively more sacred. The pillars set beneath the portico (A) are a Phoenician feature not used at Jerusalem, where the columns were free-standing. The carved lions at the base of the pillars (B) still exist at Tell Tainat, and other details are adaptations of typical Phoenician designs. In the inner holy room (C) is a statue of Baal, a fertility god, one of the many gods whom the Phoenicians worshiped.

The rocky island of Tyre, Phoenicia's greatest city, appears in another frieze at Sargon II's palace of the 8th century B.C. Two centuries before the carving was made, Tyre's King Hiram built a breakwater from the island to the mainland, improving the city's port. His ships sailed from there to Egypt, Cyprus, Sicily and Spain, with cargoes of oil, wine, timber and wheat. From this worldly city came Jezebel, wife of Israel's King Ahab, who tried to impose the gods and priests of Phoenicia on the Israelites at the time of Elijah.

Chapter 11

When he succeeds to Israel's throne, Solomon inherits a nation forged by his father and makes it rich through political alliances and trade. But the extravagance of his court and his tolerance of foreign worship sow the seeds of the kingdom's eventual dissolution.

Ruler of an Empire: Solomon

Soon after Solomon became king of Israel, he had a dream. "And God said, 'Ask what I shall give you.' And Solomon said, '. . . O Lord my God, thou hast made thy servant king in place of David my father, although I am but a little child . . . Give thy servant therefore an understanding mind to govern thy people, that I may discern between good and evil; for who is able to govern this thy great people?'" Impressed by the young king's humility, the Lord granted him wealth and wisdom. Under his rule, the Lord's temple was built in Jerusalem, and Israel experienced its first great prosperity. But the splendor of Solomon's reign also brought forced labor and taxes, the lessening of tribal power and tolerance of pagan religions in Jerusalem. Though his empire fell apart after his death, Solomon himself will be remembered as the last ruler of Israel's golden age.

When the queen of Sheba visited Solomon's Jerusalem in about 950 B.C., she must have been impressed, perhaps awed, by the splendor of the city. Surely nowhere in Sheba, a small country in southwest Arabia, were there such buildings as Solomon's temple and palace. All of Jerusalem, in fact, showed evidence of prosperity and power. Walls of massive fitted stones guarded the great city. Within these walls were hundreds of one- and two-story mud-brick houses, narrow streets and busy bazaars.

Everywhere the queen looked, it must have seemed as if another building was under construction by the king's labor force: a storehouse, perhaps, or a shrine for still another of his many wives. She may have heard that Jerusalem was a cosmopolitan city, but reports of the jealous God of the Israelites probably had not prepared her for the sight of the foreign religious ceremonies being performed in public. She might have noticed the Israelites watching the ceremonies, some with resentment but others with obvious enthusiasm for the rites.

Not far from the gates were tented markets where goods from every corner of the Near East were bought and sold. Heavily laden caravans from Syria and Egypt rested near the wells inside the city gates. Solomon allowed them to pass through the country—for a price. The queen of Sheba looked closely at these goods, for she was in Jerusalem to arrange a bargain that might prove profitable to her if she acted shrewdly. Fine cloth from Egypt, ointments from Syria, horses from Anatolia, copper from Cyprus—such goods were in demand in Sheba and other Arabian countries to the southeast of Israel.

Jerusalem's royal compound soon rose before her. This section, built on a high ridge overlooking the rest of the city, included the king's ornate cedar and stone palace and the massive rectangular stone temple of the Israelites' Lord. The palace itself was Phoenician in style, with its House of

Pomegranates were a recurring Phoenician motif in the arts of Israel during the time of Solomon, who employed many craftsmen from Tyre. Here, in a stylized form, they rim a bronze stand used to hold a bowl for ceremonial washing. The most notable use of the design was in the capitals of the temple columns at Jerusalem.

the Forest of Lebanon, and its columned entrance to the king's audience chamber. Both buildings had in fact been constructed with the help of Phoenician architects and labor.

One of the king's servants led Sheba and her entourage through the long Hall of Pillars to the throne room in the Hall of Judgment. There, seated on a high gleaming chair overlaid with gold, surrounded by scribes, attendants and officers, sat Solomon, king of Israel.

After an exchange of greetings, the queen of Sheba began to ask questions and riddles of Solomon to test his almost legendary wisdom. Her host was equal to the challenge: "And Solomon answered all her questions; there was nothing . . . which he could not explain to her. And when the queen of Sheba had seen all the wisdom of Solomon, the house that he had built, the food of his table, the seating of his officials, the attendance of his servants, their clothing, his cupbearers, and his burnt offerings which he offered at the house of the Lord, there was no more spirit in her."

The two monarchs soon began to talk of business, the true reason for the queen's visit. They probably signed some sort of treaty, ratified by an exchange of goods. "Then she gave the king a hundred and twenty talents of gold [millions of our dollars], and a very great quantity of spices, and precious stones; never again came such an abundance of spices as these which the queen of Sheba gave to King Solomon. . . . And King Solomon gave to the queen of Sheba all that she desired, whatever she asked besides what was given her by the bounty of King Solomon." Perhaps Solomon did decide to reduce his trade in the Gulf of Aqaba on Sheba's behalf. At any rate, she returned to her own country satisfied after bargaining with Solomon, and Israelite trade with Arabia continued to flourish.

David's Son and Heir

Although Solomon is perhaps the most celebrated king in Israel's history, less is known of him than of his two predecessors—Saul and David. The Bible tells us very little about Solomon's youth, except that he was the second son of David and Bathsheba. The early years of the tenth century B.C., during which he grew up in David's palace, were violent ones, marked by revolt, warfare and conquest. David had expanded Israel's territory by seizing kingdoms south and east of the Jordan River and the Dead Sea, and had added the Aramean kingdom of Zobah,

High-prowed trading ships land at Solomon's port of Ezion-geber, laden with cargoes of ivory, apes, gold and other riches from abroad. The fleet was built for Solomon in a cooperative venture with Hiram, the Phoenician king of Tyre, whose crews manned the vessels in three-year voyages to Red Sea ports. The Israelite merchants trading these goods were very successful—so much so, in fact, that the queen of Sheba may have come from southern Arabia for an agreement preventing competition with her own traders.

north of Damascus. By the time Solomon reached manhood, he was in line to inherit not just a narrow strip of Canaan's hill country, but a sizable empire that stretched from Egypt to Syria.

However, the acquisition of such an empire could not have occurred at any other time in Israel's history. David's rise to power came during a period of relative weakness of the great empires of the Near East. The Hittites in Asia Minor had fallen, the Assyrians in the Fertile Crescent had not yet become a threatening military force and Egypt was suffering from internal divisions that greatly lessened her strength. Although David had considerably strengthened the borders of his fledgling empire, there were still areas in Edom and around Damascus which had not been thoroughly subdued. During his reign they remained peaceful, perhaps because they feared Israel.

Meanwhile, Israel itself was undergoing several changes. Its population grew as its people settled into a peaceful agricultural life. There were many small towns and large cities within the nation, and a central capital, Jerusalem, where the ark of the covenant rested. The Israelite farmers' tasks were made easier by plows and tools of iron, freely available now that the Philistines' monopoly on the metal had been broken.

As the years went by, Israel's prosperity increased and the land became peaceful. And, as David aged, the matter of succession to the throne became increasingly important.

"Now King David was old and advanced in years . . ." His entire household was aware that David would soon die, particularly Nathan the prophet and Adonijah, the king's eldest son. Though no one had ever inherited the throne of Israel—both Saul and David had been anointed by Samuel—Adonijah was confident that he would become king at David's death. "He conferred with Joab the son of Zeruiah and with Abiathar the priest; and they followed Adonijah and helped him. . . . but he did not invite Nathan the prophet or Benaiah or the mighty men or Solomon his brother."

Nathan, concerned with his own fate if Adonijah became king, approached Solomon's mother, Bathsheba, with a plan. "Go in at once to King David, and say to him, 'Did you not, my lord the king, swear to your maidservant, saying, "Solomon your son shall reign after me, and he shall sit upon my throne?" Why then is Adonijah king?' Then . . . I also will come in after you and confirm your words."

Sure that both she and Solomon were in danger

from Adonijah, Bathsheba eagerly agreed to Nathan's plan. In an audience with the feeble David, she convinced him that he had privately promised her son the throne. Nathan also entered the chamber and chided the old king for not making his intentions public.

"Then King David answered . . . 'As the Lord lives, who has redeemed my soul out of every adversity, as I swore to you by the Lord, the God of Israel, saying, "Solomon your son shall reign after me, and he shall sit upon my throne in my stead"; even so will I do this day.'"

Strengthening the Throne

Nathan, Benaiah and Zadok the priest quickly "went down and caused Solomon to ride on King David's mule, and brought him to Gihon." At that spring outside Jerusalem the priest anointed the young man with oil from an ivory horn. "Then they blew the trumpet; and all the people said, 'Long live King Solomon!'"

Adonijah and his followers heard the trumpet blasts as they were feasting nearby. When Jonathan, Abiathar's son, burst into the room, they greeted him eagerly. ". . . Adonijah said, 'Come in, for you are a worthy man and bring good news.' Jonathan answered Adonijah, 'No, for our lord King David has made Solomon king . . . and Zadok the priest and Nathan the prophet have anointed him king at Gihon; and they have gone up from there rejoicing . . . This is the noise that you have heard.'" The group at the table was stunned. Now that their leader was no longer the intended king, they all became frightened. "Then all the guests of Adonijah trembled, and rose, and each went his own way."

After David's death sometime later, Solomon learned that his position as king was not unchallenged. Adonijah, the would-be king, persuaded Bathsheba to request that one of David's former concubines be given to him in marriage. "Ask for him the kingdom also," answered Solomon, outraged, for a former king's wives and concubines could be given only to the next king. "Then King Solomon swore by the Lord saying, 'God do so to me and more also if this word does not cost Adonijah his life!'"

Solomon's kingship may have been thrust on him by his mother, Bathsheba, and Nathan, but once he was king, he displayed an independence that probably shocked even his staunchest sup-

porters. Swiftly but deliberately, Solomon took several steps to secure his right to the throne.

The first step was to get rid of Adonijah. Solomon's general Benaiah did the job neatly. "When the news came to Joab—for Joab had supported Adonijah . . . Joab fled to the tent of the Lord and caught hold of the horns of the altar," claiming sanctuary. This did not stop Benaiah from completing his second assignment. He killed Joab, too, the general who was too powerful an enemy to be spared.

Abiathar the priest could not be murdered, because of the sanctity of his office, "so Solomon expelled Abiathar from being priest to the Lord," and banished him to his hometown. "The king put Benaiah the son of Jehoiada over the army in place of Joab, and the king put Zadok the priest in place of Abiathar."

One more enemy remained, an old man named Shimei who had once cursed David. Solomon ordered him to stay in Jerusalem on penalty of death. For three years Shimei obeyed the command, but when he then made a brief trip beyond the city's walls in pursuit of runaway servants, he was promptly executed. "So the kingdom was established in the hand of Solomon."

Laborers and Provisions

Upon his accession to the throne, Solomon made the first of several administrative changes: he created three new offices in his cabinet. David had governed his new empire almost single-handedly, needing only a commanding general, a chief scribe and a few secretaries. To this basic staff Solomon added Ahishar, who "was in charge of the palace." He would serve as prime minister, second only to Solomon in power. Adoniram was named the chief of forced labor— for Solomon had a tremendous building program in mind and no way to begin it without a steady supply of workers. Adoniram would supervise both foreign slave laborers (the descendants of those people who had survived the Israelite Conquest) and a newly organized, conscripted labor force of Israelites, who served one out of every three months. In addition, "Azariah the son of Nathan was over the officers [provincial governors]" of the 12 districts of Israel.

The people of Israel, in the period of the Judges and even through the reign of Saul, had been ruled largely by personal magnetism and inspi-

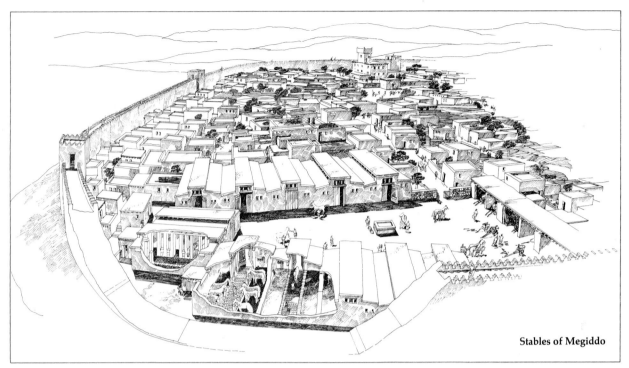

Stables of Megiddo

Solomon is known to have carried on an extensive trade in horses, buying chariots from Egypt and animals from Asia for export to Hittite and Aramean kings. The reconstruction above shows part of the vast stables at Megiddo, once thought to have been built by Solomon but now dated to the 9th-century B.C. reign of his successor King Ahab. Below, ruins of the "store-city" of Hazor, another of Solomon's royal cities, have been uncovered by the painstaking work of modern excavators.

ration from the Lord. Such leadership had been necessary to unite the 12 independent and often quarrelsome tribes during the military conquest of Canaan. But now Israel was at peace and her territory was greatly enlarged. The nation sorely needed a more efficient method of government. So Solomon divided Israel into 12 administrative districts, all comparatively equal in population and resources. To accommodate the new territory, the arbitrary divisions ignored the old tribal boundaries, and for all practical purposes the tribal distinctions were abandoned except for temple duties and genealogies.

Solomon assigned one officer to head each district; all of them were responsible to Azariah. The 12 officers were in charge of raising provisions for the king's household—each district supplied food for one month of every year. The officers in turn imposed the burden of providing food on the farmers and shepherds, and quite a burden it was. The provision needed for *one day* by Solomon's court "was thirty cors [188 bushels] of fine flour, and sixty cors [about 370 bushels] of meal, ten fat oxen, and twenty pasture-fed cattle, a hundred sheep, besides harts, gazelles, roebucks, and fatted fowl . . . And those officers . . . let

The interior of the temple at Jerusalem was adorned with "carved figures of cherubim and palm trees and open flowers" (1 Kg. 6.29). Cherubim are now understood to be winged sphinxes with human faces, borrowed from Phoenician art and often shown flanking a palm tree as guardians of the "Tree of Life" of Near Eastern mythology. These ivory plaques, one of a cherub wearing the double crown of Egypt and the other a stylized palm, were found in Syria. They were probably used to enhance a king's palace.

nothing be lacking. Barley also and straw for the horses and swift steeds they brought to the place where it was required, each according to his charge." And this was only part of the taxation.

Solomon's Temple

"Then Solomon began to build the house of the Lord in Jerusalem on Mount Moriah . . . in the second month of the fourth year of his reign." The beautiful temple took seven years to construct, and at the end of that time Solomon staged a dramatic dedication ceremony. Priests carried the ark of the covenant from the City of David, on Jerusalem's southern hill, up to the new temple, where thousands of people from all over Israel stood waiting. When the priests placed the ark inside the sanctuary of the temple, "a cloud filled the house of the Lord . . . for the glory of the Lord filled the house of the Lord."

Before the altar Solomon offered a long and eloquent prayer to the Lord. "O Lord, God of Israel, there is no God like thee, in heaven above or on earth beneath, keeping covenant and showing steadfast love to thy servants who walk before thee with all their heart . . .

"But will God indeed dwell on the earth? Behold, heaven and the highest heaven cannot contain thee; how much less this house which I have built! Yet have regard to the prayer of thy servant and to his supplication . . . that thy eyes may be open night and day toward this house, the place of which thou hast said, 'My name shall be there,' that thou mayest hearken to the prayer which thy servant offers toward this place. And hearken thou to the supplication of thy . . . people Israel, when they pray toward this place . . . and when thou hearest, forgive."

At the end of his prayer, Solomon blessed the congregation and led the ritual sacrifices—countless sheep and oxen were slaughtered before the altar. For seven days, all of the people of Israel feasted and rejoiced. "On the eighth day he sent the people away; and they blessed the king, and went to their homes joyful and glad of heart for all the goodness that the Lord had shown to . . . Israel his people."

Most of Solomon's changes eventually achieved their original purposes—his table was well supplied, he was assured of a reliable labor source, his business affairs were capably handled and now Israel had a permanent temple. But the majority of the Israelites had mixed feelings about Solomon's innovations. They could not help feeling pride in the nation and the capital Solomon was gradually strengthening. The period of peace enabled many people to settle down, build permanent homes and devote their time to their flocks, crops and families.

Despite the relative prosperity, many Israelites resented the impositions Solomon placed on them. During centuries of tribal independence, they had developed a suspicion of central authority. Samuel had predicted many years before that if the Israelites ever installed a king, he would conscript them, tax them and otherwise

Under Phoenician guidance, thousands of Israelites labored seven years on Solomon's temple. It may have been an exaggeration that "neither hammer nor axe nor any tool of iron" (1 Kg. 6.7) was used, but flooring, beams and ivory inlays could have been installed with pegs and the stones prepared elsewhere. The stones were precisely fitted together without mortar, and cedar beams were placed at intervals for strength. One feature of its advanced Phoenician design is a column capital (foreground), now considered the precursor of the Ionic style of the Greeks. Above, an architect examines some carved panels which will be placed in the interior.

interfere with their lives. That prophecy seemed to be coming true: the Israelites found themselves periodically serving in Solomon's labor force and surrendering many bushels of grain and heads of livestock to the king's officers. Now even their tribes meant little, if anything, to the government in Jerusalem, a government the Israelites often felt was too widely separated from themselves— and from the Lord.

Once the immediate problems of food-raising and labor were settled, Solomon began to establish diplomatic relations with neighboring countries. He already controlled trade between most of them, since the major caravan trails passed through his country. To prevent these nations from entertaining hopes of seizing Israel, and to insure trade agreements with them, Solomon often sealed diplomatic ties by marrying foreign princesses. His harem included Moabite, Ammonite, Edomite, Hittite and Phoenician women, among others.

The most significant of his marriages was to the daughter of the Egyptian Pharaoh. Egyptians rarely married foreigners, especially Asiatics, and even though Egypt was not the powerful nation it had been, the princess' marriage to Solomon was an important indication of the respect the king of Israel now commanded throughout the Near East. Certainly the bride's dowry was impressive. It included the Canaanite city of Gezer, over which Egypt had had nominal control for centuries—a control David did not wish to contest with his powerful neighbor.

Not all of Solomon's diplomatic ties were strengthened by marriage. A few were strictly financial relationships. Probably the most important of these was with Hiram, the Phoenician king of Tyre: "and there was peace between Hiram and Solomon; and the two of them made a treaty." Hiram had known David, and elected to continue his friendly and profitable relations with Israel when Solomon took the throne.

Cedar, Gold and Chariots

Solomon had depended on the skill of Hiram's Phoenician architects and laborers, as well as precious Lebanon cedar, to construct the most impressive buildings in Jerusalem—the temple and the royal buildings for government. From almost the beginning of Solomon's reign, ". . . Hiram supplied Solomon with all the timber of

cedar and cypress that he desired, while Solomon gave Hiram twenty thousand cors [125,000 bushels] of wheat as food for his household, and twenty thousand cors [over a million gallons] of beaten oil. Solomon gave this to Hiram year by year," on an installment plan.

The monarch also enlisted Hiram's aid in building a port and a fleet of merchant ships. "King Solomon built a fleet of ships at Ezion-geber," at the northern end of the Gulf of Aqaba. With crews of Phoenician sailors, his ships sailed regularly to Ophir, probably located in southern Arabia, returning with cargoes of almug, or sandalwood, gold and precious stones. "Once every three years the fleet used to come bringing gold, silver, ivory, apes, and peacocks," possibly from as far away as Somaliland in Africa. It was, presumably, this trade that the queen of Sheba came to Jerusalem to reach some agreement about.

Certainly Solomon did not control his financial affairs single-handedly; he probably hired a staff of skilled merchants and tradesmen to carry out the actual bargaining with their foreign counterparts. The growing number of civil servants in the king's employ formed perhaps the first bureaucracy in Israel's history.

Solomon's impressive business ventures and his control over both the routes known as the Way of the Sea and the King's Highway brought unparalleled prosperity to Israel. Solomon—ever ambitious—built four "royal cities": Hazor, Megiddo, Gezer and Jerusalem. Hazor, commanding the inland route into his kingdom, had been in ruins since Joshua destroyed it. On the acropolis a strong fortress now appeared. It was defended by double walls and a fortified gate with massive flanking towers. Megiddo had a different history. It had been continuously occupied since before Thutmose III captured it in the mid-fifteenth century. Now Solomon showered magnificence on this famous site which dominated the Way of the Sea right in the heart of Israel. Among other things a splendid, if small, palace was built for the governor who administered this area for his royal master in Jerusalem.

Gezer had been given to Solomon by the Pharaoh as part of the dowry of his Egyptian wife. The city controlled the vital Aijalon Valley and thus the road approaching Jerusalem from the northwest. Solomon's military experts realized the importance of fortifying Gezer, and the same type of walls and gates as those at Hazor soon arose. Je-

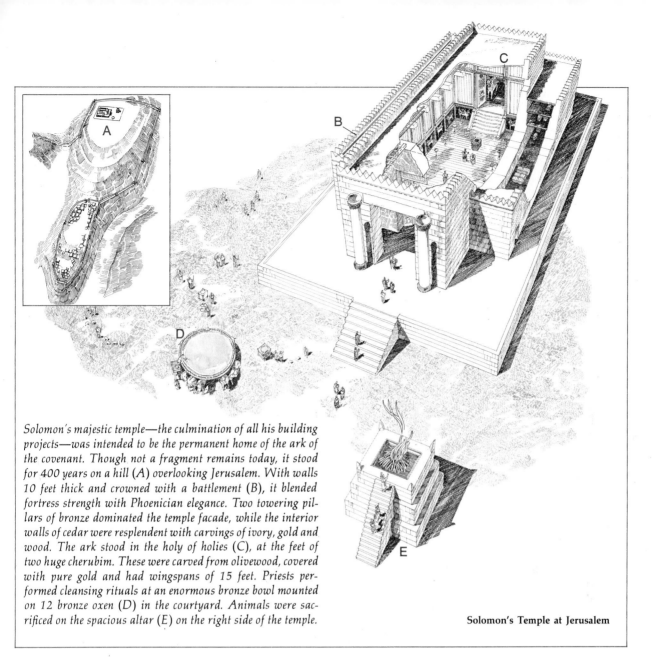

Solomon's majestic temple—the culmination of all his building projects—was intended to be the permanent home of the ark of the covenant. Though not a fragment remains today, it stood for 400 years on a hill (A) overlooking Jerusalem. With walls 10 feet thick and crowned with a battlement (B), it blended fortress strength with Phoenician elegance. Two towering pillars of bronze dominated the temple facade, while the interior walls of cedar were resplendent with carvings of ivory, gold and wood. The ark stood in the holy of holies (C), at the feet of two huge cherubim. These were carved from olivewood, covered with pure gold and had wingspans of 15 feet. Priests performed cleansing rituals at an enormous bronze bowl mounted on 12 bronze oxen (D) in the courtyard. Animals were sacrificed on the spacious altar (E) on the right side of the temple.

Solomon's Temple at Jerusalem

rusalem was, of course, the jewel of this expansive building program. It was dominated by an extraordinary palace made up of a number of striking buildings and by the temple, which was adjacent to the palace on the eastern ridge of the city overlooking the Kidron Valley.

Each of Solomon's "royal cities" served several purposes. Each was an administrative center. Each dominated a strategic route. Each served as a store-city for the agricultural goods and other items brought to the king's agents as taxes. And each served to remind everyone of the magnificence of Israel's king.

With a prime minister and a growing staff of civil servants to aid him, Solomon had time to study a wide variety of subjects ranging from human psychology—illustrated by the story of the two harlots' dispute over the child*—to natural science. "He spoke of trees, from the cedar that is in Lebanon to the hyssop that grows out of the wall; he spoke also of beasts, and of birds, and of reptiles, and of fish." His reputation for such knowledge had intrigued the queen of Sheba.

Solomon is said to have collected over 3000

* Two harlots, each claiming an infant as her own, came to Solomon asking that he settle their dispute. He called for a sword and announced that he would divide the baby in two, giving half to each woman. One woman cried out, "Oh, my lord, give her the living child, and by no means slay it," though the other agreed to his solution. Solomon awarded the baby to the first woman, knowing that no mother would permit the killing of her own child.

"Gold of Ophir, for Beth-horon, 30 shekels." This transaction, recorded on clay in the 8th century B.C., mentions the fabled source of gold visited by Solomon's trading ships. The location of Ophir is not precisely known, but it was probably in southern Arabia.

"proverbs," or folk sayings filled with practical advice, from around the Near Eastern world. The proverbs dealt with a variety of subjects. "A false balance is an abomination to the Lord but a just weight is his delight" was a warning to merchants against overcharging their customers. Child-rearing was summarized by, "He who spares the rod hates his son, but he who loves him is diligent to discipline him." Solomon's personal proverb may have been, "It is an abomination to kings to do evil, for the throne is established by righteousness."

Religious Toleration

The one thing that irritated devout Israelites more than any other of Solomon's changes was his increasing religious toleration. That toleration took several forms. As Solomon's harem grew, the number of pagan temples and their priests in Jerusalem also grew. Ostensibly, Solomon built them solely for the use of his foreign wives. Yet the pagan rites must have lured some Israelites away from the worship of the Lord, and to the Israelite priests this spelled doom for Israel.

The elaborate temple itself was an affront to some Israelites. For centuries the ark of the covenant had been carried before the 12 tribes wherever it was needed—to inspire a military victory or to sanctify an altar. It was housed in a relatively simple tent that could be dismantled at any time. The ark had belonged to all of Israel. Now, with the temple in the king's compound, it seemed that the ark had become the personal property of the king. The temple's architecture had not been dictated by the Lord, but had instead been patterned after Phoenician temples. The sight of the outwardly pagan building housing the ark was an outrage to some people.

The Rich and the Poor

Other complaints, economic ones, stirred Israelites into open defiance of their monarch. On the whole, Solomon and his administration brought Israel more national prosperity than it had ever known, but the life of the common man had been disrupted. In the past, a man's wealth had been calculated mostly by the land he owned, the number of flocks he had and the size of his family. Solomon's sweeping economic changes altered that system. Land was no longer of supreme importance—in fact, it may have become somewhat of a burden. The more land a man owned, the more crops he could grow, and thus the more he would have to turn over to the king's officers when collection time came around every 12 months. Likewise, flocks were surrendered to tax collectors and sons were forced to serve one month of every three in the king's labor force.

Now wealth was calculated not by property ownership but by the amount of money a man controlled. Certainly more and more money in gold and silver came into Israel every year, but very little of it ever filtered down to the average Israelite, who had to surrender so much of his livelihood to the king's coffers. Instead, the money was used to pay growing international debts, salaries for the full-time government officials, commissions to merchants and artisans in the king's employ, temple and palace upkeep and other expenses.

For the first time in Israel's history, there began to be a distinct difference between "rich" and "poor." The king and his household were rich; the common people were poor. In between were the salaried civil servants and the merchants and artisans, many of whom had organized craft guilds by that time. Such class separations had not been known in the Israel where a shepherd boy like David could be anointed king—only 50 years earlier.

Eventually Solomon's revenues, great as they were, became inadequate to meet his growing expenses as more and more buildings were constructed and maintained, more salaries were paid, voyages financed and wives supported. The inevitable happened: Solomon could not pay his creditors, and suddenly Israel had a national debt. The Bible reports that "King Solomon gave to Hiram twenty cities in the land of Galilee," probably mortgaging them in return for a sizable loan to ease his burden.

During the last years of Solomon's reign, the complex governmental structure he had built and controlled began to totter. Only a man with exceptional ability could have accomplished what he had and kept it operating smoothly. Nonetheless, his people were more and more discontented with the relentless taxation, the forced labor and Solomon's particular style of kingship. At the beginning of the monarchy, it was understood that a king was the anointed caretaker of the Lord's people, not their exploiter, as Solomon seemed to have become.

End of the Golden Age

There were few rules outlining the privileges and responsibilities of kings, for most of the Lord's laws were meant for a seminomadic way of life, not for the centrally governed world power Israel had become. It was believed that the Lord had given Solomon the intelligence and knowledge to rule Israel skillfully with only one stipulation—that Solomon continue to worship the Lord as his father had done. For reasons that have never been recorded, Solomon jeopardized his own throne by ignoring that one demand.

"For when Solomon was old his wives turned away his heart after other gods; and his heart was not wholly true to the Lord his God, as was the heart of David his father . . . Then Solomon built a high place for Chemosh the abomination of Moab, and for Molech the abomination of the Ammonites . . . so he did for all his . . . wives, who burned incense and sacrificed to their gods.

"And the Lord was angry with Solomon . . . Therefore the Lord said to Solomon, 'Since this has been your mind and you have not kept my covenant and my statutes which I have commanded you, I will surely tear the kingdom from you and will give it to your servant . . . However I will not tear away all the kingdom; but I will give one tribe to your son, for the sake of David my servant and for the sake of Jerusalem which I have chosen.'"

Solomon must have known that without a firm ruler Israel would probably crumble soon after his death. The last years of his reign were tense ones for Israel. His son Rehoboam was a rash young man who had inherited few, if any, of Solomon's administrative skills. Jeroboam, one of Solomon's labor officials in the north, listened sympathetically to the complaints of the northern tribes of Israel.

One day Ahijah the prophet approached him and told him privately, ". . . thus says the Lord, the God of Israel, 'Behold, I am about to tear the kingdom from the hand of Solomon, and will give you ten tribes . . . and you shall be king over Israel.'" Perhaps Solomon heard about Ahijah's prophecy and feared an open revolt during his lifetime, for "Solomon sought therefore to kill Jeroboam; but Jeroboam arose, and fled into Egypt, to Shishak king of Egypt."

After 40 years, Solomon's reign came to an end. Certainly for Israel it had been a golden age in many respects. Culture, trade and industry had developed and flourished during Solomon's reign. For the first time in history, Israel had been a respected world power, and it had had nearly a half century of peace and prosperity. Its ruler had been a man of shrewd political and business abilities but he had not respected Hebrew traditions.

It is hard to tell what might have happened to Israel if Solomon had remained true to the Lord and to his people. But now Israel was on the brink of radical change—the people were ready to revolt against the harsh measures Solomon had enacted; their potential leader, Jeroboam, was waiting for a safe time to return home from Egypt; and Solomon's son Rehoboam would be an ineffectual ruler at best.

The aged monarch himself did not live to see the developing conflict. In 922 B.C., "Solomon slept with his fathers, and was buried in the city of David his father."

The story of Solomon is told in 1 Kings 3–11 and 2 Chronicles 1–9.

Part Four

Prophets
of the Lord

In the four centuries following Solomon's death, his temple came to be symbolic of the divinely granted nationhood of the Israelites. But during these years of the great prophets, Israel witnessed ever increasing idolatry on the part of both kings and citizens. The temple court was the scene of Isaiah's conversion to the role of prophet. At the religious celebration of the solar new year, he may have watched as the ark of the covenant was borne through the temple doors in the first light of dawn. Musicians walked just behind the ark, playing lyres and blowing horns, followed by the king, and his officials and nobles. At the left was the huge ceremonial vessel called the "bronze sea," at the right a great altar. Such a scene might have prompted Isaiah's vision of "the Lord sitting upon a throne, high and lifted up" (Is. 6.1).

The great prophets of Israel and Judah—Elijah, Elisha, Isaiah and Jeremiah—often warned that their nations would fall. To these visionaries, the Assyrians and Babylonians seemed sent by the Lord against a people who had broken their covenant.

THE REIGN of King Solomon had marked the summit of Israel's power and prestige. Solomon's achievements were marred, however, by serious economic and social abuses. For years, resentment had been mounting among the northern tribes as an increasing burden of taxes and forced labor was imposed on them to support the king's lavish building projects— while the king's own tribe of Judah enjoyed preferential treatment.

Northern tribal and religious leaders had long been urging secession. The eagerness with which Solomon and his court had cultivated pagan ways was offensive to them, and many had never accepted the principle of hereditary monarchy to begin with.

The northerners did not break away, however, until Solomon's son and successor, Rehoboam, had been given a last chance to grant the needed reforms. But when asked, he arrogantly refused.

Rehoboam destroyed any chance there may have been for reconciliation. The northerners declared their independence, taking the name Israel with them. They successfully resisted Jerusalem's attempts to reconquer them, and Rehoboam was left with the much smaller kingdom of Judah, comprising only the tribal land of Judah and part of Benjamin. The northerners chose as their first king a former government official named Jeroboam, who had been forced into exile in Egypt after criticizing Solomon's policies.

For the next two generations there was sporadic and inconclusive warfare between the two states, in which neither side could win. Israel was much more populous (during the eighth century Israel had some 800,000 people and Judah some 200,000), but the northern kingdom was hampered by both domestic and external problems.

The people of Judah enjoyed a degree of social and political unity unknown to northern Israel. With a well-established religious center in Jerusalem and a line of kings who ruled steadily for three-and-a-half centuries, the tone of Judah's life was one of moderation, avoiding the extremes of discord that beset the northern kingdom.

Farmers and Craftsmen

Life on the land was hard but fairly tranquil except in times of drought or war, and the peasants (who formed the great majority of the population of Judah) were usually content to ignore the outside world. Most lived in isolated hamlets and thought mainly about weather and soil, harvests and livestock. Six days out of seven, they went at sunrise into the surrounding fields to work their land, returning home at dusk to a family meal and an early bedtime.

The agriculture of most farms in the Mediterranean world, then as now, was centered on three all-important products: grain, wine and olive oil. From mid-September to early November, people harvested olives and pressed them for oil. Then, with the onset of the winter rains, they plowed the fields and sowed wheat and barley. From midwinter until early spring they planted millet, lentils, sesame, chickpeas, cucumbers and melons. They spent part of the slack season from the end of March to the middle of April cutting down flax stalks for the fibers, used in making cloth. Then they harvested the barley crop. Harvesting the wheat took up most of May and June, and the longest days of the year were spent from dawn to dusk on the circular stone threshing floors, separating the chaff from the grain. After the harvest festival, midsummer was spent somewhat less laboriously in pruning and cleaning the grapevines while the grapes ripened in the sun. Then, August and September were given over to picking figs, dates, pomegranates, and finally, to harvesting grapes and making wine.

The cities of Judah were as hectic as the countryside was placid. Inside a city's walls every available foot of space was used for housing, until at last, in Solomon's time, the population spilled over into the fields outside the gates. The marketplaces were jammed with caravans, farmers selling their surplus crops and local artisans displaying their products.

A visitor to Jerusalem would have found hundreds of tiny workshops huddled in special quarters of the city. In the ceramic quarter, potters could be seen turning out pots and jars of every size and use. The carpenters' bazaar housed workshops specializing in the manufacture of furniture and other articles made of wood. In the cloth bazaar there were wool merchants, spinners, dyers and weavers. Smiths and metalworkers occupied the brass and iron bazaars, fashioning weapons, farming implements, musical instruments and household utensils. Then there were the workers in precious metals and jewelry. Finally, there was a Phoenician quarter composed mainly of descendants of the Tyrians brought in by David and Solomon to beautify Jerusalem. In this quarter were merchants selling cloth and garments dyed purple, as well as cabinetmakers and manufacturers of glassware.

Reform in Judah

The first decades after the division provided a severe test of Judah's ability to survive. Attacked several times by Israel and Egypt, the country's leaders neglected domestic problems, and as a result social and religious conditions gradually deteriorated. The gap between rich and poor grew wider than ever, and the erosion of religious principles continued almost unchecked. The devotees of Baal "built for themselves high places, and pillars . . . on every high hill and under every green tree; and there were also male cult prostitutes in the land" (1 Kings 14.23–24).

The moral authority of Judaism was restored, however, with the rise of King Asa and his son Jehoshaphat. Taking the throne in 913 B.C., Asa announced his support of religious conservatives, revitalized the temple priesthood and banned most forms of pagan worship. He also made peace with the northern kingdom. Jehoshaphat (873–849 B.C.) proved an equally competent ruler. He won the gratitude of his hard-pressed subjects by making broad economic and judicial reforms.

Turmoil in Israel

The northern kingdom of Israel had been turbulent and unpredictable from the beginning, with a large, diverse population who seldom agreed on anything, and an unstable government. In addition to the prophets who opposed any hereditary monarchy, there were many religious and tribal factions whose rivalries made an orderly transfer of power almost impossible. During the 200 years of its existence, the northern kingdom was ruled by 19 kings, eight of whom died violently.

In an effort to stabilize the rule of Israel, Jeroboam attempted to institute a new cult linked solely to the north. He established shrines at Dan and Bethel and strengthened the priesthood. Despite these achievements, he was unable to win over all his subjects; some still regarded Jerusalem as the center of their faith.

Following Jeroboam's death in 901 B.C., Israel entered a period of prolonged crisis. During the next generation five different men held or claimed the throne, and the resulting warfare nearly destroyed the northern kingdom.

Finally, in about 876 B.C., an army officer named Omri eliminated his last rival and began a brief but extremely successful reign. Occupying the throne for seven years, Omri strengthened the country's military position, built a splendid new capital at Samaria and founded Israel's first ruling dynasty. He also compromised with paganism to the extent that he "did more evil than all who were before him" (1 Kings 16.25).

The rise of paganism and despotism in the north reached a critical level under Omri's son Ahab (died 850 B.C.), whose wife was the strong-willed Phoenician princess, Jezebel. Ahab advertised the prosperity of his reign with elaborate building projects. However, the country's small farmers and laborers had only a marginal share in this prosperity. In Israel, as in the southern kingdom before Jehoshaphat's reforms, the gains of conquest and trade were enjoyed almost exclusively by the upper classes.

Social injustice accompanied the increasingly brutal religious policies of Ahab and Jezebel. Raised in the cosmopolitan court of Tyre, Jezebel had little liking for the rough-and-ready culture of the Israelites, and even less for their austere monotheistic religion. Following her marriage to Ahab, she arrived in Samaria with a retinue of personal attendants and priests and was permitted to establish shrines to the Phoenician gods. Fanatically devoted to the cult of Baal, she set out to make it the official state religion—in place of worship of the Lord.

The northern kingdom now faced the gravest crisis in its history. The royal court in Samaria abandoned itself totally to Phoenician ways. Though the king never officially denounced the orthodox religion, it became for many only a tradition with little effect on conduct. The true danger was in the people's willingness to go along with Jezebel's paganizing campaign.

The Prophets of Israel

At this point a man appeared who seemed to have been born to keep the spark of faith alive. An intense, lonely figure, Elijah mystified the people of his time. Dressed in a leather loincloth and a cloak of woven hair, deeply tanned, tough and lean from much fasting and outdoor exercise, he would appear without warning to challenge Israel's rulers and their pagan gods. Then he would vanish, only to reappear to carry on the struggle.

Elijah is said to have performed many brave and miraculous deeds. His greatest service was in rallying the faithful of Israel around the Lord, thus carrying on the role of prophet as established by Samuel nearly two centuries earlier. Unlike a king, priest, ambassador or general, a prophet was sustained not by birth or royal appointment, but solely by his own conviction that the Lord had chosen him as a spokesman and direct emissary to the king and people of Israel. He might advise the king on an impending battle, condemn him for apostasy or predict the destruction of the entire nation. Usually, his right to speak was considered sacred and his person in-

Excess dye was pressed out of the wool by a weighted lever. This cooperative venture was the forerunner of the trade guilds that throve under Hezekiah near the end of the century. The finest dyes came from the murex mollusk (photograph). It yielded the rich color that caused Phoenicia to be called "land of the purple."

Debir, located near vast pastures at the edge of the Negeb desert, was a center for the dyeing and weaving trades in Judah during the 8th century B.C. The town had about 30 dye works and nearly every house had a loom. Wool was dipped several times into stone vats rimmed with grooves, so not a drop of the valuable dye was wasted.

violate, because his words were believed to be the words of God. Elijah rose to heaven in a chariot of fire before the house of Omri was overthrown, but his message was remembered.

Israel found another inspirational leader in Elisha, who worked in close association with the itinerant prophets in the countryside. Scorned as fanatics by some, they would deliver spectacular public oracles, rising from an ecstatic trance-like state to a frenzy of singing and dancing in celebration of the Lord. Politically, these "sons of the prophets" were extreme traditionalists, and they played an important role in the overthrow of Ahab's son Jehoram in 842 B.C. The army feared Jehoram's military ineptitude, and the people, having borne the cost of two unsuccessful wars in Moab and Syria, were equally dissatisfied. The country was ripe for rebellion.

Elisha sent one of his disciples to the headquarters of Jehu, an army commander, where everything had been planned beforehand. Jehu was anointed king, and his enthusiastic troops quickly set out to eliminate the country's leadership, killing not only Jehoram but the visiting king of Judah, Ahaziah, and his entire entourage. The now middle-aged Jezebel was put to death, while adherents of her cult were massacred. (Ahab had died some years before.)

Jehu ruled from 842 to 815 and founded Israel's longest dynasty, but his reign was marked by continued unrest because of vast tribute paid, first to Assyria and then to the Aramean king in Damascus. After the Assyrian raid and destruction of Damascus in 803 B.C., the last two kings of the Jehu dynasty, Jehoash (801–786) and Jeroboam II (786–746), reversed Israel's fortunes, and the northern kingdom entered its greatest (and last) period of prosperity. But prosperity brought back the abuses that had characterized Omri's era. Once more, the rich immersed themselves in foreign cults and manners. The gap between rich and poor widened again. In the 10 years following Jeroboam's death in 746, Israel had five kings. Each successive revolt left the country more vulnerable to Assyrian invasion.

The Assyrians had made military forays into the west before. A century earlier they had dominated the whole of southwest Asia from Babylonia to the Mediterranean, and Israel was one of their many tributaries. Then, in the early part of the eighth century, the Assyrian Empire was weakened by domestic troubles. The fertile country between the Tigris and Euphrates rivers supported many different peoples whose allegiance to Nineveh (the Assyrian capital) could never be taken for granted, and Assyrian monarchs repeatedly had to divert troops from the empire's frontiers to deal with rebellions closer to home. Finally, after decades of instability, Tiglath-pileser III took the throne in 745 B.C. and prepared his country for serious conquest, organizing a massive, well-equipped army.

The Fall of the Northern Kingdom

In 743–742 Tiglath-pileser's Assyrians turned westward, where in northern Syria they encountered all the Syro-Palestinian coastal lands in league against them, headed by King Azariah (Uzziah) of Judah. After defeating this opposition, Tiglath-pileser demanded heavy tribute from those states (including Israel) that surrendered peaceably and crushed the rest. Amos, Hosea and the other prophets of the day saw Assyria as an instrument of God's judgment:

"Rejoice not, O Israel! Exult not . . .
for you have played the harlot,
forsaking your God. . . .
The days of punishment have come . . .
Israel shall know it" (Hosea 9.1, 7).

Under Hoshea, Israel's last king, the prophecy came to pass. Hoshea made a suicidal attempt to regain independence, and in 724 B.C. the Assyrian king, Shalmaneser V, responded decisively. In the same year the whole northern countryside was overrun and heavily fortified Samaria itself was under siege. The capital held out for more than two years, but in 721 it finally fell to Assyria's new king, Sargon II.

Of the survivors, the Assyrian annals report that 27,290 people were deported to distant parts of the Assyrian Empire, where many eventually were assimilated into native populations. Israel in turn was resettled with Assyrian captives from other conquered territories. These foreigners intermarried with the remaining Israelites, mingling their religious and cultural traditions. In time they became a new people, destined to reappear in Jewish history as the Samaritans.

Isaiah and Hezekiah

The southern kingdom had been spared, but Israel's fall was an example that Judah could not afford to ignore. Under King Hezekiah (715–687 B.C.), Jerusalem gained a leader second only to David. Celebrated as a great defender of Judah, Hezekiah was blessed with the services of one of Judaism's supreme figures: the prophet Isaiah.

Unlike earlier prophets, whose origins were humble, Isaiah was possibly born into a prominent Jerusalem family. He involved himself in politics as readily as in religious matters, for to him they were inseparable. Assyria's rise to power was no accident, he proclaimed. God had ordained it for his own purposes, and to resist would only compound Judah's sins.

Hezekiah's first crisis arose in about 713 B.C., when Judah was urged to join in an uprising against Assyria. Isaiah argued against such a move, assuring the king that God would make it known when Assyria should fall. Until then Judah must be patient. Hezekiah followed the prophet's advice and Judah was spared defeat.

A few years later, however, Hezekiah chose to ignore the prophet's counsel. In 705, following the death of the Assyrian king, Sargon II, Judah joined Egypt in a bid for independence during a new wave of uprisings. Sargon's successor, Sennacherib, took matters in hand, and by 701 Judah was overrun. Isaiah at last convinced Hezekiah to make peace and salvage what was left of the kingdom. Hezekiah sent Sennacherib a humble message and subsequently paid the huge tribute demanded of him. Then, a dozen years later, the Assyrian monarch attacked Jerusalem.

At this moment Isaiah astonished the court by reversing himself. He urged Hezekiah to resist. Sennacherib's arrogance had finally passed the limits of divine indulgence, and Isaiah saw it as a sign of Assyria's impending downfall. Within a short time, a terrible pestilence descended on the

Defensive Design Became a Fine Art

The Near East, never calm for long, was especially turbulent in the time of the prophets, when wars and invasions raged almost incessantly. These led to improvements in the design of fortified cities, parts of which are still to be found in the area today.

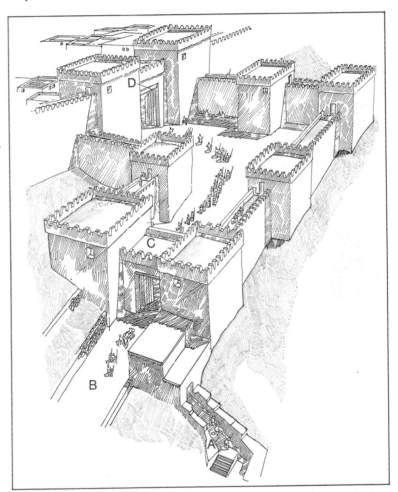

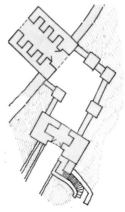

An engraving on a bronze vessel from about the 8th century B.C. (above) shows how archers defended their cities from the top of crenellated walls. Below, the city gate of Gezer—dating from the earlier time of Solomon's reign—still standing today.

Solomon's city gate at Megiddo was a truly spectacular fortification. It could be approached only by a steep stairway (A) or an exposed ramp (B) running up to a double outer gateway (C), which was covered and protected by towers. A high-walled courtyard then led to the main gate (D), likewise protected. Great double doors of wood guarded each gateway, two sets at the outer entry and four at the inner (inset, left). Soldiers could hide in bays between each set.

Assyrian camp, killing thousands of soldiers and quickly ending the siege of Jerusalem.

Isaiah's vision of history was that all nations, even the mighty Assyrian Empire, were merely tools serving God's plan for the final redemption of mankind. This millennium would not arrive, Isaiah warned, before the Jews had endured a period of trial and sufferings. But in the end "a rem-

A Judean Surgical Operation

Trepanning, or removing a section of bone from the skull to relieve pressure on the brain, was practiced by Judean surgeons during the time of Isaiah. First the patient's head was shaved

and the skin slit and drawn back, exposing the bone. Then a small surgical saw was used to remove the section, which was replaced when the drainage was completed. The hole remaining in the skull at left indicates that this particular operation killed the patient.

nant of Israel" would return to their homeland and preside over an age of perfect harmony and peace. "The wolf shall dwell with the lamb, and the leopard shall lie down with the kid . . . and a little child shall lead them" (Isaiah 11.6).

A Babylonian Threat

The final century of Judah's life was a troubled one. Hezekiah's successor was Manasseh, whose 45-year reign (687–642 B.C.) was Jerusalem's longest and one of her worst. Manasseh reestablished paganism and even permitted fertility rites and cultic prostitution to take place inside the temple. Manasseh's corrosive policy outlived him

for a while. In 640 the eight-year-old Josiah became king, and not until about 628 was he able to rule his country with a firm hand.

Assyria was steadily weakening, and the old problem of local rebellions sapped Nineveh's resources until 612 B.C. The great Assyrian capital then fell to a coalition led by the rising new power in western Asia: Babylonia.

Babylonia had first risen to eminence more than a thousand years earlier. Under Hammurabi, who produced one of history's great legal codes, Babylon was established as the most important city in Mesopotamia. Then, in about 1550 B.C., a Hittite invasion plunged the territory into a dark age. During the first millennium B.C. the Chaldeans, a Semitic people from the coast of the Persian Gulf, took over Babylonia and rose to political dominance. Chaldean Babylonia became strong enough to worry the rulers of Assyria, and in the eighth century it was incorporated into the empire by force. In about 650 B.C. a large Assyrian garrison had to be stationed in Babylon.

During the period of Assyria's disintegration, Josiah moved to eliminate pagan worship in his land. He was determined to unite north and south and reestablish a united kingdom like David's. This purge was equivalent to a declaration of rebellion. Pagan shrines throughout the country were destroyed, their priests were executed and all idolatry was forbidden on pain of death.

Jeremiah and the Fall of Jerusalem

At this time the prophet Jeremiah began his ministry. Though he supported Josiah's reforms at the outset, Jeremiah was dissatisfied with their results and soon found himself criticizing a popular cause. What he opposed above all was a growing self-satisfaction among the people of Judah—a belief that by obeying the letter of the law, they were fulfilling their spiritual obligations. They were in fact, Jeremiah believed, turning their backs to the Lord.

This was an unpopular message. The political situation in the Near East was changing again, seemingly to Judah's benefit; many believed that a triumphant new age was at hand.

The illusion did not last. The vacuum created by Assyria's collapse was filled by the energetic Babylonians. By 600 B.C. all of Syria and Palestine was under the control of Babylon. In 598 B.C. Jerusalem rebelled, and for a time there seemed some chance of success. But in December of 598, King Nebuchadnezzar arrived and, in the words of a contemporary Babylonian record, "laid siege to the city of Judah (Jerusalem) and . . . took the city on the second day of the month Addaru. He appointed in it a new king to his liking, took heavy booty from it, and brought it to Babylon." This event can now be exactly dated by Babylonian records—March 16, 597 B.C. Some thousands of Judah's important citizens, including the royal family, were taken into exile.

A number of the remaining nobles made one last attempt to fight back. They held secret meetings in Jerusalem with envoys from neighboring states to discuss a possible rebel coalition. Zedekiah, the puppet king installed by Nebuchadnez-

zar, was caught in the middle. He did his best to dissuade the plotters, but he failed. By 589 B.C. rebellion again broke out. Jerusalem was besieged and, after a full year's resistance, the exhausted city was taken in July of 587 B.C.

This time Nebuchadnezzar showed no leniency. Zedekiah was blinded and imprisoned, members of the court were executed en masse though only a few hundred people were led away in chains to Babylon. Jerusalem itself was plundered and burned to the ground.

The kingdom of Judah was dead. In time, after many years and much suffering, a few Jews would return—the "remnant of Israel" that Isaiah had foreseen. But the kingdom was gone and the course of Jewish history had been altered forever.

Disunity and Strife Divide the Empire

The Israelite empire that David had established split, and remained permanently divided, following the death of Solomon in about 922 B.C. Two rival kingdoms thus arose: Israel under Jeroboam and Judah under Solomon's son, Rehoboam. Israel was the richer and more populous of the two, but factional strife from within prevented her from mounting an effective attack against Judah. The more unified Judeans might have conquered Israel, had it not been for an Egyptian threat to their southern border. There was also the successive aggression from Syria (Aram) and Assyria to the north. The result was an inconclusive series of military conflicts, lasting until the final fall of Israel.

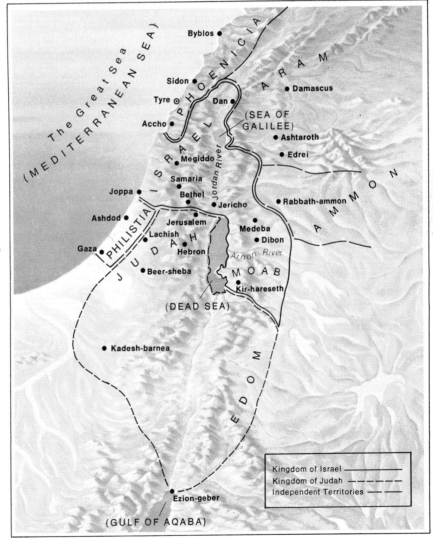

Chapter 12

Pitting himself against Queen Jezebel and her cult of Baal, a prophet affirms that the Lord is the sole God of Israel. He also condemns the despotic nature of King Ahab's rule, and lays the groundwork for the destruction of the powerful Omride dynasty.

Elijah: Troubler of Israel

The most famous of the great prophets of Israel, Elijah is remembered for his fiery words, wild appearance and opposition to the pagan cults of the infamous Queen Jezebel. Appearing suddenly in the northern kingdom sometime early in the ninth century B.C., Elijah quickly gained prominence as a spokesman for the Lord. His departure was as sudden as his appearance: "And Elijah went up by a whirlwind into heaven." His return was to be eagerly awaited by the Jews.

Elijah was born around 900 B.C. in the small village of Tishbe in the administrative province of Gilead, east of the Jordan River in northern Israel. This was a rugged, mountainous region. During the long, dry summers, temperatures hovered around 100° F. Yet, despite its harsh aspects, the land was extremely fertile, watered by the many streams flowing to the Jordan. Fields of wheat flourished on the plains of Gilead, and most of the people there—probably including Elijah's family—were farmers. Near their homes they cultivated gardens with neat rows of beans, peas, lentils, cucumbers, onions and melons. In the valleys below the hills and on terraces carved in the hillsides, they tended orchards of pomegranate, apricot and olive trees, and they planted vineyards along the slopes. Even the hills were not barren, and groves of tall oak trees shaded the mountain ridges. Gilead's greatest agricultural fame came from small plots of land filled with fragrant herbs which were marketed throughout the eastern world. The extract from these herbs,

the so-called "balm of Gilead," was a soothing, aromatic resin used in perfumes and medicines.

During his youth, Elijah may have become one of the Nazirites. These holy men lived their lives with a strict adherence to both the letter and the spirit of the Mosaic code. They symbolized their dedication to God by taking a lifelong vow never to cut their hair, own land, live in houses or drink wine. The Nazirites regarded themselves as warriors of God, always prepared to fight—and, if necessary, to kill—the enemies who undermined their religious traditions, which was treason against the Lord of Israel. Such a battle was brewing in Israel just as Elijah was reaching maturity in Gilead.

Since the original Israelite kingdom had split into Israel and Judah several decades previously, there had been friction between the two nations. Internally, Israel, the northern kingdom, experienced coups, countercoups and royal assassinations. Finally, in 876 B.C., an army commander named Omri gained enough support from the army and the general public to proclaim himself ruler of the country.

Omri brought a stable government to Israel and reestablished peaceful relations with Judah. He fortified his borders east of the Jordan, drove

"They seized them; and Elijah brought them down to the brook Kishon, and killed them there" (1 Kg. 18.40). After Elijah's ritual proved successful in a contest over who was God in Israel—the Lord or Baal—bystanders slew the defeated Baalist priests at the Kishon River, which here flows past the verdant Carmel hills.

back the encroaching Syrians, made Moab—to the south—a vassal and settled Israelites in the area north of the Arnon River. His most significant alliance was with Phoenicia, a country formed by several small, independently ruled city-states—notably Tyre, Sidon and Byblos—northwest of Israel along the Mediterranean coast. The pact between Israel and Phoenicia served as a defense against their common neighbor, warlike Syria, and as a stimulus to trade.

Omri made the alliance with Tyre even firmer by marrying his son, Prince Ahab, to Princess Jezebel, daughter of Ethbaal, the Tyrian priest-king of Phoenicia. The Israelite ruler sought greater security within his kingdom by abandoning the difficult-to-defend capital of Tirzah in favor of a location in the Ephraimite highlands, six miles northwest of Shechem. It was a hilltop site, slightly south of the fertile geographic center of Israel, on the main north-south road of the hill country. On a clear day, the Mediterranean Sea could be seen from the summit.

The city that Omri founded was a handsome and imposing citadel. Skilled Phoenician masons constructed massive walls around temple and palace; in the courtyard of the royal quarters was a large rectangular pool.

Despite Omri's extensive building plans, he did not live to see the completion of Samaria. When he died in 869, his son Ahab became king. Ahab finished the work in progress and expanded it, enlarging and tripling the strength of the site's fortifications. The royal palace, a two-story model of opulence, became known as Ahab's "ivory house" because of the extensive use of ivory wall paneling and furniture decoration—another product from Tyre, the world center of the ivory trade. Ahab built yet another palace at Jezreel, north of Samaria in the Jezreel Valley. There the weather was milder and warmer during the winter than it was in the hills of Samaria.

Worship of Baal

Jezebel worshiped Baal, a Canaanite god. As had long been customary with foreign queens, she was allowed to worship her own god, but Jezebel approached her religion with a fanatic's zeal. She was from a worldly, cultured nation, and, in her eyes, Israel—especially its religion—seemed staid and primitive and in need of stimulation. When she came to Israel, she brought along 450

Led by King Ahab and Queen Jezebel, many Israelites worshiped gods of Phoenicia during the time of Elijah. Above, some of Jezebel's priests and priestesses of Baal, the storm god, and Asherah, the mother-goddess, enact a fertility rite before an altar with images of the deities. The religion, closely related to the

priests of Baal and 400 "prophets" of Asherah, the mother-goddess. This religious cadre was luxuriously housed by the state and dined at the palace, a heavy addition to the burden of Israelite taxpayers.

When Ahab built his "ivory house," he constructed a temple of Baal with quarters for the priests next to the palace. The greater part of this sacred structure was a court, enclosed with thick walls and open to the sky. Within the court was a small sacred chapel containing symbols of Baal and the mother-goddess, Asherah. The temple priests and their attendants kept an eternal flame burning in a large dish-shaped brazier on the chapel's altar.

Since Baalism was a nature cult, worshipers joined the priests and temple prostitutes in sacred orgies before the altar, especially at the new-year celebration. Then they acted out the reproductive theme so that the gods, who controlled earth and

old Canaanite worship, sought to increase the fertility of nature. As incense burns on a horned altar, a priest and priestess pour holy wine into sacred vessels (one type is shown in photo). Others dance in a state of ecstasy, and a priest slashes himself in a plea for divine attention. Elijah fought such pagan practices.

water, would follow their example and improve the fertility of animals and man. The fertility cult was the most popular aspect of Canaanite religion, appealing strongly to subsistence farmers in an often hostile land.

The pagan religion imported by Jezebel horrified devout Israelites, but it also found many new followers. Descendants of the Canaanites who had remained in the country during David's rule paid only lip service to the Israelite God; and for centuries the Israelites themselves had often given in to the temptation to blend the Lord and local gods into a single cult. Within a few years, many of the people of Israel had embraced paganism. Although Ahab did not make Baalism the official state religion, he did nothing to curb its spread. To do so might have undermined his own power to rule.

When some Israelite prophets opposed Jezebel's policies, she had several of them executed.

She threatened others with reprisals until many gave in and spoke only what the ruling classes wanted to hear. The handful who continued to resist were persecuted, alienated from their fellow prophets and driven into hiding.

Elijah Appears

It was during this religious crisis that Elijah first appeared. Traveling from Gilead, he crossed the Jordan and headed south to Samaria, wearing only a leather loincloth, sandals and a hairy animal-hide cloak draped around his shoulders. As he climbed the hill of Samaria, the path took him past the small, rough stone houses of the common people. These were clustered tightly in the lower town that had spread down the hillside outside the wall of the citadel. At the top, on the esplanade in front of the city gate, the city elders held court, administered punishment and conducted other legal matters.

The city marketplace also occupied a large portion of the esplanade. There, shaded by a rough woolen canopy, a tradesman might be seen lifting a large clay storage jar and tipping it to measure out a portion of barley on a bronze scale for his customer. The two-handled jars were inexpensive and universally used to store grains, beans, water, wine, milk and honey. Nearby, skilled potters offered a finer grade of ceramics to those who could afford more decorative items: vases, pitchers and bowls finished with a pebblelike surface and washed with hematite, which gave it a brown-red color. When this dried, the vessels were burnished to give them a beautiful glossy sheen after baking. In the Phoenician section of the bazaar, wealthy Samaritans could choose from a dazzling display of wares: delicate glass flasks with white and yellow bands flowing over a blue background; gold rings and armbands shaped like serpents with precious jewels for eyes; deep-blue glass beads and pendants; fabrics whose metallic and multicolored yarns were intricately embroidered into complex geometric and floral patterns; bronze bowls and platters etched with pictures of winged cherubim and other mythological creatures; daggers with ivory handles carved in animal shapes, such as a snarling lion's head.

Elijah's path led him past the merchants and craftsmen, who may have stared at his odd appearance, and through the citadel's colossal covered gateway, flanked by enormous towers for defense. Inside the walls, it was a distance of several more yards to the large guard tower at the southeast corner of the wall surrounding the royal enclave, then another quarter of a mile past homes of officials and buildings for national business, to the palace itself. Once inside, Elijah passed the lavish decorations that earned the name "ivory house," such as intricate ivory wall paneling carved like a frieze in a repeating pattern of lotus buds and flowers.

The prophet was ushered into Ahab's audience hall by a royal servant. Apparently he found the king alone, possibly reclining on a cedar couch that was inlaid with ivory figures of lions, bulls, sphinxes and other beasts fighting one another. The sun glistened on ivory wainscoting sculpted in multiples of a stylized palm tree—a favorite Phoenician motif.

The king was startled when his visitor was announced. Elijah entered the room and wasted no time on formal greetings. Without hesitation, he began to condemn Ahab for the paganism that had breached Israel's sworn covenant with the Lord. "As the Lord the God of Israel lives, before whom I stand," Elijah thundered, "there shall be neither dew nor rain these years, except by my word." A long drought would demonstrate that God, not Baal, controlled the forces of fertility.

The Widow's Child

Before Ahab could recover, Elijah was gone. The king summoned his guard, but the prophet had left the city as rapidly as he had come. He recrossed the Jordan into Gilead and hid in an isolated area by the brook Cherith, a stream feeding into the Jordan a few miles south of Tishbe. There the Lord provided him with "ravens [which] brought him bread and meat" each morning and night. The drought soon began, and when the brook dried up so that he could no longer drink, Elijah returned to the Jordan and followed it many miles north, past the Sea of Chinnereth (Galilee). He then turned northwest, crossed the Phoenician border and followed the rocky coastline to the village of Zarephath, seven miles south of the port city of Sidon.

As he reached the village gate, he met an impoverished widow who was gathering twigs for a fire. Elijah approached her and said, "Bring me a little water in a vessel, that I may drink." And then he added, "Bring me a morsel of bread in your hand." The poor woman pleaded, ". . . I have nothing baked, only a handful of meal in a jar, and a little oil in a cruse . . ." It was barely enough, she said, to feed herself and her son. The prophet insisted that she "first make me a little cake of it and bring it to me, and afterward make for yourself and your son. For thus says the Lord the God of Israel, 'The jar of meal shall not be spent, and the cruse of oil shall not fail, until the day that the Lord sends rain upon the earth.'"

The widow took Elijah to her small, two-story stone home and built a fire in the kitchen area behind it. Mixing water with some of the barley meal—wheat flour was too expensive for poor people—she made dough which she flattened into a disk similar to a pancake. She then placed a griddle over the flames, poured some oil from the small clay jug over it and cooked the "cake" for Elijah on the steaming griddle.

The widow gave Elijah the "upper chamber," or attic, of the house and he lived there as the drought and famine dragged on in Israel. The small containers of meal and oil continued to provide for the household, just as the prophet had promised.

Suddenly, the widow's son became ill and died. The grief-stricken woman wailed to Elijah, "What have you against me, O man of God? . . . to cause the death of my son!" Elijah took the boy from her, carried him up the ladder to his room and placed the limp body on the woven straw mat

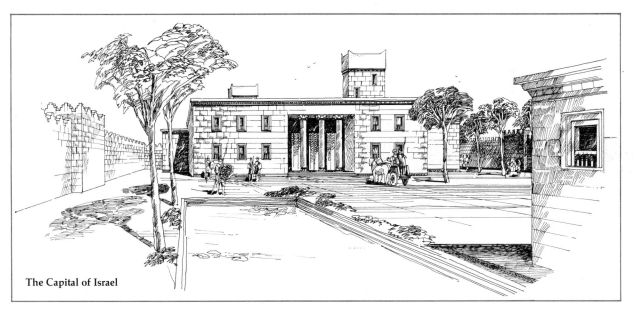

The Capital of Israel

"He bought the hill of Samaria . . . and he fortified the hill, and called the name of the city he built, Samaria" (1 Kg. 16.24). The gently rounded hill at left was uninhabited when King Omri began constructing his capital city there. On its summit, around the royal enclosure (above), were built walls whose Phoenician-style masonry was unexcelled until the 1st century B.C. The squared, unmortared stones fit so perfectly that not even a knife blade could be inserted between them. The architecture of the palace also showed Phoenician influence. It was there that Elijah first confronted Ahab. The pool (foreground) may have looked like the "pool of Samaria" at which Ahab's blood was washed from his chariot after he was killed in battle.

where he himself ordinarily slept. The prophet stretched himself out over the boy three times and prayed, "O Lord my God, let this child's soul [life] come into him again." Miraculously, the boy's eyelids fluttered and he began to breathe. Elijah brought him downstairs to his grateful mother, who cried, "Now I know that you are a man of God, and that the word of the Lord in your mouth is truth."

Soon after this, Elijah was told by the Lord to find Ahab and tell him that the three years of drought were coming to an end. He said farewell to the widow and began the long journey back to Samaria. In the capital, Ahab was steadily growing more desperate and he ordered a servant to summon Obadiah, his steward.

When the servant found him, Obadiah went immediately to the king's quarters. Ahab instructed him, "Go through the land to all the springs of water and to all the valleys; perhaps we may find grass and save the horses and mules alive, and not lose some of the animals." Obadiah was not far out of Samaria when he encountered Elijah. The prophet told the steward to go back and inform Ahab that Elijah had returned to Israel. The terrified steward pointed out that he had remained faithful to the Lord and had hidden two groups of 50 prophets in the caves around the hill of Samaria and had brought them bread and water to help them escape Jezebel's purges. Meanwhile, the king had been searching far and wide for the prophet. If Obadiah now went back to Samaria and told him that Elijah was here, and the prophet again vanished into thin air, Obadiah would be in serious trouble. Elijah assured Obadiah that he would not disappear, and followed him back to the palace.

Contest of the Gods

When the prophet entered the throne room, Ahab snapped, "Is it you, you troubler of Israel?" Elijah responded firmly, "I have not troubled Israel; but you have, and your father's house, because you have forsaken the commandments of the Lord and followed the Baals. Now therefore send and gather all Israel to me at Mount Carmel, and the four hundred and fifty prophets of Baal and the four hundred prophets of Asherah, who eat at Jezebel's table."

Ahab agreed to a test of strength between the two gods and sent out a proclamation summon-

ing all citizens to the mountain that towered over the Plain of Jezreel. The first rays of sunlight were filtering through the leaves of the oak and carob trees that gave Carmel its evergreen look, as hundreds of people streamed toward the site. Passing through thickets of bushes, they climbed the low hills to reach the long ridge stretching upward to the mountain's summit. Once they had gathered, Elijah addressed them, demanding, "How long will you go limping with two different opinions? If the Lord is God, follow him; but if Baal, then follow him."

The crowd remained silent and Elijah added, "I, even I only, am left a prophet of the Lord; but Baal's prophets are four hundred and fifty men. Let two bulls be given to us; and let them choose one bull for themselves, and cut it in pieces and lay it on the wood, but put no fire to it; and I will prepare the other bull and lay it on the wood, and put no fire to it. And you call on the name of your god and I will call on the name of the Lord; and the God who answers by fire, he is God."

The crowd agreed, "It is well spoken." The priests of Baal cut several oak trees to build a pyre, and hacked the sacrificial bull into pieces which they placed on the wood. Then they prayed to their god, repeatedly calling, "O Baal, answer us!" As the morning passed, they began a sacred dance in a limping, bobbing manner around the sacrifice. By noon, Baal had still not responded, and Elijah began to taunt them. "Cry aloud, for he is a god; either he is musing, or he has gone aside, or he is on a journey, or perhaps he is asleep and must be awakened."

The priests did call to Baal more frantically and then, grabbing swords and spears, they began to slash at their own bodies in a desperate effort to invoke his power. This sort of ritualistic gashing was common in such ceremonies but, though blood streamed down the priests' arms and legs, "no one answered, no one heeded."

By then it was late afternoon and Elijah called to the crowd to gather around him. He had an altar built of 12 large stones (symbolic of Israel's 12 tribes), and piled it high with logs and the sacrificial bull. He ordered some of the men to fill four jars with water and pour them over the offering and the wood, then to repeat the process until everything was drenched. Elijah called toward the heavens, "O Lord, God of Abraham, Isaac, and Israel, let it be known this day that thou art God in Israel . . . Answer me, O Lord, answer me, that this people may know that thou, O Lord, art God . . .''

Suddenly a bolt of fire shot down from the sky, and, in an instant, the flames consumed not only the offered bull but the wood, the water and the stone altar. The astonished people fell down with their faces to the earth, screaming, ''The Lord, he is God; the Lord, he is God.''

The triumphant Elijah ordered the crowd, ''Seize the prophets of Baal; let not one of them escape.'' The people grabbed the startled priests and, at Elijah's command, led them down the mountain to the brook Kishon and swiftly executed every one of them. By this action, Elijah declared holy war on the enemies of the Lord.

Fugitive in the Desert

Elijah turned to Ahab and told him to prepare to return to his palace at Jezreel because the drought was about to end. Clouds soon blackened the sky, and as the rain began to pour, Ahab drove his chariot horses toward Jezreel. Elijah, wild with ecstasy in the victory over Baal, ran across the plain in front of the king's chariot, splashing through puddles on the road leading from Mount Carmel to the palace entrance.

But Elijah's triumph was short-lived. As soon as Ahab dismounted in the courtyard, he rushed inside the palace to Jezebel. He told her at once of Elijah's miracle and his execution of all her priests. The outraged queen immediately sent a message to Elijah: ''So may the gods do to me, and more also, if I do not make your life as the life of one of them by this time tomorrow.''

Again the prophet became a fugitive, and he began his journey along the narrow highland running south from Jezreel, across the border into Judah. He passed through the country to the hot, dry Negeb (southland), skirting clusters of drab round hills of limestone and chalk until, after a 130-mile trip, he reached Beer-sheba on the Judean frontier.

Beer-sheba, a village of seven wells, was an oasis that had been a sanctuary since the time of the Patriarchs. Elijah remained there only long enough to revive himself with food and water, then continued south into the desert, a wilderness of hot winds and barren soil.

After a day of wandering, he reached a gully where a broom bush clung to the parched earth. This desert shrub needed little moisture to sus-

tain it and often grew to a large size, offering some protection from the relentless sun. Tired and depressed over his victory-turned-defeat, Elijah rested in the shade of the broom bush and sadly spoke: ''It is enough; now, O Lord, take away my life; for I am no better than my fathers.''

He lay down on the hard earth and slept. As he dreamed, an angel appeared, touched him and said, ''Arise and eat.'' Elijah woke to find a jar of fresh water and a cake of bread baking on a hot stone. After eating and drinking, he slept again only to have the angel appear once more in his dreams and say, ''Arise and eat, else the journey will be too great for you.''

When he opened his eyes, he found a second supper. ''And he arose, and ate and drank, and went in the strength of that food forty days and forty nights to Horeb [Sinai] the mount of God.'' There, 200 miles south of Beer-sheba, God had given the commandments to Moses. The prophet found a cave on the mountainside and prepared to spend the night. But, hearing the voice of the Lord, he went outside to witness a tremendous windstorm, followed by an earthquake and a great fire. Then the ''still small voice'' of the Lord (Hebrew: ''the sound of gentle stillness,'' within which the voice of God was heard) asked why he was there.

''I have been very jealous for the Lord, the God of hosts,'' Elijah replied, ''for the people of Israel have forsaken thy covenant, thrown down thy altars, and slain thy prophets with the sword; and I, even I only, am left; and they seek my life, to take it away.'' God told him to return to Israel to continue his work and to seek out a man named Elisha, who would be his successor.

After weeks of travel, Elijah arrived in Gilead and went to the village of Abel-meholah, some distance from Tishbe. When he found Elisha plowing his father's field, the prophet draped his hairy cloak over the young man's shoulders, thereby designating him as his successor. Elisha said farewell to his family and left with Elijah.

While Elijah was making his long journey from Mount Sinai, Ahab had been battling the ever-aggressive Syrians. After defeating them, he joined them in an alliance which was quickly forced into action. When the empire-minded Assyrians invaded Syria in 853, the armies of Israel and Syria united to block the Assyrian advance in a battle at Qarqar on the Orontes River.

With peace restored, Ahab returned to Jezreel,

"Now Naboth the Jezreelite had a vineyard in Jezreel, beside the palace of Ahab king of Samaria" (1 Kg. 21.1). Ahab's winter palace was in the lush Jezreel Valley near the area shown at left. Here, by a plot of Jezebel, Naboth was murdered and his vineyard seized. The covetous eyes of Ahab's haughty queen may have resembled those of the female figure above, found in the ruins of nearby Megiddo.

where he became interested in the large estate adjacent to the palace grounds. It was the property of a landowner named Naboth, who took great pride in the vineyards planted there. This land, an inheritance from his ancestors, produced large crops of red grapes used for the wine such as the king himself drank.

Naboth's Vineyard

From the Plain of Jezreel, the earth sloped down toward the Jordan River. Naboth, like other vineyard owners there, planted his vines on terraces dug into the stony hillsides. This was necessary to prevent the thin layer of soil from being washed away during the rainy winter months. He allowed the vine stems to grow by trailing along the ground, and once the branches were filled with clusters of grapes, his workers propped them up on forked sticks so they could ripen. This was the most common method of vine culture, though some owners in the district trained the vine stems to grow upward along sticks when they first sprouted in the spring. After the grapes had been harvested each year, Naboth's men pruned the vines so that only the trunk and a few main branches remained during the winter.

But Ahab had other ideas about this land and he went to visit his neighbor. He found Naboth in the vineyard. After they had exchanged greetings, Ahab said, "Give me your vineyard, that I may have it for a vegetable garden, because it is near my house; and I will give you a better vineyard for it; or, if it seems good to you, I will give you its value in money."

Naboth shook his head and replied, "The Lord forbid that I should give you the inheritance of my fathers." The king's proposal was unthinkable to him because Israel's long-established legal and religious custom dictated that property be forever handed down through the family that originally owned it, unless there were no heirs. The laws could not be ignored and private property could not be taken at will by the king, as it had been in Canaanite regimes.

Ahab knew that Naboth was legally correct, and he returned to the palace in a petulant mood. Going immediately to his bedchamber, he lay down on his ivory-decorated bed and turned his face to the wall. When servants brought him food, he dismissed them angrily. Learning of this, Jezebel entered and asked, "Why is your spirit so vexed that you eat no food?"

When he explained his frustration, Jezebel

smiled and said, "Do you now govern Israel? Arise, and eat bread, and let your heart be cheerful; I will give you the vineyard of Naboth the Jezreelite."

The queen had no respect for the laws and religious traditions of Israel, and she bent them to her will. Writing in Ahab's name, she sent letters, stamped with the royal seal, to the elders and noblemen of Jezreel, telling them: "Proclaim a fast, and set Naboth on high among the people; and set two base fellows opposite him, and let them bring a charge against him, saying, 'You have cursed God and the king.' Then take him out, and stone him to death." This was in accord with the rarely used law prohibiting any blasphemy or treason against the Lord.

The authorities held the event, and when the two hired informers denounced Naboth for blasphemy, he and his family were taken outside the city and stoned to death. A report was sent to Jezebel and she rushed into Ahab's room, triumphantly exclaiming, "Arise, take possession of the vineyard of Naboth the Jezreelite, which he refused to give you for money; for Naboth is not alive, but dead."

With no heirs in the way, the property was automatically vested in the king. The happy Ahab rushed to his chariot and drove to the nearby vineyard, but Elijah had also learned of Jezebel's treachery. Ahab had barely entered the property when he heard the prophet behind him angrily shouting, "Have you killed, and also taken possession?"

Ahab turned to face him and said, "Have you found me, O my enemy?" Elijah answered with the wrath of the Lord: "I have found you, because you have sold yourself to do what is evil in the sight of the Lord. Behold, I will bring evil upon you; I will utterly sweep you away, and will cut off from Ahab every male, bond or free, in Israel . . . The dogs shall eat Jezebel within the bounds of Jezreel."

The Fiery Chariot

But Ahab soon had more to worry about than Elijah's prophecy. The alliance with Syria disintegrated and, after three years of border skirmishes between the two nations, Syria invaded and took Ramoth-gilead. Ahab mustered his army and, aided by reinforcements from Judah, tried to retake the city but was killed by a Syrian archer. The sons who succeeded him were ineffectual rulers and now only Jezebel remained as the supreme adversary to Elijah.

But the aging prophet felt himself too near death to conclude that battle. Accompanied by Elisha, he made a last pilgrimage to three cities where groups of prophets lived: Gilgal, Bethel and Jericho. At each point, Elijah begged the younger prophet to stay behind but Elisha refused. From Jericho they walked to the Jordan and Elijah removed his hairy cloak. He "rolled it up, and struck the water, and the water was parted to the one side and to the other, till the two of them could go over on dry ground."

Elijah then said to his successor, "Ask what I shall do for you, before I am taken from you." Elisha replied, "I pray you, let me inherit a double share of your spirit." Elijah responded, "You have asked a hard thing; yet, if you see me as I am being taken from you, it shall be so for you; but if you do not see me, it shall not be so."

The two prophets continued to walk on and talk, when suddenly "a chariot of fire" came between them. The astonished Elisha watched as a whirlwind drew Elijah upward into heaven; he cried after him, "My father, my father! the chariots of Israel and its horsemen!" Then Elijah disappeared. Elisha sadly picked up his mentor's mantle and prepared to resume the battle against their common enemy.

The story of Elijah is told in 1 Kings 17–19, 21; 2 Kings 1, 2, 9, 10; and Malachi 4.5.

In this vicinity of the Jordan, across from Jericho, Elijah is said to have ascended into heaven. As he talked there with Elisha, "behold, a chariot of fire and horses of fire separated the two of them. And Elijah went up by a whirlwind into heaven" (2 Kg. 2.11).

Chapter 13

A new prophet arises to bring about the overthrow of the impious monarchy and to assert that there is no God in all the earth but in Israel. Yet, his avenging anger is matched by his compassion for the sick and the poor and his miraculous gift for helping them.

Elisha: Healer and Revolutionary

The prophet Elisha was the disciple and successor of Elijah. Though not as dramatic as Elijah, he was equally zealous in the Lord's service. His ministry was remembered less for angry eloquence than for benign miracles. Unlike the grim and solitary Elijah, Elisha spent his life among his fellowmen and was concerned with their everyday problems. Moreover, he involved himself directly in political and military events. Elisha instigated an army rebellion that eventually destroyed the house of King Ahab of Israel and his foreign queen, Jezebel, thus fulfilling a prophecy of Elijah. His story, like Elijah's, took place mainly in the northern kingdom of Israel. After his death his devoted followers preserved the tales of his miraculous words and deeds.

Elisha was born in the ninth century B.C., the son of a well-to-do farmer in the Jordan Valley south of the Sea of Galilee. He was a young man ploughing a field behind yoked oxen when the aged Elijah found him. The prophet had just returned from Sinai. There, where Moses received the Law, he had been commanded to anoint Elisha as his spiritual heir. Without saying a word, the stern-visaged stranger draped his goat-hair mantle over the astonished youth's shoulders. At once Elisha realized he had been chosen for holiness. After preparing a farewell feast for his parents and their household, he followed Elijah.

For several years Elisha served primarily as Elijah's attendant. Then, knowing that his end was near, Elijah made a final pilgrimage with Elisha to the communities at Gilgal, Bethel and Jer-

icho. At each place they stayed with "sons of the prophets." These were small communes of holy men and mystics of the kind the prophet Samuel had fostered. Living mainly on donations from the pious, they sought to perceive the Lord's will in their own prophecies, often falling into trances induced by music and frenzied dancing.

From the community at Jericho, Elijah and Elisha walked to the Jordan River, followed by 50 of the prophets. "Then Elijah took his mantle, and rolled it up, and struck the water, and the water was parted to the one side and to the other, till the two of them could go over on dry ground. When they had crossed, Elijah said to Elisha, 'Ask what I shall do for you, before I am taken from you.' And Elisha said, 'I pray you, let me inherit a double share of your spirit.' . . .

"And as they still went on and talked, behold, a chariot of fire and horses of fire separated the two of them. And Elijah went up by a whirlwind into heaven. And Elisha saw it and he cried, 'My father, my father! the chariots of Israel and its horsemen!' And he saw him no more."

Sorrowfully, Elisha picked up his master's mantle and struck the Jordan waters. For him, too, the waters parted. The prophets on the other bank exclaimed, "The spirit of Elijah rests on Eli-

The only known authentic portrayal of an Israelite ruler appears on the Black Obelisk of Shalmaneser III of Assyria. Here Israel's Jehu, robed and wearing the cloth cap of royalty, kisses the ground in submission to Shalmaneser. Behind him an Israelite official is holding part of Jehu's tribute of gold and silver.

sha." And they bowed down to their new leader.

At the time his ministry began (about 850 B.C.), the influence of the prophets had been weakened by Queen Jezebel's persecutions, but many holy men, at the risk of their lives, still opposed the queen and her idols. Elisha soon emerged as their leader. His first great deed, though, was in patriotic aid of his nation.

Not long after Elisha succeeded Elijah, Israel sent an army to put down the insurrection of the small vassal state of Moab, east of the Dead Sea. King Jehoram (or Joram) of Israel, son of Ahab and Jezebel, led the forces. From his capital at Samaria, he chose a long detour along the western shore of the Dead Sea, in order to attack Moab on its more vulnerable southern frontier. En route, his forces were augmented by the armies of Jehoshaphat, king of Judah, and those of the vassal kingdom of Edom. It was a long, circuitous march in relentless heat. By the time the expedition reached the semidesert region south of the Dead Sea, men and animals were weak and crazed from thirst. But the brook Zered, to which they headed for water, was bone dry.

Victory in Moab

The kings of Israel, Judah and Edom, told that Elisha was in their midst, sought him out to ask for help. Elisha rebuked Jehoram for the wickedness of his parents. "What have I to do with you?" he declared. "Go to the prophets of your father and the prophets of your mother." But he relented, saying, ". . . were it not that I have regard for Jehoshaphat the king of Judah, I would neither look at you, nor see you." Elisha then invoked the Lord's intervention. From the depths of an ecstatic trance, he promised: "You shall not see wind or rain, but that stream-bed shall be filled with water . . ." The next morning a torrent gushed through the brook. The vast expedition was refreshed and saved from disaster.

From their distant border towers, the Moabites mistook the waters splashing and shimmering over the red sandstone for blood. Thinking that the armies of the three kings were battling among themselves and were now easy prey, they raced to the scene and were killed to the last man. The victorious invaders then pushed northward, looting every Moabite city in their path, until only the fortified capital of Kir-hareseth remained. When the Israelite armies besieged that city, King

Mesha of Moab, in despair, offered the ultimate sacrifice to Chemosh, the country's god: he burned his eldest son on a pyre on the city walls, in full sight of the besiegers. Watching in horror, Jehoram and his allies were seized with dread of the alien god and ordered a hasty retreat.

Miracles in the Countryside

Back in Israel, Elisha resumed his mission, aiding the poor and afflicted. He traveled throughout the countryside on a donkey that was led by Gehazi, a man who had attached himself to the prophet as a servant.

At one place Elisha was approached by the grief-stricken widow of a holy man. Because she was unable to pay her husband's debts, creditors were about to take her two sons into slavery, a common practice condoned by the state. She was completely destitute, with nothing but a jar of olive oil in her hut. Elisha instructed her to borrow as many empty jars as possible and to begin pouring oil from her own jar into them. To her amazement, oil poured forth copiously until all the borrowed jars were filled. "Go, sell the oil and pay your debts," Elisha said, "and you and your sons can live on the rest."

Not long afterward, Elisha was staying in a prophets' commune in the hills near Bethel. There he received 20 loaves of barley bread and fresh ears of grain from a devout farmer. Told to feed the whole commune, the prophet's servant protested, "How am I to set this before a hundred men?" But Elisha was insistent. "Give them to the men . . . for thus says the Lord, 'They shall eat and have some left.'" Miraculously, the loaves and the grain multiplied until everyone was fed.

In the fertile Jezreel Valley, between Mount Gilboa and the hills of Galilee, lay the village of Shunem. There Elisha was befriended by a childless woman and her elderly husband. After he had dined with the wealthy and devout couple several times, they built a separate chamber and furnished it for his use. He soon showed his gratitude. Aware that the wife craved a child of her own, Elisha informed her, "At this season, when the time comes round, you shall embrace a son." The woman could not believe him, but eventually she conceived and gave birth to a son.

Some years later this cherished boy suffered a sunstroke while helping his father in the fields. He died in his mother's arms. The frantic woman

"And the anger of the Lord was kindled against Israel, and he gave them continually into the hand of Hazael king of Syria" (2 Kg. 13.3). This ivory plaque, framed by lotus flowers, is a contemporary portrait of Hazael. Elisha wept as he foresaw the career of this Syrian, for Hazael dreamed of extending his boundaries westward (above), beyond the Sea of Galilee. He overran Gath, took tribute from Jerusalem and routed the Judeans at Ramoth-gilead, until he was stopped in 841 B.C.

set out to find Elisha. As soon as he heard the news, the prophet returned with her to Shunem. "When Elisha came into the house, he saw the child lying dead on his bed. So he went in and shut the door upon the two of them, and prayed to the Lord. Then he went up and lay upon the child, putting his mouth upon his mouth, his eyes upon his eyes, and his hands upon his hands; and as he stretched himself upon him, the flesh of the child became warm. . . . the child sneezed seven times, and the child opened his eyes." Leaving the revived boy with his grateful mother, Elisha and his servant continued their journeys through the countryside.

Among the "sons of the prophets" settlements, Elisha apparently favored those of Jericho and Gilgal, the sites of some of his recorded miracles. Once, for instance, famine had reduced the Gilgal prophets to living on such wild roots and berries as they could forage. During one of Elisha's visits, the ingredients they had collected for a soup included some gourds from an unfamiliar wild vine. When the prophets tasted the soup, it was evident that the gourds were poisonous. "O

man of God, there is death in the pot!" they cried in alarm. Elisha asked for a little meal, sprinkled it into the cauldron, and said, "Pour out for the men, that they may eat." This was done, and to the prophets' amazement, no one became ill.

On another occasion Elisha joined a group of holy men who were cutting logs on a Jordan bank. As one of the men swung his axe, its iron head slipped from the handle and fell into the water. The man was greatly distressed, since the axe was borrowed. Elisha tossed a stick at the spot where the axehead had sunk. Instantly the heavy metal tool floated to the surface and was retrieved.

A Leper Is Cured

Soon, word of Elisha's miraculous power spread, even to neighboring lands. In the Aramean kingdom of Syria to the north, Naaman, a famous military commander, had developed leprosy. Having heard of the wonder-working Elisha, he obtained from his king in Damascus a letter to the king of Israel asking him to cure Naaman. Bearing gifts of gold and silver and embroidered festal garments, Naaman and his retinue set out for Samaria. When he read the letter, the king of Israel was angered: "Am I God, to kill and to make alive, that this man sends word to me to cure a man of his leprosy? Only consider, and see how he is seeking a quarrel with me." Elisha heard of the affair and asked to see the Syrians.

Near the prophet's house the Syrian party was met by Elisha's messenger. "Go and wash in the Jordan seven times," he told Naaman, "and your flesh shall be restored, and you shall be clean." Naaman felt himself insulted by this curt reception. Besides, he argued, were not the waters of his own country better than Israel's? Nevertheless, he finally immersed himself in the Jordan as instructed. He was cured at once.

The grateful warrior returned to Elisha, offering lavish gifts, but the prophet refused them. Convinced by the miracle that Israel's Lord was the only true God, Naaman asked for a portion of soil from Israel, so that he could worship the Hebrew God even in Damascus. (A common belief among other religions of the time was that a god's powers were effective only on his own soil.)

After the servants had left, Gehazi secretly ran after Naaman. Pretending that he was speaking for his master, he begged for a talent of silver and two festal garments. The Syrian graciously gave him *two* talents of silver and the garments. But Elisha had witnessed the fraud "in spirit." Enraged, he put a curse on Gehazi: "Therefore the leprosy of Naaman shall cleave to you, and to your descendants for ever." Gehazi departed, "as white as snow" with leprosy.

Samaria Under Siege

Before long the fragile peace between Israel and Syria broke down and warfare was resumed. Elisha used his extrasensory powers to predict the place and time of raids by the enemy. Realizing that Elisha was the source of this intelligence, the Syrian king sent a task force to kill him.

Under cover of darkness, the Syrians surrounded Elisha's house. The prophet invoked the Lord's help, and the foreigners were temporarily blinded. Then Elisha came out of his house and said to them, "'This is not the way . . . follow me,

and I will bring you to the man whom you seek.' And he led them to Samaria." When they reached the capital, Elisha, restoring their sight, placed them in the hands of the Israelite king. When Jehoram was about to have them all executed, Elisha objected: "You shall not slay them. . . . Set bread and water before them, that they may eat and drink and go to their master."

This act of clemency brought a truce in the war. But it did not last long. Ben-hadad, king of Syria, marshaled a full-scale invasion. The Israelites could offer little resistance, and Jehoram and his troops were forced to retreat behind the sturdy walls of their hilltop capital. The invaders then surrounded Samaria, preventing any supplies from entering the city. The streets of that proud, elegant city became clogged with beggars, and the moans of the dying filled the air. In desperation some people resorted to cannibalism.

That horror confronted Jehoram one day. A hysterical woman, pleading for justice, explained: "This woman said to me, 'Give your son, that we may eat him today, and we will eat my son tomorrow.' So we boiled my son, and ate

him. And on the next day I said to her, 'Give your son, that we may eat him'; but she has hidden her son."

Jehoram cursed Elisha because, as the Lord's prophet, he failed to protect his people. A royal servant sent to kill Elisha found his door barred. The king himself then arrived at the prophet's home. "This trouble is from the Lord!" cried Jehoram. "Why should I wait for the Lord any longer?" Elisha thereupon predicted that the siege would be lifted the very next day.

At twilight next evening, the Syrians heard what they took to be the sound of chariots and horses. Rumor spread that a vast army of mercenaries was approaching to relieve the Israelites. The Syrians panicked and fled, leaving behind their tents and provisions. Jehoram, suspecting a trap, sent out scouts to confirm that the enemy had run away. They soon returned with news that the Syrians had crossed the Jordan. At once the starving Israelites thronged out of the city and plundered the Syrian food and supplies. Elisha's prophecy had come true.

Now that there was peace again, Elisha journeyed from Samaria to Damascus, a trek of over 100 miles. While the capital, a great commercial center, throbbed with life, King Ben-hadad lay gravely ill. When he heard that the renowned prophet was in Damascus, he sent one Hazael to "inquire of the Lord" whether the king would recover. Hazael, bringing with him 40 camels laden with gifts, sought out Elisha.

The prophet's response was ambiguous. He told Hazael, "Go, say to him, 'You shall certainly recover'; but the Lord has shown me that he shall certainly die." Then Elisha fixed his gaze on Hazael and broke into tears. Hazael asked why he wept, and he replied: "Because I know the evil that you will do to the people of Israel; you will set on fire their fortresses, and you will slay their young men with the sword, and dash in pieces their little ones, and rip up their women with child." Hazael denied he would ever do such things, but Elisha insisted, saying, "The Lord has shown me that you are to be king over Syria."

Hazael returned to his ruler and told only the prophet's promise of recovery, but did not men-

Prophets like Elisha and his mentor Elijah were popularly credited with miraculous healing powers. Both men were said to have raised dead children by placing their bodies over the children's corpses. Such miracles were seen as proof that these prophets spoke for the Lord. Here a prophet seeks to revive the son of an Israelite woman.

tion Elisha's foretelling of the king's death. At dawn the next day he crept into Ben-hadad's bedchamber and suffocated him with a wet cloth. Then he proclaimed himself king.

As Elisha had foreseen, Hazael soon renewed the war on Israel with another invasion. Jehoram, joined by the forces of his ally and cousin, King Ahaziah of Judah, met the Syrians at Ramoth-gilead, about 25 miles east of the Jordan. Jehoram was wounded in an early skirmish, and his bodyguards carried him to his royal villa in the Jezreel Valley where his mother, Jezebel, held court. Ahaziah followed him, leaving the allied armies under the command of the Israelite general, Jehu.

Fall of the House of Ahab

Meanwhile, Elisha had decided to bring about the downfall of Ahab's idolatrous family. He dispatched a young prophet to Ramoth-gilead to find Jehu and announce: "Thus says the Lord the God of Israel, I anoint you king over the people of the Lord, over Israel. And you shall strike down the house of Ahab your master, that I may avenge on Jezebel the blood of my servants the prophets, and . . . of all the servants of the Lord. For the . . . house of Ahab shall perish . . ."

Jehu, an ambitious, battle-hardened leader, readily accepted Elisha's promise. His commanders and troops, disgusted with Jehoram's conduct of the war, at once hailed Jehu as king.

Immediately, Jehu and a band of his supporters set out in chariots for the royal villa in the Jezreel Valley. When he learned of the approaching horsemen, Jehoram sent a messenger to meet the riders and ask if they came in peace. "What have you to do with peace?" Jehu sneered. When that messenger, and then another, failed to return, Jehoram and Ahaziah rode out to confront Jehu. "Is it peace, Jehu?" Jehoram called out. The fiery general yelled back, "What peace can there be, so long as the harlotries and the sorceries of your mother Jezebel are so many?"

The two kings turned and fled, but Jehu's men pursued and slew them. After hearing of their deaths, Jezebel hurriedly "painted her eyes, and adorned her head," intending to defy the rebels. Jehu remembered the curse pronounced by Elijah many years before: "In the territory of Jezreel the dogs shall eat the flesh of Jezebel; and the corpse of Jezebel shall be as dung upon the face of the field . . ." On his orders, several of the queen's own eunuchs flung her out of a window to her death on the stone floor of the palace courtyard. Jehu and his men now took over the palace, murdering and looting. Then Jehu commanded his men, "See now to this cursed woman, and bury her; for she is a king's daughter." But when they entered the courtyard, Jehu's men found only "the skull and the feet and the palms of her hands." Dogs had devoured the rest. Such was the end of the once powerful queen.

Jehu's bloodbath had only begun. He went on to exterminate all other potential claimants to the throne, first ordering the beheading of Ahab's 70 sons and grandsons in Samaria. The severed heads were thrown into baskets and brought to him in Jezreel. On his triumphal march toward Samaria, Jehu encountered a large delegation of Ahaziah's kinsmen, who were unaware of these bloody events. He ordered them all killed.

As he neared Samaria, Jehu was greeted by Jehonadab, leader of a clan of religious extremists called Rechabites. He explained to the new ruler that his followers wished to join in a righteous crusade against Israel's sins. Jehu lifted the Rechabite into his chariot. "Come with me," he said, "and see my zeal for the Lord."

His zeal was limitless in its cruelty. He condemned to death anyone who had the remotest connection with the reign of Ahab. This done, Jehu proceeded to cleanse Israel of the worship of Baal, the fertility god of Jezebel's native Tyre. To accomplish this, Jehu resorted to trickery: he proclaimed that on a certain day he would offer a major sacrifice to Baal in the god's temple in Samaria, and commanded every priest and follower of Baal to be present or risk execution. At the appointed time, they flocked to the temple from all parts of Israel, filling the interior sanctuary and overflowing into the outer courtyard. Then the temple gates were locked. While priests of Baal were burning a ram in sacrifice, soldiers with drawn swords rushed in and slaughtered the trapped multitude, after which Jehu had the temple razed.

By provoking Jehu to rebellion, Elisha had achieved the fall of Ahab's family, as Elijah had prophesied. The bloodletting, however, left Israel isolated and weak. Both Judah and Tyre, shocked by the murders of Ahaziah and Jezebel, broke vital military and trade alliances with Israel. Moreover, Jehu made little effort to correct social and economic abuses. And though worship of

"And the driving is like the driving of Jehu the son of Nimshi; for he drives furiously" (2 Kg. 9.20). Anointed king by Elisha, Jehu became one of Israel's most zealous reformers. He carried out a purge of paganism, himself slaying King Jehoram of Israel from his chariot and ordering the death of King Ahaziah of Judah. (At left, model of a Cypriot chariot.) Jehu then rode to the house of Jezebel, and at his command the queen's attendants cast her from a window. In the Syrian ivory plaque above, an 8th-century woman is portrayed peering out of a window.

Baal was suppressed, other pagan cults flourished. Soon the very prophets who had supported Jehu were disillusioned. Elisha withdrew into the background and again roamed the countryside, aiding the people, delivering oracles and living with the prophets.

Within a short time, Syrian armies again invaded and conquered Israel's territory east of the Jordan, as far south as the Moab border. When Jehu died, about 815, his son Jehoahaz ascended the throne. He failed to stop the Syrians and was forced to become their vassal. After a humiliating reign of 17 years, Jehoahaz was succeeded as king of Israel by his son, Jehoash.

Death of Elisha

Evidently the new king and Elisha became friends, and the prophet helped him recover some of the land lost to Syria. Now old and ill, Elisha retired to await death, probably at one of the "sons of the prophets" settlements. Jehoash, learning of Elisha's illness, went to visit him.

The dying prophet summoned all his remaining strength to perform his final prophetic act. He instructed Jehoash to shoot an arrow through the window. The king did so, and Elisha assured him it was the "Lord's arrow of victory, the arrow of victory over Syria! For you shall fight the Syrians in Aphek until you have made an end of them."

This last prophecy came to pass. Not long after it was pronounced, Hazael died and Jehoash sent an army against the forces of Hazael's son. Israel defeated the Syrians three times and recovered much of its lost territory. Elisha did not live to see these victories. Soon after his last prophecy, he died and was buried in a tomb somewhere near the Moabite border.

Many years later, a group of mourners, carrying a body to the same burial ground, were surprised by Moabite raiders. Hastily they dropped the corpse into Elisha's tomb and ran, "and as soon as the man touched the bones of Elisha, he revived, and stood on his feet." Even death had not extinguished Elisha's miraculous powers. Israel would never forget his deeds.

The story of Elisha is told in 1 Kings 19.19–21 and 2 Kings 2–13.

The Assyrians: Scourge of Israel

"He will raise a signal for a nation afar off, and whistle for it from the ends of the earth; and lo, swiftly, speedily it comes!" (Is. 5.26). When Assyria drove westward in the latter half of the 8th century B.C., it destroyed the kingdom of Israel and made Judah a vassal. By repelling frequent invasions in its northern Mesopotamian homeland, Assyria had forged its army into a superb instrument of war, enabling it to conquer most of the Near East. Isaiah saw Assyria's victories over Israel and Judah as the Lord's purgation of his people, few of whom still remained faithful. He also predicted Assyria's downfall, carried out by Babylon in 612 B.C. *"When the Lord has finished all his work . . . he will punish the arrogant boasting of the king of Assyria and his haughty pride"* (Is. 10.12).

Much of what is known about the kings of Assyria comes from bas-reliefs discovered in some of their palaces. Set end to end, the reliefs found in the palace of Sargon II (722–705 B.C.) at Khorsabad would extend more than a mile. In the relief above, laborers carry Phoenician cedar used to build Khorsabad. After capturing Samaria, Sargon II deported many Israelites, some of whom may have been forced into labor.

"Of a truth, O Lord, the kings of Assyria have laid waste the nations and their lands" (2 Kg. 19.17). Ashurbanipal, the last great king of Assyria, is shown riding in his ceremonial chariot in a bas-relief (left) from his palace at Nineveh. Only the most exalted personages had canopies over their chariots. As king, Ashurbanipal was also high priest and deputy of the god Asshur, chief deity among hundreds of Assyrian gods. During his reign (669–633 B.C.) Assyrian religion was practiced in Judah alongside the worship of the Lord. Ashurbanipal's library, which has yielded more than 22,000 clay tablets, is an invaluable source for Assyria's violent history.

During the three centuries that followed the breakup of united Israel, Assyria possessed the greatest army in the Near East. The bas-reliefs on this page celebrate the subjugation of Elam, a kingdom east of Babylonia, during the reign of Ashurbanipal. At left, Elamite prisoners are fed in a military encampment. Captured soldiers made up the auxiliary units of the Assyrian army, and from some of those taken at Samaria, Sargon II manned a contingent of 50 chariots. In a policy of resettlement inaugurated by Tiglath-pileser III (745–727 B.C.), large numbers of the vanquished were scattered throughout the Assyrian Empire and their lands resettled by other deportees. This made successful revolts against the provincial administrators more difficult to win.

At right, Assyrian spearmen have scaled the double walls of an Elamite city. In addition to spearmen, archers and slingers, the Assyrians had engineers expert in siege warfare. One of their stratagems was to dig a hole under a wall and shore it up with wood—then set fire to those supports, causing the wall to collapse.

In open terrain the chariot corps (below) was the most powerful striking force of the Assyrian army. In Ashurbanipal's time, chariots were exceptionally sturdy. Their large wheels had to be strong enough to support a team of four warriors: a driver, an archer and two shield bearers. In advance of the chariot rides a cavalry archer with drawn bow. On his back he carries a full quiver of arrows.

Chapter 14

As the Assyrian forces overpower Israel and bear down on Jerusalem, Isaiah eloquently decries his people's moral weakness and guides the statesmanship of Judah's kings.

Isaiah: Prophet of Hardship and Hope

In the second half of the eighth century B.C., a spiritual leader emerged to dominate a troubled era. The man was Isaiah. Considered by some to be the greatest of the Hebrew prophets, his ministry spanned the reigns of three kings of Judah and may have ended, according to tradition, in martyrdom. It was he who foretold the coming of a Messiah, or redeemer, of Israel.

Isaiah was probably born before 750 B.C. in Jerusalem. His devout father, Amoz, named him Isaiah ("may the Lord save"). Judah was experiencing a period of relative peace and prosperity. The home of Amoz, if he was affluent, may have been a rather spacious house. The facade was probably made of rough, stucco-covered bricks, the interior walls of carefully fitted slabs of smooth, buff-colored limestone.

According to custom, Amoz took charge of the boy's education at about the age of five. The most important lessons concerned the covenant the Lord had made with the Israelites. Amoz stressed its rigid code of justice and protection in exchange for righteous conduct. Those lessons would influence Isaiah for the rest of his life as a prophet of the Lord.

As Isaiah grew older, he was tutored, either privately or with his brothers and other boys, by the priests who were custodians of the Torah. That sacred book, written on parchment scrolls and including the laws, history, poetry and other scriptures, was probably Isaiah's textbook for reading and writing. He was also taught to form numbers for basic arithmetic. Using a quill or reed pen, and ink made from carbon and gum arabic, the boy carefully copied his lessons on sheets of papyrus or strips of tanned leather.

Isaiah was a bright and serious student. But in carefree hours he would sing and dance with boys and girls of his age in the streets of his neighborhood. Sometimes he wrestled and boxed with the other youths or competed in tugs-of-war. There were also more intellectual, indoor games resembling chess and cribbage.

The years when Isaiah was maturing saw economic growth as King Uzziah began to develop Judah's resources and foreign trade. But little of the new prosperity reached the lower classes. Heartless moneylenders prevailed. Merchants cheated buyers with false weights and measures. The courts were polluted with bribery, and even the priesthood was corrupt and ignored the plight of the underprivileged. A sensitive young man, Isaiah must have been increasingly troubled by the rampant injustice and frustrated by his inability to fight it. Then, when he was in his early twenties, a profound emotional experience opened a path to action.

King Uzziah, stricken with leprosy, probably died about 742 B.C. The coronation of his son Jotham was timed to coincide with the new-year

Lachish was the strongest fortress-city in Judah until the Assyrian forces of Sennacherib breached its walls in 701 B.C. Thirteen years later they besieged the city again. Isaiah saw the Assyrian invasions as God's will: "I planned from days of old . . . that you should make fortified cities crash into heaps of ruins" (Is. 37.26).

festival. Isaiah, wearing white linen festival robes, may have been among the worshipers waiting for the eastern gates of the Jerusalem temple to open at dawn. New Year's Day, the autumnal equinox, was the only time those gates were unlocked. Only then would the rays of the rising sun pass directly through that opening and shine through the temple's doors.

A Stirring Vision

When the first light appeared in the east over the Mount of Olives, the gates swung apart. Sunlight streamed into the eastern courtyard, across the great altar near the center and the sanctuary at the western end. Jotham, in coronation robes of purple embroidered with threads of gold, led a solemn procession into the courtyard. It may have been during this ceremony that Isaiah suddenly had a soul-stirring vision of a heavenly temple. As he later described it, "I saw the Lord sitting upon a throne, high and lifted up; and his train filled the temple. Above him stood the seraphim . . . And one called to another and said: 'Holy, holy, holy is the Lord of hosts; the whole earth is full of his glory.'

"And the foundations of the thresholds shook at the voice of him who called, and the house was filled with smoke. And I said: 'Woe is me! For I am lost; for I am a man of unclean lips, and I dwell in the midst of a people of unclean lips; for my eyes have seen the King, the Lord of hosts!'

"Then flew one of the seraphim to me . . . And he touched my mouth, and said: 'Behold, this has touched your lips; your guilt is taken away, and your sin forgiven.' And I heard the voice of the Lord saying, 'Whom shall I send, and who will go for us?' Then I said, 'Here am I! Send me.' And he said 'Go, and say to the people: "Make the heart of this people fat, and their ears heavy, and shut their eyes; lest they see with their eyes, and hear with their ears, and understand with their hearts, and turn and be healed."'"

Now Isaiah understood: his mission was to speak in the Lord's name, to beseech his people to return to the laws of the covenant. If they did not heed God's words, they would be destroyed.

As Isaiah embraced his new role, those with whom he had been reared and schooled must have thought him mad. He exchanged his rich clothing for the traditional sackcloth and sandals of a prophet. "The Lord enters into judgment with the elders and princes [officials] of his people," he warned his old friends; "'the spoil of the poor is in your houses. What do you mean by crushing my people, by grinding the face of the poor?' says the Lord God of hosts."

Preaching to the People

Seeking larger audiences, Isaiah began to haunt the great bazaar that sprawled over a large part of the Lower City. In the ironworkers' quarter busy blacksmiths pumped their bellows and fired furnaces to forge threshing sledges, plowshares, sickles and axes. Metalworkers hammered copper and bronze into smoothly shaped kitchen pans and kettles, while others joined handles to pots with their mallets. The impassioned young man wearing sackcloth walked among them with a determined step. Raising his voice over the din made by the craftsmen and hucksters, Isaiah shouted, "How the faithful city has become a harlot, she that was full of justice! Righteousness lodged in her, but now murderers."

He carried the same harsh message throughout the bazaar, moving through the ceramics quarter, where perspiring potters turned their wheels to mold wet clay mixed with powdered limestone into jars, bowls, jugs and decanters. Or, pausing in the section where carpenters planed the surfaces of chairs, benches and tables, he would as-

The bucket-shaped water clock developed in Egypt was widely used in Isaiah's day. As water seeped out through a hole in the bottom of the vessel, a scale on the inner wall indicated the passage of time according to the drop in the water level. During the centuries after Isaiah, the water clock was greatly improved by the Greeks.

sail the decadence and corruption of his fellow citizens in Israel.

He reserved some of his bitterest invective for the pampered women who went to the Phoenician quarter, drawn there by jewelers from the kingdom of Tyre. These craftsmen were famous for their skill in fashioning gold and precious gems into bracelets, armbands, anklets and signet rings. Isaiah cried: ". . . the daughters of Zion are haughty and walk with outstretched necks, glancing wantonly with their eyes, mincing along as they go, tinkling with their feet . . ." Appalled by their greed for luxury, he warned of the Lord's vengeance: "Instead of perfume there will be rottenness; . . . instead of well-set hair, baldness; and instead of a rich robe, a girding of sackcloth; instead of beauty, shame."

Isaiah preached in this manner for several years. It was an inspired career to which he devoted every day of his life, except for the hours when he worshiped: "Oh Lord, thou art my God; I will exalt thee, I will praise thy name; for thou hast done wonderful things, plans formed of old, faithful and sure."

In these early years Isaiah married a woman he called "the prophetess." She gave birth to a son whom Isaiah named Shear-jashub ("a remnant shall return"). He intended the name as a symbol: if the people of Judah did not repent, only a few would remain after the Lord had punished them for breaking the covenant.

Paganism of King Ahaz

During this period Assyria, located on the upper Tigris River in Mesopotamia, had risen to great power and sent conquering armies westward. They subjugated most of the Near Eastern nations, including Israel. Judah was spared, but when King Jotham died in 735, his 20-year-old son, Ahaz, faced the threat of Assyrian aggression. The kings of Israel and Syria formed an alliance to rebel against Assyria and asked Ahaz to join them. When the new king refused, the coalition invaded Judah to force him into line.

Ahaz panicked and, his Israelite faith being weak, he appealed to pagan gods for help. He even sacrificed his own son to the Semitic deity Moloch. The king's desperate measures were futile, for the combined armies of Syria and Israel continued to advance toward Jerusalem.

To prepare his capital's defenses, Ahaz went

Playing the Game of "Hounds and Jackals"

A prosperous Judean of Isaiah's time and his son play "hounds and jackals," an Egyptian game that was enjoyed more than a thousand years before the time of the prophets. Although the exact rules of the game are no longer known, two sets of five pegs, one set with the heads of dogs and one with the heads of jackals, were moved into various positions along the rows of holes on a board. Each new move may have been decided by the casting of three knuckle-bones. The board and bones shown in the photograph below were discovered in an Egyptian tomb. The board is made of ivory, with ebony inlays and carved ivory pegs.

one morning to inspect the waterworks near the Gihon Spring accompanied by court advisors and army officers. A water shaft and an open-air reservoir had been dug in the rock there centuries before by the Canaanites.

While the king and his men were discussing ways of protecting the water supply, Isaiah came to them, leading his four-year-old son, Shear-jashub, by the hand. The prophet approached Ahaz, to assure him that faith in the Lord was his best defense. "Take heed, be quiet, do not fear," he said. Referring to the kings of Israel and Syria, he added, "and do not let your heart be faint because of these two smoldering stumps of firebrands . . . thus says the Lord God: It shall not stand, and it shall not come to pass."

A short time later, Isaiah realized Ahaz would not heed his advice. Thinking that perhaps Ahaz needed visible proof of the Lord's power, Isaiah challenged him: "Ask a sign of the Lord your God; let it be deep as Sheol [the underworld] or high as heaven." The king refused, saying, "I will not ask, and I will not put the Lord to the test."

Isaiah responded angrily, "Hear then, O house of David! Is it too little for you to weary men, that you weary my God also? Therefore the Lord himself will give you a sign. Behold, a young woman shall conceive and bear a son, and shall call his name Immanu-el [meaning "God with us"] . . . before the child knows how to refuse the evil and choose the good, the land before whose two kings you are in dread will be deserted . . .

The faithless King Ahaz, rejecting the Lord, sought help from Assyria. "I am your servant and your son," he wrote to Tiglath-pileser, the Assyrian king, pleading for help against Israel and Syria. As proof of his sincerity, he removed a large number of silver and gold utensils and other valuables from the palace and the temple and sent them to Assyria as tribute.

The Assyrian monarch responded promptly. His armies demolished the Syro-Israelite forces well before they could reach Jerusalem. Tiglath-pileser then occupied the two countries, and deported large numbers of their people to Assyria. Judah was spared, but at the cost of its independence, for heavy taxes were levied on it.

Isaiah's Seclusion

Soon afterward, the Judean king had to journey to Damascus to make a formal declaration of his allegiance to Assyria. Ahaz approached Tiglath-pileser with humility. "Ahaz . . . took the silver and gold that was found in the house of the Lord and in the treasures of the king's house, and sent a present to the king of Assyria." He was also required to pay homage to his overlord's gods by offering a sacrifice at the altar of an Assyrian god.

As a further sign of submission, Ahaz sent home an order to build an exact replica of that altar in the Jerusalem temple. On returning from Damascus, he had the bronze altar of the Lord moved to a lesser location, replacing it with

Asshur's massive altar. Thereafter, he made all his sacrifices to the pagan god.

Feeling that a true regeneration of Judah was hopeless now, Isaiah decided to remain silent until his people were more willing to heed the words of God. He withdrew to live quietly for the next 18 years (734–716), surrounded by loyal disciples who recorded his prophecies for posterity.

The northern kingdom of Israel fell to the Assyrians in 721 B.C. The southern kingdom was now the only remaining free territory left from David's empire.

In 715 Ahaz died and was succeeded by his assertive son, Hezekiah, who resolved to reclaim Judah's independence. The chance came when several revolts erupted in the eastern Assyrian Empire. Preoccupied with crushing these rebels, Sargon II (722–705), who was then king of Assyria, virtually ignored the vassal-states of Judah, Edom and Moab. Egypt, now beginning to recover from decades of weakness, offered military

"The Lord will take away the finery of the anklets . . . the pendants, the bracelets, and the scarfs" (Is. 3.18) prophesied Isaiah, making the vanity of Jerusalem's wealthy women an example of the city's decadence. Here women of the city examine necklaces and earrings amid articles of ivory, silver, glass and gold. The Phoenician craftsman is like those who worked once for David and Solomon. The human form, seldom seen in Israelite art, appears above in a clay figure of a woman who may be holding a tambourine. The rare statue is from Megiddo, and dates from 1000–600 B.C.

aid to the little nations if they would join her in open rebellion against Assyria. When Egyptian ambassadors arrived in Judah about 714, Hezekiah was tempted by their offer.

Isaiah then emerged from seclusion to proclaim that it was foolish to rely on the shaky, untried power of Egypt. The populace of Jerusalem was startled when the prophet suddenly appeared in the streets, "naked and barefoot" except for a loincloth. The Lord had told him, he explained, that "so shall the king of Assyria lead away the Egyptians captives and the Ethiopians exiles, both the young and the old, naked and barefoot, with buttocks uncovered . . ."

For three years Isaiah repeated his naked charade, while Hezekiah pondered the Egyptian offer. In that time Sargon overcame his difficulties in Assyria, and then proceeded to devastate the small nations which had allied with Egypt. But Sargon left Judah alone, apparently because Hezekiah had refused to join the alliance.

A Religious Revival

Once this crisis had passed, Hezekiah undertook a program of religious reform. Assembling the priests in the eastern courtyard of the temple, he ordered them: "Now sanctify yourselves, and sanctify the house of the Lord . . . and carry out the filth from the holy place. For our fathers have been unfaithful and have done what was evil in the sight of the Lord our God . . ."

The priests tore down the altar (like the one in Damascus) that Ahaz had built, removed all pagan idols and utensils and cleansed the temple. Hezekiah then held a ceremony of atonement, in which the priests played harps, lyres, cymbals and trumpets and offered sacrifices to the Lord. Outside Jerusalem, Hezekiah closed local pagan sanctuaries and destroyed their idols. The following spring he revived the long-neglected festival of Passover. "O people of Israel," he wrote to the northern kingdom, now an Assyrian province, "return to the Lord . . . that he may turn again to the remnant of you who have escaped from the hand of the kings of Assyria . . ." Hezekiah had hoped to reunite the two kingdoms under his rule, but his messengers were jeered, and only a handful from Israel came to Jerusalem to observe the sacrifice of the Passover lambs.

In the spirit of the religious revival, royal scribes collected a large body of proverbs and riddles teaching moral lessons. Preserved by memory through generations, dozens of the poetic maxims were at last inscribed on sheets or rolls of parchment and eventually formed a part of the Old Testament book "The Proverbs."

During these reform years, goldsmiths, potters, weavers and other craftsmen organized trade guilds to create a monopoly for themselves. There was even a guild of public scribes who wrote letters and drew up contracts at fixed prices for the majority who could not write.

Hezekiah's reign was also noted for progress in medicine and surgery. The physicians of eighth-century Judah practiced the most advanced methods of the Egyptians and Babylonians in the treatment of wounds and sores, often using Oriental narcotics to reduce pain and induce sleep during surgical operations.

As the quality of life improved, Hezekiah grew more restless with Assyrian domination and planned to reunite the country into a new Davidic state. When Sargon was killed in battle and his son Sennacherib came to the throne, about 705, Hezekiah began to form an alliance with Babylonia, Phoenicia and Egypt against Assyria. The Egyptians offered to provide military aid, and again Isaiah vehemently counseled against rebellion and reliance on the Pharaoh: "Woe to those who go down to Egypt for help . . . but do not look to the Holy One of Israel . . . The Egyptians are men, and not God; and their horses are flesh, and not spirit."

Preparation for War

This time Hezekiah ignored the prophet's advice and prepared for battle. He outfitted his army with an arsenal of thousands of new spears, swords, arrows and shields. He ordered construction crews to rebuild Judean forts that had been destroyed when Ahaz submitted Judah to Assyria, and in Jerusalem he enlisted workmen to repair the city walls.

Still Isaiah tried to dissuade Hezekiah, warning him of the Lord's plan to chastise Judah: "Ah, Assyria . . . Against a godless nation I send him, and against the people of my wrath I command him, to take spoil and seize plunder, and to tread them down like the mire of the streets."

Yet Hezekiah would not listen and, along with his allies, he declared independence. Then, anticipating the Assyrians' retaliation, he prepared his country for war. First, he sent for reports on the status of supplies in the government storehouses in Jerusalem and other large cities. These massive warehouses usually adjoined the district palace or governor's residence. Their long, narrow rooms were filled with rows of large jars containing dried grain and other foods. To protect them against spoilage, the stone walls between the rooms were exceptionally thick, and the floors were raised high above the foundations.

Hezekiah's Tunnel: Dug to Save a City

When Jerusalem's water supply was in danger of being cut off by invading Assyrians, King Hezekiah ordered a tunnel dug from the Spring of Gihon to a reservoir inside the city. Using simple tools, workers hewed their way through about 1750 feet of solid limestone.

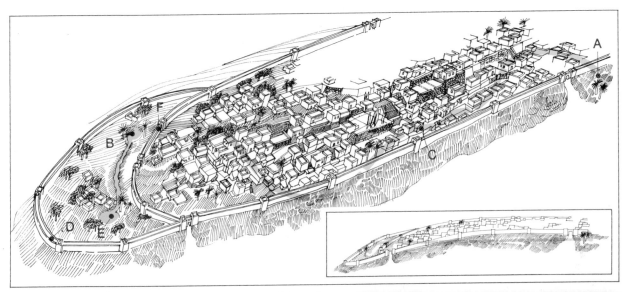

One team of tunnelers began at the Spring of Gihon (A) outside Jerusalem, and another worked from the Pool of Siloam (B) to the south, hacking through the stone until they met (C). The floor was cut out to increase the flow of water toward the lower end (inset), so the height of the waterway varies from 4 to 20 feet. The city wall was extended (D) to enclose the reservoir and its overflow (E). Water still flows through Hezekiah's tunnel (right), which was a major engineering feat for its time. The completion was described in an inscription (below) placed in the tunnel wall (F). This plaque is one of the few important surviving fragments of ancient Hebrew writing.

Hezekiah probably instituted food rationing to conserve the existing supplies. Once enough food had been accumulated, he embarked on his most ambitious project for Jerusalem. He decided to construct a new water system that would be better hidden and less vulnerable to enemy attack than the existing open aqueduct, which had been built centuries before. To accomplish this, he made plans to tunnel through the Ophel Hill to the Gihon Spring, then to dig a new reservoir, and finally, to protect the reservoir by extending the city walls around it. Guided by the most primitive surveying instruments and using only crude hand tools, small groups of men chipped away at the solid bedrock. After months, perhaps years, the two teams met near the middle of the twisting, 1750-foot tunnel within earshot of each other. Aiming toward each other's voices, the workers eagerly dug through the last five feet of rock—and then the water began to flow gently from Gihon to the new reservoir.

Assyrian Invasion

Meanwhile, Sennacherib had defeated Babylonia and turned his armies toward Jerusalem. He subdued one small state after another until by 701 only Judah remained. Hezekiah, now without any allies, gathered his army commanders in the square by one of the Jerusalem gates. "Be strong and of good courage," he told them. "Do not be afraid or dismayed before the king of Assyria and all the horde that is with him; for there is one greater with us than with him. With him is an arm of flesh; but with us is the Lord our God . . ."

Yet Isaiah's former prophecy prevailed. The smaller cities of Judah fell to Sennacherib in quick succession, and even the formidable fortress-city of Lachish was menaced. It was the main stronghold shielding Jerusalem, protecting the pass leading east to Hebron 16 miles away. Impregnable against most enemies, Lachish proved to be no match for the Assyrian war machine. Though the Judeans fought well and bravely, the city walls—nearly 20 feet thick—were breached and the Assyrians rushed in, murdering, burning and looting. The city elders knelt before Sennacherib in surrender as the captives and valuable treasures were carted off to Assyria.

The Assyrians then advanced northeast to Jerusalem. In his annals, Sennacherib later described the action against Hezekiah: "Himself I made a prisoner in Jerusalem, his royal residence, like a bird in a cage." Distressed and demoralized, Hezekiah realized that, despite all his preparations, he could not hold out for long. Without even trying to fight, he sent a message of surrender: "I have done wrong; withdraw from me; whatever you impose on me I will bear." The conqueror's impositions were severe. The former tributes of vassalage were increased and vast Judean wealth was sent to Sennacherib's capital, Nineveh, his "lordly city."

Having completed the conquest, the Assyrian monarch returned to his kingdom and ruled with relative ease until 690, when an alliance of several Mesopotamian states defeated him badly. The time seemed right for revolt, and when Egypt once again offered military aid, Hezekiah agreed to a pact. However, Sennacherib, recovered from his setback, quickly crushed the first rebels and, in 688, again invaded Judah.

While he held Lachish under siege a second time, he learned that Egyptian troops were on the way to aid Judah. To free himself to meet the Egyptians, Sennacherib demanded that Hezekiah surrender immediately. The Judean king, knowing that submission would in effect mean the end of his country, sought spiritual guidance from Isaiah. This time the aging prophet beseeched the king not to surrender.

"Therefore thus says the Lord concerning the king of Assyria: He shall not come into this city, or shoot an arrow there, or come before it with a shield, or cast up a siege mound against it. . . . For I will defend this city to save it, for my own sake and for the sake of my servant David."

A Timely Miracle

Hezekiah sent his refusal to Sennacherib, and the Assyrian drew up his army around Jerusalem. But during the night "the angel of the Lord went forth, and slew a hundred and eighty-five thousand in the camp of the Assyrians; and when men arose early in the morning, behold, these were all dead bodies." Jerusalem rejoiced over what was surely divine intervention.

"Then Sennacherib king of Assyria departed, and went home and dwelt at Nineveh." But it was only a matter of time before the Assyrians would be back. Hezekiah did not have to face the challenge again, for he died the following year, 687, and his son Manasseh assumed power. Manasseh at once bowed to the Assyrians. He seemed determined to undo his father's work and began by restoring pagan cults. He is thought to have ruled 45 years—the longest reign in Judah's history and, in the opinion of many, the worst.

After the aborted siege of Jerusalem, Isaiah, by then in his mid-sixties, disappeared from sight. A legend passed down through the centuries held that he was executed by Manasseh. No historical

corruptly! . . . Woe to those who call evil good and good evil . . . who acquit the guilty for a bribe, and deprive the innocent of his right!'"

All of Judah would suffer for the sins of those who strayed from the Lord's ways. But at the same time, Isaiah promised redemption for those few people who had kept the Lord's covenant despite the calamities visited upon them: "And the ransomed of the Lord shall return, and

Three Men Form a Two-stranded Rope

Flaxen rope had important uses in shipping, building, hunting and warfare. It was made by a three-man team (see left). The man at right walks slowly forward, whirling two stone-weighted tools which twist strands of flax attached to them. The man at left, retreating, whirls the combined strands in the opposite direction. At center, a man controls the rope's tautness with spikes. The work was done in a "rope walk."

evidence supports that story, but Manasseh's blasphemies would have placed king and prophet in sharp conflict, and martyrdom is a possibility.

Isaiah's Legacy

Throughout his ministry, Isaiah foretold with deadly accuracy the defeat and decay of Assyria, Syria and other nations bloated with pride and power. He had especially vehement words for the Babylonians: "Behold, I am stirring up the Medes against them . . . Their bows will slaughter the young men; they will have no mercy on the fruit of the womb; their eyes will not pity children. And Babylon . . . will be like Sodom and Gomorrah when God overthrew them." Indeed, Isaiah often castigated all mankind for its sins.

But the harshest judgments and threats of divine wrath Isaiah thundered against his own people: "Hear, O heavens, and give ear, O earth; for the Lord has spoken: 'Sons have I reared and brought up, but they have rebelled against me . . . Ah, sinful nation, a people laden with iniquity, offspring of evildoers, sons who deal

come to Zion with singing; everlasting joy shall be upon their heads; they shall obtain joy and gladness, and sorrow and sighing shall flee away." His faith in a Messiah's coming never wavered throughout his life: "The people who walked in darkness have seen a great light . . . For to us a child is born, to us a son is given; and the government will be upon his shoulder, and his name will be called 'Wonderful Counselor, Mighty God, Everlasting Father, Prince of Peace.'"

However he fared in his own time, Isaiah had left behind a legacy of hope for his people: "For out of Zion shall go forth the law, and the word of the Lord from Jerusalem. He shall judge between the nations, and shall decide for many peoples; and they shall beat their swords into plowshares, and their spears into pruning hooks; nation shall not lift up sword against nation, neither shall they learn war any more."

The story of Isaiah is told in 2 Kings 18–20 and the Book of Isaiah 1–39.

The Babylonians: Warriors and Builders

"Because you have not obeyed my words, behold, I will send for all the tribes of the north, says the Lord, and for [Nebuchadnezzar] the king of Babylon, my servant, and I will bring them against this land and its inhabitants, and against all these nations round about; I will utterly destroy them, and make them a horror, a hissing, and an everlasting reproach" (*Jer. 25.8–9*). *Nebuchadnezzar, ruling the Babylonian Empire, consolidated the power of Babylonian cities and the Chaldean people of the Mesopotamian lowlands. His brilliant dynasty brought Babylonia to a peak of artistic and organizational power, expanding the empire and controlling enemies by uprooting and resettling them far from their homes. Under Nebuchadnezzar was devised the massive, stately architecture of the city of Babylon. And it was here that many exiled Jews established a permanent community of their own.*

Babylon's Ishtar Gate guarded the northern entrance to the city and led into the Processional Way, a broad avenue that passed the city palace of Nebuchadnezzar. The full-sized construction at right shows the relief figures of bulls and dragons, and the facing of glazed tiles often used on the gates and walls of Babylon, where their surfaces caught Mesopotamia's bright sunlight. Brick was the standard building material of the Babylonians, whose land was almost entirely lacking in stone. The Persians left a pictorial record (above) of the Babylonians in their friezes at Persepolis, depicting Babylonian exiles after their defeat at the hands of the Persian king Cyrus in 539 B.C.

Spectacular Greenery in a Desert Setting

Trees and foliage adorning the high, walled terraces of the "hanging gardens" of Babylon were visible from a long distance across the flat landscape of the city. The series of terraces reached 75 feet in height and were watered by a system of wells and fountains. Babylon would have been a desert except for the city's irrigation, and the lavish garden built inside city walls was astonishing to visitors, who counted it among the great wonders of the ancient world. The ruins of a heavily vaulted structure, thought to have once supported earth on its arches, have been found in Nebuchadnezzar's palace complex and were the evidence for an artist's reconstruction (above) of the famous gardens.

Exiles from Jerusalem wept for their lost city by "the waters of Babylon," the Euphrates River. In the painting (right) based on excavations, the river flows past Babylon's western wall. A temple of Marduk, god of Babylon, and a huge temple tower, or ziggurat, dominated the city's sacred enclosure. Already 1000 years old when Nebuchadnezzar was king, this 300-foot tower was probably the Tower of Babel, subject of the Biblical story told in Israel since the 2nd millennium. Today raised figures are still to be seen along the high walls (above) lining the city's Processional Way.

Chapter 15

The warnings of Judah's last prophet fail to prevent the fall of Jerusalem and the exile of its people. With this calamity, the kingdom ends and the city is all but deserted.

Jeremiah: Anguished Prophet of Disaster

It was the harsh duty of the prophet Jeremiah to predict misfortunes, and his unhappy fate to witness and lament their fulfillment: the destruction of Solomon's temple, the end of the kingdom of Judah and the Babylonian captivity. A sensitive man whose ministry spanned half a century, from about 627 to about 580 B.C., Jeremiah was rejected and maligned by those he tried to save. His life was lonely and full of sorrow, but his legacy, preserved in moving and beautiful poetry, is of faith in God even in times of extreme affliction.

The village of Anathoth, where Jeremiah was born, was at the top of a broad hill about two miles northeast of Jerusalem. It had been set aside as a priestly community in the time of Joshua and since that time its priests had emphasized strict adherence to the laws of Moses. Jeremiah's father, Hilkiah, was one of those priests and his son was reared with a devout reverence for the Mosaic covenant—and, almost certainly, with the firm belief that he belonged to a more ancient and authentic priestly tradition than the one then prevailing in Jerusalem.

The surrounding countryside was hardly a pleasant playground for a young boy. Around the village itself, on the edge of Judah's central ridge, there was arable land, but to the east the rolling hills gave way to a series of sharp ridges, dropping away some 3000 feet to the Dead Sea. In this boulder-strewn wilderness there was no refuge from the desert sun, and the rare breezes were like the rush of air from a blacksmith's forge.

Images of its desolation, burned into the boy's memory, would later appear in his speeches and writings. To the south, across a deep valley, he could see Jerusalem, the city that he would come to love and chastise.

In his pious home, Jeremiah was probably shielded from the evils of the capital. He was a small child when King Manasseh died, but the corruptions of that long reign survived the monarch's passing, and as Jeremiah grew older, he became aware of them. For generations now, Judah had been a vassal of Assyria, obliged to honor its gods. But Manasseh paid far more than token homage to the Assyrians' religion. Although he did not actually prohibit the worship of the Lord, he reopened local heathen shrines, installed pagan altars and even restored the abomination of human sacrifice. Inside the Jerusalem temple he placed an image of Ishtar, the Assyrian goddess of love and war, associated with the planet Venus. In her name, priests and male worshipers engaged in ritual sex with "holy" prostitutes housed in the temple, a practice that was supposed to promote the fertility of crops, herds and families. Statues to the sun-god Shamash, the moon-god Sin and other deities representing heavenly bodies were erected within the

"Sennacherib king of Assyria came up against all the fortified cities of Judah and took them" (Is. 36.1). This sculptured wall at Nineveh records the fall of Lachish, a major Judean city, and the capture of two defenders. Assyria's army, larger than Israel's, was likely the Near East's most adept in the art of siege warfare.

temple courtyards. Although Judaism forbade sorcery, wizards and enchanters flourished. The people who openly opposed the king's practices were executed or driven underground.

In 640, less than two years after Manasseh's death, his son and successor, Amon, was murdered. Amon's eight-year-old son, Josiah, was placed on the throne. As Josiah grew to manhood, Babylonia and other vassal states were challenging Assyria's waning power, and Josiah too dared assert some independence. Defying his Assyrian overlords, in about 628 B.C. he launched a drastic religious reformation and tried almost single-handedly to cleanse Judaism of its pagan influences. Throughout Judah, Josiah's soldiers tore down pagan shrines. The temple was swept clean of idols, and the priests who practiced pagan rites, the temple prostitutes and the practitioners of witchcraft were put to death.

It was probably in 627, when he was about 18 years old, that Jeremiah first recognized his vocation. As he later wrote: "Now the word of the Lord came to me saying, 'Before . . . you were born I consecrated you; I appointed you a prophet to the nations.' Then I said, 'Ah, Lord God! Behold, I do not know how to speak, for I am only a youth.' But the Lord said to me, 'Do not say, "I am only a youth"; for to all to whom I send you you shall go, and whatever I command you you shall speak. Be not afraid of them, for I am with you to deliver you, says the Lord.' Then the Lord put forth his hand and touched my mouth; and the Lord said to me, 'Behold, I have put my words in your mouth.'"

Gloomy Portents

At the same time, God revealed to him the impending doom of Judah: "Out of the north evil shall break forth upon all the inhabitants of the land. . . . And I will utter my judgments against them, for all their wickedness in forsaking me; they have burned incense to other gods, and worshiped the works of their own hands." The divine voice forewarned Jeremiah not to be dismayed by persecution: "They will fight against you; but

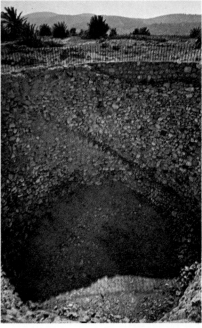

Collection of Taxes at Megiddo

"And Jehoshaphat . . . built in Judah fortresses and store-cities" (2 Chr. 17.12). From Solomon's time onward, Israelites paid taxes in the form of grain and other provisions, with each district supplying the needs of the court for one month out of the year. These were collected at special "store-cities," to which nearby farmers would bring their goods. Scribes recorded grain deposits (above, left) as they were placed in large plaster-walled pits, which probably had some type of cover. Grain and other goods were stored in thick-walled buildings on a raised earth platform, where they would keep until needed. Above: a pit from Megiddo.

they shall not prevail against you, for I am with you, says the Lord, to deliver you." God also commanded him not to take a wife, since Judah faced destruction and families would perish. Thus from the outset the prophet faced portents of loneliness, implacable enemies and his country's bitter destiny.

It was with heavy heart, therefore, that Jeremiah took up his mission in Jerusalem. Like prophets before him, he admonished the throngs of shoppers and merchants in the marketplaces and the crowds in the temple courtyard. Entering with other worshipers, he delivered his grim warnings. Dressed in a long, close-fitting priest's robe of white linen, his face youthful and his voice vibrant with anger, he must have been a startling figure as he called on the people: "Hear the word of the Lord," and cried out against pagan cults and false leaders. "As a thief is shamed when caught, so the house of Israel shall be shamed: they, their kings, their princes, their priests, and their prophets, who say to a tree, 'You are my father,' and to a stone, 'You gave me birth.'" Before long, Jeremiah was a familiar gadfly in Jerusalem, lashing out at its citizens, despite their ridicule. "They bend their tongue like a bow; falsehood . . . has grown strong in the land."

Josiah's efforts to revive religion gained impetus around 622 with the discovery of an old law book—a major portion of the book now called Deuteronomy—expounding the theology of the Mosaic covenant. In line with its Mosaic precepts, all sacrificial rituals were now performed in the Jerusalem temple, and the provincial clergy were invited to join the priestly guilds in the capital, though most of them refused to do so.

Such reforms met little popular support. Many rightly suspected Josiah of using the religious reform for political gain, and they probably feared a possible Assyrian retribution. At best most of the people obeyed Josiah's dictates without giving up their pagan beliefs and practices.

Meanwhile the Assyrian Empire was crumbling. The Babylonians' destruction in 612 of its magnificent capital, Nineveh, marked the virtual end of Assyrian power. Josiah, inspired by religious zeal and political ambition, carried his reformation into the old kingdom of Israel. Now free of Assyrian interference, he extended his political control as far north as Galilee and west to the Mediterranean Sea.

When Nebuchadnezzar besieged Jerusalem in 588 B.C., the entrapped Judeans called upon Egypt's Pharaoh Hophra for help. His army came along this strategic route west of Jerusalem. The Babylonians fell back, but returned and sacked the city when the Egyptians left.

Aiming to preserve a buffer between aggressive Babylonia and his own empire, Pharaoh Neco of Egypt decided to aid Assyria. Knowing that an Egyptian-Assyrian alliance threatened Judah's growing independence, Josiah led an army to intercept and delay the Egyptians. He met them in battle at Megiddo, about 50 miles northwest of Jerusalem, and there he was mortally wounded. He died while being rushed to the capital, after which his forces were badly routed. For a few years Judah fell under Egyptian domination. As his subjects mourned Josiah's death, his son Jehoahaz II was crowned king. But within three months Neco carried him off to Egypt, placing his brother Jehoiakim on the throne. The new ruler, in his lust for power and luxury, ignored Josiah's religious reforms, and paganism spread rapidly again.

Sermon in the Temple

Early in Jehoiakim's reign, possibly during his formal coronation in about 608 B.C., Jeremiah was instructed by God to stand in "the Lord's house" and proclaim his message. It was in September or early October, the time of the annual Feast of Booths (Tabernacles), when pilgrims from all Judah flocked to Jerusalem. Jeremiah must have been in the crowd that followed the solemn procession into the temple. As priests circled the altar, worshipers waved their lulabs—ceremonial plumes woven of branches from palm, willow and myrtle trees—and joined in the singing.

At this point Jeremiah loudly interrupted the temple ceremonies to denounce the display of superficial orthodoxy. "Thus says the Lord of hosts, the God of Israel," he cried. "Amend your ways and your doings, and I will let you dwell in this place. . . . Will you steal, murder, commit adultery, swear falsely, burn incense to Baal, and go after other gods that you have not known, and then come and stand before me in this house, which is called by my name, and say, 'We are delivered!'—only to go on doing all these abominations? Has this house . . . become a den of robbers in your eyes?"

As he went on to predict the fall of the temple itself, the furious mob, still embittered by the belief that Josiah's previous reforms had led only to Egypt's conquest of Judah, seized Jeremiah and shouted, "You shall die!" Court officials rushed to the scene and held an inquiry. An indignant priest told them, "This man deserves the sentence of death, because he has prophesied against this city, as you have heard with your own ears." Jeremiah answered: "The Lord sent me to prophesy against this house and this city all the words you have heard. Now therefore amend your ways and your doings . . . and the Lord will repent of the evil which he has pronounced against you. . . . Only know for certain that if you put me to death, you will bring innocent blood upon yourselves and upon this city and its inhabitants . . ." The officials spared Jeremiah's life and allowed him to depart.

Despite his brush with death, the prophet's threats of divine vengeance became even more vehement, and his enemies grew increasingly bitter. Even in his birthplace, Anathoth, he was warned: "Do not prophesy in the name of the Lord, or you will die by our hand."

Undeterred, however, Jeremiah soon afterwards went to Topheth, the "burning place" for human sacrifice, in the nearby Valley of Hinnom. Whether the elders and priests there were followers of a pagan cult or of a corrupt form of Judaism is unknown, but in their presence Jeremiah raised an earthenware flask and smashed it against the ground, declaring, "Thus says the Lord of hosts: So will I break this people and this city . . . so that it can never be mended."

From Topheth Jeremiah headed back to Jerusalem. He entered the temple and announced to all present: "Thus says the Lord of hosts, the God of Israel, Behold, I am bringing upon this city and upon all its towns all the evil that I have pronounced against it, because they have stiffened their neck, refusing to hear my words."

The chief priest, Pashhur, heard Jeremiah's words of doom. Outraged, he grabbed a lash and flogged the prophet. Then he had Jeremiah dragged to the Benjamin Gate in the northern wall of the city and shackled him in the stocks. When Pashhur released him the next morning, Jeremiah was unrepentant. "The Lord does not call your name Pashhur, but Terror on every side. . . . And you, Pashhur, and all who dwell in your house, shall go into captivity; to Babylon you shall go; and there you shall die, and there you shall be buried . . ."

At times Jeremiah was so humiliated by punishment and abuse that he despaired of his mission. In distress he cried, "O Lord, thou hast deceived me . . . I have become a laughingstock all the day; every one mocks me. For whenever I speak, I cry out, I shout, 'Violence and destruction!' For the word of the Lord has become for me a reproach and derision all day long." Yet he

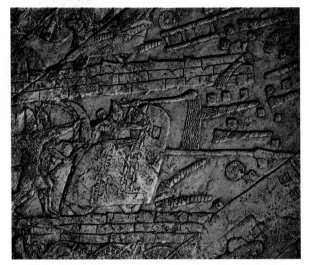

"Sennacherib king of Assyria . . . was besieging Lachish with all his forces" (2 Chr. 32.9). In 701 B.C., Assyria's war engines besieged the mighty Judean fortress of Lachish. The most powerful devices were wheeled battering rams protected by leather canopies (above and right). As their heavy beams drove wedges into the city wall, the Judeans rained missiles and firebrands on them, but the enemy doused the fires with long-handled water ladles. Judeans also poured boiling water and hot oil on enemy archers, lancers and slingers, and shored up the wall as the Assyrians undermined it. Despite these strong defenses, Lachish fell in a matter of weeks.

"A voice declares from Dan and proclaims evil . . . 'Besiegers come from a distant land; they shout against the cities of Judah'" (Jer. 4.15–16). Jeremiah's premonition referred to the extreme northern area of Israel, where the tribe of Dan had given its name to the brook above. This was the route of the Assyrian invaders.

forces at Carchemish in upper Syria. After Nebuchadnezzar's victory, Jehoiakim "became his servant" and paid him formal tribute. But then a messenger brought Nebuchadnezzar the news that his father the king had died. Nebuchadnezzar had to abandon his advantage and return to Babylon to secure the throne and to be crowned.

"In the fourth year of Jehoiakim . . . king of Judah, this word came to Jeremiah from the Lord: 'Take a scroll and write on it all the words that I have spoken to you against Israel and Judah and all the nations . . . It may be that the house of Judah will hear all the evil which I intend to do to them, so that every one may turn from his evil way, and that I may forgive their iniquity and their sin.'" To accomplish this task, Jeremiah commissioned a scribe named Baruch, to whom he dictated his most important sermons and oracles, for inscription on a papyrus scroll. Later, Baruch became Jeremiah's personal secretary.

A year later, in 604, Jehoiakim proclaimed a fast for heavenly intervention against the Babylonians, who had returned and were then advancing against the nearby Philistine city of Ashkelon. Since Jeremiah was then barred from the temple, he charged Baruch to read the scroll of prophecies on the fast day for all to hear. "It may be that their supplication will come before the Lord, and that every one will turn from his evil way . . ." Baruch joined the temple congregation and read the scroll aloud. When he acknowledged that the words were Jeremiah's, court noblemen knew they must be reported to the king. Foreseeing Jehoiakim's reaction, they told Baruch, "Go and hide, you and Jeremiah, and let no one know where you are."

On the chill evening when the courtiers brought the scroll to the king, he was warming himself before a fire in a metal brazier. Each time his secretary, Jehudi, read a portion of the writing to him, Jehoiakim angrily cut it off and tossed it into the brazier flames. When the entire papyrus was burned, he ordered the prophet's arrest. Jeremiah, safely hidden, once more dictated his oracles to Baruch, adding many other things not recorded the first time.

The First Exiles to Babylonia

When the Babylonian forces first marched through Judah in 604 B.C., King Jehoiakim submitted without a struggle and paid heavy tribute

could not restrain his compulsion to speak out: "If I say, 'I will not mention him, or speak any more in his name,' there is in my heart as it were a burning fire shut up in my bones, and I am weary with holding it in, and I cannot."

Meanwhile, King Jehoiakim ignored the prophet's tirades, probably remembering how Jeremiah had interrupted his coronation ceremonies. Taxing Judah's already strained finances and using forced labor, he built another luxurious palace in the southern outskirts of Jerusalem. Jeremiah publicly condemned him: "Woe to him who builds his house by unrighteousness, and his upper rooms by injustice; who makes his neighbor serve him for nothing . . ."

In 605, only four years after Josiah's death, Egyptian authority in Palestine was suddenly halted when the Babylonians under Crown Prince Nebuchadnezzar crushed Pharaoh Neco's to Nebuchadnezzar. In 601, the Egyptians won a major battle against the Babylonians, who then retreated to Babylon. At this time Jehoiakim unwisely rebelled against his Babylonian overlords. Nebuchadnezzar, busy refurbishing his defeated army, sent the armies of several vassal states against Judah, and for over two years they ravaged the country. Finally Nebuchadnezzar attacked with his own troops.

In Jerusalem, before any action could be taken, Jehoiakim suddenly died. His untimely death thrust his eighteen-year-old son Jehoiachin (or Jeconiah) onto the throne just in time to face the Babylonian forces as they surrounded the capital. After a three-month siege, the city surrendered on March 15, 597.

The conquerors carted off many treasures from the temple and palace, though they did not damage the capital badly. However, King Jehoiachin, his royal family, noblemen, and thousands of influential citizens, soldiers and skilled craftsmen were taken as captives to Babylonia. Nebuchadnezzar installed the king's uncle, Zedekiah, as ruler of Judah. He proved to be an indecisive vassal, under constant pressure from those eager to regain the country's independence.

As these events unfolded, Jeremiah demanded in the Lord's name that the country accept its harsh fate as a just punishment for violating the Lord's covenant. This offense to nationalist sentiment made him more unpopular than ever. His insistence that resistance was futile was regarded as treasonable. To dramatize the need to submit, he tied a wooden yoke across his shoulders and wore it for months in the streets and in the temple precincts.

One day Jeremiah sent a message from the Lord to everyone present at a conference of Zedekiah and representatives of other vassal states, who were plotting revolt. "But if any nation or kingdom will not serve this Nebuchadnezzar king of Babylon . . . I will punish that nation with the sword, with famine, and with pestilence . . ." read the message. To Zedekiah, he added, "Bring your necks under the yoke of the king of Babylon, and serve him and his people, and live." Whether through Jeremiah's influence or not, Zedekiah abandoned the conspiracy.

Jeremiah sent a letter to the Judean exiles in Babylon counseling them to abide by the Lord's judgment. In particular he warned them not to listen to prophets and diviners who proposed subversion. It was God's plan, Jeremiah told them, that they remain captive for 70 years, after which he "will restore your fortunes and gather you from all the nations" and return them to Judah. Because 70 years was reckoned a normal life span, he meant that only the children of the exiles would return to Jerusalem.

Nebuchadnezzar Attacks Judah

Within Judah, nationalist factions continued to pressure the king to resist Babylonian domination. Finally, in 589, his ninth year of rule, Zedekiah yielded. Ignoring Jeremiah's objections, he declared independence. Nebuchadnezzar's legions thereupon swept through Judah, conquering city after city until only three fortified strongholds remained: Azekah, Lachish and Jerusalem. Azekah and Lachish put up fierce resistance but were overcome, and by December 589 the Babylonian soldiers were hammering at the walls of Jerusalem.

As the siege dragged on, Zedekiah sent a delegation of priests to ask Jeremiah to intercede with the Lord. The divine word was grimly discouraging: ". . . I will turn back the weapons of war which are in your hands . . . He who stays in this city shall die by the sword, by famine, and by pestilence; but he who goes out and surrenders . . . shall live and shall have his life as a prize of war. For I have set my face against this city for evil and not for good, says the Lord: it shall be given into the hand of the king of Babylon, and he shall burn it with fire." Jeremiah lamented the prospect: "My anguish, my anguish! I writhe in pain! . . . My heart is beating wildly . . . Disaster follows hard on disaster, the whole land [of Judah] is laid waste."

Suddenly relief came. An Egyptian army invaded Judah and Nebuchadnezzar withdrew from Jerusalem to meet the new danger. Convinced that the siege would be resumed, Jeremiah persisted in urging surrender. When he tried to leave the city to visit his birthplace, he was stopped and accused of deserting to the enemy. He was hauled before palace officials, who rejected his denials and had him beaten and thrown into an underground dungeon.

"When Jeremiah had come to the dungeon cells, and remained there many days, King Zedekiah sent for him, and received him. The king questioned him secretly in his house, and said, 'Is there any word from the Lord?' Jeremiah said, 'There is.' Then he said, 'You shall be delivered into the hand of the king of Babylon.' Jeremiah also said . . . 'What wrong have I done to you or your servants or this people, that you have put me in prison? . . . Now hear, I pray you, O my lord the king: let my humble plea come before you, and do not send me back . . . lest I die there.'" The king, though disappointed, reduced Jeremiah's sentence to a sort of house arrest in the court of the guards.

Jerusalem's respite lasted about two years, until the Babylonians renewed their siege. Jeremiah's insistence on surrender provoked demands that he be executed for undermining military and civilian morale. Zedekiah agreed to the demands, and the prophet was lowered into the swamp-like mud at the bottom of a deep cistern to await his death.

However, he had not been forgotten. An Ethiopian at the court, Ebed-melech, implored Zedekiah to spare Jeremiah's life. The king relented and authorized the Ethiopian to lift the prophet out of the deathtrap.

Within a few days Zedekiah summoned Jeremiah to a private meeting near one of the temple gates, to ask if there was any hope for the city. Only after the king swore not to kill him or to deliver him to his enemies did Jeremiah repeat his advice: "If you will surrender to the princes of the king of Babylon, then your life shall be spared, and this city shall not be burned with fire, and you and your house shall live."

Destruction of Jerusalem

But Zedekiah did not heed Jeremiah's advice and the siege continued. Inside the city, suffering increased as food supplies dwindled, and thirst and hunger grew with summer's approach. Jeremiah was still imprisoned by the king, "and a loaf of bread was given him daily from the bakers' street, until all the bread of the city was gone." Jerusalem was also tormented by the summer heat. And outside her walls the Babylonians prepared to attack the city with battering rams mounted on huge armored wagons, pushed by shielded soldiers. Jerusalem was filled with the stench of rotting corpses, and disease was spreading. Food reserves were nearly exhausted, and by the sixth month of the siege, "the famine was so severe in the city, that there was no food for the people of the land." At last, the hunger-crazed people were driven to cannibalism.

By July 587 Jerusalem could hold out no longer. The walls were breached, and Nebuchadnezzar's warriors swarmed into the city. Zedekiah and some soldiers slipped out of the city that night, but were pursued and captured near Jericho. They were taken to Riblah, north of Damascus, where Zedekiah was forced to watch as his sons were killed. Then he was blinded and taken in chains to Babylon, where he later died in prison.

In August, Nebuchadnezzar sent the captain of his bodyguard to Jerusalem with orders to sack and demolish the city. This was done with cruel thoroughness. The temple and palace were stripped of all gold and silver and burned to the ground, along with other buildings. The city walls were torn down. Throughout the country most of those who had not managed to hide or to escape to other lands were slaughtered. Several hundred of Judah's more prominent citizens, however, were rounded up for deportation. In the Chronicles this is reckoned as the true start of the Babylonian captivity. Ever since, the ninth day of Ab (the fifth month of the Hebrew calendar), the day when the temple was razed, has been observed by Jews as a day of mourning.

Through the captain of his guard, Nebuchadnezzar ordered that Jeremiah should not be harmed, probably because he had counseled submission. The prophet, now close to 60 years old, was brought to Ramah, several miles north of Jerusalem. There the Babylonian official told him affably, "If it seems good to you to come with me to Babylon, come, and I will look after you well; but if it seems wrong to you . . . do not come. See, the whole land is before you; go wherever you think it good and right to go."

Jeremiah chose to remain in his homeland. The colonial government of Judah had been transferred to the town of Mizpah, about eight miles north of Jerusalem. Gedaliah, the former prime minister and member of a leading Judean family, had been appointed governor. To Mizpah, therefore, Jeremiah returned, heartbroken that his worst prophecies had come true.

Babylonian rule under Gedaliah was mild. After some months, possibly years, of peace, however, a disgruntled patriot, Ishmael, plotted with the king of Ammon to liberate Judah. In 582 Ishmael and other conspirators, while banqueting at the governor's palace, drew their swords and murdered Gedaliah and all the other guests present, including several Babylonian soldiers. The next day the rebels unleashed a swift slaughter of innocent citizens and made prisoners of others, among them apparently Jeremiah.

Loyalists, headed by a captain Johanan, succeeded in crushing the rebels, but because Ishmael and the other assassins escaped, Babylonian reprisals were feared. The best course seemed flight to Egypt, and many sought guidance from Jeremiah. After 10 days of prayer, he urged them, in the Lord's name, to remain in Judah. Fear of the Babylonians, however, prevailed over his advice. A group led by Johanan escaped to Egypt—forcibly carrying Jeremiah with them.

To avenge the murder of their officials, the Babylonians for a third time ravaged the land and carried off hundreds more Judeans into exile. Judah was placed under the authority of the Babylonian governor at Samaria. Settlers from Edom, Ammon and Moab moved in and intermarried with Judeans, so that the Israelite social order

and religious identity were all but swallowed up.

Jeremiah never saw his beloved land again. He labored to keep the Mosaic law alive among the Israelites in Egypt, and probably died in that country, far from Jerusalem.

Jeremiah's final prophecies gave renewed hope to the Jewish exiles in Babylonia and those dispersed throughout the alien world. "Therefore hear the plan which the Lord has made against Babylon . . ." he said. "Surely the little ones of their flock shall be dragged away; surely their fold shall be appalled at their fate. At the sound of the capture of Babylon the earth shall tremble, and her [Babylon's] cry shall be heard among the nations."

"For Israel and Judah have not been forsaken by their God, the Lord of hosts . . . Babylon must fall for the slain of Israel, as for Babylon have fallen the slain of all the earth."

Jeremiah's story is told in the Book of Jeremiah.

The Assyrians deported thousands of captives after their defeat of the Judeans in 700 B.C. In the frieze above is a group of men, women and children leaving Lachish after it was sacked and burned by Sennacherib's army. Some rode in ox-drawn carts, but others were forced to walk hundreds of miles to Assyria. A sudden plague stopped them at Jerusalem, but in this campaign the Assyrians captured 46 towns.

Part Five
Keepers
of the Faith

"And all the assembly of those who had returned from the captivity made booths and dwelt in [them] . . . And there was very great rejoicing" (Neh. 8.17). The conquered Jews were exiled to Babylonia, which was conquered by Persia. But within a century, they were allowed to return and rebuild the Jerusalem temple. There they held the Feast of Booths, a traditional holiday commemorating Israel's exodus from Egypt. Shelters of willow and palm branches were erected throughout the city, and in these the people lived for eight days of prayer, feasting and sacrifice. Old Testament history closed with a succession of western rulers —from Greece, Egypt, Syria and Rome—ultimately ending Jewish political sovereignty. But their religion and its holidays would sustain the nationless Jews until the founding of modern Israel, 2000 years later.

"Is not this a brand plucked from the fire?" (Zech. 3.2). *Jews returning from exile saw themselves as a remnant saved by the Lord. In the final period of Old Testament life, that remnant grew to become a nation once again, with a faith that still endures.*

NEBUCHADNEZZAR'S INVASION left the kingdom of Judah deeply scarred. Everywhere, towns were burned and looted, crops destroyed and villages deserted. Worst of all, Solomon's great temple was a charred ruin, stripped even of the ancient and sacred ark of the covenant. Ten years earlier, in 597, Nebuchadnezzar had put down a Judean revolt and taken many of the nation's leaders in captivity to Babylonia. After the destruction of Jerusalem in 587, he abducted an even larger number of Jews, and finally, in 582, deported a third group.

The impact of the captivity was crushing. The Jews taken to Babylonia were the leaders of Judah's spiritual and secular life—priests and scholars, officers, administrators, village elders, wealthy merchants and craftsmen. Without them, Judah could scarcely continue to exist politically, much less rise up again to challenge Babylonia's firm authority.

Those who remained in Judah were little better off than their captured leaders. They were still taxed by Babylonia, and the Samaritans (Israelites and foreign settlers in the old northern kingdom of Israel) were steadily encroaching upon their farmlands. Intermarriage with Gentiles became common, children were raised with no knowledge of the scriptures and Jewish rites were mingled with Babylonian and Canaanite practices. For 50 years no attempt was made to rebuild the temple. It would be left to the exiled leaders in Babylonia, more than 500 miles to the east, to someday make their way back to restore the kingdom and religion of Judah.

Despite their anguish, the day-to-day condition of the exiles was not the abject slavery that befell most prisoners of war. They were placed in their own settlements, allowed to build homes, raise crops and earn a living in virtually any way they chose. More important, they were allowed to assemble freely and maintain some sort of community and religious life. Thus, though separated indefinitely from Palestine, they managed to keep a sense of their identity as Jews and to nurture the hope that their nation would one day be restored to them.

In the meantime, large numbers of Jews left Judah to seek work and refuge elsewhere. Many made their way to Egypt and established the communities which would later make Egypt a major center of Jewry in the ancient world. Moab, Edom, Ammon, Samaria, Galilee and Transjordan also became refuges for discouraged Judeans. The emigration spurred by Nebuchadnezzar's invasion marked the beginning of a historical trend that would never be reversed. Israel had begun to be scattered among the nations.

Prophets of Redemption

After the fall of Judah even the most pious Jews were forced to question the supremacy of their God. Some feared that he had turned forever against the children of Israel for their sinfulness. Others, equally despairing, wondered whether their Lord—seemingly unable to protect one small country—was the one supreme God, after all. In these circumstances, the first task facing the Jews' religious leaders was to find an explanation for the disaster, one that would prove the Lord's power and wisdom in the face of overwhelming evidence to the contrary. There was an explanation, the scholars argued, in the writings of Ezekiel, Jeremiah and others who had prophesied God's judgment of his impious people. In the Babylonian exile that judgment was being fulfilled, but the punishment would not last forever. It was a time to purify the Israelite spirit and prepare it for redemption.

In this belief the captive Jews found hope for the future. Gradually a new religious community began to take form, no longer tied to a political state, but still defining itself through adherence to Jewish law and custom. Convinced that they were suffering for earlier sins, the Jews in Babylonia returned with special vigor to the righteous traditions of their forebears, expanding most of their scriptures, and editing the Priestly Code that would govern all services in the restored temple.

The greatest prophet of the exiles was Ezekiel, who had been brought to Babylonia during the first deportation in 597. His early writings warned those still in Jerusalem that they would soon be punished for their wickedness. After Jerusalem's destruction in 587, he turned his attention to the restoration of Judah, rallying his fellow exiles' faith in God's mercy and helping them find a concept of Judaism that depended not on a homeland or temple but on the Law of Moses.

As the exiles' religious activities progressed, so did their hope for freedom. They were encouraged by a growing instability in the Babylonian Empire after Nebuchadnezzar's death in 562. At the same time, a major uprising was taking shape in the Median Empire. The rebellion was led by Cyrus the Persian, king of a Median vassal state in southern Iran. Babylonia's leaders eagerly supported him, confident that the fighting would leave Media too weak to threaten their own security. This proved a fatal mistake. Cyrus waged a brilliant campaign, gaining the Median throne in 550 and expanding his domain with frightening speed. By 546 the new Persian Empire extended westward to the Aegean Sea, and in 539, after securing his holdings to the north and east, Cyrus moved south into Babylonia. Within months he made his triumphal entry into the capital, where the citizens welcomed him as a liberator.

From the beginning, Cyrus proved an enlightened ruler. He decreed that religious practices not be interfered with, and that social and political reforms be instituted according to the wishes of the people. Then, in 538, when all of western Asia was under his control, he issued the Edict of Restoration. This allowed all Babylonian Jews to return to their homeland and directed that the temple in Jerusalem be rebuilt at the expense of the royal treasury. Cyrus appointed Shesh-bazzar, an aristocrat of the Davidic line, to rule Judah as a semi-independent state.

The First to Return

The first group of exiles to set out with Shesh-bazzar was probably small and zealous. Work on the temple seems to have begun at once, but the project soon bogged down. The tiny community of repatriates had returned to a land that still bore the desolate marks of defeat. The rolling fields that had produced so many abundant harvests of wheat, barley, grapes and olives lay untended now, barren for many seasons, and the new settlers suffered a period of crop failures that left many of them destitute.

In addition, the new community soon had to contend with the hostility of its neighbors. The Samaritans were especially unfriendly toward the recent arrivals, for they had come to look upon Judah as part of their own territory. The Jews who had never left Judah were probably no happier than the Samaritans to see their spiritual brothers arrive and claim the landholdings of their ancestors. The situation was further aggravated by the settlers' obvious desire to set themselves apart—not only from the Samaritans but from the native Jews as well, who seemed to be practicing a pagan-influenced religion.

In such a situation, resentment and mistrust gave way to incidents of violence, ending the reconstruction of the temple and any hopes for a dramatic revival of Israel's unity. The determined leaders claimed these problems were simply the growing pains of a new Israel, but their optimism increasingly fell on deaf ears. Why, the discouraged pilgrims wondered, was the Lord not acting on their behalf? Could it be that he was not able to? New groups of the faithful continued to return from Babylonia, but the hardships persisted.

Political events outside Palestine helped the hard-pressed leaders to resume work on the temple in 520, which was 18 years after the first return from Babylonia. In 522 the Persian throne had been seized by an army officer, Darius, and a two-year epidemic of rebellions had broken out all over the Persian Empire.

In Palestine, several prophets—among them

Haggai and Zechariah—took these events as a sign that a new age was at hand. Their belief was infectious; their long-frustrated followers turned enthusiastically to the task of rebuilding the temple, and in March of 515 it was dedicated with thanksgiving and celebration. But despite the predictions and prayers, the new age did not materialize. Judah continued to enjoy relative freedom as a theocratic state, but the failure of the prophecies was deeply felt: Darius had crushed the rebels, and God's kingdom had not arrived.

Little is known of the conditions within the Jewish community during the next 70 years. The population of Judah did grow steadily as new groups of Jews resettled there, and by the middle of the fifth century had nearly doubled. Even so, the population was still far smaller than it had been before the devastating Babylonian conquest.

There was friction between the high priests in Jerusalem and Persian representatives headquartered in Samaria, and the population was still divided over many serious issues. Widespread disillusionment over Judah's continued lack of independence had brought about a gradual decline in religious devotion to the Lord, and marriage with Gentiles had become common. Sabbath laws were widely ignored by merchants struggling to make a living, workers were cheated by their employers, and unscrupulous landowners forced many small farmers to sell themselves and their families into servitude.

Even in the temple, laws of ritual cleanliness were sometimes violated, and general nonpayment of the temple tax forced many priests to

abandon their sacred duties for other forms of employment. The Judean community seemed to be collapsing.

It was at this critical point that two towering figures, Ezra and Nehemiah, appeared on the stage of Judean history. Beginning in Jerusalem in the third quarter of the fifth century, these men dramatically reversed the decline of Judean life.

Nehemiah and Ezra

The work of Nehemiah began in about 445 B.C., during the reign of the Persian monarch Artaxerxes I. In Jerusalem the Jews had begun to rebuild the city walls. Persian government officials in Samaria, always jealous of their authority, reported to the king that the Jews were planning a rebellion. Artaxerxes immediately ordered the construction stopped, prompting the intervention of one of his own attendants, Nehemiah. While loyal to the Persian king, Nehemiah was also a Jew with strong sympathy for his struggling people. He urged Artaxerxes to let him go to Jerusalem and supervise the building of the walls.

Despite Samaritan protests, the king agreed, and, according to the Bible, the walls of Jerusalem were rebuilt in an astounding 52 days. Artaxerxes was impressed enough by this to make Judah a separate province under the governorship of Nehemiah, and a new stage in Israel's history seemed to have begun.

Nehemiah's first concentrated efforts were to reform the widely unequal distribution of wealth and political influence in Judah. Later he enforced the Sabbath and marriage laws, restored a full complement of priests to the temple and required the payment of annual taxes.

During this formative period the great scribe Ezra appeared in Judah. A prominent member of the Jewish community in Babylon, he had been

"Gather wine and summer fruits and oil, and store them in your vessels" (Jer. 40.10). Olive oil was very important in Biblical life, providing food, fuel, ointments and medicines. Beaten down from their trees, the olives were first crushed in a stone basin by a heavy roller, which was turned by a man or animal. The olive pulp was then placed in a smaller vat, covered with a flat stone and pressed with a weighted lever. Oil flowed from a hole in the vat bottom. Of the finest quality was "beaten oil," obtained by gently pounding immature olives in a mortar and then straining the oil. Above are a roller and basin from the 2nd century B.C.

commissioned by Artaxerxes II to reintroduce the Law of Moses into Judah.

He brought with him a set of scrolls containing the Torah, the five books of Moses, compiled in written form during the long exile. Chapter 8 of the Book of Nehemiah gives a dramatic account of Ezra's first appearance in Jerusalem. In a public square the scholar addressed the entire population, reading the Law through the morning until the men and women of Jerusalem wept.

This burst of enthusiasm was undoubtedly heartening, but many Judeans still had a casual attitude toward their religious obligations. Drastic action was needed. One of Ezra's first decisions required all Jewish men to divorce their Gentile wives and forswear mixed marriages in the future. Such a policy provoked considerable resistance, but in Ezra's view intermarriage was endangering the religious and ethnic identity of the Jews in Palestine. His decree was finally accepted by most of the population.

Ezra's subsequent reforms demanded strict adherence to Sabbath and dietary laws, suspended cultivation of land and collection of debts every seventh year and formalized the annual half-shekel tax to maintain the temple. From then on, Israel would exist as a community bound together by the Law, and a Jew would be identified mainly by his devotion to the teachings of Moses, not by his nationality.

Almost no details are known of the last century of Persian rule in Judah. The high priests and civil governors apparently continued to rule the country as a Persian province, and relations between Jerusalem and Samaria grew steadily worse. Although there was still some social and commercial contact with the Samaritans, the theological differences between the two peoples were unreconcilable. The Samaritans recognized only the Torah as sacred, rejecting the prophetic writings and oral traditions revered by the Judeans. In turn, the Judeans condemned the Samaritans as unorthodox and excluded them from temple services. Then, although the date is unknown, the Samaritans erected their own temple on Mount Gerizim, and the split was complete.

Alexander and Hellenism

As the fourth century drew to a close, even the bitter feelings toward Samaria were overshadowed by a far more serious matter, the erosion of ancient Jewish traditions by foreign cultures. Aramaic, the official language of the Persian Empire, had already replaced Hebrew as the language of the people, and public readings from scripture were usually accompanied by a translation. But even this cultural change was slight in comparison with the flood of Greek customs and values that Alexander the Great's conquests began to release across the Near East.

In 334, Alexander, seeking to conquer all the Near East, led his armies from Greece into Asia Minor. There, in the year 333, he met and destroyed the Persian army under Darius III at Issus in one of history's most decisive battles.

Within a year the Greeks had control of Syria, Judah and Egypt, and their armies marched across Mesopotamia to subdue the remnants of Darius' forces. By 326, Alexander's empire reached India and his campaigning was over: his soldiers refused to go on. Within three years he was dead, at the age of 33.

After his death, Alexander's empire fragmented as swiftly as it had been conquered, but Hellenism, or imposed Greek culture, had made its mark. All across Mesopotamia and beyond, Alexander had followed a policy of implanting Greek civilization, conducting mass marriages between his soldiers and native women, and establishing new settlements for his troops and other Greeks. Long after his empire had broken up, thousands of Greeks continued to emigrate

"Why did I not die at birth . . . ? Why did the knees receive me?" (Job 3.11–12). Old Testament women, as this passage suggests, gave birth in a kneeling position rather than reclining. A Cypriot statue shows a woman (middle) delivering, as two women assist.

from their populous homeland to create new towns and cities in Asia Minor. Their language soon replaced Aramaic throughout most of the Near East (though not in Judea, as Judah was called in Greek), and the cities of Antioch and Alexandria became thriving centers of Hellenism.

By 312, Alexander's empire had been divided among his generals. Seleucus had established his own dynasty over Babylonia and Syria. Egypt had come under the control of Ptolemy, and his descendants ruled Judea for the next 100 years.

Jews of the Dispersion

During the century of Egyptian rule, life in Judea was probably not changed in any drastic way, though again few details are known. The Ptolemies apparently followed the Persian system, collecting taxes from the Judeans but leaving their internal affairs to the high priests. At the same time, the number of Jews living in Egypt and other places outside Judea increased substantially: Alexandria soon had the largest Jewish community of any city in the world. By the end of the third century b.c. the Jews living in foreign cities, the "Jews of the Dispersion," outnumbered the Jews still living in Judea.

As Greek became their native tongue, more and more Jews of the Dispersion found the sacred scriptures incomprehensible. In Alexandria the wealthy Jewish community sponsored a translation of the Hebrew scriptures into Greek. This translation (known as the Septuagint because 70 rabbinical scholars reputedly produced it) became the standard version of the Bible for most of the Greek-speaking Jews of the Dispersion.

The century of Egyptian rule over Judea came to an end in 198, when a Syrian army under Antiochus III defeated Egypt's forces at Panium and Palestine was added to the Seleucid Empire. The Jews, burdened by increasingly heavy taxes and deeply offended by the installation of an Egyptian garrison inside the walls of Jerusalem, had helped Syria's forces. In return, Antiochus lowered their taxes, paid for repairs to the damaged temple and guaranteed freedom of religion.

In general, the Jews of the Dispersion were sincerely loyal to the religion of their ancestors. They recognized Jerusalem as the Holy City, paid their annual taxes to the temple and whenever possible made pilgrimages there to celebrate the holy days. Nevertheless, in many synagogues outside Judea services were being conducted in Greek, mixed marriages were becoming a familiar practice again and the rite of circumcision was increasingly ignored. Among the many Hellenistic ideas that gained ground with the dispersed Jews was the popular belief that different peoples simply worshiped the same God by different names. This doctrine was anathema to the priests and scholars of Jerusalem, for it blurred the differences between Jew and Gentile.

Shortly after his victory over Egypt, Antiochus III made the suicidal mistake of challenging the legions of Rome. He was swiftly defeated, and the harsh peace terms marked the beginning of the Seleucid dynasty's decline. Antiochus died in disgrace (he was killed trying to rob a temple). In 175 after a stormy 12 years under an older son, the throne was seized by the most hated figure in ancient Jewish history: Antiochus IV.

From Antioch, the Seleucid capital of Syria, Antiochus used Hellenization as a systematic policy for exterminating Judaism. With the help of some highly placed Jewish sympathizers—mostly within the priestly aristocracy—he actively promoted Greek customs of the sort most offensive to faithful Jews. A gymnasium was built in the middle of Jerusalem, and young Jews were encouraged to participate in sports long associated with Greek gods. Among the worldly aristocrats, Greek clothing, hair styles, philosophy and drama came into vogue. Then, in 169, Antiochus and his troops plundered the temple, in reprisal for a minor uprising.

Persecutions of Antiochus

Two years later Antiochus confirmed himself as the mortal enemy of Judaism. In response to a new disturbance in Jerusalem, he dispatched a force of mercenaries who entered the city on the Sabbath, butchered thousands of Jews, looted their homes and pulled down the city walls. Subsequently they fortified the Acra, a hill that overlooked the temple, and settled a Seleucid garrison on it.

Antiochus followed this atrocity with his final attempt to destroy Judaism. Temple services were suspended, as were Sabbath observances and traditional celebrations. Circumcision was forbidden, and it became a capital crime to possess a copy of the Torah. Pagan altars were set up all over the country and Jews were forced to make sacrifices at them. Finally, in his most offensive act—the "abomination that makes desolate"—Antiochus had an altar to Zeus erected in the temple, and sacrificed the abhorred flesh of pigs on it.

At the height of Antiochus' oppression the Book of Daniel appeared. Purporting to date from

The Smith Was a Valuable Craftsman

Traveling smiths were important figures in Old Testament times, valued not only for their skill in making and repairing metal, but for the news they carried from one village to another. Here a smith lays out his tools to repair the hoe and pan of a Judean woman. With the aid of a bellows, he will heat the metal over hot coals, then hammer it on a flat rock. Most smiths were taken from Judah during the Exile, because their skills were needed by the Assyrians to make war implements.

the sixth-century Babylonian captivity, Daniel's dramatic visions unmistakably reflected the Seleucid persecution. Prophesying the tyrant's destruction and the coming of God's kingdom, the book was a rallying cry, and by the end of 167 the Maccabean revolt had begun.

Maccabees and Hasmoneans

Led by the five sons of Mattathias, a Levite priest, the rebellion mushroomed from a spontaneous guerrilla operation into full-scale warfare. Within two years, aided by Antiochus' concurrent war with the growing Parthian Empire, the Maccabees, as Mattathias' sons were known, had retaken most of Jerusalem, except for the Acra. In December of 165 the temple was restored to its rightful function by Judas Maccabeus.

For the next 12 years the fighting continued sporadically, but by 153 Judea was effectively controlled by the high priest Jonathan, one of the three surviving Maccabees. In 142 the hated stronghold on the Acra hill was finally taken and at last Judea had won its independence.

Under the Hasmonean dynasty—established by Jonathan's brother Simon and his son John Hyrcanus—Judea became a theocratic kingdom once more. John Hyrcanus, ruling from 134 to 104, enlarged Judea's borders considerably, destroying the Samaritan temple on Mount Gerizim and securing the country against attack. Subsequently, his son Alexander Janneus (104–76) continued to pursue a vigorous policy of expansion, in spite of growing opposition to the financial and physical burdens it imposed on the country. This issue finally erupted into civil war, but Janneus held onto his power and remained high priest until his death. Under his rule, Judean boundaries even exceeded those of the Israel of Solomon's reign. He was succeeded by his shrewd wife Alexandra (76–69), who gave Judea a much needed period of stability and peace.

During these extraordinary years of turmoil and success, there was a profound and historic change in the structure of Judaism. From the time of Ezra and Nehemiah, two religious factions had evolved. Following in Ezra's footsteps was a group of deeply religious and scholarly men originally called Hasidim, or "the pious ones." They strove, as Ezra had done, to redefine the Law in light of changing conditions in Judea and the rest of the world. In effect, they became the "progressive wing" of Judaism, constantly studying past interpretations of the scriptures and making new ones as the need arose.

By the time of the Maccabean revolt, the Hasidim had become the leaders of a more or less formal party, called the Pharisees. During the Hasmonean era their chief rivals were the Sadducees, organized around the aristocratic class of priests whose authority covered all activities in the temple. The Sadducees—descendants of a hereditary priesthood that arose some time after Nehemiah's temple reforms—rejected entirely the oral tradition preferred by the Pharisees. The Law of Moses, in their view, was immutable, absolute and not open to new interpretations.

Although the Sadducees were conservative in theological matters, they were far more receptive to change in secular affairs. They were a sophisticated group, in touch with international currents in politics and culture, and more at home with Greek ideas and customs than most of their less privileged countrymen.

Through the reign of Alexander Janneus, the Sadducees exercised great influence in Judean affairs, while the Pharisees were limited to an opposition role. But as the Hasmonean era drew to a close with the Roman conquest of Syria in 63 B.C., the Sadducees slipped into a decline that, with one brief interruption, proved permanent.

The Pharisees, in contrast, were not dependent on the temple or the monarchy. Their power was based on the countless small synagogues throughout Judea and the entire Dispersion. They were better equipped to survive a loss of Judean independence than was the priesthood.

This was the condition of the Jews at the close of the Old Testament period. Sooner than anyone could have expected, the entire structure of Judaism had been overturned. In the end, it was the Pharisees alone who held the key to the future. Without the leadership and continuity they later provided during the dark years after Jerusalem fell to the Romans, Israel might well have become just one more victim of history. Nor was that their last triumph. With their exhaustive oral tradition—ultimately compiled in the Mishnah and Talmud—the Pharisees gave their faith the depth and resilience not only to outlive the Roman Empire, but also to sustain itself through the next 2000 years of world history.

Persian Provinces in Syria-Palestine After the Exile

Allowed by the Persians to return to Palestine, the Jews dreamed of restoring and unifying their nation. But conditions had altered radically during the Exile. The kingdom of Judah had been made a province of fewer than 50,000 people, and Israel by now was partitioned into a number of small provinces. Also, the Persian policy of provincial home rule intensified their mutual rivalries. In about 330 B.C. the Persians fell to Alexander the Great. After he died Judah became a border state between his two successors— the Ptolemies of Egypt and the Seleucid dynasty of Syria. The former held the area for 125 years and the latter 31, until the Maccabean struggle for independence began. Fierce fighting continued until 63 B.C., when the Roman army under Pompey took decisive control.

Chapter 16

After the fall of Jerusalem, the Jewish exiles in Babylonia are inspired by a visionary prophet. He affirms the living presence of the Lord and foresees the rebuilding of Jerusalem.

Ezekiel: Priest to the Exiles

An exiled priest, Ezekiel was the great prophet of the Babylonian captivity. As a priest, he dealt with practical problems of worship in an alien land and influenced the development of the synagogue. As a prophet, he was a mystic, given to ecstatic visions and obscure symbolism. But his dream of a revived and rebuilt Jerusalem inspired hope and faith in his fellow exiles.

The prophet was born in Jerusalem, probably about 623 B.C. His father, Buzi, was a Zadokite priest, descended from Solomon's high priest Zadok. Soon after Ezekiel's birth, King Josiah of Judah, having launched an earnest religious reform, placed the Zadokites in charge of the temple to purge it of idolatry and enforce strict Mosaic laws. The boy's upbringing and education were therefore intensely orthodox.

In 609 B.C., at about the time young Ezekiel's training for priesthood began, Josiah was killed in a battle with the Egyptians at Megiddo. His successor let the reform movement lapse and paganism flourished once again. Ezekiel was deeply dismayed by the spiritual backsliding. Others, including the prophets, felt that the widespread profanation of everything holy meant that the end of Judah was near.

In the first years of the sixth century B.C., Judah finally suffered the fate Jeremiah had predicted. The nation had become a vassal of Babylonia, the dominant empire of the Near East. When it attempted to revolt, the forces of Nebuchadnezzar, king of Babylonia, invaded Judah, ravaged its

towns and countryside, and in 598 besieged Jerusalem. After three months, the city surrendered. Apart from looting temple and palace treasures, the conquerors did little damage. But they deported the young king Jehoiachin (Jeconiah), his family, officials, priests, scribes and skilled craftsmen, in all probably between 5000 and 6000 people. Ezekiel was in this first group sent to Babylonia, in the southern part of the plain between the Tigris and Euphrates rivers. The exiles must have been impressed by the country's lush fertility, the product of a system of navigable canals dug centuries before.

The exiles must have been even more impressed by the capital, Babylon, a city of some 200,000 inhabitants, made virtually impregnable by a double row of fortification walls. The city had broad avenues and sumptuous gardens; an elaborately decorated gate dedicated to Ishtar, goddess of love and war; the massive palace of the king with its famous "hanging gardens"; and the great temple of the chief god Marduk, with its seven-storied pyramidal tower.

The exiles were remarkably well treated. Though living in separate exile colonies, they were drawn into the Babylonian work force on the land and in the towns, allowed to build homes

"Behold, I am against you, O Tyre, and will bring up many nations against you, as the sea brings up its waves" (Ezek. 26.3). This jagged Lebanese coastline, near Tyre, recalls the Lord's stern words of warning. Rebuked for its worldliness by Ezekiel, the prosperous Phoenician capital fell to Nebuchadnezzar in 572 B.C.

and gardens and, most important, permitted to worship as they pleased. Ezekiel was in the group settled in the village of Tel-abib, near Babylon on the Chebar canal, with easy access by water to the capital and the cities of Nippur and Erech, farther down the Euphrates River.

Besides cultivating their own gardens, Jews worked on large plantations, where barley and sesame were the major crops, and on estates de-

Tilling a Mesopotamian Field

"He took of the seed of the land and planted it in fertile soil; he placed it beside abundant waters" (Ezek. 17.5). To the wooden, iron-tipped plow common in Egypt and Israel, the Mesopotamians added the seed drill. As shown above and in the 7th-century B.C. Assyrian relief below, the drill is simply a tube

leading downward from a seed basket to just behind the plowpoint. Seeds drop directly into the furrow and wastage is minimized. Although the Hebrews in exile must have become familiar with the seeder plow, it never became common in Israel, where seeds were scattered by hand. Both methods are still used today.

voted to palm tree cultivation. Many became shepherds, tending herds of sheep, goats and cattle. They also found employment in the cities, at their old crafts or new ones. Clay was one of the country's main natural resources, so potters were in great demand. Workers in copper and bronze

were also needed to make utensils and weapons.

As the years passed, more and more of the newcomers entered commerce, and some even became wealthy. Babylonia, unlike Palestine, had developed a complex banking system, and enterprising Jews soon learned how to deal with letters of credit, bank notes and interest rates. In Nippur, for example, some Jews dealt with the mercantile and banking firm of Murashu Sons; about two centuries later, when the area fell to Persia, Murashu would act as tax-collecting agents for the new rulers of Babylonia.

At Tel-abib the Jews built one-story houses by local construction methods, using clay bricks. The walls were made very thick for insulation against the fierce heat of the plain. There were no windows, except for small ventilation holes near the ceiling. Ezekiel, too, built himself a house and planted a garden next to it. He married a Judean woman, but nothing more is known about her.

The exiles adapted themselves to native ways of life. They slept on mats on earthen floors, squatted to eat from trays, and drank beer and wine brewed from dates. Aside from vegetables, the staple food was crisp barley bread, baked in pancake shape. Only the more affluent could afford beef and lamb, but there was plenty of fish and fowl. It is possible that the Jews shared the Babylonian taste for roasted grasshoppers.

Though free to practice their religion, the Jews had no temple or organized clergy. As they were absorbed into Babylonian society, their national and religious consciousness tended to dissolve. Ezekiel, like other priests in exile, labored to hold his community to the faith of their fathers. In part to counteract the appeal of pagan worship, he stressed Mosaic rituals such as circumcision, and prescribed ceremonies of cleanliness and the observance of the Sabbath and holidays.

A Call to Prophecy

Almost five years after the beginning of the Babylonian exile, the Jews in exile and in Jerusalem were greatly excited: popular prophets were saying that the exile would soon be over. It was at this same time, in July of 593, that Ezekiel received his call to prophecy. While he was walking in the countryside, a tremendous thunderstorm broke, the heavens opened and he beheld an apocalyptic vision. The Book of Ezekiel starts with his description of that vision—so complex

An Assyrian Home

Jewish exiles in Assyria saw homes such as these—boxlike structures with inclined roofs, grouped around a central courtyard. Reed mats alone furnished ordinary homes, but the more affluent had stools and beds. On the walls were a household altar and cooking vessels hung beyond the reach of vermin—the rats, mice, scorpions and lizards that sought refuge inside from the fierce heat of the sun.

and strange that through many centuries rabbinical scholars would seek to interpret its meanings.

Ezekiel saw four creatures in human form, each with four faces—man, lion, ox and eagle—and each with two pairs of widespread wings and the burnished hoofs of a calf. The whirring of their wings was "like the thunder of the Almighty." The four "living creatures darted to and fro, like a flash of lightning," and beside them were four great gleaming wheels, and wheels within the wheels, "their rims . . . full of eyes." Overhead he saw something like a platform, above it a chariot-throne and on the throne in human form "the glory of the Lord." The whole scene was bathed in blinding light and flames.

When he saw the Lord, Ezekiel fell upon his face as he heard the divine voice. "Son of man," it said, "I send you to the people of Israel . . . who have rebelled against me; they and their fathers have transgressed against me to this very day. . . . and you shall say to them, 'Thus says

the Lord God.' And whether they hear or refuse to hear . . . they will know that there has been a prophet among them. And you, son of man, be not afraid of them, nor be afraid of their words, though briers and thorns are with you and you sit upon scorpions . . ."

Then the Lord's hand stretched out to Ezekiel, holding a scroll upon which were written "words of lamentation and mourning and woe." Commanded to eat the scroll, Ezekiel found it honey-sweet. "And go, get you to the exiles, to your people," the voice continued. Then the Lord lifted him up, Ezekiel recorded, "and I went in bitterness in the heat of my spirit, the hand of the Lord being strong upon me . . ." Returning to his countrymen in Tel-abib, he "sat there overwhelmed among them seven days."

Thus the priest, then about 30 years old, emerged as prophet. After his seven-day shock, he again heard the Lord speak: "Son of man, I have made you a watchman for the house of Israel; whenever you hear a word from my mouth, you shall give them warning from me."

The Ordained Fate of Jerusalem

Ezekiel then set about speaking to the exiles. He told them that God was present in Babylonia and everywhere else, not just in Judah—unlike pagan gods whose supposed power was limited to certain territories—and he warned them of the consequences of disobedience. Moreover, their hopes for a speedy end to their exile were inspired by lying prophets. But many found support for such optimism in the fact that Jehoiachin was not only alive but received royal rations for his table, and in the fact that Jerusalem and the temple were still standing. False prophets had encouraged their vain hopes.

Ezekiel therefore sought to destroy the erroneous sense of security. In oracles and in symbolic actions he spoke of new and greater calamities still to come, justifying God's wrath by the continued wickedness of Judah. Once he used an earthen model of Jerusalem, complete with toy soldiers. Lying down beside the model, he ate bad food and drank little water, to indicate the misery and famine awaiting Jerusalem.

On another occasion the prophet packed a small knapsack that a fugitive might carry. After dark, he dug a hole through the clay wall of his home, crawled through it and walked away into the night. To the puzzled onlookers he explained: "This oracle concerns the prince in Jerusalem and all the house of Israel," who shall dig through their walls and slink away in the dark.

In a new vision, Ezekiel felt himself transported to Jerusalem. There he was shown 70 elders in the temple committing "vile abominations," with "all kinds of creeping things, and loathsome beasts, and all the idols of the house of Israel." Thus he was able to explain and to justify the divine vengeance still to come.

The influence of Babylonia, so powerful and prosperous, was strong upon people far from their homeland and their temple. Many must have thought the pagan deities greater than their own God, who seemed unable to save them. Ezekiel strove to convince the skeptics that the very calamities that befell them were demonstrations of the Lord's power, in that they fulfilled his warnings. The faithful should seek redemption by returning to the covenant even in captivity: "Thus says the Lord God: Though I removed them far off among the nations, and though I scattered them among the countries, yet I have been a sanctuary to them . . .''

Some exiles argued bitterly, moreover, that they were being punished for the guilt of their ancestors. Ezekiel angrily rejected this attempt to transfer guilt to their fathers. Instead, he insisted that each individual was responsible for his own actions: "The soul that sins shall die. The son shall not suffer for the iniquity of the father, nor the father suffer for the iniquity of the son . . . and the wickedness of the wicked shall be upon himself."

Merciless in denouncing his own people, Ezekiel did not spare the heathen nations, lest their present power be thought to prove their idols' influence. In a number of impassioned oracles, he pronounced the doom of Ammon, Moab, Edom, Philistia and especially Tyre and Egypt.

Roots of the Synagogue

The prophet evidently was held in high esteem. Many heard his discourses, and the elders of Jewish communities came to consult him. Because God was their sanctuary, he taught, they

Babylonian medicine combined religion, magic and science. At right a priest-physician examines the liver of a sacrificed sheep to divine the future of a patient, pegging his findings on a clay model of the liver (above) marked with magical omens. Whips, masks and a clay statuette are present to drive off disease-causing demons, who were thought to fear their own image. More practical wisdom is evident here in the foods prescribed: tear-inducing raw onion to cleanse the patient's infected eye, and a medicinal beverage. An exiled Jew takes notes, hoping to add this cure to Jewish medicine.

did not require a temple in Babylon, but needed only keep their faith. Wherever true believers came together, the Lord would be with them. In the Jewish settlements small groups began to gather for prayer and study of the writings. Such assemblies were known as synagogues—they would later replace the temple as the center of Hebrew worship. The congregation needed mainly to obey the Mosaic laws and follow the rituals, which Ezekiel and other priests codified.

The forebodings of Ezekiel, as well as the prophecies of Jeremiah in the homeland, were coming true. Zedekiah, who governed Judah for the Babylonians, was pressured by his nationalist counselors to rebel in 589. Nebuchadnezzar thereupon sent armies against Judah. They swept through the country, demolishing its cities, until they reached Jerusalem. The ensuing siege lasted about two years. Once more Ezekiel, as commanded by the Lord, acted out Jerusalem's destined fate. Into a cauldron over a fire he cast choice pieces of meat and bones and cooked them to cinders—as a symbol of the impending sack of the Holy City.

Early in the siege, Ezekiel's wife died. When people asked why he did not mourn, he quoted the Lord, saying "you shall not mourn or weep, but you shall pine away in your iniquities and groan to one another." He was setting an example of submission to God's will: Jerusalem was receiving its deserved chastisement.

In 587 news reached Babylonia that Jerusalem had fallen, thousands of its inhabitants had been slaughtered and everything in it, including the temple, had been destroyed. Again hundreds of the upper classes and skilled workers were carried off to Babylonia. The burning of the temple, on the ninth of Ab (July-August), is still observed by Jews as a day of mourning.

This second deportation is generally regarded as the definitive start of the captivity. It marked the end of the kingdom of Judah and its Jerusalem-centered cult. Israel had ceased to exist as a nation. Nebuchadnezzar would order further deportations from the remnants of the Jewish population in subsequent years. The total number of exiles to Babylonia, from the first contingent to the last, has been estimated at between 10,000 and 25,000.

Shortly after the fall of Jerusalem, Ezekiel beheld a vision of the ultimate return to Israel. In the vision, the Lord transported him to a valley filled with dry human bones, and commanded him to prophesy that they would live again: "and as I prophesied, there was a noise, and behold, a rattling; and the bones came together, bone to its bone. And as I looked, there were sinews on them . . . and the breath came into them, and they lived, and stood upon their feet, an exceedingly great host."

Then the Lord told him, "Son of man, these bones are the whole house of Israel. Behold, they say, 'Our bones are dried up, and our hope is lost; we are clean cut off.' . . . Thus says the Lord God: Behold, I will open your graves, and raise you from your graves, O my people; and I will bring you home into the land of Israel."

The New Jerusalem

Ezekiel's preaching of doom now changed to prophecies of glorious restoration. The Lord, he said, would be like a good shepherd regathering his flock into the fold. God would correct the false impression that heathen gods had overcome him, "and the nations will know that I am the Lord . . . when through you I vindicate my holiness before their eyes."

By bringing his chosen people back to the Promised Land, Ezekiel said, the Lord would prove that he was the only God. The Jews would renounce iniquity and again honor the Mosaic covenant. "Thus says the Lord God . . . I will sprinkle clean water upon you, and you shall be clean from all your uncleannesses, and from all your idols I will cleanse you. A new heart I will give you, and a new spirit I will put within you; and I will take out of your flesh the heart of stone and give you a heart of flesh. . . . You shall dwell in the land which I gave to your fathers; and you shall be my people, and I will be your God."

Ezekiel continued his work as a priest, but evidently he refrained from prophecy for about 13 years. When he resumed his inspired utterances, his themes were redemption and restoration, so that he would later be called "the prophet of reconstruction." In the year 573 B.C., another ecstatic vision transported him into a resplendent future in which a united monarchy of Israel and Judah would be governed by a messianic king of the line of David as well as an independent priesthood of the line of Zadok.

In the vision he was conducted through a restored Jerusalem by an angelic architect, "with a

line of flax and a measuring reed in his hand . . ."
The angel said, "Son of man, look with your eyes
. . . declare all that you see to the house of Israel."
The architect measured out virtually every inch
of the temple to be built. Then the Lord spoke,
giving Ezekiel a code of conduct for the city and

Gourmet Dining in Assyria

Pomegranates and certain kinds of locusts were considered delicacies by Old Testament peoples. "Among the winged insects . . . you may eat . . . the locust according to its kind" (Lev. 11.21–22). A cooling drink was made from pomegranates, and the locusts were eaten roasted or raw, or dried by threading (left) for later use. Rich in protein, locusts were ground and put into honey and date spreads, bread and other dishes. King Ashurbanipal enjoyed these foods, as this relief shows.

the new temple, the organization of the priest-hood, details of sacrifices and ritual, the layout of the city, and the apportionment of the nation's land among the 12 original tribes.

It was an ideal state and an ideal new Jerusalem in the future that Ezekiel described to the exiles. He pictured it as a theocratic state centered in the temple, and a sharp line would be drawn between the civil and the sacred authorities.

Preserving the Writings

Ezekiel's prophecies helped keep the faith alive among the captive Jews. Though some did drift away, marrying Babylonians and losing their separate identity, a large core of the faithful survived the temptations of their new surroundings. Among the generations born in Babylonia, many clung to their unique heritage. The captivity set patterns for religious survival that would preserve Judaism far outside its homeland for centuries to come.

The Babylonian exile, in addition, stimulated important and enduring literary achievements. Priests and scribes began the collection process that produced the prophetic books of the Bible. They also recorded the first five books of the Bible, the Pentateuch, as a written theological history of the world from the Creation to the giving of the laws and preparation for the Conquest. Many of the Psalms were composed in this period, among them the stirring Psalm 137, with its lament of the exile experience and its pledge of eternal allegiance to Zion:

"By the waters of Babylon,
    there we sat down and wept,
    when we remembered Zion.
On the willows there
    we hung up our lyres.
For there our captors
    required of us songs,
and our tormentors, mirth, saying,
    'Sing us one of the songs of Zion!'

How shall we sing the Lord's song
    in a foreign land?
If I forget you, O Jerusalem,
    let my right hand wither!
Let my tongue cleave to the roof of
    my mouth,
    if I do not remember you,
if I do not set Jerusalem
    above my highest joy!"

Ezekiel never saw the new Jerusalem. The latest date appearing in his chronicle is the twenty-seventh year of his exile, around 570 B.C. After about 25 years of ministry, he died in Babylonia. His efforts to keep his people together and to sustain their faith had helped the nation of Israel survive a long captivity and provided a source of hope for the future return from exile. The institutions Ezekiel helped develop in those years of captivity insured that Judaism would remain a vital force long after the Jews had been dispersed from their native land.

The story of Ezekiel is told in the Book of Ezekiel.

The Persians: Enlightened Conquerors

"Thus says Cyrus king of Persia: The Lord, the God of heaven, has given me all the kingdoms of the earth, and he has charged me to build him a house at Jerusalem" (Ezra 1.2). *Moving into a Near East exhausted by centuries of conflict, the Persians under Cyrus swept down from the Iranian mountains and easily took Babylonia in 539 B.C. Within 25 years their empire stretched from India to Ethiopia and from the Caucasus Mountains to the Arabian Sea. But as impressive as their military deeds were, of more lasting significance was the Persian philosophy of government: they strove for peaceful coexistence among the nations of the empire through a policy of toleration. This liberalism broke sharply with the usual repressiveness of conquering peoples, and cast its influence on Greek, Roman and many modern civilizations.*

Two Persian warriors—part of the king's special regiment known as "the 10,000 immortals"—appear in their brightly colored costumes on the enameled tiles of the palace at Susa, one of the empire's capitals. These experts with the bow and spear were considered the elite fighting forces of the Persian army.

The empire was composed of 20 administrative districts, each autonomous but each under a Persian "satrap," or governor, who held semiroyal status. Above is one such official, with crown and scepter, sitting behind his chariot and driver. The satrap's duties included overseeing the local finances—an important task, for with the Persians' introduction of coinage to the empire, trade was flourishing. Above the satraps were the king and his advisors, and assisting them in their governorships were the king's secretaries. One of the latter was the reformer Ezra, whose influence was vital in insuring his people's return to Jerusalem.

On the stairway of the great audience hall at Persepolis, a lion is shown killing a bull. This palace complex, which also included a large harem room and treasury, was built as the official headquarters of the king. It lay about 150 miles north of the Persian Gulf and about 300 miles southeast of the empire's winter capital at Susa. Above the stairway are remains of the tall, slender columns from the "hall of a hundred columns." The complex stood until 330 B.C., when Alexander the Great conquered the Persians and razed it.

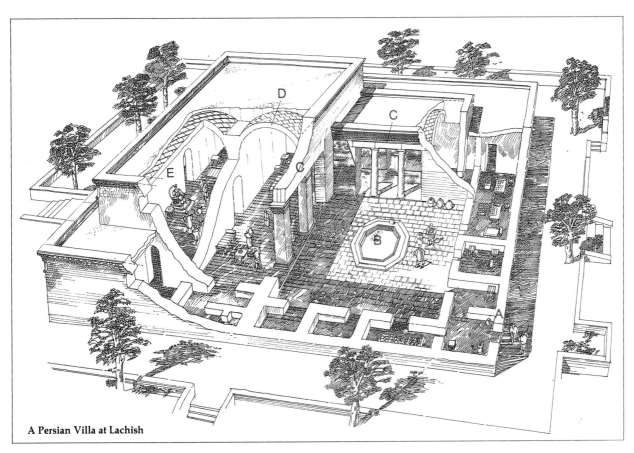

A Persian Villa at Lachish

The governors of the Persian provinces lived rather comfortably. Ruins have been found which may have been the base of one such governor's residence—a villa at Lachish, just southwest of Jerusalem. Above is an artist's rendering of the villa. It was entered through a single gateway (A) leading to an open courtyard (B) which might have contained a pool. The surrounding buildings show features new to Palestinian architecture, among them the use of columns at the two main entryways (C) and barrel-vault ceilings (D) over some of the apartments. These vaults, an innovation of Assyrian architecture, provided a way to span areas much greater than those of conventional, flat ceilings, without requiring center supports. The Romans later used the device extensively in their architecture. At the extreme interior of the villa was what appears to have been a throne room (E), where official business might have been conducted. Around the courtyard were other compartments, probably for servants, storage and guest facilities. The villa dates from the prophet Nehemiah's time, the 5th century B.C.

The famous Persian army which conquered the Near East did so without the benefit of much armor or heavy equipment. Rather, the large cavalry and infantry relied on its mobility, courage and skill as archers and spearmen. The favorite weapon was the heavy composite bow, as carried by the soldier at left. Archery was so important that the great Persian kings had themselves portrayed as archers on their coins. According to their government's policy of accommodation, the army did not usually destroy the towns of a conquered enemy. Instead, garrison troops were stationed there and the people were allowed to retain their customs and traditions.

Chapter 17

In a tale set in the time of the Persian Empire, one of the great women
of the Bible risks her life to save her people from the persecution of a hostile nation.

Esther: Heroine of the Jews

Esther, or Hadassah in Hebrew, is the heroine of an an-
cient chronicle set in the splendors of the Persian Empire
at its height, in the fifth century B.C. This is a dramatic
and rather gory tale of love, hate and palace intrigue, of
a beautiful Jewish maiden who married King Ahasu-
erus. Esther succeeded in averting a massacre of Jews,
plotted by a grand vizier named Haman, and then
avenged the plot. This story probably derives from the
many tales of persecution and deliverance in the Persian
era, handed down from generation to generation.

The tale begins with an account of a sumptuous reception staged by King Ahasuerus in his
winter palace at Susa (Shushan) "for all his
princes and servants, the army chiefs of Persia
and Media and the nobles and governors of the
provinces" to display "the riches of royal glory
and the splendor and pomp of his majesty."

(Ahasuerus' reign is often identified with that
of Xerxes, son of Darius the Great. However, at
the time Esther's story supposedly took place, he
and his army were quelling revolts in distant
parts of the empire, and probably saw little of
Susa. Furthermore, there is no record that Xerxes
might have had a Jewish wife.)

Ahasuerus had ample cause for pride in his
winter capital. Of the three cities that served as
his headquarters during the year, Susa was perhaps the finest. Persepolis, some 300 miles southeast of Susa, was the official capital, the site of
the most imposing temples and the burial place
of the kings. Occupied only in the spring months,

it was here that political and military leaders
from the entire empire—127 provinces stretching
from India to Ethiopia in one direction, to the
Mediterranean coast in the other—gathered to
pay tribute to the monarch. Ecbatana, 200 miles
north in the highlands of Media, was the royal
refuge from the fierce summer heat of Susa.

A glimpse of the opulence of the winter
palace is provided in the scriptural narrative. It
speaks of "marble pillars, and also couches of
gold and silver on a mosaic pavement of porphyry, marble, mother-of-pearl and precious
stones," and notes: "Drinks were served in
golden goblets."

Ahasuerus no doubt reveled in the magnificence of his *apadana,* or audience hall, at Susa.
Kneeling bulls sculpted in pairs topped the tall,
slender, distinctively Persian columns that supported the roof. The walls of many-colored
glazed bricks were decorated with reliefs showing fantastic winged bulls and other mythological
creatures and Persian archers and spearmen.

Materials from every corner of the empire—
ebony and silver from Egypt, gold from Asia
Minor, ivory from Ethiopia and semiprecious
stones from east of the Caspian Sea—had been
used to construct the luxurious palace. Darius

The story of Esther tells that among the hundreds of beautiful
women whom Ahasuerus (Xerxes) called to his palace, she "found
grace and favor in his sight more than all the virgins" (Est. 2.17).
This carved Persian portrait shows the same regal bearing Ahasu-
erus might have shown when he first beheld the Jewish maiden.

had brought in foreign laborers and specialized craftsmen to complete the edifice, and they embellished it with designs from their native lands.

Outside the royal quarter—containing the palace, the king's carefully guarded harem and the treasury—Susa was a bustling cosmopolitan center. Long-haired, perfumed visitors and envoys from Babylonia, itinerant Greek scientists, Jewish merchants and Persian infantrymen in coats of mail and long trousers jostled one another on the market-lined streets. The geographical center of what was then the largest empire ever assembled, Susa was a natural crossroads for travelers on the great highway system from Asia Minor to northern India.

The Persians treated most of the conquered kingdoms, including Judah and Israel, with a leniency exceptional in that period. Subject peoples were allowed to worship their own gods and live by their own customs. Countries which had not actively fought the Persians kept their own forms of government and maintained armies, though under Persian officers.

Ahasuerus saw few of his multitude of subjects face to face. In the interests of security, a curtain isolated the throne room from the rest of the hall, which was some 250 feet square, with beams of the famous Lebanon cedar. Only a select few—the seven nobles who were his closest advisers—could approach the king's person without invitation. All others, even members of his family, knew that to enter unbidden for any reason was to risk the death penalty. Only if Ahasuerus extended his golden scepter toward an intruder would he be spared.

Such was the setting in which the drama of Esther was said to have unfolded.

Ahasuerus and Mordecai

The royal reception was wound up with a seven-day banquet. On the final day, "when the heart of the king was merry with wine," he sent eunuchs to bring his queen, Vashti, to him, "to show the peoples and the princes her beauty; for she was fair to behold." Amazingly for those times, Vashti refused to come. Her husband's drunken wish to exhibit her to the male guests must have seemed humiliating. Ahasuerus was infuriated. His counselors urged him to take drastic action, lest other wives might take to disobeying their husbands. Accordingly the king banished Vashti

from his presence and sought a new queen.

"Now there was a Jew in Susa the capital whose name was Mordecai," the chronicle relates. He was one of many Jews in that city. When Cyrus conquered Babylonia some 50 years earlier, he had given all Jews there permission to return to their Palestinian homeland. But they had been well treated by the Babylonians. Many of them had prospered as merchants and craftsmen. New generations had grown up without personal memory of their fathers' country. The majority therefore had no desire to journey to the arid hills of Judah, now part of the fifth satrapy of Persia, called Abar-Nahara ("beyond the river"). With the new freedom of travel afforded under Persian rule, however, many Jews moved to other parts of the empire, including the capital Susa.

The Jews of Persia

Not much is known about the Jews outside Palestine in the Persian epoch. From earlier Biblical accounts, such as those of Ezekiel and Ezra, we know that they clung to their Mosaic faith under the Babylonians and, given the Persian tolerance of varied religious and national customs, they doubtless continued to keep their Jewish identity.

Thus their day-to-day life in Susa was not much different from the life of their fellow Jews in the homeland. Once every seven days the Sabbath was kept, perhaps in the kind of synagogues that had evolved in Babylonia. One day each spring their homes were redolent with the odors of roast lamb and bitter herbs for the ritual Passover meal commemorating the ancient exodus from Egypt. Young children still heard the tales of Israel's past heroes, triumphs and tribulations. Little suspecting that another such threat could arise in Susa, they were reminded how often their forebears had suffered persecution.

The scriptural record identifies Mordecai as one "who had been carried away from Jerusalem" by Nebuchadnezzar. The known dates, however, make this impossible; presumably he was a descendant of an exiled Jerusalem family. There is evidence that a man called Marduk, which would be Mordecai in Hebrew, held some official post in Susa. If this was indeed the Mordecai of the Esther saga, it would be one of the few authentic parts of the legend.

Mordecai had a young cousin, originally called Hadassah but later, Esther, a name based on Ishtar, goddess of love and war: "the maiden was beautiful and lovely, and when her father and her mother died, Mordecai adopted her as his own daughter." She was not to remain with him for long. At Ahasuerus' command, beautiful virgins of the empire were summoned to the palace at Susa, for the king was seeking a new principal wife to replace Vashti. "So when the king's order and his edict were proclaimed, and when many maidens were gathered in Susa . . . Esther also was taken into the king's palace and put in custody of Hegai who had charge of the women." Her prudent foster-father instructed her to conceal the fact that she was Jewish.

Baking Over an Open Fire

"Take wheat and barley, beans and lentils, millet and spelt . . . and make bread of them" (Ezek. 4.9). Bread was usually made from either wheat or barley flour, but in times of need such additional ingredients as these would be added. The simplest method of baking is shown here. The small stove is made of pottery fragments and clay, and flat stones are heating among its coals. When sufficiently hot, the stones will be swept clean of ashes and flat cakes of dough will be placed on them to bake.

The hopeful girls were placed in the harem, where the royal wives and concubines lived. It was Hegai's duty to give every promising maiden a regimen of beauty treatment—oils, perfumes, massages, hair styles—to enhance whatever attractiveness she already possessed. This process could last more than a year, after which the girl was sent to the king: "In the evening she went, and in the morning she came back to the second harem in custody of [a] eunuch who was in charge of the concubines; she did not go in to the king again, unless the king delighted in her and she was summoned by name."

Esther Becomes the Queen

For all but a few women in the harem this might be the only time they were ever to be in the monarch's company. When Esther's turn finally came, she probably expected that her first night with Ahasuerus would be the last. However, "when Esther was taken to King Ahasuerus into his royal palace in the tenth month, which is the month of Tebeth, in the seventh year of his reign, the king loved Esther more than all the women, and she found grace and favor in his sight more than all the virgins, so that he set the royal crown on her head and made her queen . . ."

To celebrate his marriage to this girl, "He . . . granted a remission of taxes . . . and gave gifts with royal liberality." This was clear indication that he loved and esteemed her, for remission of taxes was no small matter, and it brought joy to peoples throughout the empire.

Mordecai was probably a minor gatekeeper at the palace and was thus able to communicate with his cousin. One night he happened to overhear two of the king's chamberlains plotting to assassinate their sovereign. At once Mordecai reported the treachery to Esther, who in turn warned the king. "When the affair was investigated and found to be so, the men were both hanged on the gallows." The episode was duly inscribed in the official palace annals.

The prisoners were not hanged by the neck from a rope. Instead they were probably impaled. First long, sharpened poles were run through their bodies, then the blunt ends were driven into the ground, thereby suspending or "hanging" the unfortunates until they died slowly. Persian custom prescribed that political prisoners be put to death by this gruesome method.

Some time later, Ahasuerus elevated a man named Haman to the highest office, prime minister or grand vizier. If the seven nobles who counseled the king were privileged—having fine homes, riches and almost unlimited access to Ahasuerus—then Haman was even more so. Besides wealth and power, he enjoyed signs of honor especially dear to his wicked heart: "And all the king's servants who were at the king's gate bowed down and did obeisance to Haman; for the king had so commanded concerning him." Only one, the stubborn Mordecai, "did not bow down or do obeisance."

A Royal Decree

The Jew's dangerous disobedience was very likely motivated by an ancient racial feud. For Mordecai was of the tribe of Benjamin, and Haman was an Amalekite of the Agag family. Long ago their respective ancestors had fought and died for possession of Canaan. Now the Benjaminite could not demean himself to an Agagite though he be the highest official under the king.

Haman was so enraged that revenge on one Jew would not suffice: he "sought to destroy all the Jews, the people of Mordecai, throughout the whole kingdom of Ahasuerus." To obtain the king's sanction for the mass murders, Haman was forced to use all the cunning he possessed. Ever since the reign of Cyrus, his successors had adhered to his policy of winning the loyalty of conquered subjects by peaceful rather than violent means. In extreme cases it had been thought necessary to crush local dissenters, but never had they annihilated a country or a people. The grand vizier's plan went against this policy.

Knowing that before a royal decree could be issued the king was obligated to confer with his seven advisers, Haman managed to go over their heads. With a combination of flattery and bribery, he was able to act alone in the king's name.

"Then Haman said to Ahasuerus, 'There is a certain people scattered abroad and dispersed among the peoples in all the provinces of your kingdom; their laws are different from those of every other people, and they do not keep the king's laws, so that it is not for the king's profit to tolerate them. If it please the king, let it be decreed that they be destroyed, and I will pay ten thousand talents of silver into the hands of those who have charge of the king's business, that they may put it into . . . his treasuries.'"

Ahasuerus rejected the bribe—no doubt money Haman intended to steal and extort from his victims—but assented to the harsher crime. "The money is given to you," he told Haman, "the people also, to do with them as it seems good to you." Then he gave Haman his royal signet ring, enabling the vizier to validate his order.

"Let the king appoint officers . . . to gather all the beautiful young virgins to the harem in Susa the capital" (Est. 2.3). When Esther was summoned by King Ahasuerus, she might have seen an entertainment featuring acrobats and jugglers. Here members of the Persian harem, closely guarded, watch from the palace porch as musicians beat time to the performance with rattles. Jugglers were common throughout the Near East, and a painting on a bit of pottery (above) shows that acrobatic dancing was also performed. Other entertainment included boxing, wrestling and animal acts.

Haman thereupon wrote an edict commanding every official "to destroy, to slay, and to annihilate all Jews, young and old, women and children, in one day, the thirteenth day of the twelfth month, which is the month of Adar, and to plunder their goods." He had chosen this day by casting "Pur," or lots. Possibly the lots were small stones with designs carved or painted on them, like modern dice.

Preparations for the bloodbath were thorough: "A copy of the document was to be issued as a decree in every province by proclamation to all the peoples to be ready for that day." The royal couriers carried Haman's orders by a rapid relay system, riding the fleetest horses, spurring them to the limit day and night, stopping only to replace their exhausted mounts. By this method the residents of Sardis, some 1500 miles away in Asia Minor, for example, might see the posted edict within a week or two.

An ordinary traveler, on the other hand, if he covered a leisurely 18 or 20 miles a day, would probably stop each evening at one of over a hundred inns along the route. He would rest, relax with a cup of Persian wine and converse with other travelers. Normally he would have to allow himself at least three months for the same kind of journey.

"When Mordecai learned all that had been done, Mordecai rent his clothes and put on sackcloth and ashes. . . . And in every province, wherever the king's command and his decree came, there was great mourning among the Jews, with fasting and weeping and lamenting . . ."

Esther's Bravery

Mordecai asked Queen Esther to intervene at once to save their people. This was the twelfth year of Ahasuerus' reign, and she had been his

"[Esther] sent garments to clothe Mordecai, so that he might take off his sackcloth" (Est. 4.4). The garments Esther sent might have resembled those of this Persian dignitary, who wears a medium-long tunic, Persian-type trousers and a headdress like a monk's hood, called the "kyrbasia." Such clothing was usually worn for traveling. The silver figurine is from the court of Artaxerxes I (464–424 B.C.).

gather all the Jews to be found in Susa, and hold a fast on my behalf, and neither eat nor drink for three days, night or day. I and my maids will also fast as you do. Then I will go to the king, though it is against the law; and if I perish, I perish."

At the end of the fasting period Esther, wearing her royal robes, made her way toward the audience hall down a corridor which connected it with the harem. From the huge gallery's entrance she could see dozens of men waiting to present their petitions, messages and gifts to the king's seven noble advisors, who then recommended an audience or discouraged the king from granting one. Here an exhausted relay rider from Egypt was admitted to report a minor insurrection; there a Babylonian merchant in his turban and long white tunic presented 100 jars of fine-quality sesame oil to the king—but did not receive an audience. Each transaction was promptly recorded in the court annals.

Although she "had not been called to come in to the king these thirty days," Esther apparently ignored the seven advisors and proceeded directly to the inner court behind the embroidered curtain. "And when the king saw Queen Esther standing in the court, she found favor in his sight and he held out to Esther the golden scepter . . ."

Relieved that she had gained an audience, she begged her husband to dine in her quarters the following evening and to bring Haman along. Ahasuerus graciously consented. Thrilled by the invitation, Haman "went out that day joyful and glad of heart." But when he "saw Mordecai in the king's gate, that he neither rose nor trembled before him," Haman was again filled with wrath. Taking counsel with his family and friends, he ordered a gallows built on which to impale the Jewish upstart as soon as he could obtain the king's official permission.

The banquet at Esther's quarters was pleasant and her guests agreed to join her again the next day. On the night following the first meal, the king, unable to fall asleep, had some court records read to him. In one of these he came across the old entry about how Mordecai had uncovered an assassination plot. "What honor or dignity has been bestowed on Mordecai for this?" he inquired and learned that nothing had been done.

In the morning, before Haman could broach the subject of Mordecai's execution, the king asked, "What shall be done to the man whom the king delights to honor?" Supposing that the ref-

consort for five years, but apparently had not yet revealed that she was Jewish. It seems unlikely indeed that, had the king known of it, he would have so readily approved Haman's bloody plan. Evidently Esther now hesitated to disclose her secret. Besides, should she approach the king without being summoned, she risked the death penalty. But her foster-father was persuasive. "Think not," he warned, "that in the king's palace you will escape any more than all the other Jews."

So Esther agreed, saying to Mordecai, "Go,

erence was to himself, Haman proposed that the lucky man be given royal raiment, set on the king's horse and led to the city square by a high official crying, "Thus shall it be done to the man whom the king delights to honor." To Haman's horror, he was commanded to heap upon Mordecai the honors he had thought were his own.

At the second banquet Esther dramatically exposed Haman's villainy and at last revealed her own Jewish origin. She pleaded urgently: "If I have found favor in your sight, O king, and if it please the king, let my life be given me at my petition, and my people at my request. For we are sold, I and my people, to be destroyed, to be slain, and to be annihilated."

Who "would presume to do this?" Ahasuerus asked, and Esther replied, "A foe and enemy! This wicked Haman!"

The king, in a rage, stormed out of the room into the garden. Returning in a few minutes, he found Esther sitting on a couch and Haman prostrate at her feet, pleading for mercy. Misinterpreting the import of the scene, the king shouted angrily, "Will he even assault the queen in my presence, in my own house?"

One of the attendants then informed him that "the gallows which Haman has prepared for Mordecai, whose word saved the king, is standing in Haman's house . . ." And the king said, "Hang him on that." So "they hanged Haman on the gallows which he had prepared for Mordecai." For good measure, at Esther's suggestion, his 10 sons were also hanged.

Haman's possessions, including his house, were turned over to Queen Esther. More important, Mordecai was appointed grand vizier in Haman's place. He left the palace arrayed in "royal robes of blue and white, with a great golden crown and a mantle of fine linen and purple, while the city of Susa shouted and rejoiced."

The Deliverance of the Jews

The impending massacre of the Jews, however, was not yet averted. Under the law, an edict sealed with the royal signet ring could not be undone even by the king himself. Mordecai was entrusted with the signet ring and authorized to write a counterorder in the king's name. His solution was to empower the Jews to defend themselves when attacked on the appointed day. The decree was rushed to all parts of the empire by royal couriers. All who had received the original Haman order presumably realized that it need no longer be rigidly enforced.

Mordecai's edict "allowed the Jews who were in every city to gather and defend their lives . . ." Thus, "on the very day when the enemies of the Jews hoped to get the mastery over them," the Jews were ready "to lay hands on such as sought their hurt." Many of them had served in the Persian army. This training did not desert them now.

In Susa itself, on the day set for their extermination, the Jews instead "slew and destroyed five hundred men." Esther pleaded for and was granted a second day of vengeance, "and they slew three hundred men in Susa . . ." In the provinces at the same time they "slew seventy-five thousand of those who hated them . . ." Both in the capital and in the country at large, the chronicle emphasizes, "they laid no hand on the plunder"—in sharp contrast to Haman's planned confiscations.

The Jewish reprisals in self-defense took place on the thirteenth day of Adar, "and on the fourteenth day they rested and made that a day of feasting and gladness." No doubt they needed rest after the great slaughter. Awed by their prowess, "many of the peoples of the country declared themselves Jews, for the fear of the Jews had fallen upon them."

Mordecai "recorded these things, and sent letters to all the Jews . . . enjoining them that they should keep the fourteenth day of the month Adar and also the fifteenth day of the same, year by year, as the days on which the Jews got relief from their enemies . . . Therefore they called these days Purim, after the term Pur." Esther the queen also sent out letters to this effect.

A story of triumph over persecution naturally appealed to a people so often persecuted. Though the name is not Hebrew but Akkadian, and though the festival has little relevance to the worship of God, Purim became a favorite holiday among Jews, even to our day. In the synagogue services, veneration of Esther is more than matched by abuse of Haman—every mention of his name is greeted with stamping and noise.

What happened to Esther after these events, and how long she remained the queen, is not recorded. Presumably, she lived happily ever after.

The story of Esther is told in the Book of Esther.

Chapter 18

The exiled Jews begin their return to their devastated land and receive
the inspired guidance they need to build a new nation on the ruins of the old.

Leaders of a New Jerusalem: Nehemiah and Ezra

In the middle of the fifth century B.C., *some 90 years after the first exiles returned from Babylonia, Judah was a small, weak and impoverished province of Persia. Jerusalem, ravaged and defenseless, lay in ruins. Moreover, pagan practices had corrupted the religion of the Jews and debased and distorted its rituals. At this critical juncture two great leaders emerged—Nehemiah and Ezra. Born and raised to manhood in Babylonia, their labors eventually restored Jerusalem and the Jewish religion.*

After Cyrus, the Persian empire builder, defeated Babylonia in 539, he proved remarkably tolerant toward conquered peoples. He decreed that the Jews could return to their native Judah and rebuild the temple which had been burned by the Babylonians in 587. He even restored to them the temple vessels carried off by the Babylonians and promised that the cost of the new temple would "be paid from the royal treasury."

But not all the exiled Jews were interested in this offer. In the years of exile new generations had grown up. Many families had prospered in Babylonia and preferred to remain in their new homeland rather than face an uncertain future. Nor did they need to return to Judah to follow the religion of their fathers. The faith had survived better in exile than on its native soil: the center of Judaism had shifted to Babylonia.

Only a minority chose to return to Judah in 538. Others from Babylonia joined them in later years. Against the dazzling vision of restoration

prophesied by Jeremiah and Ezekiel, the actual return was a crushing disappointment. The returning exiles found Judah a wilderness and the Holy City a wasteland. Corruption was everywhere, even among the priesthood. The descendants of those who had escaped captivity were hostile to the newcomers, fearing that their Babylonian brethren might try to recover their former family properties.

The exiles eventually began to rebuild the temple, but the people of Jerusalem refused to help. Some groups even tried to halt the construction. Progress was slow, and the project was soon abandoned. It was revived after the arrival of a second band of exiles led by the new provincial governor, Zerubbabel. This time the Samaritans, who lived in the province north of Judah and practiced an adulterated form of Judaism, offered their help. Zerubbabel, who considered the Samaritans heretics, rudely rejected their offer.

The temple was finally completed in 515. Although it was not nearly as magnificent or well built as the original temple erected during Solomon's reign, the returned exiles were proud of their achievement. Its dimensions were the same as those of Solomon's temple, and its plan and style were nearly identical, though the quality of

"Whoever is among you of all his people . . . let him go up to Jerusalem . . . and rebuild the house of the Lord" (Ezra 1.3). The Jews who returned from Babylon found their homeland in ruins. For more than a century, the new Judean community they founded extended less than 25 miles south from these hills near Jerusalem.

construction and the materials used were much poorer than those used in the first temple.

Despite the restoration of the temple, the morale of the community weakened from decade to decade. At last a leader appeared to restore the Jews' sagging spirits. He was Nehemiah, an official in the Persian court who returned to Jerusalem around 444 B.C.

Nehemiah, Governor of Judah

One of many Jews who had attained positions of influence in Persia, Nehemiah held the honorable post of cupbearer to King Artaxerxes in Susa (Shushan), the Persian king's winter capital. Most men who held positions of personal service to the monarch were eunuchs, and it's probable that Nehemiah himself was one.

Nehemiah frequently heard reports about conditions in Judah, and he grew increasingly concerned about the deteriorating situation there. In December 445 a kinsman named Hanani re-

Cupbearer to the Persian King

"When wine was before him, I took up the wine and gave it to the king" (Neh. 2.1). While in exile in the 5th century B.C., Nehemiah secured the honorable position of cupbearer to the Persian King Artaxerxes. Generally a beardless eunuch, this official served the king's wine and was his trusted confidant.

Enthroned above, a Persian king holds the royal scepter with which he signals courtiers to approach. His cupbearer serves from a golden vessel like the 6th- or 5th-century one below, inscribed "Darius the Great King."

turned from a visit to Judah with a gloomy report of what he had seen. Their fellow Jews, he explained, "are in great trouble and shame; the wall of Jerusalem is broken down, and its gates are destroyed by fire."

Nehemiah was overcome with grief. "When I heard these words," he wrote later, "I sat down and wept, and mourned for days; and I continued fasting and praying before the God of heaven." In despair, he resolved to ask the king's permission to go to Jerusalem.

The king agreed and appointed Nehemiah governor of Judah. With letters of authorization, a requisition for timber from the king's own forests and a company of officers and horsemen, Nehemiah departed. He probably reached Jerusalem sometime in 444.

Upon arriving in the city, Nehemiah quickly confirmed Hanani's report: conditions were indeed deplorable. Not wishing to provoke opposition, he revealed nothing about his mission for the first few days. During that time he cautiously inspected the walls and assessed the situation. On the third evening after his arrival, he took a few men with him and slipped through the Valley Gate to make a complete circuit of the wall.

A Wall for Jerusalem

Soon afterward he announced his plans to the priests, nobles and officials: " 'You see the trouble we are in, how Jerusalem lies in ruins with its gates burned. Come, let us build the wall of Jerusalem, that we may no longer suffer disgrace.' And I told them of the hand of my God which had been upon me for good, and also of the words which the king had spoken to me." His proposal was received with enthusiasm and the people "strengthened their hands for the good work."

Fearing that the city might be attacked, Nehemiah moved quickly to make it secure. He proved to be a remarkably able organizer. Insisting that everyone work, he managed to recruit men from all walks of life and all parts of Judah. Priests, Levites, sons of district rulers, merchants, goldsmiths, perfumers, all worked side by side. Only a few refused to take part. To save time, teams of workers were assigned to work simultaneously on all sections of the wall. All around the city the building proceeded at a furious pace.

Before long the rulers of the states neighboring Judah learned of Nehemiah's effort to refortify

Limestone Blocks Are Prepared for the Rebuilding of Jerusalem

"Come, let us build the wall of Jerusalem, that we may no longer suffer disgrace" (Neh. 2.17). Limestone, which is soft to quarry but grows harder with exposure to air, was an ideal building material. Here quarriers are driving wooden wedges into crevices made by spiked tools, then wetting them. Swelling, the wedges crack loose a rough block, which is shaped by chisels and adzes. Blocks are squared with the aid of a level, a plumb rule, a square, and a line to make diagonal measures equal. Finely smoothed by a loaflike rubbing stone (at right), the block is ready for use and will fit perfectly against others without needing mortar. The photo above shows a drain near the Jerusalem wall which was rebuilt under the direction of Nehemiah.

Jerusalem. Nehemiah recorded: "it displeased them greatly that some one had come to seek the welfare of the children of Israel." Chief among them was Sanballat, governor of Samaria. His allies were Tobiah, governor of Ammon, and Geshem, leader of the Arabs to the south of Judah. The men joined in an informal coalition to hinder the reconstruction of the wall.

When Sanballat heard that work on the wall was under way, he ridiculed the efforts of the Jews. "What are these feeble Jews doing? . . . Will they revive the stones out of the heaps of rubbish, and burned ones at that?" And Tobiah the Ammonite sneered, "Yes, what they are building—if a fox goes up on it he will break down their stone wall!"

As the restoration neared completion, Sanballat and his allies became desperate enough to plan an assault on Jerusalem. Nehemiah learned of their plan and redoubled the effort to complete the wall. At the same time, he prepared for an attack by stationing men at the weakest spots.

The race to complete the wall never faltered. The men labored from dawn to dark, alternating between work on the wall and guard duty. At night they slept fully clothed, their weapons in readiness at their sides.

Meanwhile, Sanballat, Tobiah and Geshem followed the developments in Jerusalem with growing concern. They abandoned their plan for assault and sought instead to trap and kill Nehemiah, the man responsible for this sudden show of strength. Four times they sent letters full of false friendliness, urging him to meet with them, but each time Nehemiah rejected their invitation, claiming that he was still occupied with the wall.

Sanballat sent a fifth letter, threatening to inform the Persian king that Nehemiah planned to make himself king of an independent Judah. Nehemiah, confident that Artaxerxes trusted his loyalty, was not frightened by the bluff. Then Tobiah and Sanballat bribed the priest Shemaiah to lure Nehemiah to an ambush in the temple. But Nehemiah refused: "Should such a man as I flee?

And what man such as I could go into the temple and live?" He was not a priest and besides, it would be a sin for a eunuch to enter the temple.

The Task Completed

In spite of all obstacles, the wall and gates were completed in 52 days, and a great celebration began. Nehemiah summoned all the singers and musicians from the surrounding countryside. Then he organized a triumphal procession. The leading men of Jerusalem came to the Valley Gate at the southwestern corner of the wall. There they divided into two companies and marched slowly along the wall in opposite directions.

Each group was led by nobles and priests who performed rites of purification at main points along the route. They were followed by singers, accompanied by players of cymbals, harps and lyres. The two companies met on the northeastern portion of the wall, near the temple. There they "offered great sacrifices . . . and rejoiced . . . the women and children also rejoiced. And the joy of Jerusalem was heard afar off."

Nehemiah ordered that the gates always remain closed and guarded from sunset to sunrise to prevent infiltration by foes. He appointed two men to oversee the city's security and to choose

guards from among the people. He also realized that Jerusalem needed a greater population. "The city was wide and large," he said, "but the people within it were few and no houses had been built." Accordingly he took a census and ordered the people of Judah to cast lots to bring one out of every 10 to live in Jerusalem.

Now that his primary mission was fulfilled and the physical security of Jerusalem assured, Nehemiah addressed himself to the problem of morale. While the wall was being rebuilt, the farms had been neglected, resulting in a famine. The rich had exploited the crisis by illegally exacting interest on loans to the poor and foreclosing mortgages. Nehemiah forced the offenders to make restitution to their victims.

In 433 Nehemiah returned to the Persian court, perhaps at his own request. During the 11 or 12 years of his administration, Judah had gained peace and security as a result of his dedication.

Nehemiah's Second Term

Deprived of Nehemiah's vigilant leadership, the people of Judah began to return to their old ways. Reports must have reached Nehemiah at the Persian court, for he later returned to Jerusalem. The exact year of his return is uncertain, but it was sometime before 423.

Nehemiah was appalled by what he found: Tobiah the Ammonite was staying in the temple precincts; the Jews were violating the Sabbath and were marrying heathens. At once he acted to correct the situation. First he went to the temple. "And I was very angry, and I threw all the household furniture of Tobiah out of the chamber. Then I gave orders and they cleansed the chambers . . ." Then he set out to restore the sanctity of the Sabbath.

Throughout Judah people were pressing wine, harvesting crops and marketing on the Sabbath. Donkeys filed into Jerusalem on that day, laden with fresh produce, fish and wares which the city people eagerly bought. Nehemiah castigated the people for this evil and arranged to have the city gates shut on the Sabbath (beginning at sundown Friday evening). When some men attempted to set up business outside the wall he drove them off, threatening: "If you do so again I will lay hands on you." He assigned the Levites to guard the gates against violations.

Nehemiah was enraged when he learned how

"Old men and old women shall again sit in the streets of Jerusalem . . . And the streets . . . shall be full of boys and girls playing" (Zech. 8.4). Families of Jews had gone into exile in carts and on foot (above). Their descendants probably returned to Judah that way almost two centuries later (left), traveling 1200 miles from Persia to help rebuild a Jerusalem in ruins (background). This might be a family of artisans whose ancestors had been carried off by the Babylonians. Evidence of culture borrowing during the exile is seen in the old man's Persian traveling costume (far left).

many Jews had married people of Ashdod, Ammon and Moab. To his consternation, half of the children born of these marriages spoke a foreign language. He railed at the people who had acted "treacherously against our God" and reminded them how God had punished Solomon for taking foreign wives. In his rage he even beat some of the offenders and pulled their hair. When he chanced to meet the young Jew who had married Sanballat's daughter, Nehemiah chased him from his sight.

Then he gathered the princes, Levites and priests to make "a firm covenant" to obey God's laws and to make sure that the populace did likewise. Some 70 men signed the document. After that he enjoined the rest of the people to take an oath "to walk in God's law." They agreed to do so and swore they would never again permit intermarriage with nonbelievers. They pledged to support the temple and promised to make all the required offerings and to bring "the first fruits of our ground" to the temple every year.

Nehemiah felt he had done all he could to restore the house of Israel to God. He recorded what he had accomplished in his memoirs: "Thus I cleansed them from everything foreign, and I established the duties of the priests and Levites, each in his work; and I provided for the wood offering, at appointed times, and for the first fruits. Remember me, O my God, for good."

Ezra, Priest-Scholar

Another important leader returned to Judah possibly after Nehemiah's second term. He was Ezra, a member of a new group of religious scholars—the scribes—who had come into being during the exile. Ezra provided Judah with the religious guidance it badly needed in the difficult years after the exile.

The office of scribe had developed during the years in Babylonia. The Jews in captivity had worked to keep their faith alive and retain their national identity, and they organized small groups to study the Mosaic law and the history of their people. Professional scribes, men who had mastered the art of writing Hebrew, were in constant demand to prepare copies of Israel's sacred literature on scrolls of parchment for these study groups. Many scribes devoted themselves exclusively to studying and editing the scriptures. In this way a school of scribal scholars developed in

Babylonia, and the manuscripts they prepared came to make up the Old Testament.

Ezra was one of these scholars, known as "a scribe skilled in the law of Moses." He was the advisor to Artaxerxes on Jewish religious affairs. The Persian rulers encouraged conquered peoples to worship their own deities and followed religious developments in all parts of the empire.

Ezra had "set his heart to study the law of the Lord, and to do it, and to teach his statutes and ordinances in Israel." Accordingly, he asked the king for permission to return to Judah. Granting his request, the monarch prepared a letter of authorization for Ezra which read: "For you are sent by the king . . . to make inquiries about Judah and Jerusalem according to the law of your God, which is in your hand . . ." The king further instructed him to teach the written law and empowered him to appoint judges and magistrates to enforce it.

Ezra promptly gathered an entourage of leading Israelites to accompany him. Traditionally, they numbered about 5000 men. Ezra carried with him gold and silver from the imperial coffers "freely offered to the God of Israel, whose dwelling is in Jerusalem," and generous contributions from the Babylonian Jews.

Nehemiah's band of people had had the protection of a military escort for the long and dangerous journey, but Ezra and his group set forth without one. After four months the caravan reached Jerusalem. Ezra noted that he arrived in the seventh year of Artaxerxes, but whether the king was Artaxerxes I or II is not known. Scholars now hold that three different dates for Ezra's arrival are possible: 458, 428–7 or 398 B.C.

It was summer when Ezra came to Jerusalem. He immediately ordered his priests to offer sacrifices to the Lord at the temple. Then he presented his official papers to the provincial governor. When the city officials learned of Ezra's arrival, they came to him and reported that the exiles who had returned earlier had fallen away from the Lord: "The people of Israel and the priests and the Levites have not separated themselves from the peoples of the lands with their abominations . . ."

"When I heard this," Ezra wrote, "I rent my garments and my mantle, and pulled hair from my head and beard, and sat appalled." In the midst of the worshipers at the evening sacrifice, Ezra fell to his knees and wept. As he prayed for his people, the worshipers gathered around him and began to weep bitterly for their sins. Shecaniah, one of those in the crowd, proposed they "make a covenant with our God to put away all these wives and their children . . ." Ezra stood up and "made the leading priests and Levites and all Israel take oath that they would do as had been said. So they took the oath."

In the early autumn, two months after Ezra's arrival, the people gathered in the square by the Water Gate and asked him to read aloud to them from the book of the law of Moses. Standing on a wooden platform which they had built for him, "he read from it . . . from early morning until midday . . ." The book was in Hebrew, which the people of Judah imperfectly understood, for they now spoke Aramaic, the official language of the Persian Empire. The Levites in the crowd interpreted and expounded the meaning of what they were hearing. Hearing the words spoken by Ezra in the language of their forefathers must have heightened the emotions of the Jews, and they were deeply moved. Many in the crowd wept until Ezra reminded them that the day was cause for rejoicing, not for tears.

A Festival Revived

The next day the priests, Levites and others came to study the law with Ezra. As they studied they learned that the time was near for the harvest festival, the Feast of Tabernacles (Booths). Eagerly they went to the hills outside Jerusalem and brought back olive, myrtle and palm branches to build the tabernacles, small huts which farmers often built in their fields at harvest time. The celebrants were to live in these makeshift shelters during the week of the festival. All over Jerusalem the tabernacles sprang up—on rooftops, in public squares and even on the temple grounds.

The feast had a religious significance as well. It commemorated the years of Israel's wandering in the Sinai wilderness and the renewal of the covenant with the Lord. For seven days the people feasted and each day Ezra read to them and expounded the law. On the eighth day there was "a solemn assembly, according to the ordinance." Later, "the Israelites separated themselves from all foreigners" in order to make their confession. Then Ezra stood before them and made a long, public confession of sin to the Lord for all the people of Judah. "Thou art the Lord, thou alone;" he began, "thou hast made heaven, the heaven of heavens, with all their host, the earth and all that is on it, the seas and all that is in them . . ." Then he reviewed the history of his people from the time of Abraham, pointing out the steadfastness of God's love for them despite their repeated disobedience. And he recalled the severe punishment his people had received for their sins.

"Now therefore, our God," he pleaded, "the great and mighty and terrible God, who keepest covenant and steadfast love, let not all the hardship seem little to thee that has come upon us . . . since the time of the kings of Assyria until this day." As a sign of their complete repentance, the people renewed their covenant to keep the laws.

Separation of the Foreigners

Near the end of November of that year Ezra sent out a proclamation that all the heads of families of the returned exiles in Judah should assemble in Jerusalem in three days or be banished. In a heavy rain, the men gathered on the appointed day in front of the temple. Ezra came before the men and called upon them to separate themselves from their foreign wives. Reluctantly, they agreed to do so, and in three or four months all those who had married foreign women had "put them away with their children."

Ezra not only expounded the law to his contemporaries, he also took steps to insure that future generations would not fall away from their faith. He fostered efforts to provide a copy of the law to every congregation of 10 men so that they might study and live by its tenets. Before long synagogues and schools were established in Jerusalem and all the villages of Judah. In his short ministry Ezra had put the written law into the hands of his people and revived the ancient heritage of Judaism.

The scribe had averted a grave spiritual crisis among his people through his faith and knowledge of the law. Without this inspiration, Judaism might have passed into oblivion in its homeland. In subsequent years the Jews would face many serious trials, but never again would they lose sight of the law.

The stories of Nehemiah and Ezra are told in the Books of Nehemiah and Ezra.

The Greeks: Bearers of a New Culture

Alexander the Great's conquest of Persia opened the eastern world to western influence and began the Hellenistic Age. His army of "Hellenes," from Macedonia and Greece, swept across Asia Minor and claimed an empire from Egypt to India by the time he was 31. After the gifted young general died of a fever in 323 B.C., Egypt, Syria and Macedonia emerged as three great kingdoms, ruled by his former generals. Greek became the international language as Hellenistic cities were built throughout the Near East. In Judea (as the Greeks called Judah) the Jews fought to maintain their faith and ideals in the face of Greek religion and worldly culture. This fight—led by the family of the Maccabees—was only partly successful: Hellenism permeated Jewish society for many years.

"So they built a gymnasium in Jerusalem, according to Gentile custom . . . They joined with the Gentiles and sold themselves to do evil" (1 Macc. 1.14–15). Many conservatively religious Jews were offended by the naked athletic performances of the Greeks, who held the human body in high esteem and celebrated its beauty in works of art. This marble relief dating from the 6th century B.C. shows Greek wrestlers. The gymnasium was restricted to the aristocrats of Jerusalem and trained the youths in citizenship, encouraging a Hellenistic outlook. The public games also offended religious Jews because they were held in honor of foreign deities.

Alexander (above) and his heirs brought about the Hellenization of the Near East by introducing Greek religion, customs and art. From Egypt to Persia, the general won the loyalty of subject peoples by worshiping local gods and by erecting impressive new cities all along the route of his conquests.

The banqueting scene on a Greek bowl of the 5th century B.C. shows the worldliness of the Greeks, which was seductive to many Jews. In Jerusalem, a growing number of government officials, tax collectors and moneylenders became rich in the service of the Ptolemies, who ruled Judea from Egypt, and later of the Seleucid kings of Syria. Unlike the poor, who gained little from Hellenistic rule, this rising wealthy class welcomed Greek customs. The widening class differences prepared the way for the Jewish revolt against the Syrians. Here, reclining Greek men are drinking wine from bowls, attended by musicians and servants.

The art and architecture of the Jews became more elaborate and refined as a result of contact with the Greeks. In the Kidron Valley east of Jerusalem, Hellenistic Jews built large mausoleums amid the ancient burial caves and tombs that dated from the early history of the city. Hellenistic art was a blend of styles from different lands settled by the Greeks. The central tomb above has a pyramidal roof suggesting Egyptian influence, and a Greek-style portico with classical columns. It was cut from a solid block of stone from the hillside. Pottery and everyday articles, too, were changed by the introduction of Greek wares. Local artisans began to work with finer clay, making more delicately shaped vessels, and the old saucer lamp of Palestine was soon replaced by the more efficient closed Greek lamp.

A limestone ossuary from Jerusalem bears a carving of a mourning chalice similar to Greek funerary decorations. These small stone chests held the bones of the dead, once their flesh had decayed, to make room in the tombs for new burials. This one dates from the 1st century B.C.

"And the king sent letters by messengers to Jerusalem and the cities of Judah; he directed them to follow customs strange to the land, to forbid burnt offerings and sacrifices and drink offerings in the sanctuary . . . to sacrifice swine and unclean animals" (1 Macc. 1.44–47). The worst desecration in the history of the temple at Jerusalem occurred when Antiochus IV, ruler of the Seleucid kingdom which dominated Judea, enforced the sacrifice of pigs in the holy sanctuary. The priesthood in Jerusalem had long resisted the Greek attitude that their God was the same Zeus worshiped by the Greeks. When Antiochus IV attempted to unify his kingdom by imposing a uniform Hellenistic culture on his subjects, he had an altar to Zeus erected on the temple altar. For the Greeks, the pig was a common sacrificial animal, as can be seen here on this 6th century B.C. bowl. But to the Jews the offering of an "unclean" beast was an outrage. Such acts provoked the Maccabean revolt.

Chapter 19

The Syrian king Antiochus IV attempts to exterminate Judaism, and erects an altar to Zeus in the temple. But a brave group of rebels resists. Their remarkable leaders, the Maccabees, defeat the Syrians and establish an independent Israel devoted to the Lord.

Fighters for Freedom: The Maccabees

During the most intense and brutal religious repression that the Jews had ever known, a family of heroes arose to save Israel. They were called the Maccabees. Under the great Judas Maccabeus, the rebels successfully defied Syrian efforts to erase their culture. Judas' brothers continued the fight, and their descendants ruled Israel as priest-kings until the arrival of the Romans. Though by that time they had absorbed much of the Greek culture they had initially opposed, the Maccabees were revered and respected as men who would not, even under coercion, "desert the law and the ordinances."

One day in 175 B.C. a delegation of Jews returned to Jerusalem from Antioch in Syria. They had visited the Syrian king, Antiochus IV, and presented him with a revolutionary proposal concerning the government of Judea. They came back triumphant: Antiochus had granted all that they asked, and the proposal was now law. These men were the leaders of the "Hellenizers"—Jews who embraced the Greek way of life.

Their leader, Jason, was now declared high priest of the Jews. Jason's brother, Onias, the lawful high priest, was deposed and placed under arrest. The traditional government by priests and clan chiefs was abolished, to be replaced by a Greek-style city-state. Jason even planned to change the name of the Holy City from Jerusalem to Antioch, after Antiochus IV. An official list of citizens was drawn up, leaving the majority of Jerusalem's Jews with no civic status and no effective voice in public affairs.

The people were outraged: no king had ever presumed to meddle with the government of the Jews. Jerusalemites watched indignantly as the Hellenizers carried through their revolution.

To prepare their sons for citizenship, these would-be Greeks built a gymnasium within sight of the temple. Young Hellenized Jews now spent their days there, exercising in the nude, wrestling and throwing the discus. Even the young priests were forsaking the temple for the gymnasium. Before long, these young men grew ashamed of their circumcisions, which identified them as Jews in the athletic meets against the Syrians. Many of them even went through a painful operation to make it look as if they had never been circumcised.

Their dress was equally offensive to devout Jews. They walked through the streets of Jerusalem wearing abbreviated skirts, a short, fluttering cloak of bright stripes, zigzags or polka dots, and brooches at the shoulders, and (worst of all) the wide-brimmed "Greek hat," the badge of gymnasium membership. Modeled after the hat worn by the god Hermes, the Greek hat was an abominable sign to religious Jews. To the sullen majority of Israel, this charade seemed final proof of the Hellenizers' treason. The Hellenizers had "abandoned the holy covenant. They joined

These silver coins from the 4th century B.C. bear the portrait of Alexander the Great, who conquered the Near East by 331 B.C. His conquests brought Hellenistic culture to Judea and neighboring lands, an alien way of life that many Jews found so intolerable they were willing to die rather than accept it.

with the Gentiles and sold themselves to do evil.''

Within three years, fights between conservatives and Hellenizers became an everyday occurrence. The streets of Jerusalem were no longer safe for anyone. Then, to make matters worse, Jason and his followers were thrown out of office by another faction of Hellenizers who plundered the temple treasury, where many of Jerusalem's poor had deposited their life savings. Fighting increased with the threat of rebellion. When the former high priest Onias echoed the popular outcry, he was assassinated.

That was the last straw and, in 170 B.C., Jerusalem rose in revolt. A force of 3000 Hellenizers marched on the rebels, but the angry crowd stood its ground and routed them. Antiochus acted to prevent further disorder: he had Onias' assassin executed and even went so far as to sympathize publicly with the rebellious Jews. Order was temporarily restored.

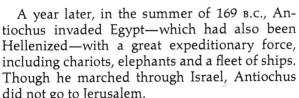

The Gymnasium at Jerusalem

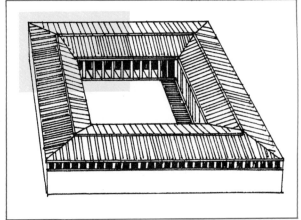

Gymnasiums, such as the one at Jerusalem (above), were centers of a city's social as well as athletic life. They were centers of Greek culture, too: 18-year-old boys spent a year studying at the gymnasium and competing naked in its open courtyard. As shown in the cutaway drawing (left) of the shaded area above, the courtyard was surrounded by rooms for dining (A), workouts (B), bathing (C) and indoor racing along an enclosed track (D). Besides athletics, the boys received Greek schooling in a lecture hall (E). Conservative Jews opposed such training as too worldly, and objected to the broad-brimmed hat of the Greek god Hermes (on coin) worn by the gymnasts.

A year later, in the summer of 169 B.C., Antiochus invaded Egypt—which had also been Hellenized—with a great expeditionary force, including chariots, elephants and a fleet of ships. Though he marched through Israel, Antiochus did not go to Jerusalem.

Jerusalem's common people were well aware of the king's grandiose plans to unite Egypt and Asia under one rule and thus become the most powerful ruler on earth, a new Alexander the Great. They had seen the coins he issued bearing the image of the Olympian Zeus (with features closely resembling his own) and stamped with his assumed title, Epiphanes, meaning "god manifest." Strange tales were told about him: his love of performing in the theater, appearing uninvited at private parties, playing practical jokes, spending his nights with prostitutes and sailors. As long as Antiochus seemed to be winning in Egypt, Jerusalem's Hellenizers supported him. But no one seemed to know exactly what was happening in the Egyptian campaign. According to one day's news, Antiochus had captured and deposed the young Egyptian king and had gone to Memphis to receive the ancient and mysterious rites of coronation as Egypt's new pharaoh. Later bulletins became confused and at last made no sense at all. Seriously alarmed, the Hellenizers split into factions, pro-Syrians against pro-Egyptians. Throughout the country, a feeling of impending disaster pervaded the air.

Civil War

During the autumn of 169 B.C., some Jerusalemites started seeing things in the sky: "for almost forty days, there appeared golden-clad horsemen charging through the air, in companies fully armed . . . all men prayed that the apparition might prove to have been a good omen."

Then came a startling rumor that Antiochus was dead. The people, incensed by the confusion and disorder, prepared to rise. Fighting broke out in the streets. At this moment the king himself, still very much alive, appeared in Jerusalem at the head of a large army. He had just been forced to abandon Egypt on a threat of war with the Romans, whose policy was to maintain a balance of power in the East. Finding Judea in turmoil, he assumed that the Jews were in revolt. His response was to order a massacre.

With Jerusalem subdued, Antiochus went on to plunder the temple. Helped by the dishonest high priest, he confiscated a sum equivalent to several million dollars. Then, after defiling and looting the sanctuary itself, he returned to Syria.

This was the beginning. Early in 167 B.C., before the people had recovered from Antiochus' first onslaught, he sent another army under a general named Apollonius. On the Sabbath, when Jews could neither work nor bear arms, the army entered the city unopposed. Apollonius' soldiers plundered and set fire to much of Jerusalem. Next they tore down the city walls and set up a heavily fortified camp on a hill overlooking the temple. This hill, called the "Acra" (citadel), would be their stronghold for 25 years.

By now, residents of Jerusalem were fleeing and taking refuge wherever they could. Hellenizers and their families started moving to safety within the Syrian garrison on the Acra, but only the rich and influential could afford to stay there. Most other Jews, whatever their allegiance, moved away if they could. The Holy City had become "a dwelling of strangers."

The Syrian Persecution

Later in the same year, Antiochus proceeded from political repression to religious persecution, something no Greek ruler had ever done before. His first step was to issue a proclamation stating that all should be united as one people and that non-Greeks should give up their ancestral customs and adopt customs prescribed by the king. He addressed this order to the entire kingdom, and throughout his lands—in Syria, Palestine, Mesopotamia, Persia and parts of Asia Minor—public officials summoned the people to assemble and hear it read.

Then Antiochus moved directly against the Jews. In hundreds of letters carried by messengers to Jerusalem and the other towns of Judea, "he directed them to follow customs strange to the land . . . to profane sabbaths and feasts, to defile the sanctuary and the priests, to build altars and sacred precincts and shrines for idols, to sacrifice swine and unclean animals, and to leave their sons uncircumcised." The decree ended with the words: "And whoever does not obey the command of the king shall die."

The king's command was enforced to the letter. In mid-December 167 B.C., Syrian authorities rededicated the temple to the Olympian Zeus. A statue of the god (which had been sculpted to look like Antiochus himself) was set up, and pigs were sacrificed in front of it on the altar of burnt offering. Thereafter, "the temple was filled with debauchery and reveling by the Gentiles, who dallied with harlots and had intercourse with women within the sacred precincts . . ."

The Jewish law itself was the chief target of Antiochus. "A man could neither keep the sabbath, nor observe the feasts of his fathers, nor so much as confess himself to be a Jew." Possession of the scriptures was made a capital offense. The members of a congregation caught secretly observing the Sabbath were all burned alive.

"He committed deeds of murder, and spoke with great arrogance" (1 Macc. 1.24). On the Greek coin is the hated Seleucid king Antiochus IV Epiphanes, whose persecution of the Jews led to the Maccabean revolt. Despite his god-king status, Greeks as well as Jews accused Antiochus of sacrilegious crimes.

"[T]wo women were brought in for having circumcised their children. These women they publicly paraded about the city, with their babies hung at their breasts, then hurled them down headlong from the wall."

When the festival of Dionysus came, conservative Jews were compelled to walk in the procession under the eyes of Syrian guards and Hellenizers. Amid the beating of drums and gongs, trumpet blasts and wild shouts honoring the wine god, they marched along, wearing wreaths of ivy (a symbol of Dionysus), their heads bowed in shame and humiliation.

Next, on pain of death for noncompliance, the entire population was summoned to eat pork. Most chose to live, and ate a morsel. "But many in Israel stood firm . . . They chose to die rather than to be defiled by [unclean] food or to profane the holy covenant; and they did die." One of these patriots, a 90-year-old scribe named Eleazar, was offered a dispensation because of his age and dignity. He would be allowed, they said, to smuggle in a portion of clean meat for himself and thus only appear to be eating the pig flesh.

"Such pretense is not worthy of our time of life," said Eleazar within the hearing of all. He was then savagely beaten to death by Antiochus' soldiers before his horrified countrymen.

Many had begun to despair of Israel's survival when a book suddenly appeared in their midst. No one knew where *Daniel* came from, but at once copies were passing from hand to hand among the faithful. Some believed it was the work of a prophet who had lived almost 400 years earlier in Babylonia. Why had no one ever heard of Daniel and his book? The book itself answered this question. It had been concealed by divine command until the moment of crisis when its message would be needed by the children of Israel. Who could doubt that the critical time was fast approaching?

Mattathias Strikes the First Blow

All over the country, people gathered in secret to listen while scribes read *Daniel* aloud, half-singing its rapturous visions. Composed in the highly colored language favored by the common folk, the message was an electrifying one. Hold out for another three years and you will cleanse the temple, it proclaimed. Keep fighting—a Messiah is coming and Israel will become God's

kingdom on earth. Throughout that year many listened and believed.

One of the many heads of families facing destruction at this time was an aged priest named Mattathias. He and his five sons—John, Simon, Judas, Eleazar, and Jonathan—lived in their an-

Wrestling Was a National Pastime
"Stand therefore, having girded your loins with truth" (Eph. 6.14). In the Greco-Roman form of wrestling in Paul's time the contestants "girded their loins" with special belts, below which holds were barred. Its great popularity made wrestling one of the major unifying forces among the peoples of the Roman Empire. Even the Jews, who abstained from many other sports, enjoyed wrestling: they had practiced it themselves for more than 2000 years. For them, as for most other nations, wrestling champions were widely admired and honored as national heroes.

cestral village of Modein, some 17 miles northwest of Jerusalem.

Antiochus' persecutions quickly spread beyond the capital, however, and soon an official arrived in Modein to enforce the royal edict. He publicly invited Mattathias, an honored elder, to set a good example by performing a small sacrifice in Greek fashion on the village altar. Mattathias vehemently refused. When another Jew advanced to fulfill the royal command, Mattathias rushed forward and killed both the Jew and the official and tore down the altar.

"Then Mattathias cried out in the city with a loud voice, saying: 'Let every one who is zealous for the law and supports the covenant come out with me!' And he and his sons fled to the hills and left all that they had in the city."

They made for the rugged hill country some 12 miles northeast of Modein, a wild area of boulders, ravines and scraggly undergrowth. Others hastened to join the rebels; among them was a group of conservative scribes known as Hasideans (the pious ones).

The rebels in the hills grew larger and stronger. They "struck down sinners in their anger and lawless men in their wrath; the survivors fled to the Gentiles for safety. And Mattathias and his friends went about and tore down the altars; they forcibly circumcised all the uncircumcised boys that they found within the borders of Israel. . . . and the work prospered in their hands."

Judas the Hammer

Mattathias was too old for the rigors of guerrilla life. Less than a year after slaying the Syrian official, he died, having named his third son, Judas, to succeed him as commander of the rebels.

Judas proved to be a genius at guerrilla warfare. He knew how to hold the loyalty of his men, how to keep them together in hard times and how to lead them in battle. When it came to the actual fighting, Judas always plunged right into the thick of it:

"He was like a lion in his deeds,
like a lion's cub roaring for prey."
People nicknamed him Maccabeus (hammer).

One day in 166 B.C. he engaged a force led by the same Apollonius who had sacked Jerusalem on the Sabbath a year earlier. Recognizing the general in the melee, Judas rushed in and killed him, taking his sword. Judas was to use that weapon in battle for the rest of his life.

The Syrians then put a large army into the field, advancing without opposition to Bethhoron, about 12 miles northwest of Jerusalem. Judas had carefully positioned his men in the surrounding hills, and they watched as the glittering Syrian battalions marched along.

Those with Judas shook their heads. How could the Syrians be withstood? Judas was firm. Numbers did not count, he said. It was surprise that would win. He waited for the precise moment when a sudden assault would throw the Syrians into disarray; then he gave the signal and led his army down the hills. The Syrians, caught by surprise, became a disorderly mass, incapable of striking back efficiently. Eight hundred were killed and the rest fled westward.

Thereafter, people talked excitedly of Judas and his brothers. His victory disturbed the king, but Antiochus had more pressing troubles. His outlying eastern provinces, hundreds of miles inland, had ceased paying their taxes. Taking an army eastward in the spring of 165 B.C., Antiochus left behind a viceroy named Lysias with half of his troops and orders to exterminate the Jews. Those fit for hard work were to be sold to slave traders, and the remainder were to be killed. Lysias quickly began his mission.

From their lookout points in the hills, Judas' scouts watched as a group of slave traders came out to meet the Syrian army. The traders had brought immense amounts of gold and silver and wagonloads of chains with which to fetter the able-bodied Jews they expected to buy.

At daybreak the next morning—after fasting and praying—Judas' army marched into position, lightly armed but confident that the Lord would defend them. Miraculously, the Syrians' main force was soundly defeated, and Judas then turned to face a detachment which had come to attack him from behind. When this rear guard saw their camp in flames, however, they fled in panic and disarray.

Rebellious Maccabeans faced a terrifying kind of warfare when the Syrians rode 32 battle-trained elephants into combat. Wearing leather armor, the wine-crazed animals charged, carrying troops in wooden towers. Eleazar, a brother of Judas, heroically killed the largest elephant, thinking it carried the Syrian king. He was crushed by the fall of the beast. An ancient oak (left) marks the place where "he gave his life to save his people" (1 Macc. 6.44).

Judas' army outsmarted the enemy again and again, until finally, early in the year 164 B.C., he defeated the Syrians in a pitched battle at Beth-zur, 16 miles south of Jerusalem. Lysias had no choice but to negotiate a truce: the Jews entered Jerusalem, but the Acra stronghold remained in Syrian hands. There, despite the truce, the fighting continued as Judas and his men entered the temple precincts.

Undeterred, Judas now carried out the greatest act of his career, the cleansing and rededication of the temple. It was a formidable task. "In the courts they saw bushes sprung up as in a thicket, or as on one of the mountains. They saw also the chambers of the priests in ruins. Then they rent their clothes, and mourned with great lamentation, and sprinkled themselves with ashes. They fell face down on the ground, and sounded the signal on the trumpets, and cried out to Heaven." During the days that followed, they rebuilt, repaired and refurnished the temple.

Then, early one morning in mid-December 164 B.C., exactly three years after the Syrian desecration, "they rose and offered sacrifice, as the law directs, on the new altar of burnt offering which they had built. At the very season and on the very day that the Gentiles had profaned it, it was dedicated with songs and harps and lutes and cymbals. All the people fell on their faces and worshiped and blessed Heaven, who had prospered them. So they celebrated the dedication of the altar for eight days, and offered burnt offerings with gladness; they offered a sacrifice of deliverance and praise. They decorated the front of the temple with golden crowns and small shields; they restored the gates and the chambers for the priests, and furnished them with doors. There was very great gladness among the people, and the reproach of the Gentiles was removed." The annual winter festival of Hannukah commemorates this event.

Death of Antiochus

Meanwhile, things were going badly for Antiochus in the East. When he learned that Jerusalem and its temple were in Jewish hands and that the Jews had taken the offensive throughout Palestine, he fell ill. In the summer of 164 B.C., he was stricken with a loathsome physical malady which affected his mind. His death followed soon afterward.

When the news reached Israel, Judas immediately besieged the Acra. Without their stronghold in Jerusalem the Syrians would not be able to retain military control of Palestine. In response, the viceroy Lysias, now acting as regent for the new king, Antiochus' eight-year-old son, raised a huge army of foreign mercenaries, the most formidable of any that had yet been used against the rebels. It even included a group of 32 battle-seasoned elephants.

In early autumn, 163 B.C., Lysias met Judas and his army 10 miles southwest of Jerusalem. After feeding the elephants wine and mulberry juice to madden them, the Syrians sounded their trumpets and moved forward. Carefully chosen horsemen and infantrymen in coats of mail and brass helmets were assigned to follow each enormous charging animal as it broke through the Jewish ranks.

"And upon the elephants were wooden towers, strong and covered; they were fastened upon each beast by special harness, and upon each were four armed men who fought from there . . . When the sun shone upon the shields of gold and brass, the hills were ablaze with them and gleamed like flaming torches."

During the battle that followed, Judas' younger brother Eleazar fought his way toward one of the elephants, one that was larger than all the rest and was arrayed with the gorgeous royal trappings. That beast, he guessed, must carry the boy-king. If he could somehow get at the king and kill or capture him, the Syrians would surely flee. He reached the elephant, darted beneath it and stabbed it from below, wounding it mortally, but the huge animal fell on top of him and crushed him to death.

Eleazar's sacrifice was in vain. The elephant did not carry the king, and the death of one elephant did not slow the relentless advance of the others. The Jews broke ranks and fled.

But Lysias could not follow up his victory. Antiochus' second-in-command during the eastern expedition had just returned to Syria with the other half of the army and was preparing to seize power. When news of the impending coup reached Lysias, he realized he must return to Syria at once. Hastily he proposed a truce and began to negotiate peace with the Jews.

Two points were at issue: the religious liberty of the Jews and their political independence. Lysias offered to yield the first if the Jews would

Antigonus, last of the Hasmoneans (40–37 B.C.), struck this bronze coin to commemorate the Maccabean revolt a century earlier. It features the seven-branched lampstand symbolic of the temple.

yield the second. Judas accepted. In principle the agreement also meant religious freedom for the Hellenizers, but Judas and his followers had no intention of tolerating their desires. Before long the civil war was on again.

Judas waged campaigns wherever the Jewish population was threatened by the Hellenizers. He would first deliver the local Jews, then kill Hellenizers and non-Jewish males regardless of age, plunder and burn their houses. In time he had rescued scores of towns from oppression.

Judas and his guerrilla bands had come a long way from their beginnings as religious rebels, but they realized that to utterly rout the Syrians they would need the help of a strong ally—the powerful republic of Rome. Judas came to admire the Romans for their patriotism, military prowess, austere way of life, and especially for their hatred of the Greeks. He sent a small delegation on the long and dangerous journey to Rome. They returned in 161 B.C. with a declaration of friendship, but not of military assistance, between the Roman Senate and the Jewish people.

Then, in 160 B.C., the Syrians managed to outmaneuver Judas, and he found himself surrounded. With a few hundred faithful comrades he made a courageous last stand and was killed in the fighting.

It was a disastrous time for Israel. With Judas dead, the Hellenizers again seized power. More-over, the year's crops had failed, and there was terrible famine. The remnants of Judas' army hid in the desolate region southeast of Jerusalem, part of the Wilderness of Judea. There Judas' younger brother Jonathan was elected leader by the small band of desperate men.

Jonathan: New Leader of the Jews

After about two years of hiding in the desert, Jonathan's guerrilla force had gathered many followers, and his army resumed its war against the Hellenizers. Alarmed Hellenizers begged the government in Antioch for help in putting down the nationalists. At the same time, they plotted to seize Jonathan and kill him. Before they could act, Jonathan captured 50 leading Hellenizers, all of them implicated in the plot, and had them executed. Meanwhile, the Syrians had sent an army to aid the Hellenizers, and Jonathan launched a series of surprise attacks against them. The Syrian heavy equipment was powerless against Jonathans' mobile and experienced guerrilla force. Bacchides, the Syrian general, turned against the Hellenizers for drawing him into this situation. He killed many of them and soon took his army back to Syria.

Jonathan immediately made a truce with Bacchides. Prisoners were exchanged, and Jonathan established his command post near Jerusalem.

In 152 B.C. civil war broke out again in Syria. Both sides now courted Jonathan's favor. By a series of adroit diplomatic moves he obtained from the winning side successive appointments as high priest, general and governor of Judea. Entering Jerusalem in triumph, Jonathan rebuilt the city and fortified the temple area. Then, at the Feast of Tabernacles that autumn, he put on the sacred robes and presented himself to the people as their new high priest.

During the next 10 years, as the Syrian crown passed from hand to hand in a series of palace revolutions and civil wars, Jonathan proved his skill in the arts of war, diplomacy and intrigue. Taking advantage of the confusion in Syria, he managed to extend his control over territories beyond Judea's borders.

But at last, in 143 B.C., he was lured into a trap and arrested by the Syrians. His brother Simon immediately took charge of Jerusalem, calling a meeting of the people and proclaiming himself their new leader. And "they answered in a loud voice, 'You are our leader in place of Judas and Jonathan your brother. Fight our battles, and all that you say to us we will do.'"

Simon acted at once to capture the Acra garrison, the last remaining Syrian outpost in Judea. His troops encircled the fortress and prepared to attack. Meanwhile, Syrian troops advanced on Jerusalem to aid the besieged soldiers. Simon learned his brother was held prisoner among the enemy ranks but was powerless to rescue him.

Finally, the Syrians planned a cavalry sweep to relieve the Acra. The night they were to start there was a blizzard, and the Syrian horses could make no headway through the snow. The frustrated enemy soldiers killed Jonathan shortly thereafter and returned to Syria.

Simon gave Jonathan a hero's burial at Modein, in the family tomb which, ironically, he enlarged and adorned in Greek style. At the same time he built seven pyramids for his parents, himself and his four brothers, and decorated them with tall columns and carved ships.

Simon: King and High Priest

Within a few months, new political upheavals in Syria made it possible for Simon to negotiate peace and independence for the Jews. In 142 B.C., ". . . the yoke of the Gentiles was removed from Israel, and the people began to write in their documents and contracts, 'In the first year of Simon the great high priest and commander and leader of the Jews.'" The following year saw the capture of the Acra, when the last of the Syrian defenders surrendered in the face of starvation. After 450 years, Jerusalem was once again the capital of a sovereign state. The stage was now set for a momentous decision: two years later, in late summer 140 B.C., the Jews made the supreme office hereditary in Simon's family, thus making him a king in all but name.

Simon was by now an old man, but like his brothers, he was fated to die a violent death. Ptolemy, his son-in-law and governor of Jericho, was plotting to kill Simon and seize power himself. On a midwinter day in 134 B.C., Simon and two of his sons stopped overnight in a little mountain stronghold called Dok, where Ptolemy maintained his headquarters.

Ptolemy "gave them a great banquet, and hid men there. When Simon and his sons were drunk, Ptolemy and his men rose up, took their weapons, and rushed in against Simon in the banquet hall, and they killed him and his two sons and some of his servants."

Simon's third son, John Hyrcanus, was in Gazara (ancient Gezer) when he heard of the murder. He went quickly to Jerusalem and seized power. Ptolemy arrived in due course, backed by

Jewelry of the Rich and Powerful

"I will take you . . . and make you like a signet ring; for I have chosen you, says the Lord of hosts" (Hag. 2.23). Signet rings, worn by kings, nobles and wealthy citizens, were valued objects in the Hellenistic world. They were engraved with

highly realistic images of their owners, who impressed them onto the seals of important documents. If lent or given away, certain powers went with them—as when Mordecai used Xerxes' ring to mobilize Jewish resisters (Est. 8). The rings above, from the 1st century B.C., are of gold set with garnet. The impression at left shows the fine portrait engraving.

the Syrian army and its king, Antiochus VII. For the next six years the Syrians controlled Judea. John Hyrcanus was able to remain in power only by paying them a heavy tribute. Then, in 128 B.C., the Syrian king was killed and Judea proclaimed its independence.

During the rest of his 30-year reign, John extended the borders of the Jewish state in all directions. Wherever he went he forcibly circumcised non-Jews and converted entire populations to the law. Conversions were carried out by scribes who traveled with the army and settled among the conquered peoples to supervise their transition to the Jewish way of life. Called Pharisees, they were the spiritual successors of the Hasideans whose zeal for the law had inspired the Maccabean heroes. Within another generation they were to become a great and influential power in the land.

At first, the Pharisees enjoyed Hyrcanus' full support. But their increasing influence led aristocrats in Jerusalem to form a new party, called the Sadducees, to oppose them. The Sadducees eventually persuaded Hyrcanus to support them, and the Pharisees soon fell into disgrace.

The estrangement had been inevitable. The Pharisees could not fail to dislike Hyrcanus: while extending his power he neglected the high priesthood. A professed aim of the war of independence had been the restoration of the ancient Jewish state, but the new order had achieved nothing of the sort. Instead the state had become a Greek-style kingdom, adapted only superficially to the life and religion of the Jews.

When Hyrcanus died, in 104 B.C., he was succeeded by his son Aristobulus, who claimed his throne by imprisoning his mother and brothers. His mother later starved to death in her cell. People called him the "Greek-lover." He invaded Galilee in northern Palestine and like his father forcibly circumcised and converted the conquered heathen population. A year later he died.

His 37-year-old widow, Alexandra, released the imprisoned brothers and married one of them, the 22-year-old Janneus. Like his forebears, Janneus was an energetic but brutal man. He ordered his remaining brothers put to death and then assumed the title of king. On his accession he took the name Alexander.

King Alexander Janneus

Janneus extended the borders of Judea to the Mediterranean coast, and during his reign the Jews became a maritime people for the first time since Solomon. Although the kingdom prospered, Alexander Janneus grew unpopular. An uncouth, hard-drinking soldier, he was guilty of negligent and scandalous behavior in his performance of the duties of high priest.

Finally, in 94 B.C., the people rebelled, led by the Pharisees. After six years of indecisive civil war, the Pharisees made an incredible mistake.

They called on the Syrians to intervene. The people, stunned at seeing the successors of the Hasideans in league with the hated Syrians, withdrew their support and went over to Janneus in time to repel the Syrian invasion.

Once reinstated in Jerusalem, Janneus had 800 leading Pharisees crucified and their wives and children killed in front of them. Reclining on couches set up nearby, Janneus and his concubines held a Greek-style drinking party and watched the bloody spectacle. One of the Dead Sea Scrolls comments on this event: "He hanged living men on wood . . ."

As in the days of the revolt against Antiochus, many fled to the hills and desert. The Wilderness of Judea once again became the refuge of those zealous for the law. Some set up monastic communities there, and among them were the Essenes, the messianic sect who produced the Dead Sea Scrolls.

When Janneus died in 76 B.C., his widow Alexandra took over the government, installing her half-witted elder son, John Hyrcanus II, as high priest. The Pharisees were recovering their lost influence over the people, and Alexandra wisely reversed her late husband's policy. With her support, the Pharisees supplanted the Sadducees as political leaders of Judea. The ensuing reign was to be remembered in Pharisaic tradition as a golden age—grains of wheat the size of kidneys, barleycorns as big as olives, lentils like gold pieces. If it was so, then Alexandra must have been even richer than her predecessors, because the crown was entitled to one-third of all sown crops as well as half of the harvests of all orchards and vineyards. This prodigious tax burden was the heaviest in that part of the world, worse even than that borne by the Egyptian peasantry. A salt tax, a head tax and various indirect taxes bore down on the people as heavily under Alexandra as they had under Antiochus.

After Alexandra's death in 67 B.C., the fierce struggle for the succession between her two sons led to civil war. After four years a Roman army under Pompey intervened, and in 63 B.C. Jerusalem fell after heavy fighting. A 500-year period of Roman domination had begun.

The story of the Maccabees is told in the First and Second Books of the Maccabees.

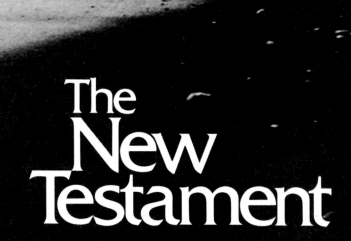

The New Testament

It was by the restless waters of the Sea of Galilee that Jesus first began to preach, almost 2000 years ago. After his death, his followers came to believe that Jesus' ministry had marked a new covenant, or testament, with the Lord.

IN THE LAST DECADES before the birth of Jesus of Nazareth, the Jews of Palestine experienced a profound change of belief and of mood. Outwardly, this change was not easily recognized. The temple at Jerusalem still represented the center of their faith. The priests there still sacrificed to the Lord, while the Levites sang holy psalms. In the surrounding city and all over Palestine, a great building program was being carried out by Judea's king, Herod the Great. Judea itself was now subject to Rome and was part of that great empire.

The Jewish nation had rarely seemed more peaceful or prosperous. In fact, it had been impoverished by Herod's extravagance and the people were in a rebellious frame of mind. Many hoped for a leader who would free them of Roman rule. Others believed the end of the world was near and eagerly awaited the coming of the Messiah, the God-sent leader who would signal the approaching end of the world and pronounce the judgment of God. This Messiah had been predicted by the prophets, notably Isaiah: "Therefore the Lord himself will give you a sign. Behold, a young woman shall conceive and bear a son, and shall call his name Immanuel [God with us]" (Isaiah 7.14).

Along with the growing expectation of the Messiah, relatively new religious ideas had gained wide acceptance. The most dramatic of these ideas was that of the resurrection of the dead. As early as the time of the prophet Ezekiel in the sixth century B.C., the concept of a future symbolic resurrection had been present in the Jewish faith: ". . . Thus says the Lord God: Behold, I will open your graves, and raise you from your graves, O my people; and I will bring you home into the land of Israel" (Ezekiel 37.12).

Now, many Jews—especially the devout sect called the Pharisees—believed that the Lord would actually raise the dead on the Day of Judgment. The good would be rewarded with everlasting life in the kingdom of the Lord and his angels, while the wicked would be punished eternally in the hell of Satan and his demons. These ideas, too—heaven, hell, angels, demons—while not new, had never before been so prominent in Jewish thought. But they were widely discussed by the Jews of Palestine in the years following the total conquest of their country by the Romans.

New Masters

In 63 B.C. the Roman general Pompey took over the old Seleucid Empire of Syria. After he defeated the forces of Antioch, Pompey turned toward Jerusalem. The city had been nominally independent since the Maccabean revolt against Syria and chose to resist.

Jerusalem was in turmoil by the time Pompey and his army broke through its walls after a siege of three months. Thousands of Jews had been killed during the siege, and by then they were even killing each other in the confusion. Hardly anyone, save a few valiant priests, was left to resist Pompey as, surrounded by his guard, he rode through the city to the temple courtyards and then entered the temple itself.

Just what Pompey expected to see when he flung aside the embroidered curtain that shielded the holy of holies, no one knows. He may have heard that the Jews refused to pay homage to images or idols, but he was still surprised when he discovered that the dark, airless cubicle held nothing of value—for that matter, nothing at all. He abruptly left the building, taking care not to defile it, and ordered that the ritual sacrifices of the Jews be resumed.

Thus began the turbulent Roman rule of Judea. The Romans confirmed John Hyrcanus II as High Priest and appointed Antipater, an Idumean and royal official, as minister of Palestine under the Jewish high priest. Through adroit political maneuvering he managed to secure exemptions from taxes and military service, as well as religious tolerance for the Jews. But soon after Julius Caesar's murder in 44 B.C., Antipater himself was poisoned, and his sons and other hopeful successors vied for the favor of Rome's new leaders.

Meanwhile, Antigonus, son of the last Hasmonean king, attempted to reestablish the dynasty. His action provoked a civil war. In 40 B.C., to restore order, the Romans named Herod "king of Judea," meaning almost all of Palestine. In 37 B.C. Herod gained complete control of the country, and the Romans executed Antigonus. Rome would rule Palestine through puppet kings and governors for four centuries more.

Ruled by an Idumean, taxed by both Rome and the temple, surrounded by thousands of "Gentiles" in their ancestral land, the Jews began to turn inward and examine their faith and history for signs of deliverance. The Lord had saved them more than once before and he would certainly do so again. But when? In hundreds of synagogues throughout Judea and Galilee, the holy scriptures were searched, studied and interpreted for signs of the Lord's purpose.

It was in this atmosphere that many Jews became more certain that the long-predicted judgment of the Lord was approaching. And it was in this time that Jesus of Nazareth was born.

Jesus and the Jews

The story of Jesus, his disciples and the development of Christianity, is directly connected with the story of the Old Testament. The crucial link between the two is Jesus himself. Jesus experienced his life, ministry and faith within the context of Jewish life and religion. Though he was probably aware of the universality of his message, and certainly aware of the many Gentiles in Palestine, he spoke as a Jew and addressed himself to Jewish audiences. His disciples saw him as a new prophet, a divine messenger of the Lord of Israel who re-interpreted the traditional faith—not one who would inspire a new religion.

According to the Gospel writers, Jesus' "transfiguration" took place in the presence of Moses and Elijah, and the apostles heard the Lord say: "This is my beloved Son, with whom I am well pleased; listen to him" (Matthew 17.5). Opposition to Jesus' followers came not from Jews who denied the possibility of a Messiah (there were few, if any, who did), but from those who did not believe that Jesus was the Messiah.

Jesus and his disciples, as Jews, often spoke in synagogues. The synagogue was a place of both worship and discussion and it was there that Jesus' teaching made its initial impact. Without that forum, it would have been much more diffi-

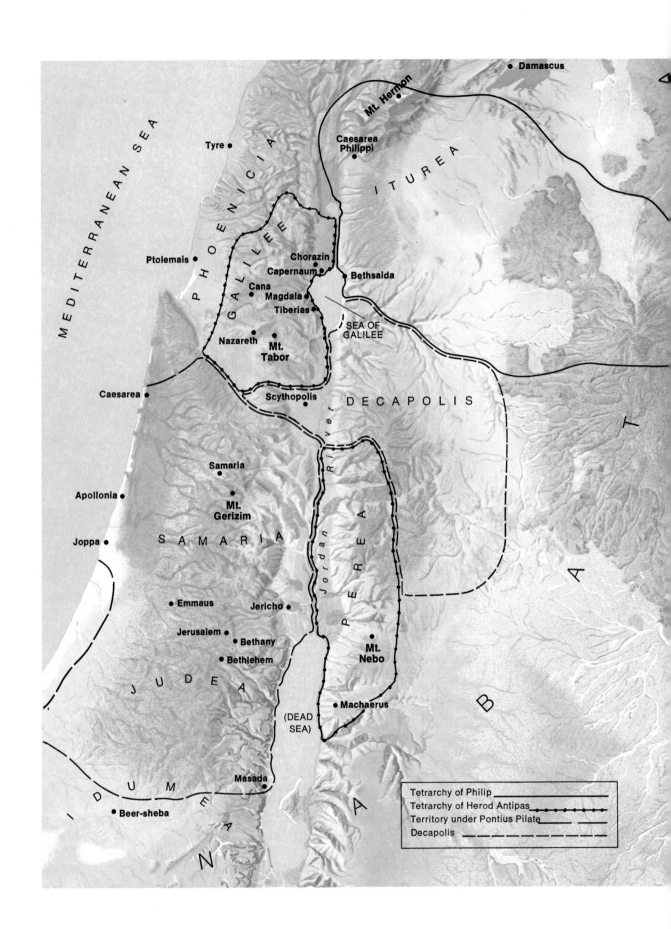

Damascus

Mt. Hermon

Caesarea
Philippi

I T U R E A

MEDITERRANEAN SEA

Tyre

P H O E N I C I A

Ptolemais

G A L I L E E

Chorazin

Capernaum

Bethsaida

Cana

Magdala

Tiberias

SEA OF
GALILEE

Nazareth

Mt.
Tabor

Caesarea

Scythopolis

D E C A P O L I S

Samaria

Mt.
Gerizim

Apollonia

S A M A R I A

Joppa

J o r d a n   R i v e r

P E R E A

Emmaus

Jericho

Jerusalem

Bethany

Mt.
Nebo

Bethlehem

J U D E A

Machaerus

(DEAD
SEA)

Masada

I D U M E A

Beer-sheba

Tetrarchy of Philip	————
Tetrarchy of Herod Antipas	•—•—•—•—
Territory under Pontius Pilate	— — —
Decapolis	– – – – –

cult to spread the gospel. Only when Paul and his fellow apostles were finally barred from the synagogues, years later, did they begin to bring their message to the Gentiles.

How the Story Was Written

"Inasmuch as many have undertaken to compile a narrative of the things which have been accomplished among us, just as they were delivered to us by those who from the beginning were eyewitnesses and ministers of the word, it seemed good to me also, having followed all things closely for some time past, to write an orderly account for you, most excellent Theophilus, that you may know the truth concerning the things of which you have been informed" (Luke 1.1-4). Thus begins the third Gospel.

Modern scholars believe that the method described by Luke was essentially that used in writing the Gospels of Matthew and Mark as well as Luke. The writers of these Gospels were probably not themselves witnesses of the life of Jesus; rather they based their narratives on both oral and written accounts of those who had actually known Jesus. There must have been a variety of such accounts to draw from: only one miracle of the many performed by Jesus, the feeding of the 5000, is recorded in all four Gospels.

Jesus' various sermons—such as the Sermon on the Mount—were also apparently not delivered on specific occasions, as the Gospels relate them, but are collections of related sayings of Jesus arranged by the Gospel writers into coherent themes. The purpose of these writers was re-

Palestine in the Time of Jesus

When Jesus was born, in 6 B.C., Palestine had been under Roman control for more than half a century. In 63 B.C., Pompey put the area under the control of the new Roman province of Syria, and in 40 B.C. Rome designated Herod king of Judea—which meant nearly the whole of Palestine. Herod reigned until his death in 4 B.C., at which time the territory was divided among his three sons. One of them, Herod Antipas, received Galilee and Perea. A second, Philip, ruled the northeastern province of Iturea, which bordered on the north with Syria. The third, Archelaus, with the title of Ethnarch, reigned over the areas most heavily populated with Jews: Samaria, Judea and part of Idumea. Because of the Jews' complaints against him, however, Rome replaced Archelaus with a series of prefects, or governors. The fifth of these was Pontius Pilate, whose tenure lasted from A.D. 26 to 36.

ligious, not historical. They sought to preserve the spirit of Jesus' teachings—the incidents of Jesus' life are told only in relation to the Gospel writers' belief that Jesus was the Christ, or Messiah, sent by the Lord to redeem mankind.

The greatest of the apostles, Paul, made no references to the life of Jesus in his many letters. It was enough for Paul that Jesus was the Christ who had died for man's sins, had been resurrected and would return again to earth. In fact, given the totally religious attitude of all the early Christian writers, it is amazing how much they tell of Jesus' life and background.

From the four Gospels it is possible to construct the outline of Jesus' life in some detail. The narrative in this book draws upon all of them. The details of Jesus' youth are found only in Luke, while the account of Jesus' ministry in Galilee is based on all four Gospels. The account of the final ministry in Judea is taken mainly from the Gospel of John. It seems likely that, as John asserts, Jesus spent considerably more time in Judea than the other writers imply.

The account of the arrest, trial, crucifixion and resurrection is based on all of the Gospels, as well as on the book of Acts. The latter book, believed to have been written by Luke, is rich with details of life in Jesus' time. It is also the main source of the account of the lives and work of the apostles after Jesus' death.

For many centuries much research and debate has gone into the question of when the various Gospels were written. Today, most authorities believe that they were all written some time during the last third of the first century A.D.

The Gospel of Mark is believed to have been written first—some scholars hold that it was completed in Rome just prior to the fall of Jerusalem (A.D. 70). The Gospel of Mark is thought to have been the primary source for the Gospels of Matthew and Luke. Because all three of these Gospels have so many incidents in common, they are called the "synoptic" Gospels (from the Greek word *synopsis*, a seeing together).

The Gospel of John, on the other hand, has none of the parables mentioned in the other Gospels and presents a much more mystical interpretation of Jesus' ministry. It also concentrates more on the Judean ministry. It was written later than the other Gospels, possibly at the end of the first century A.D.

The various letters to the early churches, including those of Paul, were written as instructions to the young Christian communities that the apostles left in the wake of their missionary journeys. They contain many valuable insights into the thoughts and lives of the early Christians. These, too, date mostly from the end of the first century and some of them were probably written even earlier than the Gospels.

Equally important to the spread of Jesus' gospel and the rise of Christianity was the fact that Greek was widely spoken throughout the Roman Empire. The Old Testament had been translated into Greek a few centuries earlier, and many pagans had been exposed to Hebrew tradition. The Gospels, Acts, Paul's letters and the book of Revelation were also written in Greek. Thus, the whole New Testament as well as the Old Testament background of Jesus' faith and message of salvation were expressed in terms comprehensible to most inhabitants of the Roman Empire.

Archaeology of the New Testament

The archaeological evidence from the New Testament period is limited compared to that of the Old Testament era. The time span was much shorter (only a century) and the principal characters left no physical monuments behind. Jesus and the apostles were not kings or builders of cities but men who lived simple lives and devoted themselves to preaching the new gospel and organizing the early Christian communities.

Almost all the synagogues in which Jesus and his disciples preached were destroyed in the course of the Jewish war with the Romans from A.D. 66 to 73. The ruins of a synagogue found at Capernaum (where Jesus began his ministry) date only from the end of the third or fourth century A.D.; traces of an earlier identifiable synagogue have yet to be found.

The city of Jerusalem was destroyed by the Romans. The grandiose buildings which the Herods had built for the ages barely outlived their creators. In the Gospel of Mark, Jesus himself predicts the destruction of the temple: "Do you see these great buildings? There will not be left here one stone upon another, that will not be thrown down" (Mark 13.2).

Archaeologists have found the paved streets of Jesus' day. Stones from the temple platform wall still lie on them as silent witness to the Roman destruction.

The main archaeological remnant of Jesus' time is the retaining wall of the temple area. The famous "Wailing Wall" is part of the western portion of that wall. Only a few years ago, the south wall (where the main gate and stairway were) was uncovered. Houses and other buildings of Jesus' time are also being found under the destruction debris of the wall. Another site of the New Testament period uncovered in Jerusalem is the floor of the Antonia fortress where Jesus may have stood before Pontius Pilate. The paving stones

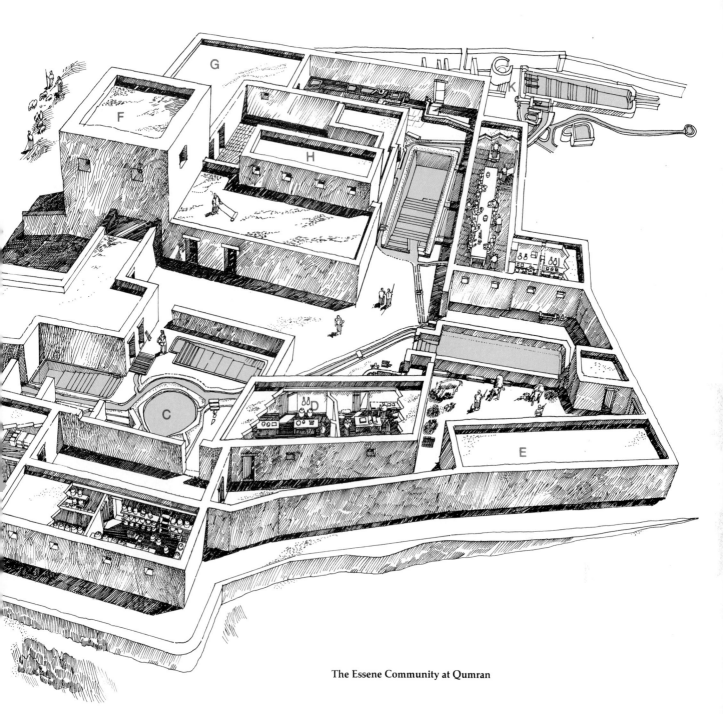

The Essene Community at Qumran

On a barren promontory on the northwestern coast of the Dead Sea lie remains of a unique settlement—Khirbet Qumran, enclave of the Essenes, or "Holy Ones." Near the end of the 2nd century B.C. these Jewish dissenters left a Jerusalem they felt was too worldly and settled here. Within their walls they prayed, meditated and took frequent ritual baths to purify themselves for the coming of a Messiah. Here they also worked as scribes, copying religious writings on long leather scrolls. Discovered only recently, these transcriptions are now known as the Dead Sea Scrolls (see p. 389). Qumran consisted of a cluster of buildings grouped around a canal system specially designed for the baptism rituals of the Essenes. As shown above in blue, water entered the compound by way of a broad aqueduct (A) from a waterfall to the west. It flowed through a bathing pool (B) and into conduits supplying seven major cisterns (C), other pools and certain buildings. Bread for the members' ceremonial meals was made in a mill and bakery (D), adjacent to which was a stable (E). Here pack animals were kept for use in hauling supplies from a farm about two miles to the south. There was also a tall watchtower (F) and a kitchen (G). Nearby was a scriptorium (H) where the holy texts were copied. The largest room in the compound was the refectory/assembly hall (I), and in a pantry (J) adjoining it about a thousand dishes have been found—suggesting that pilgrims may have come on occasion. At a pottery works (K) clay jars were made in which to store the scrolls. Qumran fell to the Romans in the Jews' revolt of A.D. 68, and was abandoned until excavations were begun there in 1951.

still bear the marks carved by Roman soldiers to make a game board for their garrison. Today the floor of the Antonia lies beneath a convent.

The main source of knowledge of the New Testament period outside the Bible itself is not archaeological but literary. Such documents as the Dead Sea Scrolls, the writings of Josephus—a Jewish officer in the war with the Romans (A.D. 66–73)—and the works of the Roman historian Tacitus offer valuable information and insights into Jesus' time. Tacitus, who wrote some 40 years after Jesus' death, described the attitude of a typical Roman toward the early Christians. In his description of the mad Emperor Nero's persecution, Tacitus wrote: ". . . Nero fastened the guilt and inflicted the most exquisite tortures on a class hated for their abominations, called Christians by the populace. Christus, from whom the name had its origin, suffered the extreme penalty during the reign of Tiberius at the hands of one of our procurators, Pontius Pilatus, and a most mischievous superstition, thus checked for the moment, again broke out not only in Judea, the first source of the evil, but even in Rome, where all things hideous and shameful from every part of the world find their center and become popular" (Tacitus, Annals 15.44).

Jesus' followers probably wrote little, if anything, themselves. Since they expected the world to end very soon, they felt no need to record Jesus' thoughts and actions. Besides, most of them were probably illiterate—the ability to read and write was rare until modern times. But the authors of the Gospels apparently did rely on accounts written very soon after the crucifixion. And our story is based on theirs. This, in summary, is the story of the New Testament as told in the chapters that follow.

The Life of Jesus

The story of Jesus began with his birth in Bethlehem in Judea in 6 B.C., during the last years of the reign of Herod the Great. (We now know that the date formerly accepted for his birth was inaccurate and that he was actually born some six years earlier.) A few weeks after his birth, his parents, Mary and Joseph, learned of Herod's plan to murder all the male infants in Bethlehem and fled to Egypt. At Herod's death, they returned to Joseph's hometown of Nazareth, where Jesus spent his childhood and young manhood.

When Jesus reached the age of 12, he traveled to Jerusalem for the Passover holiday and was fascinated by the learned rabbis in the temple. Some years later, Jesus heard of a remarkable prophet named John. Eagerly, he joined the crowds flocking to hear John and was baptized by the prophet. After this profound spiritual experience, Jesus spent 40 days in the wilderness. Then he returned and spent several months as a disciple of John before beginning his own mission.

Returning to Galilee, Jesus gathered disciples and began healing and preaching in synagogues, proclaiming: "The time is fulfilled, and the kingdom of God is at hand; repent, and believe in the gospel." Many came to hear his message. In time, his popularity, his tolerance of sinners and his outspoken manner began to arouse the opposition of the influential Pharisees.

After learning of the death of John the Baptist, Jesus redoubled his efforts to gather followers and spread the gospel. He appointed the 12 apostles and sent them out to preach and heal the sick. Meanwhile, Herod Antipas, ruler of Galilee, hearing rumors of Jesus' miracles, feared that Jesus might be the Messiah, or perhaps John the Baptist returned to life. With some Pharisees, he plotted to arrest and kill Jesus, but, warned of these plans, Jesus and the apostles fled to Judea.

After preaching to the Judeans for several months, Jesus made his final journey to Jerusalem for Passover. A large procession accompanied Jesus to the temple, where he overturned the tables of the moneychangers and drove out the vendors of sacrifical animals. On the eve of Passover, Jesus and the apostles celebrated their last meal together. Late that night he was arrested.

He was taken before the Sanhedrin, the Jewish high court, and tried and convicted of blasphemy. Since the Sanhedrin could not give the death sentence, they brought him before the Roman governor, Pontius Pilate, who sentenced Jesus to die by crucifixion. The order was carried out and Jesus died a painful death on the cross.

Paul and the Apostles

Less than two months after the crucifixion, the apostles returned to Jerusalem to found a community of believers in the Messiahship of Jesus. Led by Peter and inspired by visions of the resurrected Jesus, they gathered a group of the faithful and preached the gospel in Jerusalem's synagogues and temple. Among the new followers were a group of Greek-speaking, or Hellenist, Jews. Their leader, Stephen, was stoned to death by an angry mob for blasphemy. Paul of Tarsus was involved in the persecutions of Hellenist Christians that followed. The Hellenists fled to cities in Samaria, Egypt, Cyprus and Syria and founded churches. Intent on destroying the new sect, Paul traveled to Damascus, but on the way a vivid vision of the resurrected Jesus transformed him into a zealous Christian.

Rome's Cruel Way with Rebels

Crucifixion, a common practice in Jesus' time, was the penalty for robbery, tumult and sedition. It was reserved for slaves and foreigners, and was intended to be a form of public humiliation. The victim was nailed to a T-shaped cross through the wrists and ankles, as the hands and feet would not support the body. Ropes under the arms and a heavy peg between the legs gave additional support. Death came slowly, usually from heart failure or asphyxiation rather than loss of blood. Though many written accounts of crucifixions exist, our only tangible evidence are the heel bones (right) of a 30-year-old man, found with the spike still in them. The victim was crucified in the 1st century.

Largely through the tireless and inspired missionary work of Paul, Christianity grew from a small Jewish sect into a new religion, whose converts were mainly Gentiles. With Barnabas, Paul joined an established Christian community at Antioch in Syria. From there he launched three extensive missionary journeys, founding Christian communities in major cities throughout Asia Minor and Greece. Along the way he met opposition and persecution from both pagans and fellow Jews. The church in Jerusalem at first opposed his mission to the Gentiles, but later reluctantly agreed to it.

Returning from his third journey, Paul was imprisoned in Jerusalem at the insistence of hostile Jews, taken to Caesarea and finally to Rome to await trial. There he is said to have worked with the aged apostle Peter and (like Peter) to have met his death during Nero's persecutions. His legacy included a vital network of Christian churches and an extensive Christian theology, beautifully expressed in his letters, which conveyed the full richness of his experience of Christ.

The Message of Jesus and Paul

Jesus had preached a gospel of love, promising men that the kingdom of heaven was near. After Jesus' death, when it seemed that the Lord's judgment would not come very soon, the apostles put more emphasis on the role of the risen Christ as the Redeemer. Judgment would come in God's own time, but meanwhile men must prepare for it. Paul in particular, taught his listeners to see in Jesus a man like themselves who was at the same time uniquely the Son of God, prepared to share with them his kinship with the Father. Religion then became a deep *personal* experience, no longer a matter of fate, duty or fear but a doctrine of personal grace and love addressed to all men. Moreover, it was not centered in a temple or shrine but in men's hearts.

Paul preached that the gospel, crucifixion and resurrection of Jesus signified a new covenant with the Lord, complementing the old covenant, or testament. He believed that the prophet Jeremiah had foreseen this: "And no longer shall each man teach his neighbor and each, his brother, saying, 'Know the Lord,' for they shall all know me, from the least of them to the greatest, says the Lord; for I will forgive their iniquity, and I will remember their sin no more" (Jeremiah 31.34).

Part Six
Seekers
of the Messiah

"In those days a decree went out from Caesar Augustus that all the world should be enrolled" (Lk. 2.1).
For this special census, Jews from all over the empire returned to their ancestral homes—like Bethlehem,
above—to be counted. During the busy period they took shelter at the caravansary or inn at left, on the
rooftops of private homes or in caves in the outlying hills. Here shopkeepers, their markets lining the
bustling square, hawk their wares as a constant stream of travelers enters the town. Women carry jars of
water from the well for themselves and their guests, as the men from each household file past the Roman
census takers' table to report family size and worth. This was the setting in which Jesus was born, as Joseph,
along with other Jews, submitted to the rule of Rome. Jesus' death would change that world forever.

Soldiers and officials of imperial Rome imposed an uneasy peace in Palestine. Armed garrisons controlled the countryside, and even the sacred temple bore Caesar's emblem. But promises of a Messiah gave the oppressed Jews new hope.

PALESTINE on the eve of Jesus' birth was a crossroads of cultures and peoples. Its 2,000,000 people—ruled by Rome—were divided by geography, religion and politics. In a day's journey a man could travel from rural villages where farmers still tilled their fields with primitive plows to bustling cities where men enjoyed the comforts of Roman civilization. In the Holy City of Jerusalem, Jewish priests offered sacrifices to the Lord of Israel, while at Sebaste, only 30 miles away, pagan priests held rites in honor of the Roman god Jupiter. Only half of Palestine's population was now Jewish. The remainder was a mixture of pagan Greeks, Romans, Syrians, Egyptians, Arabs, Persians and Babylonians. The Jews themselves were split into many rival, and sometimes hostile, sects.

The Romans had divided Palestine into five provinces: from north to south were Galilee, Samaria, Judea and Idumea; to the east of Judea, across the Jordan River, was Perea. Most Jews lived in rural sections of Galilee, Perea and Judea or in the Holy City of Jerusalem. The Samaritans and Idumeans (Edomites), followers of Judaism who were regarded as heretics by the Jews, also lived primarily in rural areas. Most others lived in the prosperous new cities located along the coast and the main routes of travel. These beautiful towns, with their colonnaded avenues and graceful, pillared buildings, were showplaces of Greek and Roman culture.

Most Jews despised their foreign overlords and deeply resented the presence of a pagan culture in their ancient homeland. Yet they disagreed about how to oppose it. In the hills of Galilee, bands of Jewish patriots plotted armed rebellion, but only a few hours away, in their Dead Sea sanctuary, the Essenes patiently awaited a "heavenly Deliverer." For many other Jews, too, it was a time of hope and expectation as well as despair. They believed they were about to witness the dawn of a new age.

Promises of the Prophets

For centuries the prophets and holy men of Israel had foreseen the coming of a day when the Lord would deliver his people from their pagan rulers and establish his kingdom over the entire earth. On that day he would send a savior to bring an end to the corrupt world of the present and replace it with an eternal earthly paradise. He would resurrect the dead and judge their actions in this world. The wicked would be punished, but the righteous would be rewarded with eternal life in the new kingdom of God.

According to the Book of Daniel and other popular Jewish writings, the Lord's kingdom would be established only after a final, cosmic struggle between the forces of evil, led by Satan, and the forces of good, led by the Lord. It would end with the destruction of the existing world and the creation of a paradise in which evil would be unknown and peace would reign forever. This belief, along with ideas about the resurrection of the dead and the last judgment, were not mentioned in the books of Moses, but had developed among the exiled Jews in Babylonia and Persia. In Jesus' day, however, they were very much a part of common Jewish belief. Only the Sadducees rejected them, on the grounds that these things did not appear in the scriptures.

Most people were uncertain about the details of the kingdom's arrival. Some believed that the prophet Elijah, who had ascended to heaven without dying, would return to earth to herald its approach. Others felt that the Lord would send an agent, a Messiah, to establish his benevolent rule on earth. This Messiah, many believed, would be a descendant of Israel's beloved King David. Descriptions of the Messiah's arrival, like the one in the Book of Daniel, fired the popular imagination: "I saw in the night visions, and behold, with the clouds of heaven there came one like a son of man . . ." (Daniel 7.13).

With a sense of urgency such Jews looked for ways to prepare themselves for the coming of the new age. The Essenes withdrew into isolated communities of prayer and contemplation. (The Dead Sea Scrolls were written by these men.) A lone, fiery leader named John the Baptist urged his followers to repent of their sins and to be baptized with water as preparation for membership in the coming kingdom.

Jesus was among those baptized by John in the Jordan River, and soon afterward he began his own mission, proclaiming: "The time is fulfilled, and the kingdom of God is at hand; repent, and believe in the gospel" (Mark 1.15).

The Jews of Galilee

The subject of the kingdom of God was a burning issue among the Jews during Jesus' lifetime and played a major role in the political hopes of the people of Palestine. The Jews of Galilee, Judea and Perea were essentially a rural people, living in hundreds of small towns and villages scattered throughout the countryside. They worked the land, tended flocks, practiced trades and seldom ventured more than a day's journey from home. They might see the Holy City occasionally—traveling there as Joseph and his family did to celebrate Passover—but otherwise their world was limited to their own village and surrounding fields.

Such a village might claim no more than several hundred inhabitants who lived in modest, one-story houses of mud brick clustered together on the side of a hill. Between the houses, narrow unpaved streets and alleyways wound toward a dusty square at the center of town. There women came daily to shop in the open-air market and to draw water from the communal well, while older men gathered to chat and pass the time of day.

Each town had a handful of local craftsmen, usually including a carpenter, potter, weaver, blacksmith and shoemaker. Their small one-room shops stood at the edge of the marketplace. Most of these craftsmen worked with the help of an assistant or a young apprentice, generally their own sons, to whom they taught their trade. Young Jesus probably served as an apprentice to his father, Joseph the carpenter.

Every morning the men of the village went out to the fields to till, sow, prune or harvest the crops on which their existence depended. For these men, as for the generations who had worked the land before them, life was a long, difficult struggle against the elements. The plows, sickles and other tools they used were generally makeshift devices, little better than those the Patriarchs used. At dusk they returned to their homes, wearily driving their few oxen before them.

Most families also kept a few sheep and goats for food, leather and wool. At sunrise each day shepherds could be seen leading the village flocks to nearby hillsides for pasturage.

After dinner the men were expected to gather in the village synagogue for evening services. Following prayers, the local rabbi (Hebrew for "teacher") or another member of the congregation would read a passage from the scriptures (holy writings) and comment on it, inviting discussion.

During the day the synagogue served as the schoolhouse for the young boys of the village. Their teacher was a respected figure in the town and absolute master of his one-room school.

Most of the boys learned the ancient Hebrew language in the synagogue classroom, because at home and among themselves most of them spoke Aramaic, a language related to Hebrew that had come into use since the Exile. Each region in Palestine had developed its own particular dialect of Aramaic, and a man from Judea could easily identify a Galilean by his distinct accent.

Larger towns and cities were often fortunate enough to have a scribe (sometimes called a doctor of the law) as a teacher and religious adviser to the community. These influential men had spent most of their lives studying and copying the sacred scriptures. Their primary concerns were preserving and teaching the scriptures and interpreting the laws of the Torah, the five books containing the laws and commandments the Lord gave to Moses. They and they alone could decide

Herod the Great built a network of hilltop fortresses in Palestine, each within signaling distance of at least one other. One of the most impressive of these engineering feats was the citadel south of Bethlehem called Herodium (left). The hill itself was made higher, and three concentric walls and four round towers were erected on the summit, reached by 200 marble steps. Remains of a colonnaded courtyard (right) show Hellenistic influence. Herod was buried in Herodium amid spectacular funeral rites, in which the army escorted his solid gold bier.

whether it was lawful for a man to divorce his wife because she was flirtatious; whether a man could lawfully repair his leaky roof on the Sabbath; or how many threads must be on each tassle of a prayer shawl.

Most scribes were affiliated with a particular school of thinking, headed by a famous rabbi who was surrounded by a circle of disciples, or devoted followers. There were many scribal schools in Palestine in the first century A.D., most of them based in Jerusalem. It was not unusual for followers of different schools to engage in heated public discussions over a particular point of the law. The courtyard of the temple and other public places were often the scenes of such discussions.

Days of Worship and Celebration

From sundown every Friday until sundown on Saturday, all work ceased in Jewish towns and villages throughout Palestine. This was the Sabbath, the day given over to the worship of the Lord. (The Jewish day began at sunset rather than at daybreak; their months began with the new moon.) According to rabbinical law, 39 kinds of work were forbidden on the Sabbath. These in-

cluded almost every kind of labor, except that absolutely necessary, like saving a person's life.

Besides the weekly Sabbath observances, there were a number of special religious festivals. The most popular of these were the feasts of Passover, Weeks and Booths. On these occasions throngs of pilgrims traveled to Jerusalem from all parts of Palestine and the Roman Empire to take part in elaborate ceremonies. There were colorful processions and numerous sacrifices at the temple.

The Passover, commemorating the deliverance from Egypt, was celebrated in late March or early April. The Feast of Weeks, marking the end of the grain harvest, took place in late May or early June. The Feast of Booths (Succoth), held in the early fall, celebrated the grape harvest and commemorated Israel's wandering in the wilderness.

Other religious festivals included the Feast of the New Moon, which marked the first day of each month; the Feast of Lights, commemorating the purification of the temple by Judas Maccabeus; and the Feast of Purim, celebrating the deliverance of the Jews by Esther and Mordecai. These festivals often had a joyous, carnival-like atmosphere, with much merriment and feasting.

One festival, though, was most solemn. This

was the Day of Atonement, a time of repentance and expiation for the sins of the nation of Israel. No food was eaten, no liquid drunk and no pleasures indulged in on that day. The high priest of the temple offered special sacrifices and then entered the holy of holies, an empty, windowless room at the innermost part of the temple building. There he prayed to the Lord for forgiveness of the nation's sins and uttered aloud the name of the Lord—*Yahweh*—a name so sacred no one else dared say it aloud. Even the high priest spoke it only on the Day of Atonement.

The People of the Lord and Rome

To the Jews whom Jesus lived among, their religion represented more than a form of worship. It gave them their unique identity as a people. While other nations worshiped pagan gods in the visible form of "graven images" (idols), the Jews alone worshiped a single, invisible God, believed more powerful than all the other gods together.

The Jews believed their Lord had given them a special place in history. At the time of the Exodus, he had revealed himself to Moses and made a covenant with the people of Israel. The terms of the covenant were demanding: the Lord promised to give the Israelites a land and a prosperous future if they would give him their steadfast love and abide by his laws and commandments. Throughout their history the Jews had failed repeatedly to keep their side of the covenant, and national disasters had invariably followed: foreign invasions, civil dissension, occupation and even exile. Time and again, the prophets and holy men exhorted the Jews to return to the covenant and to obey the laws and commandments. The Lord, they preached, would reward the faithful.

By the time of Jesus, though, many Jews (the Sadducees excepted) despaired of any hope of reward in their present unjust world, and concentrated on the expectation of reward in a world to come. Their recent history had been one of almost continuous calamity and foreign rule. For the last eight centuries, they had been subject successively to Assyria, Babylonia, Persia, Greece, Egypt, Syria and Rome.

Most Jews viewed their new masters with hostility and suspicion. For their part, the Romans found these people among the most difficult to govern in the entire empire. Palestine's political stability was especially important to Rome be-

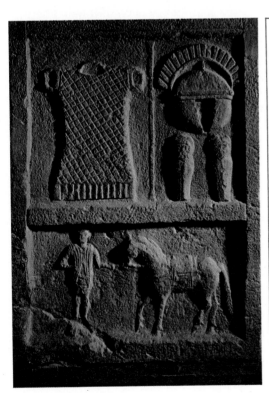

An Empire Builder's Arms and Armor

The policemen of Jesus' world were the legions of the Roman army—contingents of 6000 foot soldiers who were supplemented by cavalrymen and smaller auxiliary units. At far left is the tombstone of a Roman cavalryman who served on the Danube. Carved on it are his horse, leg armor, spear, crested helmet and metal-reinforced jerkin. At left, a legionnaire wears a short suit of leather armor covered with bronze. His weapons are a javelin and double-edged sword. The Roman javelin was an innovation, barbed to stick fast in its target. The shaft bent on impact, so the weapon was too damaged to turn back against the thrower. Their superior weapons and surpassing strategic knowledge made the Romans invincible for centuries.

cause the country straddled a vital commercial and military highway, linking Asia, Africa and Europe by land and sea. Moreover, it shared a common border with two of Rome's potential enemies: the powerful kingdom of Parthia, which controlled a large empire east of the Euphrates; and the kingdom of the Nabateans, a strong desert people who dominated important overland commerce between Arabia, India and the Mediterranean countries.

Rome devised an elaborate defense system to maintain security in Palestine. A string of garrisons and fortresses protected the eastern border, and additional strongholds stood at strategic spots throughout the country. This military presence provided the Jews with a constant reminder of their nation's subjugation to Rome.

Another odious aspect of Roman rule was taxation. Rome appointed officials to make an annual circuit through the country to collect a head tax, based on the value of each household's income and personal property. To keep track of the total number of households, the Romans made a periodic census of the population. Such an enrollment brought Joseph and Mary back to their ancestral town of Bethlehem.

Taxes were gathered by the infamous publicans, or tax collectors, so often mentioned in the Gospels. Required to pay only a fixed amount to the imperial treasury each year, they were free to collect as much from the public as they could. In Jesus' lifetime the publicans were among the most corrupt and despised figures in Palestine. Yet Jesus made a point of befriending these and other social outcasts. His disciple Matthew had originally been such a tax collector.

A Conflict of Cultures

Although the Jews disliked Rome's military controls and heavy taxation, their resentment of Roman rule was much more deep-seated. In the eyes of devout Jews, the Romans were not just another in a long series of alien conquerors. They were representatives of a hated way of life. Imperial rule again brought to Palestine the Hellenistic culture which the Syrians had tried to impose forcibly on the Jews over a century before.

Most Jews, especially the Jewish peasantry, stubbornly refused to accept Roman rule and Hellenization. More than ever, they emphasized those traditions and practices that set them apart from pagan cultures. They became intolerant of people they considered unclean (ritually impure), and extremely sensitive about small details of religious observance. Thus the mere presence in Jerusalem of Roman guards bearing imperial standards (poles with insignia on their tops) could touch off riots because the emblems violated the Lord's commandment against graven images.

Politically, pious Jews were represented by the influential sect called the Pharisees. These men lived apart from other men (their name means "separated ones") and adhered scrupulously to every detail of Jewish law. Their piety made them respected among the common people of the land. After Herod the Great became king, they refused his demand that his subjects take a personal oath of allegiance to him. This act was in line with their view that the holy life was separate from and above politics.

Not all Jews found Roman rule distasteful. The hundreds of thousands in the Roman Empire outside Palestine welcomed it. They benefited considerably from Roman improvements in commerce, transportation and technology. Living in large urban centers in Syria, Egypt, Asia Minor, Greece and Italy, they had gradually become accustomed to Hellenistic ways and had adopted many superficial aspects of Greek culture. Yet they held to their traditional religious beliefs, and every Jew living outside Palestine looked forward to making at least one pilgrimage to the Holy City during his lifetime.

In Palestine itself certain Jews found Roman support tolerable and at times advantageous. Among them were members of Jerusalem's aristocracy. From this small group of wealthy, pedigreed families came the high priest and the lesser priests of the temple. Many of them found the sophisticated manners and fashions of Greco-Roman culture to their liking and some even took Greek names. Their interests were represented by the conservative political group known as the Sadducees. At the time of Jesus, these men still controlled the high Jewish council, or Sanhedrin, but they had little influence among the common people. They were engaged in bitter rivalry with the increasingly powerful Pharisees for control of the Jerusalem temple.

The Romans tried to appease their temperamental Jewish subjects as much as they could without losing the upper hand. They retained the important office of high priest, for example, but

"When Herod's birthday came, the daughter of Herodias danced before the company"(Mt. 14.6). The scene below might be a typical Roman-style feast at Herod Antipas' palace at Machaerus. Such occasions began with exotic appetizers like jellyfish and fungi and ended with pastries and fruit. Elaborate main courses were served, such as flamingo tongues, wild boar, and lobster with truffles. Here revelers enjoy an exotic professional dancer.

Good roads and military patrols made travel easy and safe in the Roman world by the early 2nd century. Travelers and mail could go anywhere in the empire by means of a highway system branching out from the forum in Rome. Sturdy carriages such as the one in the relief above also hauled baggage, foodstuffs and spoils of war.

in effect he was a Rome-appointed official and his ceremonial garments were in Roman custody. He was given them only on religious holidays. They allowed the Jews complete freedom of worship, but they were careful to station extra guards in Jerusalem during the major religious festivals, when huge throngs of pilgrims filled the streets and tempers ran high. They even forbade the use of the emperor's portrait on coins and public buildings in Jewish sections of Palestine, in deference to the first commandment.

Herod the Great

Rome needed a shrewd and capable agent in Palestine, and in Herod the Great they felt they had found such a man. Young, ambitious and brutal when necessary, Herod was not a true Jew but an Idumean, whose forefathers had been forced to convert to Judaism a century before. He had first come to Rome's attention when, as governor of Galilee, he quickly put down a minor Jewish rebellion in 47 B.C. Seven years later, when civil war disrupted the country, Herod fled to Rome and persuaded the Romans to name him king of Judea in order to restore peace.

During his long reign, which lasted until his death in 4 B.C., Herod kept an uneasy peace by dealing ruthlessly with suspected rivals and troublemakers. He systematically killed off all living claimants to the Hasmonean kingship, in-

cluding his young brother-in-law, the high priest Aristobulus. He even ordered the execution of his favorite wife, Mariamne, and her mother because he believed they were plotting against him. Shortly before his death, he had three of his own sons killed because of rumors that they had designs on his throne. It is easy to imagine such a man ordering the massacre of all male infants in Bethlehem for no better reason than a vague rumor that one had been born "King of the Jews."

Herod never succeeded in winning the loyalty of most Jews in his realm. To them he was a pagan and a usurper. He had been crowned in a pagan ceremony and, by taxing the Jews, had financed the building of pagan temples in Palestine and in other locations throughout the empire. Moreover, though Herod had married a woman of the Hasmonean family, he himself had no legitimate claim to Jewish royalty.

With what many saw as a callous disregard for Jewish tradition, Herod actively fostered the growth of Hellenistic culture in Palestine. He invited scholars from all parts of the empire to his court to discuss the ideas of Greek philosophy and science, and he sent most of his sons to Rome to receive a classical education. In Caesarea he inaugurated an international athletic competition modeled on Greece's Olympic Games, to be held every ten years.

The most visible aspect of Herod's encouragement of Hellenism was a tremendous building program that literally changed the face of Palestine. He constructed whole new cities throughout his realm and enlarged existing ones, adding pagan temples, gymnasiums, aqueducts, amphitheaters, theaters, public baths, gardens and hippodromes (racing stadiums).

The king also transformed Jerusalem with the construction of a magnificent palace and gardens, the reconstruction of fortifications, a huge palace-fortress (the Antonia), impressive public buildings and a spectacular new temple complex.

Herod had hoped that rebuilding the temple area would at last win the trust and loyalty of his Jewish subjects, but even this extravagant display of good will failed. Most Jews openly hoped for his death, but when it finally came in 4 B.C., conditions did not improve. Herod's kingdom was divided among three of his remaining sons, Philip, Herod Antipas and Archelaus, and for the most part, they continued the policies of their father.

Philip ruled the lands north and east of the Sea

of Galilee, where he built the beautiful Greek-style city of Caesarea Philippi. Herod Antipas, who received the districts of Galilee and Perea, was almost as ambitious a builder as his father. His reign spanned Jesus' youth and ministry, and it was he who ordered the execution of John the Baptist. Archelaus was named Ethnarch of Judea, which included Samaria and Idumea, but he was removed from office in A.D. 6. Rome made Judea an imperial province.

The arrival of the first Roman governor set off riots in Jerusalem. This unrest soon spread to other parts of the country, especially unruly Galilee. In Sepphoris, capital of Galilee, the revolt was led by a zealous Jew known as Judas. Although the outbreak was quickly and ruthlessly suppressed, the fierce dedication of Judas and his followers inspired other Jews to form a clandestine rebel group known as the Zealots. During Jesus' lifetime these men engaged in sporadic guerrilla warfare in the hills of Galilee. They were to play a leading role in the unsuccessful Jewish rebellion against Rome in A.D. 66–73.

Such was the Jewish nation Jesus knew, a proud, stubborn people ruled by hated alien masters. As the years passed with no sign of relief from their affliction, they concentrated more and more on their visions of a world to come. They sought reassurance in the inspired writings of prophets like Isaiah, who promised them:
"Say to those who are of a fearful heart,
    'Be strong, fear not!
Behold, your God
    will come with [vindication],
with the recompense of God.
    He will come and save you' " (Isaiah 35.4).
Impatiently, the Jews waited for a sign that their Lord had not forgotten them.

The Travels of Jesus During His Ministry in Galilee and Judea

Born in Bethlehem, carried as an infant to Egypt and raised in Nazareth of Galilee, Jesus may have traveled more in his youth than during his ministry. After his baptism and 40 days in the Judean desert he returned to Galilee, where he spent most of his ministry. From his lakeside headquarters in Capernaum he visited Cana, Nain and Bethsaida—traditional sites of his miracles. Always he and his disciples stayed on the move, to gather followers and, when necessary, elude hostile authorities. In the last months of his ministry Jesus taught in Jericho, and for Passover went to Jerusalem, where he was tried and crucified.

The Romans: Architects of Order

Jesus' Palestine was a border province in a Roman Empire which, at its height, stretched from Egypt to Britain and from the Black Sea to Gibraltar. Rome's brilliantly conceived—and firmly imposed—legal and military administration brought economic prosperity to most areas of the Mediterranean world. At the same time, local customs and religions were officially tolerated, because the Romans sought to unify and pacify conquered peoples. The empire's diverse nations were also encouraged to adopt the Hellenistic culture of ancient Greece, and to adore the emperor as a sign of loyalty. But in Jesus' time and the ensuing century of Roman rule, efforts to impose such policies in Palestine met stout resistance from the Jews, who were determined never to relinquish their national and religious identity.

"Render to Caesar the things that are Caesar's, and to God the things that are God's" (Mk. 12.17). Tiberius Caesar (A.D. 14–37), the emperor who ruled during Jesus' ministry, appears on this 1st-century cameo. Tiberias, Galilee's new capital built in A.D. 25, was named after this detested ruler.

The Jews found many aspects of Roman religion distasteful, including their pantheon of gods (many borrowed directly from the Greeks) and the practice of emperor worship. Augustus ("The Exalted One"), Rome's first emperor, was worshiped as a god and officially deified after his death. Above, he officiates as a bull is sacrificed to the imperial gods.

A network of 50,000 miles of highways linked Rome's 43 provinces by the early 2nd century A.D. Many are still in use today. Straight, level and wide, they provided safe overland transport for travelers, wagons, caravans and armies. Rome's engineers extended these vital arteries into each newly conquered area. They first excavated down to bedrock, then added rubble and concrete filler and a smooth surface of fitted paving blocks. Most roads also had shoulders and drainage ditches. At right is a Roman road in Judea.

Aqueducts were favorite building projects of the provincial kings and governors of the Roman Empire. Remains of them have been found in Africa, Spain, France, England, Germany and Asia Minor. Above is one that provided Caesarea, on Palestine's Mediterranean coast, with water from the Carmel hills over 20 miles away. Basically, an aqueduct was a channel to conduct water from a higher, distant source to a town without a local water supply. They could be elevated on arches, as above, or subterranean. Dropping an average of one foot for every 200 feet of length, these aqueducts were as much as 30 miles long. The channels were concrete-covered, and so efficient that the flowing water could be siphoned upward over short spans.

Rome's invincible legions enforced the peace throughout the empire. These tough units of 6000 professional soldiers—all Roman citizens— were aided by auxiliary troops from Gaul, Germany and other provinces. In the province of Syria, Rome stationed three or more legions, but most soldiers in Palestine were noncitizen, provincial auxiliaries. There were military colonies at Sebaste (former site of Samaria) and at Caesarea, and guard posts and fortresses at strategic points throughout Judea. Legionnaires and auxiliaries were frequently transferred, and the two infantrymen shown on this German relief from Mainz, legion headquarters on the Rhine River, might also have been among the auxiliaries in Judea.

Chapter 20

*A son is born to a Galilean carpenter and his wife at a time when
many Jews are awaiting a sign of the coming of the Lord. The boy grows up
among pious farmers and craftsmen and learns his religious heritage.*

A Family of Nazareth:
Joseph, Mary and Jesus

*Only two of the Gospel writers, Matthew and Luke, tell
of Jesus' birth. They include in their accounts supernatural occurrences and signs which have become part of
the Christian tradition: the conception of Jesus as a miraculous gift of the Holy Spirit, the angel's announce-
ment of the birth to the shepherds and the visit of three
wise men, or magi, to the infant. These lend support to
the belief that the child was indeed the Messiah sent by
the Lord to redeem Israel and all humanity. Yet beyond
this miraculous aura, there is also the probable life of
Jesus as a child in Galilee, living, playing and learning
as thousands of Jewish boys were doing 2000 years ago.*

Jesus of Nazareth was probably born in the
Roman year 747, or 6 B.C. by our calendar. According to Luke, his parents, Joseph and Mary,
had traveled from Nazareth to Bethlehem, the
home of Joseph's forefathers, to be counted as
part of a Roman census: "In those days a decree
went out from Caesar Augustus that all the world
should be enrolled. This was the first enrollment,
when Quirinius was governor of Syria. And all
went to be enrolled, each to his own city." As the
young couple made their way toward Bethlehem,
they passed hundreds of Jews from throughout
the Empire who, like themselves, were returning
to their ancestral homes for the census.

In appearance, Bethlehem, four-and-a-half
miles south of Jerusalem, was no different from
dozens of other hamlets in the stony hill country
of Judea. A traveler approaching the town would
have seen a cluster of boxlike, whitewashed

houses on the top of a low but rather steep ridge.
Perhaps 300 people lived there.

Although small, Bethlehem was a busy place.
Caravans traveling to Egypt often stopped there,
and a caravansary, the Palestinian version of a
hospice or inn, had been built there in the time of
King David, nearly a thousand years earlier. Repaired and rebuilt, it had remained in use over
the centuries. The tomb of Ruth was in the little
town, and in the valley below lay the field of
Boaz. Most important, Bethlehem was the birthplace of David, Israel's beloved shepherd-king.

For Jews of the time, Bethlehem had a very
special significance. It was the place where—
according to the prophet Micah—the savior of
Israel, the Messiah, would be born: "But you, O
Bethlehem . . . from you shall come forth for me
[God] one who is to be ruler in Israel, whose origin is from of old, from ancient days. . . . And he
shall stand and feed his flock in the strength of
the Lord, in the majesty of the name of the Lord
his God. And they shall dwell secure, for now he
shall be great to the ends of the earth."

Late in the afternoon of the fifth day of their
journey, Joseph and Mary approached Bethlehem. They had walked the 90 miles from Nazareth, their provisions loaded on the back of a

*"And Joseph also went up from Galilee, from the city of Nazareth,
to Judea, to the city of David, which is called Bethlehem" (Lk. 2.4).
Over this Galilean tableland lay the rough road taken by Joseph
and his young wife, Mary, as they journeyed south to be enrolled
in the Roman census. Traveling by day and sleeping in tents by
night, they probably took almost a week to make the 90-mile trip.*

donkey. Joseph, a carpenter by trade, was a husky man in the prime of life. His young wife, probably still in her teens, was apprehensive for she knew she would soon be in labor.

Lodging in Bethlehem

As they passed through the entrance to the town, where helmeted Roman sentries stood guard, they came upon a scene of noisy confusion. The dusty square that served as Bethlehem's marketplace was jammed with people of every description: uniformed Roman soldiers and officials; wealthy Jews from Egypt, Greece and Rome; aristocratic families from Jerusalem; peasants and craftsmen from rural Judea, Galilee and Perea. Merchants elbowed their way through the crowd, noisily hawking food and provisions.

The caravansary, which stood at the edge of the square, was bustling with activity, and Joseph quickly realized that he would have to look elsewhere for lodging. The courtyard was crowded with caravaneers unsaddling their camels and donkeys and bedding them down for the night. Upstairs the rooms were overflowing with weary guests. Even the flat roof was fully occupied.

Ordinarily, Joseph could have found a room in a private home, but a few inquiries showed that every available space had already been taken. A helpful villager suggested he might find shelter in one of the caves in the hillside near Bethlehem, used by local herdsmen as stables.

Because of Mary's urgent condition, one peasant agreed to let Joseph use his cave stable and gave him a bundle of straw for bedding and a lighted clay lamp filled with olive oil. Joseph made a comfortable bed for Mary from the straw, and gave her his woolen cloak for a blanket. Near the back of the cave he found a feeding trough, or manger, which had been hollowed out from the wall. He filled it with straw so that it could serve as a cradle for the expected child.

A Child Is Born

That night or perhaps early the next morning, Mary began to feel the first pangs of labor. Joseph probably found a female servant or midwife in Bethlehem to assist at the birth. As soon as the wailing male infant had been born, the midwife cut the umbilical cord. Then she fetched water from a nearby well and gently bathed him. She probably also rubbed salt over the baby's body to guard against infection.

Mary then lovingly wrapped him in swaddling clothes, binding the long strips of linen so tightly that he could not move his arms or legs. This ancient custom was based on the belief that the child's limbs would not grow straight and strong unless they were bound so they could not move freely for at least six months.

Mary nursed her son and then carefully placed him in the manger. She and Joseph decided to name him Jeshua, a common Hebrew name meaning "the Lord is salvation." The Greek form of Jeshua is Jesus. In keeping with Jewish law, Joseph had his son circumcised with a metal knife eight days after the birth.

The day after Jesus' birth, Joseph went into the town to register with the census officials, but Mary remained behind. She could not mingle with other people because by Hebrew law a mother was considered unclean until 40 days after the birth of a son. (If the child had been a daughter, the mother would have been isolated for 40 more days.)

Flight to Egypt

At the end of that period, Joseph and Mary, cradling her infant son in her arms, trudged up the winding road to Jerusalem. There they would visit the temple to make the required offering marking the official end of Mary's confinement. They soon caught sight of the huge walled city with its enormous temple area, the temple itself gleaming gold and white. Entering through the Dung Gate, they made their way through the narrow unpaved streets of the commercial district and up to the temple.

Unable to afford the more prestigious offering of a lamb, they bought two doves from a dealer in the vast and crowded Court of the Gentiles. Joseph then left Mary in the Court of Women and ascended the stairs to the Court of Israel, where he handed the doves to the officiating priest. The priest placed the doves on the slaughtering table and solemnly slit their throats with a special knife. Then he collected the blood in a bronze basin, took the birds in his hands, climbed to the top of the great stone altar and placed them on the sacrificial fire. As the smoke rose upward, the voices of chanting Levites filled the air with psalms in praise of the Lord. A priest spoke the appropriate words for Mary, who was then officially cleansed and could begin to associate with other people again.

Shortly after Jesus' birth, King Herod, the ruler of Judea, learned of three wise men who followed a star from the east to Palestine, where they believed the Messiah had been born. Fearful that his throne might be in danger, Herod ordered that all male children in Bethlehem under the age of two were to be slaughtered. Joseph and Mary had been forewarned of Herod's plans and fled to Egypt with their infant son.

The Birthplace of Jesus

"And she gave birth to her first-born son . . . and laid him in a manger, because there was no place for them in the inn" (Lk. 2.7). The actual birthplace of Jesus is not told in the Gospels, but it may well have been one of the numerous caves surrounding Bethlehem.

"*You will find a babe wrapped in swaddling cloths and lying in a manger*"(Lk. 2.12). Like most Palestinian peoples, the Jews thought that swaddling an infant, or binding it with long cloth strips, would ensure straight limbs. (The practice was also used for mending broken bones.) This early nativity scene shows how the wrappings were actually used.

Most of Bethlehem's caves, like those at right, were originally formed by erosion of the area's soft limestone. For Mary and Joseph to seek refuge in one of them would not have been unusual, since some show signs of human and animal habitation dating from the Stone Age. Even today the caves provide natural manger space and shelter from Judea's winter climate, which at night averages a chilly 44 degrees.

Situated not far from Bethlehem's lush grasslands, these caves were excellent shelters for livestock and beasts of burden. As illustrated above, herdsmen often carved out niches in the cave wall and used them as feeding troughs. This man is dressed in clothes typical of Jesus' time: heavy-soled sandals, woolen tunic and sleeveless robe.

When Jesus was nearly two years old, news reached Joseph and Mary that Herod had died. The aged tyrant had spent his final years in agony, his mind and body wracked by disease.

Joseph decided it would now be safe to return to his native Galilee. This region, where Jesus was to spend most of his life, was probably the most beautiful and fertile in Palestine. Each spring the fields of Galilee were covered with a fresh mantle of wildflowers. Its gentle hills and grassy plains were ideally suited for growing grain and grazing flocks; grapes, figs, olives, pomegranates and many other fruits flourished in its pleasant climate. The clear blue waters of the Sea of Galilee, which is really an inland lake, contained myriads of fish, and supported whole villages of fishermen along its shores.

Galilee's natural beauty and abundance had attracted a large, racially mixed population. About half of them were Jews, like Joseph and his small family, who lived in rural towns and villages scattered throughout the hills and along the shores of the lake. Other Jews described their Galilean brothers as industrious, gay, kindly and optimistic people. They (and Jesus) spoke Aramaic, a Semitic language closely related to Hebrew. Most of the remaining Galileans were Greek or Greek-speaking.

Though peaceful now, Galilee would shortly see open and bloody battle between the Jews and the Romans. Jesus and his parents were probably untouched by this rebellion—quickly and brutally suppressed by the Romans—but they must have been aware of it. The discontent that produced it was never far below the surface.

The small village of Nazareth to which Mary and Joseph returned lay in a sheltered basin in the hills at the northern edge of the fertile Plain of Esdraelon. Its squarish houses were huddled close together on the side of a small hill, some distance from the main road. At the highest point stood a simple one-story synagogue, which had been built some time earlier. This building and the open marketplace at the entrance to Nazareth were the focal points of village life. At that time there were probably no more than 100 inhabitants. Most of the men were farmers, but a few, like Joseph, worked as craftsmen.

No doubt the people of Nazareth gave the returning travelers a warm welcome. Everyone in the village knew everyone else, and the young couple was recognized at once. Joseph, Mary and Jesus were soon home, where Joseph had his carpenter's tools in a corner of the house. Dressed in the short linen tunic of an artisan, he went about the narrow streets of Nazareth, telling old friends and relatives that he was again available for work.

A Housewife's Day

While Joseph worked, Mary was occupied with household chores. The young Jesus stayed by her side, sometimes helping with simple tasks. Their home was small and unpretentious, probably a square, flat-roofed building made of dried mud bricks. The exterior was whitewashed but the inside walls had been left their drab natural color. There was only one room.

The doorway opened directly onto the street. Most of the time the door stood open; a thin linen curtain hung across it to keep out dust. If there were windows, they were cut into the walls and veiled by curtains. The floor was hard-packed dirt mixed with clay and ash to make it hard as cement, and covered with a few straw or leather mats. Furnishings were sparse, probably only wooden stools and a low wooden table.

Outside, a wooden ladder led up to the roof, which was made of a hardened mixture of mud, straw and lime laid over the ceiling beams. A parapet about 1½ feet high was built around the edge. After a rainstorm Joseph had to roll the roof with a heavy stone cylinder to repack the surface and prevent leakage. Such rooftop areas provided useful space for doing chores, drying clothes and flax, and even sleeping and eating during the hot, rainless summer.

Mary's day began at sunrise. After a simple

"She seeks wool and flax, and works with willing hands" (Pr. 31.13). In Jesus' time spinning was still done in the home. First raw fiber was rolled on the thigh to form a strand of yarn, which was made into thread by the twisting motion of a weighted shaft, or spindle. Two threads were spun at once by using a yarn bowl (left) with guides to separate the strands. This woman spins as a helper rolls yarn and her child plays with a rag doll. The simple home has a grain mill, lamp, bedroll and roof ladder.

meal of curds and bread, she wrapped herself in a rough linen mantle, probably edged with two stripes of red or blue. She draped part of the mantle modestly over her long dark hair. Underneath she wore a simple linen tunic, caught up at the waist with a wide leather belt. On her feet were sandals with leather thongs. Her young son, now able to walk, wore either a short linen tunic or a knee-length kilt and shirt.

Carrying an earthenware jug, Mary led Jesus the short distance to the marketplace, where they exchanged greetings with other housewives and children. At the village well they filled the jug with fresh water for the day's needs and then returned home. On one or two special days each week, the marketplace was jammed with temporary stalls and booths where local farmers and merchants sold their wares. On those days Mary stopped to buy provisions for the week, paying with coins she carried in a purse at her waist.

Baking the Daily Bread

Back home, Mary began her most important task, baking the day's bread. First she took some unground barley from one of the large storage pots and ground the kernels between two millstones. The coarsely ground meal gradually filled a large bowl. Then she poured water into a smaller bowl and crumbled in a small piece of fermented dough she had saved from the day before. This day-old dough was used as leaven, and a fistful would be enough for the day's bread. On feast days or for a special treat, she added mint, cumin or cinnamon for flavoring.

Little Jesus watched with interest as his mother mixed the liquid with the meal, kneaded the dough in a special kneading trough and left it to rise for a few hours. Later Mary shaped the dough into several large flat disks, carefully reserving a bit for the next day's leaven, and baked them in the household oven.

Meanwhile, there were countless other chores to be done. When the weather permitted, Mary worked on the roof, where there was more light and sometimes a breeze. Her daily routine included spinning, weaving, mending, washing, and making curds from goat's milk in a goatskin churn. In the afternoon she went inside again to prepare the evening meal and light the oil lamp.

Their dinners were simple but tasty. Besides the staples, bread and wine, there would some-times be dried, salted fish from the Sea of Galilee or boiled chicken from a local farm. Only the rich —of whom there were few in Nazareth—ate meat regularly, and Jesus' family probably tasted roast lamb or goat only on holidays. They ate a variety of vegetables, though, including beans, lentils, cucumbers, leeks and onions. For dessert there might be nuts, melons, figs, grapes or pomegranates, depending on the season. Sometimes they also had sweet fried cakes. There was no sugar, but there was wild honey and thick grape or fig syrup for sweetening. Curds or goat cheese often completed the meal.

Before dinner began, the family washed their hands in accordance with prescribed ritual and Joseph gave the blessing. Then they took their places on mats, grouped around the large dinner pots. They helped themselves by hand from communal dishes, using as scoops the bread baked that morning.

While they ate, Joseph possibly recited the stories of their Hebrew ancestors, a custom traditionally begun in the time of the Patriarch Abraham, some 2000 years earlier. Joseph also taught his son the duties required of every faithful Israelite. These laws and commandments, given to Moses by the Lord as conditions of Israel's covenant, had been vastly expanded by customs accumulated through the centuries. By Jesus' time there were over 600 written and oral observances regulating nearly every aspect of the Jews' daily life.

Toward the end of the day, Joseph went to the synagogue for the evening meeting. Jesus often accompanied his father, but Mary stayed at home. Before retiring, she lit the fire in the oven. The mats they used at meals probably served as beds each night.

Day of the Sabbath

This domestic routine varied little from day to day, and the family looked forward to the Sabbath, when all work was put aside. At the appearance of the first evening star on Friday night, the *hazan* (cantor) announced the beginning of the Lord's day of rest with three sharp blasts of a *shofar* (ram's horn trumpet) from the roof of the synagogue. By that time Mary and the other women of Nazareth had completed their weekly chores. They had already cooked the three Sabbath meals, made sure the lamps were filled with olive oil and the jugs filled to the brim with freshly drawn water.

Meanwhile, Joseph and the men of the village put away their tools and cleansed themselves. After ritual ablutions and perfuming of their bodies with scented olive oil, they put on clean tunics and prepared for the evening synagogue service. The Friday evening meal was a joyful occasion, and wives prepared special treats in honor of the Lord. They too, and their children, dressed in freshly laundered tunics and turned their thoughts away from everyday cares. This mood of quiet joy and thanksgiving continued through the next day until sunset, when the hazan's trumpet announced the end of the Sabbath.

Just after his sixth birthday, Jesus began to go to school. Classes were held regularly at the synagogue six days a week, and every boy was required to attend. In the morning Jesus and his classmates, each carrying a lunch of bread and wine, walked to the simple, one-story synagogue. As they entered the building, they were greeted by their schoolmaster, the rabbi, a stern figure dressed in a long white belted tunic with a tasseled prayer shawl draped over his head.

Their schoolroom was the same austere, rectangular hall their fathers used for evening and Sabbath services. Along three sides were wooden benches and stools, and at the far end stood a curtained chest containing the sacred scrolls of the scriptures. In front of the chest, or ark, were lamps which burned continuously.

Learning the Scriptures

While the boys arranged themselves in a semicircle on the hard floor, the rabbi went back to the ark and solemnly took out one of the scrolls. Carefully he removed its linen wrapping and leather case and took his seat in the center of his pupils. The scrolls, each of which contained one of the books of the Old Testament, were the primary texts he used for his lessons.

The boys listened attentively as the rabbi began to recite passages from the scroll. He spoke slowly and distinctly, giving the words a rhythmic cadence, which made them easier to memorize. The best of the older students could already repeat many passages by heart without omitting or adding a single word. In time, Jesus would be able to do the same.

Most of the youngsters had already become accustomed to this method of learning in their homes, when their fathers had acquainted them with the laws and history of Israel. Their fathers had spoken in Aramaic, but in the classroom the language was Hebrew.

Later they also learned to write, first copying the 22 letters of the Hebrew alphabet. (Their everyday Aramaic language used the same alphabet, which had no vowels, only consonants.) Each student had a wax-covered wooden tablet on which he wrote with a pointed stylus of bone, bronze or wood. When the youths had mastered the letters and short passages, they were allowed to copy longer lessons on sheets of parchment, using reed pens dipped in black ink.

Nazareth and Beyond

After school Jesus and the other boys probably assisted their fathers at farm chores or various trades. In free hours they wandered through the streets of the village or explored the surrounding countryside. No doubt one of their favorite spots was the busy marketplace, where they could watch the craftsmen at work. At one of the shops, they could see the potter and his assistants molding large lumps of clay into jugs, pitchers and pots. Next door the weaver was making a length of linen cloth on his large horizontal loom. Not far away, the dyers plunged clean, uncolored fabrics into big stone vats filled with brilliant red and blue liquid dyes.

On sunny afternoons the boys may have gone into the fields to watch the farmers planting or harvesting or to talk with the shepherds. The rolling hills around Nazareth were a wonderful playground and offered spectacular views: from the crests of nearby hills, Jesus could see for miles. Nearby stretched the enormous Plain of Esdraelon, where heroes like Barak, Gideon, Saul and the Maccabees had battled Israel's enemies and across which the conquering armies of Assyria, Babylonia, Persia and Greece had marched in earlier centuries.

One day soon he too would leave Nazareth and travel to the Holy City. That journey would mark his official entry into manhood, and Jesus looked forward to it eagerly. "And the child grew and became strong, filled with wisdom; and the favor of God was upon him." In the spring of his twelfth year Jesus was allowed to accompany his parents to Jerusalem for Passover.

Chapter 21

In an inspiring prelude to his ministry, Jesus meets a charismatic religious leader who proclaims that "the kingdom of heaven is at hand." At his baptism, Jesus feels the presence of the Holy Spirit and realizes his mission.

John the Baptist: Prophet in Judea

None of the Gospels tells of Jesus' life in the almost 18 years that elapsed between his visit to the temple in Jerusalem and his baptism by John the Baptist. Yet during those important years Jesus completed his formal education and acquired the skills of a carpenter. No doubt he also spent much time studying and contemplating the scriptures. The account of Jesus' early visit to the temple with his parents appears only in Luke, but all four Gospels relate the story of his baptism and the profound spiritual experience that marked his ministry.

Each spring Joseph and Mary and the other families of Nazareth journeyed to Jerusalem for the Passover celebration. Every highway in Palestine was then crowded with throngs of joyous pilgrims heading toward the Holy City. For weeks road crews were busy making repairs along the way. Innkeepers and homeowners had extra shelters prepared for the travelers.

When he was 12 years old, Jesus too was allowed to make the festive pilgrimage to the Holy City. At sunrise four days before the Passover, the travelers set out. Most of them went on foot, carrying the traditional pilgrim's staff, and wearing thin-soled leather sandals. Their food and provisions were strapped on donkeys. Along the way they sang favorite psalms and prayers.

Other travelers joined their group as the long, colorful caravan trekked southeastward across the grassy Plain of Esdraelon and passed through Beth-shan. This was a prosperous city located in a fertile, well-watered site at the meeting point of the Jezreel and Jordan valleys. Some caravans using the main trade route between Mesopotamia and Egypt passed through it. In the recent centuries Beth-shan, renamed Scythopolis, had become a wealthy center of Greek culture.

Here Jesus encountered the pagan culture of Greece and Rome in all its richness. It was a different world from the one he had always known. Along the wide, paved main thoroughfare were huge stone temples to Rome's gods, colonnaded public buildings of pure white marble and a Roman-style marketplace with shops crowded beneath a stone archway. Above the city were the massive towers of a Roman garrison.

Only in the small Jewish quarter, where the pilgrims probably stayed overnight, did Jesus find any resemblance to the world he knew. Even here, though, people dressed in Greek-style clothes and spoke Greek rather than Aramaic.

Early the next morning they left Scythopolis and headed southward, using the highway under the western hills. This enabled them to follow a straight and level road rather than the twisting, turning course of the Jordan, some three miles to the east. To the east and west rose the stark, tree-

"The Spirit immediately drove him out into the wilderness. And he was in the wilderness forty days, tempted by Satan; and he was with the wild beasts; and the angels ministered to him" (Mk. 1.12–13). The setting for Jesus' dramatic temptation by the devil was this somber-looking landscape which lies to the west of the Jordan Valley.

less mountains of Gilead and Ephraim. There were no towns along the way, only occasional stone fortresses manned by Archelaus' soldiers. That night the pilgrims slept under the stars in encampments near the road.

Passover in Jerusalem

Toward evening on the third day the monotonous brown landscape of the valley was relieved by the lush palm trees of the oasis of Jericho, the ancient caravan city. Just southwest of Jericho lay the dazzling white summer palace built by Herod the Great, with its Roman-style pleasure gardens, pools, theater and gymnasium. In palm groves around it were pastel-colored vacation villas built by wealthy citizens of Jerusalem.

After resting overnight in Jericho, the travelers resumed their journey, ascending the steep, rugged limestone ridge rising sharply through the bleak Judean desert. The road, which was guarded by Roman watchtowers, was now crowded with other travelers. As they neared Jerusalem, the countryside changed to cultivated fields, vineyards and groves of olive trees.

Rounding the curve of the southern foot of the Mount of Olives, they caught sight of the Holy City. Never before had Jesus seen such huge, awesome buildings. Excitedly Joseph pointed out the massive white and gold temple, which dominated the panorama. Directly behind it, to the north, stood the Antonia fortress. In one of the four towers of the Antonia, he explained, the magnificent robes of the Jewish high priest were kept in Roman custody. They were given to him only on special feast days. A stairway led directly from the fortress to the adjacent temple courts, so that soldiers on duty in the Antonia could rush down to quell disturbances below. Across from the temple, and linked to it by a viaduct, rose the grandiose palace built by Herod the Great on the western hill of the city.

The pilgrims crossed the Kidron Brook in the eastern valley below Jerusalem and entered the city through the Golden Gate. The population of the rapidly growing city was greatly swollen by huge throngs of pilgrims from all over Palestine, from Babylonia and from every part of the Roman Empire. Many of them wore strange costumes and spoke unfamiliar languages. To the young boy from Nazareth, the noisy, colorful scene must have been fascinating.

The pilgrims' first task was to rent a room or rooftop where they could stay during the festival. This done, Mary set out to buy the required wine and herbs and returned to prepare the Passover meal. Meanwhile, Joseph and Jesus went up to the temple. On the way Joseph purchased a live, year-old male lamb from a merchant. The outer courtyard of the temple, the Court of the Gentiles, was jammed with pilgrims, vendors, money changers and guards. Pushing through the crowd, Joseph led the boy through a huge gateway to the Court of Women and then up the stairs to the Court of Israel, into which only male Jews were allowed to enter. Directly before them rose the enormous stone altar of sacrifice, and behind it the gleaming white marble and gold facade of the sacred sanctuary.

Ceremony of the Priests

At three P.M. three blasts on silver trumpets signaled the official beginning of the Passover sacrifices. The many pilgrims looked on as a long, solemn procession entered the upper courtyard. At its head was the high priest, who wore a magnificent blue ceremonial robe decorated with blue, purple and scarlet pomegranates and golden bells which jingled softly as he moved. His waist was girded with a band of blue, purple and scarlet threads interwoven with spun gold. Across his chest was a breastpiece of the same material, adorned with 12 precious stones, each representing one of Israel's tribes. On his head was a fine linen turban wreathed with blue and encircled by a golden crown which bore in relief the inscription, "Holy to the Lord."

Behind him came the lesser priests dressed in spotless white linen tunics and turbans. Around their waists were white linen sashes embroidered with threads of blue, purple and scarlet. At the

Using a bow drill, a carpenter of Joseph's time makes a cattle yoke in his shop. In villages like Nazareth such a respected craftsman proudly wore a chip of wood behind his ear to indicate his trade. Among his tools were the adze (like the one photographed at left, from Beth-shemesh), awl, mallet (by his foot), saw and compass (hanging on the wall behind his head). By the doorway is a newly made plow, and stacked in the corner are door and window frames. Across the unpaved street some boys have just finished their studies for the day in the synagogue.

rear came the Levites, lesser temple officials, playing lyres and chanting the Hallel: "O give thanks to the Lord, for he is good; his steadfast love endures forever!"

When the high priest signaled that it was time for the sacrifices to begin, Joseph and the other pilgrims handed their lambs to the priests, who slaughtered them. As some of the Levites collected the blood in special gold and silver trays, others skinned and dressed the lambs. Meanwhile, the priests solemnly splashed the blood against the sides of the huge horned altar and then ascended the stairs to its top. There they placed the entrails and fat on the sacrificial fire.

Joseph explained this ancient mysterious ritual

A Pharisee Shows Religious Zeal
"The Pharisee . . . prayed thus with himself, 'God, I thank thee that I am not like other men'" (Lk. 18.11). Jesus often condemned the ostentatious piety of the Pharisees. Here one such man reads from the Law in a loud voice. His prayer shawl is adorned with exceptionally long tassels, and his phylacteries —boxes containing passages from scripture—are bound to his left arm and forehead with characteristic wide leather straps.

to his son. In essence, the sacrifice was a gift to the Lord of something men valued. The blood, which was said to contain all the life of the animal, was collected and dashed against the altar because it belonged to God alone. The remainder of the animal was eaten during a sacred meal by the fami-

ly who had offered it to the Lord for sacrifice.

When they had received their slaughtered lamb from the priests, Joseph and Jesus left the temple. While Mary roasted the lamb over a fire, using a pomegranate branch as a spit, Joseph dipped a hyssop branch in the lamb's blood and daubed it against the doorposts, as Moses' people had done long ago. Some friends from Nazareth soon joined them, and Joseph, lifting his wine goblet, gave the traditional Passover blessing. When everyone had drunk, they ate the lamb with unleavened bread and bitter herbs. Then they drank a second glass of wine.

Jesus turned to his father and asked the ritual question: "Why is this night different from all other nights?" In reply Joseph recited the miraculous story of the Lord's deliverance of Israel from Egypt and other tales of crisis and redemption throughout the nation's history. He concluded with a fervent plea to the Lord for deliverance from the present oppression of the Jews by their Roman overlords.

Doctors of the Law

During the remaining days of the feast, Jesus and Joseph visited the temple many times. At almost any hour of the day the huge outer Court of the Gentiles was buzzing with activity. Anyone, Jew or pagan, could enter the splendid colonnaded court, which closely resembled the public squares of Athens, Rome and Alexandria. People from all walks of life came there to discuss religious or political questions, to exchange bits of news and gossip or merely to pass the time of day. Many of Jerusalem's learned scribes, or doctors of the law, came there to teach and debate.

Set apart from this din and clamor were the inner temple courts and, within them, the holy sanctuary itself. Only adult male Jews were allowed in the innermost court, and only priests could enter the sanctuary.

Jesus was particularly attracted to the doctors of the law in the outer courtyard, and he probably listened to their debates with great interest. He actually entered into discussions with them and became so absorbed that he stayed there. His family, assuming he was in the caravan, left Jerusalem. When they discovered his absence, they returned and searched Jerusalem for him.

"After three days they found him in the temple, sitting among the teachers, listening to them and asking them questions; and all who heard him were amazed at his understanding and his answers. And when they saw him they were astonished; and his mother said to him, 'Son, why have you treated us so? Behold, your father and I have been looking for you anxiously.' And he said to them, 'How is it that you sought me? Did you not know that I must be in my Father's house?' And they did not understand . . .''

Both parents were probably so pleased to have found their son and so surprised at his remarkable display of knowledge that they did not scold him very severely. Taking him by the hand, they led him from the temple and made their way back to Nazareth, following the same Jordan Valley route by which they had come.

Carpenter of Nazareth

Once they were back in Nazareth, Joseph took Jesus into his carpenter's shop and began to teach him the skills of his trade. By now he may have been prosperous enough to have his own shop in the marketplace, alongside the shops of the potter, weaver, dyer and blacksmith. Like the other shops, Joseph's was probably open on one side to let in light and air. On the walls hung his tools: axes, hatchets, saws, knives, adzes, planes, hammers and bow drills. Planks of wood were stacked in piles near the rear.

At first Jesus must have spent most of the day just watching his father work. Sometimes he would fetch supplies of wood or help saw a tree trunk into boards, but it would be a while before he could master more intricate tasks. Joseph's work included building entire houses, as well as making and repairing stools, tables, benches, cabinets, door and window frames, plows and yokes, and many other essential items.

In a typical day, he might repair a neighbor's plow and contract with another man to build an upstairs room on the roof of his house. Later, a local housewife might stop in to ask him to make her a new kneading trough, and another villager might come to order a door frame.

Although Jesus no longer went to school, he almost certainly continued to study the sacred scriptures with other youths under the guidance of a local teacher. Though he was an exceptional student, he does not seem to have studied under one of the famous rabbis teaching in Jerusalem or in one of the larger towns of Galilee.

During these years, the political situation in Palestine was tense, and Jewish resentment of Roman rule grew ever stronger. Jews remembered with sorrow the tragic revolts that had broken out in the years following King Herod's death. In 4 B.C., when Jesus was a small child,

The Shofar's Blast Heralds the Sabbath

The shofar, or ceremonial ram's horn, was used since Joshua's time to announce important events. Though it could produce only two notes, players combined them in many ways to convey a variety of messages. Here a rabbi of Jesus' time blows three sharp blasts to signal the start of the Sabbath. He would do so each Friday at sunset from atop the synagogue, and signal the end of the Sabbath in the same manner the next evening. Among the other events heralded by the shofar were the approach of danger, the death of an elder or priest, appearance of the new moon, and Passover. As a Jew, Jesus would have understood each signal.

during the Passover celebration in Jerusalem Jewish pilgrims had massed threateningly in the temple and stoned the soldiers sent to restrain them. Reinforcements soon arrived and stormed the sacred precincts, killing some 3000 pilgrims.

Several weeks later, during the Feast of Weeks, Jewish rebels seized control of Jerusalem. Meanwhile, revolt spread throughout the countryside as self-styled deliverers proclaimed their rule. At Sepphoris, capital of Galilee, a man named Judas gathered a considerable rebel force. In Perea and Judea, other rebel leaders rose to fight. Varus, the Roman governor of Syria, sent his legions into Palestine to quell the revolt. One contingent subdued Galilee and burned Sepphoris to the ground. The flames and smoke of the burning city must have been visible from Nazareth, only four miles away. In Perea and Judea, Roman troops plundered and burned rural villages and then marched on Jerusalem. There the rebels were rounded up and some 2000 were crucified.

The Roman army had crushed the revolt, but it

could not destroy the spirit that had provoked it. Tighter security measures were taken to keep the unruly Jews under control and prevent a recurrence of rebellion. Ten years later Judea came under the direct rule of a Roman governor. Though there were no major rebellions for nearly 50 years, incidents occurred from time to time.

Talk of rebellion was still heard, but the chances of success seemed remote. More and more, the contemporaries of Jesus became convinced that their present oppression resembled the ordeal described by the prophets as the necessary prelude to the final deliverance. The Lord was waiting until evil had become rampant. Then he would unleash his mighty power and destroy Israel's enemies. He would establish the rule of righteousness on earth, and peace and love would reign forever.

Thus, to many, the present humiliation became a sign of hope rather than despair, because the miraculous event seemed to be near at hand. They began to prepare themselves spiritually for the inevitable deliverance: only the righteous would be chosen to live in the Lord's kingdom. Some set themselves apart from their fellow Jews in order to "prepare the way of the Lord," who

"In those days Jesus came from Nazareth of Galilee and was baptized by John in the Jordan. And . . . he saw . . . the Spirit descending upon him like a dove" (Mk. 1.9–10). Although ancient tradition places the site of Jesus' baptism near Jericho, some scholars believe it took place on the upper Jordan (above) near the Sea of Galilee. This area could also have produced the crowds that John preached to.

would soon relieve the oppressed. The Pharisees lived in strictest adherence to the laws of the Torah as well as to the vast body of traditional laws which had accumulated over the centuries. They avoided men who failed to observe the laws as strictly as they did, because they feared religious contamination.

Although the Pharisees looked down on Jews outside their ranks, "the people of the land," as they called them, they disliked the Romans more and had stubbornly refused to take the loyalty oath to Rome. This attitude made them popular among the common people, who accepted their claims to religious and moral superiority because of their outspoken patriotism.

Another important religious group, the Essenes, had little or no interest in politics. Instead, one major group of them withdrew into the Judean wilderness. There, in isolated monastic communities, they studied the scriptures and prepared themselves for the Lord's kingdom.

John the Baptist

Other ascetics also withdrew into the wilderness, gathering disciples around them to await the coming age. The Israelites had always thought of the desert as a fitting place for religious thinkers, and in Jesus' time many men believed the Messiah would appear there first.

"In those days came John the Baptist, preaching in the wilderness of Judea, 'Repent, for the kingdom of heaven is at hand.' For this is he who was spoken of by the prophet Isaiah when he said,

'The voice of one crying in the wilderness:
Prepare the way of the Lord, make his paths
  straight.'

Now John wore a garment of camel's hair, and a leather girdle around his waist; and his food was locusts and wild honey. Then went out to him Jerusalem and all Judea and all the region about the Jordan, and they were baptized by him in the river Jordan, confessing their sins."

John had been born in the hill country of Judea, not far from Jerusalem. The son of an elderly priest and his wife, he was still very young when his parents died, and he went to live in the wilderness of Judea. He stayed there for many years, possibly alone or in a community like that of the Essenes at Qumran.

When he finally inaugurated his public minis-try, it was in one of the busiest parts of the wilderness: at the ford of the Jordan, just north of the Dead Sea. Soon huge crowds of Jews from all over Palestine were flocking to the Jordan to see and hear this remarkable man, who looked and spoke like the prophets of old.

His eyes ablaze, he stood on the riverbank and exhorted all who came to repent of their sins and prepare for the coming day of judgment. "You brood of vipers!" he thundered. "Who warned you to flee from the wrath to come? Bear fruits that befit repentance . . . Even now the axe is laid to the root of the trees; every tree therefore that does not bear good fruit is cut down and thrown into the fire."

To those who asked what they should do, he replied, "'He who has two coats, let him share with him who has none; and he who has food, let him do likewise.' Tax collectors also came to be baptized, and said to him, 'Teacher, what shall we do?' And he said to them, 'Collect no more than is appointed you.' Soldiers also asked him, 'And we, what shall we do?' And he said to them, 'Rob no one by violence or by false accusation, and be content with your wages.'"

Many believed John must be the Messiah, but he vehemently denied all claims to such a role. "I baptize you with water; but he who is mightier than I is coming, the thong of whose sandals I am not worthy to untie; he will baptize you with the Holy Spirit and with fire. His winnowing fork is in his hand, to clear his threshing floor, and to gather the wheat into his granary, but the chaff he will burn with unquenchable fire."

Baptism in the Jordan

At the height of his sermon, he called upon his listeners to confess their sins and to be purified by baptism in the waters of the Jordan. Men baptized by him, John said, entered a completely new existence as members of the community of the righteous, who would form the core of the coming kingdom of God.

Most of the men who were baptized by John returned to their homes to await the Messiah, but a few stayed behind and became John's disciples. John taught these followers to pray and to fast periodically.

Soon after John began his public ministry, the news reached Nazareth that a prophet had appeared in the wilderness, proclaiming that the long-awaited kingdom was at hand and preaching the repentance of sins. Jesus listened in rapt attention as the townsmen discussed this remarkable figure. Could it be, he must have wondered, that the time was actually near at hand? He determined to go and see for himself the man many said was the resurrected prophet Elijah.

With a group of fellow Galileans, Jesus journeyed south along the bank of the Jordan to where John was preaching to a large crowd. Jesus took his place quietly among the people as John talked with priests who had come down from Jerusalem to settle the question of John's identity.

"Who are you?" they asked.

"I am not the Christ [Messiah]," John replied.

"What then? Are you Elijah?" they persisted.

"I am not," he answered.

"Who are you?" they asked again impatiently. "Let us have an answer for those who sent us. What do you say about yourself?"

"I am the voice of one crying in the wilderness, 'Make straight the way of the Lord,' as the prophet Isaiah said."

Unable to get a satisfactory answer, the men departed in anger. Later, when John began baptizing, Jesus came forward and slowly entered the shallow, muddy river. John placed his hands on Jesus' shoulders and gently immersed him in the water. After emerging, he knelt with the others on the riverbank and began to pray.

"And when he came up out of the water, immediately he saw the heavens opened and the Spirit descending upon him like a dove; and a voice came from heaven, 'Thou art my beloved Son; with thee I am well pleased.'"

All at once the world was transformed for him. Light and understanding burst upon his soul, driving away all uncertainty. Suddenly Jesus knew what he must do and saw with amazing clarity the truth he had been seeking. He could not join his friends who were returning to Nazareth to await the end of the age. Instead, he would go out alone to preach to all Jews the beautiful vision he had beheld. He would share his divine inspiration with all who would listen. For a time he withdrew into the wilderness, where he is said to have been tempted by the devil:

"The Spirit immediately drove him out into the wilderness. And he was in the wilderness forty days, tempted by Satan; and he was with the wild beasts; and the angels ministered to him."

The movement John had begun was growing

"And [Jesus] went throughout all Galilee, preaching in their synagogues" (Mk. 1.39). Jesus began his ministry in a modest synagogue like this one. Here men sit on the stone benches along the walls, listening attentively to the scriptures. Following the usual custom, a visitor has been invited to read. Two Pharisees (center), known by their ornate prayer shawls, await the guest's interpretation of the text. He stands at a wooden lectern, the sacred scroll lit by a seven-branched lampstand, or menorah. The menorah in the relief above was from just such a synagogue in Galilee.

rapidly. His disciples were active in various parts of the Judean wilderness, and he himself was now baptizing as far away as Samaria, close to large, populous cities. Herod Antipas, the ruler of Galilee and also Perea, a district east of the Jordan where John had begun his ministry, became alarmed that John's movement would breed a new rebellion among his volatile subjects. His fears were increased when John denounced his illicit marriage to Herodias, wife of Antipas' half brother, and challenged his worthiness as ruler.

Hoping to silence John and to put an end to his movement, Antipas sent soldiers to arrest him. John was imprisoned in the remote fortress of Machaerus on the cliffs above the Dead Sea in southern Perea, but he was not killed, because

Antipas feared the prophet's popularity. If he killed John, he might provoke a serious uprising among the prophet's countless followers.

In fact, John's arrest did not achieve the intended purpose. Instead, it increased the determination of his disciples to spread John's message, and they continued to preach. His most faithful disciples stationed themselves near Machaerus to keep in touch with John and carry out his instructions.

For Jesus, John's imprisonment meant it was time for him to begin his mission. He returned at once to his native Galilee and began preaching in the synagogues, proclaiming, "The time is fulfilled, and the kingdom of God is at hand; repent, and believe in the gospel."

Galilee: Homeland of Jesus

The thriving cities and fertile hills of Galilee were ideally suited to receive the ministry of Jesus. The populous district lay to the west of the Sea of Galilee, and there an active trade in fish, oil, grain and wine was carried on that reached to Damascus and across the Mediterranean. The Judeans disdained Galilee's Jews, who made up only one third of their area's mixed population. These northern Jews were mostly farmers of the rich table-lands, whose simple customs characterized the district. Among them, the theological issues raised by more austere and orthodox Judeans were unpopular. In the towns of Galilee Jesus first began to preach freely, and in the countryside his words found an enthusiastic audience.

"The grass withers, and the flower falls, but the word of the Lord abides for ever" (1 Pet. 1.24–25). The images in this passage reflect the grassy slopes (left) and abundant flowers (above) of the Galilean landscape. Although rainfall is not heavy, the fertile soil receives generous moisture from the nearby mountains of Lebanon.

"Again he began to teach beside the sea" (Mk. 4.1). Life around the Sea of Galilee was concentrated mostly in this region, on its northern and western shores. Lakeside villages were the setting for most of Jesus' ministry, and he performed several miracles here. Many fishermen dwelt in the area. Their livelihood prospered on the great variety of fish—including carp, sardines, mullet and tilapia—found in the lake.

"He took with him Peter and John and James, and went up on the mountain to pray. And as he was praying, the appearance of his countenance was altered, and his raiment became dazzling white" (Lk. 9.28–29). The Gospels do not name the place of Jesus' transfiguration, but traditionally it is thought to be the heights of Mt. Tabor (above), overlooking the Jezreel Valley about six miles southeast of Nazareth. Several churches and monasteries were built here by early Christians.

"Get away from here, for Herod wants to kill you" (Lk. 13.31). The apostles encouraged Jesus to preach by the shore of Galilee, so they could row him to safety on the eastern side if Herod attempted to sieze him. There he would be in another district, outside Herod's jurisdiction. Above is a view from Magdala, on the western shore of the Sea of Galilee. At left is a view from the east.

Chapter 22

In the simple synagogues of his native province, the young man from Nazareth

begins to tell his gospel, or "good news," of the coming of the Lord. Some of his listeners

are hostile, but most are impressed by his learning and enthralled by his message.

Jesus: The Gospel in Galilee

The first months of Jesus' ministry in Galilee were a time of excitement and revelation. Ranging tirelessly throughout the sunny countryside from his base at Capernaum, Jesus soon became known as a teacher and miracle worker. In rural synagogues and open-air meetings, he delivered his message about the kingdom of God to increasingly larger crowds. But even as he attracted loyal disciples and other followers, the storm clouds of opposition gathered, for some Pharisees and Sadducees thought his gospel was nothing but blasphemy.

After John the Baptist was arrested by Herod Antipas, Jesus left Judea for Galilee to begin his own ministry. He had decided to preach there, rather than in Judea, because it was his home. He knew Galilee's roads, towns and villages, and he understood his fellow Galileans. In this lovely land of gentle hills and warm, green valleys Jesus experienced his first triumphs—but he also suffered his first serious setback here, in Nazareth, the town of his upbringing.

Unlike John, Jesus did not conduct a ministry of baptism. Instead, he healed the sick and urged those who heard him to repent of their sins because the kingdom of God was near. His early teachings were concerned almost entirely with describing that imminent kingdom. Whereas John had been fiery and impassioned, Jesus was gentle and persuasive. His message was joyous.

During those early weeks and months Jesus traveled from village to village throughout Galilee, preaching in synagogues in the evenings and on the Sabbath. Carrying a bundle of bread, a wineskin and a walking stick, he walked along the dusty highways. He was probably dressed like any other traveler, in a rough linen tunic covered by a heavier red or blue mantle.

On a typical day Jesus would set out at dawn and walk many miles. Toward sunset, he would enter a village and go up to its synagogue. There he probably received a warm welcome from the townspeople, who often had no resident rabbi and relied on the services of wandering teachers like Jesus. When the lamps had been lit and the men of the village had taken their places, Jesus would seat himself on the raised central platform and begin reading a passage from one of the sacred scrolls. Invariably, he chose a passage concerning the coming kingdom of God. When he had finished, he would look up, his face full of joy and conviction. In a clear, forceful voice, he would announce that the fulfillment of the scriptures was taking place at that very moment.

His proclamation provoked a variety of responses from his astonished listeners. Some marveled at his wisdom and eagerly questioned him about the meaning of his words. In answer, Jesus spoke in parables. These were brief stories, using explicit examples from everyday life, and they gave his preaching a simplicity and directness most men had not heard before.

"And they went into Capernaum; and . . . [Jesus] entered the synagogue and taught" (Mk. 1.21). In Galilean synagogues Jesus first proclaimed the coming of the kingdom of God. Worshipers sat on stone benches, like these from a Capernaum synagogue built about A.D. 400—perhaps near the one in which Jesus taught.

"The kingdom of God," he would explain, "is as if a man should scatter seed upon the ground, and should sleep and rise night and day, and the seed should sprout and grow, he knows not how. The earth produces of itself, first the blade, then the ear, then the full grain in the ear. But when the grain is ripe, at once he puts in the sickle, because the harvest has come."

In such stories he tried to convey a sense of the mystery and inevitability of the approach of God's kingdom. Just as seeds quietly and quickly grew to be grain, the present world would soon be transformed into another. As yet, most men could not see the process the Lord had begun, but just as the seeds grew secretly and mysteriously, so did the kingdom. Its final coming would be joyous and as inevitable as the harvest.

Preaching and Healing

Not everyone who heard Jesus' words accepted them. Men who had studied the scriptures were often very critical of his audacity in claiming to know what the prophets themselves had not known. Others thought he was claiming that he himself was the long-awaited agent of the Lord who would announce the new age.

One of the worst receptions Jesus received was in his own hometown of Nazareth. "And on the sabbath he began to teach in the synagogue; and many who heard him were astonished, saying, 'Where did this man get all this? What is the wisdom given to him? What mighty works are wrought by his hands! Is not this the carpenter, the son of Mary . . . ?' And they took offense at him. And Jesus said to them, 'A prophet is not without honor, except in his own country, and among his own kin, and in his own house.'" According to Luke, the people of Nazareth were so enraged that they dragged Jesus from the synagogue and tried to throw him off a nearby cliff.

The most popular aspect of Jesus' early ministry was his healing, and stories of his remarkable powers soon spread from town to town. Men at that time were convinced that evil spirits caused all diseases and infirmities as well as insanity.

They were said to lurk everywhere, waiting for an opportunity to enter living bodies and take possession of them. It was, for example, considered unsafe for a man to sleep alone in a house because Lilith, the she-devil, might appear and seduce him. Evil spirits were thought to be par-

ticularly powerful in dark places because Satan, their ruler, was lord of darkness. For this reason, people avoided the shade of certain trees, marshlands and other murky places. Many wore charms or amulets containing locusts' eggs or foxes' teeth to ward off the spirits' presence.

Jesus was convinced that such charms were powerless against evil and that only a positive trust in the Lord would protect a person. His method of driving the spirits away was unlike that of common wonder-workers and exorcists, who recited incantations and magic formulas. He merely touched his patients and addressed the demons with the unflinching authority of the Lord, and the demons were seen to flee.

Once, for example, he cured a man of leprosy (a term then used to describe many skin diseases): "and behold, a leper came to him and knelt before him, saying, 'Lord, if you will, you can make me clean.' And he stretched out his hand and touched him, saying, 'I will; be clean.' And immediately his leprosy was cleansed."

Another time he restored two madmen to sanity. "And when he came to the other side [of the lake], to the country of the Gadarenes, two demoniacs met him . . . And behold, they cried out, 'What have you to do with us, O Son of God? Have you come here to torment us . . . ?' Now a herd of many swine was feeding at some distance from them. And the demons begged him, 'If you cast us out, send us away into the herd of swine.' And he said to them, 'Go.' So they came out and went into the swine; and behold, the whole herd rushed down the steep bank into the sea, and perished in the waters."

Jesus saw his miraculous success at healing as an outward sign that the Lord's kingdom was beginning to triumph over the realm of Satan. Yet he feared that his cures would be misinterpreted, that people would see him as just another magician (there were many such men at this time); and he cautioned those he healed to be silent.

The Wedding at Cana

Of course, the news spread, and before long people in every town and village in Galilee were talking excitedly of the new wonder-worker who could cure the blind, the lame and the sick with the power of his voice and the mere touch of his strong carpenter's hands. Soon large crowds gathered wherever he spoke, and people pressed forward eagerly, pitifully begging to be healed.

Early in Jesus' ministry, the people of Galilee heard reports that he had miraculously turned ordinary water into wine during a wedding feast he had attended at Cana. Apparently Jesus and his mother had gone to the wedding of a relative in the village of Cana, about nine miles north of Nazareth. It was a festive occasion which probably lasted seven days. The reclining guests ate on floor mats and, in the course of the week-long celebration, consumed large quantities of food and drink. There was rhythmic music, lively dancing and general merriment.

In the midst of the festivities the supply of wine was used up, and Jesus, at his mother's request, had taken charge of this potentially embarrassing situation. "Now six stone jars were standing there, for the Jewish rites of purification, each holding twenty or thirty gallons. Jesus said to them [the servants], 'Fill the jars with water.' And they filled them up to the brim. He said to them, 'Now draw some out, and take it to the steward of the feast.' So they took it. When the steward of the feast tasted the water now become wine, and did not know where it came from (though the servants who had drawn the water knew), the steward . . . called the bridegroom and said to him, 'Every man serves the good wine first; and when men have drunk freely, then the poor wine; but you have kept the good wine until now.'"

During most of his Galilean ministry, Jesus' main base was the fishing village of Capernaum, on the northwest shore of the Sea of Galilee. Capernaum's population was predominantly Jewish, made up of native families and others from different lakeside towns or from villages throughout Galilee. It stood near the border between the territories of Herod's sons, Antipas and Philip, and a custom house and Roman military outpost were located near the edge of town. Arab caravans, Jewish pilgrims, Roman soldiers and townspeople created a constant flow of traffic across the border and along the main streets.

The town was famous for its large, prosperous fishing industry. The fresh blue waters of the lake abounded with a variety of fish, including perch, carp, sardines and catfish. During the day the fishermen mended their nets and repaired their boats along the shore, but at sunset, when the wind had died down and the water was more tranquil, they launched their wooden crafts and set out to take their daily catch. In the fading late afternoon light, their muscular, suntanned figures could be seen casting huge nets out over the water and hauling them back in, filled with fish.

To the south and west of Capernaum stretched the fertile Plain of Gennesaret, with its abundant grainfields, orchards of date palms, olive groves,

An Essene Baptism Ceremony

"For John baptized with water, but before many days you shall be baptized with the Holy Spirit" (Acts 1.5). Baptism was a daily ritual for the Essenes, a religious group and community of Jesus' time. In specially built pools they purified themselves repeatedly for the coming of a Messiah. Here an Essene priest reads from one sacred text while a follower bathes. Some Biblical scholars now think that John the Baptist was an Essene.

vineyards, walnut and sycamore trees. There, tireless Galilean peasants spent long days sowing, harvesting and pruning their crops.

The Gospels do not provide many details of Jesus' everyday life in Capernaum, but he seems to have lived there in a house that he shared with some of his followers. It was probably a simple one-room structure built of dark stone or whitewashed mud bricks, much like his childhood home in Nazareth. Most likely it was located along one of the steep, narrow streets that wound upward from the busy lakeshore.

Before long, Jesus had begun to attract a small group of disciples, mostly from the region around Capernaum. Among them were James and John, brothers who came to be nicknamed the "sons of thunder," perhaps because of their quick tempers. They were fishermen from Capernaum, where their father, Zebedee, owned a sizable fleet of boats. James and John often fished with two of the other disciples, Simon Peter and Andrew, brothers from the nearby lakeside town of Bethsaida. Peter was strong-willed and impetuous, and his enthusiasm endeared him to Jesus.

Philip, another fisherman from Bethsaida, was just the opposite: even-tempered and down-to-earth. It was he who introduced Jesus to a sixth disciple, Nathanael (sometimes called Bartholomew), from Cana, an earnest and sincere man who, like many Jews, was awaiting the coming Messiah. Another fisherman, Thomas, sometimes called "doubting" Thomas, was a loyal follower noted for his skepticism.

The disciples accompanied Jesus on his travels throughout Galilee. By now his reputation preceded him wherever he went. People came out in great numbers to hear his words and to be healed. It was often impossible to teach in local synagogues because of the size of the crowd, so Jesus would preach in the open air. Sometimes he even had to board a fishing boat and row out a slight distance so that all who came could see him and hear his message from the shore.

Preaching to the Multitudes

Seated on the grass or in a fishing boat, he would speak in parables to the large crowd of farmers, housewives, artisans and other humble people who had come to see him. "With what can we compare the kingdom of God, or what parable shall we use for it?" he once asked. "It is like a grain of mustard seed, which, when sown upon the ground, is the smallest of all the seeds on earth; yet when it is sown it grows up and becomes the greatest of all shrubs, and puts forth

large branches, so that the birds of the air can make nests in its shade."

Everyone there knew and understood the remarkable nature of mustard seeds; they had all seen those tiny seeds grow to be sizable plants. Now, as they listened to Jesus' inspired parable, they understood more clearly what the kingdom of God would be like. It too would have small beginnings and would grow mysteriously. Yet in the end it would appear in all its magnificence.

Soon, Jesus' growing fame and popularity began to arouse controversy. The Pharisees were particularly disturbed to see the people flocking to hear a man who had never studied under the learned scribes, and they began to question his authority openly. Their hostility is easy to understand. To these men, who saw themselves as the guardians of Jewish heritage, Jesus was something of a heretic. His proclamation of a kingdom of God open to all Jews who would repent sounded like a bold challenge to the Pharisaic ideals. They believed that men would be allowed to enter the Lord's kingdom only if they had proven their devotion by obeying every one of the hundreds of religious laws that had accumulated over the centuries. Some even went so far as to avoid all contact with people they considered to be sinful or ritually impure by Jewish law. Yet, they also represented the most liberal trend of Judaism, and their teachings were rejected by the Sadducees.

The Pharisees were feared and respected by average men, who relied on their scribes to settle their problems about what was lawful. Jewish law had become so complicated and extensive that only very learned men could master all its details. A learned scribe could explain, for example, whether it was in violation of the Sabbath law for a man to pick a fruit on the Sabbath or whether pouring wine from an unclean pitcher into a clean one rendered the second pitcher unclean as well.

Some Pharisees went to extremes to emphasize their piety. Such men wore bleached white tunics rather than the natural flaxen tunics of other men.

"Now six stone jars were standing there . . . each holding twenty or thirty gallons. Jesus said to them, 'Fill the jars with water'" (Jn. 2.6–7). Jesus performed his first miracle at a marriage feast at Cana, by changing water into wine. Such celebrations, which sometimes lasted a week, began with a dance led by the bride and groom, wearing wreaths of flowers. Then the company joined in, with much eating, drinking and lively music. Arriving guests ritually washed their hands and feet at the door with water from stone vessels, like those above from Jesus' time. The feast ended with preparation of a bridal chamber.

The phylacteries (small leather prayer cases) they wore on their foreheads and left forearms when they prayed were larger than those worn by other Jews. The tassels on their prayer shawls were also longer than average. They would wash their hands and bathe several times a day to remove all impurities. Such Pharisees fasted at least twice a week and prayed many times a day, often in public so all could observe their piety.

Jesus believed that such ostentatious piety was hypocritical. He preached that men's sins could be forgiven, and he freely associated with social outcasts. In fact, one of his closest followers was a tax collector named Matthew, who worked in Capernaum's customhouse, collecting duties on all goods entering and leaving the city. The Pharisees and other righteous Jews looked down on tax collectors, equating them with the lowliest sinners because they often collected more money than was rightfully theirs, handled unclean pagan currency and dealt closely with the occupying Roman forces. Jesus' association with Matthew infuriated certain of the Pharisees.

John's Doubts

The Pharisees were not the only people who questioned Jesus. John the Baptist himself was disturbed by rumors reaching his prison cell at Machaerus about Jesus' unorthodox methods. Despite his radical appearance and harsh manner, John had always emphasized strict obedience to Jewish law. Like the Pharisees, he and his disciples fasted two days a week.

When he heard that Jesus and his disciples did not fast, John sent some of his followers to ask the reason. "And Jesus said to them . . . 'no one puts a piece of unshrunk cloth on an old garment, for the patch tears away from the garment, and a worse tear is made. Neither is new wine put into old wineskins; if it is, the skins burst, and the wine is spilled, and the skins are destroyed; but new wine is put into fresh wineskins, and so both are preserved.'"

Jesus was simply saying that fasting and self-denial might be all right for John and his disciples, but that they did not fit the new road he himself had taken. His path called for entirely new principles, not patched-up old ones.

Not long thereafter, John received even more startling news about Jesus. According to the story his disciples excitedly related, Jesus had restored a dead girl to life! John was amazed at their words, and he sent men to Capernaum with a question for the young man he had baptized.

Jesus was at home, instructing a group of his disciples, when John's delegation arrived. He invited them in and politely inquired why they had come. They explained that they had been sent by John to ask, "'Are you he who is to come, or shall we look for another?' And Jesus answered them, 'Go and tell John what you hear and see: the blind receive their sight and the lame walk, lepers are cleansed and the deaf hear, and the dead are raised up, and the poor have good news preached to them. And blessed is he who takes no offense at me.'" Jesus knew that John would recognize this prediction concerning the Messiah from the prophet Isaiah.

When John's disciples had gone, Jesus' friends may have begun to speak critically of John. No doubt angered by their attitude, Jesus scolded: "What did you go out into the wilderness to behold? A reed shaken by the wind? Why then did you go out? To see a man clothed in soft raiment? Behold, those who wear soft raiment are in kings' houses. Why then did you go out? To see a prophet? Yes, I tell you, and more than a prophet. This is he of whom it is written, 'Behold, I send my messenger before thy face, who shall prepare thy way before thee.' Truly, I say to you, among those born of women there has risen no one greater than John the Baptist; yet he who is least in the kingdom of heaven is greater than he. . . . For all the prophets and the law prophesied until John; and if you are willing to accept it, he is Elijah who is to come."

Jesus Instructs His Disciples

By now the disciples were growing used to their master's sometimes enigmatic statements and had learned to wait patiently for an explanation. This time, however, he did not explain further, leaving his disciples to puzzle over the implication of what he had just said. If John was Elijah reincarnated, they mused, was Jesus himself the Messiah? Had the new age already begun?

During these months, Jesus devoted much of his time to private instruction of and discussions with his disciples. It was to them that he revealed his innermost thoughts, related his beliefs and gradually unveiled his own awareness of his role and mission. These men were robust outdoorsmen and rugged individualists. They were not learned men like many Pharisees, but their trust of and loyalty to their teacher were strong. To Jesus, they possessed that unquestioning faith in the Lord's purposes which men would need to enter the kingdom of God.

Gradually they began to understand more and more what Jesus meant by the kingdom of God and how he envisaged the new community which would populate it. He explained these ideas most clearly in the teachings called "the Sermon on the Mount," which he probably delivered privately to his inner circle of followers and not to a huge public assembly.

"Seeing the crowds, he went up on the mountain, and when he sat down his disciples came to him. And he . . . taught them, saying:

"'Blessed are the poor in spirit, for theirs is the kingdom of heaven. Blessed are those who mourn . . . the meek . . . those who hunger and thirst for righteousness . . . the merciful . . . the pure in heart . . . the peacemakers . . . Blessed are those who are persecuted for righteousness' sake, for theirs is the kingdom of heaven.

"'Blessed are you when men revile you and persecute you and utter all kinds of evil against you falsely on my account. Rejoice and be glad, for your reward is great in heaven, for so men persecuted the prophets who were before you. . . .

"'Think not that I have come to abolish the law and the prophets; I have come not to abolish them but to fulfil them. For truly, I say to you, till heaven and earth pass away, not an iota, not a dot, will pass from the law until all is accomplished. Whoever then relaxes one of the least of these commandments and teaches men so, shall be called least in the kingdom of heaven . . . For I tell you, unless your righteousness exceeds that of the scribes and Pharisees, you will never enter the kingdom of heaven.

"'You have heard that it was said to the men of old, "You shall not kill; and whoever kills shall be liable to judgment." But I say to you that every one who is angry with his brother shall be liable to judgment . . . You have heard that it was said, "You shall not commit adultery." But I say to you that every one who looks at a woman lustfully has already committed adultery with her in his heart. . . . You have heard that it was said, "An eye for an eye and a tooth for a tooth." But I say to you, Do not resist one who is evil. But if any one strikes you on the right cheek, turn to him the other also . . . You have heard that it was said, "You shall love your neighbor and hate your enemy." But I say to you, Love your enemies and pray for those who persecute you . . . For if you love those who love you, what reward have you? Do not even the tax collectors do the same? And if you salute only your brethren, what more are you doing than others? Do not even the Gentiles do the same? You, therefore, must be perfect, as your heavenly Father is perfect.

"'Beware of practicing your piety before men in order to be seen by them; for then you will have no reward from your Father who is in heaven. . . . And in praying do not heap up empty phrases as the Gentiles do; for they think that they will be heard for their many words. Do not be like them, for your Father knows what you need before you ask him. . . .

"'Therefore I tell you, do not be anxious about your life, what you shall eat or what you shall drink, nor about your body, what you shall put on. . . . Look at the birds of the air: they neither sow nor reap nor gather into barns, and yet your heavenly Father feeds them. . . . Consider the lilies of the field, how they grow; they neither toil nor spin; yet I tell you, even Solomon in all his glory was not arrayed like one of these. But if God so clothes the grass of the field, which today is alive and tomorrow is thrown into the oven, will he not much more clothe you, O men of little faith? Therefore do not be anxious, saying, "What shall we eat?" or "What shall we drink?" or "What shall we wear?" For the Gentiles seek all these things; and your heavenly Father knows that you need them all. But seek first his kingdom and his righteousness, and all these things shall be yours as well.'"

Here was the heart and core of the old faith, stripped of the legalistic concerns certain Pharisees were teaching. Thus it came as fresh, simple, new—so that it was said of him that he taught as one with inner authority, not as one of the scribes. Yes, the Lord would provide for his disciples, as he did for all his creatures. They need not concern themselves with material things but with leading righteous lives. In every action and thought they would have to strive to reach a higher level of selflessness and understanding. Anything less than that would not merit the final reward of the Lord's eternal kingdom on earth, the central quality of which was *shalom*, a word much richer than our word "peace."

Chapter 23

In the hills and towns along the Sea of Galilee, Jesus preaches in parables to increasingly larger crowds. Gathering twelve disciples around him, he instructs them in the Lord's will and prepares them to carry on his message.

Fishers of Men: The Twelve Apostles

After the murder of John the Baptist, Jesus began to work intensely to spread his message and instill knowledge and zeal in his 12 disciples. More and more he spoke of his need to go to Jerusalem and there suffer persecution and death before God would bring to pass the radical new earthly order of which the prophets had spoken. But Jesus' disciples resisted this part of his teaching. They would accept it ultimately only after his death. In the meantime, as the opposition of the Pharisees increased daily, Herod Antipas himself became concerned about the miracle-worker who many claimed was the "Son of man," and decided to send agents to spy on him.

Jesus' ministry in Galilee lasted nearly three years. Toward the end of that time, he received distressing news from John's disciples. They came to him dressed in sackcloth, their bodies strewn with ashes, the traditional garb of mourning. When he saw them approaching, he guessed their news at once: John the Baptist was dead. Sadly, they told the bizarre story of his murder.

John had been beheaded by Herod Antipas as a result of a drunken promise. On his birthday Antipas had given a lavish banquet at his palace fortress at Machaerus. John was imprisoned in a lonely cell far below the festively appointed main hall, where the banquet was being held. The guests, all men, wore sleeveless white tunics and floral garlands in their hair, and reclined on cushioned couches around long banquet tables. In the course of the evening they had eaten many rich dishes of game, fish and meat and had drunk large quantities of wine from silver goblets. Musicians played softly on tambourines, flutes and zithers, and beautiful professional dancers had provided entertainment between the courses.

Late in the night, Antipas, who was very drunk, had summoned Salome, his voluptuous young stepdaughter, and asked her to perform a dance for him. As a reward he had promised to give her anything she desired. "Ask me for whatever you wish, and I will grant it," he had boasted. "Whatever you ask me, I will give you . . ."

The idea of a royal princess dancing in public was a daring, even shocking one. Salome went to her mother, Herodias, and inquired, "What shall I ask?" Herodias, who still bitterly remembered John's accusation that she was an adulteress, replied, "The head of John the baptizer."

Salome ran back to Antipas with her request. "I want you to give me at once the head of John the Baptist on a platter." Antipas, trapped by his own reckless words, gave the order. "And immediately the king sent a soldier of the guard and gave orders to bring his head. He went and beheaded him in the prison, and brought his head on a platter, and gave it to the girl; and the girl gave it to her mother. When his disciples heard of it, they . . . took his body, and laid it in a tomb."

"And he awoke and rebuked the wind, and said to the sea, 'Peace! Be still!' And the wind ceased, and there was a great calm" (Mk. 4.39). Jesus' calming of the storm was one of several miracles he performed in the days of his Galilean ministry. During those days he also faced a storm of events, including the death of John the Baptist and growing opposition from the Pharisees and Herod.

The news affected Jesus deeply. When John's disciples had gone, he went out and walked slowly to a lonely spot outside of town. There he prayed and meditated in solitude. He had known his ministry would involve conflict and danger, but perhaps not until that moment did he realize the true implication of his continued work. Now he knew that like John, he too would suffer and die for proclaiming the coming kingdom.

Conflict on the Sabbath

Despite the great popularity John had enjoyed among the Jews, in the end he had been deserted by all but a handful of his most loyal disciples. No powerful men among the Jews had interceded on his behalf. No one had attempted to rescue him. For perhaps the first time, Jesus had to face the grim realization that if he continued his work he risked a similar fate.

When Jesus returned to Capernaum, he redoubled his efforts. The crisis was deepening, and he had to finish his work before the authorities caught up with him. He sought more and more to dramatize his conflicts with the Pharisees by direct confrontation. One Sabbath, for example, as he and some of his disciples were walking through a grainfield, some of them plucked a few ears of grain to eat. A group of Pharisees saw this and accused them of violating the laws of the Sabbath, which forbade most kinds of work, including plucking grain.

"And he said to them, 'Have you never read what David did, when he was in need and was hungry, he and those who were with him: how he entered the house of God . . . and ate the bread of the Presence, which it is not lawful for any but the priests to eat, and also gave it to those who were with him? . . . The sabbath was made for man, not man for the sabbath . . .'"

On another Sabbath he was attending services at the synagogue at Capernaum. "And behold, there was a man with a withered hand. And they [the Pharisees] asked him, 'Is it lawful to heal on the sabbath?' so that they might accuse him. He said to them, 'What man of you, if he has one sheep and it falls into a pit on the sabbath, will not lay hold of it and lift it out? Of how much more value is a man than a sheep! So it is lawful to do good on the sabbath.' Then he said to the man, 'Stretch out your hand.' And the man stretched it out, and it was restored, whole like

the other. But the Pharisees went out and took counsel against him, how to destroy him."

The lines of battle had been drawn, and the dangers for Jesus were increasing daily. Yet he persisted in his campaign, deciding now to attack on an additional front. He would send out his 12 closest followers (the Twelve) to help spread the word. Besides the eight men who had earlier formed the inner core, four others had become close associates of Jesus. They included James, the son of Alphaeus, and his good friend Thaddeus, and two more-radical figures—Simon the Zealot, who may have belonged to the numerous guerrilla group called the Zealots, and Judas Iscariot, the only non-Galilean among the disciples, who was from the village of Kerioth in Judea. Judas was the treasurer of the disciples' meager common fund.

Mission of the Twelve

Jesus called these men together and explained their mission to them. "Go nowhere among the Gentiles, and enter no town of the Samaritans,

"Follow me, and I will make you fishers of men" (Mt. 4.19). At least six of the twelve disciples were fishermen on the Sea of Galilee (left), a lake supporting a sizable fishing industry. Men who fished its waters were husky and weathered from long hot hours of casting their nets and hauling in fish. The best time to fish was late at night, when the still waters abounded with fish. During the day they repaired their sturdy wooden sailboats and mended their nets and sails. At dawn they gathered their night's catch in baskets, to be sold fresh or salted and dried for export as far as Spain.

but go rather to the lost sheep of the house of Israel. And preach as you go, saying, 'The kingdom of heaven is at hand.' Heal the sick, raise the dead, cleanse lepers, cast out demons. You received without pay, give without pay. Take no gold, nor silver, nor copper in your belts, no bag for your journey, nor two tunics, nor sandals, nor a staff . . . And whatever town or village you enter, find out who is worthy in it, and stay with him until you depart."

Then he warned them of the grave dangers they would face. "Behold, I send you out as sheep in the midst of wolves; so be wise as serpents and innocent as doves. Beware of men; for they will deliver you up to councils, and flog you in their synagogues, and you will be dragged before governors and kings for my sake . . . When they deliver you up, do not be anxious how you are to speak or what you are to say; for what you are to say will be given to you in that hour; for it is not you who speak, but the Spirit of your Father speaking through you. . . . When they persecute you in one town, flee to the next; for truly, I say to you, you will not have gone through all the towns of Israel, before the Son of man comes."

The note of urgency deepened as he went on. "Do not think that I have come to bring peace on earth; I have not come to bring peace, but a sword. For I have come to set a man against his father, and a daughter against her mother, and a daughter-in-law against her mother-in-law; and a man's foes will be those of his own household. He who loves father or mother more than me is not worthy of me . . .

"He who receives you receives me, and he who receives me receives him who sent me. He who receives a prophet because he is a prophet shall receive a prophet's reward, and he who receives a righteous man because he is a righteous man shall receive a righteous man's reward."

At daybreak the next day, the Twelve, filled with self-assurance and a sense of purpose, left Capernaum. Meanwhile, Jesus continued his attacks against the Pharisees. A few days later a hostile group of them confronted Jesus on a street in Capernaum and accused him of being in league with the devil and of casting out demons with powers given by Satan. Jesus at once pointed out the absurdity of their accusation. "Every kingdom divided against itself is laid waste, and no city or house divided against itself will stand; and if Satan casts out Satan, he is divided against

himself; how then will his kingdom stand? And if I cast out demons by Beelzebul [another name for the devil], by whom do your sons cast them out? Therefore they shall be your judges. But if it is by the Spirit of God that I cast out demons, then the kingdom of God has come upon you."

Still skeptical, they asked him to give them a sign to prove that his powers against demons came from the Lord and that the kingdom was at hand. He retorted irately: "An evil and adulterous generation seeks for a sign; but no sign shall be given to it except the sign of the prophet Jonah. . . . The men of Nineveh will arise at the judgment with this generation and condemn it; for they repented at the preaching of Jonah, and behold, something greater than Jonah is here. The queen of the South [Sheba] will arise at the judgment with this generation and condemn it; for she came from the ends of the earth to hear the wisdom of Solomon, and behold, something greater than Solomon is here."

Hearing his words, the Pharisees became angrier than ever. Unable to find a fitting rejoinder, they went their way. When Jesus returned to his house, he found a group of his disciples waiting for him and a crowd gathered outside. "Your mother and your brothers are outside, asking for you," the disciples explained. His family had probably come from Nazareth to warn him of the increasing danger he was facing.

Jesus, however, seems to have decided that he must break his family ties if he was to continue his work, perhaps hoping to protect them from persecution. "And he replied, 'Who are my mother and my brothers?' And looking around at those who sat about him, he said, 'Here are my mother and my brothers! Whoever does the will of God is my brother, and sister, and mother.'"

Jesus Instructs His Disciples

As opposition from the Pharisees increased, Jesus began to concentrate more and more on private instruction of his closest disciples, and his public preaching became less frequent. When the Twelve returned from their mission with optimistic reports of their success, of large crowds coming to hear them and of many healings, he cautioned them against being overly confident of their lasting effects.

"Listen!" he explained. "A sower went out to sow. And as he sowed, some seed fell along the

"And he told them many things in parables, saying: 'A sower went out to sow'" (Mt. 13.3). *For centuries crops have been raised on the Plain of Gennesaret, one of the most fertile areas in Galilee. It lies on the northwest shore of the Sea of Galilee, near Capernaum. Jesus often spoke to large crowds in these fields, and the plain's abundance inspired many of his parables about the nature of God's kingdom.*

path, and the birds came and devoured it. Other seed fell on rocky ground, where it had not much soil, and immediately it sprang up, since it had no depth of soil; and when the sun rose it was scorched, and since it had no root it withered away. Other seed fell among thorns and the thorns grew up and choked it, and it yielded no grain. And other seeds fell into good soil and brought forth grain, growing up and increasing and yielding thirtyfold and sixtyfold and a hundredfold."

When they asked him what he meant, he replied impatiently, "Do you not understand this parable? How then will you understand all the parables? The sower sows the word. And these are the ones along the path, where the word is sown; when they hear, Satan immediately comes and takes away the word which is sown in them.

And these in like manner are the ones sown upon rocky ground, who, when they hear the word, immediately receive it with joy; and they have no root in themselves, but endure for a while; then, when tribulation or persecution arises on account of the word, immediately they fall away. And others are the ones sown among thorns; they are those who hear the word, but the cares of the world, and the delight in riches, and the desire for other things, enter in and choke the word, and it proves unfruitful. But those that were sown upon the good soil are the ones who hear the word and accept it and bear fruit, thirtyfold and sixtyfold and a hundredfold."

On another occasion, as they sat discussing Jesus' teachings, one of the disciples asked, "Who is the greatest in the kingdom of heaven?" Jesus called to a child who was playing nearby and asked him to join them. "Truly, I say to you," he explained, holding the child before him, "unless you turn and become like children, you will never enter the kingdom of heaven. Whoever humbles himself like this child, he is the greatest in the kingdom of heaven."

Sometime later, John reported a problem to Jesus. "Master," he explained, "we saw a man casting out demons in your name, and we forbade him, because he does not follow with us." Gently Jesus rebuked him, saying, "Do not forbid him; for he that is not against you is for you."

Meanwhile, Jesus' enemies were joining forces against him. It seems that some of the most hostile Pharisees had gone to Herod Antipas and urged him to put this cocksure radical in prison before his popularity got out of hand. His talk of a kingdom sounded dangerously like subversion, they hinted. Antipas became alarmed at the mention of possible political upheavals. Yet he also feared that if he arrested Jesus, he might provoke an uprising. Instead, he sent agents to observe Jesus' activities and to report back to him.

Jesus, however, had decided to escape the crowds and the growing opposition of the Pharisees in Capernaum. He and his disciples traveled to Bethsaida, a small fishing village about three miles east of Capernaum, which was the home of Philip, Andrew and Simon Peter. Bethsaida was located just inside the territory of Antipas'

"The scribes and the Pharisees sit on Moses' seat" (Mt. 23.2), a carved stone chair reserved for a visitor or for the most distinguished elder of a synagogue. This one is from Chorazin, one of the three towns Jesus inveighed against for their citizens' unbelief.

brother Philip, and Jesus may have felt safer there, away from Antipas' political control.

Before long, word spread throughout Bethsaida and neighboring towns that the famous miracle-worker was there, and again crowds gathered to hear his words and be healed. One balmy spring afternoon Jesus preached to a large gathering on a grassy slope near the shore of the lake. It was near the time of Passover, and the meadow was bursting with bright blossoms and new growth. The air was filled with the songs of birds and the fresh smells of wildflowers and clover. As was his habit, Jesus was seated high up on the slope, his disciples grouped around him. The crowd, which was made up of fishermen, farmers, craftsmen and merchants, had gathered on the grass around and below them.

Feeding the 5000

Perhaps because of the mild weather or the magnetism of Jesus' words, no one noticed that the hour was getting late. "And when it grew late, his disciples came to him and said, 'This is a lonely place, and the hour is now late; send them away, to go into the country and villages round about and buy themselves something to eat.' But he answered them, 'You give them something to eat.' And they said to him, 'Shall we go and buy two hundred denarii [one denarius was a day's wages for a skilled worker] worth of bread, and give it to them to eat?' And he said to them, 'How many loaves have you? Go and see.' And when they had found out, they said, 'Five, and two fish.' Then he commanded them all to sit down by companies upon the green grass. So they sat down in groups, by hundreds and by fifties. And taking the five loaves and the two fish he looked up to heaven, and blessed, and broke the loaves, and gave them to the disciples to set before the people; and he divided the two fish among them all. And they all ate and were satisfied."

The next day everyone was talking excitedly about how Jesus had fed a crowd of as many as 5000 people with only two fishes and five loaves of bread. Some claimed it was actually the predicted Messianic banquet that was to be held at the dawn of the new age. Others hailed Jesus as Elijah reborn; still others spoke of John the Baptist raised from the dead. According to some reports, the crowds had been so affected by Jesus' powers that they had wanted to make him king.

"Think not that I have come to abolish the law and the prophets; I have come . . . to fulfil them" (Mt. 5.17). The ark of the covenant symbolized the Mosaic covenant that Jesus came to fulfill. This chest with doors and wheels, a decorative relief from a 3rd-century synagogue in Capernaum, probably represents the ark.

In his columned throne room at the lakeside capital of Tiberias, Herod Antipas listened to these reports with mounting concern. Although he could not believe that this man was actually the expected Messiah, the fact that his followers believed he was, made him a dangerous rival. His fears deepened when he heard that some of Jesus' disciples claimed their master had walked upon the waters of the Sea of Galilee and had calmed a sudden storm.

Antipas could no longer afford to let this man remain free. Sooner or later Jesus would lead an uprising against him. He called his council together at once to discuss the safest means of eliminating this troublesome character.

The Son of Man

Jesus meanwhile had withdrawn with his disciples into the region of Caesarea Philippi. They began to ask him if he really was the long-awaited Messiah. "Who do men say that I am?" he asked. "And they told him, 'John the Baptist; and others say, Elijah; and others one of the prophets.' And he asked them, 'But who do you say that I am?' Peter answered him, 'You are the Christ [the Messiah].'" And Jesus charged his disciples to tell no one about him.

"And he began to teach them that the Son of man must suffer many things, and be rejected by the elders and the chief priests and the scribes, and be killed, and after three days rise again. And he said this plainly. . . . And he said to them, 'Truly, I say to you, there are some standing here who will not taste death before they see the kingdom of God come with power.'"

Puzzled, the disciples continued to question him. "Then why do the scribes say that first Elijah must come?" they asked. Jesus replied, "Elijah does come, and he is to restore all things; but I tell you that Elijah has already come, and they did not know him, but did to him whatever they pleased. So also the Son of man will suffer at their hands." Then the disciples understood that he was speaking to them of John the Baptist.

More and more frequently now, Jesus spoke of himself as the "Son of man." The term had several meanings, and he may have purposely been ambiguous about which one he meant. The famous vision in the popular Book of Daniel described the Messiah coming to judge the world as "one like a son of man," stressing the fact that the Lord's agent would look just like other men. Jesus may, however, have used the term in a much broader sense, for all men were sons of men.

When they returned to Capernaum, a group of Pharisees who had befriended Jesus came to the house at night with an urgent warning to leave Galilee: "'Get away from here, for Herod wants to kill you.' And he said to them, 'Go and tell that fox, "Behold, I cast out demons and perform cures today and tomorrow, and the third day I finish my course. Nevertheless I must go on my way today and tomorrow and the day following; for it cannot be that a prophet should perish away from Jerusalem."'"

"Then he began to upbraid the cities where most of his mighty works had been done, because they did not repent. 'Woe to you, Chorazin! woe to you, Bethsaida! . . . And you, Capernaum, will you be exalted to heaven? You shall be brought down to Hades. . . . For if the mighty works done in you had been done in Sodom, it would have remained until this day. But I tell you that it shall be more tolerable on the day of judgment for the land of Sodom than for you.'"

Soon afterward Jesus and his small band of disciples left Capernaum and headed southward toward Judea and Jerusalem, where he had already prophesied he would meet his death. Yet there was still a little time to spread his message throughout Judea, and he was determined to work with renewed vigor until the inevitable end.

Part Seven

Jesus
and Jerusalem

"After this there was a feast of the Jews, and Jesus went up to Jerusalem" (Jn. 5.1). In his final months Jesus walked from Jericho to preach and pray at Jerusalem's temple. The temple, built by Herod the Great, was the religious center for Jews throughout the Roman world. Before the towers of Herod's palace, the courtyard outside the temple's south wall teems with Persian, Babylonian and Hellenist Jews who have returned to Jerusalem, as Jesus did, for the Passover. They trade their foreign currency for silver shekels at the moneychangers' tables and buy food, drink and sacrificial lambs at brightly colored booths. A long limestone stairway leads past vigilant Roman guards and through the gates into the Court of the Gentiles, where Jesus often taught large holiday crowds. One day, these crowds would shout for his crucifixion.

"O Jerusalem, Jerusalem, killing the prophets and stoning those who are sent to you!" (Mt. 23.37). Thus Jesus decried the great city in which he knew he was to meet his fate. There, at Passover, his enemies awaited him.

THE JERUSALEM Jesus knew bore little resemblance to the city David conquered in the tenth century B.C. Then, it had been a small, isolated hill fortress, valued more for its location than its size or splendor. Yet from that time on it was known as the City of David, and the kings of David's dynasty, especially his son Solomon, had enlarged and enriched it.

In the sixth century B.C., the army of Nebuchadnezzar razed Jerusalem and drove its citizens into exile. During the long years of captivity in Babylon, the exiles' prayers and longings focused on the distant Holy City. But the city rebuilt by the Jews who returned a century later was far inferior to its predecessor. It was, ironically, the hated tyrant Herod the Great who restored Jerusalem to its former grandeur.

In the 33 years of his reign (37–4 B.C.), Herod transformed the city as had no other ruler since Solomon, building palaces and citadels, a theater and an amphitheater, viaducts and public monuments. These ambitious building projects, some completed long after his death, were part of the king's single-minded campaign to increase his capital's importance on the political and cultural map of the Roman Empire.

No visitor seeing Jerusalem for the first time could fail to be impressed by its visual splendor. The long, difficult ascent from Jericho to the Holy City ended as the traveler rounded the Mount of Olives, and suddenly caught sight of a vista like few others in the world. Across the Kidron Valley, set among the surrounding hills, was Jerusalem, "the perfection of beauty," in the words of Lamentations, "the joy of all the world."

The view from the Mount of Olives was dominated by the gleaming, gold-embellished temple, the most hallowed spot in the Jewish world. This was the Lord's earthly dwelling place, the focal point of the Jews' most solemn rites and celebrations. It stood high above the old City of David, at the center of a gigantic white stone platform.

To the south of the temple was the lower city, a sea of limestone houses, buff-colored from years of sun and wind. Narrow, unpaved streets meandered among the houses and sloped downward toward the Tyropean Valley, which ran through the center of the city. Rising upward to the west was the Upper City, where the white marble villas and palaces of the very rich stood out like patches of snow. A large arched passageway spanned the valley, crossing from Herod's palace in the Upper City to the temple.

A high, thick, gray stone wall encircled Jerusalem. It had been damaged, repaired and enlarged over the centuries, and in Jesus' day it was about $3\frac{1}{2}$ miles in circumference, compressing about 25,000 people into an area of less than a square mile. At intervals along the wall were located massive gateways. Just inside each gate was a customs station, where publicans collected taxes on all goods entering or leaving the city.

Commerce of the Lower City

Once past one of the gates, the visitor faced a bewildering maze of dusty streets and alleyways, running uphill and down in every direction. As he slowly made his way toward the temple, his senses were assaulted by oppressive dust and heat, sounds of voices raised in anger or song, the clatter of hooves and odors of cooking food.

Along the Small Market street in the Lower City, he would pass open-air shops where Jerusalem's craftsmen sat at work: the city's weavers, dyers, potters, bakers, tailors, carpenters and metal-workers. Farther along he would enter the colorful bazaar, where merchants sold fruits and vegetables, dried fish, sacrificial animals, clothes, perfumes and jewelry.

The market street was always crowded and busy, expecially on Mondays and Thursdays, the main market days, when citizens and visitors came there to buy goods or souvenirs. Perishable goods were on sale every day. Only on the Sabbath was the street empty and quiet.

A weary traveler could always stop to rest or refresh himself at one of Jerusalem's many taverns or restaurants. There he might select from a menu offering fresh or salted fish, fried locusts, vegetables, soup, pastry and fruit. He could drink local wine or imported beer.

The farmers of Jerusalem, like their rural cousins, went out each morning to tend their crops. Most of them worked in the rich olive groves that covered the surrounding hillsides and provided the city's only major export.

Jerusalem's numerous craftsmen had long been organized into guilds and most of them worked in communal shops. The members of each guild lived in a cluster of houses in a particular section of the city and they usually had their own synagogue. In Jesus' time, there were at least 480 synagogues in Jerusalem.

Splendor of the Upper City

Most of Jerusalem's working people lived in the crowded, noisy precincts of the Lower City. Their one- and two-story houses stood packed closely together like bricks in a very crooked wall. In contrast, the broad fashionable avenues of the Upper City were laid out in an orderly grid pattern like the stately cities of Greece and Rome. This part of Jerusalem was the home of the rich and powerful Jewish families and high-ranking Roman officials. Comfortably removed from the rest of the population, they lived in spacious white marble mansions and palaces built around courtyards with formal gardens and pools. The magnificent royal palace of Herod the Great—later used by the Roman governor of Judea during his visits to Jerusalem—was situated in the uppermost northwest corner of the city.

Directly in front of the palace stood the Upper Market, with its Roman-style arcades along three sides and an open court for market booths in the center. Here were the shops of the dealers in luxury goods: the distillers of expensive oils and perfumes; the master tailors and silk merchants; the goldsmiths and silversmiths; the dealers in ivory, incense and precious stones. Household slaves went there to buy expensive imported foods for their masters' banquet tables.

Not far away was the palace of the Jewish high priest. (The high priest at the time of Jesus' ministry in Jerusalem, Caiaphas, did not live there but in another section of the Upper City. Jesus' trial before the Sanhedrin probably took place in one of the large halls of his palace.)

Herod the Great had also built a theater in the Upper City. It was a large, open-air auditorium with semicircular rows of seats ascending from a central stage. Wealthy Jews came there to watch the best of Greek and Roman drama. Most traditional Jews, however, scorned this and other outgrowths of Greco-Roman culture as immoral.

Herod's Temple

Directly across the Tyropean Valley from the Upper City, in the northeastern corner of Jerusalem, stood the incomparable temple, the city's crowning jewel. Built by Herod as a goodwill gesture toward his hostile Jewish subjects, it was reputedly one of the finest religious structures in the world. The central sanctuary was approached through a series of spacious outer courts, each court progressively more exclusive.

The outermost was the Court of the Gentiles, a huge rectangular area about 35 acres in size. It was paved with colored stones and enclosed by tall, stately columns.

Visitors entered through a number of immense double and triple gates, which stood at intervals along the outer court. As its name suggests, the Court of the Gentiles was open to Gentiles as well as Jews, and it was usually crowded with people from many backgrounds and walks of life. On a typical day a visitor would encounter Jewish pilgrims from all over Palestine and the Roman Empire; merchants selling doves, young sheep and cattle for sacrifice; moneychangers converting foreign currency into Tyrian shekels; Jewish scribes and rabbis discussing points of Mosaic law; and others simply passing the time of day.

At the center of the Court of the Gentiles stood a second enclosed compound, posted with notices in Greek that proclaimed: "No foreigner is allowed within the balustrades and embankment about the sanctuary. Whoever is caught will be personally responsible for his ensuing death." Only Jewish men and women could venture beyond this point, which led, through three large gates, into the Court of Women. This court too was surrounded by ornate columns.

At the western side of the Court of Women was a curved flight of 15 stairs, which ascended to the Nicanor Gate, so named because its magnificent bronze doors had been donated by a rich Alexandrian Jew named Nicanor. Beyond them lay the Court of Israel, a long and narrow area where the Jewish men assembled during temple services. No women were allowed here.

A low balustrade separated this section from the Court of Priests, accessible only to the priests

and Levites who served in the temple. In the center of this court was the great horned altar of sacrifice with a long ramp leading to the top.

Dominating the entire complex was the majestic sanctuary itself, which stood at the rear of the Court of Priests. It was built of perfectly tooled and fitted white marble stones, covered with plates of heavy gold. Golden spikes rose from the roof, which soared to a height of about 165 feet. At the back of a large porch were immense gilded doors covered by a Babylonian tapestry of blue, purple, crimson and gold, depicting the heavens. Above was a golden vine, symbol of the nation of Israel. It was said that there was so much gold covering the building that no one could look directly at it in bright sunlight.

Inside the sanctuary were two rooms. The first, the holy place, was a large hall paneled in cedar. It contained a golden altar for incense, a golden table for the bread offering and a golden menorah, a seven-branched candelabrum lit by seven lamps burning purest olive oil. The second room, the holy of holies, was separated from the first by a heavy linen curtain embroidered with spun gold. Only the high priest was allowed to enter this sacred spot, and he only on the annual Day of Atonement. Within this mysterious chamber, believed to be the earthly dwelling place of Israel's Lord, there was nothing at all. The very absence of objects symbolized the intangible and invisible presence of God.

Begun in 20 B.C., the construction of the temple was one of Herod's most ambitious projects. The old temple mount first had to be cleared and enlarged to about twice its original size. The new area was roughly 1000 by 1500 feet, girded by a massive retaining wall of huge fitted stones, each more than 15 feet long and 13 feet thick. As Solomon had done earlier, Herod imported the best stone masons and architects from abroad to direct the construction. Only the finest materials were used: cedar from Lebanon, the purest marble and limestone and the finest gold.

"One of his disciples said to him, 'Look, Teacher, what wonderful stones and what wonderful buildings!'" (Mk. 13.1) When Herod the Great rebuilt Jerusalem's temple in 20 B.C., he erected a great retaining wall to extend the temple's base. Taking thousands of workers many years to build, the huge wall was made of limestone blocks—some of them over 30 feet long—hauled from a quarry on rollers and hoisted aloft by wooden cranes. Its fine masonry is apparent in unweathered, newly excavated portions (left), where the unmortared stones still show their smooth original facing.

The project required the services of more than 10,000 laborers. Herod had 1000 priests specially trained as carpenters and masons to work on the sanctuary building: by law no layman was allowed to handle the sacred building materials. The sanctuary was completed in 18 months, but the outer courtyards were not finished for another 80 years, in A.D. 64. During this entire time the temple ritual was never interrupted.

Guardians of the Sanctuary

Along the northern side of the temple courtyard stood the massive palace-fortress of Antonia, another of Herod's landmarks. A porticoed stairway connected the Antonia Palace with the Court of the Gentiles, and the 600 soldiers stationed there were always on the alert for disturbances in the temple precincts. The precious ceremonial robes of the high priest were kept in one of its four guard towers and were released only on important religious feast days.

The Romans had taken custody of the garments as a precautionary measure. Realizing the tremendous power of the high priest's office, they sought to limit it by restricting the use of the robes, which symbolized its authority. In the century before the Roman occupation in 63 B.C., the king of Israel had also been the high priest, and both offices had been hereditary. The Romans had abolished the kingship and had made the office of high priest appointive, always subject to their approval. Nonetheless, in Jesus' day the high priest remained the most powerful figure in the Jewish nation.

The office of high priest carried with it a number of unique privileges and responsibilities. He alone was permitted to enter the holy of holies on the Day of Atonement to atone for the sins of the entire nation. As head of the Sanhedrin or Jewish high court, he presided over the nation's highest administrative and judicial body. His daily life was governed by the strictest rules of ceremonial purity. His death was viewed as an act of atonement and was marked by the release of a condemned murderer. Even if he retired from office he continued to wield great influence.

The high priest stood at the apex of an elaborate hierarchy of temple personnel. Directly beneath him in rank were the chief priests, an exclusive group of about 200 highborn Jews. The most important of them was the captain of the temple, second only in rank and power to the high priest. His duties included supervision of the whole body of priests and of all temple activities. Other chief priests had charge of the daily and weekly temple services, the temple treasury and the maintenance of the sacred vessels.

Below the chief priests were the ordinary priests of the temple. There were probably about 7200 of them in Jesus' time. They formed an exclusive hereditary community of men who could trace their descent back to Aaron, Moses' brother and the first high priest. Unlike the chief priests, most of them lived outside Jerusalem in the towns and villages of Judea and Galilee. They were divided into 24 priestly clans, each of which served a week at a time at the temple. Their duties included lighting the altar fires, attending to the offerings of incense and unleavened bread and killing the sacrificial animals.

The lowest-ranking temple officials were the Levites. These men were descendants of Levi, the patriarch of the priestly tribe. Aaron and all Israel's priests had been members of this tribe. There were some 9600 Levites in the first century B.C. Like the majority of priests, they comprised 24 clans, each clan serving one week at a time as guards, policemen, doorkeepers, singers, musicians and servants of the temple. They were forbidden, on pain of death, to enter the holy sanctuary or approach the altar of sacrifice.

The daily temple ritual required the services of nearly 1000 chief priests, priests and Levites. On feast days all 24 clans were required to come to Jerusalem to participate in the elaborate ceremonies and sacrificial rites. This meant that there were nearly 18,000 temple personnel on hand during each of the three great pilgrim festivals: Passover, Weeks and Booths.

Pilgrims and Priests

During these times the enormous influx of pilgrims into the Holy City swelled its population of 25,000 to at least four or five times that number. Their presence provided an important stimulus to the city's economy. Besides creating a huge demand for food, lodging and sacrificial animals, the incoming Jews were required to spend a tenth of their annual income—after taxes—within Jerusalem. This "second tithe" was in addition to the tithe they had to pay directly to the temple.

Many pilgrims found lodging in one of Jerusalem's inns or in private homes. Some of the foreign Jewish communities had built hospices for their citizens to use when they visited the Holy City. The Essenes and Pharisees also provided lodging for fellow members. But the vast majority stayed in tents outside the city or in private homes in the villages of Bethphage or Bethany, where Jesus and his disciples stayed during his last months of ministry.

The overcrowding and the excitement of the festivals frequently led to outbreaks of violence and anti-Roman rebellion. On more than one occasion the huge mass of pilgrims had been stirred up by zealous nationalists or would-be Messiahs.

The Fortress Where Jesus Was Scourged

Jesus' trial before Pilate may have taken place in the Antonia, a fortress overlooking the Jerusalem temple. Though the temple had its own police force—a small army of Levites— Roman soldiers of the Antonia stood by as a constant reminder of Rome's presence.

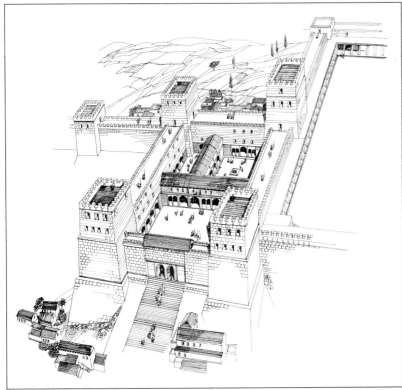

Originally a Maccabean fortress, the Antonia (above) was rebuilt on a grand scale by Herod the Great and named for Mark Antony. It stood on a precipice 75 feet high at the temple's northwest corner. Stairs led to the Court of the Gentiles. Symbols of Roman authority were common in the empire, such as the headless porphyry statue (upper right) of the Emperor Hadrian found at Caesarea, seat of Roman government in Palestine.

"When Pilate heard these words, he brought Jesus out and sat down on the judgment seat at a place called The Pavement" (Jn. 19.13). The stones at lower right are thought to have been part of "The Pavement" in the Antonia—a central court where a Roman governor might adjudicate at public trials. Games have been scratched in the stones, perhaps by some of the 500 to 600 Roman soldiers who made up the cohort stationed there. The chief duty of the garrison troops was to be ready for any emergency in the Court of the Gentiles. During major Jewish religious festivals, when this court was thronged, the garrison was increased.

For this reason, the Roman governor made a point of being present during these occasions, and extra soldiers were stationed at strategic locations throughout the city.

Besides attracting large crowds of pilgrims three times a year, the temple provided a constant demand for supplies from local merchants. Its requirements provided the mainstay of the city's economy, and more than one fortune had been amassed by families who had obtained monopolies on supplying certain items. The wealthy family of Garmo, for example, had the exclusive right to bake the offertory loaves of bread for the temple. Other merchants wove the priestly vestments, supplied incense, carried wood for the altar fires and fashioned the sacred ornaments and golden vessels.

The high priest and the chief priests formed an elite religious nobility within Jerusalem. Their members were selected from a small number of wealthy families who traced their descent back to Zadok, the high priest during Solomon's reign.

In the time of Jesus, however, the dominant priestly families constituted an illegitimate aristocracy whose members were not of pure Zadokite blood. The powerful clans of Boethus, Annas, Phiabi and Kamith, all members of the illegitimate priesthood, supplied all the high priests in the temple. The house of Annas was especially powerful. Annas had been high priest from A.D. 6–15, and five of his sons, his son-in-law Caiaphas and his grandson Jonathan also held that important post.

A Ruling Elite

These men controlled not only the temple, but a large number of seats on the Sanhedrin, the supreme judicial body of the Jewish nation. Its 71 members were divided into three groups, the chief priests, the elders and the scribes. The high priest served as its presiding officer. Although in theory the Sanhedrin had executive and legislative functions as well as judicial authority, its powers had been curbed by the Roman rulers. In Jesus' day, the Sanhedrin did not have the authority to carry out the death sentence.

There was also an influential lay nobility within Jerusalem, represented by the elders who sat on the Sanhedrin. They were the descendants of ancient ruling families whose powers had originated in the days following the Conquest.

After the return from exile in Babylon they had functioned as representatives of the people in dealing with the Persian, Egyptian and Syrian rulers. Many elders were wealthy merchants and landowners.

These two powerful ruling elites, the priestly and lay aristocracy of Judaism, made up the party known in Jesus' time as the Sadducees. They constituted a tightly closed circle of influential families who wielded great political power by virtue of their control of the Sanhedrin and their favored status in the eyes of the Roman rulers. They had found that they could best maintain their position by following a policy of cooperation with Rome. Their political and religious outlook was conservative, aimed at preserving both the temple and their own authority.

Scribes of Jerusalem

In the decades just before and during the time of Jesus, the dominant role of the Sadducean families was being overtaken by a new and dynamic ruling class of scribes. These men came from all classes. Some were priests, but the vast majority were merchants, artisans and laborers. Among the most famous scribes in Jesus' day, Shammai was a carpenter and Hillel a laborer.

Unlike the hereditary ancestral and financial status of the Sadducees, the authority of the scribes rested upon their learning. Anyone who wished could try to become a member of this venerated class, but he had to devote years of study to that end. A would-be scribe had already mastered the law and achieved a thorough familiarity with the scriptures by the age of 14. Thereafter he spent years in close association with a recognized scribal teacher, receiving lengthy instruction in personal conduct and application of the law in everyday situations.

Such teachers were so venerated that pupils often observed not only their teachings but their actions as well. When a student reached the point where he could make his own personal decisions on points of law and justice, he became a non-ordained scholar. Only at about the age of 40 would he be formally ordained as a scribe in his own right, and from that time on he could be addressed as rabbi.

In the time of Jesus, young Jews came to Jerusalem from all over the Roman Empire to sit at the feet of the rabbis. At any given time there might have been 10 scribal schools in the Holy City. The venerated sage Hillel had as many as 80 pupils at a time. Much of the teaching took place in the precincts of the temple, but there were probably classrooms elsewhere in the city.

The scribes were held in great awe and respect throughout the Jewish world. Like the prophets of old, they were thought to possess vast, secret

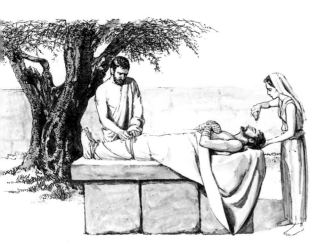

Preparation for a Jewish Burial

"They took the body of Jesus, and bound it in linen cloths with the spices" (Jn. 19.40). Family and friends of a dead person washed the body and anointed it (as above) with scented oils. Then, beginning with the hands and feet, they wrapped it in strips of linen and sprinkled fragrant spices between them. (The Pharisee Nicodemus, a secret follower of Jesus, brought a scented resin from India for this purpose.) Finally, the body was interred in a cave or family plot as soon as possible.

knowledge of the workings of the Lord's power. In many ways they might be viewed as the legitimate heirs of the prophetic tradition. They could be recognized on the streets by their long, flowing robes, fringed at the corners with very long tassels. When a scribe passed, ordinary people rose as a sign of respect. They were given the place of honor at important feasts and in synagogues.

Models of Perfect Piety

Closely linked with the scribes were the Pharisees, a group of laymen who had chosen to live in strictest adherence to scribal tradition and law. Although the scribes were numbered among the ranks of the Pharisees and were often leaders of

their communities, the majority of Pharisees were also well educated in the law. Yet it was their extreme piety rather than wisdom that set them apart from others, and they often went to great lengths to demonstrate that piety.

In Jerusalem the Pharisees lived in several communities. Membership was limited to men who had demonstrated their ability to follow scribal teachings. Each community had a leader and followed a stringent set of rules. Members were required to fast twice a week, to observe fixed daily hours of prayer and to take part in a weekly communal meal. The Pharisees saw themselves as practicing the ideal way of life and were convinced that their communities would form the core of the community of the righteous in the Lord's kingdom. They were often contemptuous of the masses of people who did not live as they did. The masses, on the other hand, looked up to them as models of perfect piety.

In the time of Jesus there was much hostility between the Pharisees and the Sadducees. In many ways these two groups conflicted with each other. The Sadducees represented the privileged, conservative, traditional elite of Judaism. The Pharisees were the democratic, progressive new party of the common man. The Sadducees controlled the temple and its rituals, but the Pharisees controlled the synagogues.

These newcomers openly challenged the privileged status of the Sadducees and criticized their easy tolerance of foreign rule. For their part, the Pharisees opposed Roman rule, refused to take the oath of allegiance to the emperor and more than once participated in short-lived revolts against Rome. (In A.D. 66 many of them would take part in a great rebellion against Roman rule.) Though the Pharisees were represented on the Sanhedrin by the scribal members, the power there still rested with the Sadducees. Pharisaic influence was most strongly felt in the realm of religious thinking and daily ritual.

During his last months in Judea and Jerusalem, Jesus brought about an uneasy alliance between these two groups. By threatening the privileged position of the Sadducees and at the same time challenging the basic scribal and Pharisaic precepts, he caused them to unite against him. For their own very separate reasons, both parties saw this self-styled prophet from Galilee as a dangerous enemy, and together they concluded that he must be brought to trial and condemned to death.

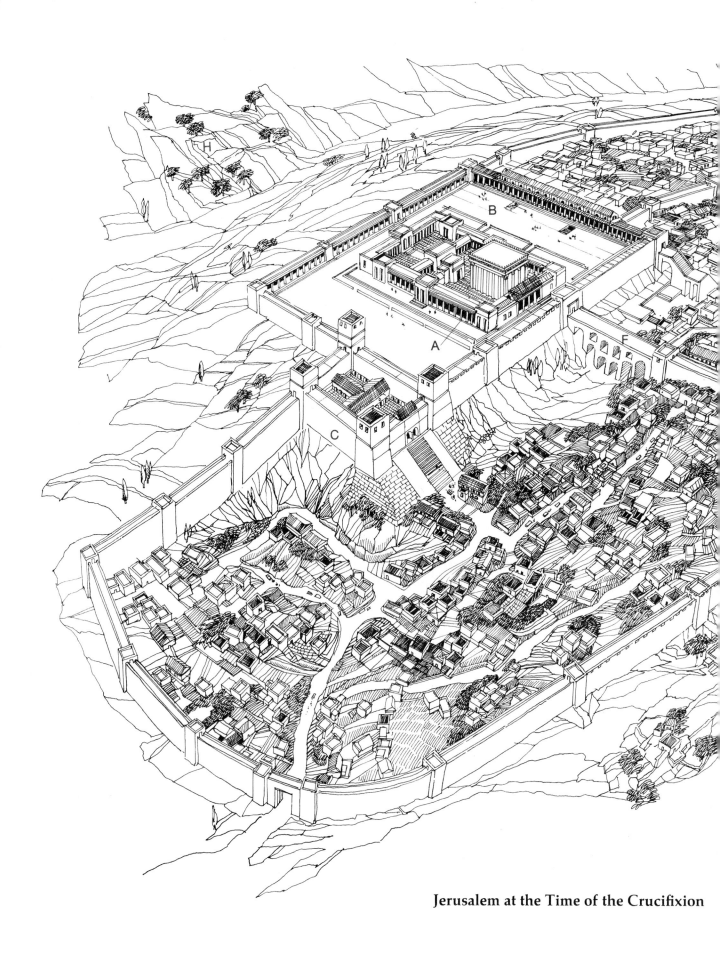

Jerusalem at the Time of the Crucifixion

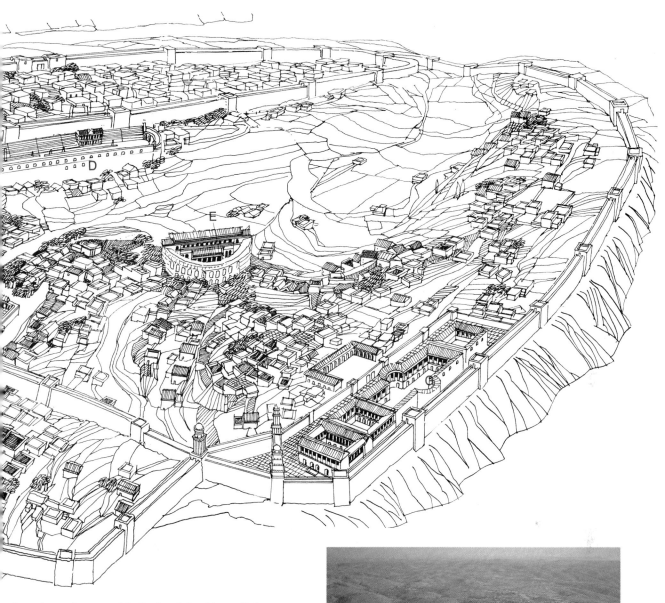

Jerusalem as Jesus saw it in the days before his crucifixion was still the city created by Herod the Great, although the hated ruler had been dead for three decades. Herod had admired Greek culture and Roman power, and wanted to make his kingdom a notable cultural and political province of the Roman Empire. He had sought, too, the allegiance of his Jewish subjects, and he considered the temple (A) at Jerusalem his finest achievement. Jesus preached in the Court of the Gentiles (B) which Herod's builders had doubled in size and surrounded with an elaborate Hellenistic portico. Herod's palace-fortress, named the Antonia (C) for his benefactor Mark Antony, was the place where Jesus may have been tried before Pontius Pilate. The sports hippodrome (D), theater (E) and viaduct (F) linking the temple with Herod's grand fortified palace (G) were similar to ones built by Herod in other cities. The Mount of Olives (H) where Jesus prayed was outside the city, opposite the eastern wall of the temple. We can only speculate on the appearance of Jerusalem then, since building enterprises could go on for years. The temple complex was actually completed only a few years before the Romans destroyed it in 70 A.D. The contours of Jerusalem today (right) are much the same as they were in Jesus' time.

Chapter 24

Jesus leaves Galilee for the last time and journeys south to Judea. There

he continues his ministry, despite the opposition of Pharisees and Sadducees.

As his time grows nearer, he finds comfort in loyal followers.

Friends in Judea:
Lazarus, Mary and Martha

The final ministry of Jesus was not in his native Galilee, but in Judea and in Jerusalem itself. There, in the region where John the Baptist had baptized him, Jesus began to prepare himself and his loyal disciples for the time of the Passover feast. Then, he knew, his enemies would arrest him, and he would meet his death. Yet throughout this period, he continued to preach his message of the kingdom of God, and to perform such miracles as that related by John: the raising of Lazarus from death.

Jesus spent nearly seven months in Judea, making several journeys to Jerusalem for important feasts. On those occasions he spoke to large crowds in the temple courtyard during the day and spent the nights in the nearby village of Bethany. The rest of the time he preached and healed in the vicinity of Jericho, the busy oasis city at the edge of the Judean wilderness.

During these final months, Jesus became more outspoken in his attacks on the scribes and Pharisees and more explicit about his role in the coming kingdom of God. At times he seemed to provoke hostility deliberately. Yet he never tried to incite rebellion. He sought instead to persuade the people of Judea to repent of their sins and prepare for the new age.

Knowing that his days were numbered, Jesus had decided to leave his native Galilee and journey to Judea and Jerusalem, the seat of Jewish authority and tradition. As he and his disciples hastened southward toward Judea from Capernaum, they probably joined the crowds of pilgrims who

were traveling to Jerusalem for the Feast of Tabernacles. Amid the throngs Jesus was less likely to be detected by Antipas' soldiers, who had orders to arrest him. Even if he was recognized, they would probably not seize him for fear of provoking a riot.

The travelers did not continue south along the highway through Samaria, the home of the hated Samaritans. Most pilgrims avoided this direct route to Jerusalem, traveling eastward instead and then taking the highway southward along the Jordan Valley. This well-traveled route was level and avoided the central hills of Samaria.

It was said that the Samaritans were descended from foreign colonists who had been sent there after the Assyrians conquered the northern kingdom of Israel in the eighth century B.C. and deported most of the Israelites. Actually, they were of mixed Israelite and alien blood. The Samaritans arrogantly regarded themselves as the only true Jews, refusing to worship at the temple in Jerusalem. They claimed that their temple on Mount Gerizim was the only authentic place of worship, and they followed a separate liturgical calendar. Their version of the Torah differed insignificantly from that of Jesus' people, but the Samaritans rejected all other Old Testament

"When the days drew near for him to be received up, he set his face to go to Jerusalem" (Lk. 9.51). The way there from Bethany, where Jesus spent the final days of his ministry, was along this road, past the Mount of Olives. His triumphal last entrance into the Holy City was made through the eastern gate, at upper left.

books, including the writings of the prophets.

Jesus does not seem to have shared his countrymen's bitterness toward the Samaritans. On one occasion, Jesus and his disciples stopped to rest at an ancient well in Samaria. The well, said to have been dug by the Patriarch Jacob, stood outside the town of Shechem, which at the time of Jesus was a small village. (The large city which had stood there for centuries had been destroyed in about 100 B.C.)

The Samaritan Woman

It was noontime and probably very hot. Jesus sat down on the edge of the well while his disciples went into the village to buy some bread and wine. As he was sitting there, a woman came up to the well to draw water. "Give me a drink," he said to her. "The Samaritan woman said to him, 'How is it that you, a Jew, ask a drink of me, a woman of Samaria?' . . . Jesus answered her, 'If you knew the gift of God, and who it is that is saying to you, "Give me a drink," you would have asked him, and he would have given you living water.'"

Puzzled by these strange words, the woman exclaimed, "'Sir, you have nothing to draw with, and the well is deep; where do you get that living water?' . . . Jesus said to her, 'Every one who drinks of this water will thirst again, but whoever drinks of the water that I shall give him will never thirst . . .'" Still failing to perceive the meaning of Jesus' words, the woman said eagerly, "Sir, give me this water, that I may not thirst, nor come here to draw."

"Jesus said to her, 'Go, call your husband, and come here.' The woman answered him, 'I have no husband.' Jesus said to her, 'You are right in saying, "I have no husband"; for you have had five husbands, and he whom you now have is not your husband; this you said truly.' The woman said to him, 'Sir, I perceive that you are a prophet.'

". . . So the woman left her water jar, and went away into the city, and said to the people, 'Come, see a man who told me all that I ever did.'" The people of the town came out to the well and listened to Jesus' words. At their request he and his disciples stayed there a few days, teaching the villagers about the Lord's kingdom, and many of them became his followers.

This time, however, Jesus and his disciples bypassed Samaria. When they reached Jericho, Jesus restored sight to a blind man, and large crowds gathered to hear him speak. It may be that the people of Jericho had already heard of the Galilean prophet, or perhaps this remarkable teacher reminded them of John the Baptist. One of those who came to hear Jesus "was a man named Zacchaeus; he was a chief tax collector, and rich. And he sought to see who Jesus was, but could not, on account of the crowd, because he was small of stature. So he ran on ahead and climbed up into a sycamore tree to see him, for he was to pass that way. And when Jesus came to the place, he looked up and said to him, 'Zacchaeus, make haste and come down; for I must stay at your house today.' So he made haste and came down, and received him joyfully.''

At the Feast of Tabernacles

The next day, Jesus left Jericho with his disciples and ascended the steep highway leading westward through the Judean wilderness to Jerusalem. There he would attend the Feast of Tabernacles, or Booths, the fall harvest feast commemorating the 40 years of wandering in the Sinai wilderness. Tabernacles was then the most sacred and important of the major Hebrew feasts. Solomon was said to have dedicated his temple during Tabernacles, and the prophet Zechariah had associated the feast with the coming triumph of the Lord: "Then every one that survives of all the nations that have come against Jerusalem shall go up [to Jerusalem] year after year to worship the . . . Lord of hosts, and to keep the feast of booths."

According to later rabbinic writings, each morning of the seven-day festival a procession of barefoot priests and Levites clad in white linen robes descended from the temple to the spring of Gihon in the Kidron Valley. There the officiating priest filled a golden pitcher with water while a choir of Levites sang, "With joy you will draw water from the wells of salvation." The priests and the worshipers who accompanied them carried "lulabs," branches of myrtle and willow tied together with palm fronds, in their right hands and citrons or lemons in their left hands. (The lulabs and lemons were symbolic of the harvest.) As they walked, they sang psalms of praise and thanksgiving to the Lord.

Then the procession ascended from the spring to the city and entered the sacred precincts of the temple. The priests marched around the huge stone altar once, waving the lulabs and singing, "Save us, we beseech thee, O Lord, we beseech thee, give us success!" Meanwhile, the officiating priest mounted the ramp and poured pitchers of water and wine through silver funnels onto the altar fires.

Each night of the festival the entire temple area was lit by four huge candelabra called menorahs. For most of the night the celebrants danced before the menorahs with burning torches, while Levites chanted psalms accompanied by the music of flutes. At dawn every morning the priests gathered at the east gate of the temple. As the first rays of the sun appeared, they turned westward and faced the temple sanctuary, chanting, "Our fathers [ancestors] when they were in this place turned their faces toward the east, and they worshiped the sun toward the east; but as for us, our eyes are turned [westward] toward the Lord."

During the day Jesus and his disciples came to the temple precincts, which were crowded with pilgrims from all parts of Palestine as well as Jews from throughout the Roman Empire. Many rabbis were in the habit of teaching in the large Court of the Gentiles, and Jesus too came there to teach. Sitting cross-legged in customary rabbinical fashion under one of the temple porticoes, his disciples grouped around him, he would speak about the nature of the Lord's kingdom.

Those who heard him were often surprised by the wisdom and simplicity of Jesus' words. "How is it that this man has learning, when he has never studied?" they wondered. Every rabbi had to study diligently under another recognized rabbi for many years before he could teach on his own. Most rabbis based their opinions on those of famous teachers from the past, citing lengthy arguments to support their views. Jesus spoke without such justification, which indicated that he had not been formally trained as a rabbi.

"My teaching is not mine," he explained, "but his who sent me." Then he proceeded to attack those venerated scholars who based their teachings on their own or past authority: "if any man's will is to do his [the Lord's] will, he shall know whether the teaching is from God or whether I am speaking on my own authority. He who speaks on his own authority seeks his own glory; but he who seeks the glory of him who sent me is true, and in him there is no falsehood."

The implication of his words was not lost on the rabbis, Pharisees and priests in the crowd. Like the prophets of old, Jesus was questioning the authenticity of all teaching that was not directly inspired by the Lord. As the crowds who came to hear him increased daily in size, the anger of these learned men increased. Who was this arrogant, uneducated Galilean who dismissed their proud traditions so scornfully?

Jesus and the Adulteress

Jesus arrived at the temple at daybreak on each day of the feast, and "all the people came to him, and he sat down and taught them. The scribes and the Pharisees brought a woman who had been caught in adultery, and placing her in the midst, they said to him, 'Teacher, this woman has been caught in the act of adultery. Now in the law Moses commanded us to stone such. What do you say about her?' This they said to test him, that they might have some charge to bring against him. Jesus bent down and wrote with his finger on the ground. And as they continued to ask him, he stood up and said to them, 'Let him who is without sin among you be the first to throw a stone at her.' And once more he bent down and wrote with his finger on the ground. But when they heard it, they went away, one by one, beginning with the eldest, and Jesus was left alone with the woman standing before him. Jesus looked up and said to her, 'Woman, where are they? Has no one condemned you?' She said, 'No one, Lord.' And Jesus said, 'Neither do I condemn you . . .'"

On the last day of Tabernacles, according to later rabbinic accounts, the priests made their customary procession to the spring of Gihon and returned to the temple. Then they walked around the altar seven times, chanting psalms and beating the ground with their lulabs while the officiating priest poured the water and wine over the altar. At this most sacred moment of the feast, Jesus stood up and cried out in a loud voice, "If any one thirst, let him come to me and drink. He who believes in me, as the scripture has said, 'Out of his heart shall flow rivers of living water.'"

"When they heard these words, some of the people said, 'This is really the prophet.' Others said, 'This is the Christ [Messiah].' But some said, 'Is the Christ to come from Galilee? Has not the scripture said that the Christ is descended from David, and comes from Bethlehem, the village

where David was?' So there was a division among the people over him. Some of them wanted to arrest him, but no one laid hands on him.''

Opposition of the Authorities

Such talk of a Messiah alarmed and frustrated the temple authorities. They feared that a popular hero like Jesus might arouse another revolt against the Roman government, yet they were hesitant to arrest him for fear of provoking a riot. Many of these men were members of the aristocratic priestly party known as the Sadducees, the most powerful group within Judaism at that time. The high priest and all the lower priests of the temple belonged to this elite. They controlled the wealthy treasury and the temple ceremonies.

A man like Jesus presented a real danger to the Sadducees, who held their privileged position with the support of the Roman authorities. Anyone who aroused talk of a Messiah undermined the peoples' allegiance to the established religious and political order. Moreover, he endangered the relationship the Sadducees had with the

Romans. Such a man must be silenced, they reasoned, before he sparked an uprising, which the Romans would crush with characteristic brutality. If that happened, the Sadducees stood to lose their privileges. In fact, the Romans might even forbid them to practice their religion except under the most stringent controls.

Their common fear of Jesus brought about an unusual alliance between the Sadducees and their rivals, the Pharisees. Many of the Pharisees had grown to dislike this man, who made such pointed attacks on their teachings and their chosen way of life. Jesus, who openly violated the Sabbath laws and questioned the validity of other laws, seemed to be undermining the authority of the Jewish religion. They failed to understand his call for reform of the traditional laws, seeing instead a blasphemous desire to invalidate the fundamental doctrines of their faith. At a time when their religious beliefs were threatened by pagan influences on the one hand and internal dissension on the other, a man like Jesus presented yet another danger. Like the Sadducees, the Pharisees concluded that Jesus must be silenced.

Yet Jesus had a few followers who were Pharisees. One of them was Nicodemus, a wealthy citizen of Jerusalem and a member of the Sanhedrin, the Jewish high court. He is said to have spoken in Jesus' defense on the last day of Tabernacles, when the temple authorities were discussing how to arrest him.

One night Nicodemus met secretly with Jesus in Jerusalem. He was curious to learn more about this remarkable man, but at the same time he was afraid he would lose his influence in the Sanhedrin if he lent Jesus public support. "Rabbi" he said to Jesus, "we know that you are a teacher come from God; for no one can do these signs that you do, unless God is with him."

Jesus explained that "unless one is born anew, he cannot see the kingdom of God." Puzzled, the Pharisee questioned him further, but his reply again seemed enigmatic: "Do not marvel that I say to you, 'You must be born anew.' The wind blows where it wills, and you hear the sound of it, but you do not know whence it comes or whither it goes; so it is with every one who is born of the Spirit." Still puzzled, Nicodemus departed. But he must have been impressed, for he became one of Jesus' supporters.

Friends and Enemies

In the small village of Bethany, just outside of the Holy City, a man named Lazarus lived with his two sisters, Mary and Martha. Jesus and his disciples were frequent guests in their home. Like most of Jesus' devoted followers, these people were humble, pious Jews.

Mary and Martha each tried to show their devotion toward Jesus in her own way. Martha prepared elaborate dinners for him, while Mary spent long hours sitting at his feet, listening to his teaching. One evening Martha complained to Jesus that Mary wasn't helping her with the dinner. "Lord, do you not care that my sister has left me to serve alone?" she asked in annoyance. "Tell her then to help me."

To her surprise, Jesus rebuked her gently for her impatience. "Martha, Martha, you are anxious and troubled about many things; one thing is needful. Mary has chosen the good portion, which shall not be taken away from her."

Jesus left Bethany with his disciples at the end of the Feast of Tabernacles and returned to Jericho, where he continued to preach and gather

"And he entered the temple and began to drive out those who sold, saying to them, 'It is written, "My house shall be a house of prayer"; but you have made it a den of robbers'" (Lk. 19.45–46). Scripture required every Jewish man to offer a half-shekel to the temple during Passover. But profiteering had arisen among the moneychangers at the temple, who received a fee from incoming Jews for converting their local coins into the prescribed Tyrian silver. Excessive rates were also charged for unblemished lambs and doves used for sacrifice. In the colonnaded Court of the Gentiles above, vendors and moneychangers do business while a rabbi lectures to a group of Jewish pilgrims. Only Jews were allowed entry to the sacred inner-temple courts, as announced by the inscription below.

The Art of Perfume-Making

"Now when Jesus was at Bethany . . . a woman came up to him with an alabaster jar of very expensive ointment, and she poured it on his head" (Mt. 26.6–7). Jesus was anointed with nard, a precious ointment from India made from the

roots and stems of a fragrant herb. Perfumes served a variety of uses, and were made in the three ways shown above. At left a woman drops flower seeds and petals into hot olive oil, which she will strain before it cools. The other woman makes a sweet pomade by spreading layers of fresh petals on a dish of animal fat, which will absorb the scent. The man uses a bag press to wring the oils from flower petals. Left: an alabaster vial of Jesus' time.

---

followers. Meanwhile, the Jewish authorities in Jerusalem were meeting to discuss ways of getting rid of him. They decided to try to trap him into uttering a blasphemy, an offense for which he could be arrested. Accordingly, a group of Pharisees traveled to Jericho to question him.

"And Pharisees came up to him and tested him by asking, 'Is it lawful to divorce one's wife for any cause?' He answered, 'Have you not read that he who made them from the beginning made them male and female, and said, "For this reason a man shall leave his father and mother and be joined to his wife, and the two shall become one"? So they are no longer two but one. What there-

fore God has joined together, let no man put asunder.' They said to him, 'Why then did Moses command one to give a certificate of divorce, and to put her away?' He said to them, 'For your hardness of heart Moses allowed you to divorce your wives, but from the beginning it was not so. And I say to you: whoever divorces his wife . . . and marries another, commits adultery.'"

Instead of suggesting that Mosaic law was too strict, as the Pharisees hoped, Jesus offered the view that it might be too lenient because it permitted divorce in cases other than adultery. Discouraged, the Pharisees returned to Jerusalem, where they probably reported that it would not be an easy task to catch Jesus in a verbal trap.

This encounter may still have been in Jesus' thoughts when he went up to Jerusalem a few months later for the Feast of Dedication (Hanukkah), commemorating the cleansing of the temple by Judas Maccabeus in the second century B.C.

It was now winter, and Jesus taught in Solomon's Portico, where he was sheltered from the cold east wind. By this time the people who came to hear him were increasingly preoccupied with the question of whether Jesus was the Messiah. He was careful to make his answers ambiguous. Apparently, the temple authorities tried again to arrest him, but Jesus managed to elude them.

Returning to Jericho, he resumed his work. He may even have sent his disciples out to other parts of Judea to proclaim the advent of the Lord's kingdom and to heal the sick and insane.

Treasure in Heaven

One day a man came up to him and asked, "'Good Teacher, what must I do to inherit eternal life?' And Jesus said to him, 'Why do you call me good? No one is good but God alone. You know the commandments: "Do not kill, Do not commit adultery, Do not steal, Do not bear false witness, Do not defraud, Honor your father and mother."' And he said to him, 'Teacher, all these I have observed from my youth.' And Jesus looking upon him loved him, and said to him, 'You lack one thing; go, sell what you have, and give to the poor, and you will have treasure in heaven.' At that saying his countenance fell, and he went away sorrowful; for he had great possessions.

"And Jesus looked around and said to his disciples, 'How hard it will be for those who have riches to enter the kingdom of God! . . . It is easier for a camel to go through the eye of a needle than for a rich man to enter the kingdom of God.'" The disciples were surprised by his words, for riches were said to be a sign of the Lord's favor.

The Raising of Lazarus

Some weeks later Jesus was preaching on the eastern side of the Jordan near the place where John had baptized him. A messenger came hastily toward him with an urgent message from Mary and Martha. "Lord," he said, "'he whom you love is ill.' But when Jesus heard it he said, 'This illness is not unto death . . .' So when he heard that he was ill, he stayed two days longer in the place where he was. Then . . . he said to the disciples, 'Let us go into Judea again.'

"Now when Jesus came, he found that Lazarus had already been in the tomb four days. . . . Then Jesus, deeply moved again, came to the tomb; it was a cave, and a stone lay upon it. Jesus said, 'Take away the stone.' Martha, the sister of the dead man, said to him, 'Lord, by this time there will be an odor, for he has been dead four days.' Jesus said to her, 'Did I not tell you that if you would believe you would see the glory of God?' So they took away the stone. And Jesus lifted up his eyes and said, 'Father, I thank thee that thou hast heard me. . . .' When he had said this, he cried with a loud voice, 'Lazarus, come out.' The dead man came out, his hands and feet bound with bandages, and his face wrapped with a cloth."

The news of the raising of Lazarus soon reached nearby Jerusalem. The citizens talked more and more excitedly about Jesus and many spoke openly of him as the Messiah. Tension mounted as the time of Passover approached; the Sanhedrin met to discuss how they could deal with the problems Jesus would almost certainly cause if he appeared during the feast.

"So the chief priests and the Pharisees gathered the council, and said, 'What are we to do? For this man performs many signs. If we let him go on thus, every one will believe in him, and the Romans will come and destroy both our holy place and our nation.' But one of them, Caiaphas, who was high priest that year, said to them, 'You know nothing at all; you do not understand that it is expedient for you that one man should die for the people, and that the whole nation should not perish.' . . . So from that day on they took counsel how to put him to death."

Meanwhile, Jesus realized the danger of remaining in the open. Quietly he and his disciples withdrew to the tiny town of Ephraim, in the countryside about 15 miles north of Jerusalem. A few days before the Passover he announced that he planned to go up to Jerusalem to preach during the feast. The disciples tried to dissuade him, knowing he would almost certainly be arrested or killed if he entered the Holy City again.

But Jesus insisted that he must go, and he set out on foot for Bethany. With stubborn determination he walked ahead of his disciples, a man ready to face whatever danger lay ahead. Solemnly, he again explained to them, "Behold, we are going up to Jerusalem; and the Son of man will be delivered to the chief priests and the scribes, and they will condemn him to death, and deliver him to the Gentiles; and they will mock him, and spit upon him, and scourge him, and kill him; and after three days he will rise." For the first time, perhaps, they began to realize the meaning of his prediction.

At Bethany they stayed again with Lazarus and his sisters. "There they made him a supper; Martha served, and Lazarus was one of those at table with him. Mary took a pound of costly ointment of pure nard [a very rare and aromatic balm] and anointed the feet of Jesus and wiped his feet with her hair; and the house was filled with the fragrance of the ointment. But Judas Iscariot, one of his disciples . . . said, 'Why was this ointment not sold for three hundred denarii [almost 10 months' wages for a skilled laborer] and given to the poor?' . . . Jesus said, 'Let her alone, let her keep it for the day of my burial. The poor you always have with you, but you do not always have me.'"

The next day was the beginning of the Passover, and Jesus knew he would not live out the week. Yet he was determined to use the precious time that remained to make a final, dramatic attack on the men and institutions he believed were leading the people away from the Lord.

"The next day a great crowd who had come to the feast heard that Jesus was coming to Jerusalem. So they took branches of palm trees and went out to meet him, crying, 'Hosanna! Blessed is he who comes in the name of the Lord, even the King of Israel!' And Jesus found a young ass and sat upon it; as it is written,

'Fear not, daughter of Zion;
behold, your king is coming,
sitting on an ass's colt.'"

Chapter 25

Among the crowds of Passover pilgrims in Jerusalem, a man is arrested and condemned. Derided as the "King of the Jews," he is executed by the Romans at the demand of the temple authorities.

Jesus Called Christ: His Arrest, Trial and Crucifixion

In the last days of his life, Jesus returned to Jerusalem to confront the fate he had foreseen. His disciples accompanied him, still not fully comprehending the meaning of his predictions. In the great city itself, Jesus' enemies prepared to play their roles, too. The final dramatic events, set amidst the crowded celebration of the Passover, were the arrest, trial and crucifixion of the "Jesus who is called Christ." It was both an end and a beginning.

Jesus entered Jerusalem in a triumphal procession a few days before Passover, accompanied by his disciples and a sizable crowd of followers from Bethany and other pilgrims who had come for the festival. "And when he entered Jerusalem, all the city was stirred, saying, 'Who is this?' And the crowds said, 'This is the prophet Jesus from Nazareth of Galilee.'" Winding its way through the teeming, narrow streets, the procession headed uphill toward the temple. There, in an act of protest reminiscent of the prophets of the Old Testament, ". . . Jesus entered the temple of God and drove out all who sold and bought in the temple, and he overturned the tables of the moneychangers and the seats of those who sold pigeons. He said to them, 'It is written, "My house shall be called a house of prayer"; but you make it a den of robbers.'"

His action was not an attempt to denigrate the temple as an institution but rather a zealous protest against its desecration by commercial interests. He was forcefully reminding the Jews that the Court of the Gentiles was not a market place or bazaar but an important part of the Lord's temple. Business transactions like selling sacrificial animals and exchanging foreign coinage for temple shekels had no place there.

News of this dramatic event quickly swept through Jerusalem, and people began flocking to the temple, hoping to catch a glimpse of Jesus. Rumors spread of the appearance of the Messiah and the imminent destruction of the temple. The worst fears of Caiaphas, the Jewish high priest, and the Sanhedrin were confirmed. They could no longer tolerate such acts of religious fanaticism. The situation had become so volatile that rebellion might erupt at any moment.

Once again the Jewish authorities tried to ensnare Jesus in a verbal trap, hoping to establish a legitimate ground for arresting him, but his replies remained elusive. When he came to preach in the Court of the Gentiles the next day, temple officials came up to him and asked, "'By what authority are you doing these things, and who gave you this authority?' Jesus answered them, 'I also will ask you a question; and if you tell me the answer, then I also will tell you by what authority I do these things. The baptism of John, whence was it? From heaven or from men?' And they argued with one another, 'If we say, "From

Pontius Pilate, the governor of Judea who sentenced Jesus, is named in the inscription at right from Caesarea, the Roman capital of Judea. Caesarea was Pilate's official residence, but at the time of Jesus' trial he had traveled to Jerusalem to help in maintaining order during Passover. Jewish resentment, always a problem for the Romans, ran especially high during national or religious holidays.

Traditionally, Jesus ate his last supper with his disciples on the eve of Passover, the week-long festival commemorating the Jews' deliverance from Egypt. They gathered near midnight in an upper room in Jerusalem to eat the Passover lamb, which had been slaughtered in the temple that day. Above, a group of celebrants, wearing white linen tunics, recline in the Roman style around a low table. Before them are set the traditional foods: lamb, unleavened bread, bitter herbs and rice. The host lifts his wine goblet for the opening toast. Later the men will eat nonritual foods from communal dishes of everyday pottery like those pictured below.

heaven,'' he will say to us, "Why then did you not believe him?'' But if we say, "From men,'' we are afraid of the multitude; for all hold that John was a prophet.' So they answered Jesus, 'We do not know.' And he said to them, 'Neither will I tell you by what authority I do these things.'"

Not long thereafter a second group came up to Jesus and asked, "'Is it lawful to pay taxes to Caesar, or not? Should we pay them, or should we not?' But knowing their hypocrisy, he said to them, 'Why put me to the test? Bring me a coin, and let me look at it.' And they brought one. And he said to them, 'Whose likeness and inscription is this?' They said to him, 'Caesar's.' Jesus said to them, 'Render to Caesar the things that are Caesar's, and to God the things that are God's.'"

Jesus had not only won the argument, he had also outsmarted and publicly humiliated his opponents. Their frustration increased as they realized the futility of their attempt to entrap him.

Meanwhile, Jesus seized upon the incident to make a public attack on the authority of the Pharisees and the learned scribes. Turning back to the assembled crowd, he said, "The scribes and the Pharisees sit on Moses' seat; so practice and observe whatever they tell you, but not what they do; for they preach, but do not practice. They bind heavy burdens, hard to bear, and lay them on men's shoulders; but they themselves will not move them with their finger. They do all their deeds to be seen by men; for they make their phylacteries broad and their fringes long, and they love the place of honor at feasts and the best seats in the synagogues, and salutations in the market places, and being called rabbi by men. But you are not to be called rabbi, for you have one teacher, and you are all brethren. And call no man your father on earth, for you have one Father, who is in heaven."

His voice grew louder as he continued, "But woe to you, scribes and Pharisees, hypocrites! because you shut the kingdom of heaven against men; for you neither enter yourselves, nor allow those who would enter to go in. . . . Woe to you, blind guides, who say, 'If any one swears by the temple, it is nothing; but if any one swears by the gold of the temple, he is bound by his oath.' You blind fools! For which is greater, the gold or the temple that has made the gold sacred?"

Those who heard Jesus' words were divided in their reactions. The scribes and Pharisees were venerated figures in the Jewish world, and many people accepted their authority without question. They could not accept the suggestion that their piety was an affectation or that their teachings might not be sincere. On the other hand, many ordinary Jews had come to believe that they could never hope to gain entrance to the Lord's kingdom because they did not always follow the difficult laws and rituals of the scribes

Jesus' betrayer, Judas, was paid in silver Tyrian shekels like the ones above with eagles and portraits. The three shekels in the foreground are from the first Jewish Revolt. They had the same silver content as the Tyrian shekels (14 grams).

and Pharisees. To them, Jesus' words brought comfort and hope, but the rabbis and Pharisees who heard his accusations were infuriated.

The Coming of the Son of Man

When he had finished, Jesus left the temple with his disciples and returned to Bethany, where they were staying. Late that night he quietly left the house and went alone to a spot on the nearby Mount of Olives. When his disciples saw that he was gone, they went looking for him. In the shadows of an olive grove, they saw their teacher sitting alone, deep in thought.

As they had done so often in the past, they gathered at his feet and spoke of things that were troubling them. One disciple was curious about the rumor that had circulated all afternoon that the temple would soon be destroyed. "Tell us," he asked, "when will this be, and what will be the sign of your coming and of the close of the age?"

In a low voice, Jesus answered, "Take heed that no one leads you astray. For many will come in my name, saying, 'I am the Christ,' and they will lead many astray. And you will hear of wars and rumors of wars; see that you are not alarmed; for

this must take place, but the end is not yet. For nation will rise against nation, and kingdom against kingdom, and there will be famines and earthquakes in various places: all this is but the beginning of the sufferings. . . . For then there will be great tribulation, such as has not been from the beginning of the world until now, no, and never will be. . . . Immediately after the tribulation of those days the sun will be darkened, and the moon will not give its light, and the stars will fall from heaven, and the powers of the heavens will be shaken; then will appear the sign of the Son of man in heaven, and then all the tribes of the earth will mourn, and they will see the Son of man coming on the clouds of heaven with power and great glory; and he will send out his angels with a loud trumpet call, and they will gather his elect from the four winds, from one end of heaven to the other.

"But of that day and hour no one knows, not even the angels of heaven, nor the Son, but the Father only. As were the days of Noah, so will be the coming of the Son of man. For as in those days before the flood they were eating and drinking . . . and they did not know until the flood came and swept them all away, so will be the coming of the Son of man. . . . Therefore you also must be ready; for the Son of man is coming at an hour you do not expect."

Looking around at their attentive faces, he must have felt a twinge of sadness at the thought that he would soon leave them. Would these men, with whom he had shared his most private thoughts, be able to carry on his mission without him? He must have feared that perhaps even then they did not fully understand that he must die, for he added, "You know that after two days the Passover is coming, and the Son of man will be delivered up to be crucified."

As he uttered these words, the chief priests and elders of the Sanhedrin were gathering at the palace of Caiaphas, the high priest, to discuss Jesus' fate. They decided that they could not arrest him on legitimate grounds because he was too clever for them. Instead they would have to invent a fraudulent charge and take him at night. During the day they ran the risk of provoking an outbreak among the holiday crowds.

Later that night, for reasons that remain a mystery, one of Jesus' disciples, Judas Iscariot, volunteered to help the chief priests make their stealthy arrest. "What will you give me if I deliver him to you?" he demanded. With his aid they could arrest Jesus secretly, without provoking a riot; so "they paid him thirty pieces of silver," nearly four months' wages for a skilled worker.

The Last Supper

The next day was the first day of Passover, and Jesus and his disciples prepared for the ritual dinner that evening. At sundown they gathered secretly at the appointed place. Their mood was solemn as they ate the meal, commemorating the Exodus of the Jews from Egypt. Reclining on couches arranged around a low table, they drank wine and consumed the Passover lamb with bitter herbs and unleavened bread.

"And as they were at table eating, Jesus said, 'Truly, I say to you, one of you will betray me, one who is eating with me.' They began to be sorrowful, and to say to him one after another, 'Is it I?' He said to them, 'It is one of the twelve, one who is dipping bread in the same dish with me. For the Son of man goes as it is written of him, but woe to that man by whom the Son of man is betrayed! It would have been better for that man if he had not been born.'

"And as they were eating, he took bread, and blessed, and broke it, and gave it to them, and said, 'Take; this is my body.' And he took a cup, and when he had given thanks he gave it to them, and they all drank of it. And he said to them, 'This is my blood of the covenant, which is poured out for many. Truly, I say to you, I shall not drink again of the fruit of the vine until that day when I drink it new in the kingdom of God.'"

Later they sang a hymn together and then walked to their accustomed meeting place at the foot of the Mount of Olives, an olive grove known as Gethsemane. There was a full moon, and the grove was bathed in soft light. A gentle breeze stirred the leaves.

Jesus looked regretfully at his twelve followers seated around him. "Then Jesus said to them, 'You will all fall away because of me this night . . .' Peter declared to him, 'Though they all fall away because of you, I will never fall away.' Jesus said to him, 'Truly, I say to you, this very night, before the cock crows, you will deny me three times.' Peter said to him, 'Even if I must die with you, I will not deny you.' And so said all the disciples."

Then Jesus said to his disciples, "'Sit here, while I go yonder and pray.' And taking with him Peter and the two sons of Zebedee [James and John], he began to be sorrowful and troubled. Then he said to them, 'My soul is very sorrowful, even to death; remain here, and watch with me.' And going a little farther he fell on his face and prayed . . . And he came to the disciples and found them sleeping; and he said to Peter, 'So, could you not watch with me one hour? . . .' Again, for the second time, he went away and prayed . . . And again he came and found them sleeping, for their eyes were heavy. So, leaving them again, he went away and prayed . . . Then he came to the disciples and said to them, 'Are you still sleeping and taking your rest? Behold, the hour is at hand, and the Son of man is betrayed into the hands of sinners. Rise, let us be going; see, my betrayer is at hand.'"

The Arrest and Trial

"And immediately, while he was still speaking, Judas came, one of the twelve, and with him a crowd with swords and clubs, from the chief priests and the scribes and the elders. Now the betrayer had given them a sign, saying, 'The one I shall kiss is the man; seize him and lead him away safely.' And when he came, he went up to him at once, and said, 'Master!' And he kissed him. And they laid hands on him and seized him. . . . And Jesus said to them, 'Have you come out as against a robber, with swords and clubs to capture me? Day after day I was with you in the temple teaching, and you did not seize me.'"

Making no reply, the guards, who were probably part of the temple police force, dragged Jesus away to the palace of Caiaphas in the western section of Jerusalem. Inside the splendidly appointed mansion, the 70 members of the Sanhedrin had gathered to try Jesus on the charge of blasphemy. When the guards had brought Jesus before the court, the high priest called on witnesses to testify against him. Many came forward, but only two witnesses had serious evidence. Pointing to Jesus, they said, "This fellow said, 'I am able to destroy the temple of God, and to build it in three days.'"

Apparently satisfied with this accusation, Caiaphas stood up and addressed Jesus, asking, "'Have you no answer to make? What is it that these men testify against you?' But Jesus was silent. And the high priest said to him, 'I adjure you by the living God, tell us if you are the

Christ, the Son of God.' Jesus said to him, 'You have said so. But I tell you, hereafter you will see the Son of man seated at the right hand of Power, and coming on the clouds of heaven.' Then the high priest tore his robes, and said, 'Why do we still need witnesses? You have now heard his blasphemy. What is your judgment?' They answered, 'He deserves death.'"

As this dramatic scene was taking place, Peter waited outside in the courtyard for news of his teacher's fate. The other disciples, fearing that they too might be arrested, had fled in confusion. Some servants of Caiaphas came to Peter and asked him if he was with Jesus. Three times he denied knowing the man. After the third denial, a cock crowed. Only then did Peter remember Jesus' prediction, and he wept bitterly.

Pilate's Decision

As the first rays of sunlight appeared, Jesus was led out of Caiaphas' palace and escorted to the Antonia, a palace-fortress where the Roman governor, Pontius Pilate, was staying during the Passover. Pilate's official residence was at Caesarea on the coast, but he came to Jerusalem for the great pilgrim festivals to keep a close eye on potential troublemakers. Since the Sanhedrin was not empowered to carry out the death sentence, the members had to present their case against Jesus to Pilate.

The man in whose hands Jesus' fate rested was a controversial figure. Shrewd, hot-tempered, stubborn and aristocratic, he was no more than a few years older than Jesus. Pilate's rule as governor of Judea (A.D. 26–36) was punctuated with civil unrest, and he was finally removed from office for his excessive brutality in suppressing sporadic uprisings.

A messenger entered the sumptuous chambers of the Antonia to summon Pilate, while the council members and their prisoner waited below in the paved courtyard of the fortress. A few minutes later the governor appeared. He wore a red toga draped over a white tunic in customary Roman fashion, the distinctive mark of a Roman citizen. At once Caiaphas began to state his case.

"'We found this man perverting our nation, and forbidding us to give tribute to Caesar, and saying that he himself is Christ a king.' And Pilate asked him, 'Are you the King of the Jews?' And he answered him, 'You have said so.' And Pilate said to the chief priests and the multitudes, 'I find no crime in this man.' But they were urgent, saying, 'He stirs up the people, teaching throughout all Judea, from Galilee even to this place.'"

The Roman governor pondered the situation. It seemed to him that the chief priests had approached him to settle a petty religious dispute, and to convict Jesus during the festival could surely spark at least a minor uprising. Yet if he ignored their accusations and this Galilean eventually proved to be a traitor to Rome, his own position would be endangered. Meanwhile, a belligerent crowd had gathered outside the Antonia, clamoring for Pilate's decision.

"Now at the feast the governor was accustomed to release for the crowd any one prisoner whom they wanted. And they had then a notorious prisoner, called Barabbas. So when they had gathered, Pilate said to them, 'Whom do you want me to release for you, Barabbas or Jesus who is called Christ?' . . . And they said, 'Barabbas.' Pilate said to them, 'Then what shall I do with Jesus . . . ?' They all said, 'Let him be crucified.'

"So when Pilate saw that he was gaining nothing, but rather that a riot was beginning, he took water and washed his hands before the crowd, saying, 'I am innocent of this man's blood; see to it yourselves.' Then he released for them Barabbas, and having scourged Jesus, delivered him to be crucified." This was a brutal death sentence usually reserved for political criminals.

"The King of the Jews"

Pilate's soldiers led Jesus to a cell to wait while preparations were made for his crucifixion. "And they stripped him and put a scarlet robe upon him, and plaiting a crown of thorns they put it on his head, and put a reed in his right hand. And kneeling before him they mocked him, saying, 'Hail, King of the Jews!' And they spat upon him, and took the reed and struck him on the head. And when they had mocked him, they stripped him of the robe, and put his own clothes on him, and led him away to crucify him."

At about 9 A.M. a small procession left the Antonia and slowly made its way to Golgotha ("place of a skull"), a hill outside the walls of Jerusalem where prisoners were executed. It was so named because its contour resembled a human skull. Jesus was accompanied by two other prisoners, a centurion and a few Roman soldiers.

When they reached Golgotha, the soldiers stripped the clothes off the men and divided them among themselves as the crosses were assembled. Each prisoner was then placed on his cross. Jesus suffered in silence as the soldiers nailed his hands to the crosspiece with large iron spikes and drove another spike through both feet. As they lifted his cross upright, his weight was supported by a peg jutting out from the cross between his legs. The soldiers placed a sign on the cross, proclaiming, "This is Jesus the King of the Jews." As was customary, they then offered him some wine mixed with gall to dull the pain.

It was a slow and painful death. Jesus hung there helplessly for long hours as the hot sun beat down on his body and insects buzzed about his limbs. Curious passersby paused to watch his agony and to read the sign describing his offense. Gradually he weakened, his body tortured by muscle cramps, hunger and thirst. From afar, a small group of his despairing followers watched in silence as his life slipped away.

"And about the ninth hour [3 P.M.] Jesus cried with a loud voice, 'Eli, Eli, lama sabach-thani?' that is, 'My God, my God, why hast thou forsaken me?' And some of the bystanders hearing it said, 'This man is calling Elijah.' And one of them at once ran and took a sponge, filled it with vinegar [a cheap, sour wine], and put it on a reed, and gave it to him to drink. But the others said, 'Wait, let us see whether Elijah will come to save him.' And Jesus cried out again with a loud voice and yielded up his spirit."

Later that afternoon, one of Jesus' wealthy Jerusalem followers, Joseph of Arimathea, went to Pontius Pilate and asked him for Jesus' body, so that he might give him a proper burial. After making sure that Jesus was in fact dead, Pilate agreed to let Joseph take the body. The kind man removed Jesus' corpse from the cross and prepared it for burial. He bound the body from head to foot in clean, white linen strips, sprinkling fragrant spices between the layers.

When he had finished, Joseph carried Jesus' body into his garden, where there was a tomb that had been hewn out of a large rock. Inside near the rear of the tomb was a couch, also of stone, and Joseph gently placed the corpse upon it. Then he rolled a heavy stone across the entrance and returned to his home.

Sometime early in the next morning, or the day after, some of Jesus' women followers, Mary Magdalene, Mary the mother of James and Joseph, and another woman named Salome, went to the tomb to sprinkle more spices on the corpse. "And very early on the first day of the week they went to the tomb when the sun had risen. And they were saying to one another, 'Who will roll away the stone for us from the door of the tomb?' And looking up, they saw that the stone was rolled back . . . And entering the tomb, they saw a young man sitting on the right side, dressed in a white robe; and they were amazed. And he said to them, 'Do not be amazed; you seek Jesus of Nazareth, who was crucified. He has risen, he is not here; see the place where they laid him. But go, tell his disciples and Peter that he is going before you to Galilee; there you will see him, as he told you.'"

"And Joseph [of Arimathea] took the body . . . and laid it in his own new tomb, which he had hewn in the rock; and he rolled a great stone to the door of the tomb" (Mt. 27.59–60). *This 1st-century sepulchre near Jerusalem, owned by a wealthy family, resembles the one in which Jesus was buried. It too was sealed with a stone.*

"And Peter said to them, 'Repent, and be baptized every one of you in the name of Jesus Christ for the forgiveness of your sins; and you shall receive the gift of the Holy Spirit'" (Acts 2.38). From the first days of the church, the rite of baptism was the means of entering the community of believers in Jesus. It signified repentance of sins and the beginning of a new spiritual life. The apostles and their followers met secretly in house-churches which were rooms in the homes of well-to-do brethren. In these they shared a common meal, prayed and baptized new converts. The oldest known house-church, at Dura-Europus in Syria, had a separate baptistry with a columned baptismal font and vivid murals of scenes from Jesus' life. Along with the paintings in Rome's catacombs, these murals are the earliest examples of Christian art.

Within one generation after the crucifixion of Jesus, the apostles succeeded in spreading the gospel throughout the Roman world, despite hostility. Foremost among them was Paul, who lived to see the establishment of Christianity from Jerusalem to Rome.

THE 35 YEARS after the death of Jesus, an uneventful period in most of the Roman Empire, marked one of the great turning points of history: the birth of the Christian church. During these years Jesus' followers—so few and humble that they were scarcely noticed—formed a community in his name and began to spread his message. By A.D. 64 a network of small Christian congregations had been founded in cities from Damascus to Rome through the determined labors of the apostles and their disciples.

In the initial period, the death of Jesus had little visible effect on life in Palestine. Pontius Pilate remained governor until A.D. 36. Except for the brief kingship (41–44) of Herod Agrippa I, grandson of Herod the Great, Palestine continued to be ruled by Roman governors until the abortive Jewish rebellion of 66–73. The Pharisees and Sadducees continued to debate religious problems, and ordinary Jews continued to pay their taxes to the temple and to Rome.

After the crucifixion the eleven apostles fled Jerusalem in fear. They had hoped that Jesus was the Messiah sent by the Lord to redeem Israel, but his death seemed to prove that he was only another false prophet. Even the reports that his tomb was found empty failed to revive their hopes. Yet in the next few weeks Jesus appeared to the eleven startled apostles, and explained: "All authority in heaven and on earth has been given to me. Go therefore and make disciples of all nations, baptizing them in the name of the Father and of the Son and of the Holy Spirit, teaching them to observe all that I have commanded you; and lo, I am with you always, to the close of the age" (Matthew 28.18–20).

When the apostles returned to Jerusalem to celebrate the Feast of Weeks (Pentecost), seven weeks after the crucifixion, they gathered together with renewed confidence and faith that Jesus was the Messiah. Excitedly they reported to the small band of followers in Jerusalem that Jesus was truly the long-promised redeemer of Israel. His victory over death marked the start of a new age.

Community of the Faithful

The small band of apostles and disciples, among them Mary and some kinsmen of Jesus, formed the nucleus of a new community held together by belief in Jesus' message that the kingdom of God was at hand. They were led by the eleven apostles with Peter at their head. They soon chose a twelfth apostle, Matthias, to replace Judas Iscariot, who had committed suicide soon after the crucifixion.

The members of the new community remained loyal to Jewish law and continued to worship in synagogues and at the temple. Their life-style resembled that of other Jewish sects of the time. They shared property and food in accordance with Jesus' injunctions of charity and brotherhood. New members were expected, but not compelled, to contribute to a common fund to help destitute members, and those with houses opened them to all who needed shelter. Evening meals were taken together in memory of the last supper with Jesus.

The disciples termed their new movement "The Way," emphasizing their belief that Jesus' teaching would lead his followers to the kingdom of God. Outsiders called them Nazarenes, meaning followers of Jesus of Nazareth. Before long the Jerusalem community came to call itself by an Old Testament term used to refer to the assembly of Israel. The Greek equivalent, *ekklesia* ("church" in English), means a gathering of people.

The majority of those who joined the new church were members of the working classes. Others included Pharisees and even some temple priests. Theirs was a simple, idealistic congregation, nourished by a steady flow of new believers. From the start Peter assumed leadership of the embryonic group.

At first the temple authorities, uneasy about the existence of the community, arrested Peter and the eleven other apostles. It was only a token arrest, however, and they were forced to release the Twelve the next day for lack of grounds. The Sanhedrin chose to be tolerant, partly because the followers of Jesus attended temple services regularly and strictly observed Jewish laws and rituals. They did not as yet seem a challenge to Jewish doctrines or the authority of the temple.

Some of the brethren, as they called themselves, worked at their old trades or collected alms. The rest preached to all who would listen, speaking to small groups in the temple courts and in city streets. Every Sabbath they preached in any Jerusalem synagogue that would admit them, as Jesus also had done. Within two years their ranks had grown to several thousand. The words and deeds of Jesus again became a popular topic of conversation. New converts told others about the apostles, and disciples who had actually seen Jesus shared their memories with eager listeners.

"Hebrews" and "Hellenists"

Thus began the oral traditions later compiled and preserved in the gospel narratives. Groups of incidents and sayings were memorized and passed on, often altered and embellished in the retelling. The result was not conventional history or biography but, like the tales of the Patriarchal age, narratives which emphasized spiritual meaning rather than literal details.

The rapid growth of the community of believers in Jerusalem brought with it the first tremors of internal discord. More and more of the new converts were recruited from among Hellenist Jews, who had returned from all parts of the Roman Empire to settle in the Holy City. Many of them had come on pilgrimages, then decided to remain permanently. Like immigrants everywhere, they lived in separate communities. They spoke Greek and used the Greek version of the Old Testament (the Septuagint).

The Hellenistic Jews were faithful to their religion, but in the world beyond Palestine—Egypt, Asia Minor, Europe—they had long been exposed to Greek culture. They mixed more easily with Gentiles and were more responsive to new ideas than were their Palestinian cousins.

At first the apostles welcomed the Hellenists into their Jerusalem community. But the spirit of fraternity was marred by a growing rivalry between the Hebrew and Hellenist members. In an attempt to allay these resentments, the apostles created a council of seven Hellenist disciples, among them Stephen and Philip. These men were called deacons (in Greek, *diakonoi*), meaning "servants" or "ministers." The apostles themselves concentrated on preaching and ministry.

The First Christian Martyr

Before long, however, Stephen began preaching in Jerusalem's Hellenist synagogues. His audiences were so enraged by his unorthodox preaching that they complained to the Sanhedrin. Though that council could not inflict the death penalty, Stephen was subsequently stoned to death by a crowd that included the brilliant young Pharisee, Saul of Tarsus, later to be known by his Roman name of Paul. Stephen was the first Christian martyr. His death heralded a wave of persecution in Jerusalem, during which vigilantes seized and imprisoned suspected Nazarenes.

This first Christian bloodletting, in about A.D. 36, had significant consequences. Though the Hebrew apostles were not molested, the Hellenist disciples' lives were endangered. They fled Jerusalem, seeking refuge in Samaria and in Syria, where they founded Christian communities. Other unnamed Hellenist Christians founded churches at Damascus, Antioch and Tarsus in Syria, on the island of Cyprus and in Egypt. In each city they visited, the first converts were usually fellow Jews.

At that time there were millions of Jews living outside Palestine in cities throughout the Roman Empire, from Spain to southern Arabia and from Egypt to the Danube. Collectively, these foreign Jewish communities were called the "Diaspora," a Greek term indicating their widespread settlement or dispersion. As a whole their number was probably equal to or greater than the Jewish population of Palestine. In Alexandria alone there were hundreds of thousands, and it was said there were a million Jews in all of Egypt.

In their foreign environments the Jews held to their ancestral religion and customs. Each dispersion community lived in its own section of the city and worshiped in its own synagogue. Living in the midst of pagan cultures, however, they had adopted at least some of the surface manners of their Gentile neighbors. More important for the future of the Christian missionary efforts, they tended to be more receptive to new ideas than their Palestinian brethren.

Most Gentiles looked upon the Jews with a mixture of scorn and resentment. They did not understand these people who stubbornly refused to recognize any gods but their own Lord and observed peculiar personal and dietary laws. Some Gentiles, however, were attracted to the Jewish religion and admired its strict moral code. Known as "God-fearers," these men and women attended synagogue services and worshiped the Jewish God but did not observe all the Jewish laws—for instance, those concerning circumcision and diet. These "partial Jews" were particularly responsive to the new creed preached by the Hellenists.

News of the activities of the Hellenists filtered back to Jerusalem, and the church soon sent delegates to establish ties with the new Christian centers. Peter and John went to Samaria to confer with Philip; and Barnabas, a Jew from Cyprus who was among the earliest Jerusalem converts, traveled to Antioch in Syria, where unnamed "men of Cyprus and Cyrene" had founded a successful Christian movement.

Antioch was the administrative capital of the Roman province of Syria. With a population of half a million, it was also the third largest city in the empire, after Rome and Alexandria. Antioch was a busy, cosmopolitan metropolis; its racially mixed population was overwhelmingly Gentile, but there was also a large Jewish community. At Antioch the followers of Jesus were first called Christians. The term was originally used by opponents of the church as a derogatory reference to the "devotees of the Anointed One" (in Greek, *Christianoi*), but the movement soon adopted it.

Antioch was gradually to succeed Jerusalem as the center of Christian activity. This was largely due to the work of Paul, who joined Barnabas there about A.D. 44. The former leader of the anti-Christian persecution in Jerusalem, Paul had been miraculously converted to the new faith and had become one of the most zealous apostles of Christianity. Paul's missionary journeys carried the message of Jesus westward from Antioch to the major cities of the Roman Empire, to Ephesus, Thessalonica, Corinth and finally to Rome. Under his leadership Christianity bridged the gap between the Jewish and Gentile worlds.

Paul was uniquely qualified for this task. A Jew from the Syrian city of Tarsus, he had grown up amid the Greco-Roman culture of his fellow citizens. Though he had been educated in the strictest Jewish tradition and had studied under the famous rabbi Gamaliel in Jerusalem, he spoke Greek fluently and was familiar with Greek thought and literature. This meant that he could

"The Brethren [of Rome] . . . came as far as the Forum of Appius and Three Taverns to meet us" (Acts 28.15). Roman taverns in Paul's day were frequented by workingmen and soldiers who ate, drank, gamed and often brawled there. Wines from throughout the empire were shipped in amphoras made of porous, unglazed clay. These heavy amphoras were set into holes in the bar, where the seeping wine evaporated and cooled the vessels. Adjacent pouring blocks eased transfer of the wine into serving pitchers.

express the doctrines and teachings of Jesus, many of which were based on Old Testament beliefs completely alien to the Gentiles, in ways that the pagan mind could grasp.

The Roman Empire

The work of Paul and his followers was aided considerably by the peace and unity of the Roman Empire. Stretching from Britain in the north to the Sahara in the south and from Cappadocia in the east to the Spanish peninsula in the west, the Roman Empire embraced the entire Mediterranean world.

Founded in 753 B.C., according to legend, the original settlement of Rome on the Palatine Hill had grown to be the most important city in the world. Rome had earlier been a republic, governed by a senate. As its boundaries expanded, a strong centralized authority was needed, and in 27 B.C. Augustus assumed the new rank of emperor. The senate's powers were reduced to ad-

ministering the city of Rome and certain of the older provinces. During the period between Jesus' ministry and Paul's death in Rome, there were four emperors: Tiberius (A.D. 14–37), Caligula (37–41), Claudius (41–54) and Nero (54–68).

The city of Rome, which the apostles Peter and Paul later visited, was truly the center of the civilized world. Its population was over 1,500,000, possibly the largest concentration of people on earth and probably the most diverse—Romans, Greeks, Syrians, Arabs, Jews, Egyptians, Gauls and Spaniards. The great majority were poor, living in densely packed disease-ridden tenements. The government, however, supplied them with free grain and, at little or no cost, with theaters, circuses, gladiatorial shows and public baths.

The Roman aristocracy lived in luxury, but it was no longer the high-born caste that had been dominant under the republic only a century before. A new elite had risen, based more on service than birth. Its ranks included successful businessmen, high government officials, military

leaders and nobles from the provinces. These were the core of a minority holding the privileged status of hereditary Roman citizens. The benefits of citizenship included various tax exemptions and the precious legal right—invoked more than once by Paul, who was a citizen—to be tried before Roman courts and to appeal the verdict directly to the emperor.

The granting of citizenship was an effective device for fostering loyalty among a diverse population. It was conferred upon soldiers completing 25 years of service and upon others who had made valuable contributions to the state. In several instances citizenship was conferred on an entire city as part of a program of pacification.

By the first century A.D. the Mediterranean world had been largely united by the language and culture of Greece and the politics of Rome. The imperial provinces paid heavy taxes to Caesar, but under the *Pax Romana* (Roman peace) their international commerce flourished, aided by superb roads and military patrols that made travel quick and safe.

The vast realm was administered from Rome as a confederation of provinces, sometimes governed semi-independently by a native prince, as in the case of Herod the Great, but more often by an official sent from the capital. Some provinces were controlled directly by the emperor, the others by the senate through a provincial governor or proconsul. Senatorial provinces included the more thoroughly Romanized areas—among them Greece, Cyprus and parts of Asia Minor, all visited by Paul and his associates—where large military establishments were unnecessary. The imperial territories, which for political or geographic reasons required greater military control, were governed directly by the emperor. In the early apostolic period Judea's governor was under the authority of the legate of Syria, the ranking imperial official in the East.

Mission to the Gentiles

The itineraries of Paul's great journeys were planned to reach the largest number of people, whether Jews or pagans. On his first journey he visited the island of Cyprus and the main cities in the province of Galatia in central Asia Minor: Pisidian Antioch, Iconium, Lystra and Derbe. On his second journey he revisited the congregations he had founded earlier. Then he traveled across western Asia Minor to Troas, where he decided to carry his mission to Europe. The missionary sailed to Macedonia, where he set foot for the first time on European soil. From Philippi in northern Macedonia, Paul traveled to Thessalonica and Beroea. Then he visited Athens, the birthplace of western civilization.

Paul's task of carrying the gospel of Jesus to the Gentiles was difficult but not impossible, for the Gentile world was far from irreligious. Aside from allegiance to a pantheon of Greek gods, adopted and renamed by the Romans, every town and village had its own deity. In his travels Paul encountered most major pagan beliefs.

In particular, a group of so-called mystery cults had developed in different regions in the empire. They were local cults based on legends of gods who were reborn every spring: Hercules, Dionysus, Isis, Mithras and others. Although their central beliefs were based on the fertility cycle of nature, the mystery cults embraced a number of sophisticated ideas, including those of immortality, resurrection and the struggle between good and evil. This superficial similarity to Christian belief was useful to Paul in explaining the message of Jesus to pagans.

In Athens Paul entered into debate with followers of the two major philosophies of his day, the Stoics and Epicureans. The Stoics believed the universe was governed by reason, or *logos.* They taught that the greatest virtue was wisdom, which consisted in making one's will conform to the destiny governing the universe. The Epicureans, who scorned Paul's teaching about the resurrection, believed the goal of life was happiness.

From Athens Paul traveled to Corinth, where he founded a sizable Christian community. A year and a half later he returned to Syrian Antioch. On his third missionary journey, Paul founded a church at Ephesus and preached and taught there for more than two years. When he returned to Jerusalem at the end of his journey, he was arrested and imprisoned. He spent the next two years under house arrest at Caesarea, the Roman capital of Judea, until he finally exercised his right as a Roman citizen to appeal his case directly to the emperor.

Thus Paul finally journeyed to Rome. He spent the final years of his life awaiting trial. Allowed to continue his preaching, he probably won over many converts. Paul was never heard from again after the Emperor Nero's persecution of Chris-

The Holy Scriptures in Jesus' Time

In 1947 the first fragments of over 600 manuscripts were found in the Qumran region of the Wilderness of Judea. These are the Dead Sea Scrolls—a priceless collection of ancient texts offering new insights into the Old Testament, Judaism and the origins of Christianity.

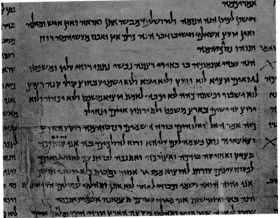

The scrolls were transcriptions made by the Essenes in their scriptorium at Qumran (see page 303). Here one of the sect's 12 priests reads from one scroll while a scribe, seated at a plaster table, copies his words with a reed pen. Both wear white tunics, symbolic of the spiritual purity that was central to Essene belief.

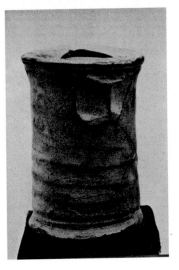

While herding sheep among these caves near the Dead Sea, south of Jericho, a young Arab threw a stone into a hole on the cliff face, and heard a jar shatter. Investigating, he found several more sealed jars containing ancient Hebrew writings on long leather scrolls: The Dead Sea Scrolls. Written mostly during the three centuries before the fall of Jerusalem in A.D. 70, they had been hidden in these caves by the Essenes just before the Romans destroyed their community at nearby Qumran. At right is a terra-cotta inkpot—still bearing traces of dried ink—actually used by the Essene transcribers.

The contents of the scrolls include fragments of all books of the Old Testament except Esther; two relatively complete scrolls of Isaiah; apocryphal and apocalyptic works in Hebrew and Aramaic; and original material on the tenets of Essene doctrine. As in the sample above, the careful transcriptions were done on animal skins marked with horizontal lines for writing and verticals for margins. The Biblical texts—the earliest known—predate the next oldest Hebrew manuscripts by 1000 years; yet the two versions show remarkably few discrepancies. The Scrolls are now under study by Biblical scholars in Israel, Europe and America.

tians in Rome, which began in A.D. 64. No doubt he, along with the apostle Peter, was executed as part of the general bloodbath.

By that time, most or all of the original apostles were dead, and the church was left to the leadership of men who, though devout, had never known Jesus. The communities founded by Paul in every large center of the Roman Empire be-

Traveling by Freighter in Paul's Day

Ships built exclusively for passenger travel were nonexistent in Paul's day, so he sailed in trading ships. Many were quite large: an Alexandrian grain ship (above) might be 180 feet long and carry 1200 tons of cargo and several dozen passengers. But the cumbersome ships were hard to maneuver, and, as Paul discovered off Malta's coast, shipwrecks were frequent.

came bases for expansion into neighboring areas. At Paul's death the number of Christians in the empire was still very small in proportion to the number of pagans, but the new religion would continue to grow, thanks to the apostle's inspiration and foresight.

Fate of the Jerusalem Church

The Hebrew faction of the church did not fare as well. This was partly due to the great success of Paul's missionary activities among the Gentiles. The admission of non-Jews to the church had provoked controversy from the start. Most Jewish Christians were opposed to admitting men and women who did not observe Jewish law, but Paul persuaded the Jerusalem church to admit Gentiles who had been baptized but had not converted to Judaism. The coming of Jesus, he argued, signaled the birth of the new age under the

new law he had come to proclaim, and the old laws of Judaism were no longer binding.

While Paul was gathering Gentile followers throughout the pagan world, the church in Jerusalem continued its strict adherence to Jewish orthodoxy. In about A.D. 41, James, the son of Zebedee, long one of Jesus' closest followers, was murdered at the order of Herod Agrippa I, king of Judea from 41 to 44. James' brother John, the beloved disciple, may have then fled Jerusalem. Peter was arrested shortly after James' death, but he escaped and embarked on an extensive missionary journey in which he visited Antioch, Corinth and other cities in Asia Minor. Toward the end of his life he traveled to Rome, where he was probably martyred during Nero's persecution. Nothing is known for sure of the fate of the other apostles.

After Peter left Jerusalem, the leadership of the church passed into the hands of James, "the brother of the Lord." A devout, law-abiding Jew, he was revered by his followers, but in A.D. 62 he was murdered by command of the Jewish high priest. His death left the Jerusalem church leaderless and demoralized.

Meanwhile, tensions between the Jews and their Roman overlords were growing ever stronger. The completion of the Jewish temple in 64 put thousands of laborers out of work, adding to the general discontent. Finally in 66 the Jews revolted, signaling their intent by refusing to perform the daily sacrifice for the emperor.

The tragic, bloody war that followed cost more lives than any previous war. The Jews held out against overwhelming odds for four years, but they could not withstand the power of Rome. In A.D. 70 the Emperor Vespasian's forces, led by Titus, broke through the walls of Jerusalem, looted and burned the temple and carried off the spoils to Rome. The Holy City was totally destroyed. In the reprisals that followed, many synagogues were also destroyed.

At the start of the revolt, the leaders of the Jerusalem church were advised in a vision to flee the city. Their flight was seen by pious Jews as an act of treason, and it sealed the fate of the church in the Jewish world. With the decision to bar Christian Jews from synagogue services some years later, the break was complete. Any Jew who wished to remain faithful to his religion could not also be a Christian. The new faith had become and would remain a Gentile movement.

Less than 50 years after the death of Jesus, the religion he had founded had undergone profound, far-reaching and unexpected changes. Beginning with the missionary work of the Hellenist disciples, the gospel had spread to communities throughout Palestine and Syria, and to cities in Egypt. Then Paul had carried Jesus' message westward to the cities of Asia Minor, Greece and Rome. At Paul's death there were churches in every major center of the empire.

The apostles had expected Jesus to return to earth and usher in the kingdom of God during their lifetime, and they had awaited the Second Coming in a mood of joyous expectation. When it failed to arrive, however, the movement did not disintegrate, as some had predicted, because the apostles had gradually come to understand the true meaning and promise of the resurrection.

By A.D. 70 the apostolic age was at an end. All the original apostles had died, and the churches they had founded had passed into new hands. Through their tireless activity a powerful new force had been introduced into the Mediterranean world. More lasting and resilient than the forces that opposed it, the Christian religion preached by the apostles would endure persecution and opposition, emerging centuries later as the dominant faith of the Roman Empire.

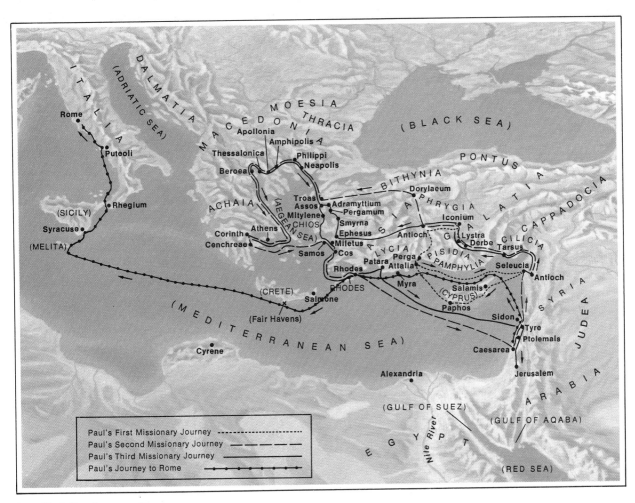

Paul's Missionary Journeys

In four epic journeys Paul brought the gospel of Jesus to the major cities of the Roman Empire and established a strong international network of Christian churches. His first journey (A.D. 47–48) was to Cyprus and Asia Minor, where he often received hostility from the Jews. Undaunted, he returned on a second visit. Then he continued to Macedonia and westward, establishing a major church at Corinth (50–52). On another mission (53–57), Paul set up a church at Ephesus, a notorious pagan city. A voyage to western Europe was prevented in 57 by his arrest in Jerusalem and by his subsequent imprisonment in Rome.

Chapter 26

Transformed by the death and resurrection of Jesus, his disciples remain in Jerusalem to found a community. They are persecuted by the authorities, but persist in preaching the gospel to all who will listen.

Followers of the Way: The Disciples in Jerusalem

Within 15 years after the death of Jesus, his apostles had founded a vigorous community of the faithful in Jerusalem. The message he had preached had begun to spread outward from the Holy City to Judea, Samaria, Phoenicia and Syria. Working with tireless devotion and zeal, the apostles laid the foundations of a movement destined to become worldwide. Behind all their efforts lay an unshakable belief that their teacher, Jesus of Nazareth, was indeed the Son of God sent to redeem the people of Israel. For them the ultimate proof of his power was his victory over death in the resurrection.

Jesus' death at the hands of the Romans had little immediate impact on the lives of most of the citizens of Jerusalem and Judea. The man who only a week before had been hailed as the Jewish Messiah had been crucified like a common criminal, and to many it seemed that Jesus the Galilean was only another in a series of false prophets proclaiming the advent of the kingdom of God.

Most of the residents of Jerusalem were skeptical of the disciples' claims that Jesus had actually risen from the dead. Rumors had begun three days after his death that his tomb had been found empty, but they were quickly stifled. The chief priests and elders had bribed the guards to say, "His disciples came by night and stole him away while we were asleep." For many, this was enough explanation.

The apostles themselves had not understood the significance of the empty tomb. Discouraged and disheartened, some had left Jerusalem and returned to Galilee. Other followers, including a man named Cleopas, remained near Jerusalem. As he explained it, "we had hoped he was the one to redeem Israel." The true Messiah, he might have added, would not have died on the cross.

Then, unexpectedly, Jesus appeared to his closest followers and convinced them that he had overcome death and would return soon to usher in the kingdom of God. The Gospel of Luke recounts no less than five occasions on which he appeared to his startled disciples.

With a new sense of dedication the eleven apostles gathered in Jerusalem, determined to carry on Jesus' work. As he had commissioned them, they would gather together a community of the righteous, baptized in the Holy Spirit, to form the core of the kingdom Jesus would soon return to inaugurate. The apostles included Peter, James and John, Andrew, Philip, Thomas, Bartholomew, Matthew, James son of Alphaeus, Simon the Zealot and Judas son of James. They chose a disciple named Matthias to become the twelfth apostle, replacing Judas Iscariot, who had committed suicide soon after the crucifixion.

Pentecost marked the traditional start of the apostolic age and the birth of the Christian church (in Greek *ekklesia*, or "assembly of peo-

"I am the good shepherd; I know my own and my own know me . . . and I lay down my life for the sheep" (Jn. 10.14–15). The paternal figure of Jesus as the good shepherd, a popular motif of early Christian art, is shown in this sculpture from a 4th-century church. At times, Jesus likely wore a short tunic rather than long robes.

According to tradition, during Nero's persecution of the Christians both Peter and Paul were held captive in Rome's Mamertine Prison (above). The lightless interior cell of this prison was 12 feet underground, and as originally designed it could be reached only through a hole in the ceiling. Prisoners were so often chained during confinement that publica vincula *("public chains") was a synonym for "jail."*

disciple Mark. There many of the Jerusalem brethren had gathered to pray for his safety. When he suddenly appeared at the door, they were astounded at his miraculous escape. After telling them what had happened, Peter warned the brethren to reveal his escape only to James (the "brother of the Lord") and the other apostles. Then he fled the city to avoid being captured.

The Bible makes only vague reference to Peter's life after he left Jerusalem. For the next 20 years he apparently traveled from one city to another, from Palestine to Asia Minor, preaching to the small Christian communities. He was said to have reached Rome near the end of his life, and there he became an important figure in the Roman church. Most likely he was martyred in A.D. 64 during the persecution of Nero.

After Peter's flight from the Holy City, the leadership of the Jerusalem church passed to James (the "brother of the Lord"), who was more conservative than Peter. Though lenient concerning the mission to the Gentiles, he himself strictly observed Jewish laws and rituals.

From that time on, the Jerusalem church began to lose its authority over the rapidly growing religion. It would always be revered as the birthplace of the Christian religion, and it would continue to administer funds for needy Christian communities. "But the word of God grew and multiplied" as the Gentile mission became more important to the church. Antioch had become the true center of the new religion.

From Antioch, the apostles to the Gentiles—men like Barnabas and Paul—departed on journeys throughout the Roman Empire. In time, the message of the Jerusalem apostles evolved into a faith that was neither Jewish nor Gentile but incorporated elements of both.

The story of the disciples is told in the Gospels and the Acts of the Apostles.

Cities of the Gentiles: The World of Paul

"To me, though I am the very least of all the saints, this grace was given, to preach to the Gentiles the unsearchable riches of Christ" (Eph. 3.8). Though isolated groups of Hellenist Christians also carried out the Gentile mission, Paul was by far the most determined and energetic apostle of all. A Roman citizen familiar with Hellenistic ways, Paul was well qualified to translate Jesus' message—rooted in Jewish tradition—into one with universal appeal. Accompanied at times by Barnabas, Silas, Mark and other disciples, he traveled on four epic journeys throughout the eastern world. He and his assistants established churches in 20 cities of the Roman Empire during the 30 years between his conversion and his death in Rome. These efforts helped Christianity to become, within a few decades of Jesus' crucifixion, fully established as the most vital and persuasive new religion of the age.

"Great is Artemis of the Ephesians!" (Acts 19.28). With this shout, angry citizens of Ephesus pursued and nearly killed Paul's assistants during his second visit to that city. The port of Ephesus, whose ruins are shown above, was the commercial and administrative center of the Roman province of Asia, and famed for its temple of Artemis, a many-breasted fertility goddess (left). Pilgrims who might otherwise have flocked to the spectacular temple were dissuaded by Paul's dynamic preaching, however, and local tradesmen blamed him for a decline in tourism, their major source of income. Despite their resentment Paul continued, and within two years he and his helpers had established a thriving Christian church within that pagan city.

"And at Antioch the disciples were for the first time called Christians" (Acts 11.26). *The once-great city of Antioch, in northern Syria, became a Christian center in Paul's time. From here he began his three missionary journeys. Among the few remains of the early Christian city are these 6th-century citadel walls.*

"Agrippa the king . . . arrived at Caesarea . . . [And] Festus laid Paul's case before the king" (Acts 25.13–14). *For two years Paul awaited trial at Caesarea for inciting a riot in Jerusalem. Then he used his citizen's right to appeal to Caesar, and from Caesarea's harbor (above) he sailed for Rome—where he helped found a new church.*

Paul's first missionary journey was to the Mediterranean island of Cyprus, where Hellenist Christians had founded a Christian community. With his colleagues Mark and Barnabas, a native of the island, Paul walked from the port of Salamis through the whole island as far as Paphos, possibly crossing plains like the ones shown at left. At Paphos, Cyprus' most important port, Paul succeeded in converting the Roman proconsul, Sergius Paulus. From there he left the island, and journeyed to Asia Minor.

Chapter 27

"But if we have died with Christ, we believe that we shall also live with him"

(Rom. 6.8). Thus, Paul proclaims Jesus' message of salvation to the Roman world.

The former scourge of the Christians becomes their greatest apostle.

Paul:
Bearer of Christianity

The man most responsible for carrying the Christian faith to the Greco-Roman world beyond Palestine was Paul. Beginning his career as a fierce persecutor of the earliest followers of Jesus, he experienced a miraculous conversion, and from that time on he practiced Christian evangelism so zealously and successfully that he went down in history as the revered "apostle to the Gentiles."

Paul was born into a devout Jewish family in the city of Tarsus, capital of the small Roman district of Cilicia in Asia Minor. His father, a member of the ancient tribe of Benjamin, named him Saul, after Israel's first king. (Later in life, Saul became better known by his Roman name, Paul.) A man of standing in the community, he held the privileged status of Roman citizen, an honor rarely conferred upon Jews. His son inherited this legal advantage.

Paul's father was also a Pharisee, a member of a religious group dedicated to strict observance of Jewish laws and customs. Accordingly, Paul received detailed instruction in Jewish law from an early age, and he studied under the most respected rabbis in Tarsus.

Like all pious Jews, Paul scorned the pagan religion of the majority of the people of Tarsus. But unlike most young Jews, he was attracted by Greek culture, the prevailing culture in the Near East at that time. He learned to speak and read Greek and became familiar with the most influential philosophy of the time: Stoicism. The Stoics taught that men should strive to become one with nature and the universe, which was governed by the power of reason.

Every Jewish boy was taught a useful trade, and so Paul learned to fashion tent material from goat's hair or tanned goatskins. The foothills of the Taurus Mountains were ideal goat-raising country, and the goat-hair fabrics woven there were in wide demand throughout the Roman Empire. In fact, the region of Cilicia was so closely identified with their production that the Latin name for goat-hair cloth was *cilicium*.

When Paul was about 13, he left home for Jerusalem to study under the famous rabbi Gamaliel, the head of the most influential school of Jewish learning at that time. Like his grandfather and mentor, the noted teacher Hillel, Gamaliel favored a liberal interpretation of Jewish law. He was a Pharisee and a member of the Sanhedrin, the Jewish high court.

In Jerusalem Paul lived with relatives, apparently in the home of a paternal aunt. Dark-complexioned, small of build, with bowlegs and a large nose, the young scholar was unimpressive physically; but his brilliant mind and intense piety attracted attention. In his own words, ". . . I advanced in Judaism beyond many of my own age among my people, so extremely zealous was I for the traditions of my fathers."

"Many of the Corinthians hearing Paul believed and were baptized" (Acts 18.8). Paul founded his most beloved church in the Greek city of Corinth and wrote some of his most eloquent letters to Christians there. The column-lined road at right leads to the open square where Paul's teachings were denounced by traditional Jews.

At this time Hellenists of the Christian sect in Jerusalem were being persecuted relentlessly by the Jewish authorities. Paul felt obliged to defend the purity of his faith against these heretics. In due time, he was engaged in bitter debates in the synagogues and on Jerusalem's street corners with preachers of the Christian "heresy." Paul was particularly infuriated by the controversial preaching of the deacon Stephen. When Stephen was arrested on charges of blasphemy and stoned to death by a mob of angry Jews, Paul looked on with approval.

In the months that followed Stephen's martyrdom, Paul became one of the most active leaders in the rising persecution of the followers of the new faith. Meanwhile, many Hellenist disciples fled Jerusalem and began preaching in Samaria and cities in Syria.

On the Road to Damascus

Reports that Christians were active in Damascus caused some alarm among the Jewish hierarchy of Jerusalem. Damascus was a busy commercial center, and they feared that the heresy would spread quickly from there to other cities. Paul asked the high priest, to whom the Romans had granted authority over the Jews of Damascus, for permission to travel there to arrest any followers of Jesus and bring them to Jerusalem for trial.

It was a long journey, about 150 miles, and Paul traveled with a caravan, partly on foot, partly by donkey. As the caravan neared Damascus, he experienced a vision that transformed him: "suddenly a light from heaven flashed about him. And he fell to the ground and heard a voice saying to him, 'Saul, Saul, why do you persecute me?' And he said, 'Who are you, Lord?' And he said, 'I am Jesus, whom you are persecuting; but rise and enter the city, and you will be told what you are to do.' The men who were traveling with him stood speechless, hearing the voice but seeing no one. Saul arose from the ground; and when his eyes were opened, he could see nothing; so they led him by the hand and brought him into Damascus. And for three days he was without sight, and neither ate nor drank."

Then he was visited by a Christian convert named Ananias, who announced that he had been sent by Jesus. "And laying his hands on him he said, 'Brother Saul, the Lord Jesus who appeared to you on the road by which you came, has sent me that you may regain your sight and be filled with the Holy Spirit.' And immediately something like scales fell from his eyes and he regained his sight." Overwhelmed by his amazing experience, Paul asked Ananias to baptize him.

Soon afterward, Paul traveled to the desert of Arabia, where he spent some three years in solitude and meditation, preparing himself for his new life. Then he joined the disciples of Jesus who were preaching in Damascus. Before long he was proclaiming in the synagogues that Jesus was the Son of God. "And all who heard him were amazed, and said, 'Is not this the man who made havoc in Jerusalem of those who called on this name? And he has come here . . . to bring them bound before the chief priests.'" Many Jews refused to believe Paul was sincere and they plotted to kill him. When Paul learned of the plot, he fled from Damascus to Jerusalem.

There the disciples, remembering his eager persecutions, suspected that he might be a secret agent seeking to infiltrate their ranks. But Barnabas believed Paul's story and brought him to Peter and to James, the "brother of the Lord." They too were convinced that Paul's conversion was genuine, and Paul remained with them in the Holy City for about two weeks. The apostles began to fear that the temple authorities might persecute the new convert, so they induced Paul to return to his native Tarsus and preach his newfound faith to the Jewish community there.

The Church at Antioch

Paul spent the next few years in Tarsus. During that time the leaders of the Jerusalem church were worried by reports from Antioch, the capital of Syria; it seems that the Greek-speaking Jews who had founded a church there had accepted non-Jews into their congregation. The apostles sent Barnabas to investigate. When he found that the church at Antioch was thriving as a result of its open policy, he remained in Antioch and became a leader of the Christian movement. As the community grew, Barnabas felt he needed an able associate, and in about A.D. 44 he went to Tarsus to summon Paul. Together they returned to Antioch, where they worked with both Jewish and Gentile converts for about a year.

Antioch was not far from Tarsus. It was located in northwestern Syria, on the Orontes River, some 16 miles upstream from the Mediterranean

Sea. Surpassed in size and wealth only by Rome and Alexandria, Antioch had grown enormously under Roman rule. The original city on the south bank of the Orontes was matched on the opposite bank by a new section of many splendid temples and private villas. Between them, an island in the river was transformed into a civic center linked with the other parts of town by five bridges. The

A Tentmaker Plies His Craft

"Because [Paul] was of the same trade he stayed with them . . . for they were tentmakers" (Acts 18.3). Usually, Jewish boys learned a craft, and the apostle Paul's was tentmaking. Here a tentmaker scrapes one side of a goatskin, which he will sew to other skins on the wall. His tools include bone or metal needles, combs, awls and knives. Paul's native Cilicia was famed for its goat-hair cloth, a material also used in tents.

Romans had also built magnificent theaters, stadiums and public baths.

The Jewish population, though large, was only a small minority in a pagan Greek society. Among the number of local deities was Astarte, a fertility goddess, whose worship involved orgies which even the Romans looked upon with disgust. The sanctuary to Apollo at nearby Daphne was a notorious center of immorality. When Juvenal, a first-century writer, satirized Rome's increasing corruption, he wrote that the Orontes had overflowed and polluted the Tiber.

While the gospel preached by Paul and Barnabas appealed to some Jews in Antioch, the majority of the new converts came from the ranks of the "God-fearers." These were Gentiles who had adopted the Jewish faith and code of morality and attended synagogue services, but who were not full converts. Most likely they found the requirements of full conversion too strict. (These were circumcision, full knowledge of the scriptures and sacrificial offerings at the temple in Jerusalem.) Instead, they chose to remain on the fringe of the Jewish community, retaining many of their pagan customs while worshiping Israel's Lord.

These men and women were deeply impressed by the Christian message that the long-awaited Messiah (*Christos* in Greek) had already lived on Earth, suffered for the sins of mankind, died and been raised from death by the Lord. Paul could offer his own first-hand vision as compelling proof of the power of Jesus. He was so completely convinced of the truth of his belief that he persuaded many to believe too.

In vivid terms Paul would describe his dramatic conversion and tell of the supernatural events that would soon take place when Jesus returned to earth in glory: "the Lord himself will descend from heaven with a cry of command, with the archangel's call, and with the sound of the trumpet of God. And the dead in Christ will rise first; then we who are alive, who are left, shall be caught up together with them in the clouds to meet the Lord in the air; and so we shall always be with the Lord. Therefore comfort one another with these words."

Especially attractive to the God-fearers was the idea that they could become members of the Christian community merely by confessing their sins and submitting to baptism. Before long hundreds of Gentiles had joined Antioch's church.

The citizens of Antioch soon took notice of the new community, whose members they scornfully called *Christianoi* (partisans of the Messiah). The name became popular, and in time the Christians accepted their appellation as a badge of honor.

The Christian brotherhood flourished so well in Antioch and its environs that before long it began to overshadow the mother church in Jerusalem. But the bond between them remained strong. During a famine in the Holy City, about A.D. 45, the Antioch Christians sent a relief fund to the Jerusalem church, attesting their desire for friendly relations. Paul and Barnabas personally presented their contributions to the apostles and reported on their activities in Antioch.

On this visit, his first in more than a decade, Paul found the situation much altered. A few years earlier the apostle James, son of Zebedee, had been executed by King Herod Agrippa, who ruled Palestine from 41 to 44. The apostle Peter had been arrested and imprisoned at the same time, but he had escaped and fled Jerusalem. He may have visited Paul and Barnabas in Antioch. Meanwhile, the Jerusalem church had continued its conservative policy of accepting only Jews and full Jewish converts into its ranks. The leader of the community at the time of Paul's visit was James, the "brother of the Lord."

Soon after Paul and Barnabas returned to Antioch, certain Christian prophets brought them a message from the Holy Spirit: "Set apart for me

A Daughter Is Sold into Slavery

In Philippi Paul drove a "spirit of divination" from a slave girl. Her irate owners persecuted him for her loss of this profitable talent. In Biblical times debtors often sold their children, or themselves, into slavery. But the law dictated that

they receive decent treatment. Above, a poor man brings his daughter to a wealthy citizen in a public bath. She carries a palm-frond basket like that at left. This 2nd-century bag was found in Israel, still filled with the personal belongings of a young Jewish woman.

Barnabas and Saul for the work to which I have called them." Both men had discussed plans for missionary efforts in other parts of the empire, and they took the message as a signal for action.

First Missionary Journey

Probably at the suggestion of Barnabas, the two missionaries set out for the island of Cyprus, Barnabas' birthplace. Mark, the young cousin of Barnabas, accompanied them. The third largest island in the Mediterranean, Cyprus was fertile and prosperous. Its famous copper mines supplied most of the Roman Empire.

At Seleucia, the seaport near Antioch, the three men arranged for passage to Cyprus, some 50 miles distant. There were no passenger ships at that time; travelers by sea were often carried on square-rigged cargo ships, which regularly plied the Mediterranean sea lanes between Africa, Asia and Europe. Most of the space on the ships was taken up by cargo and crew, but there were limited accommodations for passengers.

The men came ashore at Salamis, a large port city on the eastern shores of Cyprus. An influential Jewish colony had been founded there centuries earlier, and the men preached to the Jews in their synagogues. There may even have been a small Christian group as well, founded by Hellenist disciples who had fled Jerusalem. From Salamis the three traveled overland to Paphos, a prosperous city on the southwestern coast.

Paphos was the seat of Roman government in Cyprus and an important naval station. The local Roman proconsul, Sergius Paulus, was curious about Christianity—many cultivated Romans, in fact, wanted to hear about new religions. He invited the three strangers to his palace, where they clashed with a Jewish magician named Bar-Jesus. Eager to keep his influence with the proconsul, Bar-Jesus tried to prevent the visitors from proclaiming their faith. Paul glared at him and said, "You son of the devil . . . will you not stop making crooked the straight paths of the Lord? And now, behold, the hand of the Lord is upon you, and you shall be blind . . . for a time."

The terrified magician was led away sightless. Triumphantly Paul turned to Sergius Paulus and told him of the life, death and resurrection of Jesus. Already impressed by the power Paul's God had shown over Bar-Jesus, the proconsul was even more affected by Paul's promises of salvation through Jesus. Before the day was over, he asked to be baptized. He was the first Roman of rank to become a Christian.

From Paphos the missionaries sailed northward to Pamphylia, a Roman province to the west of Cilicia on the coast of Asia Minor. They landed near Perga, the provincial capital. It was a fortress town with a huge acropolis a thousand yards long and 650 yards wide. Unfortunately, the surrounding countryside was full of coastal marshes that bred malaria-carrying mosquitos. In fact, Paul may have fallen ill there, alternately sweating and shivering with malarial chills.

Mark, frightened and disheartened, pleaded that they abandon the expedition, and he himself left for Jerusalem. But Paul was determined to persevere. With Barnabas' help, he struggled a hundred miles north from Perga to Pisidian Antioch, located in the Roman province of Galatia. This city lay at the western edge of the Anatolian Plateau. In its dry climate, high above sea level, he slowly recuperated.

As soon as Paul was able, he resumed his missionary task. As in Cyprus, he initially proclaimed his gospel in the synagogues on the Sabbath. It was customary in synagogues throughout the empire to invite visiting Jews to address the congregation after the main part of the service. "After the reading of the law and the prophets, the rulers of the synagogue sent to them, saying, 'Brethren, if you have any word of exhortation for the people, say it.' So Paul stood up, and motioning with his hand said:

"'Men of Israel, and you that fear God, listen. . . . God has brought to Israel a Savior, Jesus, as he promised. . . . what God promised to the fathers, this he has fulfilled to us their children by raising Jesus . . . Let it be known to you therefore, brethren, that through this man forgiveness of sins is proclaimed to you . . .'"

His words caused a great stir among the congregation, and after the service many Jews and God-fearers sought out the two visitors, asking to know more about Jesus and his message. The next Sabbath a large crowd gathered to hear Paul and Barnabas. The leaders of the synagogue, skeptical of Paul's claims concerning Jesus and alarmed at his growing popularity, stood up and tried to disprove his statements. "And Paul and Barnabas spoke out boldly, saying 'It was necessary that the word of God should be spoken first to you. Since you thrust it from you . . . behold, we turn to the Gentiles.'" The leaders of the synagogue urged their people to attack the missionaries with clubs and stones, and an angry mob drove Paul and Barnabas out of the city.

From there they traveled eastward along the Roman road through the very heart of Asia Minor. At Iconium, a busy trading center, the two missionaries won a following among both Jews and Gentiles, but hostile opponents threatened them and drove them away.

Adventures in Lystra

At Lystra, a small city about 20 miles south of Iconium, they encountered an unexpected problem. An ancient and well-known Greek legend told of the visit of the gods Zeus and Hermes to a humble Galatian couple. When Paul cured a lame man in the marketplace of Lystra, the witnesses were convinced that the two strangers were the same two gods in disguise. "The gods have come down to us in the likeness of men!" they proclaimed. The tall, bearded Barnabas they called Zeus, and the more articulate Paul they called Hermes.

Unable to understand the local language, the missionaries did not realize at first that the priest of Zeus was preparing to offer sacrifices at their feet. When they did, they stopped the ceremony and Paul cried out in Greek, "Men, why are you doing this? We also are men, of like nature with you, and bring you good news, that you should turn from these vain things to a living God who made the heaven and the earth and the sea and all that is in them." Reluctantly, the people abandoned their sacrifices, and Paul began to proclaim his gospel to them.

A short while later a group of Jews from Iconium and Pisidian Antioch, still nursing their resentments from the recent missionary visits, converged on Lystra. They persuaded the people there that the preachers were both liars and traitors, since Jesus had been crucified by the Romans. Convinced by them, the crowd "stoned Paul and dragged him out of the city, supposing that he was dead." At night, Barnabas and a few men who had believed Paul's message carried him back into the city. The next morning before dawn the two headed to the city of Derbe, a day's journey to the southeast. There Paul's wounds healed, and he gathered many followers.

Undaunted, Paul and Barnabas revisited the

cities where they had been persecuted. This time they avoided the local synagogues, meeting instead in the private homes of their new followers. There they instructed the converts in the faith and appointed elders to carry on the work in their absence. One of the most zealous converts was a young man from Lystra named Timothy.

After retracing their steps they set sail for Syrian Antioch. By any standards their first journey had been a success. In less than three years' time, the two men had covered a distance of nearly 1400 miles and had established small but strong Christian communities in major cities of Cyprus and Asia Minor.

Council at Jerusalem

The congregation at Antioch was elated by the news of their activities and their success among the Gentiles, but certain disciples from the Jerusalem church questioned them sharply. "Unless you are circumcized according to the custom of Moses," they argued, "you cannot be saved." The issue soon became so heated that the Antioch community decided to send a delegation including Paul and Barnabas to Jerusalem to settle the question of Gentile converts.

In the Holy City the delegates were warmly received by the church leaders. At a large gathering of the Christian community, Paul and Barnabas eloquently presented their case. "After they finished speaking, James replied, 'Brethren, listen to me. Symeon [Peter] has related how God first visited the Gentiles, to take out of them a people for his name. And with this the words of the prophets agree . . . Therefore my judgment is that we should not trouble those of the Gentiles who turn to God . . .'"

On his advice the council prepared a resolution stating that it was not necessary for Gentile converts to follow the entire body of Jewish law. At best the resolution was a fuzzy compromise, outlining separate paths for Jewish and Gentile Christians. From that time on, the Antioch church would carry its main thrust into the Gentile world, while the Jerusalem church would remain small, conservative and exclusively Jewish.

Paul and Barnabas returned to Antioch in Syria and continued their work for several months. In the spring of the following year (A.D. 50), they decided to revisit the churches they had founded in Cyprus and Asia Minor. Barnabas insisted they

take Mark along; but Paul refused to travel with "one who had withdrawn from them in Pamphylia, and had not gone with them to the work." Instead, Paul chose Silas, a young disciple from Antioch, to accompany him. Barnabas and Mark sailed to Cyprus, and Paul and Silas headed overland to Galatia.

At Lystra the missionaries were joined by Timothy, and together they revisited the small Christian communities at Iconium and Pisidian Antioch. Then they headed northwest across the rugged interior of Asia Minor to the city of Troas, near the site of ancient Troy. (It was in that city that Paul was joined by Luke, the evangelist who would eventually tell the story of Paul in his Acts

This portrait of a Greek shows the kind of Gentile to whom Paul and the other apostles preached the gospel. It was painted in Egypt while that country was under the domination of Rome and its Hellenistic culture. In the realistic style of the time, the subject's complexion, hair style and clothing are meticulously painted.

"We piped to you, and you did not dance" (Mt. 11.17). *Using this vivid image, recorded in the Gospels of Matthew and Luke, Jesus chided unbelievers for their thoughtless wilfulness. Pipers and other musicians, like these on a mosaic from Pompeii, were common in the Roman world. Paul, too, knew how to teach through striking imagery, and often drew upon scenes from street life to make a point or draw a moral.*

of the Apostles.) Paul had been uncertain about which direction his mission should take, but at Troas he received a fateful vision telling him to cross over into Europe.

The next day Paul, Silas and Timothy boarded a cargo ship at Troas and sailed across the Aegean Sea. Landing at the north Aegean port of Neapolis, they traveled 10 miles inland to Philippi along the Via Egnatia, the great military highway linking Rome with Asia. As elsewhere, they first sought out members of the local Jewish community and told them about Jesus. One of the listeners, a woman named Lydia who sold costly purple cloth, asked to be baptized along with her en-

This frieze is from the Arch of Titus, named for the Roman general who quelled the Jews' revolt of A.D. 66–73. It shows a sacred menorah (candelabrum), a table of gold and the silver trumpets taken as booty from the temple. Titus savagely razed the city, ending the temple's influence as the center of Judaism. The Christian community also fled, and in later years Antioch became a center of the fledgling church.

tire household and eagerly offered her home to the two missionaries.

Paul's mission at Philippi soon ran into difficulties. Paul exorcised a demon from a slave girl reputed to have prophetic powers. The owners of the girl were furious at the loss of her gift of prophecy, which meant they could no longer earn money for her services. They brought Paul and Silas before the city magistrates, charging them with unlawful practices. The two were beaten severely by the magistrates and other enraged citizens, thrown into prison and placed in stocks. Roman stocks were designed to force a victim's legs apart as far as possible, causing intense pain. Paul suffered from the effects of this torture for the rest of his life.

After their release, Paul and Silas paid a brief visit to Lydia and other followers, appointed leaders to carry on their work and, with Timothy, hastily departed. Heading westward on the Via Egnatia, they soon reached Thessalonica, the largest port city of the north Aegean. There Paul preached for three weeks in the local synagogue before he was driven out of town.

Then, he and his companions fled westward to Beroea, where they were warmly welcomed in the synagogue. But Jews from Thessalonica soon pursued Paul there, and he was again forced to flee for his life. Silas and Timothy remained at Beroea and later returned to Thessalonica and Philippi. Paul meanwhile journeyed south to the famed city of Athens.

Three centuries earlier Athens had been the center of the civilized world. Though it had lost its political and economic leadership to Rome, it was still a splendid city, its intellectual glories undimmed. Everywhere one looked there were brightly painted marble temples dedicated to the gods. Colonnades, lifelike statues of gods and heroes and stately public buildings recalled the days of Athens' political glory and independence. High above the city was the sacred hill of the Acropolis, its complex of temples and shrines dominated by the magnificent Parthenon.

In Athens Paul preached not only in the synagogues but also in the public marketplace to all who would listen. Among the curious bystanders who engaged him in debate were philosophers of the Stoic and Epicurean schools. They asked Paul to appear before the Areopagus, the city's highest council, and explain his new teaching.

Surrounded by pagan statues, altars and temples, the apostle began to speak. "Men of Athens, I perceive that in every way you are very religious. For as I passed along, and observed the objects of your worship, I found also an altar with this inscription, 'To an unknown god.' What therefore you worship as unknown, this I proclaim to you. The God who made the world and everything in it, being Lord of heaven and earth, does not live in shrines made by man . . . Being then God's offspring, we ought not to think that the Deity is like gold, or silver, or stone, a representation by the art and imagination of man. The times of ignorance God overlooked, but now he commands all men everywhere to repent, because he has fixed a day on which he will judge the world in righteousness by a man whom he has appointed, and of this he has given assurance to all men by raising him from the dead."

Most of the listeners were skeptical of Paul's claims and mocked his talk of the resurrection of the dead. A few wanted to hear more, and invited Paul to speak further. He agreed to meet with them and won a handful of converts. A few days later, Paul left Athens and went to Corinth, where he had arranged to rejoin Silas and Timothy.

Among the Corinthians

Corinth, a great commercial center, was located west of Athens on the narrow isthmus joining the Peloponnesus to the Greek mainland. In earlier centuries Corinth had been renowned for its temple to Aphrodite, goddess of love, which was served by cult prostitutes. Long after the temple had been destroyed by the Romans (146 B.C.), the city's reputation for immorality lingered.

Yet in this predominantly pagan city, Paul founded his most successful church. He was aided considerably by the efforts of two Jewish converts, Aquila and Priscilla. They had possibly come there from Rome, where the Emperor Claudius had issued an edict in 49 or 50 expelling all Jews. There had been rioting in the city over one "Chrestos," presumably provoked by a disagreement between Rome's Jews and Christians over Jesus.

The apostle stayed at Corinth for 18 months. In that time he gathered a sizable community of believers, drawing its membership mainly from the lower classes and slaves. As Paul wrote some years later in his first Letter to the Corinthian church, "not many of you were wise according to worldly standards, not many were powerful, not many were of noble birth . . ." Such humble people grasped Paul's message of Jesus much more readily than the philosophers of Athens.

The faith Paul preached to them was concerned with basic human problems such as love, guilt, grief and death. "When I came to you, brethren," he wrote later, "I did not come proclaiming to you the testimony of God in lofty words or wisdom. For I decided to know nothing among you except Jesus Christ . . . my speech and my message were not in plausible words of wisdom, but in demonstration of the Spirit and power, that your faith might not rest in the wisdom of men but in the power of God."

When he was not preaching, Paul worked with Aquila and Priscilla, weaving tentcloth and preparing animal hides for tents. Their small open-air shop was probably located in the arcade along the Lechaion Road in Corinth, just outside the monumental gateway to the marketplace. They worked there during the early morning and late afternoon, stopping at midday from eleven to four, when the heat was too intense.

At length Paul decided it was time to return to Syrian Antioch. He sailed with Aquila and Priscilla to the large eastern Aegean port of Ephesus. There he left his companions and continued to Caesarea, perhaps visiting Jerusalem briefly before finally returning to Antioch.

His second journey had covered 2800 miles, twice the distance of the first journey, and had lasted nearly three years. Most important, Paul had brought the message of Jesus to the continent of Europe and the centers of western civilization. The dedicated disciples at Corinth would help spread the gospel into the Gentile world.

Paul's Third Journey

Paul stayed in Antioch briefly before embarking on a third missionary journey to Ephesus, a great city in the province of Asia. It was a wealthy metropolis, ranking in commercial im-

portance with Alexandria and Antioch. In Paul's day the city had a population of some 250,000.

Ephesus was especially famed for its magnificent temple to Artemis (known to the Romans as Diana). One of the seven wonders of the ancient world, the enormous white-marble temple stood at a distance from the city. Its 100 tall, stately columns rose to a height of more than 55 feet and supported a roof that spanned an area measuring 160 by 340 feet. The entire building was adorned with gold leaf, bright paint and beautiful sculpture. There was a huge altar before the temple entrance, and within stood a many-breasted statue of the fertility goddess. At the very center of the temple was a sacred stone, possibly a meteorite, which had fallen from the sky and was thought to resemble the goddess' image.

The cult of Artemis was popular throughout Asia Minor, and thousands of pilgrims went to Ephesus annually to participate in sacred rites in her honor. A large staff of eunuchs, priests and temple virgins was associated with the cult. Magical arts flourished around the shrine to such an extent that books on magic were often called "Ephesian writings."

At Ephesus, as at Corinth, Paul supported himself by making tentcloth. During the five-hour midday siesta, he preached in a hall he rented with the help of some well-to-do converts. Paul remained at Ephesus for more than two years. His mission was so successful that the temple priests noted a distinct decline in the

"And he lived there two whole years . . . and welcomed all who came to him, preaching the kingdom of God and teaching about the Lord Jesus Christ" (Acts 28.30–31). While living in Rome, Paul may have stayed in an apartment house like one replicated in the model above. Group housing developed in response to the city's growing middle-class population, and apartments were built from 4 to 8 stories high. Followers could have listened to Paul teach in the spacious court of such a place while he was under house arrest.

number of pilgrims, and merchants and innkeepers complained of a loss of business. Equally alarmed were the magicians and healers, who did a brisk business with the pilgrims.

One of the merchants, a silversmith named Demetrius, who made a living by selling small, expensive images of Artemis, aroused the people against Paul. An angry mob of merchants and innkeepers gathered to protest both their loss of business and the threat to the worship of Artemis. After a near riot, a town clerk quieted them, urging those with grievances against Paul to bring them before the courts. Reluctantly, Paul left. Through his efforts the city had become the third most important center of the faith, after Antioch and Jerusalem. On leaving Ephesus, Paul made a detour through Macedonia and Greece, visiting the churches he had founded and collecting alms for the Jerusalem church. Finally he made his way back to Judea with a stopover at Miletus, not far from Ephesus. There he summoned the elders of the Ephesus church to bid them farewell.

Imprisonment in Judea

When Paul reached Judea, late in A.D. 57, he found a nation on the brink of chaos. Jewish hatred and resentment of Roman rule was seething, and only a spark was needed to set off a full-scale revolt. Under the Roman governor Cumanus (A.D. 48–52) there had been several minor revolts, and the frustrated rebels had formed outlaw guerrilla bands known as the *sicarii* (assassins).

Cumanus' successor, Felix (c. 52–59), was no more successful at restoring order, despite his ruthless policies. Early in his reign a false prophet from Egypt came to Judea, gathered a large group of followers and marched on Jerusalem. A Roman infantry unit dispersed the mob, killing many in the process, and the would-be Messiah fled back to Egypt.

Paul arrived in Jerusalem in time for the Feast of Pentecost and was greeted warmly by James and the Jerusalem brethren. His gifts bestowed, he went up to the temple. As he made his way through the pilgrim throng, a group of Asian Jews recognized Paul and seized the opportunity to have him arrested. They must have been from one of the cities Paul had visited in his travels. In loud voices they accused him of bringing pagans into the inner courts of the temple, an offense punishable by death. Only the arrival of Roman troops saved him from being beaten to death by the infuriated mob.

The Roman tribune in command at Jerusalem sent Paul to Caesarea for trial before the Roman governor Felix. There, a delegation of Jews, headed by the high priest Ananias, accused him of blasphemy and treason and demanded his execution. The wily Felix, anxious to avoid trouble, refused to pass sentence. For the next two years, however, he held Paul prisoner in Caesarea.

Paul's friends were allowed to visit him, and he busied himself writing letters to the Christian churches he had founded. These epistles, like others he had dispatched earlier, exhorted Christians to keep their faith, settled internal disputes among their members and warned them repeatedly not to yield to the luxury and sensuality of their pagan environment.

In his Letters, Paul expounded the basic tenets of his theology. Unlike the Gospel writers, Paul was less concerned with the life and teachings of Jesus than with his death and resurrection and their meaning for mankind. For Paul the ultimate manifestation of God's power and love for undeserving mankind was in the resurrection, Jesus' victory over sin and death.

Journey to Rome

During the years of Paul's detention, Felix faced a major outbreak of violence. An attempt by Jews to drive the Greek-speaking citizens out of Caesarea provoked warfare in which Felix' soldiers slaughtered hundreds. The Jews petitioned Rome, and the new emperor, Nero, replaced Felix with Porcius Festus.

Festus was eager to placate the Jews. When Ananias and his group renewed the demand that Paul stand trial in Jerusalem, Festus was inclined to agree. Paul, however, invoked his legal privilege as a Roman citizen: the right to a trial before the emperor. "I appeal to Caesar," he declared.

In the autumn of the year A.D. 60, when Paul was in his late fifties, he and other prisoners sailed for Rome, under the guard of a centurion named Julius. Accompanying Paul was the disciple Luke, author of the third Gospel and the book of Acts. Luke, who had gone to Philippi with Paul some years earlier, traveled with the apostle on several of his missions.

The group boarded a small cargo ship at Caesarea and sailed along the coastline of Asia Minor. At Myra they changed ships, embarking on a large grain ship bound for Italy. Their next stop was to be the port of Fair Havens in southern Crete. Finding it unsuitable for anchorage, the captain tried to reach the more sheltered harbor of Phoenix, west of Fair Havens. En route their ship was driven off its course by a winter storm, and after two weeks of sailing helplessly before the wind, they were shipwrecked on Malta, a small island south of Sicily and nearly 600 miles west of Crete. At Paul's urging the captain and passengers swam ashore. The people of Malta offered them food and shelter, and they remained there for the winter. Paul was able to heal and teach during those months.

In the spring of 61, Paul and his companions set out once more for Rome. Boarding another grain ship, they sailed north to Sicily and then to the Italian port of Puteoli, whence they completed the journey on foot. A small group of Roman Christians met Paul at the Forum of Appius, some 40 miles south of Rome. Together they traveled along the Appian Way to the capital.

The Appian Way led into Rome through the Porta Capena. Directly inside was the Circus Maximus and above it the Palatine Hill, where the palace of Nero stood. Beyond lay the center of the city, with its grandiose temples, monuments and forums. The large, open, colonnaded forums served as gathering places and centers of commerce for the people of Rome. Above the main forum rose the Capitoline Hill, the most ancient seat of power in Rome and the symbolic center of the empire. At its foot was the milestone from which all roads in the empire were measured.

On the lower hills to the east of the Capitoline Hill were the gleaming white villas and gardens of wealthy Romans. There and elsewhere were public baths, theaters and sports arenas. Beyond the stately forums stood another Rome, the blocks of large, often makeshift apartment buildings that housed the Roman masses.

In Rome Paul was placed under house arrest for two years while awaiting trial. This meant that he was free to come and go about the city but could not go beyond the city limits. The apostle used this valuable time to strengthen the small Christian church in Rome. He also kept in touch with the churches he had founded in other cities. It may be that he was joined in his efforts by his aides Aquila and Priscilla, who had returned to

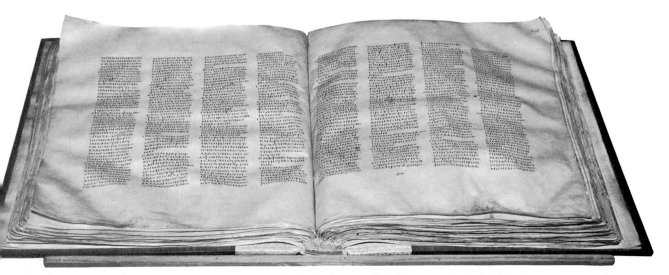

The earliest known complete text of the New Testament is in the Codex Sinaiticus (above), written in Greek. This 4th-century manuscript was found in 1859 in a monastery on Mt. Sinai. Its "codex" form, using separate pages bound with stitching on one side, rather than unwieldy scrolls, helped people read and refer to the Bible more easily. It was also the forerunner of the modern book. The Sinaiticus consists of 346½ sheets of vellum, each 15 by 13½ inches, and besides the New Testament it contains most of the Old Testament up to Ezra.

Rome after the death of the Emperor Claudius in 54. The apostle Peter may also have been there, along with Mark.

During these years news must have reached Paul of the worsening situation in Judea. Events were building toward a tragic climax as hostility between Jews and Romans became more and more open. Jewish intolerance of the Christians was growing as well. After the death of Festus in 62, the Jewish high priest, Ananias, took advantage of the brief vacuum of power to order the murder of James, the "brother of the Lord."

Sometime later a harsh fate befell the Christians in Rome. On a hot summer night in A.D. 64 a great fire broke out at the northern end of the Circus Maximus. Fed by the flimsy wares in the surrounding shops and fanned by a strong wind, the flames spread. The fire raged for five days, completely destroying most of the city. Rome's citizens suspected the fire had been set at the order of the Emperor Nero so that he could rebuild the capital on a grander scale.

To direct suspicions away from himself, Nero accused the Christians of Rome of starting the fire. A widespread persecution followed this accusation. Suspected Christians were systematically rounded up, interrogated and executed in cruel public games. Some became human torches to light Nero's pleasure gardens; others were wrapped in animal hides and tossed to wild beasts in the arenas. Peter was probably among the victims of this vicious campaign. He is said to have been crucified with his head downward because he felt unworthy of dying as Jesus had.

Paul was also caught up in this whirlwind of depraved persecution. Apparently he had been released from house arrest after two years, since no one from Jerusalem had appeared to press charges. He then left Rome and called on churches in Greece and Asia Minor. It is likely that foes of Christianity seized Paul and accused him of treason. Once more Paul appealed for trial in Rome and returned to the capital, where he swiftly became another victim of Nero's irrational hatred.

As a Roman citizen, Paul received the courtesy of a trial. He was judged guilty and a few hours later was beheaded outside the city gates, the customary execution for a citizen. Christian friends reverently carried his body and head to a nearby cemetery for burial. His tomb and shrine are today at the Roman basilica of St. Paul's outside the city walls.

The Pharisee from Tarsus had become the most impressive figure of early Christianity, dominating the apostolic age. Martyrdom ended his earthly mission, but his immortal Epistles, the first Christian theological writings, and the dozens of churches he founded survived as foundations of a great universal religion.

The story of Paul is told in the Acts of the Apostles 7.58–60; 8-28 and in his Letters.

In three hundred years, the early Christian faith grew to become the dominant religion of the Roman Empire. Meanwhile the Jews, deprived of their homeland, carried their own faith into communities around the world.

Founders of the Church

Christianity, which began as a tiny offshoot of Judaism early in the first century, became the official religion of the entire Roman Empire only three centuries later. Despite widespread and determined efforts to eliminate the new faith, it had survived. From the outset its growth had been hindered by hostility and persecution, but the church founded by the apostles emerged from its early struggles as a dynamic, expanding faith. By the reign of Constantine (312–337), the first Christian emperor, there were Christian churches in every large town in the empire and in places as distant from each other as Britain, Carthage, Armenia and Persia.

The century after the death of the apostles and Paul was a decisive one for the church. With the passing of the first generation of missionaries, the leadership came into the hands of local leaders who had been selected by the men who had actually known Jesus. Thus began a tradition of apostolic succession which survives to this day. The loose organization established by Paul, varying from one place to another, gradually evolved into a uniform hierarchy of bishops, elders and deacons. At the head of each church was a bishop (from the Greek word *episcopos*, "supervisor").

Jewish–Christian Schism

Another development which was of tremendous consequence to the church's future was the Jewish revolt of A.D. 66 and the subsequent destruction of Jerusalem by the Romans in 70. The leaders of the Jerusalem church, the headquarters of the Christian movement at the time, fled Jerusalem at the outbreak of the rebellion. The Jews saw this action as a betrayal, and from that time on grew increasingly hostile to the Christians. For their part, the Christians viewed the destruction of Jerusalem as God's punishment of the Jews for rejecting Jesus. Before the end of the first century, Jewish Christians were barred from synagogues.

From then on, Christianity was destined to be a separate religion, neither Jewish nor pagan but incorporating elements of both into its own unique doctrine. After the fall of Jerusalem, the center of the movement gravitated to Antioch, and later to Ephesus and Rome. The event was even more decisive for Judaism. With the destruction of the Jerusalem temple, the synagogues became the centers of worship and the development of modern Judaism began. The breach between Jew and Christian was complete.

A second Jewish revolt was led by Bar-Kochba in 132. Bar-Kochba, who was hailed as the long-awaited Jewish Messiah, began the revolt after the Roman Emperor Hadrian announced plans to build a new city, dedicated to Jupiter, on the site of Jerusalem. The rebels held Jerusalem for three years, but their resistance was broken in 135. Thereafter all Jews were barred from their Holy City, and again synagogues in the Holy Land were destroyed. Judea was renamed Palestine, after the ancient enemies of Israel, the Philistines.

Until the destruction of Jerusalem, the Christians had been regarded as Jews by the Romans. As such, they enjoyed the special legal status the emperor had granted to the Jewish nation, which permitted them to celebrate their Sabbath as a day of rest, excused them from service in the imperial army and honored their right to observe their religion. Despite Christian claims that they were the only true Jews, the empire came to regard them as an entirely new and separate sect, and therefore illegal. From then on, Christians had no protection under Roman law.

Blood of the Martyrs

Lack of legal status made the Christians vulnerable to imperial whim, and they suffered sporadic waves of persecution for their refusal to worship the emperor as a god. The first of these occurred under Domitian (reigned 81–96), and all who refused to offer sacrifices to the emperor-god were tortured and executed. The emperors Trajan (98–117) and Hadrian (117–138) also hunted down Christians who denied the ruler's divinity.

It was an age of great martyrs and heroic acts of faith. Bishop Ignatius of Antioch, for example, while being taken across Asia Minor in chains to face certain death in Rome, stopped at cities along the way to encourage fellow Christians to stand fast. "Do not hinder me from being martyred," he begged the church fathers in Rome. Courageous to the end, Ignatius was devoured by wild beasts in the arena. Some writers claimed he even urged the animals on.

Another famous martyr was Polycarp, bishop of the church at Smyrna in Asia Minor. Polycarp was burned at the stake in the stadium at Smyrna in A.D. 155. When given a final chance to recant, he replied, "For eighty-six years I have served Christ, and he did me no wrong. How am I to blaspheme my King and Savior?"

As the theologian Tertullian of Carthage observed late in the second century, "The blood of martyrs is the seed [of the church]." The steadfast faith of the martyrs was an example to all.

Another important source of inspiration and encouragement during these trying years was the book of Revelation, written by John of Patmos about A.D. 95. John seems to have written Revelation to prepare the churches of Asia for the impending persecutions. At the heart of his message was his complete trust in the words of Jesus, "Be faithful unto death, and I will give you the crown of life" (Revelation 2.10).

Despite persecution, the Christians continued to meet together, sometimes in secret, and to attract converts. No doubt many who embraced the faith were inspired by the zeal of the martyrs. Others were attracted by Jesus' simple and direct message of salvation to all who would repent.

The majority of the converts were from the poorer classes. They included small tradesmen, artisans, craftsmen, farmers, domestic servants and slaves. Yet Christianity also won over a number of high-born converts. When a man or woman decided to become a Christian, he or she underwent a period of initiation followed by a solemn and joyous ceremony of baptism. Through this rite they entered a new life as members of the Messianic community of Jesus. They were thereby cleansed of their sins, and received the gift of the Holy Spirit.

In the early years of the church, when many members were Jewish, the services centered around simple gatherings to commemorate the Last Supper. Christians attended synagogue services in the evening and on the Sabbath.

Yet a distinctively Christian service soon began to emerge. Not only the supper but also baptism became regular parts of Christian ritual. Hymns were sung. And Christians met on the first day of the week—Sunday—to celebrate Jesus' resurrection. Indeed, Gentile converts would not have known any other holy day. There were regional variations in worship, but common elements gave unity.

By 150 the service had taken on definite form. After the faithful had taken their places in the church, usually a converted private home, they would read passages from the scriptures. Then the leader of the congregation would exhort the people to follow the ways of the Lord, and the group would stand to offer private prayers. When they had finished, the leader offered prayers of thanksgiving, and the congregation indicated its assent with a vigorous "Amen" ("So be it" in Aramaic). The most sacred part of the service was an offertory of bread and wine, the Eucharist (thanksgiving), which symbolized the body and blood of Jesus.

House–Church and Catacombs

The earliest example of a Christian house-church has been found at Dura-Europus, a city in eastern Syria on the Euphrates River. The building was built about 232, and in size it was somewhat larger than an average house. One small room, used as a chapel, had a small space at one end with an arched roof above it. This may have been a baptismal font. A larger room was probably used for services and could hold about 100 people. At one end was a raised platform for the bishop or minister. Both rooms were decorated with colorful murals of scenes of Jesus' miracles.

The catacombs in Rome and other cities were also built during the early centuries of Christianity. They were extensive underground corridors and chambers, where the dead were buried in niches along the walls. Christians gathered there in times of persecution for secret services and held communal meals there to honor the dead. Like the church at Dura-Europus, the chambers of the catacombs were decorated with vivid frescoes of Biblical scenes. A common motif of such early Christian art was the fish. The Greek word for fish, *ichthus,* was formed from the first letters of the Greek words meaning "Jesus Christ, Son of God, Savior."

In many cities the secrecy and mystery surrounding Christian gatherings aroused suspicion and hostility. Rumors of all sorts circulated about their peculiar rites. "Brothers and sisters" were reputed to exchange "kisses of peace" during the ceremony and to consume the flesh and blood of their God. To the uninitiated, such rites sounded incestuous and cannibalistic.

Many regarded the Christians' refusal to recognize other gods as atheism. They feared that the gods would be angered and would punish the community for such blasphemy. In times of official persecution, the public joined the hunt.

Christians and Pagans

Nonetheless, the congregations continued to grow. One reason for this success was that, superficially at least, Christianity had certain similarities to pagan beliefs, especially to the Late Hellenistic mystery religions. These cults were built around the myth of a dying and rising god. Only the initiated were allowed to participate in their secret rituals, involving baptism in the blood of a goat or a bull, sacred meals and dramatic re-enactments of the myth of the god.

Like Christianity, the mystery cults of Orpheus, Dionysus, Mithras and others sought to assure the ultimate triumph of life over death. Though Jesus was not a mythical figure, the spring celebration of his resurrection seemed to satisfy those who had worshiped pagan gods.

The adaptability of the gospel caused a direct clash with a popular philosophy known as Gnosticism. This philosophy maintained that flesh and matter were evil and that man could be saved only by releasing his spirit from its imprisonment in his corrupt body.

Many Gnostic thinkers seized upon the gospel story as the ultimate example of the triumph of the spirit over matter. They claimed that Jesus had not actually been a man but a manifestation of the spirit, which had taken on material form in order to bring his message to men. The God who sent Jesus, they maintained, was not the God of the Old Testament, who had created the evil material world, but the true God, the lord of spirit.

Such ideas varied radically from the teaching of Jesus and the doctrines of the church. Jesus had been a real man, and his triumph had been not over the flesh but over death. His life and death represented the fulfillment of the prophecies of the Old Testament, and his God was the same God who had created the entire universe.

The New Testament

In the face of such heresies, the church was forced to reaffirm its faith in the historical events surrounding Jesus' life and to preserve his teachings. For the first few decades after Jesus' death, his gospel had spread by word of mouth. No one felt that a more permanent form was needed.

As the years passed and the men who had known the Master died, others decided to give the gospel written form. The earliest of these was Mark, who had known both Peter and Paul. He wrote his Gospel about A.D. 65 or 68, during Nero's persecutions in Rome. A few years later the Gospel of Matthew was written. Its author may have been the disciple Matthew, but more probably it was based on an earlier document written by Matthew. At about the same time, the Gospel of Luke was composed. A fourth Gospel, that of John, appeared about A.D. 100.

These four books, the book of Acts by Luke, the letters of the apostles and the book of Revelation eventually came to be accepted as the New Testament. Contrary to Gnostic teaching, the church also included the entire Old Testament as part of its scripture. At the same time, the church fathers worked together to codify the basic tenets of their faith. Their efforts were frequently hindered by heated controversy over the question of Jesus' relationship to God. This problem was not resolved until 325, when an ecumenical council at Nicea adopted the doctrine of the Trinity, the Nicene Creed: "I believe in one God . . . and in one Lord Jesus Christ, the only-begotten Son of God . . . of one substance with the Father . . . and in the Holy Spirit . . ."

The Church at Rome

By the end of the second century the church at Rome had begun to assume preeminence over other churches. This development is easy to understand. Rome was the center of the empire, the city from which communication radiated to all parts of Europe, Asia and Africa. Moreover, Peter, upon whom Jesus had placed the responsibility of founding the church, and Paul had both been martyred there. The Roman church was led by influential and powerful bishops.

Until the time of the Emperor Decius (249–251), persecution of Christians was sporadic and usually localized. But by the middle of the third century the empire was suffering from a rapid decline in military power, and its political framework was beginning to weaken. A series of military emperors came to power and attempted to restore Rome to its former glory.

As part of this attempt, Decius initiated a revival of the old imperial gods under whom Rome had risen to power. When the Christians refused to offer sacrifices to the imperial gods, Decius set out to eradicate them as enemies of the empire. His reign of terror ended with his death in 251, but a successor, Valerian, revived it in 253.

Gallienus (258–268) issued an edict of toleration in 261, granting freedom of worship to all sects. For the next 40 years the Christians enjoyed an interval of peace. During that time they continued to expand into the far reaches of the empire. Churches were established in England, western Gaul, Mauretania and beyond the eastern borders of the empire. They formed an international network of Christian communities linked together by a common faith.

Another savage wave of persecution was begun by the Emperor Diocletian. This was to be the last empire-wide campaign against the new faith and it proved to be fiercer than all earlier ones. In February of the year 303, Diocletian announced the beginning of his campaign by burning to the ground the church at Nicomedia in Asia Minor. The following day he issued an edict outlawing Christianity. First he rounded up the clergy and killed all who refused to renounce Jesus. Then he confiscated churches and church property and

Ruins of an ancient church at Nicea, in Asia Minor, site of the first Christian ecumenical council. Emperor Constantine called all bishops there to settle a dispute over the divinity of Jesus. The 300 attendants, many still bearing scars of persecution, drew up the Nicene Creed, stating that Jesus and God are of one substance.

executed all Christians who refused to sacrifice to the official Roman gods.

The Roman world fell into chaos after Diocletian's abdication in 305. He had divided the unwieldy empire into two parts, one in the east and one in the west. It seemed that the once mighty empire would never again rise to greatness, but a new leader soon appeared who revived Rome's sagging strength. That man was Constantine, the first Christian emperor.

Constantine, Champion of the Faith

According to legend, Constantine had seen a vision of a burning cross on the eve of an important battle and at once became converted to Christianity. As sole emperor of the western empire (312–337), he championed religious freedom for all, granting the Christians legal status and official protection for the first time. In 324 Constantine conquered the eastern empire and united East and West under the standard of the cross. Six years later he moved his capital from Rome to Byzantium, a strategic port on the shore of the Bosporus. The city was hailed as the new Rome and was dedicated to "the God of the martyrs."

Christianity had conquered the Roman world. A new era of one empire, one emperor, one church, one Lord (Jesus) *and* one God had begun. Soon millions would eagerly embrace the new faith, and the inspiration of Jesus would sustain countless generations of the faithful.

Index

Boldface numbers indicate illustrations, captions and maps. *Italic* numbers indicate main references.

U

Ugarit, 27
  map, **16–17**
Upper City (Jerusalem), 356, 357
Ur, 26, 27, 28
  map, **33**
Uriah, 174
Urmiah, Lake, **16–17**
Ussher, Archbishop, 16
Uzziah (king of Judah), 224

V

Valerian, 421
Van, Lake, **16–17**
Varus, 331
Vashti, 268
Vaux, Roland de, 18

W

"Wailing Wall," 302
Walls, **20, 109**
  around homes, 62, **155,** 156, **209**
  Jericho's, 104, 106
  Jerusalem's, 173, 182, 251, 276–79, 356
  temple, **191,** 302, 358–59
  town and city, **23,** 36, 38, **107,** 111, 190,
    201, 223, 232, **234, 236–37,** 240
Wars, *see* Battles
Water, 36, 37, 39, 75, **84–85,** 88–89, 216, **231,**
    232
  aqueducts, **317**
  cisterns, 60, 96, **162, 303**
  droughts, **48, 126,** 208
  floods, **34–35,** 50, 73
  irrigation, **23,** 26, 64, 66, 73
  to wine, miracle of, 341, 342–43
  See also Bathing; Oases; Springs; Wells

Wealth
  classes of society, 102, 192–93, 197–98, 200,
    224, 251, **282,** 312
  Jesus' view of, 372–73, 394
  See also Money
Weapons, 18, 38, 62, **96–97,** 100, 152, 157,
    160, 167, 174, 197, **223,** 230, **240–41,** 311
  armor, 62, **96–97,** 116, **150, 311**
  bows and arrows, 30, 50, 51, 62, 80, **92–93,**
    116, 156, 161, **223, 264,** 265
  daggers, **96,** 108, 116
  javelins, **311**
  slings, **40–41,** 58, 80, **92–93,** 116, 156, 166,
    223
  spears, 30, **40–41,** 80, **92–93, 96,** 116, **223,**
    264
  swords, 108, 116, 119, **150,** 161, **311**
  See also Chariots, military use
Weaving, 50, **82, 98,** 197, **198–99,** 325, 404
  basket for Moses, 73
Weddings, *see* Marriage
Weeks, Feast of, 310, 331, 360, 384, 394
Wells, 37, 42, 44–45, 50, **51,** 53–54, **69,** 75, 96,
    164, **168, 307,** 309, 324, 368
Wheat, **38,** 40, 42, **91, 126–27,** 196, 295. *See*
    also Grain
Wheels, **32,** 122
Wildgoats' Rocks, 160
Wine, 29, 66, **142–43,** 196, 197, 258, **282,** 292,
    357, 381, **386–87**
  cupbearers, 276
  Jesus' miracle of, 341, **342–43**
  at Last Supper, **376–77,** 379
  See also Dionysus; Grapes
"Wisdom school," 150
Witchcraft, 141, 161, 171, 238
Worship
  as personal experience, 30, 305
  use of shofars, 324, **331**
  use of trumpets, 80, 106, 230, 328, **412**
  See also Altars; Churches; God; Gods;
    Priests; Sacrificial offerings; Temples
Wrestling, 224, **282, 289**
Wright, G. Ernest, 18

Writing, art of, 21, **31,** 50, **56,** 73, 173, 224,
    231, 242, **302–3,** 304, 325, **389.** *See also*
    Language; Literature; Oral traditions;
    Scribes (secretaries)

X

Xerxes, *see* Ahasuerus

Y

Yadin, Yigael, 18
Yehud, *see* Judah

Z

Zacchaeus, 368
Zadok, 147, 173, 186, 256, 262, 362
Zarephath, 208
Zealots, 315, 348
Zebedee, 342
Zebulun (son of Jacob), 55, 60–62, 64–67
Zebulun (tribe), 121, 172. *See also* Tribes of
    Israel
Zechariah, 250, 368
Zedekiah, 203, 243–44, 262
Zerubbabel, 274
Zeus, 254, **283,** 287, 288, 409
Ziggurats, 26, **28,** 235
Ziklag, 145, 170, 171
Zilpah, 54
Zilu, **81**
Zin, Wilderness of, **84**
  map, **81**
Ziph, Wilderness of, 160
Zipporah, 75
Zion, 356, 357
Zithers, 346
Zobah, 184–85
  map, **151**
Zorah, 123

CONTRIBUTING ARTISTS

Kenneth Bald 31, 32, 38, 43, 50, 51, 55, 63, 66, 67, 82, 90, 98, 99, 100 *from a Megiddo ivory, Palestine Archaeological Museum,* 122, 129, 133, 139, 146, 147, 166, 170, 176, 177, 202, 227, 233, 238, 254, 258, 263, 269, 276, 277, 289, 305, 311, 321, 330, 331, 341, 363, 372, 389, 390, 396, 407, 408.

Tom Beecham 60–61, 65, 72–73, 76–77, 120–121, 137, 149, 184–185, 198–199, 229, 241, 250–251, 270–271, 291, 313, 323, 329, 334–335, 349.

Neil Boyle 158, 175, 178–179, 376–377, 399.

Paul Calle 28–29, 36–37, 41, 44–45, 52–53, 56, 88–89, 97, 105, 117, 130–131, 189, 218–219, 261, 342–343, 359.

Jean Leon Huens 306–307.

Robert Lavin 142–143, 194–195, 354–355.

Victor Lazarro 20–21 *based on drawing by Daniel S. Wright,* 23, 39, 47 *based on drawing by Daniel S. Wright,* 83, 107 *based on drawing by Daniel S. Wright,* 109, 113, 140, 155, 168 *based on drawing by G. A. Naterna,* 181 *based on drawing by Carney E. S. Gavin, Harvard University,* 187, 191, 201, 209, 231, 235, 259 *based on reconstruction by Walter Andrae,* 265, 286–287, 302–303, 361, 364–365.

Robert McGinness 24–25, 92–93, 246–247, 382–383.

Harry Schaare 206–207, 278, 370–371, 386–387, 414.

PHOTOGRAPHY CREDITS

All photographs are by Erich Lessing (L), Magnum Photos, unless otherwise indicated.

The initials BC are for the Bronfman Collection, Israel Museum, Jerusalem; BM for the British Museum, London;
OI for the Oriental Institute, University of Chicago;
RAM for the Rockefeller Archaeological Museum, Jerusalem;
SC for the Norbert Schimmel Collection, New York; UM for the University Museum, University of Pennsylvania.

Page 10 Photri; 12–13 L; 19 L except lower left; 19 lower left Frank Schreider / Photo Researchers; 23 upper Jericho Excavation Fund, courtesy Kathleen Kenyon; 23 lower L; 28 OI; 30 L (Kunsthistorisches Museum, Vienna); 31 middle Mission Archéologique de Mari; 31 lower OI; 35 L; 38 UM; 39 Bullaty-Lomeo; 40 Lee Boltin (UM); 43 Metin Ergin; 44 Cast in Louvre Museum, Paris; 46 left L (Louvre Museum, Paris); 46 right, upper & lower L (RAM); 47 L; 49 L; 53 L (Louvre Museum, Paris); 55 UM; 59 George Holton / Photo Researchers; 61 L (SC); 62 OI (line drawing by Virginia Wells); 63 OI; 64 L (SC); 68 left, upper & lower L (Cairo Museum); 68 right F. L. Kennett © George Rainbird Ltd., 1963; 69 upper OI; 69 lower L (Luxor, Egypt); 71 L; 72 OI; 74 L; 75 L (Egyptian Museum, Turin, Italy); 77 L; 78 Courtesy Service des Antiquités, Cairo; 80 L (Louvre Museum, Paris); 84–87 L; 90 OI; 91 L (SC); 96 L (RAM); 99 left Courtesy OI / Cairo Museum; 99 lower right L (RAM); 103 L; 104 L; 107 L (Louvre Museum, Paris); 109 UM; 110 L; 112 left L (Medinet-Habu, Egypt); 112 upper right Israel Department of Antiquities, Israel Museum, Jerusalem; 112 lower right L (RAM); 113 L (RAM); 115 L; 116 UM; 118 L; 120 BM; 123 L; 127 L; 128 L (RAM); 129 Sir Flinders Petrie, from Gerar; 135 L; 136 L (RAM); 139 L (RAM); 140 L; 147 L (SC); 148 OI; 150 L (RAM); 153 L; 155 R. L. W. Cleave, Audio-View (Mideast) Ltd., Jerusalem; 157 L (Israel Museum, Jerusalem); 159 L (RAM); 161 L (RAM); 162–163 L; 165 L; 166 L; 168 L; 171 L; 172 L (Kunsthistorisches Museum, Vienna); 174 L; 176 L (RAM); 177 UM; 179 L (BC); 180 left & lower right L (Louvre Museum, Paris); 180 center L (BC); 180 upper right L (RAM); 181 L (Louvre Museum, Paris); 183 L (Louvre Museum, Paris); 185 L; 187 L; 188 upper L (E. Borowski Collection, Israel Museum, Jerusalem); 188 lower L (E. Borowski Collection, Basel, Switzerland); 192 L (Israel Museum, Jerusalem); 198 Edith Alston; 201 upper L (E. Borowski Collection, Basel, Switzerland); 201 lower L; 202 J. L. Starkey (courtesy Institute of Archaeology, University of London); 205 L; 207 L (RAM); 209 L; 212 left L; 212 right L (RAM); 213 L; 215 L (BM); 217 left L (Louvre Museum, Paris); 217 right L; 221 L (Louvre Museum, Paris); 222–223 L (Louvre Museum, Paris); 225 L; 226 OI; 227 Metropolitan Museum of Art, New York, gift of E. S. Harkness, 1926; 228 L (RAM); 231 left L (BC); 231 right L; 234 left OI; 234 right L (reconstruction, State Museums, Berlin); 235 left Photri; 235 right OI; 237 L (BM); 238 L; 239 L; 240 L (BM); 242 L; 245 L (BM); 251 Marvin Newman; 252 Department of Antiquities, Cyprus; 257 L; 258 BM; 260 Michael Holford Library, London; 263 BM; 264 left L (Louvre Museum, Paris); 264 upper right L (Istanbul Archaeological Museum); 264 lower Photri; 265 Photri; 267 L (Louvre Museum, Paris); 270 Egyptian Museum, Turin, Italy; 272 L (State Museums, Berlin); 275 Ted Speigel / Rapho-Guillumette; 276 Metropolitan Museum of Art, New York, H. B. Dick Fund, 1954; 227 L; 279 L (cast in RAM from original in BM); 282 left L (Louvre Museum, Paris); 282 upper right L (Athens National Museum); 282 lower L (Kunsthistorisches Museum, Vienna); 283 upper L; 283 middle L (RAM); 283 lower right L (Louvre Museum, Paris); 285 L (BC); 287 Hirmer Fotoarchiv, Munich; 288 Hirmer Fotoarchiv, Munich; 290 L; 293 L (E. Reifenberg Collection, Israel Museum, Jerusalem); 294 upper OI; 294 lower OI, gift of Chester D. Tripp; 296–297 L; 302 R. L. W. Cleave, Audio-View (Mideast) Ltd., Jerusalem; 305 L (BC); 310 left R. L. W. Cleave, Audio-View (Mideast) Ltd., Jerusalem; 310 right L; 311 L (Museum Carnuntum, Deutsch Altenburg, Austria); 314 L (Kärtner Landesmuseum, Klagenfurt, Austria); 316 left L (Temple of Vespasian, Pompeii Excavations); 316 upper right L (Kunsthistorisches Museum, Vienna); 316 lower L; 317 upper L; 317 lower L (Römisch-Germanisches Zentralmuseum, Mainz, Germany); 319 L; 321 upper L (Byzantine Museum, Athens); 321 lower L; 322 UM; 327 L; 328 UM; 332 L; 334 L (from the ruins of the Synagogue of Aphek, Golan Heights, Israel); 336–337 L; 339 L; 343 L (Israel Department of Antiquities, Israel Museum, Jerusalem); 347 L; 348 L; 351 L; 352 L (from the Synagogue of Chorazin, Israel); 353 L; 358 Ted Spiegel / Rapho-Guillumette; 361 L; 365 R. L. W. Cleave, Audio-View (Mideast) Ltd., Jerusalem; 367 L; 371 L (Istanbul Archaeological Museum); 372 L (RAM); 375 L (Israel Museum, Jerusalem); 376 L (RAM); 378 L (RAM); 381 L; 389 upper left L; 389 lower left L (École Archéologique Française); 389 right L (Israel Museum, Jerusalem); 393 L (San Clemente); 395 L; 401 L; 402 left L (Archaeological Museum, Ephesus, Turkey); 402 right Fred J. Maroon / Louis Mercier; 403 upper A. F. Kersting; 403 lower left & right L; 405 L; 408 Yigael Yadin; 410 OI; 411 L (National Museum, Naples); 415 Velio Cioni / Rome's Press Photo; 417 Angelo Hornak (BM); 421 Metin Ergin.

432